FOURTH EDITION

SPORT IN CONTEMPORARY SOCIETY

An Anthology

D. STANLEY EITZEN
Colorado State University

St. Martin's Press
NEW YORK

Editor: Louise H. Waller
Manager, publishing services: Emily Berleth
Project management: East End Publishing Services
Production supervisor: Edith H. Riker
Cover design: Nadia Furlan-Lorbek
Cover photo: © E. Alan McGee/FPG International Corporation

Library of Congress Catalog Card Number: 92-50037

Manufactured in the United States of America.
76543
fedcba

For information, write:
St. Martin's Press, Inc.
175 Fifth Avenue
New York, NY 10010

ISBN: 0-312-08033-6

Preface

Most Americans are at least somewhat interested in sport, and many are downright fanatical about it. They attend games, read the sport pages and sport magazines, and talk endlessly about the subject. But even those fans who astound us with their knowledge of the most obscure facts about sport—who the opposing pitcher was when Don Larsen pitched his perfect no-hit World Series game or how many winning seasons the football team of Slippery Rock has had—do not necessarily *understand* sport.

Do sport buffs know how sport is linked to other institutions of society? Do they understand the role of sport in socializing youngsters in American values? Do they know how much racial discrimination continues to exist in American sport, and why? Do they know how often or how seldom it is really the case that sport enables its participants to rise in the American social structure? Do they know that the assumption that sport builds character is open to serious question? What about the relationship of violence in sport to the structure of society? What about the ways in which sport has perpetuated sex-role stereotypes in society? How do owners, coaches, and other sport authorities exercise power to maintain control over athletes? These are some of the issues this book examines.

There are two fundamental reasons for the ignorance of most Americans about the role of sport in society. First, they have had to rely mainly on sportswriters and sportscasters for their information, and these journalists have usually been little more than describers and cheerleaders. Until recent years journalists have rarely looked critically at sport. Instead, they have perpetuated myths: "Look what baseball did for Jackie Robinson" or "Football helped a whole generation of sons of coal miners escape the mines."

The second reason for our sports illiteracy is that sport has been virtually ignored by American academics. Only in the past twenty years or so have American social scientists and physical educators begun to employ scientific research methods to investigate the social aspects of sport. Previously, as with sports journalism, academic research in the field of sport tended to be biased in support of existing myths. In particular the early research by physical educators was aimed at proving that sports participation builds character. In this limited perspective such phenomena as cheating, violence, and failure were, for the most part, simply ignored.

Today, however, not only academics but also a new breed of sports journalists—though the latter are still a minority—are making insightful analyses of sport's role in society. They are examining the positive *and* the negative consequences of sport. They are substituting facts for myths. Most significantly, they are documenting the reciprocal impact of sport and the various institutions of society: religion, education, politics, and economics. There is no danger that sport will suffer from such examination. On the contrary, sport is revealed as a subject far more complex and far more interesting than most of us have imagined.

This book is a collection of the writings representing this new era of critical appraisal. It includes contributions from both journalists and academics. The overriding criterion for inclusion of a particular article was whether it critically examined the role of sport in society. The praise of sport is not omitted, but such praise, as with condemnation, must be backed by fact, not mythology or dogma. (Occasionally, a dogmatic piece has been included to challenge the critical faculties of the reader.) The selection of each article was also guided by such questions as, Is it interesting? Is it informative? Is it thought-provoking? Does it communicate without the use of unnecessary jargon and sophisticated methodologies?

In short, the selections presented here not only afford the reader an understanding of sport that transcends the still prevalent stereotypes and myths; they also yield fascinating and important insights into the nature of American society. Thus, this book has several groups of potential readers. First, it is intended to be the primary or supplementary text for courses in the sociology of sport, sport and society, and foundations of physical education. Second, the book can be used as a supplemental text for sociology courses such as the introduction to sociology, American society, and American institutions. A third audience for this book is general readers who wish to deepen their understanding and appreciation of sport.

The fourth edition of *Sport in Contemporary Society*, while retaining much of the structure of the earlier editions, has undergone extensive revision. One part from the previous edition has been dropped, and two new parts have been added: "Sport and Violence," and "Mass Media and Sport." Only ten of the selections from the previous edition have been retained, making it possible to include twenty-five more up-to-date essays. The result is a collection of lively and timely essays that will sharpen the reader's analysis and understanding of sport *and* American society.

My choices in these revisions have been guided by the valuable suggestions of my editor, Louise Waller, and the suggestions of reviewers of this edition of the book. These reviewers include: John Fuller, West Georgia College; David Furst, San Jose State University; David Hastings, University of Tennessee; Thomas Jable, William Paterson College; and Linda S. Trapp, Ohio Wesleyan University.

My greatest debt is to the authors found in this volume. My thanks to them for their scholarship and, most significant, for their insights that help us to unravel the mysteries of this intriguing and important part of social life.

D. Stanley Eitzen

Contents

Part One

Toward an Understanding of Sport

The sociologist who gives scholarly attention to sport, as is the case with the investigation of all social phenomena, is guided by a theoretical perspective. The focus of attention, the questions asked, the relationships sought, the interpretations rendered, and the insights unraveled are rooted in a theoretical base. This is because "the way one approaches the study of sport . . . will depend on the questions one is asking, and ultimately on one's assumptions about what it is possible to question."[1] And, of course, these assumptions are determined by where one stands in the theoretical firmament.

The three selections in this introductory part illustrate two fundamental ways to view and interpret social life—the functionalist and conflict theoretical perspectives. The selection by Garry J. Smith looks at spectator sport from the functionalist perspective.[2] His interpretation of this phenomenon is positive—sport socializes spectators; sport is a mechanism of social integration; sport inspires; and sport provides a legitimate means of escape and excitement from an otherwise humdrum existence of the spectators. In a much different vein, because it comes from a different theoretical perspective, D. Stanley Eitzen's essay is critical of the way sport is organized. It looks at the "dark side of sport"—deviance—from the conflict perspective.

The final selection, by sociologist Jay J. Coakley, enhances our understanding of sport by elaborating on these two contrasting theoretical approaches—functionalist and conflict—that guide much of the work of sport sociologists. The understanding of both of these perspectives is vitally important to the analyst of society. It is crucial to note that each approach offers significant insights about society. However, the theoretical approach guiding the structure of this book and the choice of selections is the conflict perspective. As I stated in the preface to Eitzen and Sage's *Sociology of North American Sport:*

> [The] goal is to make the reader aware of the positive and negative consequences of the way sport is organized in American society. We are concerned about some of the trends in sport, especially the move away from athlete-oriented activities toward the impersonality of what we term "corporate sport." We are committed to moving sport and society in a more humane direction, and this requires, as a first step, a thorough understanding of the principles that underlie the social structures and processes that create, sustain, and transform the social organizations within the institution of sport.[3]

NOTES

1. Whitson, David J., "Research Methodology in Sport Sociology," *CAHPER Sociology of Sport Monograph Series* (Ottawa: CAHPER, no date).
2. For a critique of Smith, see: Meier, Klaus V., "The Ignoble Sports Fan," *Journal of Sport and Social Issues* 13 (Fall 1989):111-119.
3. Eitzen, D. Stanley, and George H. Sage, *Sociology of North American Sport*, 5th ed. (Dubuque, Iowa: Wm. C. Brown, 1993), p. xi.

1. *The Noble Sports Fan*

GARRY J. SMITH

INTRODUCTION

The interest in mass appeal spectator sport has never been greater in any society past or present than it is in North America today. Certainly older societies also had a passion for watching athletes perform, but until recently there was not the sophisticated technology to deliver the sporting events to a wider audience. One might suspect that we are nearing the saturation point in our enthusiasm for following sport, yet indicators such as attendance figures and television ratings show that, for most commercial sports, fan fervor is not subsiding (Figler, 1981).

This fascination with sport continues despite the well publicized troubles that have plagued sport over the past few years. Some of these difficulties include: (a) player strikes, as happened in 1981 and 1985 in major league baseball, and in 1982 and 1987 in the National Football League; (b) drug scandals, in professional baseball, basketball and football; (c) lack of league competitive balance and overall low quality of play, especially as evidenced in the Canadian Football League and the National Hockey League; (d) mis-management of individual franchises, such has been the case with Vancouver in the N.H.L., Atlanta and Tampa Bay in the N.F.L., and New Jersey in the N.B.A. to name only a few; (e) problems in intercollegiate sports which have become epidemic in major American universities, such as recruiting, drug abuse, sexual assaults, and acceptance of bribes to shave points.

Certainly sport sociologists realize that spectator sports are immensely popular, but what is not known is how commercial sports are able to retain this public acceptance during periods of upheaval. A related matter that has perplexed scholars is whether or not the sport follower role has utility either for the individual or society as a whole.

This paper features a critical examination of various prominent sport sociology theories which attempt to explain and interpret the sport follower role. The position taken is that the sport follower role is a worthwhile leisure pursuit that enhances as individual's quality of life in addition to having a cohesive effect on society.

SOURCE: *Journal of Sport and Social Issues* 12 (Spring 1988), pp. 54-65. Reprinted by permission of the *Journal of Sport and Social Issues*.

The term sport spectator, sport fan and sport follower are used interchangeably in this paper. All three labels refer to individuals who have a strong emotional involvement in the actual outcome–who wins and loses. In addition, this particular type of fan spends considerable time, effort, and money to read about, listen to, and watch sporting events.

Naturally there are gradations of being a sports fan, ranging all the way from minimal interest to addiction. An enthusiastic sports follower ranks high on the following criteria established by McPherson (1975, p. 256): "(1) The person has knowledge of sports performers, sport statistics, sports lore and sports strategies; (2) The person experiences mood changes while consuming a sport event; (3) The person employs sport as a major topic of conversation; (4) The person sometimes arranges his or her lifestyle around . . . sports."

WHAT IS THE ATTRACTION?

The primary difference between the sports fan and the non-fan is that the fan accepts the illusion that the result of the contest matters, while the non-fan is indifferent to the result. Intellectually, most of us know that it is not important in the grand scheme of things whether Washington beat Denver in Super Bowl XXII. Yet, if one allows oneself to have an emotional stake in the outcome, the game becomes a pleasurable form of recreation.

Those individuals most wedded to this illusion are males from the middle and upper social strata. Edwards (1973, p. 246) has advanced a proposition which attempts to explain this phenomena; he avers "that the greater the individual's involvement in instrumental pursuits, the greater the interest in sport." Instrumental pursuits refer to the striving for socially approved goals such as status, power and security. Since it has been males, particularly those from the middle and upper social strata, who have been involved in these pursuits, it follows that these same people would be most interested in sport. Edwards' explanation may have some validity but it is quite general. Whether a particular individual becomes a sport follower is the result of a complex web of causal factors which, besides gender and socioeconomic status, include ethnicity, family size, opportunity set, the influence of the extended family, and past experiences as a sport participant (Loy, McPherson and Kenyon, 1978).

An intricate socialization process takes place which channels certain individuals into a sport follower role. A nascent interest in sport is aroused and nourished by certain attributes which exist in the sports realm and which are not found to the same extent in other forms of entertainment. Koppett (1981) suggests the following characteristics as being the building blocks of the sport follower foundation: comprehensibility, continuity, readability and coherence. By Koppett's reckoning most sports are easily understood; even the uninitiated can grasp the object of the game and develop a rooting interest rather quickly. This is not the same as with opera, abstract art or a Fellini movie, for example, where a taste must be cultivated for one to fully appreciate the form. Continuity in sport is provided through the copious amounts of information on past events. Halls of Fame, player biographies, and statistics manuals are only a few means of recognizing past achievements and allowing comparisons with contemporary performers. An interest in today's game is intensified by the knowledge of how this particular rivalry has fared before and what records are at stake.

Another reason why sport can be so absorbing is that a person can experience pleasure by following the action after the fact. Roger Angell (1972), the celebrated baseball writer, submits that the reading of a baseball box score provides him with an aesthetic joy equivalent to that which a musician might experience in reading a score of sheet music by a gifted composer.

Part of the traditional appeal of following sport has been that sport was perceived as an oasis of stability in a turbulent society. In the sporting contest itself it is relatively clear cut: who wins, who loses; does the ball go into the hoop or not; was the player in or out of bounds? In the larger society there is often confusion about government economic policies, the value of nuclear power, the Middle East situation and so forth. These problems are complicated and depressing and sport, as a counterpoint, represents a tidy, regulated environment that serves as a tranquil retreat from the complexities of everyday life. Of course, what happens off the field is another matter. With labor disputes, drug charges and cheating allegations the sports realm is nearly as chaotic as other areas of society. One might expect that if this trend continues, fan interest will sharply deteriorate.

Epstein (1985, p. 265) finds sport "intrinsically interesting" because it enables us to observe experts performing their craft at a high level. Sport differs from other domains such as politics, journalism and show business in that the athlete must produce under pressure, in full view of everyone. The athlete cannot go back and change what was done. He, rarely is "she" of interest to the male fan, is beyond image manipulation and public relations. He has only the energy and ability that he can muster here and now. Epstein states that, for the observer, there is something about this struggle "that is elemental and greatly satisfying."

Loy (1981, p. 265) concurs that sport has an intrinsic appeal for the spectator. He suggests two main reasons why this is so: "the uncertainty of the outcome and the opportunity for sanctioned display." We know that evenly matched competition produces maximal fan enthusiasm, whereas "sanctioned display" refers to our need to represent and identify with heroic actions and characteristics that are valued in the broader society.

The preceding has been a brief description of how the sports follower role evolves to the point where it is integrated into a person's daily routine. What follows in the next section is an explanation of how and why this role has beneficial consequences for both individuals and society.

BENEFITS OF THE SPORT FOLLOWER ROLE

Sport sociology literature contains several theories which attempt to explain the motivation for a person being a sports fan. Three of these theories which focus on the functional aspects of the sports follower role are examined in greater detail.

The Social Integration and Socializing Factor

Durkheim (1960) postulated that the division of labor plays a central role in integrating society; he also warned that extreme specialization in occupational roles could lead to disruption of social cohesion. This condition was labelled "the economic division of labor," and it signified a situation where individuals become isolated from one another due to a narrowing of their interests brought on by their specialized occupational roles. When this happens there is a resultant breakdown in interpersonal communication and growing feelings of alienation. Modern day industrialized societies have already reached this stage of ultra-specialization. To counter the negative effects of this process society has invented a wide variety of symbols, rituals and ceremonies which have shared meaning for the masses.

Spectator sport is especially important in this context because it purportedly integrates schools, communities, ethnic groups, cities and even countries (Smith, 1974). The following quote typifies the support given by scholars to the premise that sport is a social integrator: "Common interests, common loyalties, common enthusiasms—those are the great integrating factors in any culture. In America, sports have provided this common denominator in as great a degree as any other single factor" (Cozens and Stumpf, 1951, p. 229).

At the personal level, an interest in sport is stoked by participating in sport, being a spectator at the sports events, and by consuming the sports information that is conveyed by the mass media. Following sport in this fashion leads to the development of team loyalties and an identification with sports heroes, both of which help to satisfy our need for affiliation.

The sports setting itself is also a source of enjoyment because it affords an opportunity for people with common interests to interact. Sports fans invariably watch sports events with someone, usually a family member or a close friend (Smith, 1974). Sports promoters capitalize on this need to socialize by creating special family nights, as well as by forming fan or booster clubs (Offen, 1975).

Favorite teams, favorite players and a knowledge of sports lore all provide grist for conversation. Stone (1970) considers sport to be a universal; that is, it is a subject that nearly everyone knows something about, and unlike most other subjects, it is a topic of conversation that involves little risk. An interest in sport, then, is a catalyst which brings people together on common ground. No matter how ephemeral, or how mundane, these interactions create a sense of community. Epstein (1985, p. 177) provides a poignant example to illustrate this point:

> . . . in a wider sense, sport is culture. For many American men it represents a common background, a shared interest. It has a binding power that transcends social class and education. Some years ago I found myself working in the south among men with whom I shared nothing in the way of region, religion, education, politics or general views: we shared nothing, in fact, but sports, which was enough for us to get along and grow to beome friends, in the process of showing how superficial all the things that might have kept us apart in fact were.

The Escape and Excitement Factors

These two factors are not synonymous but they are dealt with together here because the search for excitement represents one of the most familiar means of escape. Klapp (1972, p. 347) noted that there is a condition of banality that is prevalent in modern society. Banality is defined as: "A restriction of awareness, a shallowness of meaning, the feeling that something is missing from a person's environment." Boredom is the main symptom of banality and, as a way of coping with this situation, we develop ways of disassociating ourselves from our humdrum daily routines. For some, an involvement is sport is chosen as an escape route which is used to seek fulfillment and liberation. This response to banality can be a healthy coping strategy, to the extent that the escape is seen as temporary, and that the escape attempt itself does not become the paramount reality (Cohen and Taylor, 1978).

Spectator sport engenders feelings of tension, stress and risk that we do not face in everyday life (Elias and Dunning, 1970). The stimulation and variety derived from following sport makes life more enjoyable for many people. Koppett (1981, p. 22) explains why sport is so appealing for excitement seekers: "Sports titillate that response to danger in a way or at least to an extent, that other entertainments don't. Once we make an emotional investment by choosing to root for one of the contestants, the nervous excitement that accompanies each step toward victory or defeat is an exhilaration quite different from our everyday equilibrium." Heinegg (1985, p. 457) characterizes an interest in sport as "a flight from the pain of existence," whereby the committed fan finds a haven from the perpetual whirl of "worldly cares and crises." While engrossed in the sporting event a fan's mood may fluctuate, but any pain is temporary and minor compared to the relief of gaining a respite from a wearisome existence.

The Aesthetic Factor

Committed sport fans say that one of the reasons they follow sport is that they are fascinated by the excellence, beauty, and creativity in an athlete's performance. Watching those who are the best perform any craft, but particularly an athletic feat, can be energizing, euphoric experience for the fan. Devotees will speak rapturously, years later, of great moments they witnessed; a Gretzky goal, a Dr. J move, or a Nadia Comaneci perfect routine. A splendid athletic performance rivals any great work of art; but, unlike "a concert where the musician normally interprets the work of the composer, the athlete is an innovator, responding to each situation as it comes along" (Heinegg, 1985 p. 458).

On a more prosaic level, even ordinary plays or actions may evoke an aesthetic response. The tight spiral of a football, a crisp body check, or a well timed feint, may exude a simple elegance which forges a bond between the player and the audience. In his incisive analysis of modern sport, Novak (1976) poses the rhetorical question: "Can an enlightened person be a fan?" Many fans would be surprised at the question, and would respond by saying that being a fan helps one to become enlightened.

Following sport can be inspiring, since it makes us aware of our human potential by giving us fleeting glimpses of perfection. Loy (1981, p. 274) expands on this theme by noting that for the devoted sports fan, following sport may actually cause the individual to "consciously or unconsciously address the existential questions of self-construction: What am I? Who am I? Am I what I ought to be?"

The sports follower role can have favorable consequences for both the individual and society. For the individual, an interest in sport is a pleasurable and innocuous way to fill leisure time, and is seen as a major contributor to one's own quality of life. Society benefits from the sports follower role too, because an interest in sport promotes personal interaction which leads to social cohesion and a strengthening of major social values.

The term "quality of life" is a rather vague catch-phrase, which refers to a person's level of happiness, life satisfaction, and psychological well-being (Iso-Ahola, 1980). Smith, Patterson, Williams and Hogg (1981) studied the heavily committed male sports fan and found that eighty-one percent of the sample claimed that their interest in sport contributed to their quality of life, while seventeen percent said that it made some contribution, and only two percent said that it made no contribution at all to their quality of life.

Recently, publications have emerged that rank communities on a quality of life index, using criteria such as climate, education, transportation, crime rates, housing cost, or undesirable places to live (Boyer and Savageau, 1985). When judging a location's recreational opportunities one of the main parameters is the presence of professional sports teams and NCAA Division 1 football and basketball teams. All of the cities that were ranked in the top ten had major league professional sports franchises or access to top level college sports or both.

The point to be made here is that the existence of elite sports teams in a community is deemed a major positive factor in determining whether or not an area is a desirable place to live. The city of Oakland made this very case in its attempt to persuade the courts to force the Raiders football team to remain in that city. The argument put forth was that the city had lost a cultural asset and that the quality of life had deteriorated because of it.

While this paper stresses the value of the sports follower role, it must be noted that the role is not without its hazards. No one can be sure on an absolute basis just when the disadvantages of an activity start to outweigh the advantages. At one stage it is a healthy habit, while one step further it becomes an addiction. The actual amount of time spent on the activity is not necessarily the critical factor but when the activity begins to have a negative effect on family life or job performance, one would suspect the activity is becoming addictive. On the other hand, if an involvement in the activity is a source of pleasure which does not adversely affect personal health or do harm to others, it could be viewed as a healthy habit (Peele, 1981).

Whether or not the sport follower role is better or worse than other leisure pursuits is a matter of debate. While some scholars may not rate the sports follower role highly they would be hard pressed to disagree with the comments of Zillman, Sapolsky and Bryant (1979, p. 310): "If spectatorship produced no effects other than enjoyment, and even if such enjoyment were branded as 'superficial,' it would still be an experience of some value and preferable to many others."

TRADITIONAL CRITICISMS OF THE SPORT FOLLOWER ROLE

This final section will feature a critical analysis of the main arguments which are in opposition to the sports follower role. The sport follower role has been disparaged by a variety of sources, but most notably by conservative intellectuals and conflict theorists. The conservative intellectuals are elitists who view all popular entertainment forms as being cheap and vulgar, whereas conflict theorists see the masses as innocents who are duped and victimized by the sports and T.V. moguls. Even cartoonists have had an impact on the public image of the sports fan. The fan is usually depicted as being a slackjawed, overweight male with a 5 o'clock shadow and several tattoos, who lives to drink beer and watch sports events. While no doubt there are fans who fit the cartoonists' stereotype, research evidence shows the profile of the ardent sports fan to be the antithesis of this representation. Committed sports fans tend to be well educated professionals who were former high school and university athletes, and who still participate in sports on a regular basis (Smith et al., 1981).

Sport Spectating as an Opiate

The essence of this position is that spectator sport narcotizes individuals who might otherwise be active in striving to change social and political conditions. Spectator sports ostensibly act as a tranquilizer which takes people's minds off their serious problems, and while people are in this state they are susceptible to manipulation by those in power. Sports fans are considered as inactive bystanders, whose passivity in this leisure activity contaminates other areas of their lives, such as their voting or purchasing behavior. According to this thesis, the sports fan is a pitiful creature who is tricked into being entertained by a trifling, time wasting activity.

Conflict theorists perceive this scenario as a Machiavellian scheme by the state to dominate the masses. While recreationists, like Nash (1938), concur that "spectatoritis" is a societal malady, they do not view it as a part of some ruling class master plan. To what extent is this criticism of the sport follower role valid? Research findings do not support the sport-as-an-opiate theory. Numerous studies have indicated that viewing sports events, either in person, or on film, has anything but a soporific effect on the spectators. The evidence does suggest, however, that watching sports events may increase a person's tendency toward aggressive behavior (Sloan, 1979). This finding is counter to the conflict theorists' notion that watching sports events "renders the spectator apathetic" (Guttman, 1981, p. xxvi).

Studies conducted in a variety of cultures have repeatedly shown that it is well educated males, from the middle and upper socioeconomic strata, who have the greatest interest in sport. If sport watching were an opiate, it would have the greatest effect on those who need it least. The disadvantaged individuals in society generally have the least interest in following sport.

Perhaps the best ammunition against the sport as an opiate thesis is that committed sports fans are much more physically active than the population at large (McPherson and Kenyon, 1975; Smith et al., 1981). For the keen sports fan an interest in following sport is often a stimulant to be physically active, rather than the anesthetic that conflict theorists submit. Not only are sports followers physically active, but they also claim that their interest in following sport contributes greatly to their quality of life (Smith et al., 1981). Conflict theorists contest this statement with the hackneyed "false consciousness" argument: the notion that sports fans are locked into the capitalist mentality to such an extent that they are being victimized. The problem with false consciousness as a concept is that it is untestable; there is no way to refute, or verify, its existence. It is akin to a religious faith: one is a believer or a non-believer; either way, it is a sterile scientific concept.

One final comment may help lay to rest the sport as an opiate metaphor. A true opiate is a depressant which lessens feelings of pain and discomfort. The opiate user experiences what Peele and Brodsky (1976, p. 45) call "total drive satiation," that is, "the user's appetite and sex drive are suppressed and his motivation to achieve, or his guilt at not achieving like-wise disappear." It is hardly appropriate to compare a sports fan to an opiate user. In the first instance, sex drive and appetite are not ordinarily reduced because one is a sport follower, and, secondly, sports followers experience their share of discomfort as well as pleasure. Over seventy percent of the respondents in a study by Smith et al. (1981), claimed that they had mood swings when their favorite team lost. It is difficult to support the assertion that following sport dampens a person's motivation to achieve. Profiles of committed sports fans indicate that they were already experiencing success in most areas of their life; they tended to be well educated, had good jobs, and were satisfied with their quality of life (Smith et al., 1981).

Sport as a Transmitter of Distorted Values

Zillman et al. (1979, p. 302) noted in the literature they surveyed that there was "nearly a universal condemnation of sport spectatorship." Most of the comments knocking sport spectating were moral or philosophical in nature, with no substantive proof to support them. The following thoughts are representative of this mode of thinking: viewing sport is a useless activity, a waste of time (Nash, 1938); sport watching appeals to man's coarser instincts, and renders one prone to violence (Beisser, 1969); sports spectators become inculcated with negative values because racism, sexism and cheating are pervasive in this setting (Hoch, 1972).

Each of these utterances has a grain of truth in it when taken to the extreme. Some fans are violent, some are glassy-eyed cretins who watch sport on T.V. for hours, and some negative behavior can be learned or reinforced by following sports. There is, however, no concrete evidence to indicate that any more than a small percentage of sports fans are affected in these ways.

Is sport a repository of negative values? Do sports fans learn to accept violence, sexism, hypocrisy and other evils that purportedly have infiltrated sport? We know that sport is certainly not immune to the social problems and injustices that infest other spheres of society, yet the questions of whether and to what extent particular values are conveyed by sport is paradoxical. On the one hand, scholars such as Zillman et al. (1979) say that sport settings are an effective model for teaching the virtues of fairness and justice to both players and fans. On the other hand, authors like Cullen (1974) and Vaz (1979) claim that following sport may produce individuals who are undisciplined and lacking in character. Edwards (1973) adds to the ambiguity by pointing out that there is no conclusive proof that following sport fosters either positive or negative values.

One recent study using a sample of committed male sports fans may help to resolve this stalemate. This study demonstrated that avid fans were strongly opposed to cheating or dirty play (Smith et al., 1981). When respondents were asked which sports figures they most admired, and why, they invariably selected outstanding athletes who personified traditional values. Athletes like Wayne Gretzky, Dr. J and Gordie Howe were mentioned frequently because of their dedication, leadership, modesty and community involvement. When respondents were asked if there were any prominent athletes that they especially disliked, they tended to choose athletes from two main categories: hockey goons and tennis brats. Athletes such as Bobby Clarke, John McEnroe and Ilie Nastase were seen as unsportsmanlike, immodest and undisciplined. This sample of sports fans claimed to be uplifted by the positive values displayed by their favorite athletes, while renouncing what they perceived as intemperate behavior in the athletes they disliked.

Sport as Lowbrow Culture

Nash (1938, p. 5) devised the term "spectatoritis" to describe " . . . all kinds of passive amusement, an entering into the handiest activity merely to escape boredom. Instead of expressing he is willing to sit back and have his leisure time pursuits slapped on to him like mustard plaster—external, temporary and, in the end, dust in the mouth."

Implicit in this statement is the value judgement that if the person could develop new standards or a higher level of taste he or she could be more fulfilled and could make a greater contribution to society. Cultural elitists recognize the existence of a hierarchy where there are at least three tiers. Sails (1964) labels these tiers as superior, mediocre and brutal. These are broad categories which represent degrees of quality based on aesthetic, intellectual and moral standards. Invariably sport is consigned to the lowest level because it is not seen by the elitists as a serious subject matter. Further, elitists do not believe that penetrating insights into the human condition can be made through sport, as is the case with other cultural forms.

Modern day cultural elitism can be traced back to Thorstein Veblen (Diggins, 1978). His famous put down of those who follow sport, "it marks an arrested development of man's moral nature," is still used as a battle cry by the tiny aristocracy that tries to impose these artificial standards on the masses. In capsule form, they view spectator sport as lowbrow culture because it is for the masses and therefore lacking in refinement. It follows then, that watching a sports event is several notches below so-called more discriminating leisure pursuits like visiting an art gallery, attending an opera, or listening to a symphony concert.

This line of thinking is merely a continuation of the mind-body dualism that has permeated the western intellectual tradition. This tradition seems *passé* now as it is taken for granted by most leisure behavior scholars that sport is a legitimate art form. Mahue (1962) was among the first to crystallize the similarities between a sport and an artistic performance. As he explained, both are products of leisure, both are forms of play, both engage an audience and are vehicles for escaping reality, and both have elements of grace, beauty and elegance.

We can exist without sport or art, but both are something we create to enrich our lives. They are forms of expression to be cultivated, appreciated, mastered and displayed. There seems to be little defense for separating them and even less for ranking one above the other. As a final point the following quote provides a trenchant summary of the position taken in this paper.

> In watching sports, I seek not so much a golden mean or even a silver one but will settle for something akin to a tarnished bronze mean. Achieving anything like real moderation here is now well beyond me. If I never watch another game, I have already seen many more than my share, but I fully intend to watch another game, and another and another and another. My justification is that doing so gives me great delight; my defense is that is causes no known harm, and, on occasion, I learn a thing or two from it (Aristides, 1985, p. 22).

REFERENCES

Angell, R. 1972. *The Summer Game.* New York: The Viking Press.

Aristides. 1985. *The Sporting Life.* The American Scholar.

Beisser, A. R. 1967. *The Madness in Sports.* New York: Appleton-Century-Crofts.

Boyer, R. & Savageau, D. 1985. *Places Rated Almanac.* Chicago: Rand-McNally and Co.

Cohen, S. & Taylor, L. 1978. *Escape Attempts: The Theory and Practice of Resistance to Everyday Life.* Harmonds-worth: Penquin Books Ltd.

Cozens, F. W. & Stumpf, F. S. 1953. *Sports in American Life.* Chicago: University of Chicago Press.

Cullen, F. T. 1974. Attitudes of players and spectators toward norm violation in ice hockey. *Perceptual and Motor Skills,* 3:38.

Diggins, J. P. 1978. *The Bard of Savagery: Thorstein Veblen and Modern Social Theory.* New York: The Seabury Press.

Durkeim, E. 1960. *The Division of Labor in Society*, (G. Simpson, Trans). Glencoe, IL: The Free Press.
Edwards, H. 1973. *Sociology of Sport*. Homewood, IL: Dorsey Press.
Elias, N. & Dunning, E. 1970. The quest for excitement in unexciting societies. In G. Luschen (Ed.), *The Cross Cultural Analysis of Sport and Games*. Champaign, IL: Stipes.
Epstein, J. 1985. Obsessed with sport, In D. L. Vanderwerken & S. K. Wertz (Eds.), *Sport Inside Out*. Fort Worth: Texas Christian University Press.
Figler, S. K. 1981. *Sport and Play in American Life*. Philadelphia: Saunders Publishing.
Guttmann, A. 1981. Introduction. In Rigauer, B., *Sport and Work*. New York: Columbia University Press.
Heinegg, P. 1985. Philosopher in the playground: Notes on the meaning of sport. In D. L. Vanderwerken & S. K. Wertz (Eds.), *Sports Inside Out*. Fort Worth: Texas Christian University Press.
Hoch, P. 1972. *Rip Off the Big Game*. New York: Doubleday Anchor Books.
Iso-Ahola, S. E. 1980. *The Social Psychology of Leisure and Recreation*. Dubuque, IA: Wm. C. Brown Company.
Klapp, O. E. 1972. *Currents of Unrest: An Introduction to Collective Behavior*. New York: Holt Rinehart and Winston, Inc.
Koppett, L. 1981. *Sport Illusion, Sports Reality*. Boston: Houghton Mifflin.
Loy, J. W., McPherson, Berry D., & Kenyon, G. 1978. *Sport and Social Systems*. Reading, MA: Addison-Wesley.
Mahue, R. 1962. Sport and culture. *International Journal of Adult and Youth Education* 15(4).
McPherson, B. D. 1975. Sport consumption and the economics of consumerism. In D. W. Ball & J. W. Loy (Eds.), *Sport and Social Order: Contributions to the Sociology of Sport*. Reading, MA: Addison-Wesley.
Nash, J. B. 1938. *Spectatoritis*. New York: A. S. Barnes.
Novak, M. 1976. *The Joy of Sports*. New York: Basic Books.
Offen, N. 1975. *God Save the Players*. Chicago: Playboy Press.
Peele, S. 1981. *How Much is Too Much*. Englewood Cliffs, NJ: Prentice Hall.
Peele, S. & Brodsky, A. 1976. *Love and Addiction*. Scorboroug, Ont: Signet.
Schrank, J. 1977. *Snap, Crackle and Popular Taste: The Illusion of Free Choice in America*. New York: Delta Books.
Sails, E. 1964. in N. Jacobs (Ed.), *Culture for the Millions? Mass Media in Modern Society*. Boston: Beacon Press.
Sloan, L. R. 1979. The function and impact of sports for fans: A review of theory and contemporary research. In J. H. Goldstein (Ed.), *Sports, Games, and Play: Social and Psychological Viewpoints*. Hillsdale, NJ: John Wiley & Sons.
Smith, G. J. 1979. *Sport and Social Integration*. Unpublished Ph.D. thesis, University of Alberta.
Smith, G. J., Patterson, B., Williams, T., & Hogg, J. 1981. A profile of the deeply committed sports fan. *Arena Review*, 5(2).
Stone, G. P. 1969. Some meanings of American sport: An extended view. In, G. Kenyon (Ed.), *Sociology of Sport*. Chicago: The Athletic Institute.
Vaz, E. W. 1979. Institutionalized rule violation in professional hockey: Perspective and control systems. In A. Yiannakis et al. (Eds.), *Sport Sociology: Contemporary Themes*. Dubuque, IA: Kendall Hunt.
Zillman, D., Sapolsky, B. S., & Bryant, J. 1979. The enjoyment of watching sports contests. In J. H. Goldstein (Ed.), *Sport Games, and Play: Social and Psychological Viewpoints*. Hillsdale, NJ: John Wiley & Sons.

2. *Conflict Theory and Deviance in Sport*

D. STANLEY EITZEN

The purpose of this essay is to elaborate the conflict paradigm with emphasis on its insights for understanding deviance in sport using the American case for illustrative purpose. To accomplish this the discussion is organized to: (1) enumerate the assumptions of the conflict perspective; (2) define deviance and establish its parameters as dictated by the conflict model; and (3) examine the structural roots of deviance in sport.*

THE ASSUMPTIONS OF CONFLICT THEORY

The conflict perspective has a long tradition in sociology with such early giants as Marx and Weber and later theorists such as Mills, Dahrendorf, Habermas, Collins, Chambliss, Domhoff, Zeitlin, and Useem. These theorists and others have provided a unique and important paradigm for understanding social structure, the social sources of social problems, and social change.

A problem in applying this perspective to social phenomena is that the vision and emphasis of conflict theorists vary considerably. Conflict theorists may be Marxists, neo-Marxists, or nonMarxists. Critical theorists from the Frankfurt school are included as are some phenomenologists. The analytical focus of conflict theorists may be on power structures, the role of institutions in legitimizing the status quo, how individuals are dominated through the shaping of their consciousnesses and world views, the connection between the personal troubles of individuals and the structure of society, or the efforts by the advantaged to retain power and the disadvantaged to increase theirs.

The conflict perspective, while not a unified theory, does have a unique way of interpreting social life that unites its somewhat diverse adherents. In this section I will present the general principles common to conflict theorists (taken in part from Collins, 1975; Chambliss, 1976;

SOURCE: *International Review for the Sociology of Sport* 23 (1988), pp. 193-203. Reprinted by permission of Institut für Soziologie, Universitat Hamburg.

Lenski, 1966; Reasons and Perdue, 1981; Johnson, 1981; Turner, 1974; Hansen, 1976; Bowles and Gintis, 1976; and Parenti, 1978).

Foremost the conflict perspective is sociological. The primary unit of analysis is social structure as a totality. The focus is not on individual behavior or social interaction but on patterns of action and networks of interaction in social organizations. The social organizations may be friendship groups, voluntary associations, or athletic teams, but typically conflict theorists concentrate on large scale social organizations such as bureaucracies and communities, and most often total societies and their institutions. To the extent that conflict theorists are concerned with individual behavior, it is always as these behaviors are affected by the conditions of social structure. Explanation, then, is never reduced to psychological variables but remains at the structural level, thereby retaining sociological purity.

A major premise of the conflict perspective is that conflict is endemic in social organizations resulting from social structure itself. The things that people desire such as property, prestige, and power are not distributed equally in social organizations, resulting in a fundamental cleavage between the advantaged and the disadvantaged (Marx and Engels, 1951; and Dahrendorf, 1959).

Related to the above is the assumption of conflict theorists that group interests are the basic elements of social life. Those persons in a similar social condition will organize to maximize their effectiveness in the struggles to preserve or promote vital group interests.

Next, there is the assumption that the powerful use their power to keep themselves in power. They are effective in controlling the powerless in three fundamental ways. Foremost, they claim a monopoly on the legitimate power including the use of force. Any threat to this power is considered illegitimate and the dissenters coerced to conform or face punishment. Next, directly or indirectly, the powerful control the decision-making apparatus. At the societal level, for example, they claim that the state and the law are instruments of the powerful (Wolfe, 1978). Finally, the powerful control the production and distribution of information thus achieving ideological conformity among members (Bagdikian, 1983). In Marx's memorable words, "The ideas of the ruling class are in every epoch the ruling ideas . . ." (1947:39). At the societal level, this ideological hegemony is accomplished by controlling the media, schools, churches, and other institutions (Ingham, 1976:246-247). Through the socialization process individuals are taught the cultural norms, values, and ideologies and thus to accept the status quo as normal and right, thereby preserving the interests of the dominant (Parenti, 1978; Bowles and Gintis, 1976). This last process is a most effective social control mechanism, even resulting in individuals defining conditions against their interests as appropriate—a condition that Marx called false consciousness (Marx, in Johnson, 1981:130-131).

Another assumption common to conflict theorists is that the inequities in wealth, power, and prestige plus the coercion and exploitation by the powerful aimed at the disadvantaged inevitably lead to conflicts between them. There is a dynamic tension between the haves and have nots with discrimination and power plays. A wide variety of street politics develop to change power and class relations. This tension and the resulting struggles shape the relations within the social organization and the direction and magnitude of social change within it (Chambliss and Ryther, 1975:55-56).

A prominent assumption of the conflict perspective is that the understanding of society or any of its institutions requires the analysis of the political economy. Power and wealth are inextricably intertwined and they dominate the rest of society. Social relations are the consequence of society's economic organization. Therefore, the analyst must consider the type of economy, the ways that members are organized for production and consumption, the distribution of material goods, the way decisions are made, and the distribution of power (Hoch, 1972:1-15). In short, although conflict theorists may be interested in a number of social institutions, they show a distinct preference in their description, analysis, and explanation for the two "master" institutions of the economy and the polity (Forcese and Richer, 1975:92-101).

Another assumption of the conflict perspective has to do with the consequences of social structure for individuals. Conflict theorists believe that the conditions of social organization, domination, and exploitation are not impersonal forces but have alienating, repressive, and frustrating effects on individuals. The important concept here is alienation, which refers to estrangement resulting from the lack of control over the conditions of one's own life (see, Marx 1962; and Horton, 1966). The individual may be alienated from work, the products of labor, from others, and from oneself. Relations of powerlessness and estrangement prevail in social organizations characterized by impersonal bureaucracy, undemocratic decision-making, class inequality, and where system needs supersede individual needs.

The final assumption of the conflict perspective is that human beings are the architects of social organization and history. Individuals as members of groups define their form and content. The extent to which the powerless are able to accomplish radical change depends on their understanding of the bias of the system and their ability to mobilize others in the same condition (Anderson and Gibson, 1978:7). Poor theory produces bad politics; however, pre-theoretical resistance and rebellion entail such destructive responses as crime, capitalist religion, petty tyranny in the home, or psychological anguish. Social conditions, then, are subject to the collective actions of human actors, which may have good or bad consequences (Flacks and Turkel, 1978:193-194).

TOWARD A DEFINITION OF DEVIANCE IN SPORT

Typically, sociologists define deviance as behavior that violates the norms. The rules are taken as morally correct and the focus is on what kinds of people deviate. Conflict theorists interpret deviance quite differently. They assume that the rules are instruments of the ruling class to maintain and perpetuate the existing social order and therefore its advantage (Quinney, 1974; 1977). Society's rules are believed to be not based on a consensus of the members but rather express the interests of those powerful who make the rules (McCaghy, 1985:88). Conflict theorists argue that the traditional view of taking the rules of the social order as the foundation of what is and what is not deviance, results in an analysis that supports the social order (Braithwaite and Wilson, 1978:4). To do so ignores the pernicious consequences of power, privilege, domination, and opposition.

Conflict theorists, then, do not focus on rule breakers but rather on rule makers. They do not focus on troublemakers but rather on the troubles caused by the macro structural forces of the larger society (Miller, 1976). Thus, conflict theory directs our attention to the covert, institutional, and normal activities in society that do physical and psychic harm (Liazos, 1972; Thio, 1973). The conflict theorist, then, focuses, for example, on the law, the quality of life, the economy, and institutional racism and sexism. We ask: How does the economy, the educational system, or the organization of sport really work? Who benefits from these arrangements and who does not (Eitzen, 1984b:11)?

Implicit in this discussion is the assumption by conflict theorists that there are objective conditions, regardless of the rules, that do harm and are therefore deviant (see Eitzen, 1984a; 1988). I believe that conflict theorists would tend to agree that the following principles should be applied to assess right or wrong behavior by organizations and individuals in the sports context.

1. Athletes must always be considered ends and not means. In other words, the outcome for the participants in sport is infinitely more important than the outcome of the contest, the money generated, or other extraneous consideration. In practice this means that athletes must be treated by coaches and administrators with dignity and respect; they must not be exploited; and they must not be demeaned or dehumanized. This means, further, that athletes must respect their opponents and not condone or engage in tactics of intimidation or willful injury. As philosopher Paul Weiss has argued: "Sports should begin and be carried out with a concern for the rights of others" (1969:180).

Obviously this principle is violated and deviance occurs when:

- Athletes are physically and mentally abused by coaches as Gary Shaw has documented in his description of the football program at the

University of Texas (1972), and as Feinstein (1986) described of the basketball program under Coach Bob Knight at Indiana University.
- Coaches encourage disrespect for opponents as the legendary Vince Lombardi did when he counseled "To play this game [football] you must have that fire in you, and nothing stokes that fire like hate" (quoted in Kramer, 1971:x).
- Athletes are expected by their superiors to use excessive violence to intimidate opponents and to injure them.
- Injured athletes are administered pain killing drugs so that they can return to action sooner than is prudent for their long-term health.
- Administrators and owners insist on using artificial turf regardless of the evidence that it increases the probability of injuries to athletes (Johnson, 1985).
- Especially strong teams schedule the especially weak to enhance their records and the weak do so to make money, although often at the expense of their players' health.
- College athletes are exploited through low pay, excessive demand on their time and energies, ignoring their educational goals, treating them as interchangeable parts, and by a system of rules and enforcements that punishes athletes more than those who coax them to break the rules (Sack and Thiel, 1985; Purdy, Eitzen, and Hufnagel, 1982; and Underwood, 1984).

2. *The competition must be fair.* The administration of leagues and the supervision of contests must be governed by rules applied impartially to all parties. There must be no taint of bias.

An implication of this fairness principle has to do with the nature of sport itself. Sport, by definition, is a competition involving physical prowess. Thus, athletic contests, true to the ideals of sport, must be decided only by differences in physical skills, motivation, strategy, and luck. This rules out those activities that give an athlete or team an unfair advantage such as cheating (Luschen, 1976) or the use of drugs to enhance performance artificially. Obvious, too, is that efforts to fix the outcome of athletic contests by gamblers and corrupt athletes violates the spirit of sport.

The temptation to cheat by individuals and sports organizations is great because the psychic and material rewards for winning are so great. For the athletes winning brings adulation, fame, records, and, depending on the sport, the possibility of great material gains. For coaches winning translates into celebrity status, contracts with shoe manufacturers, gifts from generous fans, television contracts, and ever higher salaries. For team owners winning increases gate receipts, brings invitations to lucrative tournaments and bowl games, and raises television revenues.

In short, sport is not a pristine activity in a utopia but rather one that occurs in a society where only the fittest survive. The doctrine of "winning is the only thing" means that the end justifies the means. As one football coach stated:

> Until three years ago we obeyed every rule and where did it get us? We finished last in the conference. Since that time there isn't a rule we haven't broken. And where are we now? This year we're playing in the Orange Bowl (quoted in Shea 1978:145).

One might argue that when unethical practices such as cheating are widespread, then they do not constitute deviance. If "everyone is doing it" how can it be deviance? Most big-time college sports programs break the rules in recruiting. Most offensive linemen illegally hold their opponents. Every major league baseball team probably has at least one pitcher who illegally applies a foreign substance to the baseball for an unfair advantage. And, most world class weight lifters use illegal anabolic steroids to increase bulk, strength, and muscle definition. Does a majority flaunting a rule negate it? Does the rationale that "everyone is doing it" justify it? Conflict theorists would argue that if a widespread practice in sport provides an unfair advantage in athletic contests, then it is deviant no matter how many are doing it. Rules intended to provide equity for all participants and teams are unconditional and thus constitute imperatives (Shea, 1978:149).

3. Participation, leadership, resources, and rewards must be based on achievement rather than ascribed characteristics. This means that sports activities must be characterized by equal access and equal opportunity. Thus ability coupled with motivation shall decide who participates rather than race, creed, gender, or social position. Sport, however, has a long and sordid history in violating this principle. The structures of class, gender, and racial privilege have always dominated sport with the rules guiding amateur sport and in the societal wide practices that denied equal opportunity in sport to women and people of color.

The battle for equality in sport continues. Unequal opportunity structures still deny access to the poor. Blacks remain virtually absent from some sports. Where blacks do participate and even dominate on the field in a sport, they are vastly underrepresented in leadership roles as players, coaches, and administrators (Eitzen and Sage, 1986). The patriarchal power structures in sport remain in power, resisting for the most part, efforts to achieve gender equality whether it be equal resources, equal and nonsexist media coverage, or whatever.

THE STRUCTURAL ROOTS OF DEVIANCE IN SPORT

How are we to understand the cheating, the exploitation, and the other forms of deviance so commonplace in sport? Obviously, there are some bad people who, when given an option, gravitate toward these behaviors, but this explanation is shallow and does not get at the source. The conflict approach to rule-breaking and other deviant acts locates them not in original sin, in the genes, or in the psyches of evil persons, but in the structural conditions of society and in the organization found therein.

Deviance in American sport does not occur in a vacuum. Deviance is rooted in the political economy of society. The insights of the conflict theorists within the Marxist tradition are especially instructive in aiding our understanding of deviance in sport. They argue that society in monopoly capitalism is dominated by two structural conditions—massification and commodification—both of which help to explain why individuals *qua* individuals and as decision-makers in organizations make deviant choices in all areas of social life including sport.

Massification refers to the transformed social relations in society resulting from a more specialized division of labor, large-scale commodity production and consumption, the widespread use of technology to increase industrial and administrative efficiency, and an increasingly authoritarian state (Hargreaves, 1982:6). In short, the massification of society is the consequence of the increased bureaucratization, rationalization, and routinization found therein. Sport reflects this as it has become increasingly technocratic, specialized, controlled by elites, and impersonal. The apt descriptions of contemporary sport as work, sport as big business, sport as spectacle (Hughes and Coakley, 1984), and sport as power politics suggest how sport mirrors the massification of the larger society.

Two related elements of massification that are manifested in sport increase the likelihood of deviant behavior by the participants. As the tasks in sport become more complex and specialized, the anonymity of the participants increases. This even occurs on a single team, as in football, for example, the offensive and defensive units often practice separately and meet independently with their specialized coaches. Social contact is minimized and the norms of reciprocity that are essential to community are evaded even among these members of the same team (Young and Massey, 1980:88).

Anonymity is also enhanced among sports participants as their interactions are short-term and episodic (Young, 1972). Interactions are segmentalized so that participants rarely encounter each other in different roles. Thus, coaches and players, opponents, and other actors in the sports drama evade knowing each other as whole persons. Such segmentalized and impersonal relationships in a competitive setting such as in sports fosters a “me-first/goals regardless of the means” attitude in individuals. Thus, cheating, manipulation, fraud, exploitation, and excessive violence flourish.

Commodification refers to the social, psychological, and cultural uses of social structures for the commercial needs of advanced monopoly capital (Young, 1984:7). The human consequences of commodification are dramatic. Human beings are objects–interchangeable parts–in their role as workers in the production process and they are objects to be manipulated in their roles as consumers. In the sports realm, owners and administrators allow profit maximizing decisions to take precedence over humane considerations. Sports enterprises produce what they can sell and sports spectaculars attract customers. Thus, sports performances become activities of dis-play.

When sport becomes an activity of *dis*-play, it destroys what is valuable in sport altogether. Sport becomes transformed into a spectacle, played for and shaped into a form which will be "consumed" by spectators searching for titillating entertainment Sewart, 1981:49).

Violence attracts spectators even more and is therefore encouraged. Sport, because of its attractiveness to so many in mass society, is a particularly effective vehicle for advertising. Many athletes, male and female, are objectified as sex objects to sell products. As Brohm has put it: "They [athletes] are very often advertising 'sandwich-board' men" (1978:176). Today's top-level athletes, whether so-called amateur or professional, are workers who sell their labor power–their ability to draw crowds–to employers. Thus, players are purchased, bought, and sold for profit. So, too, are franchises leaving fans feeling abused and used. As a final example, athletes are treated like machines, as instruments, for producing victories and income. This is seen in the total mobilization of the athletes to produce maximum performance.

Every sport now involves a fantastic *manipulation of human robots* by doctors, psychologists, bio-chemists and trainers. The "manufacturing of champions" is no longer a craft but an industry, calling on specialized laboratories, research institutes, training camps and experimental sport centers. Most top-level athletes are reduced to the status of more or less voluntary guinea pigs. "Hopefuls" are spotted young, the less talented are methodically weeded out and those that remain are then systematically oriented according to their potential . . . The specialists in this sporting Gulag stop at no human sacrifice in their drive to push back the limits of human capacity and transcend biological barriers (Brohm, 1978:18-19).

In short, sport and its participants are like any other commodity– "something to be marketed, packaged, and sold . . . The consequence of the process of commodification is that the multifarious forms of human activity lose their unique and distinct qualities to the principles of the market" (Sewart, 1981:47-48).

Under the social conditions resulting from the massification and commodification of sport, coaches, athletes, and spectators are increasingly objects to be manipulated and exploited. Winning is the all consuming goal and participants will be judged exclusively in terms of instrumental rationality. The unsuccessful will be replaced, just as the defective parts in a machine. Under these circumstances opponents *are* enemies. So, too, are teammates since they compete among themselves for starting positions. Under these conditions the human actors view themselves as objects and others as objects to be used.

In viewing himself as an object, the worker increasingly relates to other people as objects; he is alienated from the species whereby instead of celebrating his existence through meaningful interaction, he is isolated, asocial and ultimately, like the market within which he exists, amoral (Sugden, 1981:59).

Under these conditions, then, the actors are alienated individuals who are exploited and see others as means to their ends. Thus, the common *modus operandi* of "whatever it takes to win."

Organizational deviance. We have seen that conflict theory points to the structural sources of deviance. In American society the rewards for winning are so great that coaches, athletes, and others often use and abuse others for personal gain. But deviance is not just the behavior of unethical individuals. Organizations, too, may be deviant (Santomier et al., 1980; Santomier and Cautilli, 1985). Some deviant acts are perpetrated by individuals concerned with achieving organizational goals. The owners of professional baseball, for example, once conspired to keep the sport racially segregated. Throughout their histories professional leagues have worked to retain their power over athletes through the reserve clause, Rozelle Rule, the player draft, and other unfair mechanisms. Some universities have repeatedly been found guilty of "buying" athletes regardless of the personnel. When Clemson University was found guilty of multiple violations, its president, William Atchely, wanted to clean up the program. The Board of Regents fired him for advocating such a plan.

The controlling body of intercollegiate sport, the National Collegiate Athletic Association (NCAA) is, in many respects, a deviant organization. The NCAA has monopolistic control over big-time college athletic programs. Most significantly, this monopoly is used to the one-sided detriment of the worker-athletes and to the benefit of the member schools. Four examples forcefully make this point: (1) scholarship athletes make a four-year commitment to a school, yet the schools only make a commitment to the athletes on a year-to-year basis; (2) athletes must wait a year to play if they change schools even if the coach they signed to play for has left the institution; (3) athletes are paid only for room, board, tuition, and books yet they may be in a sport generating many millions of dollars to the school; and (4) by insisting that an athletic scholarship is not pay, the NCAA has helped keep injured athletes from receiving workers' compensation (Porto, 1985).

The NCAA is also deviant, I would argue, when it resists government regulations that would move toward gender equality in school sports. The NCAA maintains that big-time athletic programs are revenue-producing businesses and that sacrificing these revenues for gender equality is bad business. The NCAA argues that the schools are businesses but the athletes generating the income are not workers but amateurs engaged in an educational experience. Somehow this twisted logic is permitted by its member institutions to justify the continued second class status of women's sports (Sack, 1981).

To conclude, this essay has demonstrated how sport is a microcosm of society and how the origins of deviance in sport are structural. The conflict perspective, however, does not stop with these insights. This theoretical stance demands that we *not* accept "the way things are" (Birrell, 1984). Rather, we must work to improve the human condition and this requires not reform but the transformation of society and its institutions, in this case the institution of sport.

NOTE

*Portions of this paper are adapted from Eitzen (1981a; 1984a; 1984b; and 1988).

REFERENCES

Anderson, Charles H. and Jeffry R. Gibson, 1978: *Toward a New Sociology*, third edition. Homewood, IL: Dorsey.

Bagdikian, Ben, 1983: *The Media Monopoly*. Boston: Beacon Press.

Birrell, Susan, 1984: "Separation as an Issue in Women's Sport," *Arena Review* 8, (July):21-29.

Bowles, Samuel and Herbert Gintis, 1976: *Schooling in Capitalist America*. New York: Basic Books.

Braithwaite, John and Paul R. Wilson, 1978: "Pervs, Pimps, and Powerbrokers," *Two Faces of Deviance*, Paul R. Wilson and John Braithwaite (eds.). Queensland, Australia: University of Queensland Press, pp. 1-12.

Brohm, Jean-Marie, 1978: *Sport: A Prison of Measured Time*. London: Ink Links.

Chambliss, William J., 1976: "Functional and Conflict Theories of Crime: The Heritage of Emile Durkheim and Karl Marx," *Whose Law? What Order? A Conflict Approach to Criminology*, William J. Chambliss and Milton Mankoff (eds.). New York: John Wiley & Sons, pp. 1-28.

1984: "Crime and Conflict Theory," *Criminal Law in Action* second edition. New York: John Wiley & Sons, pp. 1-9.

Chambliss, William J. and Thomas E. Ryther, 1975: *Sociology*. New York: McGraw-Hill.

Collins, Randall, 1975: *Conflict Sociology*. New York: Academic Press.

Dahrendorf, Ralf, 1958: "Out of Utopia: Toward a Reorientation of Sociological Analysis," *American Journal of Sociology* 64:115-127.

1959: *Class and Class Conflict in Industrial Society*. Stanford, CA: Stanford University Press.

Eitzen, D. Stanley, 1981a: "Athletes and Higher Education: A Conflict Perspective," paper presented at the annual meeting of the North American Society for the Sociology of Sport, Fort Worth, Texas (November, 12-15).

1981b: "Sport and Deviance," *Handbook of Social Science of Sport*, Gunther R. F. Luschen and George H. Sage (eds.). Champaign, IL: Stipes.

1984a: "Teaching Social Problems: Implications of the Objectivist-Subjectivist Debate," *Society for the Study of Social Problems Newsletter* 16(Fall):10-12.
1984b: "Conflict Theory and the Sociology of Sport," *Arena Review* 8 (November):45-54.
1988: "Ethical Dilemmas in Sport," *Journal of Sport and Social Issues* (forthcoming).
Eitzen, D. Stanley and George H. Sage, 1986: *Sociology of North American Sport*, third edition. Dubuque, IA: Wm. C. Brown.
Feinstein, John, 1986: *A Season on the Brink*. New York: Macmillan.
Forcese, Dennis and Stephen Richer, 1975: *Issues in Canadian Society*. Scarborough, Ontario: Prentice Hall.
Flacks, Richard and Gerald Turkel, 1978: "Radical Sociology: The Emergence of Neo-Marxian Perspectives in U.S. Sociology," *Annual Review of Sociology* 4:193-238.
Hasen, Donald A., 1976: *An Invitation to Critical Sociology*. New York: Free Press.
Hargreaves, John, 1982: "Theorizing Sport," *Culture and Ideology*, John Hargreaves (ed.). London: Routledge & Kegan Paul.
Hoch, Paul, 1972: *Rip Off the Big Game*. Garden City, New York: Doubleday.
Horton, John, 1966: "Order and Conflict Theories of Social Problems in Competing Ideologies," *American Journal of Sociology* 71 (May):701-713.
Hughes, Robert and Jay J. Coakley, 1984: "Mass Society and the Commercialization of Sport," *Sociology of Sport Journal* 1(1):57-63.
Ingham, Alan G., 1976: "Sport and the 'New Left'; Some Reflections Upon Opposition without Praxis," *Social Problems in Athletics*, Daniel M. Landers (ed.). Urbana: University of Illinois Press, pp. 238-248.
Johnson, William Oscar, 1985: "The Tyranny of Phony Grass," *Sports Illustrated* 63 (August 12):34-44.
Johnston, Doyle Paul, 1981: *Sociological Theory*. New York: John Wiley & Sons.
Kramer, Jerry (ed.), 1981: *Lombardi: Winning Is the Only Thing*. New York: Pocket Books.
Lenski, Gerhard E., 1966: *Power and Privilege: A Theory of Social Stratification*. New York: McGraw-Hill.
Liazos, Alexander, 1972: "The Poverty of Sociology of Deviance: Nuts, Sluts, and 'Preverts,'" *Social Problems* 20 (Summer):103-120.
Luschen, Gunther R. F., 1976: "Cheating in Sport," *Social Problems in Athletics*, Daniel M. Landers (ed.). Urbana: University of Illinois Press, pp. 67-77.
Marx, Karl, 1947: *The German Ideology*. New York: International Publishers (originally published in 1846).
1963: "Economic and Philosophical Manuscripts," *Karl Marx Early Writings*, T. B. Bottomore (ed.). New York: McGraw-Hill.
Marx, Karl and Friedrich Engels, 1951: *The Communist Manifesto*, volume 1. Moscow: Foreign Languages Publishing House (originally published in 1848).
McCaghy, Charles H., 1985: *Deviant Behavior: Crime, Conflict, and Interest Groups*, second edition. New York: Macmillan.
Miller, S. M., 1976: "The Political Economy of Social Problems: From the Sixties to the Seventies," *Social Problems* 24(October):131-141.
Parenti, Michael, 1978: *Power and the Powerless*. New York: St. Martin's Press.
Porto, Brian L., 1985: "Athletic Scholarships as Contracts of Employment: The Rensing Decisions and the Future of College Sports," *Journal of Sport and Social Issues* 9 (Winter/Spring):20-37.
Purdy, Dean A., D. Stanley Eitzen, and Rick Hufnagel, 1982: "Are Athletes Also Students?" *Social Problems* 29 (April):439-447.
Quinney, Richard, 1974: *Critique of Legal Order*. Boston: Little, Brown.

1977: *Class, State and Crime.* New York: David McKay.

Reasons, Charles E. and William D. Perdue, 1981: *The Ideology of Social Problems.* Sherman Oaks, CA: Alfred.

Sack, Allen L., 1981: "College Sports Must Choose: Amateur or Pro?" *The New York Times* (May 3):2S.

Sack, Allen L., and Robert Thiel, 1985: "College Basketball and Role Conflict: A National Survey," *Sociology of Sport Journal* 2 (September):195-209.

Santomier, James P. and Peter Cantelli, 1985: "Controlling Deviance in Intercollegiate Athletics," *Sport and Higher Education*, Donald Chu, Jeffrey O. Segrave, and Beverly J. Becker (eds.). Champaign, IL: Human Kinetics, pp. 397-403.

Santomier, James P., William G. Howard, Wendy L. Pilz, and Thomas J. Romance, 1980: "White Sock Crime: Organizational Deviance in Intercollegiate Athletics," *Journal of Sport and Social Issues* 4 (Fall/Winter):26-32.

Sewart, John J., 1981: "The Rationalization of Modern Sport: The Case of Professional Football," *Arena Review* 5 (September):45-53.

Shaw, Gary, 1972: *Meat on the Hoof: The Hidden World of Texas Football.* New York: St. Martin's Press.

Shea, E. J., 1978: *Ethical Decisions in Physical Education and Sport.* Springfield, IL: Charles C. Thomas.

Sugden, J. P., 1981: "The Sociological Perspective: The Political Economy of Violence in American Sport," *Arena Review* 5 (February):57-62.

Thio, Alex, 1973: "Class Bias in the Sociology of Deviance," *The American Sociologist* 8 (February):1-12.

Turner, Jonathan H., 1974: *The Structure of Sociological Theory.* Homewood, IL: Dorsey.

Underwood, John, 1984: *Spoiled Sport.* Boston: Little Brown.

Weiss, Paul, 1969: *Sport: A Philosophic Inquiry.* Carbondale, IL: Southern Illinois University Press.

Whitson, David J., n.d.: "Research Methodology in Sport Sociology. *CAHPER Sociology of Sport Monograph Series.* Ottawa, Canada: CAHPER.

Wolfe, Alan, 1978: *The Seamy Side of Democracy: Repression in America.* New York.

Young, T. R., 1972: *New Sources of Self.* London: Pergamon Press.

1984: "The Sociology of Sport: A Critical Overview," *Arena Review* 8 (November): 1-14.

Young, T. R. and Garth Massey, 1980: "The Dramaturgical Society: A Macro-Analytic Approach to Dramaturgical Analysis," *Qualitative Sociology* 1(2): 78-98.

3. *Sport in Society: An Inspiration or an Opiate?*

JAY J. COAKLEY

People in American society generally see sport in a very positive way. Not only is sport assumed to provide a training ground for the development of desirable character traits and good citizens, but it is also believed to reaffirm a commitment to societal values emphasizing competition, success, and playing by the rules.

Does sport really do all these things? Is it as beneficial and healthy as people believe? These questions have generated considerable disagreement among sport sociologists. It seems that most of us in the sociology of sport are quick to agree that sport is a microcosm of society—that it mirrors the values, structure, and dynamics of the society in which it exists (Eitzen and Sage, 1978). However, we often disagree when it comes to explaining the consequences or the functions of sport in society. This disagreement grows out of the fact that sport sociologists have different theoretical conceptions of how society works. Therefore, they differ on their ideas about how sport functions within society. A description of the two major theoretical approaches used in the sociology of sport will illustrate what I mean.

THE FUNCTIONALIST APPROACH

Sport Is an Inspiration

The majority of sport sociologists assume that society is most accurately conceptualized in terms of a *systems model.* They see society as an organized system of interrelated parts. The system is held together and operates because (1) its individual members generally endorse the same basic values and (2) the major parts in the system (such as the family, education, the economy, government, religion, and sport) all fit together in mutually supportive and constructive ways. In sociology, this theoretical approach is called *functionalism.*

SOURCE: Excerpt from *Sport in Society: Issues and Controversies*, 2nd ed., (St. Louis: C. V. Mosby, 1982), pp. 16-30.

When the functionalists describe and analyze how a society, community, school, or any other system works, they are primarily concerned with how the parts of that system are related to the operation of the system as a whole. For example, if American society is the system being studied, a person using a functionalist approach would be concerned with how the American family, the economy, government, education, religion, and sport are all related to the smooth operation of the society as a whole. The analysis would focus on the ways in which each of these subparts of society help to keep the larger system going.

The functionalists also assume that a social system will continue to operate smoothly only if the four following things happen:

1. The members of the system must learn the values and the norms (i.e., the general rules or guidelines for behavior) that will lead them to want to do what has to be done to keep the system in operation. This process of shaping the feelings, thoughts, and actions of individuals usually creates some frustration and tension. Therefore, there must also be some channels through which people can let off steam in harmless ways.
2. The system must contain a variety of social mechanisms that bring people together and serve as catalysts for building the social relationships needed for coordinated action. Without a certain degree of cohesion, solidarity, and social integration, coordinated action would be impossible and the social system would stop functioning smoothly.
3. The members of the system must have the opportunity to learn what their goals should be within the system and the socially approved ways of achieving those goals.
4. The social system must be able to adjust to the demands and challenges of the external environment. It must have ways of handling and coping with changes in the social and physical environments so that it can continue to operate with a minimal amount of interference and disruption.

According to those using a functionalist approach, these four "system needs" are the basic minimum requirements for the smooth operation of any social system whether it be a society, community, club, large corporation, or neighborhood convenience store (Parsons and Smelser, 1965). These four basic system requirements are referred to as:

1. The need for pattern maintenance and tension management.
2. The need for integration.
3. The need for goal attainment.
4. The need for adaptation.

When you start with a functionalist conception of how society works, the answer to the question of what sport does for a society or community is likely to emphasize the ways in which sport satisfies the four basic needs of the social system. A brief review of how sport is related to each of these needs is a good way to summarize this approach.

PATTERN MAINTENANCE AND TENSION MANAGEMENT

The functionalists generally conclude that sport provides learning experiences that reinforce and extend the learning occurring in other settings. In other words, sport serves as a backup or a secondary institution for primary social institutions such as the family, school, and church. Through sport people learn the general ways of thinking, feeling, and acting that make them contributing members of society. They become socialized so that they fit into the mainstream of American life and therefore reaffirm the stability and continued operation of our society (Schafer, 1976).[1]

The pattern maintenance function of sport applies to spectators as well as those who are active participants. Sport is structured so that those who watch or play learn the importance of rules, hard work, efficient organization, and a well-defined authority structure. For example, sociologist Gunther Luschen (1967) shows how sport helps to generate the high levels of achievement motivation necessary to sustain the commitment to work required in industrialized countries. Along similar lines, Kleiber and Kelly (1980) have reviewed a number of studies concluding that participation in competitive games helps children learn how to handle adult roles in general and competitive relationships in particular. In fact, some recent discussions of sex roles have suggested that women may be at a disadvantage in business settings partly because they have not been involved in competitive sports to the same degree as their male counterparts (Hennig and Jardim, 1977; Harragan, 1977; Lever, 1978).

Sport has also been thought to serve tension management functions in society by providing both spectators and participants with an outlet for aggressive energy (Vanderzwaag, 1972; Proctor and Eckard, 1976; Marsh, 1978). This idea prompted two widely respected sociologists, Hans Gerth and C. Wright Mills (1954), to suggest the following: "Many mass audience situations, with their 'vicarious' enjoyments, serve psychologically the unintended function of channeling and releasing otherwise unplacable emotions. Thus, great volumes of aggression are 'cathartically' released by crowds of spectators cheering their favorite stars of sport—and jeering the umpire." The idea that sport may serve tension management functions is complex and controversial.

INTEGRATION

A functionalist approach also emphasizes how sport serves to bring people together and provide them with feelings of group unity, a sense of social identification, and a source of personal identity. In short, a functionalist explains how sport creates and reaffirms the linkages between people so that cooperative action is possible. Luschen (1967) outlines how this occurs in the following: "Since sport is also structured along such societal subsystems as different classes, males, urban areas, schools, and communities, it functions for integration. This is obvious also in spectator sport, where the whole country or community identifies with its representatives in a contest. Thus, sport functions as a means of integration, not only for the actual participants, but also for the represented members of such a system."

Sport has been seen to serve integration functions in countries other than the United States also. For example, others have discussed how sport contributes to unity and solidarity in Switzerland (Albonico, 1967), France (Bouet, 1969), Germany (Brockman, 1969), China (Chu and Segrave, 1979), the Soviet Union (Riordan, 1977), and Brazil (Lever, 1981).

Andrzej Wohl (1970), a sport sociologist from Poland, has argued that competitive sport could not exist if it recognized "local, nation or racial barriers or differences of world outlook." He points out that sport is so widely used to serve integration functions that it "is no secret for anybody any more."

GOAL ATTAINMENT

Someone using a functionalist approach is likely to see sport as legitimizing and reinforcing the primary goals of the system as well as the means to be used to achieve those goals. In the United States, for example, sport is organized so that successful outcomes are heavily emphasized, and success is generally defined in terms of scores and win-loss records. Just as in the rest of society, the proper way to achieve success in sport is through a combination of competition, hard work, planning, and good organization. Therefore, the sport experience not only serves to legitimize the way things are done in other sectors of society but also it prepares people for participation in those sectors.

In other countries, different aspects of the sport experience are emphasized so that it serves as a supportive model for their goal priorities and the proper means to achieve goals. Capitalist countries are more likely to emphasize output and competition in sport while socialist countries will be more likely to emphasize cooperation and the development of a spirit of collectivism (Morton, 1963). Sport seems to be amazingly flexible in this respect; it has been shaped and defined in a variety of ways to serve goal attainment functions in many different social systems. This point has been developed and explained by Edwards (1973): "Most sports have few, if any, intrinsic and invariably social or political qualities . . . and those qualities which such activities do possess are sufficiently 'liquid' to fit comfortably within many diverse and even conflicting value and cultural traditions."

ADAPTATION

In preindustrial societies it is easy to see how sport serves a system's need for adaptation. Since survival in such societies depends on the development and use of physical skills, participation in games and sport activities is directly related to coping with the surrounding environment (Luschen, 1967). Dunlap (1951) makes this case in her study of the Samoans. Additionally, she found that the "factors of physical strength and endurance which were essential for success in their games were also essential for success in their wars."

In industrial societies, it is more difficult to see how sport satisfies the adaptation needs of the social system. However, in two articles on the functions of sport, Wohl (1970, 1979) has suggested that it is in this area that sport makes its most important contributions. He points out that in any society with technologically advanced transportation and communications systems, sport becomes the only sphere of activities in which physical skills are developed and perfected. Through sport it is possible to measure and extend the range of human motor skills and to adapt them to the environments we have created. Without sport it would be difficult to maintain a population's physical well-being at the levels necessary to keep an industrial society operating efficiently. Sport is so crucial in this regard that Wohl (1979) calls for the use of all the sport sciences to plan and control its development. In this way the contributions of sport to satisfying adaptation needs could be maximized.

In concluding our review of the functionalist approach to sport it should be pointed out that social scientists are not the only ones who use such an approach in explaining the relationship between sport and society. Most people view society and the role of sport in terms very similar to those used by the functionalists. They look for the ways in which sport contributes to the communities in which they live. They see sport providing valuable lessons for their children and opportunities for themselves to release the tensions generated by a job or other life events. Sport gives them something to talk about with strangers as well as friends and it provides occasions for outings and get-togethers. Many people believe that sport can serve as a model of the goals we should strive for and the means we should use in trying to achieve those goals. Finally, sport is viewed as a healthy activity for individuals as well as the entire country; it can extend life and keep us physically prepared to defend our country in case of war.

These beliefs about sport have led to policy decisions on Little League programs, the funding of high school and college athletics, the support of professional teams and the Olympic movement, the development of physical education programs in schools, and the use of sport activities in military academies to prepare young men and women to be "combat ready." The widespread acceptance and the pervasive influence of the functionalist approach make it necessary for us to be aware of its weaknesses.

Limitations of the Functionalist Approach

Using a functionalist approach to answer the question of how sport is related to society can provide us with valuable insights, but it is not without its problems. Such an approach tends to emphasize the positive aspects of sport. This is because those using it often assume that if some part or component of a social system has existed for a long time, it is likely to be contributing to the system in a favorable way; if it were not, it would have been eliminated or gradually faded out of existence on its own. Since sport has been around for some time and is an increasingly significant component of our social system, most functionalists conclude that it *does* make positive contributions to society. This conclusion leads them to ignore or underemphasize the negative aspects of sport. After all, it is also possible that sport could distort values and behavioral guidelines (norms). Sport could destroy motivation, create frustration and tensions, and disrupt social integration. It could impede goal attainment and interfere with methods of coming to terms with the external social and physical environment by diverting a group's attention away from crucial personal and social issues.

Another problem with the functionalist approach is that it is based on the assumption that the needs of the individual parts of a social system overlap with the needs of the system as a whole. The possibility of internal differences or basic conflicts of interests within a social system is inconsistent with the assumption that any system is held together by a combination of common values and an interrelated, mutually supportive set of parts. If the needs of the total system were in serious conflict with the needs of the individual parts, the validity of the functionalist approach would be called into question.

This is one of the major weaknesses of functionalism. Although we may agree that many people in our society hold similar values, can we also argue that the structure of American society serves the needs of everyone equally? It would be naive to assume that it does. In fact, it may even frustrate the needs of certain groups and individuals and generate conflict. To conclude that sport exists because it satisfies the needs of the total system overlooks the possibility that sport may benefit some segments of the population more than others. Furthermore, if the interests of some groups within the system are met at the expense of others, the consequences of sport could be described as positive only if you were viewing them from the perspective of those privileged groups. Unfortunately, a functionalist approach often leads to underemphasizing differences of interests as well as the possibility of exploitation and coercion within the social system. It also leads to ignoring the role of sport in generating conflict and maintaining a structure in which at least some relationships are based on exploitation and coercion.

In sociology the theoretical approach that calls attention to these unpleasant characteristics of social systems and how sport is related to them is called conflict theory.

CONFLICT THEORY

Sport Is an Opiate

Conflict theory is not as popular as functionalism. It does not fit with what most people think about how society is organized and how it operates. Instead of viewing society as a relatively stable system of interrelated parts held together by common values and consensus, conflict theorists view it as an ever-changing set of relationships characterized by inherent differences of interests and held together by force, coercion, and subtle manipulation. They are concerned with the distribution and use of power rather than with common values and integration. Their analysis of society focuses on processes of change rather than on what is required for a social system to continue operating smoothly.

Most beginning students in the sociology of sport are not very receptive to the use of conflict theory in explaining the relationship between sport and society. They say that it is too negativistic and critical of our way of life and the institution of sport. They prefer the functionalist approach because it fits closely with what they have always believed and because it has implications that do not threaten the structure of either society or sport. My response is that although functionalism is useful, it can often lead us to look at the world unrealistically and ignore a dimension of the relationship between sport and society that should be considered. Neither American society nor sport is without problems. Awareness and understanding of these problems require critical thought, and conflict theory is a valuable stimulus for such thought.

Conflict theory is based primarily on an updated revision of the ideas of Karl Marx. Those who use it generally focus their attention on capitalist countries such as the United States but it has also been used to describe and understand any social system in which individuals are perceived as not having significant control over their own lives. According to many conflict theorists this includes capitalist systems along with fascist or military/police regimes and socialist systems controlled by centralized, bureaucratic governments (Brohm, 1978).

In order to understand how conflict theorists view the role of sport in society, we will start with a simplified description of capitalism and how contemporary organized sport fits into its structure. Any capitalist system requires the development of a highly efficient work process through which an increasing number of consumer goods can be mass produced. Industrial bureaucracies have been created to meet this need. This means that in the interest of efficiency and financial profit, workers end up performing highly specialized and alienating jobs. These jobs are generally in the production, marketing and sales, or service departments of large organizations where the workers themselves have little control over what they do and experience little or no excitement or satisfaction in their day-to-day work lives. This situation creates a need for escape and for tension-excitement in their nonwork lives. Within capitalist systems, people are subtly manipulated to seek the satisfaction they need through consumerism and mass entertainment spectacles. Sport is such societies has emerged as a major form of entertainment spectacle as well as a primary context for the consumption of material goods. Additionally, the structure of sport is so much like the structure of work organizations and capitalist society as a whole that it serves to stabilize the system and promote the interests of people who are in positions of power.

Conflict theorists see sport as a distorted form of physical exercise that has been shaped by the needs of a capitalist system of production. A specific example of how sport has developed in this manner has been outlined by Goodman (1979) in an analysis of the history of playground and street life in one of New York City's working class neighborhoods. Goodman shows how the spontaneous, free-flowing play activities of children in New York were literally banned from the streets in order to force participation in organized playground programs. The original goals of the playgrounds are best described through the words of one of the influential playground supervisors early in this century (Chase, 1909): "We want a play factory; we want it to run at top speed on schedule time, with the best machinery and skilled operatives. We want to turn out the maximum product of happiness." Thus the organized activities and sport programs became a means for training the children of immigrants to fit into a world of work founded on time schedules, the stopwatch, and production-conscious supervisors.

For the parents of these children the playground and recreation center programs had a different goal. It was clearly explained in the following section of a 1910 New York City Department of Education report (cited in Goodman, 1979): "The great problem confronting the recreation center principal and teachers is the filling of the leisure time of the working men and women with a combination of recreation and athletic activities which will help make their lives more tolerable." As Goodman points out, the purpose of the centers was to provide controlled leisure activities to take the people's minds off the exploitation and poor working conditions experienced in their jobs. The supervised activities were meant to pacify the workers so that they could tolerate those conditions and continue contributing to the growth of the economy.

When they needed to be replaced, the organized playground activities would have prepared their children to take their roles.

Other conflict theorists have not limited their focus to a local community setting. They have talked in more general terms about the relationship between sport and society. Their discussions emphasize four major aspects of the role of sport. These include:

1. How sport generates and intensifies alienation
2. How sport is used by the state and the economically powerful as a tool for coercion and social control
3. How sport promotes commercialism and materialism
4. How sport encourages nationalism, militarism, and sexism

The following sections summarize the discussions of the conflict theorists on each of these four topics.

ALIENATION

According to the conflict theorists sport serves to alienate people from their own bodies. Sport focuses attention on time and output rather than on the individual. Standardized rules and rigid structure destroy the spontaneity, freedom, and inventiveness characteristic in play. Jean-Marie Brohm (1978), a French sport sociologist, explains how sport affects the connection between athletes and their bodies: "[In sport the body is] experienced as an object, an instrument, a technical means to an end, a reified factor of output and productivity, in short, as a machine with the job of producing maximum work and energy." In other words, sport creates a setting in which the body is no longer experienced as a source of self-fulfillment and pleasure in itself. Pleasure and fulfillment depend on *what is done* with the body. Satisfaction is experienced only if the contest is won, if a record is set or a personal goal achieved, and if the body performs the way it has been trained to perform. When this happens sport becomes a "prison of measured time" and alienates athletes from their own bodies (Brohm, 1978).

Mumford (1934) extends the idea of alienation even further. In a classic analysis of contemporary civilization he describes the sport stadium as an "industrial establishment producing running, jumping or football playing machines." Building on this notion conflict theorists argue that commercialized sport (any sport in which profits are sought) reduces athletes to material commodities (Hoch, 1972). Thus the body becomes a tool not only for the setting of records but also for generating financial profits for nonparticipants—from team owners and tournament sponsors to concession operators and parking lot owners. The athletes may also benefit, but their rewards require them to forfeit the control of their bodies and become "gladiators" performing for the benefit of others.

Conflict theorists have pointed to the use of drugs and computer technology in sport as support for their analysis of how sport affects the definition of an athlete's body (Brohm, 1978). When the body is seen as an instrument for setting records and the improvement of times is defined as the measure of human progress, then the use of drugs, even harmful drugs, will be seen as a valuable aid in the quest for achievement. Computer technology used to analyze and improve the body's productive capacity further separates the physical act of sport participation from the subjective experience of the athlete. Just as on the assembly line, efficiency comes to be the major concern in sport and the worker (athlete) loses control over the means of production (the body).

COERCION AND SOCIAL CONTROL

Goodman's (1979) study of the working class neighborhood in New York City led him to conclude that sport in that city was used as a means of making the lives of shop workers more tolerable. Other conflict theorists expand this notion and describe sport as an opiate interfering with an awareness of social problems and subverting collective attempts to solve those problems. According to Hoch (1972), sport perpetuates problems by providing people with either "(1) a temporary high . . . which takes their minds off problem[s] for a while but does nothing to deal with [them]; or (2) a distorted frame of reference or identification which encourages them to look for salvation through patently false channels."

Hoch's description of the personal and social impact of sport is similar to Marx's description of religion in society. To Marx, religion focuses attention on the supernatural, provides people with a psychological lift, and emphasizes improvement through changing the self rather than changing the social order. Religion destroys awareness of material reality and promotes the maintenance of the status quo by giving priority to the goal of spiritual salvation. Marx further concluded that organized religion can be exploited by people in positions of power in society. If the majority of individuals in a society believe that enduring pain, denying pleasure, and accepting their status in this life gains them spiritual salvation, those in power can be reasonably sure that those under their control will be hard working and docile. If those in power go so far as to manifest their own commitment to religion, their hold over the people can be strengthened even further. Such a manifestation would, after all, show that they had something in common with the masses.

Conflict theorists make the case that in an advanced capitalist society where people are not likely to look to the supernatural for answers and explanations, religion may be supplemented by other activities with similar narcotic effects. Hoch points out that these contemporary "opiates" include "sport spectacles, whiskey, and repressively sublimated sex." These combined with other opiates such as nationalism, racism, and sexism distort people's perspectives and encourage self-defeating behavior. Among these, sport stands out as an especially powerful opiate. Unlike the others, sport spectatorship is often accompanied by an extremely intense identification with players, teams, and the values perceived to be the basis for success in athletics. According to Hoch, this identification brings sport further into the lives of the spectators and captures their attention on a long-term basis. When the game ends, fan involvement does not cease, but carries on between games and into the off season. This means that workers think about and discuss the fate of their teams rather than the futility of their own lives. Thus they are less likely to become actively involved in political or revolutionary organizations. Petryszak (1978), in a historical analysis of sport, makes the case that the "ultimate consequence of . . . spectator sports in society is the reduction of the population to a position of complete passivity."

Beyond occupying people's time and distracting their attention and energy, sport helps maintain the position of those in power in other ways. Conflict theorists note that the major contact sports, such as football, hockey, and boxing, promote a justification for the use of "official" violence by those in authority positions. In other words, sport shapes our values in ways that lock us into a social system based on coercion and the exploitive use of power. The more we witness violent sports, the more we are apt to condone the use of official violence in other settings—even when it is directed against us.

Sport also serves the interests of those in power by generating the belief that success can be achieved only through hard work and that hard work always leads to success. Such a belief encourages people to look up to those who are successful as being paragons of virtue and to look down of the failures as being lazy and no good. For example, when teams win consistently their success is attributed to hard work and discipline; when they lose consistently, losing often is blamed on a lack of hustle and poor attitude. Losses lead the fans to call for new players and coaches—not a restructuring of the game or its rules. Hoch (1972) points out that this way of looking at things blinds people to a consideration of the problems inherent in the social and economic structure and engenders the notion that success depends only on attitude and personal effort. It also leads to the belief that failure is to be blamed on the individual alone and is to be accepted as an indication of personal inadequacies and of a need to work harder in the future.

Conflict theorists see sport as a tool for controlling people and maintaining the status quo. It is structured to promote specific political ideas (Helmes, 1978) and to regiment and organize the lives of young people so that they will become productive workers. For adults, the role of spectator reinforces a passive orientation toward life so that they will remain observers rather than the shapers of their own experience (Aronowitz, 1973).

COMMERCIALISM AND MATERIALISM

The conflict theorists emphasize that sport is promoted as a product to be consumed and that it creates a basis for capitalist expansion. For example, increasing numbers of individuals and families are joining athletic clubs where they pay to participate and pay for the lessons teaching them how to participate correctly and efficiently. Creating and satisfying these expanding interests have given rise to an entire new industry. Summer sport resorts, winter sport resorts, and local athletic clubs are all part of this profit-generating industry.

Furthermore, sporting goods manufacturers have found that effective advertising can lead more and more equipment to be defined as absolutely necessary for successful and healthy involvement. Potential consumers have been convinced that if they want to impress other people with their knowledge about the sport experience they have to buy and show off only top-of-the-line equipment. It has come to the point where participants can prove themselves in sport through their ability to consume as well as their ability to master physical skills. Thus sport has been used to lead people to deal with one another in terms of material images rather than in terms of the human quality of experience.

Sport not only creates direct profits but also is used as an advertising medium (Brohm, 1978). Sport spectacles serve as important settings for selling cars, tires, beer, soft drinks, and insurance. The tendency for people to personally identify with athletes is also used to sell other products. The role of athlete, unlike most adult occupational roles, is highly visible, prestigious, and relatively easy to emulate. Therefore, the attachment to sport heroes serves as the basis for the creation of an interest in sport along with a general "need" for consumer goods.

This process affects young people as well as adults. Children are lured into the spectator role and the role of consumer by trading cards, Dallas Cowboy pajamas, Yankee baseball caps, NBA basketball shoes, and a multitude of other products that ultimately create adulthood desires to become season ticket purchasers. Participation in highly specialized sport programs leads children to conclude that the proper equipment is always necessary for a good time and that being a good runner, tennis player, and soccer player depends on owning three different pairs of the best shoes on the market.

NATIONALISM, MILITARISM, AND SEXISM

Conflict theorists point out that sport is used by most countries as the showplace for displaying their national symbols and military strength. In many developing countries, national sport programs are administered by the defense department; in industrialized countries sport is symbolically linked with warfare and strong militaristic orientations. The conflict theorists claim that the collective excitement generated by sport participation and mass spectator events can be converted into unquestioning allegiance to political beliefs and an irrational willingness to defend those beliefs. Nationalistic feelings are fed by an emphasis on demonstrating superiority over other countries and other political systems. Furthermore, sport provides a model of confrontation, which polarizes groups of people and stresses the necessity of being militarily prepared.

Finally, the conflict theorists argue that sport divides the sexes and perpetuates distorted definitions of masculinity and femininity. The organization of contemporary sport not only relegates women to a secondary, supportive role, but also leads people to define masculinity in terms of physical strength and emotional insensitivity. In fact, the model of the successful male is epitomized by the brute strength and the controlled emotions of the athlete. Sport further reinforces sexism by focusing attention on performance differences in selected physical activities. People then use those differences to argue that male superiority is grounded in nature and that the sexes should continue to be separated. This separation obscures the characteristics men and women have in common and locks members of both sexes into restrictive roles.

Conflict theorists see much of contemporary sport as a source of alienation and a tool of exploitation and control serving the needs of economic and political systems rather than the needs of human beings. They generally argue that it is impossible for sport to provide humanizing experiences when the society in which it exists is not humane and creative (Hoch, 1972).

Limitations of the Conflict Theory Approach

Like the functionalist approach, conflict theory has some weaknesses. The conflict theorists make good use of history but they tend to overemphasize the role of capitalism in shaping all aspects of social reality since the Industrial Revolution. Capitalism has been a significant force, but other factors must be taken into account in explaining what has happened during the last two centuries.

The emergence and growth of modern sport is a good case in point. Sport has been strongly influenced by capitalism but the emergence of contemporary sport can be explained in terms of factors that existed prior to the Industrial Revolution. Guttmann (1978) has argued that modern sport is a product of a scientific approach to the world rather than of the needs of capitalist economic systems. This scientific approach to the world grew out of seventeenth-century discoveries in mathematics and is characterized by a commitment to quantification, measurement, and experimentation. According to Guttmann this scientific world-view has given rise to contemporary sport. This is the reason why sport is also popular in noncapitalist countries including China, Cuba, Czechoslovakia, and the Soviet Union.

In their analysis of sport, many conflict theorists are too quick to conclude that sport inevitably creates alienation and serves as an "opiate of the masses." They tend to ignore the testimonials of athletes who claim that sport participation, even in a capitalist society, can be a personally creative, expressive, and liberating experience (Slusher, 1967; Spino, 1971; Bannister, 1973; Csikszentmihalyi, 1975; Sadler, 1977). This possibility, of course, is inconsistent with the idea that the athlete's body automatically becomes a tool of production controlled and used for the sake of political and economic goals.

The argument that sport is an opiate also has some weaknesses. It is probably true that athletes and fans are more likely than other people to have attitudes supportive of the status quo. However, it is not known if their involvement is sport caused these attitudes or if the attitudes existed prior to their involvement and caused them to be attracted to sport. It may be that sport attracts people who are already committed to the status quo. If this is the case, it is difficult to argue that sport provides an escape from reality for those who might otherwise be critical of the social order. Research suggests that the most alienated and the most dissatisfied people in society are the least likely to show an interest in sport. In fact, interest and involvement are greatest among those who are the most economically successful (Sillitoe, 1969; Edwards, 1973a; Anderson and Stone, 1979).

Another weakness of conflict theory is that it often overemphasizes the extent to which sport is controlled by those in positions of power in society. The people who control the media, sport facilities, and sport teams do have much to say about the conditions under which top level sport events are experienced and viewed by players and spectators alike. However, it is difficult to argue that all sport involvement is a result of the promotional efforts of capitalists or government bureaucrats. This is especially true when attention is shifted from professional level sport to sport at the local recreational level. Active sport participation generally occurs at levels where the interests of the participants themselves can be used as the basis for creating and developing programs.

Furthermore, certain sports have characteristics making them difficult to control by those who are not participants. Surfing is a good case in point; it does not lend itself to scheduling or television coverage, equipment needs are not extensive, and it does not generate much long-term spectator interest among those who have never been surfers. Therefore, the development of surfing and other similar sports has not been subject to heavy influence from outsiders whose main concerns are generating profits and creating sport spectacles.

SUMMARY AND CONCLUSION: WHO IS RIGHT?

Now that we have looked at the relationship between sport and society (see Table 3-1 on page 42 for a review) from two different perspectives, which explanation is most correct? Is sport an inspiration or an opiate? I have found that the way people answer this question depends on what they think about the society in which sport exists. For example, those who are generally uncritical of American society will tend to agree with the functionalist approach when they look at sport in the United States. Those who are critical of American society will side with the conflict theorists. However, when the country in question is East Germany or China rather than the United States, some people may shift perspective. Those who do not agree with the way of life in East Germany or China will quickly become conflict theorists in their discussions of sport in these countries; those supportive of socialist systems will tend to become functionalists. It can be confusing to say that sport is an inspiration in one country and an opiate in another.

In order to eliminate some of the confusion on this issue we need detailed research on how the structure of physical activities is related to the subjective experiences of participants (players and spectators). We also need to know how those experiences are related to attitudes and behavior patterns. We can assume that under certain circumstances the consequences of sport will be constructive, and under other circumstances they will be destructive. Our task is to be able to clearly describe the circumstances under which these different consequences occur and to explain why they occur the way they do. This means that studies cannot be limited to specific countries or to specific groups of people. We need cross-cultural and comparative research focusing on all dimensions of the phenomenon of sport.

In developing research and exploring these issues we need to be aware of the ideas of both the functionalists and the conflict theorists. Each of their explanations of the relationship between sport and society alerts us to questions that must be asked and hypotheses that must be tested. Unless these and other theoretical perspectives are used our understanding of sport will be needlessly restricted.

Unfortunately, research will never be able to show us what the relationship between sport and society *should* be. It only alerts us to the possibilities and provides us with a starting point for shaping what it will be in the future.

NOTE

1. Although the focus in this [selection] is the United States, the pattern maintenance function of sport has been described in other countries, including the Soviet Union (Morton, 1963; Riordan, 1977), East Germany (Santomier and Ewees, 1979), China (Johnson, 1973a,b; Chu and Segrave, 1979), Finland (Olin, 1979), Australia (Murray, 1976), and Samoa (Dunlap, 1951).

TABLE 3-1 Functionalism and Conflict Theory: A Summary of Their Assumptions about the Social Order and Their Explanations of the Relationship between Sport and Society

Functionalist Approach	*Conflict Theory*
Assumptions about the social order	
Social order based on consensus, common values, and interrelated subsystems	Social order based on coercion, exploitation, and subtle manipulation of individuals
Major concerns in the study of society	
What are the essential parts in structure of social system?	How is power distributed and used in society?
How do social systems continue to operate smoothly?	How do societies change and what can be done to promote change?
Major concerns in the study of sport	
How does sport contribute to basic social system needs such as pattern maintenance and tension management, integration, goal attainment, and adaptation?	How does sport create personal alienation?
	How is sport used to control thoughts and behavior of people, and maintain economic and political systems serving interests of those in power?
Major conclusions about the sport-society relationship	
Sport is valuable secondary social institution benefiting society as well as individual members of society	Sport is distorted form of physical exercise shaped by needs of autocratic or production-conscious societies
Sport is basically a *source of inspiration* on personal and social level	Sport lacks creative and expressive elements of play; *it is an opiate*
Goals of sport sociology	
To discover ways in which sport's contribution to stability and maintenance of social order can be maximized at all levels	To promote development of humane and creative social order so that sport can be source of expression, creative experiences, and physical well-being
Major weaknesses	
Assumes that existence and popularity of sport prove that it is serving positive functions	Assumes that structures and consequences of sport are totally determined by needs of political and economic order
Ignores possibility of internal differences and basic conflicts of interest within social systems and therefore assumes that sport serves needs of all system parts and individuals equally	Ignores factors other than capitalism in analyzing emergence and development of contemporary sport
	Focuses too much attention on top-level spectator sport and overemphasizes extent to which all sport involvement is controlled and structured by power elite

REFERENCES

Albonico, R. 1967. Modern University Sport as a Contribution to Social Integration. *International Review of Sport Sociology* 2:155-162.

Anderson, D., and G. P. Stone. 1979. A Fifteen-Year Analysis of Socio-Economic Strata Differences in the Meaning Given to Sport by Metropolitans. In M. L. Krotee, ed. *The Dimensions of Sport Sociology*. Leisure Press, New York.

Aronowitz, S. 1973. *False Promises*. McGraw-Hill, New York.

Bannister, F. T. 1980. Search for "White Hopes" threatens Black Athletes. *Ebony* 34(4):130-134.

Brockmann, D. 1969. Sport as an Integrating Factor in the Countryside. *International Review of Sport Sociology* 4:151-170.

Brohm, J-M. 1978. *Sport: A Prison of Measured Time*. Ink Links. London.

Chase, J. H. 1909. How a Director Feels. *Playground* 3(4):13.

Chu, D. B., and J. O. Segrave. 1979. Physical Culture in the People's Republic of China. *Journal of Sport Behavior* 2(3):119-135.

Csikszentmikhalyi, M. 1975. *Beyond Boredom and Anxiety*. Jossey-Bass. San Francisco.

Dunlap, H. L. 1951. Games, Sports, Dancing, and Other Vigorous Recreational Activities and their Function in Samoan Culture. *Research Quarterly* 22(3):298-311.

Edwards, H. 1973. *Sociology of Sport*. Dorsey Press, Homewood, IL.

Eitzen, D. S., and G. H. Sage. 1978. *Sociology of American Sport*. Wm. C. Brown. Dubuque, IA.

Gerth, H., and C. W. Mills. 1953. *Character and Social Structure*. Harcourt Brace Jovanovich, New York.

Goodman, C. 1979. *Choosing Sides*. Schocken, New York.

Guttmann, A. 1978. *From Ritual to Record: The Nature of Modern Sports*. Columbia University Press, New York.

Hennig, M., and A. Jardim. 1977. *The Managerial Woman*. Anchor, New York.

Hoch, P. 1972. *Rip Off the Big Game*. Doubleday, New York.

Johnson, W. O. 1973. Faces on a New China Scroll. *Sports Illustrated* 39(14):42-67.

Kleiber, D. A., and J. R. Kelly. 1980. Leisure, Socialization and the Life Cycle. In S. Iso-Ahola, ed. *Social Psychological Perspectives on Leisure and Recreation*. Charles C. Thomas, Springfield, IL.

Lever, J. 1978. Sex Differences in the Complexity of Children's Play. *American Sociological Review* 43(4):471-483

Lever, J. 1980. Multiple Methods of Data Collection: A Note on Divergence. Unpublished manuscript.

Luschen, G. 1967. The Interdependence of Sport and Culture. *International Review of Sport Sociology* 2:127-139.

Marsh, P. 1978. *Aggro: The Illusion of Violence*. J. M. Dent, London.

Morton, H. W. 1963. *Soviet Sport*. Collier, New York.

Mumford, L. 1934. *Technics and Civilization*. Harcourt Brace Jovanovich, New York.

Murray, L. 1979. Some Ideological Qualities of Australian Sport. *Australian Journal of Health, Physical Education and Recreation* 73:7-10.

Olin, K. 1979. Sport, Social Development and Community Decision-Making. *International Review of Sport Sociology* 14(3-4):117-132.

Parsons, T., and N. J. Smelser. 1965. *Economy and Society*. The Free Press, New York.

Petryszak, N. 1978. Spectator Sports as an Aspect of Popular Culture—An Historical View. *Journal of Sport Behavior* 1(1):14-27.

Proctor, R. C., and W. M. Echard. 1976. "Toot-Toot" or Spectator Sports: Psychological and Therapeutic Implications. *American Journal of Sports Medicine* 4(2):78-83.

Riordan, J. 1977. *Sport in Soviet Society*. Cambridge University Press, New York.

Sadler, W. A. 1977. Alienated Youth and Creative Sports Experience. *Journal of the Philosophy of Sport* 4(Fall):83-95.

Santomier, J., and K. Ewees. 1979. Sport, Political Socialization and the German Democratic Republic. In Krotee, M. L. (ed.), *Dimensions of Sport Sociology*. Leisure Press, West Point, N.Y.

Schafer, W. E. 1976. Sport and Youth Counterculture: Contrasting Socialization Themes. In D. M. Landers, ed. *Social Problems in Athletics*. University of Illinois Press, Urbana, IL.

Sillitoe, K. 1969. *Planning for Leisure*. University of Keele, London.

Slusher, H. S. 1967. *Man, Sport and Existence*. Lea & Febiger, Philadelphia.

Spino, M. 1971. Running as a Spiritual Experience. In J. Scott, *The Athletic Revolution*. The Free Press, N.Y.

Vanderzwaag, H. J. 1972. *Toward a Philosophy of Sport*. Addison-Wesley, Reading, MA.

Wohl, A. 1970. Competitive Sport and Its Social Functions. *International Review of Sport Sociology* 5:117-124.

Wohl, A. 1979. Sport and Social Development. *International Review of Sport Sociology* 14(3-4):5-18.

■ FOR FURTHER STUDY

Caillois, Roger. "The Structure and Classification of Games." *Diogenes* (Winter 1965):62-75.

Coakley, Jay J. "Sociology of Sport in the United States." *International Review of the Sociology of Sport* 22 (1987):63-79.

Coakley, Jay J. *Sport in Society: Issues and Controversies*, 4th ed. St. Louis: Times-Mirror/Mosby, 1990.

Eitzen, D. Stanley, and George H. Sage. *Sociology of North American Sport*, 5th ed. Dubuque, IA: Wm. C. Brown, 1993.

Frey, James H., and D. Stanley Eitzen. "Sport and Society." *Annual Review of Sociology* 17 (1991):503-522.

Guttmann, Allen. *From Record to Ritual: The Nature of Modern Sports*. New York: Columbia University Press, 1978.

Guttmann, Allen. *Sports Spectators*. New York: Columbia University Press, 1986.

Guttmann, Allen. 1988. *A Whole New Ball Game: An Interpretation of American Sports*. Chapel Hill: University of North Carolina Press, 1988.

Harris, Janet C. "Suited Up and Stripped Down: Perspectives for Sociocultural Sport Studies." *Sociology of Sport Journal* 6 (December 1989):335-347.

Huizinga, Johan. *Homo Ludens: A Study of the Play Element in Culture*. Boston: Beacon Press, 1950.

Lapchick, Richard E., ed. *Fractured Focus: Sport as a Reflection of Society*. Lexington, MA: D. C. Heath, 1986.

Lever, Janet. *Soccer Madness*. Chicago: University of Chicago Press.

Loy, John W. "The Nature of Sport: A Definitional Effort." *Quest* 10 (May 1968):1-15.

Loy, John W., Barry D. McPherson, and Gerald S. Kenyon. *The Sociology of Sport as an Academic Specialty.* CAHPER monograph (no date).
Luschen, Gunther. "Sociology of Sport." *Annual Review of Sociology* 6 (1980):315-347.
Luschen, Gunther, and George H. Sage. "Sport in Sociological Perspective." In *Handbook of Social Science of Sport,* ed. Gunther Luschen and George H. Sage. Champaign, IL: Stipes, 1981, pp. 3-21.
McKay, Jim. "Marxism as a Way of Seeing: Beyond the Limits of Current 'Critical' Approaches to Sport." *Sociology of Sport Journal* 3 (September 1986):261-272.
McPherson, Barry D., James E. Curtis, and John W. Loy. *The Social Significance of Sport: An Introduction to the Sociology of Sport.* Champaign, IL: Human Kinetics, 1989.
Meier, Klaus V. "The Ignoble Sports Fan." *Journal of Sports and Social Issues* 13 (Fall 1989):111-119.
Melnick, Merrill J. "The Sports Fan: A Teaching Guide and Bibliography." *Sociology of Sport Journal* 6 (December 1989):167-175.
Morgan, William J. "'Radical' Social Theory and Sport: A Critique and a Conceptual Emendation." *Sociology of Sport Journal* 2 (March 1985):56-71.
Nixon, Howard L., II. "Sport Sociology That Matters: Imperatives and Challenges for the 1990s." *Sociology of Sport Journal* 8 (September 1991):281-294.
Rees, C. Roger, and Andrew W. Miracle, eds. *Sport and Social Theory.* Champaign, IL: Human Kinetics, 1986.
Roberts, Randy, and James S. Olson. *Winning Is the Only Thing: Sports in America Since 1945.* Baltimore: The Johns Hopkins University Press, 1989.
Sage, George H. *Power and Ideology in American Sport: A Critical Perspective.* Champaign, IL: Human Kinetics, 1990.
Sage, George H. "Pursuit of Knowledge in the Sociology of Sport: Issues and Prospects." *Quest* 39 (December 1987):255-281.
Sociology of Sport Journal. "Functionalism Theory and Sport: Annotated Bibliography." *Sociology of Sport Journal* 8 (September 1991):299-305.
Sociology of Sport Journal. "Symbolic Interaction Theory and Sport: Annotated Bibliography." *Sociology of Sport Journal* 8 (December 1991):391-398.
Young, T. R., ed. "Critical Perspectives on Sport." *Arena Review* 8 (November 1984):entire issue.

Part Two

Sport and Socialization

The involvement of young people in adult-supervised sport is characteristic of contemporary American society. Today, millions of boys and girls are involved in organized baseball, football, hockey, basketball, and soccer leagues. Others are involved in swimming, skating, golf, tennis, and gymnastics at a highly competitive level. School-sponsored sports begin about the seventh grade and are highly organized, win-oriented activities.

Why do so many parents in so many communities strongly support organized sports programs for youth? Primarily because most people believe that sports participation has positive benefits for those involved. The following quotation from *Time* summarizes this assumption.

> Sport has always been one of the primary means of civilizing the human animal, of inculcating the character traits a society desires. Wellington in his famous aphorism insisted that the Battle of Waterloo had been won on the playing fields of Eton. The lessons learned on the playing field are among the most basic: the setting of goals and joining with others to achieve them; an understanding of and respect for rules; the persistence to hone ability into skill, prowess into perfection. In games, children learn that success is possible and that failure can be overcome. Championships may be won; when lost, wait until next year. In practicing such skills as fielding a grounder and hitting a tennis ball, young athletes develop work patterns and attitudes that carry over into college, the marketplace and all of life.[1]

However parents often ignore the negative side of sports participation, a position that is summarized by Charles Banham:

> It [the conventional argument that sport builds character] is not sound because it assumes that everyone will benefit from sport in the complacently

prescribed manner. A minority do so benefit. A few have the temperament that responds healthily to all the demands. These are the only ones able to develop an attractively active character. Sport can put fresh air in the mind, if it's the right mind; it can give muscle to the personality, if it's the right personality. But for the rest, it encourages selfishness, envy, conceit, hostility, and bad temper. Far from ventilating the mind, it stifles it. Good sportsmanship may be a product of sport, but so is bad sportsmanship.[2]

The problem is that sports produce positive and negative outcomes. This dualistic quality of sport is summarized by Terry Orlick:

> For every positive psychological or social outcome in sports, there are possible negative outcomes. For example, sports can offer a child group membership or group exclusion, acceptance or rejection, positive feedback or negative feedback, a sense of accomplishment or a sense of failure, evidence of self-worth or a lack of evidence of self-worth. Likewise, sports can develop cooperation and a concern for others, but they can also develop intense rivalry and a complete lack of concern for others.[3]

The first selection in this part, by sociologist Jay J. Coakley, describes the organized youth sports of today and compares them with the spontaneous games more characteristic of youth in previous generations. The second selection by Del Stover is critical of what school sports have become. In effect, high school sports are becoming like big-time college sports programs where winning is an obsession. The final selection is an excerpt from H. G. Bissinger's book about football at Permian High School in Odessa, Texas. It demonstrates, forcefully, how football takes precedence over education in one high school.

NOTES

1. "Comes the Revolution: Joining the Game at Last, Women are Transforming American Athletics," *Time* (June 26, 1978), p. 55.
2. Charles Banham, "Man at Play," *Contemporary Review*, 207 (August 1965), 62.
3. T. D. Orlick, "The Sports Environment: A Capacity to Enhance—A Capacity to Destroy," paper presented at the Canadian Symposium of Psycho-Motor Learning and Sports Psychology (1974), p. 2.

4. *Play Group versus Organized Competitive Team: A Comparison*

JAY J. COAKLEY

One way to begin to grasp the nature and extent of the impact of participation in sport is to try to understand the sport group as a context for the behavior and the relationships of youngsters. In a 1968 symposium on the sociology of sport, Gunther Luschen from the University of Illinois delivered a paper entitled "Small Group Research and the Group in Sport." While discussing the variety of different group contexts in which sport activities occur, he contrasted the spontaneously formed casual play group with the organized competitive team. He was primarily interested in the social organization and the amount of structural differentiation existing in sport groups in general, but some of his ideas give us a basis for comparing the characteristics of the spontaneous play group and the organized competitive Little League team in terms of their implications for youngsters. In general, any group engaging in competitive physical activity can be described in terms of the extent and complexity of its formal organization. Simply put, we can employ a continuum along which such groups could be located depending on how formally organized they are. Figure 4-1 illustrates this idea.

The spontaneous play group is an example of a context for competitive physical activities in which formal organization is absent. Its polar opposite is the sponsored competitive team in an organized league. It follows that the amount of formal organization has implications for the actions of group members, for their relationships with one another, and for the nature of their experiences. Table 4-1 outlines the characteristics of the two groups that would most closely approximate the polar extremes on the continuum.

Before going any further, I should point out that the two descriptions in Table 4-1 represent "ideal type" groups. In other words, the respective sets of characteristics represent hypothetical concepts that emphasize each group's most identifiable and important elements. Ideal types are necessarily extreme or exaggerated examples of the phenomenon under investigation and as such are to be used for purposes of comparison rather

SOURCE: Excerpt from *Sport in Society: Issues and Controversies* (St. Louis: C. V. Mosby, 1978), pp. 96-103.

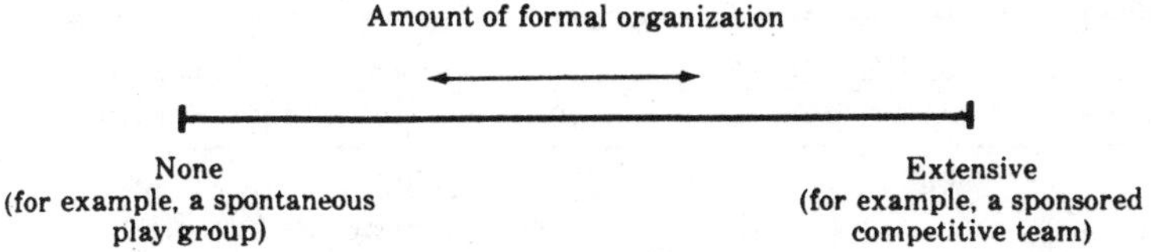

FIGURE 4-1 A formal organization continuum for groups in competitive physical activities.

than as depictions of reality. Our concern here is to look at an actual group in which youngsters participate and to compare the actual group with the ideal types in order to make an assessment of what the real group might be like as a context for experience. Of course, the real group will not be an exact replica of either of the ideal types, but will more or less resemble one or the other.

GETTING THE GAME STARTED

The characteristics of each group suggest that the differences between the spontaneous play group and the organized competitive team would be quite apparent as soon as initial contact between the participants occurs. In the spontaneous play group, we might expect that the majority of time would be spent on dealing with organizational problems such as establishing goals, defining means to those goals, and developing expectations of both a general and a specific nature for each of the participants. Being a member of a *completely* spontaneous play group would probably be similar to being involved in the initial organizational meeting of a group of unacquainted college freshmen who are supposed to come up with a class project. Both would involve a combination of some fun, a good deal of confusion, much talking, and little action. For the context of the organized competitive team, we might imagine a supervisor (coach) blowing a whistle that brings a group of preselected youngsters of similar ages and abilities running to fall into a routine formation to await an already known command. This would resemble a "brave new world" of sport where there would be some action, a good deal of listening to instructions, much routinization, and little fun. Fortunately, most group contexts for youngsters' sport participation fall somewhere between these two extremes. The trick is, of course, to find which points on the continuum would have a maximization of both fun and action along with the other characteristics seen as most beneficial to the young participants' development.

From my observations of youngsters in backyards, gyms, parks, and playgrounds, I have concluded that, for the most part, they are quite efficient in organizing their sport activities. The primary organizational

TABLE 4-1 Comparison of Two Groups*

The Spontaneous Play Group: No Formal Organization	*The Sponsored Competitive Team: High Formal Organization*
Action is an outgrowth of the interpersonal relationships and of the decision-making processes of participating members.	Action is an outgrowth of a predesignated system of role relationships and of the role-learning abilities of group members.
Rewards are primarily intrinsic and are a function of the experience and the extent of the interpersonal skills of the group members.	Rewards are primarily extrinsic and are a function of the combined technical skills of group members.
Meanings attached to actions and situations are emergent and are subject to changes over time.	Meanings are predominantly predefined and are relatively static from one situation to the next.
Group integration is based on the process of exchange between group members.	Group integration is based on an awareness of and conformity to a formalized set of norms.
Norms governing action are emergent, and interpretation is variable.	Norms are highly formalized and specific, with variability resulting from official judgments.
Social control is internally generated among members and is dependent on commitment.	Social control is administered by an external agent and is dependent on obedience.
Sanctions are informal and are directly related to the maintenance of action in the situation.	Sanctions are formal and are related to the preservation of values as well as order.
Individual freedom is high, with variability a function of the group's status structure.	Individual freedom is limited to the flexibility tolerated within role expectations.
Group is generally characterized by structural instability.	Group is generally characterized by structural stability.

*A study of the game-playing behavior of elementary school children done by Sylvia Polgar (1976) provides empirical support for the comparison made in this table.

details are often partially worked out by physical setting, available equipment, and time of the year, all of which influence the choice of activity and the form the activity will take. To the extent that the participants know one another and have played with each other before, there will be a minimum amount of time devoted to formation of norms—rules from previous games can be used. But despite the ability of most youngsters to get a competitive physical activity going, there seems to be a tendency for adults to become impatient with some of the "childish" disagreements of the young participants. Adults often become impatient because they do not understand the youngsters' "distortions" of the games–games the adults know are supposed to be played another way. Adults who want to teach youngsters to play the game the *right way* and to help young players avoid disagreements and discussions in order to build up more action time seem to be everywhere. These adults see a very clear need for organization, that is, establishing regular practice times, scheduling contests, and giving positive rewards and encouragement to those whose performances are seen as deserving. Although their motives may be commendable, these adults usually fail to consider all of the differences between the informally organized group and the formally organized team.

Most importantly, the game in the park is in the control of the youngsters themselves, whereas the organized competitive team is supervised and controlled by adults (Polgar, 1976). In the play group, getting the game under way depends on the group members being able to communicate well enough to make organizational decisions and to evoke enough cooperation so that a sufficient amount of the group's behavior is conducive to the achievement of the goals of the game, however they have been defined. In this situation, interpersonal skills are crucial, and youngsters will probably be quick to realize that playing the game depends on being able to develop and maintain positive relationships or, at least, learning to cope with interpersonal problems in a way that will permit cooperative action. This constitutes a valuable set of experiences that become less available to participants as the amount of the group's formal organization increases. It is a rare adult coach who allows youngsters to make many decisions on how the game should be organized and played. In fact, most decisions have been made for the coach; the availability of the practice field has been decided, the roles defined, the rules made, the sanctions outlined, the team colors picked, the games scheduled, etc. Occasionally the players are allowed to vote on their team name, but that happens only if the team is new and does not already have one. In all, *the emphasis in the organized setting is on the development of sport skills, not on the development of interpersonal skills.*

PLAY OF THE GAME

Differences between the two groups do not disappear once the game begins. For the spontaneous play group, the game experience is likely to be defined as an end itself, whereas for the organized team, the game is a means to an end. In the play group, the game is unlikely to have implications beyond the setting in which it occurs, and the participants are primarily concerned with managing the situation so that *action* can be preserved for as long as possible. To this end, it is quite common for the participating youngsters to develop sets of norms accompanied by rather complex sets of qualifications and to establish handicaps for certain participants. These tactics serve to compensate for skill differences and to ensure that the game proceed with scores close enough so that excitement and satisfaction can be maximized for as many of the players as possible. For example, if one of the pitchers in an informal baseball game were bigger or stronger than the rest of the youngsters, he/she would be required to pitch the ball with "an arch on it" to minimize the ball's speed and to allow all the batters a chance to hit it. Exceptionally good batters might be required to bat left-handed (if they were right-handed) to minimize the chances of hitting a home run every time they came to bat. A youngster having a hard time hitting the ball might be given more than three strikes, and the pitcher might make a special effort to "put the ball over the plate" so that the batter would have a good chance of hitting the ball rather than striking out. Since a strikeout is a relatively unexciting event in a game where the primary goal is the involvement of all players, one of the most frequently made comments directed to the pitcher by his/her teammates in the field is "C'mon, let'em hit it!"

Similar examples of norm qualifications and handicap systems can be found in other sport groups characterized by a low degree of formal organization. Sometimes these little adaptations can be very clever, and, of course, some participants have to be warned if they seem to be taking unfair advantage of them. This may occur in cases where a young player tends to call time-outs whenever the opposition has his team at a disadvantage or when someone begins to overuse an interference or a "do-over" call to nullify a mistake or a failure to make a play. Although the system of qualifications and handicaps may serve to allow the participants to have another chance when they make mistakes and to avoid the embarrassment associated with a relative lack of skills, the major function of such systems seems to be to equalize not only the players, but also the teams competing against one another. Through such techniques, scores will remain close enough that neither team will give up and destroy the game by quitting. In a sense, the players make an attempt to control the competition so that the fun of all will be safeguarded. Adults do the same thing when given the chance. None of us enjoys being overwhelmed by an opponent or overcoming an opponent so weak that we never had to make an effort.

For the formally organized competitive team, however, the play of the game may be considerably different. The goal of victory or the promotion of the team's place in the league standings replaces the goal of maximizing individual participant satisfaction. The meanings and rewards attached to the game are largely a function of how the experience is related to a desired outcome—either victory or "a good show." Players may even be told that a good personal performance is almost always nullified by a team defeat and that to feel satisfied with yourself without a team victory is selfish (as they say in the locker room, "There is no 'u' in team" or "Defeat is worse than death because you have to live with defeat").

Since victories are a consequence of the combined skills of the team members, such skills are to be practiced and improved and then utilized in ways that maximize the chances for team success. Granting the other team a handicap is quite rare unless any chance for victory is out of their grasp. If this is the case, the weaker players may be substituted in the lineup of the stronger team *unless*, of course, a one-sided score will serve the purpose of increasing the team's prestige or intimidating future opponents.

Also, if one player's skill level far exceeds that of the other participants, that player will often be used where he can be most effective. In the Little League game, it is frequently the bigger youngster with the strongest arm who is made the pitcher. This may help to ensure a team's chances for victory, but it also serves to nearly eliminate the rest of the team's chances for making fielding plays and for being involved in the defensive play of the game. In a 6-inning game, the fact that a large number of the 18 total outs for the opponents come as strikeouts means that a number of fielders may never have a chance to even touch the ball while they are out in the field. A similar thing happens in football. The youth-league team often puts its biggest and strongest players in the backfield rather than in the line. The game then consists of giving those youngsters the ball on nearly every play. For the smaller players on the defensive team, the primary task may be getting out of the way of the runner to avoid being stepped on. Thus on the organized team, intimidation may become a part of playing strategy. Unfortunately, intimidation increases apprehension and inhibits some of the action in the game as well as the involvement of some of the players. Generally, it seems that on the organized team the tendency to employ the skills of the players to win games takes precedence over devising handicaps to ensure fun and widespread participation.

One way to become aware of some of the differences between the informal play group and the formally organized competitive team is to ask the participants in each group the scores of their games. In the formally organized setting, the scores are often one-sided with members of the winning team even boasting about how they won their last football game 77 to 6, their last baseball game 23 to 1, or their last soccer game 14 to 0. Such scores lead me to question the amount of fun had by the players. In the case of the losers, it would be rare to find players who would be able to maintain an interest in a game when they are so completely beaten. If the winners say they enjoyed themselves, the lesson they may be learning through such an experience should be seriously questioned. It may be that the major lesson is if your opponents happen to be weak, take advantage of that weakness so totally that they will never be able to make a comeback. Such experiences, instead of instilling positive relationships and a sincere interest in sport activities, are apt to encourage distorted assessments of self-worth and to turn youngsters off to activities that, in modified forms, could provide them with years of enjoyment.

In addition to the differences in how the game is organized and how the action is initiated, there are also differences in how action for the two groups is maintained. In the informally organized group, the members are held together through the operation of some elementary processes of exchange that, in a sense, serve as the basis for the participants obtaining what they think they deserve out of the experience (Polgar, 1976). When the range of abilities is great, the older, bigger, more talented participants have to compromise some of their abilities so that the younger, smaller, and less talented will have a chance to gain the rewards necessary to continue playing. The play of the game depends on maintaining a necessary level of commitment among all participants. This commitment then serves as a basis for social control during the action. Although there are some exceptions, those in the group with the highest combined skill and social prestige levels act as leaders and serve as models of normal behavior. For these individuals to deviate from the norms in any consistent manner would most likely earn them the reputation of being cheaters or bad sports. In fact, consistent deviation from the group norms by any of the participants is likely to be defined by the others as disruptive, and the violator will be reminded of his/her infraction through some type of warning or through a threat of future exclusion from group activities. When sanctions are employed in the informal play group, they usually serve an instrumental function—they bring behavior in line so that the game can continue. Sanctions are usually not intended to reinforce status distinctions, to preserve an established social structure, or to safeguard values and principles. Interestingly, self-enforcement of norms in the play group is usually quite effective. Deviation is not totally eliminated, but it is kept within the limits necessary to preserve action in the game. The emphasis is not so much on keeping norms sacred, but on making sure that the norms serve to maintain the goal of action. In fact, norms may change or be reinterpreted for specific individuals or in specific situations so that the level of action in the play activities can be maximized. The importance of maintaining a certain level of action is demonstrated by the informal sanctions directed at a participant who might always be insisting on too rigid an enforcement of norms. This is the person who continually cries "foul" or who always spots a penalty. To be persistent in such a hard-nosed approach to norm enforcement will probably earn the player the nonendearing reputation of being a baby, a crier, or a complainer.

In the informally organized play group, the most disruptive kind of deviant is the one who does not care about the game. It is interesting that the group will usually tolerate any number of different performance styles, forms, and individual innovations as long as they do not destroy action. Batting left-handed when one is right-handed is okay if the batter is at least likely to hit the ball, thus keeping the action going. Throwing behind-the-back passes and trying a crazy shot in basketball or running an unplanned pass pattern in football are all considered part of the game in the play group *if action is not destroyed.* Joking around will frequently be tolerated and sometimes even encouraged *if action can continue.* But if such behavior moves beyond the level of seriousness required to maintain satisfying action for all the participants, commitment decreases, and the group is likely to dissolve. In line with this, usually those participants with the highest amount of skill are allowed the greatest amount of freedom to play "as the spirit moves them." Although such behavior may seem to indicate a lack of seriousness to the outsider, the skill of the player is developed enough to avoid a "disruptive" amount of mistakes. At the same time, such freedom gives high-ability participants a means through which their interest level can be maintained. Similar free-wheeling behavior by a low-ability participant would be viewed with disfavor, since the behavior would frequently bring the action level below what would be defined as acceptable by the rest of the group.

In contrast to the play group, the maintenance of action on the formally organized team depends on an initial commitment to playing as a part of the team. This commitment then serves as a basis for learning and conforming to a preestablished set of norms.[1] The norms apply equally to everyone, and control is administered through the coach-supervisor. Regardless of how priorities are set with respect to goals, goal achievement rests primarily on obedience to the coach's directives rather than on the generation of personal interests based on mutually satisfying social exchange processes. Within the structure of the organized competitive team, deviation from the norms is defined as serious not only when it disrupts action, but also when it *could* have been disruptive or when it somehow challenges the organized structure through which action occurs. Thus sanctions take on a value-supportive function as well as an instrumental function. This is demonstrated by the coaches who constantly worry about their own authority, that is, whether they command the respect of their players.

In the interest of developing technical skills, the norms for the formally organized competitive team restrict not only the range of a player's action, but also the form of such actions. Unique batting, throwing, running, shooting, or kicking styles must be abandoned in the face of what the coach considers to be correct form. Joking around on the part of any team member is usually not tolerated regardless of the player's abilities and the demonstration of skills is usually limited to the fundamentals of the game.

If commitment cannot be maintained under these circumstances, players are often not allowed to quit. They may be told by the coach that "We all have to take our bumps to be part of a team" or "Quitters never win and winners never quit." Parents may also point out that "Once you join a team, it is your duty to stick it out for the whole season" or "We paid our money for you to play the whole season; don't waste what we've given you." With this kink of feedback, even a total absence of personal commitment to the sport activity may not lead to withdrawal from participation. What keeps youngsters going is a commitment to personal honor and integrity or obedience to a few significant people in their lives.

WHEN THE GAME IS OVER: MEANING AND CONSEQUENCES

The implications of the game after completion are different for the members of the informal play group than they are for the members of the formally organized competitive team. For the latter, the game goes on record as a win or a loss. If the score was close, both winners and losers may initially qualify the outcome in terms of that closeness.[2] But, as other games are played, all losses and wins are grouped respectively regardless of the closeness of scores. In the informal play group, the score of a game may be discussed while walking home; however, it is usually forgotten quickly and considered insignificant in light of the actions of individual players. Any feelings of elation that accompany victory or of let-down that accompany defeat are shortlived in the play group—you always begin again on the next day, in the next game, or with the next activity. For the organized competitive team, such feelings are less transitory and are often renewed at some future date when there is a chance to avenge a previous loss or to show that a past victory was not just a fluke. Related to this is the fact that the organized team is usually geared to winning, with the coaches and players always reminding themselves, in the Norman Vincent Peale tradition, that "We can win . . . if we only play like we can." This may lead to defining victories as the expected outcomes of games and losses as those outcomes that occur when you do not perform as you are able. When this happens, the elation and satisfaction associated with winning can be buried by the determination to win the next one, the next one, and so on. Losses, however, are not so quickly put away. They tend to follow you as a reminder of past failures to accomplish what you could have if you had executed your collective skills properly. The element of fun in such a setting is of only minor importance and may be eliminated by the seriousness and determination associated with the activity.

The final difference between the two groups is related to the stability of each. The informal play group is characteristically unstable, whereas the opposite is true of the organized team. If minimal levels of commitment cannot be maintained among some members of the play group, the group may simply dissolve. Dissolution may also result from outside forces. For example, since parents are not involved in the organization of the play group, they may not go out of their way to plan for their youngster's participation by delaying or arranging family activities around the time of the group's existence. When a parent calls a youngster home, the entire group may be in serious jeopardy. Other problems that contribute to instability are being told that you cannot play in the street, that someone's yard is off limits, that park space is inaccessible, or that necessary equipment is broken or unavailable. These problems usually do not exist for the organized team. Consent by parents almost guarantees the presence of a player at a scheduled practice or game, space and equipment are reserved in advance, and substitute players are available when something happens to a regular team member. Because the team is built around a structure of roles rather than a series of interacting persons, players can be replaced without serious disruption, and the action can continue.

NOTES

1. In some cases, "commitment" may not be totally voluntary on the part of the player. Parents may sign up a son or daughter without the youngster's full consent or may along with peers, subtly coerce the youngster to play.
2. Such qualifications are, of course, used for different effects. Winners use them to show that their challengers were able or that victory came under pressure. Losers use them to show how close they came to victory.

5. *What to Do When Grown-Ups Want to Spoil the Fun of School Sports*

DEL STOVER

Whatever happened to the notion that school sport ought to be fun? That's a question a lot of school board members are asking these days as they watch high school (and even junior high) sports become more competitive and demanding of coaches and students.

Just count the hours some young athletes spend in physical training. Then take a look at the hundreds of fans screaming for victory at a Friday night football game, and consider the extensive local press coverage some athletes and their teams receive. Add the lure of college scholarships and professional contracts for top athletes, and you easily can see why some observers question whether–somehow–priorities haven't gotten out of kilter.

In theory, school sports is supposed to be educational and good, clean fun. Winning should be a treasured goal but not an obsession. Passion for victory can cause a ripple effect that travels farther than you might think: Young athletes seeking to excel devote all their efforts to one sport and miss out on others; students of average athletic ability are squeezed out of participation; parents demand that a losing coach be fired. This is fun?

If all this sounds more than vaguely familiar, it might be because you've heard it before–about college sports. Some school people now fear that the troubles afflicting college athletic programs now threaten high schools.

That potential certainly exists, says Richard Lapchick of the Center for the Study of Sport in Society at Northeastern University. "Winning has become everything," he says. "It's a reflection of everything else in society. Our society puts a high premium on winning. Unless you get the brass ring, you have nothing."

Fortunately, nobody is suggesting that the situation with high school sports has reached crisis proportions. At the National Federation of State High School Associations (N.F.S.H.S.A.), Assistant Director Dick Fawcett

---

says most coaches consider themselves educators "first and foremost" and that any problems must be sought out on a school-by-school basis or even sport-by-sport. Yet he acknowledges there are "strong forces" promoting increased competitiveness, and he recommends all school board members be alert to the potential for problems in their school.

A look at your athletic program probably will reassure you that no serious problems exist. But you'll likely find the seeds—pressure placed on coaches to win, athletes specializing in one sport at an early age, some students feeling shut out. Your task is to keep these seeds from sprouting.

TURNING PRO AT 15

Talented young athletes who once changed sports with the seasons are finding it either an advantage or a necessity to specialize in one sport. "Finding a multidimensional player is increasingly rare," says Lapchick. "The demands of the sport, the desire for increased competitive levels by coaches and players—it's put people in the position where specialization is a requirement."

Several factors have played a role in this development, but one unavoidable influence on students has been society's adulation of athletic prowess, starting early. Star school athletes are featured on local sports pages and often hold high social status among their peers. College scholarships await those who excel. "It's how our society works," says Steve Scovic, who as superintendent of the Fairborn (Ohio) Public Schools has taken a strong interest in the role of school sports. "We pay our entertainers and athletes more than we'll ever think to pay our teachers, doctors, or engineers. We're leading kids to believe it's a way to be successful and famous."

Acquiring such acclaim takes work. In the past decade, observers of high school sports say, students have started specializing at an earlier age, honing their skills in sports camps and local sports leagues and lifting weights to develop muscle strength. As skill levels increase, students must specialize merely to stay competitive. In some school systems, competition is so great that a student must begin serious training before he reaches junior high school. And sports such as ice hockey or swimming can demand that students train 11 months a year.

Because winning teams provide job security, coaches sometimes contribute to this problem by encouraging students to train during the off-season. A school's coaches even can begin competing with one another for top athletes, says N.F.S.H.S.A.'s Fawcett, who also is a school board member in the Park Hill (Missouri) R-5 School District. He tells of one basketball coach who told his players not to go out for football lest they be injured and have to miss basketball season. "Some coaches want to take over the lives of students," he says.

Specialization costs kids the opportunity to experience different sports and experiment with their athletic skills. The danger is that students will specialize too early, says Jack Roberts, executive director of the Michigan High School Athletic Association, who complains coaches forget some students fail to mature physically until their late teens. "Youngsters are being pressured into specializing in one sport . . . before they know what they're good at," he says. "They're being shortchanged."

Critics also complain that specialization takes some of the fun out of sports. Concentrating on improvement in one sport is hard work, and athletes literally can "burn out"—eventually dropping sports altogether or at least avoiding other sports so they can "take a break." That doesn't hurt just students: "If you keep athletes involved in different sports, it strengthens your whole program." Roberts says. "You've got more depth, more top athletes for [various] sports."

Some school people are trying to discourage specialization. In Michigan, the state athletic association limits the amount of off-season contact coaches may have with players—allowing coaches to provide individual training to no more than three students during the off-season and forbidding full-scale team practices. In Illinois, school athletes cannot participate in a club sport (a community basketball league, for example) if the same sport is in season at school—a rule designed to prevent kids from spending too much time on one sport. "Students should be in several sports until they're seniors," says Frank Pitol, athletic director at Collinsville (Illinois) High School. "If they have a chance at a scholarship, then it's fine to specialize in the last year. But we recommend they participate in three sports and enjoy a whole year of competition.

That's a policy some critics endorse. "I sense that the schools are breeding a star system," says Nancy Karweit, a principal research scientist at the Center for Social Organization of Schools at Johns Hopkins University. "We're seeing two classes: students who excel [in athletics], and an awful lot of kids who are doing nothing. The incidence of obesity among young people is growing, yet we have the other syndrome of super athletes at age 11. The balance isn't there."

NOT MAKING THE CUT

With specialization comes another problem: Some students who want to participate don't get the opportunity. Students at small schools might find it easier to make the team, but competition at larger schools can be so stiff that even good athletes consider themselves lucky to warm the bench. For the average student, participation in school athletics can end as early as elementary school.

The trend upsets people like Fawcett: "A good school athletic program ought to create options for kids rather than close them down. If we're shutting kids out, then something's wrong."

Coaches counter that limiting participation is the last thing they want to do. Some factors, they say, simply are out of their control: Gymnasium space is limited for indoor sports, and many schools do not have the equipment or staff to handle large turnouts for sports. Finding coaches also is a problem. At Collinsville High School, Pitol says a teacher from a neighboring school system had to be recruited to serve as an assistant coach.

On the surface, nationwide student participation in sports appears strong. According to N.F.S.H.S.A., more than 5.2 million students were involved in high school athletics during the 1986-87 school year. Although below the all-time high of 6.5 million in 1977-78, participation is the highest in four years and, Fawcett says, seems to follow enrollment trends. Also, he says, high schools have added new sports in the past ten years, many organized for girls in response to Title IX.

But not everyone is convinced. Some school observers worry that tight budgets are forcing schools to cut back on intramural and low-profile sports—leaving only the expensive "glamour" sports of football and basketball untouched. But even if schools are adding new sports, that doesn't necessarily create opportunities for students who hadn't participated before. Only so many students will jump at the chance to join the swimming team or golf team, for example, and boys hoping to play basketball aren't helped by the addition of girls' soccer. Also, many coaches limit varsity football teams to 35 or 45 players, and most basketball teams suit up an average of only 15 players.

Both students and school sports programs in general can be hurt when prospective athletes are shut out. Students lose the opportunity to participate, and athletic programs lose out on those kids whose skills develop later—long after they've given up any hope of playing. "We never know when a student is going to mature," says Dick Fawcett. "Some won't hit their stride until twelfth grade." Adds Roberts: "I think it's a tragedy how many kids we lose . . . , how many we exclude as early as ninth grade."

Some schools refuse to cut students. At Collinsville High School, Pitol has added junior varsity and freshman varsity teams to expand participation. And in varsity football, he assigns less-able students to specialty teams rather than turn them away. In Fairborn, Ohio, school officials say they've worked hard to find sufficient athletic facilities to accommodate intramural as well as varsity teams. Says Steve Scovic: "We've had basketball teams playing from Saturday morning to late afternoon. Other athletic programs have gone on after school to ten o'clock at night."

Of course, such commitment requires the support of your board. Expanding an athletic program requires additional equipment and coaches, and board members must decide what priority to place on athletics. Otherwise, you might find yourself in the position of one Colorado school, where 80 students tried out for the soccer team and fewer than one-third were chosen because only one soccer coach was available. Scovic points out that taxpayers might be disturbed by the inequities in some programs: "On extracurricular activities, the expenditure per pupil is almost $100 a child, yet not all children participate. Parents don't know how much of their school funds aren't getting spent on their children."

THE SPIRIT OF VINCE LOMBARDI

Ultimately, what determines whether a school athletic program strays from its educational objectives is the subtle–and not so subtle–pressure put on school administrators, coaches, and students to produce a winning season. To some degree, such pressure is normal: Athletes always will want to win for themselves and their classmates. But pressure can build.

Asked about the sources of this negative pressure, school administrators point first to parents. Some parents push kids as young as 7 years old into community sports leagues–putting their youngsters through the hectic pace of as many as three sports programs at the same time. In Georgia, the state board of education years ago had to take steps against red-shirting–in which parents hold young athletes back a grade to give them time to mature physically so they will be bigger and stronger than the kids they compete against.

Other factors feed the victory-at-all-costs mentality. Local newspapers long have ballyhooed the exploits of local sports heroes ("The smaller the town, the more the pressure," says Ross Merrick of the American Alliance for Health, Physical Education, Recreation and Dance), and now the national press is expanding coverage of high school sports: *USA Today* and *Sports Illustrated* regularly cover high school sports and occasionally profile high school athletes.

But a much more proximate problem is overzealous fans. Unrestrained enthusiasm can turn ugly, with fans and even parents attacking student athletes. Scovic says he's dismayed by what parents yell from the stands. "It amazes me how people can criticize young people who are trying the best they can. A kid who's at a formative age doesn't purposely try to mess up a football game or basketball game." Allowing such behavior to gain acceptance has repercussions beyond the damaged psyches of athletes. It's not uncommon to hear of school games where fans throw soda cans or toilet paper at players, and in Union City, N.J., school officials last year banned fans from a Hoboken-Emerson high school football game because of the rival schools' history of violence in the heat of the game.

"Spectators have brought unacceptable standards of behavior to high school sports," says Jack Roberts. "They've watched how college and professional athletes and fans behave, and they're starting to behave like them."

The effect of such pressures touches everyone: Unless a coach has a "well-developed value system," Fawcett says, the temptation to make small concessions—scheduling additional days of training or overlooking bad grades—to gain a competitive edge is likely to win out. That's only natural, says Richard Lapchick, who speculates that the turnover rate for losing coaches probably is high: "At the college level, in basketball, it's 20 percent a year; in football, it's 24 percent. I'm sure [the numbers are similar] in the high schools."

Some school leaders are taking steps to avoid these problems. At Collinsville High School, coaches meet with parents and athletes to discuss sportsmanship and spectator etiquette, and national high school athletic rules require basketball coaches to stay seated during matches to prevent what Roberts calls "the pacing and yelling of those silly college and professional coaches." Coaches say state adoption of no-pass, no-play rules also have helped everyone keep school sports in perspective.

PUTTING THE FUN BACK

Protecting your athletic program from the problems that touch other schools isn't always easy. But many observers say your board has options—if you put educational objectives above the short-term interests of players, coaches, and fans. Some suggestions:

- *Start a program to educate people about the purposes of school sports.* Articulating the objectives of your sports program—and ensuring that participants and fans are familiar with those objectives—can help put the brakes on excessive efforts to excel in sports. "I think our biggest problem is failing to extol the virtues and educational values of athletics," says Ed Joseph of the Texas High School Coaches Association. "We must remind people that the primary purpose of the program is not to win state championships but to offer these children an educational experience." Another goal should be clearly to outline what is acceptable behavior from students, parents, and spectators. At Missouri's Park Hill, Fawcett says, high school coaches meet with athletes and their parents to discuss team rules, sportsmanship, and fan behavior.
- *Add junior varsity and intramural programs.* Although some school people question whether students are interested in intramural programs, many coaches say these programs can go a long way toward solving the participation issue. "If you give me a school, and I like marbles, I'll have 500 kids playing with marbles," says Ross Merrick.

"If I'm not excited about intramurals, no one will come out." In Illinois, Pitol says expansion of junior varsity teams in his area has allowed the expansion of interscholastic competition for students.

- *Encourage student participation.* A little encouragement from coaches might be all that's needed to persuade less-talented students to participate—and to encourage top athletes to experiment with different sports. So your board must make your expectations clear to coaches and athletic directors. "A school board must have a philosophy; it must put a strong premium on participation," says Fawcett. "And you've got to ask, 'Are we willing to back that philosophy up?' A no-cut policy is great . . . but it's a considerable expense."
- *Set financial priorities.* Expanding intramural sports and adding junior varsity or freshmen varsity teams might boost participation, but such programs require additional funding for coaches, equipment, and transportation. If you provide only enough funds to support big-time football and basketball programs, Fawcett says, "You send a message to your coaches and athletic department about what you really value."
- *Establish an athletic council.* In the Park Hill schools, the school board established an athletic council of administrators, athletic directors, and coaches to help board members resolve athletic program issues. The council recommends board policies and serves as an appeals body—hearing complaints from students and parents about board policies. In addition to serving as a "tremendous buffer" between critics and board members, Fawcett says, the athletic council also "provides a larger perspective for making decisions."
- *Hire a coach who will teach.* When hiring a new coach, select a good teacher who puts education before winning and who will instill the values you expect to be taught in an athletic program. "We hire a teacher first and a coach second, and that message gets heard by coaches," Fawcett says. Adds Scovic: "We'd like to win more, but I want good coaches who are role models for my athletes. I'll take a good role model who keeps our kids competitive [rather] than a jerk who'll win 90 percent of his games."
- *Protect your coaches.* When losses start to mount, community members can forget the reasons behind your athletic program and put heavy pressure on coaches, administrators, and board members to replace a losing coach. But experts say succumbing to such pressure only puts more pressure on the next coach. Your best move is simply to refuse, "As an administrator, I want to protect my coaches from people breathing down their necks," says Scovic, who refuses to discuss a coach's performance during the sports season.
- *Evaluate coaches as teachers.* To reduce the pressure on coaches, let everyone know that evaluations are heavily weighted toward teaching ability. And mean it. Scovic suggests a four-point evaluation: (1) Is the coach a positive role model? Does he serve as a good repre-

sentative of the school system? (2) Is the coach knowledgeable about his sport? Can he ensure student safety, help students improve their athletic skills, and make them feel good about themselves? (3) Can the athletic program be enjoyed by all family members who attend as spectators? Is it fun? (4) Are teams competitive? (In answering this question, Scovic says, evaluators must remember that talented athletes aren't always available.)

- *Survey your athletes.* Except by looking at win/loss records and participation figures, schools boards have few ways to gauge the value of athletic programs. One possibility is to distribute a questionnaire asking student athletes what they think of the program. Among the questions you might ask: "What are you learning? Are you treated well by coaches? Do coaches spend sufficient time with you? Are the coach's expectations explained to you? Do you feel good about your progress?" (Such a survey is available from N.F.S.H.S.A., 11724 Plaza Circle, Kansas City, MO 64195.)

Despite the challenges facing school athletic programs, school leaders aren't pessimistic about the future. "We're not without problems, but I think school sports programs continue to be a model of educational activity in the schools," Roberts says. "I think we can be really proud of what takes place in athletics."

Still, adds Fawcett, more needs to be done to keep the educational objectives of school sports uppermost in everyone's mind: "Athletics at its best can be an experience where young people learn what it means to be mentally and physically tough. Ideally, that should take place in a value system [in which] coaches and fans and parents are all supporters of the kind of growth that we really value–how to win gracefully and lose gracefully, emphasizing teamwork and proper training, avoiding drugs and alcohol. This is the context that should surround all our athletic activities."

6. *High School Football and Academics*

H. G. BISSINGER

I

If school was boring, Don Billingsley nevertheless did his best to get through it. When the food science teacher made the fatal mistake of asking the class if it knew the meaning of the word *condiment,* Don immediately answered with "lambskin, sheepskin." All joking aside, Don was becoming something of a food science scholar. He had scored a superb 99 on the fill-in-the-blank worksheet on cakes and frostings, not to mention a 96 on his poultry worksheet. The "preparation and service" worksheet was coming a little more slowly; he had gotten only a 60, but there seemed little doubt that Don would eventually get a handle on it. And, of course, when the occasion arose to write out a menu for a black-tie dinner party in Odessa, he would know exactly what to do.

In English, where one of the blackboard panels had a list of questions about *Macbeth* and another a reminder to bring a flashlight to the pep rally, Don had uncovered one of the great secrets of the class with the discovery that if he angled his chair in a certain way behind the other students, the teacher could not see him fall asleep. "Do you like to sleep? This is where I sleep," he said just before he entered the classroom.

A worksheet was due that day deciphering the meaning of some lines from *Macbeth,* and Don was handed a copy of the homework by someone else so he could copy down the answers. The class time was supposed to be spent doing a little crossword puzzle on the play, but Don didn't do much of it and it didn't seem to matter. The instructor for her part believed that the text the students used, *Adventures in English Literature,* which contained selected works by Shakespeare, Edmund Spenser, and Daniel Defoe among others, was too hard for them. She said also that they absolutely hated any assignment in which they had to interpret what they had read. If they had to think about anything, make critical judgments and deliberations, the cause was hopeless. The best they could be expected to do was regurgitate.

SOURCE: Excerpt from *Friday Night Lights: A Town, A Team, and a Dream.* 1990, by H. G. Bissinger. Reprinted with permission of the Addison-Wesley Publishing Company.

In sociology, Don generously passed around his bag of cookies. He and the other students watched eagerly as accounts of one gruesome murder after another passed over the tiny VCR screen, accompanied by the hushed melodrama of Geraldo Rivera. The teacher gave no instruction the entire period, except to applaud the actions of a man who, in broad daylight at an airport, killed a manacled criminal suspect accused of molesting the man's son.

Don, of course, was a football player, which gave him special status among his peers regardless of how he performed in class. In the hierarchy of the school, where girls and partying and clothes and fancy cars were as important as academics, being a football player opened doors that other students could only dream of. All other achievements seemed to pale in the face of it.

Eddie Driscoll, a wonderfully articulate student ranked number two in the senior class, loved to read and debate and throw out ideas. He stood out in class like a sore thumb. There were some who admired him and others who considered him a pompous windbag. Despite all his academic accomplishments, Eddie himself often wondered what it would be like to sit in those two rows at the front of the pep rally each Friday in a brotherhood as supremely elite as Skull and Bones at Yale or the Porcellian Club at Harvard. Such musings didn't make him resentful of the football players; he liked them. He just felt a little envious. No matter how many books he read, no matter how exquisite his arguments in government class about gun control or the Sandinistas or the death penalty, he never got the latest scoop on who was having the weekend parties. Only the football players were privy to that sacred knowledge.

"The football identity is so glorious," he said. "I always wondered what it would have been like if I had been a football player. I think it would be great to be in the limelight and be part of the team, have a geisha girl bring me candy three times a day."

Roqui Pearce, who had graduated from Permian in 1988 and was going out with starting defensive cornerback Conni Dean, said there was definitely a mystique in the school about dating a Permian football player. "Everybody's into football. Football is *the* sport. I wouldn't say it's an honor or anything but it's looked up to: 'Wow, you're going out with a football player, a Permian football player.'"

Roqui had been chosen a Pepette her senior year. Lots were drawn to see which player each Pepette would be assigned to for the season. Some of the players were obnoxious and egotistical, but Roqui didn't really mind as long as it was a football player she got and not one of the student trainers. "Nobody wants a trainer. You want a football player."

She had ended up being assigned to Coddi, who was then a junior. At the Watermelon Feed that year, she hadn't worn his number on her jersey, which angered him. But they hit it off well. "I liked him, plus I wanted to be a real good Pepette. I didn't want him to think I was a bad

Pepette. I wanted to be a good Pepette." She brought Coddi an ice cream cake in the shape of a football field from Baskin-Robbins. She baked him cakes and brownies. She got him a black trash can and filled it with popcorn balls. She gave him a towel and pillowcase decorated with the insignia of Mojo and Texas. After several months they went on a date and then started going out steadily.

From time to time the role of the Pepette became controversial. A stinging editorial in the school newspaper, the *Permian Press*, applauded a new rule prohibiting Pepettes from placing candy in players' lockers every Friday. "Though losing a tradition, Pepettes have gained much respect," said the editorial. "No longer will a member be the personal Geisha girl of a player. Instead, she can focus more on the organization's original purpose, boosting morale. And in so doing she will carry the image of professionalism she deserves for her work bolstering the famous Mojo spirit." But the Pepettes still spent time baking players cookies and making them signs. Since they could no longer put goodies in the lockers of the players, they just handed the stuff to them instead or dropped it off at their houses.

Their role was symptomatic of the role all girls played at Permian. "You hate to admit it in this day and time, but a lot of girls are conditioned towards liberal arts courses rather than engineering and science," said Callie Tave, who found herself perpetually buried under a blizzard of forms and recommendation requests since she was the only college counselor for the seven-hundred-member senior class.

The attitude that girls at Permian seemed to have about themselves was reflected during an economics class one day when Dorothy Fowler, a spirited and marvelous teacher, tried to wake students up to the realities of the world in West Texas where the days of the fat-paying blue-collar job were over.

"Think about your jobs. Where do you want to be in five years?" asked Fowler of a female student.

"Rich," the student replied.

"How are you going to achieve that?"

"Marry someone."

On the SAT exam, boys who took the test during 1988-89 at Permian had a combined average score of 915 (433 verbal, 482 mathematical), 19 points below the national average for boys. Girls had a combined score of 840 (404 verbal, 436 mathematical), 75 points below their male counterparts at Permian and 35 points below the national average for girls. Of the 132 girls who took the test during the 1988-89 school year, there wasn't one who got above a 650 in either the math or verbal portions of the exam.

"It's very revered to be a Pepette or a cheerleader," said Julie Gardner, who had come to Odessa from a small college town in Montana as a sophomore. "It's the closest they can get to being a football player." Gardner found the transition to Permian enormously difficult. She was utterly unprepared for her first pep rally, for all those fanatical cheers, all those arms pumping so frantically up and down, and she found the girls cliquey and obsessed with appearance. At first she dressed up like everyone else, but then she began to reject it. And because she was intelligent (she graduated from Permian in 1986 and went on to become an honors English major at Swarthmore College), she also felt ostracized.

"It was very important to have a boyfriend and look a certain way. You couldn't be too smart. You had to act silly or they put you in a category right away. It was the end of your social life if you were an intelligent girl." The pressure to conform was so intense, said Gardner, that she knew girls who privately were quite intelligent and articulate, but were afraid to show it publicly because of the effect it would have on their social lives.

Her father, H. Warren Gardner, vice president of the University of Texas of the Permian Basin, a branch of the University of Texas system located in Odessa, believed the disparities in performance between boys and girls were a result of the social hierarchy of the school. Gardner said it was clear to him that girls had to "dumb down" at Permian or else run the risk of being excluded from dating and parties because the boys considered them too smart. "It's not appropriate [for a girl] to be intelligent," he concluded. "It's not popular to be bright."

And being a Pepette, despite the restriction making candy off-limits to the locker room, still carried status. "I hate football players, especially at Permian," said senior Shauna Moody. "They're the most egotistical . . . they think they're God's gift." But for a girl at Permian, the only thing worse than being a Pepette was not being one. Or as Moody explained her own reasoning for having joined, "Well, *everybody's* a Pepette."

Cheerleading had a special cachet for girls at Permian as well. Just as the football players walked down the school halls in their game jersies on Fridays, so did the cheerleaders in their uniforms. There were five girls on the cheerleading squad, all of them white, and they had enormous visibility.

The most popular of them was Bridgitte Vandeventer, who had always wanted to be a cheerleader. "Everyone knew who Permian was and who Mojo was, and I thought it would be neat to be a Permian cheerleader," said Bridgitte, who had lived with her grandparents since she was eight.

The most wonderful moment of her life, she said, was being crowned Homecoming Queen, and she had vivid memories of it—changing from her cheerleading uniform into a black velvet dress, wearing a fantastic spread of mums adorned with black and white streamers and trinkets in the shape of little footballs that one of the players had given her, dutifully waiting in line with the other finalists at halftime and then hearing her name called, holding the hand of her best friend as she walked around the oval of the stadium with tears in her eyes, receiving four dozen red roses afterward from admirers. Because of her status at school and her friendliness, she had no lack of them.

For a while she went out with Brian Chavez, and it was hard not to feel proud when she saw him on the football field. "It was neat to say, that's my boyfriend out there, that's who I'm dating. The time Brian scored a touchdown, I was never so excited. . . ."

Brian was Hispanic, but that didn't make her uncomfortable. "My grandmother says, 'whites are for whites, Hispanics are for Hispanics, blacks are for blacks.' I don't think blacks are for whites, whites for blacks. I think Hispanics are fine because they're as close to whites as you can get."

She had many ambitions for her life. She wanted to go into the medical field. She wanted to be Miss Universe. She wanted to open a dance studio. She wanted to be famous. She wanted to write a book about her life.

But for the immediate future, her plans included going to the junior college in town, Odessa College. A main reason she was going there was her failure to take the college boards, a requirement for admission at most four-year-schools. Bridgitte said she had been advised by a teacher at Permian not to take the SAT exam until after the football season because of her myriad duties as a cheerleader. But she didn't seem upset about it, and one thing was obvious—her popularity at school was unrivaled. Not only was she crowned Homecoming Queen, she was also voted Miss PHS by her classmates. Clearly she was a role model.

"I just want to be known," said Bridgitte in summing up her hopes in life. "I want everybody to know me, but not in a bad way. My dream is to be known, to be successful, and to help people. I love to help people."

"I look forward to getting out on my own and tryin' the world. They say it's a real rat race and I hope to win it."

With his dark, pouty looks, it was hard not to think of Don Billingsley as a movie star when he walked down the halls of Permian, gently fending off female admirers in his black football jersey, except for those two or three or four or five who seemed to have a certain special something. The way he talked to them, with his head ducked low and the words coming out in a sweet, playful cadence, suggested a certain self-recognition of his aura. Sophomore girls fantasized over having him in the same class so they could catch a glimpse of his buttocks in a tight-fitting pair of jeans. He received inquiries about his availability for stripteases. The characterization used by girl after girl to describe him was the same, said with the wistfulness of irrepressible infatuation: "He's so fine!"

Aware of his image as the best-looking guy at Permian and fortunate enough not to have school interfere with the responsibilities that came with such a title, much of his day was spent flirting either silently with his eyes or with his benign naughtiness in the classroom. He might not be learning anything, but school was a blast and everywhere he looked he was fending off girls—the one who sat behind him in government and wanted a relationship (Don had to explain to her gently but firmly that he didn't "do" relationships), the one who sat behind him in food science (he went out with her for a while but it wasn't what he was looking for), the one who came up to him in the hallway.

Then there was the girl who had been dubbed the "book bitch." So desperate was she to ingratiate herself with the football players that she bought one of them a brand-new backpack and then offered him fifty dollars to sleep with her. When that didn't work, she offered to bring the books of several of them to class. Dutifully, she waited in the hallway, whereupon Don and some others loaded her down with books so she could trudge off to class with them with a slightly chagrined smile on her face, as if she knew that what she was doing was the price you paid for trying to gain the acceptance of the football players when you had blemishes on your face and didn't look like Farrah Fawcett.

Don was clearly not motivated to be a scholar. His class rank at Permian going into his senior year was the second lowest of any senior on the football team, 480 out of 720. He reveled in playing the Sean Penn role in his own version of *Fast Times at Ridgemont High*, but beneath all that was a witty, personable kid. During the fall he was voted Mr. PHS, an honor that delighted his classmates and stunned the hell out of his teachers and coaches. The nondemanding, lethargic nature of the classes he was in made it difficult to fault his attitude about school. Left to his own devices, he did what any high school senior in America would do: he took advantage of it.

Asked what the purpose of school was at Permian, Don had a simple answer. "Socializing," he said candidly. "That's all senior year is good for." That, and playing football. If there was any angst about school, it was over the number of girls who desired to spend at least some part of their lives with him. They were everywhere. Girls in short leather skirts. Girls in expensive designer jeans. Girls who spent the last five minutes of class carefully applying rouge and lipstick to their faces because the teacher had run out of things to say. The perplexity of it all gnawed at him a great deal more than the meaning of *Macbeth*. Or as he put it in a line probably not inspired by Shakespeare's play, "There's so much skin around, it's hard to pick out one."

There were other football players who had light schedules. One of his teammates, Jerrod McDougal, had taken senior English the previous summer so that he wouldn't have to grapple with it during the football season. There was something wonderfully soulful about Jerrod. He was unusually sensitive and spoke with pained and poignant sorrow about the confusion of growing up in a world, in an America, that seemed so utterly different from the one that had spawned the self-made success of this father. His class rank was in the top third, but because of football Jerrod wanted as little challenge as possible his senior year. With English out of the way, he was taking government and the electives of sociology, computer math, photography, and food science.

"That's why I took all my hard courses my sophomore and junior year, so I wouldn't have to worry about any of that stuff," he said one afternoon after food science, where Billingsley and he had just spent sixty minutes on a worksheet containing 165 fill-in-the-blanks on the uses of a microwave. "Maybe that's a bad deal. I don't know."

Permian's best and brightest, those ranked in the top ten, reported few demands made of them in the classroom as well. Eddie Driscoll, who would end up attending Oberlin College, said he had never been pushed at Permian and generally had half an hour's worth of homework a night. Scott Crutchfield, another gifted student ranked in the top ten who would end up going to Duke, said he had two to three hours of homework a week, "I think I'd probably learn more if I had to do more work. As it is, I still learn a lot, I guess. In general, I don't do a lot."

II

In computer science, Brian Chavez wore faded blue jeans and black Reeboks. The number 85 jersey around his expansive chest nicely matched his earring with the numeral 85 embossed in gold. He had a fleshy face in need of a shave and his hair looked a little like that of a main character in *Eraserhead*, high and square on top like an elevated putting surface. It came as no surprise that he held the Permian record for the bench press with 345 pounds.

The way he looked, five eleven and 215 pounds, the way he loved to hit on a football field, the way the words came so slowly out of his mouth sometimes as if he had a two-by-four stuck in there somewhere, it was hard to think he had any chance of making it past high school unless he got a football scholarship somewhere.

He fit every stereotype of the dumb jock, all of which went to show how absolutely meaningless stereotypes can be. He was a remarkable kid from a remarkable family, inspired by his father, whose own upbringing in the poverty of El Paso couldn't have been more different.

Ranked number one in his class at Permian, he moved effortlessly between the world of the football and the academic elite. On the field he was a demon, with a streak of nastiness that every coach loved to see in a football player. Off the field he was quiet, serene, and smart as a whip, his passivity neatly hiding an astounding determination to succeed. "He's two different people," Winchell said of him. "He's got a split personality when he puts on that helmet."

From computer science he made his way to honors calculus, where a black balloon from the Friday pep rally floated casually from his knapsack. On the way there he was handed a note by Bridgitte that read, "Have fun at lunch and I either will see you before lunch or after lunch. Okay! Smile! Love you!" In calculus class he casually scribbled his answers in a white notebook, an exercise that seemed as mentally strenuous to him as trying to see whether he still remembered the alphabet. While others strained and fretted he just seemed to glide, and inevitably several classmates gathered around him to watch him produce the right answer. After calculus it was off to honors physics and then honors English and then honors chemistry. These courses came easily to him as well. Part of that had to do with what was asked of him—with the exception of English, he said he had almost no homework.

If he wasn't a typical brain filled with anguish and neurosis, he wasn't a typical Permian football player either. He was lucky, but he always knew in the back of his mind that if he failed in football it didn't really matter anyway.

He had become as indoctrinated into the cult of football in Odessa as anyone. After all, it was something he had lived, eaten, and breathed since seventh grade. But as he headed into his senior year he also realized that he wanted something more. No matter how glorious and exciting the season was, he also knew it would come to an end.

In his own private way, he found far more inspiration in the classroom than he did on the football field. And nowhere did he seem more determined than in English class, under the spell of a special teacher named LaRue Moore.

She saw in him a metamorphosis his senior year, a fascination with vocabulary and literature and trying to write essays with perception and clarity. He was striving for something she hadn't quite seen before, and when he told her he was interested in going to Harvard she joyously encouraged him as much as she could and agreed to read his application essays.

It was simply part of her style. Whenever she could, she tried to show students the bountiful world that existed past the corporate limits of Odessa and how they should not be intimidated by it but eager and confident to become a part of it. On five different occasions, she and her husband, Jim, the former principal of Ector High School before it closed, had taken students to Europe to let them see other cultures, other lands. What she aspired to as a teacher was embodied by a written description she prepared of her senior honors English class for a group of observers:

> I work not only for the gathering and assimilation of knowledge, but also to teach the fact that one can be brilliant without being arrogant, that great intellectual capacity brings great responsibility, that the quest for knowledge should never supplant the joy of learning, that one with great capacities must learn to be tolerant and appreciate those with lesser or different absolutes, and that these students can compete with any students at any university anyplace in the world.

A teacher such as LaRue Moore should have been considered a treasure in any town. Her salary, commensurate with her ability and skill and twenty years' teaching experience, should have been $50,000 a year. Her department, of which she was the chairman, should have gotten anything it wanted. She herself should have been given every possible encouragement to continue what she was doing. But none of that was the case, of course. After all, she was just the head of the English department, a job that in the scheme of natural selection at Permian ranked well behind football coach and band director, among others.

As Moore put it, "The Bible says, where your treasure is, that's where your heart is also." She maintained that the school district budgeted more for medical supplies like athletic tape for athletic programs at Permian than it did for teaching materials for the English department, which covered everything except for required textbooks. Aware of how silly that sounded, she challenged the visitor to look it up.

She was right. The cost for boys' medical supplies at Permian was $6,750. The cost for teaching materials for the English department was $5,040, which Moore said included supplies, maintenance of the copying machine, and any extra books besides the required texts that she thought it might be important for her students to read. The cost of getting rushed film prints of the Permian football games to the coaches, $6,400, was higher as well, not to mention the $20,000 it cost to charter the jet for the Marshall game. (During the 1988 season, roughly $70,000 was spent for chartered jets.)

When it came to the budget, Moore did have reason to rejoice this particular year. The English department had gotten its first computer. It was used by all twenty-five teachers to keep grade records and also to create a test bank of the various exams they gave to students.

The varsity football program, which had already had a computer, got a new one, an Apple IIGS, to provide even more exhaustive analyses of Permian's offensive and defensive plays as well as to keep parents up to date on the progress of the off-season weight-training program. At the end of the year the computer would be used to help compile a rather remarkable eighty-two-page document containing a detailed examination of each of the team's 747 defensive plays. Among other things, the document would reveal that Permian used sixty-six different defensive formations during the year, and that 25.69 percent of the snaps against it were from the middle hash, 67.74 percent of which were runs and 32.26 percent of which were passes.

Moore's salary, with twenty years' experience and a master's degree, was $32,000. By comparison, she noted, the salary of Gary Gaines, who served as both football coach and athletic director for Permian but did not teach any classes, was $48,000. In addition, he got the free use of a new Taurus sedan each year.

Moore didn't object to what the football program had, nor did she object to Gaines's salary. She knew he put in an enormous number of hours during the football season and that he was under constant pressure to produce a superb football team. If he didn't, he would be fired. She had grown up in West Texas, and it was obvious to her that high school football could galvanize a community and help keep it together. All she wanted was enough emphasis placed on teaching English so that she didn't have to go around pleading with the principal, or someone else, or spend hundreds of dollars out of her own pocket, to buy works of literature she thought would enlighten her students.

"I don't mind that it's emphasized," she said of football. "I just wish our perspective was turned a little bit. I just wish we could emphasize other things. The thing is, I don't think we should have to go to the booster club to get books. I don't think we should have to beg everyone in town for materials."

But that was the reality, and it seemed unlikely to change. The value of high school football was deeply entrenched. It was the way the community had chosen to express itself. The value of high school English was not entrenched. It did not pack the stands with twenty thousand people on a Friday night; it did not evoke any particular feelings of pride one way or another. No one dreamed of being able to write a superb critical analysis of Joyce's *Finnegan's Wake* from the age of four on.

LaRue Moore knew that. So did Dorothy Fowler, who fumed to a visitor one day, "This community doesn't want academic excellence. It wants a gladiatorial spectacle on a Friday night." As she made that comment a history class that met a few yards down the hall did not have a teacher. The instructor was an assistant football coach. He was one of the best teachers in the school, dedicated and lively, but because of the legitimate pressures of preparing for a crucial game, he did not have time to go to class. That wasn't to say, however, that the class did not receive a lesson. They learned about American history that day by watching *Butch Cassidy and the Sundance Kid* on video.

■ FOR FURTHER STUDY

Dubois, Paul E. "The Effect of Participation in Sport on the value Orientations of Young Athletes." *Sociology of Sport Journal* 3 (March 1986):29-42.

Fine, Gary Alan. "Team Sports. Seasonal Histories, Significant Events: Little League Baseball and the Creation of Collective Meaning." *Sociology of Sport Journal* 2 (December 1985):299-313.

Fine, Gary Alan. *With the Boys: Little League Baseball and Preadolescent Culture.* Chicago: University of Chicago Press, 1987.

Foley, Douglas E. *Learning Capitalist Culture: Deep in the Heart of Tejas*. Philadelphia: University of Pennsylvania Press, 1990.

Hill, Grant M., and Jeffrey Simon. "A Study of Sport Specialization on High School Athletics." *Journal of Sport and Social Issues* 13 (Spring 1989):1-13.

Lever, Janet. "Sex Differences in the Games Children Play." *Social Problems* 23 (1976):479-487.

Lever, Janet. "Sex Differences in the Complexity of Children's Play and Games." *American Sociological Review* 43 (August 1978):471-483.

Lidz, Franz. "BMXing It Up with the Rad Crowd." *Sports Illustrated* (December 8, 1966):28-36.

Looney, Douglas S. "Bred to be a Superstar." *Sports Illustrated* (February 22, 1988):56-63.

Morris, G. D., and James J. Stiehl. *Changing Kids' Games.* Champaign, IL: Human Kinetics, 1989.

Nixon, Howard L., II. "Rethinking Socialization and Sport." *Journal of Sport and Social Issues* 14 (Spring 1990):33-47.

Rees, C. Roger, Frank M. Howell, and Andrew W. Miracle. "Do High School Sports Build Character?" *The Social Science Journal* 27 (1990):303-315.

Sage, George H. "Sports Participation as a Builder of Character?" *The World and I* 3 (October 1988):629-641.

Smoll, Frank L., Richard A. Magill, and Michael J. Ash, eds. *Children and Sport*, 3rd ed. Champaign, IL: Human Kinetics, 1988.

Snyder, Eldon E. "Athletic Dressing Room Slogans as Folklore: A Means of Socialization" *International Review of Sport Sociology* 7 (1972):89-102.

Waid, R. "Child Abuse: Reader's Forum." *Runner's World* (September 1979):16.

Weiss, Maureen R., and Daniel Gould, eds. *Sport for Children and Youths.* Champaign, IL: Human Kinetics, 1986.

Weiss, Maureen R., and Becky L. Sisley. "Where Have All the Coaches Gone?" *Sociology of Sport Journal* 1 (December 1984):332-347.

Yablonsky, Lewis, and Jonathan J. Brower. *The Little League Game.* New York: Times Books, 1979.

Part Three

Sport and Violence

Of the many questions concerning violence in sport, one takes precedence: Why are violent sports so popular in some societies and less so in others? Is it because aggressive activities have a cathartic effect, releasing pent-up hostility in a socially healthy way? Thus, they are needed in those societies where tensions are high. Research shows again and again, however, that aggression actually produces more aggression. In the first selection, anthropologist Richard Grey Sipes provides evidence for a related explanation—that violent societies have violent sports. There is ample evidence that America is a violent society (for example, the history of slavery; the forcible taking of land from Native Americans; vigilante law in the West; a foreign policy of Manifest Destiny; our contemporary crime rates, which tend to be about ten times greater than those found in Great Britain, France, Sweden, and Japan; our high imprisonment rate; and the popularity of violence in literature, movies, and television). Similarly, violent sports are popular in American society.

Violence is inherent to many sports. Athletes hit, tackle, block, and collide as they engage in various sports. Even some non-contact sports such as basketball have become very "physical." In these sports settings some violence is "normative" while other aggressive acts go beyond the acceptable. The second selection by sociologist Michael Smith, helps us to sort out the differences by providing a typology of sports violence.

The third selection is by Rick Telander, a sports journalist and a former football player from Northwestern. Telander describes the essence of football—violence.

7. *Sports as a Control for Aggression*

RICHARD GREY SIPES

From as early as our first recorded thoughts of man, we have been attempting to control what we call aggression. We haven't tried to eliminate it, but rather to have it manifest how, when and where we wish it and to have it absent in all other situations. Most of the time, on a day-to-day basis, we succeed, but we become quite concerned when our control fails and results in muggings, fist fights, child abuse, riots, police brutality or a war not to our benefit.

Can we significantly improve the precision of our control of aggression? I do not think so. My opinion is based on research results[1,2,3] indicating that, with massive effort, we could raise or lower the *general* aggressiveness of a society and its members, but that we cannot control manifestations of aggression much more precisely than we presently do.

Sport has been seen as an activity that can be used to at least influence the manifestation of aggression on the social and individual levels. It is true that sport is theoretically and practically more controllable by social institutions, up to and including the governmental level, than virtually any other widespread activity. How we would use our control of sports, though, depends on which of two opposing models of human behavior we use in our thinking.

TWO MODELS OF BEHAVIOR

According to what I have called the *Drive Discharge Model* of human behavior, there is a certain level of aggression in every individual and in every society. The aggression is like a liquid substance generated by an innate drive or by interaction with the environment. Although its level may vary somewhat from time to time, and from one society to another and one person to another, it generally is higher than desired, and must be discharged along acceptable paths. This is the model with which most psychiatric and psychological writers work, and it is the one most com-

SOURCE: *The Humanistic and Mental Health Aspects of Sports, Exercise and Recreation*, Timothy T. Craig (ed.) (Washington, DC: American Medical Association, 1976), pp. 46-49.

monly used by the layman. According to this model, we can decrease unwanted manifestations of violence and other aggressive behavior by encouraging its manifestations in innocuous behavior. Simplistically, we can reduce the frequency of fistfights by increasing the frequency of attendance at boxing matches, and decrease the likelihood of war by increasing combative sports.

The alternative model, which I label the *Culture Pattern Model*, assumes something quite different about human behavior. It stresses the fact that we learn our individual patterns of behavior, and that our culture supplies us with these patterns. It sees individuals and entire societies as fundamentally consistent in most of their behavior patterns, with similar generalized modes manifesting themselves in divergent arenas of action. According to this model, we can decrease unwanted violence and other aggressive behavior by reducing the aggressive component of culture patterns wherever this component is found. Simplistically, we would reduce the frequency of fistfights if we eliminated the sport of boxing, and could reduce the likelihood of war by not engaging in combative sports.

The "treatments" indicated by these two models, then, are mutually exclusive—indeed opposite.

But both models, if we stop here, are only unsubstantiated speculations . . . informed opinions. They must survive rigid, controlled tests if they are to pass to the category of substantiated theories, and they must be in this category before we are justified in acting on them.

TESTING THE MODELS

Both models have been tested through hypotheses logically derived from them. The *Drive Discharge Model* predicts that as the incidence of one form of aggression goes up, the incidence of other forms will go down. We should find a lower incidence of combative sports in societies that are more warlike, and within any given society a lower incidence during periods of increased military activity. So with other forms of aggressive behavior. More warlike societies should have a lower need for—and consequently have a lesser occurrence of—such venting behavior as the practice of malevolent magic, harsh punishment of deviants or body mutilation. More peaceful societies, on the other hand, denied the release of aggression in the form of warfare, should show a higher occurrence of these aggressive outlets. More generally, we could predict that the more any one or more of these aggressive channels are used, the less the remainder are likely to be needed by the society.

The *Culture Pattern Model*, on the other hand, predicts that the above channels, including warfare, are likely to vary directly. That is, a society low in one is most likely going to be low in all and a society high in one probably will be high in all, since the same general orientation or cultural motif will govern these and many other behaviors of, and within, the society.

METHODOLOGY

I subjected these hypotheses to test, using the cross-cultural correlation method. This method has been accepted and employed by anthropologists, sociologists, psychiatrists and psychologists to test numerous hypotheses.[4] It has been brought to a high level of confidence and rigor in recent years.[5]

A cross-cultural correlation study utilizes a representative sample of societies from the universe of human societies. Within this sample it tests for Variable A relative to Variable B. If A and B tend systematically to occur or otherwise vary together (correlation studies are statistical–not mechanical–in orientation and admit of discomformity), it is assumed that there is some functional relationship, direct or indirect, between A and B. A biological parallel is the correlation between the presence (or absence) of certain parasitic protozoans in the bloodstream of humans and the periodic manifestation (or absence) of symptoms we term malaria. The correlation is not unity, but it is strong enough and statistically significant enough to suggest an important functional, perhaps causal, connection between the two phenomena.

THE TEST AND RESULTS

I randomly selected ten warlike and ten peaceful societies throughout the world and ethnographically coded them for the presence or absence of combative type sports.[1] A combative type sport was defined as one involving the acquisition of disputed territory, generally symbolized by the placing of an object in a guarded location (a hockey puck in the cage, a basketball through the ring, or a football at the opponent's end of the field), the subduing of an opponent (as in some–but not all–forms of wrestling), or patently combat situations (fencing, dodging thrown spears, karate). If a society had even one combative sport, it was coded as having combative sports. Of the ten warlike societies, nine had combative sports and one did not. Of the ten peaceful societies, only two had combative sports and eight lacked them. This indicates that warlikeness and combative sports tend to occur together. The *phi* value of this distribution is 0.7035. The Fisher Exact Test shows that the probability of getting this, or a rarer distribution of cases in the same direction, by chance alone is less than 0.0028, or about three in a thousand tries. The test supports the *Culture Pattern Model* and vitiates the *Drive Discharge Model.*

To verify my cross-cultural results, I conducted a temporal-variation study in the United States. The level of military activity was measured by the percent of the adult male population in the United States Armed Forces each year between 1920 and 1970. This spanned three periods of active combat. I used two relatively combative sports: hunting (a participation sport) and attendance at football games (spectator activity). I also used two relatively noncombative sports: race-track betting (participant) and attendance at baseball games (spectator). Yearly measures of activity in these sports were correlated with yearly level of military activity. Technical reasons led me to divide the data into two periods: pre-1946 and post-1946. Of the eight resulting correlation tests, six showed a non-significant—often insignificant—relationship between sports and military activity, of which five were direct. The only significant *inverse* relationship was between military activity and betting in the period following 1946. This was balanced by an equally significant *direct* relationship between military activity and betting in the pre-1946 period. This also is the least sport-like of the four sports used, according to common interpretations. Moreover, if graphed, it becomes evident that the eight-fold increase in betting between 1942 (in the midst of World War II) and 1970 probably was due to increasing affluence, and may have nothing to do with the fact that the percent of males in the military shrank from twenty-five to five in the same period. (During the actual World War II and Korean periods of conflict, there is a strong rise in betting, providing a direct correlation between betting and warfare for that specific time span.)

The *Drive Discharge Model* predicts a negative dischronic relationship between sports and war, whereas the *Cultural Pattern Model* predicts a positive *or no* dischronic relationship over this length of time. The case study test results, therefore, confirm the results of the synchronic cross-cultural study and tend to support the *Cultural Pattern Model* at the expense of the *Drive Discharge Model.*

AN ETHNOSCIENTIFIC STUDY OF SPORTS AND CONFLICT

Professor Kendall Blanchard has conducted a comparative ethnoscientific linguistic analysis and emic conflict-model study of "perceived conflict"—fights, wars, aggressive displays and sports—in the contemporary Choctaw Indian and "Anglo" societies. (This approach studies, in depth, the terms grammar, values and logic used by the members of a culture themselves, to arrive at the *meaning* of behavior in the cultural context.[6]) Through personal correspondence he informs me that his unpublished results[7] support my findings that sports, especially combative team sports, do not serve as functional alternatives to other forms of aggression, such as warfare. Sports and war would appear to be components of a broader cultural pattern.

MALEVOLENT MAGIC, MUTILATION, AND PUNISHMENT

I anticipated the objection that the choice and test of merely two alternative channels of aggression discharge might not give a valid or sufficiently complete picture of the situation. This prompted me to later test three other activities, using the same sample societies and the cross-cultural method.[3] I selected the practice of malevolent magic as a way in which an individual could secretively aggress upon a fellow community member. Cosmetic/status mutilation was chosen because it has been claimed to represent a turning-inward of aggression against one's self (although this claim certainly can be disputed). The punishment of deviants was used because it represents aggression of society against the individual.

Three indicator variables were used to measure malevolent magic: (1) how important such magic looms in the minds of most members of the society (importance), (2) roughly what proportion of misfortunes are attributed to it (scope), (3) the amount of harm it can produce (intensity).

Body mutilation was broken down into tattooing, scarification, piercing, shape molding and amputation. The *measure of mutilation* was the sum of measures of (1) how many different types of mutilation were practiced for cosmetic reasons, by what proportion of the population, and by either male or female or both; and (2) the occasions at which mutilation was used to mark changes in the social status or role (adulthood, marriage, widow[er]-hood) of the individual, male or female or both, and the proportional incidence of such mutilation.

Punishment of deviants was measured as the sum of coding values for the severity of usual punishment for (1) murder, (2) major theft, and (3) forbidden sexual intercourse.

Each of the above three theoretical (indirectly measured) variables, and their indicator (directly measured) variables, was tested against the warlikeness of the societies, and the results of the correlation tests are shown in Table 7-1. (Results of the earlier combative-sports test also are shown for comparison and completeness.) A nonwar summarized aggression value for each society also was computed from all four theoretical variable scores (sports, magic, mutilation and punishment) and tested against warlikeness, with the result of that test also shown. Note that all directly-measured indicator variables show a positive correlation with warlikeness. The more warlike societies are more likely to have higher "aggressiveness" in each of these variables. The results are somewhat more impressive when we look at the theoretical variables—the correlations tend to be more significant. The overall aggressive measure is

TABLE 7-1 Warlikeness versus Other Traits

	*Phi**	*CumP***
Malevolent Magic	0.6710	0.0070
Importance	0.4725	0.1002
Scope	0.5164	0.0593
Intensity	0.7135	0.0038
Punishment	0.6250	0.0305
Murder	0.4910	0.0835
Theft	0.5006	0.1186
Sex	0.5774	0.0468
Body Mutilation	0.4000	0.0900
Cosmetic	0.2041	0.3257
Male	0.2182	0.3142
Female	0.2182	0.3142
Status	0.2000	0.3258
Male	0.1005	0.5000
Female	0.1155	0.5000
Sports	0.7035	0.0028
Combined	0.8000	0.0005

**Phi* is a statistical measure of strength of association between two dichotomized variables. The higher the value, the stronger the association.

***CumP*, computed with Fisher's Exact Probability Test, represents the probability of getting the observed distribution, or one more rare, in the direction predicted by chance alone. The lower the value, the more significant the association.

singularly impressive, with the probability of finding that correlation by chance alone being about five in ten thousand.

These results emphatically support the *Culture Pattern Model* and invalidate the *Drive Discharge Model.* The functional relationship between various aggression-containing activities is one of mutual support, not one of alternative discharge paths.

DISCUSSION

Sports and war (and other "aggressive" forms of behavior) obviously do not, as often claimed, act as alternative channels for the discharge of accumulable aggressive tensions.

The *Cultural Pattern Model* seems better able to predict and explain human behavior. It says that each society and its culture (and perhaps each individual?) is characterized by one or more motifs or themes. The consistency typical of any culture leads us to expect to find similar attitudes, orientations and behaviors manifesting themselves in different activities. If indifference to suffering, zero-sum games, bravery, aggressiveness or other generalized characteristics are found strongly present in one activity, they most likely will be found throughout the culture rather than be limited to that one activity.

COMMENT

The hope would seem dim of using sports to influence warfare, or any of the other forms of undesirable aggressive behavior. Aggression by society, or by components thereof, or a manifested in the individuals who make up society, is an integral part of the total cultural configuration. To significantly attenuate one form of aggression would require us to simultaneously attenuate most or all forms; that is, to overhaul our entire culture.

Modification of behavior—individual or social—is difficult at best. If we wish to take on this task, though, my research would indicate that aggressive behavior is best reduced by eliminating combative or conflict-type sports. Attempting to siphon off aggressive tension by promulgating the observation of or participation in aggressive sports is more than a futile effort; to the degree that it had any effect at all, it most likely would raise the level of aggression in other social and individual behavior patterns.

REFERENCES

1. Sipes, R. G.: War, sports and aggression: an empirical test of two rival theories. *American Anthropology* 75 (1):64-86, 1973.
2. Sipes, R. G.: War, combative sports and aggression: A preliminary causal model of cultural patterning, in Nettleship, M. A. (ed): *War: Its Causes and Correlates*. The Hague, Mouton Press, 1975.
3. Sipes, R. G., Robertson, B. A.: Malevolent magic, mutilation, punishment, and aggression. Read before the American Anthropological Association, San Francisco, 1975.
4. Naroll, R.: What have we learned from cross-cultural surveys? *Am Anthrop* 72:1227-1288, 1970.
5. Sipes, R. G.: Rating hologeistic method. *Behav Sci Notes* 7:157-198, 1972.
6. Tyler, S. A.: *Cognitive Anthropology*. New York, Holt, Rinehart, and Winston, 1969.
7. Blanchard, K.: Team sports and violence: an anthropological perspective. Read before the Association for the Anthropological Study of Play, Detroit, 1975.

8. *A Typology of Sports Violence*

MICHAEL D. SMITH

> No rules or practice of any game whatever can make that lawful which is unlawful by the law of the land; and the law of the land says you shall not do that which is likely to cause the death of another. For instance, no persons can by agreement go out to fight with deadly weapons, doing by agreement what the law says shall not be done, and thus shelter themselves from the consequences of their acts. Therefore, in one way you need not concern yourself with the rules of football. (Hechter, 1977:444)

These were Lord Justice Bramwell's instructions to the jury in an 1878 British court case, *Regina* v. *Bradshaw.* A soccer player was accused of manslaughter after he charged and collided with an opposing player, who subsequently died, in a game played under Football Association rules. The defendant was acquitted, but the judge's pronouncement has been cited of late in North America by those who wish to make the point that sports should not be exempt from the laws that govern our behaviour elsewhere.

Seventeen years later, in 1895, Robert Fitzsimmons engaged in a public boxing exhibition with his sparring mate, Riordan, in Syracuse, New York. Riordan was knocked unconscious by a punch to the head and died five hours later. Fitzsimmons was indicted for manslaughter. The judge directed the jury as follows:

> If the rules of the game and the practices of the game are reasonable, are consented to by all engaged, are not likely to induce serious injury, or to end life, if then, as a result of the game, an accident happens, it is excusable homicide . . . (Hechter, 1977:443)

Fitzsimmons was acquitted. What is noteworthy about this case is that the rules and practices of the game were taken into account in determining criminal liability, a precedent directly contrary to that established in *Regina* v. *Bradshaw.* It is the Fitzsimmons ruling that has more or less held ever since.

The fact is, sports violence has never been viewed as "real" violence. The courts, except for isolated flurries of activity, have traditionally been reluctant to touch even the most outrageous incidents of sports-related

---

SOURCE: Excerpt from *Violence and Sport* (Toronto: Butterworths, 1983), pp. 8-14, 17-21. Reprinted by permission.

bloodletting; legal experts still flounder in their attempts to determine what constitutes violence in sports. The great majority of violence-doers and their victims, the players, even though rule-violating assaults often bring their careers to a premature close, have always accepted much of what could be called violence as "part of the game." Large segments of the public, despite the recent emergence of sports violence as a full-blown "social problem," continue to give standing ovations to performers for acts that in other contexts would be instantly condemned as criminal. An examination of sports violence that fails to consider these perspectives "does violence," as it were, to what most people, not to mention those involved with criminal justice systems, regard as violence.

Following is an attempt to answer the question: what is sports violence? I shall go about this task by constructing a typology. A typology is a device for categorizing a phenomenon into at least two types on each of one or more dimensions. In the present case, sports violence will be divided into four types, ranging roughly from greater to lesser, on a scale of *legitimacy*, as shown in Table 8-1. I shall take into account the viewpoints of the law, the players, and the public in so doing. This exercise is confined to acts performed by players during the game, or in its immediate context.

BRUTAL BODY CONTACT

This category of sports violence comprises all significant (i.e., high magnitude) body contact performed within the official rules of a given sport: tackles, blocks, body checks, collisions, legal blows of all kinds. Such

TABLE 8-1 A Sports Violence Typology

Relatively Legitimate	
Brutal body contact Conforms to the official rules of the sport, hence legal in effect under the law of the land; more or less accepted.	**Borderline violence** Violates the official rules of the sport and the law of the land, but widely accepted.
Relatively Illegitimate	
Quasi-criminal violence Violates the official rules of the sport, the law of the land, and to a significant degree informal player norms; more or less not accepted.	**Criminal violence** Violates the official rules of the sport, the law of the land, and players' informal norms; not accepted.

contact is inherent in sports such as boxing, wrestling, ice hockey, rugby, lacrosse, football, and to lesser degrees in soccer, basketball, water polo, team handball, and the like. It is taken for granted that when one participates in these activities one automatically accepts the inevitability of contact, also the probability of minor bodily injury, and the possibility of serious injury. In legal terms players are said to "consent" to receive such blows (*volenti non fit injuria*—to one who consents no injury is done). On the other hand, no player consents to be injured intentionally. Suppose a blitzing linebacker levels a quarterback with a ferocious but legal tackle; the quarterback is severely injured; a civil court case ensues. Theoretically, the law suggests, if it can be shown that the linebacker foresaw that his blow would severely injure the quarterback, hence *intended* to injure him, the linebacker is culpable. The probability of such a legal outcome, however, is close to zero. If effect, any blow administered within the formal rules of a sport is legal under the law of the land (Lambert, 1978).

Legal body contact is nevertheless of interest as violence when it develops (or as some might prefer, degenerates) into "brutality." A rising toll of injuries and deaths, followed by public expressions of alarm, then demands for reform, typically signal this condition. An "intrinsically brutal" sport like boxing always hovers not far from this point; for this reason, boxing is almost everywhere regulated by the state, albeit often inadequately. When body contact assumes an importance out of proportion to that required to play the game—when inflicting pain and punishing opponents are systematized as strategy, and viciousness and ferocity are publicly glorified—a stage of brutality can be said to have been reached. Such practices may strain the formal rules of sports, but they do not necessarily violate those rules.

Sports brutality is not a new phenomenon. The history of football, to take probably the best example, is in part a chronicle of intermittent waves of brutality, public censure, and reform. In 1893 indignation against alleged viciousness in American college football, smouldering for some time, erupted across the country. A campaign led by the magazines *Saturday Evening Post* and *The Nation* caused several institutions to drop the game, including Harvard, one of the first schools to play it on a regular intercollegiate basis. (Parke Davis [1911:98], then the University of Wisconsin coach and later a historian of the game, wrote that the reports of brutish play were somewhat exaggerated. Among the most hysterical must have been that appearing in a German publication, *Münchener Nachrichten*. This report, quoted by Davis, described the Harvard-Yale game of 1893 as "awful butchery," seven participants reportedly being carried in "dying condition" off the field with broken backs, broken legs, and lost eyes.) A popular vaudeville ditty of the day is revealing (Betts, 1974:244):

Just bring along the ambulance,
And call the Red Cross nurse,
Then ring the undertaker up,
And make him bring a hearse;
Have all the surgeons ready there,
For they'll have work today,
Oh, can't you see the football teams
Are lining up to play.

Antifootball sentiment swept the United States again in 1905. In a report somewhat more measured than the one above, a Chicago newspaper published a compilation for the 1905 season showing 18 players dead, 11 from high schools and 3 from colleges, and 159 more or less serious injuries. President Roosevelt called representatives of Yale, Harvard, and Princeton to the White House and threatened to ban the game unless its brutality was eliminated. Stormed Teddy "Rough Rider" Roosevelt, "Brutality and foul play should receive the same summary punishment given to a man who cheats at cards" (Stagg, 1927:253). Rule changes resulted, including the outlawing of the notorious V formation, and the furor abated.

Roughing up and intimidating opponents as a legal tactic, however, seems to have gained new life of late. Football is still in the vanguard. Consider the "hook," a sort of on-field mugging, whereby a defensive back in the course of making a tackle flexes his biceps and tries to catch the receiver's head in the joint between the forearm and upper arm. Professional player Jack Tatum (Tatum and Kushner, 1979:18), who likes to think that his hits "border on felonious assault," fondly recalls a well-executed hook (the tactic was outlawed soon after):

> I just timed my hit. When I felt I could zero in on Riley's head at the same time the ball arrived in his hands, I moved. . . . Because of the momentum built up by the angles and speed of both Riley and myself, it was the best hit of my career. I heard Riley scream on impact and felt his body go limp.

The casualty rates, the ultimate result of this type of play, are not insignificant. The rate in the National Football League is said to be 100 per cent—at least one serious injury per player per season (Underwood, 1979). About 318,000 football injuries annually require hospital emergency room treatment in the United States (Philo and Stine, 1977). In the Canadian Football League, according to a survey conducted by the *Toronto Star* (November 25, 1981), 462 man-games were lost in the 1981 season owing to injury (down slightly from the year before). Observers seem to agree that the high injury rates at all levels of the game are attributable in significant measure to the way football is taught and played: brutishly.

BORDERLINE VIOLENCE

In this category are assaults that, though prohibited by the official rules of a given sport, occur routinely and are more or less accepted by all concerned. To wit: the hockey fist-fight, the late hit in football, the high tackle in soccer, the baseball knock-down pitch, basketball "body language," the sometimes vicious elbowing and bumping that takes place in track and road races. Such practices occasionally produce serious injuries, but these are usually dismissed as unfortunate accidents. Borderline violence is essentially the province of referees, umpires, and other immediate game officials, higher league officials and law enforcement authorities seldom becoming involved. Sanctions never exceed suspension from the game being played, and perhaps a fine.

Borderline violence is nonetheless illegal under civil law, as the U.S. *Restatement of Torts* makes clear (Rains, 1980:800):

> Taking part in a game manifests a willingness to submit to such bodily contacts or restrictions of liberty as are permitted by its rules or usages. Participating in such a game does not manifest consent to contacts which are prohibited by rules or usages of the game if such rules or usages are designed to protect the participants and not merely to secure the better playing of the game as a test of skill. This is true although the player knows that those with or against whom he is playing are habitual violators of such rules.

Thus a football lineman who goes offside and injures his opposite number with a legal block has broken a rule designed to "secure the better playing of the game" and is not legally liable under civil law for his action. But a defensive back who hits a ball carrier just after the whistle has blown has broken a safety rule, a rule designed "to protect the participants," and *is* liable on grounds of negligence or recklessness. Playing football does not, in the eyes of the law, include "consenting" to be the recipient of a late hit. Yet the law almost never intervenes in such cases, for reasons that will begin to emerge shortly.

Borderline violence is tolerated and justified on a number of grounds, most of which boil down to some version of the "part of the game" argument. Take hockey fisticuffs. A National Hockey League player, one of sixty interviewed in 1976-77 by the author (see Smith, 1979c), provides this familiar (non) explanation:

> I don't think that there's anything wrong with guys getting excited in a game and squaring off and throwing a few punches. That's just part of the game. It always has been. And you know if you tried to eliminate it, you wouldn't have hockey any more. You look at hockey from the time it was begun, guys get excited and just fight, and it's always been like that.

Naturally because fist-fighting is considered legitimate it is not defined by its practitioners as "violence." Also nobody gets hurt in a punch-up, players insist. (This is not precisely true. Of 217 "minor injuries" suffered by players on a Southern Professional Hockey League team over a three-year period in the mid-1970s, most involved the hand or forearm [fractures, sprains, lacerations, etc.] and were usually incurred during fights [Rovere et al., 1978:82].) To the majority of professional players interviewed by the author the periodic public fuss over hockey fighting is simply a product of the rantings of publicity-hungry politicians:

> I think it's really blown out of proportion. A lot of these politicians trying to get somewhere are just trying to crack down on fighting to get their name in the paper. Most of the guys that say things like that don't know anything about hockey, and they're trying to talk about violence, and they don't even know what they're talking about. I don't think a punch in the head is going to hurt you, unless it's, you know, a sick thing where a guy pummels a guy into the ice and things like that.

There are, or course, more elaborate folk theories in circulation. Apologists are prone to claim, for example, that hockey fisticuffs are safety valves for aggressive impulses (usually described as "frustration") that inevitably accumulate due to the speed, the contact, the very nature of the game. Because these aggressive urges must be vented, the argument goes, if not one way then another, prohibiting fist-fighting would result in an increase in the more vicious and dangerous illegal use of the stick. In the words of John Ziegler, President of the NHL (*Toronto Star*, December 13, 1977:C2): "I do not find it unacceptable in a game where frustration is constant, for men to drop their sticks and gloves and take swings at each other. I think that kind of outlet is important for players in our games."

The logic is shaky. Would Ziegler argue that the pugnacious Philadelphia Flyers, NHL penalty leaders nine years in a row, get more penalties than other teams because they get more frustrated? Or that the Flyers are somehow compelled to respond to frustration with aggression, whereas other teams are not? Hockey may well have its frustrating moments (what sport does not?), but as researchers have repeatedly shown, human beings may or may not respond to frustration with aggression. Like most human behaviour, responses to frustration are shaped by culture and learning. "Frustration" seems more an excuse for, than a cause of, violence in hockey.

Belief in the inevitability of hockey violence generally is so entrenched, that a judge in the famous Ted Green-Wayne Maki assault trials (stemming from a stick-swinging duel during a 1969 game in Ottawa that nearly ended Green's life) concluded that the game "can't be played without what normally are called assaults." Both players were acquitted, needless to say (*New York Times*, September 4, 1979:31).

As for public opinion, polls have revealed that substantial minorities find the hockey fist-fight more or less acceptable. Just months after the Green-Maki episode, almost 40 per cent of the respondents in a Canada-wide survey sponsored by *Maclean's* magazine said they "liked to see fighting at a hockey game"; among males the figure was 46 per cent (Marshall, 1970). In a 1972 *Canadian Magazine* reader survey (over 30,000 questionnaires were returned), 32 per cent of all respondents and 38 per cent of the male respondents thought NHL players should *not* be given automatic game penalties for fighting (Grescoe, 1972). In the United States a state-wide survey of Minnesota residents conducted by Mid-Continent Surveys of Minneapolis, shortly after the 1975 assault trial in Minnesota of Boston hockey player David Forbes, found that 61 per cent of Minnesotans thought punishment for fighting in professional sports should be left to the leagues. Twenty-six per cent preferred court punishment, and 5 per cent preferred both (Hallowell and Meshbesher, 1977). More recently, 26 per cent of over 31,000 Ontario residents surveyed in 1979 responded "No" to the general question, "Do you feel there is too much violence in professional hockey?" (McPherson and Davidson, 1980).

QUASI-CRIMINAL VIOLENCE

Quasi-criminal violence is that which violates not only the formal rules of a given sport (and the law of the land), but to a significant degree the informal norms of player conduct. It usually results, or could have resulted, in serious injury, which is what brings it to the attention of top league officials and generates public outrage in some quarters. This in turn puts pressure on legal authorities to become involved. League-imposed penalties for quasi-criminal violence usually go beyond the contest in question and range from suspensions from several games to lifetime bans, depending on the sport; each league seems to decide how much and what types of violence it will tolerate. Increasingly, civil legal proceedings follow, though perhaps less often than thought; up to 1978 only about ten civil suits involving personal injury in the National Football League took place; in the National Basketball Association, there were perhaps two (Horrow 1980). Criminal proceedings, rare in the past, are occurring more frequently, but convictions remain few and far between. In 1976 the Attorney General of Ontario, after several public warnings, ordered a crackdown on violence in amateur and professional sports in the province. According to an internal memorandum provided by the Director of Regional Crown Attorneys, sixty-eight assault charges were laid in less than a year (sixty-seven in hockey, one in lacrosse), but only ten convictions were obtained, although sixteen cases were still pending at the time of the memorandum. Apparently all the convictions, and almost all the charges, were against amateur athletes. . . .

Still, a small number of episodes of quasi-criminal violence in professional sports have resulted in litigation, and it is these cases that have generated the greatest publicity. Several civil disputes have received continent-wide attention. One of the first in sport's modern era took place in baseball during a 1965 game between the San Francisco Giants and the Los Angeles Dodgers. Giant batter Juan Marichal felled Dodger catcher John Roseboro with his bat following an acrimonious verbal exchange. Roseboro sustained considerable injury; Marichal was fined $1,750 by the League and suspended for eight games. Roseboro filed a $110,000 civil suit for damages against Marichal and the San Francisco club; it was reportedly settled out of court for $7,500 (Kuhlman, 1975).

A decade and a half later, in 1979, Houston Rocket basketball player Rudy Tomjanovich was awarded the whopping sum of $3.25 million dollars in a civil suit for injuries received as a result of a single, devastating punch thrown by Kermit Washington of the Los Angeles Lakers during a 1977 game, a blow described by a Laker assistant coach as "the hardest punch in the history of mankind." Tomjanovich suffered a fractured jaw, nose, and skull, severe lacerations, a cerebral concussion, and was not surprisingly out for the season. The League Commissioner suspended Washington for sixty days and fined him $10,000. The jury, in making an award of more than half a million dollars above what Tomjanovich's attorneys had demanded found that Washington had acted "intentionally," "maliciously," and "with reckless disregard for the safety of others." The Lakers as an organization were deemed negligent because they "failed to adequately train and supervise Washington," even though they were aware that "he had a tendency for violence while playing basketball" (nine fights in four years, according to the plaintiff's attorneys). The Lakers paid (Horrow, 1981; Rains, 1980).

A similar case is one that began in 1975, *Hackbart* v. *Cincinnati Bengals Inc.* This litigation arose out of an incident in a National Football League game in 1973 in which the plaintiff, Dale Hackbart of the Denver Broncos, was given an illegal forearm blow on the back of the head by an opposing player, Charles Clark of the Cincinnati Bengals, in a "malicious and wanton" manner five seconds after the play had been whistled dead. The referees did not see the action, and no penalty was called. Hackbart returned to the sidelines, but later discovered he had suffered a career-ending spinal fracture. The district court ruled that Hackbart had taken an implied risk by playing a violent game and that "anything" happening to him "between the sidelines" was part of that risk. The case was dismissed. But an appeals court reversed this decision, stating that although Clark may not have specifically intended to injure, he had engaged in "reckless misconduct"; the accountability of his employer (the Cincinnati Bengals) could therefore now be legally considered (Gulotta, 1980; Rains, 1980). New proceedings have apparently been scheduled. The way now seems clear for a professional sports team, as an employer, to be held accountable under civil law for the actions of the players, its employees. (An alternative approach, the Sports Violence Arbitration Act of 1983, is now before the U.S. Congress. This act would force each major professional sports league to establish an arbitration board with the power to discipline players for using "excessively violent conduct" and to make their teams financially liable for injuries suffered by the victims.)

In none of the above cases were criminal charges laid. Why this near immunity to criminal prosecution and conviction? First, most players seem reluctant to bring charges against another athlete. Based on a mail survey of 1,400 major-league basketball, football, and hockey players (no response rate is given), Horrow (1980) concludes that professional athletes, in particular, tend to believe that player disputes are best settled privately and personally on the field of play; that team management does not appreciate "troublemakers" who go "outside the family" (i.e., the league) for justice, and contract difficulties or worse probably await such individuals; that the sheer disruptiveness of litigation can ruin careers, and so on. Bolstering these beliefs is the apparent willingness of most players to dismiss virtually any during-the-match assault short of using a gun or a knife as part of the game.

From the point of view of the law, says Horrow, based on information obtained from twenty United States county prosecutors, in whose jurisdiction most of the country's major professional teams operate, many officials are reluctant to prosecute sports violence because they believe that they have more important things to do, like prosecuting "real" criminals; that the leagues themselves can more efficiently and effectively control player misbehaviour; that civil law proceedings are better suited than criminal for dealing with an injured player's grievances; that most lawyers do not have the expertise to handle sports violence cases; and that it is almost impossible to get a guilty verdict anyway.

There are two other more subtle, nonlegal reasons for the hands-off policy of criminal justice officials. One is the "community subgroup rationale." As explained by Kuhlman (1975), this is the tacit recognition by law enforcement authorities that certain illegal activities by members of some social groups ought more or less to be tolerated because they are widespread within the group and because group members look upon them as less serious than does society in general. Moreover, it would be unfair to single out and punish an individual member when almost everyone else in the group behaves similarly. In other words, the illegal conduct is rendered less criminal because everybody does it. This rationale sometimes arises in connection with the issue of differential law enforcement for minority groups. In some tough police jurisdictions,for instance, police rarely make an arrest for felonious assault involving family members and neighbours, even though such assaults are frequent. Police in these areas tend to define domestic violence as a mere "disturbance," whereas officers in other jurisdictions are more inclined to define it as genuine violence. It seems that certain assaultive practices in sports are looked upon with the same benevolent tolerance. At the very least, the severity of the penalties for violence provided by the law are widely regarded within the legal community, as well as the sports community, as out of proportion to the seriousness of the illegal acts.

The "continuing relationship rationale" applies in assault cases where offender and victim have an ongoing relationship. Legal authorities may wish to avoid straining the relationship further by prosecuting one or both parties. Husbands and wives may wish to continue living together; neighbours may have to; athletes typically compete against each other at regular intervals (Kuhlman, 1975). Criminal prosecution in sport could exacerbate already-present hostility to the point where league harmony is seriously threatened. The 1976 prosecutions on various assault charges of four Philadelphia Flyers hockey players, arising out of a game in Toronto, caused considerable strain between the Philadelphia and Toronto Maple Leafs hockey clubs, and even a public squabble between the Philadelphia District Attorney and the Ontario Attorney General (*Toronto Star*, April 22, 1976). The assumption underlying this rationale is that society has an interest in maintaining such social relationships, that professional sport in this instance serves some socially useful purpose.

Finally there is the premise of "legal individualism"—the notion that the individual is *wholly* responsible for his or her own criminal acts—which has resulted in a virtual immunity to criminal charges of sports organizations in cases where an individual member of the organization has been indicted for assault. The leading case is *State* v. *Forbes*, apparently the only criminal prosecution ever of a professional athlete in the United States.

On January 4, 1975, during an NHL game in Bloomington, Minnesota, an altercation occurred between David Forbes of the Boston Bruins and Henry Boucha of the Minnesota North Stars. Both players were sent to the penalty box, where Forbes repeatedly threatened Boucha verbally. As they left the box at the expiration of the penalties—Boucha first and Forbes seconds later—Forbes skated up behind Boucha and struck him with the butt end of his stick just above the right eye. Boucha fell to the ice stunned and bleeding (with a badly damaged eye, it turned out). Forbes jumped on him, punched him on the back of the head, then grabbing him by the hair, proceeded to pound his head into the ice. Eventually another Minnesota player separated the two. The President of the NHL suspended Forbes for two games, but shortly afterward a Minnesota grand jury charged him with the crime of aggravated assault by use of a dangerous weapon. Forbes pleaded not guilty. The jury, after a week and a half of testimony and eighteen hours of deliberation, was unable to reach a unanimous verdict. The court declared a mistrial, and the case was dismissed (Flakne and Caplan, 1977).

Described in law journals as a "landmark" case because it focused so much legal and public attention on the issue of violence in sports, *State* v. *Forbes* also raised the important and still unanswered question of legal individualism as it applies to the occupational use of violence; namely, who should be held responsible in such cases, the individual or the group?

Should not only Forbes, but the Boston Bruins and even the League, have been on trial? Was Forbes merely doing his job, his duty, as a good hockey soldier? The defence counsel tried to ask these questions during the trial, to instruct the jury to consider, for example, the "context" in which the assault took place, but the judge demurred, insisting the indictment applied only to Forbes, the individual (Hallowell and Meshbesher, 1977).

The public, too, is divided on legal individualism, if an opinion poll conducted shortly after Forbes' trial, and regarding accountability in the trial of Lieutenant Calley of My Lai massacre notoriety, is any indicator. As reported by Hallowell and Meshbesher (1977), 58 per cent of the respondents in this survey disapproved of criminal sanctions being applied to an individual acting in a legitimate role and following what that individual believed to be "at least implicit orders." Are orders to perform acts of violence implicit in professional hockey? The question should be: how explicit are such orders?

As for legally raising (let alone demonstrating) criminal liability on the part of an employer in sports violence disputes, Kuhlman (1975) suggests that although problems of proof are substantial (the burden of proof on the prosecution in a criminal trial is heavier than in a civil trial), the most promising route is probably via the statutes on conspiracy; that is, the prosecution should attempt to prove that the organization and the individual conspired to commit an assault. Owners, coaches, and teammates—all members of the "system"—are thus potentially implicated; sociological reality becomes legal fact.

By way of a footnote to *State v. Forbes*, the author was engaged in 1980 by the Detroit law firm of Dykema, Gossett, Spencer, Goodnow, and Trigg as a consultant and "expert witness" in a civil suit being brought by Boucha against the Boston Bruins and NHL. (After several only partly successful eye operations, Boucha's career had ground to a halt.) The charge was, in effect, "creating an unsafe work environment." The case was settled out of court for an undisclosed amount two days before the trial was to begin in Detroit.

CRIMINAL VIOLENCE

This category consists of violence so serious and obviously outside the boundaries of what could be considered part of the game that it is handled from the outset by the law. Death is often involved, as in the 1973 Paul Smithers case, which received world-wide publicity. Smithers, a seventeen-year-old black hockey player, was convicted of manslaughter after killing an opposing player in a fight in a Toronto arena parking lot following a game (Runfola, 1974). Almost always such incidents, though closely tied to game events, take place prior to or after the contest itself. (One suspects that if Smithers' attack had occurred during the game he would have received a five-minute or match penalty, and the victim's death would have been dismissed as an "unfortunate accident.") On the extreme fringe of this category are assaults and homicides only incidentally taking place in a sports setting.

An extended, first-hand account of another hockey incident provides an illustration of a typical episode of criminal violence in sports, while at the same time conveying something about a social milieu that encourages such misbehaviour. This assault took place in a Toronto arena after the final game of a Midget playoff series that had been marred by bad behaviour in the stands and on the ice,including physical and verbal attacks on opposing players by the assailant in question. The victim was the coach of the winning team. He had been ejected from the game for making a rude gesture at the referee and was standing against the boards some distance from his team's bench when the assault took place. He also happened to be a student at York University. Three days after the incident he came to my office seeking some advice, his face barely recognizable. He left promising to lay an assault charge, which he had not yet done, and to write down in detail his version of what happened. He did both. (The offending player was later convicted of assault.)

REFERENCES

Betts, J. R. (1974). *America's Sporting Heritage: 1850-1950.* Reading, MA: Addison-Wesley.

Flakne, G. W., and A. H. Caplan (1977). "Sports violence and the prosecution." *Trial* 13:33-35.

Grescoe, P. 1972). "We asked you six questions." *Canadian Magazine,* January 29:2-4.

Gulotta, S. J. (1980). "Torts in sports–deterring violence in professional athletics." *Fordham Law Review* 48:764-93.

Hallowell, L. (1978). "Violent work and the criminal law: An historical study of professional ice hockey." In J. A. Inciardi and A. E. Pottieger, eds., *Violent Crime: Historical and Contemporary Issues.* Beverly Hills: Sage.

Hallowell, L., and R. I. Meshbesher (1977). "Sports violence and the criminal law." *Trial* 13:27-32.

Hector, W. (1977). "The criminal law and violence in sports." *The Criminal Law Quarterly* 19:425-53.

Horrow, R. B. (1980). *Sports Violence: The Interaction between Private Law-Making and the Criminal Law.* Arlington, VA: Carollton Press.

R. B. (1981). "The legal perspective: Interaction between private lawmaking and the civil and criminal law." *Journal of Sport and Social Issues* 5:9-18.

Kuhlman, W. (1975). "Violence in professional sports." *Wisconsin Law Review* 3:771-90.

Lambert, D. J. (1978). "Tort law and participant sports: The line between vigor and violence." *Journal of Contemporary Law* 4:211-17.

Marshall, D. (1970). "We're more violent than we think." *Maclean's,* August:14-17.

McPherson, B. D., and L. Davidson (1980). *Minor Hockey in Ontario: Toward a Positive Learning Environment for Children in the 1980s.* Toronto: Ontario Government Bookstore.

Philo, H. M., and G. Stine (1977). "The liability path to safer helmets." *Trial* 12:38-42.

Rains, J. (1980). "Sports violence: A matter of societal concern." *Notre Dame Lawyer* 55:796-813.

Rovere, G. D., G. Gristina, and J. Nicastro (1978). "Medical problems of a professional hockey team: A three season experience." *The Physician and Sports Medicine* 6:59-63.

Runfola, R. T. (1974). "He is a hockey player, seventeen, black and convicted of manslaughter." *New York Times*, October 17:2-3.

Smith, M. D. (1979). "Towards an explanation of hockey violence." *Canadian Journal of Sociology* 4:105-24.

Stagg, A. A. (1927). *Touchdown*! New York: Longmans, Green.

Tatum, J., with B. Kushner (1979). *They Call Me Assassin*. New York: Everest House.

Underwood, J. (1979). *The Death of an American Game: The Crisis in Football*. Boston: Little, Brown.

9. *Football and Violence*

RICK TELANDER

The one part of football that separates it from all other sports is tackling. Tackling is the primitive, essential element that both thrills and terrifies the game's participants and viewers. I know the Chicago Bears' Mike Singletary fairly well, and I wrote a feature on him before Chicago played in Super Bowl XX in 1986. Singletary, several times the NFL's Defensive Player of the Year, began describing some of his helmet-busting, guided-missile tackles in a near-rapturous tone that sprang from his Zen-like immersion in the chaos of the game. One brutal hit on running back Eric Dickerson stuck out in his mind.

"I don't feel pain from a hit like that," he said. "What I feel is joy. Joy for the tackle. Joy for myself. Joy for the other man. You understand me; I understand you. It's football, its middle-linebacking. It's just . . . good for everybody."

The clarity and reward for a hit like that are deeply rooted in the dark essence of the game. But the type of tackling we see now—"I try to visualize my head all the way through the man," says Singletary, "my whole body through him"—is relatively new and different from the way tackling was done in the past, and the main reason is the advent a couple of decades ago of the hard-shell, air- and water-filled helmet with the increasingly large and protective face mask. Modern-day helmets allow face-first tackles, burying "your nose on his numbers" as the coaches say, so that the helmet is now less a protective device than a weapon, a rock-hard spear point that is almost always the first part of a defensive player's uniform to touch the ballcarrier. Don Cooper, the team physician at Oklahoma State, calls the helmet "the damnedest, meanest tool on the face of the earth." And if you've ever been hit by one, with someone else's head inside it, moving at a high rate of speed, you know what the doctor means.

I was reading former Oakland Raider and Buffalo Bills wide receiver Bob Chandler's book, *Violent Sundays,* a few years ago when I came to a part that grabbed my attention. I remembered covering Chandler when he played for Southern Cal and our teams met in the Coliseum in Los Angeles. "My junior year, we played Northwestern in our opening game,"

SOURCE: Excerpt from *The Hundred Yard Lie: The Corruption of College Football and What We Can Do to Stop It* (New York: Simon & Schuster, 1989), pp. 168-181. Reprinted by permission of Simon & Schuster.

he wrote. "I went down to catch a low ball, and the halfback speared me in my lower back. I wasn't sure what was damaged, but I couldn't feel my right leg, which scared the hell out of me. I hobbled off the field. Later, back at my apartment, I was in such agony that by the middle of the night my roommate Gerry Mullins literally had to pick me up, carry me to his car, and take me to the hospital. After a battery of X rays, [Coach] John McKay came in and said matter-of-factly, 'Looks like you broke your back.'"

Chandler said he was hit by a "halfback," which meant it had to have been either Jack Dustin or I who had done the damage, since we were the two cornerbacks who played for Northwestern that night. I remembered Chandler as a shifty, glue-fingered little white guy, but my biggest concern that game had been trying to stay with 6'3", lightning-bolt split end Sam Dickerson. I didn't remember hitting anybody particularly hard or making much of an impact on the game in any way, but the fact was, I might have broken an opponent's back with my helmet and not even realized I had done so. I asked Dustin, who is now a physician, if he remembered hitting Chandler in the back. He said he couldn't recall.

I finally ran into Chandler himself in the press box at an NFL game. Chandler was working as a sportscaster for a TV station in L.A., and he looked about the same as I remembered him from college. I asked him if it could have been I who had broken his back years ago, if he remembered the player's number. He said he didn't remember the number, but for some reason, he didn't think I was the man. Why, he couldn't say. Probably, it was because I just looked too harmless standing there with my notebook in my back pocket and press ID hanging from a shirt button. Still, the incident haunts me. The thought that any player could do such damage to an opponent with his helmet and not even know it is an indictment of some fundamental part of the game.

A friend of mine, sportswriter Don Pierson, who covers the NFL for the *Chicago Tribune*, recently loaned me a notebook of his from his undergrad days at Ohio State. The notebook is from a credited course Pierson took in 1966 called The Coaching of Football, taught by one Woodrow Wilson Hayes, and open to all students at the university. The maintaining of a notebook was the main work for the course, and at the back of Pierson's notebook is written in red ink: "'A' Excellent! W.W.H." The reason Pierson wanted me to take a look at the notes was to see the section on tackling. Hayes called in his right-hand man to class that day, defensive coordinator Lou McCullough, and let him explain the proper way to stick an opponent. McCullough, who would later become the athletic director at Iowa State, had a Southern drawl, Pierson informed me, and I needed to keep that in mind as I read the text. Herewith:

> We don't like to see a kid making a tackle like he is trying to hug the man down. We want to give him cancer of the breast by knocking his titty off. We want to knock his anus up through his *haid*.

That's verbatim, and I still howl every time I read it. But I think you can see why the helmet now comes with a product liability sticker on it, one that must remain on the helmet during play, as if players might stop to casually peruse the warning during lulls in the action. The label reads, "Do not use this Helmet to butt, ram or spear an opposing player. This is in violation of the football rules and such use can result in severe head or neck injuries, paralysis or death to you and possible injury to your opponent. No helmet can prevent all head or neck injuries a player might receive while participating in football."

In other words, the way coaches teach their players to tackle, face-first, may be damaging to their health. But that's how the game is played—if such a harmless word as "play" can be applied to this increasingly violent spectacle.

Worse, some players feel invincible once they strap on their headgear, at least partly because the helmets themselves make the players feel like Kralite-hulled gladiators. Back in November 1987, I read something in the newspaper that haunted me as I went about covering college football. A boy named Doug Mansfield, a 5'10", 165-pound senior noseguard at Humboldt High School in Tennessee, had run headfirst into a brick wall in frustration after a loss to Lexington High and was now paralyzed from the neck down. The wire service report stated that moments after the game ended, the youth had run in full football gear directly into the wall outside the dressing room. The blow broke his neck and severed his spinal cord and left him in critical condition. "The doctors said there is nothing we can do, that he won't ever get any better," his mother, Susan Mansfield was quoted as saying. "We're just praying and waiting it out."

I thought about the incident so much as the months went by, wondered what it was that had forced such a horrible fate on the football player, that a year and a half after the accident I decided to track down young Mansfield himself. I heard from Billy Reed, an *SI* writer in Kentucky, that Mansfield had been an "A" student and apparently had been offered an academic scholarship to Mississippi State or some other large southern school before the tragedy.

I spoke with Jim Potee, the principal and athletic director at Humboldt High. "I was within twenty-five to thirty yards of him when it happened," said Potee. "He was going up the hill where the dressing room is, and he had his helmet in his hand. He put it on, buckled both chin straps, lowered his head, and ran straight into the wall. That was the last time he moved."

The only question I could ask was, why?

"He was frustrated. It was the first round of the state playoffs, and we had the game won but gave it away when we had a touchdown called back and then fumbled to let them score. We lost, fourteen to thirteen. He had nothing to do with the loss, but he was a fierce competitor. What he had, he gave you. He was a great person, too—a fine student and a great artist. We still use some of his paintings in our yearbook."

I asked the principal if he thought the boy had been trying to hurt himself.

"Oh, no, it was not intentional," Potee answered. "He had no concept of the danger. It was like if you would kick a car tire or hit a door with your fist in anger. In that uniform and helmet you think you're protected against all elements."

I remembered the old football cliché that tells players that with enough heart and guts a kid can run right through a brick wall. Coaches love to expound on that. I wondered if that myth had played a role in Doug Mansfield's tragedy.

I asked Potee how the boy was doing now, if there was any hope for recovery.

"Oh," said the man. "You didn't know. He's dead. He died at the spinal injury center in Atlanta three months after the game."

Pete Gent once wrote, "Psychotic episodes are a daily occurrence in a business where the operative phrase is, 'Stick your head in there.'" And he is right. The use of the head–the thinking center, the housing (scientists and philosophers now suspect, for the soul), the very thing that contains that which separates us from beasts–as the primary weapon in football tends to warp logic and reward people on the fringes of sanity. It's not enough to say that the sport rewards aggressiveness. The best players often are those who are the most reckless with their own well-being, the most willing to do crazy, dangerous things with their own bodies and, consequently, to other people's bodies. "Nobody will know what I'm talking about unless they strap on a helmet and run forty yards downfield and hit a guy who doesn't see you coming," says Phoenix Cardinals special-teams player Ron Wolfley on the joys of football. "Now that's comedy to me." Is anybody laughing?

I think about the profile I had to do for *SI* on Detroit Lions linebacker Jimmy Williams two years ago. Williams can be almost rabid on the field, fighting and swearing like a man possessed, though off the field he is quiet and retiring, a Sunday school teacher at a Baptist church in Pontiac, Michigan, among other things. Of course, such Jekyll and Hyde behavior is pretty normal for high-level football players. But I asked Williams specifically if he liked hurting people on the field. "If it's between getting an interception and putting a hit on the receiver," he said, "I'll always hit the receiver. I like to hit a man and hear that . . .'"

He smiled warily, afraid that maybe he had revealed too much.

Hear what, I asked.

"Hear that little . . ."

Yes?

He thought a moment. His smile grew. "That little moan."

When Auburn linebacker Aundray Bruce, the first player taken in the 1988 NFL draft, was in college, he sometimes worked himself into such a frenzy of malevolence at the line of scrimmage that tears would stream down his face. There has been at least one study done that shows that in certain adolescent boys the line between aggression or violence and sexual stimulation is so thin that young football players have been known to achieve orgasm from the excitement of the game. The craziness of the sport sometimes affects players' ability to think rationally about their own safety. Last season Bears safety Shaun Gayle fractured the seventh vertebra in his neck when his helmet collided with teammate Singletary's hip during a tackle in a game against Detroit. Singletary had to come out of the game because of the collision, but Gayle stayed in, even though his neck was broken and his hands were numb. He dropped a ball he should have intercepted because he couldn't grip with his fingers, and still he remained in the game. He made another hit, on Lions fullback Garry James, and promptly lost feeling in his right arm. Still, he stayed in the game. Later, after he had been diagnosed and put on injured reserve for the rest of the season, he started working out at health club I sometimes visit. I ran into him at the club and asked him how in the world he could have taken his own potential paralysis so lightly.

He laughed. Gayle is a bright man; he has a degree from Ohio State in recreation education and is one of the most well-spoken NFL players I have ever interviewed. But he just chuckled with the question.

"I didn't think it was that serious," he said.

Later I would read in the paper that Gayle was eagerly awaiting the 1989 season now that his neck had healed. "I will wear a built-in neck brace with my shoulder pads," he said. "It will allow me movement so I can see the ball but not much movement forwards or backwards. It should be interesting. I'll become a human missile."

I remember visiting Ohio State during the summer of 1987 to talk to all-American linebacker Chris Spielman about the coming season. Spielman, I knew, had been called "the most intense player I've ever coached" by then-head coach Earle Bruce. His father, Sonny Spielman, a high school football coach, recalled that when Chris was five years old he had tackled his own grandmother. "A perfect-form tackle," Dad said. "He broke her nose. He wiped her out on the spot. That's when I knew I had a maniac on my hands."

So I wanted to sit for a few minutes and just observe this athlete who against Iowa the previous year had broken his helmet, tossed it aside since there wasn't time to fix it, and dived into a pile headfirst. He sat in a coach's office at St. John's Hall and simply twitched. He was like a bug on a needle. I asked him what his style of play was and he said, "Controlled insanity." He added that what's important "is not how you play the game, it's whether you win or lose." He looked at the floor, avoided eye contact, bounced his knees. Playing Michigan, he said, was like freedom versus communism. "Football is almost a life or death situation for me," he said. Later, Chicago Bears quarterback Mike Tomczak, a teammate of Spielman's at Ohio State, would tell me that before each season Spielman would rent a room in a Cincinnati flophouse and simply lie on a bed for a day or two, staring at a bare light bulb hanging from the ceiling, getting his mind right for football.

I asked Spielman now if maybe things might not be a little easier for him if he weren't so totally focused on this violent game. He looked up.

"Easier for me, or the people around me?" he asked with an edge in his voice. "I have blinders on. I'm in a tunnel, a train is coming, and I don't see anything but the light approaching. That's how I want it."

A few years ago I was at the University of Pittsburgh to write about the Pitt team's response to the untimely death of sophomore linebacker Todd Becker. Becker was a special-teams demon, a 6'2", 214-pound live wire with a tattoo on his left calf of a grinning Sylvester the Cat hanging Tweety Bird by the neck and whose favorite pastime, according to the Pitt press guide, was lifting weights. The young man had climbed out a third-story window at a dorm toga party to avoid detection by campus police who had raided the party, and when he tried to jump to the pavement thirty-five feet below, he spun in midair, hit his head on the cement, and died instantly. Becker was drunk at the time, but he also didn't think he could be hurt by the fall. "He had no fear," said head coach Foge Fazio. "I'm sure he thought, 'This is easy for me. I can do this.'" Becker's father, Al, a long-distance trucker, said, "He was such a good football player. He was a killer."

But that same aggressiveness that delighted every coach Becker ever had got him into a lot of problems off the field. The reason Becker was jumping was that he had already been banned from the Pitt dorms for causing disturbances there and he didn't want to jeopardize his football career by getting caught again. In the course of researching my story, I spent some time with Pitt athletic director Ed Bozik, a former Air Force colonel, and during one interview he grew philosophical about the tragedy.

"Football training is very much analogous to military training," he said. "In both cases young men are trained to do things they instinctively would not do. This has to condition your psyche, but the question is, can you convert that training and use its positive elements in normal life? In the military we have what we call 'war lovers,' the ones who can't turn it off. But everyone is constantly trained to act like gentlemen when not in a battle situation."

"Basically, I believe in the Aristotelian philosophy of striking a median, a balance. Any characteristic taken to an extreme becomes a vice. After all, getting into trouble, doing stupid things—that's not really the province of football players. It's traditional for *young people* to get into trouble."

This is true, but when football players get into trouble, they just seem to do it a little harder, to take things a little further than other kids do, and this may be because the sport attracts, trains, conditions, and develops men who are predisposed to wildness and encourages them to push themselves beyond their limits. Perhaps Todd Becker would have done something equally stupid and self-destructive if he'd never heard of football. But were it not for football, he certainly wouldn't have been so praised and prized for these self-destructive tendencies, and he wouldn't have been so doggedly sought out by universities, by institutions of learning, eager to reward him for the qualities that led to his death: recklessness, fearlessness, aggressiveness.

Syndicated columnist Stephen Chapman has suggested getting rid of hard-shell helmets and imposing weight limits on players to lessen the violence of the game and the resulting injuries and unhealthy behavior such violence causes. But the helmets have been around for too long to downgrade, and ironically, they do prevent many of the head injuries that players in the olden days sometimes died from. And limiting the size of players would not be particularly effective in reducing violence, either, since speed is at least as devastating as weight in collisions. And in truth, many of the smaller players are the meanest players anyway. Safety Jack Tatum weighed just over 200 pounds when he paralyzed wide receiver Darryl Stingley with a vicious blow. And Detroit cornerback James Hunter weighed only 195 pounds when he nailed the Vikings' Ahmad Rashad and broke his back in 1982, ending Rashad's final season prematurely. Ironically, Hunter hit another Minnesota receiver in almost the same fashion later in the game and injured his own neck so severely from the blow that he himself was forced to retire.

I tried to get hold of Hunter after the '82 season to see what he thought about ending two careers in one game, but he wouldn't take my calls. I caught up with Rashad a year or so later in Miami, where he was preparing to work a Dolphins game as a TV reporter, and asked him what he felt about the incident.

"It was the weirdest pain I've ever had," he said. "I couldn't feel my legs for about five minutes. I was just like paralyzed. I told the trainer, 'When you get this helmet and these pads off me, I'll never play this game again.'"

What did he think of Hunter's blow to his back?

"I never thought it was too violent," Rashad answered. "I just got a good shot is all."

And there is the twisted truth that injuries are not only a part of the game, but a welcome part. One of the very reasons players play the game is to have the chance to give and receive injuries. You think I'm kidding? I remember lying in bed after a college game with my own ankle throbbing, my shoulder aching, and feeling very . . . comfortable . . . about it all. The pain signified something. It wasn't the gratuitous pain of a disease or chronic illness, but a friendly, masculine reminder of my accomplishments as a player, and subliminally, as a man, in a dangerous sport.

"It's that instant when . . . artistry is threatened by violence and the outcome is in doubt, that epitomizes the game's attraction," wrote Oregon State English professor Mike Oriard in an essay on football violence in the *New York Times* a few years ago. "Injuries are not aberrations in football, or even a regrettable byproduct. They are essential to the game." He then added that any efforts to make the game safer must grapple first with the "ideological underpinning" of the game itself, since "it's not possible to have the (desired) danger without the injuries to confirm that the danger is real." Oriard had been a captain of the Notre Dame football team and had played four season with the Kansas City Chiefs in the early seventies. He was a center, and I remembered him from my brief stay with the Chiefs in 1971 as being a tall, quiet, observant man who did not seem to fit in with the rowdier, veteran Chiefs. If I had known the thinking going on in his brain, I might have made it a point to get to know him a little better before Hank Stram unceremoniously booted me out of pro football.

Pain itself is a funny bird. In an article on the matter in the June 11, 1984, edition of *Time*, pain researcher Dr. Ronald Dubner of the National Institutes of Health stated that "pain is a complex experience that involves emotions, previous experiences with pain, and what the pain means to us at any given time." "In short," concluded the article's author, "the borderline between the physiology and psychology of pain is a blurry one." Thus it is that, to a football player, pain can be something akin to rapture. I am reminded here of the saints of the Middle Ages, who likewise often got off on the self-inflicted pain that brought them closer to their God. One who stands out in particular was Henry Suso, a fourteenth-century saint who carved religious symbols in his chest with a stylus, wore a hair shirt, a heavy iron chain, and a tight-fitting hair undergarment with 150 nails imbedded in the straps, the points directed inward. Suso wore this gear at night, too, and when he picked at the outfit in his sleep, he had leather gloves made, fitted over with brass tacks, so that he could not enjoy the pleasure of touching himself. Suso mutilated himself to such an extent that according to historian Richard Kieckhefer, writing in *Unquiet Souls: Fourteenth-Century Saints and Their Religious Milieu*, "suffering became for Suso almost an end in itself, or more precisely, a token of divine favor, such that an absence of suffering was for him the greatest cause of suffering."

I can compare that nut to former Chiefs all-pro middle linebacker and center E. J. Holub, who, when I wrote about him for *Esquire* in 1980, was believed to have had more knee operations, twelve, than any other athlete in the world, with more cuttings scheduled for the future. Holub, a cowboy from West Texas, had undergone seventeen operations in all, including two on his hands, two on his elbows, and one on a hamstring, yet missed only eleven games in his eleven-year pro career. At forty-two, he walked like a man twice his age. Forget running. Holub destroyed his knees partly by coming back from the initial surgeries way too soon, once tearing off a cast almost three months before it was due to be removed. He would drain his knee joints himself, using a 16-gauge needle or sometimes a plain old razor. For a year with the Chiefs he wore a sanitary napkin on one knee to absorb the liquid that seeped out constantly.

"People are always asking me if it was worth it, the operations and all," he said to me cheerily. "Yep, it sure was, I tell 'em. I enjoyed the hell out of football."

There are many other players like Holub in the game, at all levels. Trust me. Tommy Chaikin told me one night about how he and some of his South Carolina teammates started drinking in his home while he was an undergrad and ended up carving each other's arms with a butcher knife in the kitchen, just for the hell of it, just to show pain was no big deal. They got a little carried away, stabbing one of the players pretty hard in the forearm. They went to bed after that, leaving the knife and blood on the table, forgetting that it might not be the pleasantest of sights for Tommy's parents in the morning. I found myself laughing, thinking back on some of my own lunacies in college. Looking back, I'm not particularly proud of that response.

Last fall I received a letter from a *Sports Illustrated* reader, and after reading it, I wrote back to its author, G. Bruce Mills of Lexington, North Carolina, asking him if I could print the letter in a book on college football that I was considering writing. Mills wrote back that he would be flattered to have his letter printed. Here it is:

Dear Mr. Telander:

After reading your story about Tommy Chaikin, I'm left asking a question to which I can't provide the answer: "What is it about football that drives participants to total disregard for their well-being in the quest for success?" Perhaps it's peer acceptance, or just a way to impress the girls. At my son's high school practice today I watched a player who was last in sprints (gasping for breath) struggled through drills, was hammered in the scrimmage, was the object of his teammates' ridicule, and will never get any better or make any contribution to his team. He's not alone, for practically every team at every level of amateur football has a player like him. Why do they do it? Why do the Tommy Chaikins of today risk their lives with drugs to achieve success in football?

They're really no different from players of days gone by. I, like you, played college football in the late sixties and early seventies. As an all-conference player at Duke University, I wasn't aware of this "edge" called steroids. But I, too, had an abusive addiction, which was playing with pain. At one time or another every player has been asked to "suck it up," and doing anything less is unacceptable. Nobody wants to be told "you can't cut it." I'll skip the details, but let it suffice to say that I've had four operations on my left knee, one on my right knee, two on my right ankle with the third scheduled in for January. I must visit the chiropractor regularly for back pains, I walk club-footed and struggle with inclines and rough terrain. I haven't been able to do anything resembling a jog or a run in four years, and my athletic sons are growing up without the benefit of playing backyard ball with their father.

The scariest thing, Rick, is that knowing what I've gone through and will continue to endure . . . **I'D DO IT ALL OVER AGAIN!** What is this mystical hold that football has over me and thousands like me?

I don't think anybody knows.

FOR FURTHER STUDY

Bredemeier, Brenda Jo, and David L. Shields. "Values and Violence in Sports Today." *Psychology Today* 19 (October 1985):23-32.

Bredemeier, Brenda Jo, and David L. Shields. "Athletic Aggression: An Issue of Contextual Morality." *Sociology of Sport Journal* 3 (March 1986):15-28.

Dunning, Eric. "Sociological Reflections on Sport, Violence and Civilization." *International Review for the Sociology of Sport* 25 (1990):65-82.

Eitzen, D. Stanley. "Violence in Professional Sports and Public Policy." In *Government and Sport*, ed. Arthur T. Johnson and James H. Frey. Totowa, NJ: Rowman and Allanheld, 1985, pp. 95-116.

Goldstein, Jeffrey H., ed. *Sports Violence*. New York: Springer-Verlag, 1983.

Hersch, Hank. "It's War Out There!" *Sports Illustrated* (July 20, 1987):14-17.

Hillsbery, Kief, "Clockwork Orange County." *Outside* (August/September 1982):55-59, 72-74.

Horrow, Rick, ed. "Violence in Sport." *Arena Review* 5 (February 1981):entire issue.

Lang, Gladys E. "Riotous Outbursts in Sports Events." In *Handbook of Social Science of Sport*, ed. Gunther Luschen and George H. Sage. Champaign, IL: Stipes, 1981, 415-536.

Messner, Michael A. "When Bodies Are Weapons: Masculinity and Violence in Sport." *International Review for the Sociology of Sport* 25 (1990):203-219.

Miedzian, Myriam. *Boys Will Be Boys: Breaking the Link between Masculinity and Violence*. New York: Doubleday, 1991.

Poliakoff, Michael B. *Combat Sports in the Ancient World: Competition, Violence, and Culture*. New Haven: Yale University Press, 1987.

Rostaing, Bjarne, and Robert Sullivan. "Triumphs Tainted with Blood." *Sports Illustrated* (January 21, 1985):12-21.

Royce, Joseph. "Play in Violent and Non-Violent Cultures." *Anthropos* 75 nos. 5-6 (1980):799-822.

Schneider, John and D. Stanley Eitzen. "The Structure of Sport and Participant Violence." *Arena Review* 7 (November 1983):1-16.

Smith, Michael D. *Violence and Sport*. Toronto: Butterworths, 1983.

Sugden, John P. "The Sociological Perspective: The Political Economy of Violence in American Sport." *Arena Review* 5 (February 1981):57-62.

Wulf, Steve. "Brawl Game!" *Sports Illustrated* (August 27, 1990):12-17.

Young, Kevin. "Violence in the Workplace of Professional Sport from Victimological and Cultural Studies Perspectives." *International Review for the Sociology of Sport* 26 (1991):3-14.

Zimmerman, Paul. "The Agony Must End." *Sports Illustrated* (November 10, 1986):16-21.

Part Four

Sport and Deviance

Sport and *deviance* would appear on the surface to be antithetical terms. After all, sports contests are bound by rules, school athletes must meet rigid grade and behavior standards in order to compete, and there is a constant monitoring of athletes' behavior because they are public figures. Moreover, sport is assumed by many to promote those character traits deemed desirable by most in society: fair play, sportsmanship, obedience to authority, hard work, and commitment to excellence.

The selections in this part show, to the contrary, that deviance is not only prevalent in sport but that the structure of sport in American society actually promotes deviance. Players and coaches sometimes cheat to gain an advantage over an opponent. As we saw in Part 3, some players engage in criminal violence on the playing field. Some players use performance-enhancing drugs. Some players are sexually promiscuous, as the tragic example of Magic Johnson illustrates. Not only did he contract the HIV virus from his sexual escapades, but he, in turn, may have infected many of his sexual partners with the fatal virus.

The first selection, by D. Stanley Eitzen, provides an overview of deviance in sport by examining the ethical dilemmas faced by athletes, coaches, administrators, team doctors, fans, and the media. The consequence of immorality in sport and the structural roots of these unethical behaviors are also addressed.

Next, sociologists John R. Fuller and Marc J. La Fountain focus on a major problem in sport—drug use by athletes. Just like other members of their age cohort, they may take recreational drugs. They also take what might be called "vocational" drugs—that is, drugs taken to enhance sport performance.

The final selection, by journalist Jill Neimark, summarizes what is known about the serious problem of gang rape by athletes.

10. *Ethical Dilemmas in Sport*

D. STANLEY EITZEN

There is a country tune sung by Kris Kristofferson in which he decries the lack of ethical standards common today. He says, in effect, that it's getting harder to know wrong from right and to separate the winners from the losers. Although the songwriter was referring to alienation in American society in general, the lyrics can be applied to sport. Why are so many big-time sports celebrities often in trouble with the law? Why is the outrageous behavior of coaches not only overlooked but generously rewarded? Why is big-time sport permitted to corrupt our universities? Why is gratuitous violence glorified in sport? Many believe that these problems exist because the world of sports has declined morally—moral values are confused with dollar values, and the win-at-any-price ethic controls the conduct in much of sport (Spander, 1985; Lamme, 1985).

Clearly, it is time for scholars of sport and sports-program administrators to reexamine what sport has become and what it should be, to determine the distorted values that now drive sport, and to consider appropriate alternatives. This essay addresses these issues by considering (1) the need to develop ethical principles to guide sport, (2) the ethical dilemmas that confront sport's various constituencies, (3) the ethical consequences of sport's prevailing and distorted code of ethics, and (4) the structural sources of unethical behavior in sport.

ETHICAL PRINCIPLES

My position is that the following ethical principles must be applied to assess the behavior of coaches, players, spectators, and others involved in sport. The principles represent not only the ideals for which we should strive but also our obligation to sport and its participants.

1. *Athletes must be considered ends and not means.* The outcome for the participants in sport is infinitely more important than the outcome of the contest, the money generated, or other extraneous considerations. Athletes must be treated by coaches and administrators with dignity

SOURCE: *Journal of Sport and Social Issues* 12:1 (1988), pp. 17-30. Reprinted by the permission of the *Journal of Sport and Social Issues*.

and respect; they must not be exploited; and they must not be demeaned and dehumanized. Further, athletes must respect their opponents and not condone or engage in tactics of intimidation or willful injury. Also, the equipment, procedures, and rules of sport must provide for the relative safety of the participants. As philosopher Paul Weiss has argued, "Sports should begin and be carried out with a concern for the rights of others" (1969:180).

2. *Competition must be fair.* (a) The administration of leagues and the supervision of contests must be governed by rules impartially applied to all parties. (b) Sport, by definition, is a competition involving physical prowess. Thus, if athletic contests are to be true to the ideals of sport, they must be decided only by differences in physical skill, motivation, strategy, and luck. By doing so we would rule out such activities as cheating or drug use to enhance performance artificially that give an athlete or team an unfair advantage. Efforts made by gamblers and corrupt athletes to fix the outcome of athletic contests violate the spirit of sport.
3. *Participation, leadership, resources, and rewards must be based on achievement rather than on ascribed characteristics.* Sports activities must be characterized by equal access and equal opportunity. Thus, ability and motivation shall decide who participates rather than race, creed, gender, or social position.
4. *The activity must provide for the relative safety of the participants.* The rules of the sport and the required equipment must be designed to protect the athlete. The health and safety of athletes must be considered by coaches and administrators as more important than team performance. Coaches must avoid creating situations that lead to physical ailments such as dehydration and heat prostration. Further, athletes must not purposefully act to injure their opponents except in explicitly pugilistic sports, such as boxing, which themselves may be unethical.

Although these principles are difficult to rebut, there are a few counterarguments that should be mentioned. First, although big-time sport is something that many Americans are proud of, its value is diminished when we consider that winning is the primary objective of most coaches and fans. Sport is an activity that occurs in a society where only the fittest survive. The "win-at-any-cost" ethic means that the end justifies the means. As one football coach stated: "Until three years ago we obeyed every rule and where did it get us? We finished last in the conference. Since that time there isn't a rule we haven't broken. And where are we now? This year we're playing in the Orange Bowl" (quoted in Shea, 1978:145). Many coaches emulate the legendary football coach Vince Lombardi who argued that hatred of opponents should be used to inspire athletes to a higher level of intensity and increased performance. In Lombardi's words, "To play this game you must have that fire in you, and nothing stokes fire like hate" (quoted in Kramer, 1971). However, such tactics create a disrespect for opponents and a greater likelihood of purposeful injury. Further, by practicing the doctrine of "winning is everything" we diminish or even negate the intrinsic rewards of sports participation (Simon, 1983).

Another counterargument questions the so-called "unethical" nature of sport practices that are so widespread. If everyone is doing it, how can it be wrong? For example, many big-time college sports programs commonly break rules when recruiting; most offensive linemen illegally hold their opponents; many major-league baseball teams have at least one pitcher who illegally applies a foreign substance to the baseball for an unfair advantage; and the majority of world-class weight lifters use illegal anabolic steroids to increase their bulk, strength, and muscle. Therefore, if the majority ignores the rules, are the rules negated? Are these activities truly unethical if "everyone is doing them," and does their common use make them justified? To the contrary, ethics applies to how people *should* behave and not to how they *do* behave (Shea, 1978:148). If a widespread practice in sport provides an unfair advantage in athletic contests, then it is immoral no matter how often it is practiced. Rules intended to provide equity for all participants and teams are unconditional (Shea, 1978:149).

Still another counterargument is that universal principles cannot be successfully applied to sports participation because many of its situations and conditions cannot be ethically categorized. In essence, each ethical principle is a continuum with varying degrees of ethical purity. The question is where to draw the line dividing proper from improper conduct if the distinctions are unclear. For example, we can determine easily that Kermit Washington acted improperly when he gave Rudy Tomjanovich a powerful punch that ended his professional basketball career. But how can we evaluate legal acts of mayhem encouraged by coaches and fans as part of the game? For example, we know that when an athlete takes a bribe to affect the outcome of a contest that action is immoral and illegal. Bowyer has characterized such behavior as ". . . a violation of the cathedral" (1982:301). But is it a "violation of the sports cathedral" when in basketball a slow home team wets the nets to tighten them and thus decelerate a visiting fast-breaking team by giving the defense artificially gained time to set up their defense? Defenders of such an act would call it "getting a competitive edge," but is the act ethical? The following section examines these questions and others.

ETHICAL DILEMMAS

Several common but questionable practices in sport need to be examined more closely in terms of their ethical meaning and consequences. Such practices include cheating and excessive violence, spectator behavior that violates the ethical principles in varying degrees, and the questionable behavior of coaches, athletes, administrators, sports medicine personnel, and the media. Although space does not permit an exhaustive coverage of all areas of ethical concern in sports, the following discussion highlights many ethical dimensions present in the sports world today.

Cheating and Excessive Violence

The *sine qua non* of sport is competition. The goal is to win. But to be ethical the quest to win must be done in a spirit of fairness. Fairness tends to prevail in certain sports such as tennis and golf, but in other sports the dominant mood is to achieve an unfair advantage over the opponent. Obtaining a competitive edge unfairly is viewed by many participants and others involved as "strategy" rather than cheating (Figler, 1981:72; Avedon, 1971). In such instances cheating takes two forms—normative and deviant (Eitzen, 1981). *Normative cheating* refers to illegal acts that are, for the most part, accepted as part of the game—coaches encourage or overlook them, impose minimal penalties, or ignore them altogether. *Deviant cheating* refers to illegal acts that are not accepted and that are subject to stern punishment, such as drugging a race horse, accepting a bribe, and tampering with an opponent's equipment.

Our interest here is with normative cheating and how it violates the ethical principles of sport even though it is practiced and deemed acceptable by the majority. Following are some examples of normative cheating—commonly accepted practices for achieving an unfair advantage:

- Basketball players pretend to be fouled in order to receive an undeserved free throw and give the opponent an undeserved foul.
- Basketball players are often coached to bump the lower half of a shooter's body because referees are more likely to be watching the ball and the upper half of the shooter's body.
- Offensive linemen in football are typically coached to use special but illegal techniques to hold or trip the opponent without detection. The Oakland Raiders once were accused of greasing the jerseys of their defensive linemen so that blockers could not hold them so easily—"a clear case of one rulebreaker seizing an edge from another" (Axthelm, 1983).
- Coaches sometimes use loopholes in the rules to take unfair advantage of an opponent. For example, during a 1973 football game between the University of Alabama and the University of California, Alabama had the ball on the California 11 yard line. Alabama sent in their field goal kicker with a tee but a player did not leave the field. California countered by sending in its defensive team against the kick. As the huddle broke, the field goal kicker picked up his tee and dashed off the field, leaving the defense at a distinct disadvantage. Alabama

scored on the play and the NCAA Rules Committee later declared such plays illegal because a team cannot simulate a substitution designed to confuse an opponent.

- In baseball it is common for the home team to "doctor" its field to suit its strengths and minimize the strengths of a particular opponent. For example, a fast team can be neutralized or slowed down by digging up or watering the basepaths or by placing sand in the takeoff areas (Ostrow, 1985).
- In baseball the pitcher's application of a foreign substance to the ball in order to disadvantage the hitter is a common but illegal occurrence.
- In baseball a practice called "corking the bat" often occurs in which a bat is hollowed out and the wood replaced with various substances that make it more powerful (Bowyer, 1982:308-309).
- In ice hockey the blades of the sticks are sometimes curved beyond legal limits to make them more effective.

Many people are fascinated by acts of normative cheating such as these. As sportswriter Pete Axthelm has said, "The next best thing to the home team getting an edge is a game that is on the level. . . . Sports fans love the rules—and the chance that somebody will figure out a way to break them" (1983). There exists a fundamental irony of sport—rule-bounded activities where rule breaking is deemed acceptable. Obviously, a stronger application of ethical principles must be applied if sport is to be rid of this hypocrisy.

Also of ethical concern is normative violence in sport. Many popular sports such as hockey and football encourage player aggression—not only is the very nature of these sports to strike an opponent but they encourage excessive violence with little or no penalty. Hockey is well known for its minimal penalties and its tendency to condone crowd-pleasing violence. Hockey players' fights routinely result in cuts, concussions, and fractures. But why do these athletes participate in violence? Smith (1983) has argued that violence in hockey, as in war, is a socially rewarded behavior. The players believe that aggression (body checking, intimidation, and the like) is vital to winning, and their behavior is approved by fans, coaches, and peers. Young athletes idolize the professionals and attempt to emulate their aggressive behaviors at their level of play, thereby perpetuating violence in the sport.

Normative violence is also an integral part of football (Underwood, 1978; 1984). Players are expected by their peers, coaches, and fans to be "hitters." They are taught to lower their heads to deliver a blow to the opponent and gang tackle—to make the ball carrier "pay the price." By physically punishing their opponents the football team attempts to increase the opponent's likelihood of failure—by causing fumbles, a lack of concentration, exhaustion, or player replacement by less-talented substitutes. These win-at-any-cost tactics are almost universally held among coaches, players, and fans in the United States even though they result in a significantly higher injury rate. How unethical is such within-the-rule but excessive violence? According to John Underwood these practices should be neither tolerated nor condoned: "Brutality is its own fertilizer. From 'get away with what you can' it is a short hop to the deviations that poison sport. . . . But it is not just the acts that border on criminal that are intolerable, it is the permissive atmosphere they spring from. The 'lesser' evils that are given tacit approval as 'techniques' of the game, even within the rules" (1984:85).

Spectator Behavior

Certain spectator behaviors during sports events can be excessive, such as rioting and throwing objects at players and officials. But do we need also to evaluate other common but unsportspersonlike practices of spectators? For example, the booing of officials or opponents; the cheering of an opponent's injury; and such cheers as "kill Bubba kill" or "blood, blood, blood . . . blood makes the grass grow." Spectators can distract opponents in various ways–by making unusual noises, shouting racial/ethnic slurs, chanting "air ball" when an opponent attempts a free throw,or parading signs that demean visiting athletes (such as those that plagued basketball superstar Patrick Ewing throughout his college career at Georgetown University–"Patrick Ewing Can't Read This Sign," or "Patrick Ewing Is the Missing Link").

The Behavior of Coaches

Coaches commonly engage in a number of ethically questionable acts in their quest for a successful team. Many coaches have been found guilty of offering illegal inducements to prospective athletes, providing illicit payments to athletes, and altering the transcripts of athletes to retain their eligibility. Coaches may deliberately attempt to intimidate officials by inciting a home crowd. They may encourage violence toward opponents, such as in the celebrated case in Iowa where the coach of a high school team playing a team called the "Golden Eagles" spray painted a chicken gold and encouraged his players to stomp it "to death" in the locker room before the contest.

In assessing the ethics of coaches, we might ask the following questions (adapted from Eitzen, 1984c:199-200):

- Are coaches being ethical when they run practice sessions like a marine boot camp?
- Are coaches being ethical when they physically or verbally assault athletes?

- Are coaches being ethical when they treat adult players like children?
- Are coaches being ethical when they encourage athletes to use drugs to enhance their performances artificially?
- Are coaches being ethical when they encourage athletes to cheat?
- Are high school and college coaches being ethical in their lack of regard for the athletes' educational goals and achievements?
- Are coaches being ethical when they refuse to "blow the whistle" on their coaching peers whom they know to be violating the rules?

The Behavior of Athletic Directors and Other Administrators

The administrators of sport have the overall responsibility of ensuring that their athletic programs abide by the rules and that their coaches behave ethically. They must provide safe conditions for play, properly maintained equipment, and appropriate medical attention. However, are they showing adequate concern for players when, for example, they choose artificial turf over grass, knowing that the rate and severity of injury is higher with artificial turf? There are four other areas where athletic directors and administrators may be involved in questionable ethics:

- Are athletic directors being ethical when they "drag their feet" in providing equal facilities, equipment, and budgets for women's athletic programs?
- Are athletic directors being ethical when they schedule teams that are an obvious mismatch? That is, strong teams are often matched with weak teams to enhance the former team's record and to maintain a high ranking, while the weak teams are encouraged to schedule matches with the strong teams to make more money.
- Are administrators being ethical when they refuse to schedule legitimate opponents? For example, boxing champions often ignore their stiffest competition and fight much easier opponents. In college some powerful teams have refused to play other teams because they did not want to legitimate the latter's status.
- Are administrators being ethical when they make decisions regarding the hiring and firing of coaches strictly on their win-loss record? For the most part school administrators do not fire coaches guilty of shady transgressions *if they win*. As John Underwood has characterized it: "We've told them it doesn't matter how clean they keep their program. It doesn't matter what percentage of their athletes graduate or take a useful place in society. It doesn't even matter how well the coaches teach the sports. All that matters are the flashing scoreboard lights" (1981:81).

The Behavior of Team Doctors and Trainers

There are essentially two ethical issues facing those involved in sports medicine, especially those in the employ of a school or professional team. Most fundamentally, team doctors and trainers often face a dilemma in terms of their ultimate allegiance; that is, is their responsibility to the employer or to the injured athlete (Eskenazi, 1987)? The employer wants athletes on the field, not in the training room. Thus, the ethical question arises–should pain-killing drugs be administered to an injured player so that he or she can return to action sooner than would be otherwise recommended for the long-term health of the athlete?

The other ethical issue for those in sports medicine is whether they should dispense performance-enhancing drugs to athletes. There may be pressures to do so from coaches and players because "everyone is doing it."

The Behavior of the Media

The media, which devote so much attention to sport, are partly to blame for the unethical behaviors found in sport for several reasons. The media often glorify violence; for example, by showing in slow motion bone-crushing hits accompanied by exclamations of glee and wonder; or by their use of such terms as "assassins" and "enforcers" in referring to violence among players. The media also use violence in the promotions of upcoming telecasts to increase the number of viewers. Although less common today than in the past, the media tend not to report the negative side of sport and athletes. For instance, reporter Joe Falls, in discussing the fall of former pitching great Denny McLain, who was found guilty of loan sharking, extortion, bookmaking, and possession of cocaine, commented: "As guilty as he [McLain] is, I don't hold him entirely to blame for the way his life turned out. I also blame the people who allowed him to get away with his irresponsible acts. They allowed it because he was Denny McLain, the famous pitcher. Some of these people were in the media. They knew Denny was doing wrong, but they grabbed his coattails and thought they would go for a wild ride" (1985:18). Sports media persons are faced with an ethical dilemma–that is, what information about athletes should be made public and what is best left alone? Rick Telander of *Sports Illustrated* has written perceptively of this ethical problem facing sports reporters:

> For writers the ethical course is tricky but not impossible. *Milwaukee Journal* sports editor Jim Cohen sums it up thus: "A reporter's job is simply to report accurately and fairly–accurately in the sense that what he writes must be true, and fairly in the sense that what he writes must be relevant and told in the proper perspective. If that's not good enough for the people he's writing about, that's too bad. If it offends the reader, that also is too bad."

> The key work here is "fairly." The days when sports writers were "housemen"—bought-off flunkies for the owners—are long gone. But even though independent, writers still must be aware of the effect of their work. They must remember that athletes are real people living in the real world with families, friends, and acquaintances, and that what goes into print about the athlete affects all these people. A writer can call an athlete a bum or a crybaby or a coward, if he is sure it is warranted, and at times it is. But to be sure of that, a writer always has to be thinking, always examining his motives. He must not take cheap shots for laughs or deal meanness out of vengeance (1984:11).

Another area of ethical concern is the media's role in reinforcing negative stereotypes of racial minorities and women. For example, studies have shown that articles in magazines such as *Sports Illustrated* (Corrigan, cited Gerber et al., 1974), *Young Athlete* (Rintala and Birrell, 1984), and others (Hilliard, 1984; Bryant, 1980) underrepresent female athletes, focus their attention on women athletes' physical appearance, and often use sexist language.

Finally, it has been suggested by many that the media legitimate gambling in sports by reporting point spreads (Kaplan, 1983; Straw, 1983; D'Angelo, 1987) and by accepting advertising for betting-sheet touts (Frey and Rose, 1987). But is it unethical to do so? The question is debatable. Because readers seek information about sports and athletes, the media often argue that the First Amendment gives them the freedom to provide that information to the public. On the other hand, in states where gambling is illegal, the media are in effect encouraging an illicit activity.

THE ETHICAL CONSEQUENCES OF UNETHICAL PRACTICES IN SPORT

A widely held assumption of parents, educators, and editorial writers is that sport helps youths to understand and accept the moral ideals of society. However, this is not always the case and oftentimes sport, as it is presently conducted in youth leagues, schools, and at the professional level, does not enhance positive character traits. As philosopher Charles Banham has noted, although many do benefit from the sports experience, for others sport "encourages selfishness, envy, conceit, hostility, and bad temper. Far from ventilating the mind, it stifles it. Good sportsmanship may be a product of sport, but so is bad sportsmanship" (Banham, 1965:62).

The "win-at-any-cost" philosophy guides every level of sport in American society and often leads to cheating by coaches and athletes, to the dehumanization of athletes (Shaw, 1972; Feinstein, 1986), and to their alienation from themselves and their competitors. In view of this, it is not surprising that research has consistently revealed that athletes who participate in sport for long periods of time, who face higher levels of competition, and who are more central to their teams have more negative character traits (Eitzen, 1984b). For instance, Bredemeier (1983; 1984) and Bredemeier and Shields (1986) have shown that reasoning about moral issues in sport is significantly higher for nonathletes than for athletes and for female athletes than for male athletes.

However, we cannot infer with confidence that these studies prove the longer athletes are exposed to sport, the less morally sound they become, in that sport is not only a molding process but also a rigid selection process (Ogilvie and Tutko, 1971). We can conclude, though, that unethical practices in sport do not lead to positive moral development of the participants. Gresham's law would seem to apply to sport—bad morality tends to defeat good morality; unfairness tends to encourage unfairness (Heinila, 1974:13). Melvin Tumin's principle of least significant morality also makes this point: "In any social group, the moral behavior of the group as an average will tend to sink to that of the least moral participant, and the least moral participant will, in that sense, control the group unless he is otherwise restrained and/or expelled. . . . Bad money may not always drive out good money, though it almost always does. But 'bad' conduct surely drives out 'good' conduct with predictable vigor and speed" (1964:127).

THE STRUCTURAL ROOTS OF UNETHICAL BEHAVIOR IN SPORT

How can we begin to understand why cheating, exploitation, and other forms of immoral behavior have become so commonplace in sport? Obviously, there are people who seek unethical options, but they alone cannot account for the present situation. Rather, the sociological approach to rule-breaking and other unethical acts locates them not in the original sin, in the genes, or in the psyches of evil persons, but in the structural conditions of society.

The ethical problems of American sport have their roots in the political economy of society. Critical theorists of the Marxist tradition argue that capitalistic society is dominated by two structural conditions—massification and commodification—that help to explain why people make unethical choices in all areas of social life including sport.

Massification refers to the transformed social relations in society that have been caused by a more specialized division of labor, large-scale commodity production and consumption, widespread use of technology to increase industrial and administrative efficiency, and an increasingly authoritarian state (Hargreaves, 1982:6). In short, the massification of society is the consequence of the society's increased bureaucratization, rationalization, and routinization. The massification of sport is seen it its increasingly technocratic, specialized, controlled-by-the-elite, and impersonal nature. The apt descriptions of contemporary sport as work, big business, spectacle (Hughes and Coakley, 1984), and power politics suggest how sport mirrors the massification of the larger society.

Two related elements of massification that are manifested in sport increase the likelihood of unethical behavior by its participants. As the tasks in sport become more complex and specialized, the anonymity of the participants increases. This occurs even on a single team, as in football, for example, when the offensive and defensive units practice separately and meet independently with their specialized coaches. Social contact is minimized and the norms of reciprocity that are essential to community are evaded even among teammates (Young and Massey, 1980:88).

Anonymity among sports participants is also enhanced by short-term and episodic interaction (Young, 1972). Interaction is segmentalized so that participants rarely encounter each other in different roles. As a result, coaches and players, opponents, and other sport participants experience only impersonal relationships, which, in a competitive setting such as in sports, foster a "me-first/goals-regardless-of-the-means" attitude among them. This, in turn, causes unethical acts such as cheating, manipulation, fraud, exploitation, and excessive violence to occur more freely.

Commodification refers to the social, psychological, and cultural uses of social structures for the commercial needs of monopolies (Young, 1984:7). The commodification process views human beings as objects, or interchangeable parts, that can be manipulated. In the sports realm, team owners and administrators allow profit-maximizing decisions to take precedence over humane considerations. Sports enterprises seek to produce what they can sell, and spectacular sports events attract customers. As a result, sports performances become activities of dis-play. "When sport becomes an activity of *dis*-play, it destroys what is valuable in sport altogether. Sport becomes transformed into a spectacle, played for and shaped into a form which will be 'consumed' by spectators searching for titillating entertainment" (Sewart, 1981:49).

Violence is encouraged by sport administrators because it attracts spectators. Further, sport's popularity in society makes it a particularly effective vehicle for advertising. Male and female athletes are often portrayed as sex objects to sell products. As Brohm has put it: "They [athletes] are very often advertising 'sandwich-board' men" (1978:176). Today's top-level athletes, whether so-called amateurs or professionals, are viewed as workers who sell their labor—their ability to draw crowds—to employers. Thus, players and franchises are purchased, bought, and sold for profit. Athletes are treated like machines or instruments that are used to produce victories and income. They are manipulated to produce maximum performance:

> Every sport now involves a fantastic *manipulation of human robots* by doctors, psychologists, bio-chemists and trainers. The "manufacturing of champions" is no longer a craft but an industry, calling on specialized laboratories, research institutes, training camps and experimental sport centers. Most top-level athletes are reduced to the status of more or less voluntary guinea pigs. "Hopefuls" are spotted young, the less talented are methodically weeded out and those that remain are then systematically oriented according to their potential. . . . The specialists in this sporting Gulag stop at no human sacrifice in their drive to push back the limits of human capacity and transcend biological barriers (Brohm, 1978:18-19).

In short, sport and its participants are like any other commodity—"something to be marketed, packaged, and sold. . . . The consequence of the process of commodification is that the multifarious forms of human activity lose their unique and distinct qualities to the principles of the market" (Stewart, 1981:47-48).

Under the social conditions resulting from the massification and commodification of sport, coaches, athletes, and spectators are objects to be manipulated and exploited. Winning is the all-consuming goal, and participants are judged exclusively in terms of their ability to meet that goal. The unsuccessful are replaced like the defective parts of a machine. Under these circumstances, opponents *are* enemies. So, too, are teammates, in that they compete for starting positions. "In viewing himself as an object, the worker increasingly relates to other people as objects; he is alienated from the species whereby instead of celebrating his existence through meaningful interaction, he is isolated, asocial and ultimately, like the market within which he exists, amoral" (Sugden, 1981:59). Under these conditions, where athletes are alienated from one another and exploited by the system, they view one another as means to their ends, reinforcing the "win-at-any-cost" ethic.

CONCLUSION

Sport has the potential to ennoble its participants and society. Athletes strain, strive, and sacrifice to excel. But if sport is to exalt the human spirit, it must be practiced within a context guided by fairness and humane considerations. Most important, the competitors must respect and honor each other—in effect, there should be a bond uniting them and their common sacrifices and shared goals. Those intimately involved in sport—athletes, coaches, administrators, and fans—have critical choices to make. When the goal of winning supersedes other goals, they and sport are diminished, and sport does not achieve its ennobling potential. It is time for those who care about sport to recognize the problems of contemporary sport and to strive for changes.

John Underwood, in writing about the excessive violence in sport, presents an insightful analysis of sport:

> True sportsmanship is not compatible with a win-at-all-cost philosophy. . . . I think it is clear enough that the time is ripe in American sport to realize that a stand for sportsmanship and fair play *without* intimidation or brutality will not tilt the axis on which this planet spins. Competitive sports, in the end, must go beyond sportsmanship. They must reach all the way to "fair play." The essential difference is that fair play involves taking a stand above the legalities of the game. A stand that places winning at a risk but at the same time preserves the dignity and value of sport. It is a moral issue, not a political one. It must be based on the inner conviction that to win by going outside the rules and the spirit of the rules is not really to win at all (1984:87).

If we fail to heed Underwood's admonition, then we, as in Kris Kristofferson's lament, will find it hard to "separate the winners from the losers" and "to know what's wrong from right."

REFERENCES

Avedon, E. "The Structural Elements of Games." In *The Study of Games*, edited by E. Evendon and B. Sutton-Smith. New York: John Wiley & Sons, 1971.

Axthelm, P. "Psst, Somebody May be Cheating." *Newsweek* (August 8, 1983):74.

Banham, C. "Man at Play." *Contemporary Review* 207 (August 1965):60-65.

Bowyer, J. B. *Cheating: Deception in War & Magic, Games & Sports, Sex & Religion, Politics & Espionage, Art & Science*. New York: St. Martin's, 1982.

Bredemeier, B. J. "Athletic Aggression: A Moral Concern." In *Sports Violence*, edited by J. Goldstein. New York: Springer-Verlag, 1983.

Bredemeier, B. J. "Sport, Gender, and Moral Growth." In *Psychological Foundations of Sport*, edited by J. M. Silva, III, and R. S. Weinberg. Champaign, IL: Human Kinetics Publishers, 1984.

Bredemeier, B. J., and David L. Shields. "Athletic Aggression: An Issue of Contextual Morality." *Sociology of Sport Journal* 3 (March 1986):15-28.

Brohm, J. M. *Sport: A Prison of Measured Time*. London: Ink Links, 1978.

Bryant, J. "A Two Year Selective Investigation of the Female in Sport as Reported in the Paper Media." *Arena Review* 4 (May 1980).

D'Angelo, Raymond. "Sports Gambling and the Media." *Arena Review* 11 (May 1987):1-4.

Eitzen, D. S. "Sport and Deviance." In *Handbook of Social Science of Sport*, edited by G.R.F. Luschen, and G. H. Sage. Champaign, IL: Stipes, 1981.

Eitzen, D. S. "Teaching Social Problems: Implications of the Objectivist-Subjectivist Debate." *Society for the Study of Social Problems Newsletter* 16 (Fall 1984a):10-12.

Eitzen, D. S. "The Dark Side of Coaching and the Building of Character." In *Sport in Contemporary Society*, 2nd ed., edited by D. S. Eitzen. New York: St. Martin's 1984b, pp. 189-192.

Eitzen, D. S. "School Sports and Educational Goals." In *Sport in Contemporary Society*, 2nd ed., edited by D. S. Eitzen. New York: St. Martin's, 1984c, pp. 199-202.

Eskenazi, G. "Team Doctors: Operating in a Quandary." *The New York Times* (April 15, 1987):44.

Falls, J. "Indulgence's Child: McLain's Faults were Worsened by Excuse." *The Sporting News* (March 18, 1985):18.

Feinstein, John. *A Season on the Brink: A Year with Bob Knight and the Indiana Hoosiers*. New York: Macmillan, 1986.

Figler, S. K. *Sport and Play in American Life*. Philadelphia: Saunders, 1981.

"The Fraud Merchants" [editorial]. *The Sporting News* (March 18, 1983):8.

Frey, James H., and I. Nelson Rose. "The Role of Sports Information Services in the World of Sports Betting." *Arena Review* 11 (May 1987):44-51.

Gerber, E. R., J. Felshin, P. Berlin, and W. Wyrick. *The American Woman in Sport.* Reading, MA: Addison-Wesley, 1974.

Gilligan, C. *In a Different Voice.* Cambridge, MA: Harvard University Press, 1982.

Hargreaves, J. "Theorizing Sport." In *Sport, Culture and Ideology*, edited by J. Hargreaves. London: Routledge and Kegan Paul, 1982, pp. 1-29.

Heinila, K. *Ethics in Sport.* Jyvaskyla, Finland: University of Jyvaskyla, Department of Sociology, 1974.

Hilliard, D. C. Media Images of Male and Female Professional Athletes: An Interpretative Analysis of Magazine Articles. *Sociology of Sport Journal* 1 (no. 3, 1984):251-262.

Hughes, R., and J. Coakley. "Mass Society and the Commercialization of Sport." *Sociology of Sport Journal* 1 (no. 1, 1984):57-63.

Kaplan, H. R. "Sports, Gambling and Television: The Emerging Alliance." *Arena Review* 7 (February 1983):1-11.

Kramer, J., ed. *Lombardi: Winning is the Only Thing.* New York: Pocket Books, 1971.

Lamme, A. J. III. "How Big-Time Athletics Corrupt Universities." *The Christian Science Monitor* (February 25, 1985):12.

Luschen, G. R. F. "Cheating in Sport." In *Social Problems in Athletics: Essays in the Sociology of Sport*, edited by D. M. Landers. Urbana, IL: University of Illinois Press, 1976, pp. 67-77.

Ogilvie, B., and T. Tutko. "Sport: If You Want to Build Character, Try Something Else." *Psychology Today* 5 (October 1971):61-63.

Ostrow, R. "Tailoring the Ballparks to Fit Needs." *USA Today* (March 21, 1985): C1.

Ramsey, F., and F. Deford. "Smart Moves by a Master of Deception." *Sports Illustrated* (December 9, 1963):57-63.

Rintala, J., and S. Birrell. "Fair Treatment for the Active Female: A Content Analysis of *Young Athlete* Magazine." *Sociology of Sport Journal* 1 (no. 3, 1984):231-250.

Sewart, J. J. "The Rationalization of Modern Sport: The Case of Professional Football." *Arena Review* 5 (September 1981):45-53.

Shaw, G. *Meat on the Hoof: The Hidden World of Texas Football.* New York: St. Martin's, 1972.

Shea, E. J. *Ethical Decisions in Physical Education and Sport.* Springfield, IL: Charles C. Thomas, 1978.

Simon, I. "A Humanistic Approach to Sports." *The Humanist* 43 (July/August 1983): 25-26, 32.

Smith, M. D. *Violence and Sport.* Toronto: Butterworths, 1983.

Spander, A. "Blame Civilization for Win-at-All-Costs Code." *The Sporting News* (March 18, 1985):11.

Straw, P. "Pointspreads and Journalistic Ethics." *Arena Review* 7 (February 1983):43-45.

Sugden, J. P. "The Sociological Perspective: The Political Economy of Violence in American Sport." *Arena Review* 5 (February 1981):57-62.

Telander, R. "The Written Word: Player-Press Relationships in American Sports." *Sociology of Sport Journal* 1 (no. 1, 1984):3-14.

Tumin, M. "Business as a Social System." *Behavioral Science* 9 (no. 2, April 1964):120-130.

Underwood, J. "An Unfolding Tragedy." *Sports Illustrated* (August 14, 1978):69-82; (August 21, 1978):32-56; and (August 28, 1978):30-41.

Underwood, J. *Spoiled Sport.* Boston: Little, Brown, 1984.

Weiss, P. *Sport: A Philosophic Inquiry.* Carbondale, IL: Southern Illinois University Press, 1969.

Young, T. R. *New Sources of Self.* London: Pergamon Press, 1972.

Young, T. R. "The Sociology of Sport: A Critical Overview." *Arena Review* 8 (November 1984):1-14.

Young, T. R., and G. Massey. "The Dramaturgical Society: A Macro-Analytic Approach to Dramaturgical Analysis." *Qualitative Sociology* 1 (no. 2, 1980):78-98.

11. *Performance-Enhancing Drugs in Sport*

JOHN R. FULLER AND MARC J. LA FOUNTAIN

The growing concern in the United States about drug abuse among young people is mobilizing teachers, parents, law enforcement officers, and youth-serving professionals in an effort to educate, treat, and prevent the recreational use of drugs. Laudable as these efforts are, they can have only a minimal effect without some major rethinking about which substances should be sanctioned, the approaches (criminal or medical) that should be used to discourage drug use, and the level of threat from drug use that can offset violation of civil rights which some popular remedies (i.e., drug testing) may imply. A logical, coherent drug policy to deal with recreational drugs has yet to emerge despite the universal concern of those who deal with the problems of youth. In the spirit of broadening the examination of drugs in our society, this article looks at another form of drug abuse that is frequently overlooked. Young athletes are using anabolic steroids and a substance called human growth hormone to increase the size and strength of their bodies. Because this form of drug use is potentially more harmful to the body of a young person than almost any of the popular recreational drugs, it deserves greater attention.

The purposes of this paper are (1) to discuss the seriousness and prevalence of the use of performance-enhancing drugs, and (2) to report the results of a series of interviews with steroid users to determine their rationales for drug use.

PERFORMANCE-ENHANCING DRUGS: THE HEALTH PROBLEMS

In the summer between his junior and senior years in high school, Bob (not his real name), an all-city, 205-lb. linebacker, works out with weights at a local gym amid a number of older football players, body builders, and competitive weight lifters. When he returns to school in the fall, his coach is delighted to see the changes in Bob. Not only is he now 235 lbs. of lean

SOURCE: *Adolescence* 22 (Winter 1987), pp. 969-976. Reprinted by permission of Libra Publishers.

muscle, but he also has gained an intense attitude and killer instinct which are sure to make him all-state and possibly an all-American. The transformation in Bob's body and demeanor makes the coach marvel at the advances in body shaping available to almost every young athlete. If the coach had looked more closely, he would not have been so delighted at some of the other changes that occurred in Bob: He is in a constant state of anxiety; he cannot concentrate on his studies; he is constantly arguing with his parents; and he is having problems with his girlfriend–jealousy, pressuring for sex, and much to her surprise, beating her up when he gets frustrated.

Bob's unusual behavior should be a sign to parents, coaches, and teachers that he may have a serious drug problem. In addition to his aggressive attitude, he is suffering damage to his heart, liver, reproductive system, and stomach as a result of taking performance-enhancing anabolic steroids. The medical case against the use of anabolic steroids, human growth hormones, and erogenic aids in sport is clear (Brubaker, 1985; Stone & Lipner, 1980; Goldman, 1984; Taylor,1982, 1985a, 1985b; Todd, 1984). The real question is why anyone who has heard about the harmful effects of these drugs would expose himself to heart attacks, sterility, ulcers, and liver tumors, not to mention psychological and emotional instabilities. Perhaps the current "win at all costs" mentality costs too much.

INTERVIEWING THE MESOMORPHS: WHY THEY USE STEROIDS

In an effort to understand the rationale and motivation of those who use performance-enhancing drugs we interviewed 50 athletes who admitted to steroid use. With the help of some key informants we were introduced to several steroid-using weight lifters, football players, wrestlers, and bodybuilders. These athletes ranged in age from 15 to 40 years, with an average age of 19. Since this is considered a self-selected sample, any claims of generalization are offered with qualifications. No systematic differences between the high school and college-level athletes were found and the type of sport did not seem to play a major role in the decision to use steroids.

We were interested in how these athletes rationalized engagement in three types of deviant behavior: (1) taking unfair advantage in sport (using performance-enhancing drugs is prohibited by all sport-sanctioning bodies), (2) breaking the law (with the exception of one athlete who had received a doctor's prescription for his steroids, all the athletes interviewed received their drugs through black market purchase), and (3) exposing the body to health risks (these athletes were all aware of the risks). They were asked quite directly why they used the drugs, how they had learned about them, and the values they associated with this form of drug use.

In order to understand human behavior, the meanings people attach to their own behavior must be considered (Mills, 1940). Researchers interested in deviant behavior have examined how a justificatory vocabulary has been developed to explain involvement in homicide (Luckenbill, 1977), rape (Scully & Marolla, 1984), child molestation (McCaghy, 1968), and gang violence in prisons (Jacobs, 1977). In order to analyze the motivations of steroid-using athletes, Sykes and Matza's (1957) "techniques of neutralization" were used as the basis for the interviews. These are the techniques juvenile delinquents use to rationalize responsibility for their crimes. Sykes and Matza labeled the techniques as denial of victim, denial of injury, condemnation of condemners, and appeal to higher loyalties.

DENIAL OF VICTIM

Athletes who use steroids do not believe they are causing harm to anyone. They view their drug use as a "victimless crime"—one that should not be the concern of other people. Those interviewed felt that the serious athlete is required to use steroids if he wants to be competitive nationally and internationally. Most of them said that if the athletes against whom they competed did not use drugs, they would consider not using steroids themselves. One recurrent theme in the rationalization of steroid use is finger-pointing at the Eastern-block nations. Steroid use was justified as an act of patriotism, and as paying the price necessary to be competitive:

> We should be allowed to take them because all those other countries take them. Those guys from East Germany, Bulgaria, and Russia all use steroids. The women too. If we don't take them you can kiss off ever winning an Olympic medal for America.

> You have no choice if you want to compete in the big-time. Everyone does from other countries so we should also. If you want to dance you have to pay the fiddler. I wish they would outlaw them but at most meets all of them are juiced up so you have to be too.

The consistent paranoia that other athletes use steroids seem to be pervasive in the weight-lifting and football subcultures. When athletes look around the gym and see steroid use among their peers, they are quick to attribute drug use to all athletes who achieve a high degree of success. It is clear that this is not the case since some of the best athletes have demonstrated that they are drug-free (Todd, 1984).

DENIAL OF INJURY

The athletes interviewed were not very concerned with the potential health problems that are linked to steroid use. In discounting the health risks they displayed a remarkable lack of knowledge about the effect on their bodies. Many had little interest in sorting out the conflicting evidence on the health risks and seemed to view their bodies as simply a tool or machine that could be manipulated for results. They picked up their attitudes toward steroid use and the techniques for administering them from the more experienced athletes at the gyms where they worked out. These served as "gym gurus" who advised athletes as to the type of drug to use, how often to use it, and which drugs could be used in combination—called "stacking" in the weight lifters' argot. The athletes do not see steroid use as being injurious to their health, employing a variety of rationalizations to discount the potential risks:

> Every drug has side effects. Did you ever read the printed matter that comes with Tylenol? There is a long list of side effects. Steroids have less side effects than other drugs.
>
> You can abuse anything. Even aspirin. I don't think there is any proven test that says steroids really do hurt you. I know you hear a lot of talk but I know of nothing conclusive. A lot of us who use them are walking around but none of us have any health problems. Some may develop health problems because we do it on a hit or miss basis, not like the Russians who have it down to a science. We have these local gym gurus who make money off these guys and sell them too much, but even then I don't see any harmful effects.
>
> I use small doses. I don't use that much. I only know of about three people who have had trouble. One guy almost died. He was really good and had a chance to go to the L.A. Olympics but he took too much. If I ever have trouble I'll come off it.
>
> I see so many bodybuilders who take ungodly amounts and they never have problems. Only one guy got messed up and that's because he went off his cycle.
>
> The one I was on they give to people recovering from surgery, so how bad can that be for your body. It's not like they are poison or anything bad like that. It's like medicine. They help you grow. Besides I only take two a day so I don't feel I take enough to harm myself.

Few of the athletes considered the aggressive behavior associated with steroids as cause for concern. The emotional and psychological mood changes that result from taking hormonal drugs are dismissed as unimportant. They do not consider their behavior toward parents and girlfriends as injurious. It should be noted, however, that the girlfriends of a few of these athletes sought us out to complain about aggressive behavior and implored us to convince the athletes to quit using the drugs.

None of the athletes we talked to had done any reading or research on the potential health risks of steroid use. Most of their information was derived from muscle magazines or from peers at the gym.

CONDEMNATION OF CONDEMNERS

Another way steroid-using athletes deflect responsibility for their deviant behavior is by condemning the condemners, i.e., they question the knowledge, motives, and integrity of their critics.

> The people who do those studies are not athletes and don't really know what's going on. Those studies are not valid because they lasted only a couple of weeks and were done on rats. American studies are not sophisticated and I don't believe them because so many athletes say it works and that proves the studies false.
>
> People just don't understand what it means to be an athlete. Why don't they raise hell when they see all the knee operations done on football players. Sports eat up the body for those who reach the top and all those loudmouth purists don't blink an eye especially where big money is involved. Rules should not be made and enforced by people who don't know what they are talking about.

APPEAL TO HIGHER LOYALTIES

The athletes commonly spoke of what can be described as an appeal to higher loyalties–a vague, loosely defined "code of commitment" to sport. The dominant normative system is not repudiated by the appeal of higher loyalties technique of neutralization, but rather is violated with reluctance and with the justification that other norms are more pressing. The patchwork of rules and regulations which are inconsistently enforced are viewed as impediments–not guidelines for the practice of sport. Warnings about health risks, appeals to the ideals of fair play, and the threat of arrest are all dismissed as secondary to the code of commitment as expressed by these athletes. Steroid use is equated with having a dedicated attitude. For many of the athletes, steroid use was the only feature of their sport-related behavior that suggested sacrifice.

> I think you should take care of your body. I have not always taken care of mine but I do now. I get a lot of fun and enjoyment from powerlifting. It gives me a chance to achieve for myself and I do all I can to make my body stronger. I don't use drugs or drink or smoke and if my coach says steroids will make me stronger I will use them.
>
> I enjoy being with athletes more than with other people. I have changed my social life since we got into weightlifting. I don't like negative-thinking people, and being on steroids makes me feel very positive. I live fast. I had

> one hour of sleep last night, and I'm still going strong. If your mind is thinking positive you can do anything you want.
>
> I use them because they give me the White Moment (defined as a mystical, ecstatic feeling). If you have never experienced the high, then you don't know what I'm talking about. I load up on roids and take a hit of speed and I'm on top of the world.

The appeal to higher loyalties rationale had an additional aspect worth noting. According to the reports of almost all the athletes interviewed, the chemical reaction resulted in an intensification of the sex drive. Several reported having personal problems with girlfriends during steroid cycles. One bodybuilder said he took only oral steroids because of threats of abandonment by his girlfriend. The increased sex drive results from the increase in excitability, aggressive behavior, and irritability. Thus, this side effect of taking hormonal drugs is not surprising. However, the athletes' perception and consequent lauding of the aphrodisiac effects of the drugs is disturbing. If these drugs become more widely used as a result of the perceived sexual effect, we may see even greater abuse.

DISCUSSION

The interviews revealed several problems. First, from the ease with which our sample was collected, and from the comments of the athletes, it appears that performance-enhancing steroid use is widespread. Thought at one time to be the province of only the world-class athlete, we are now seeing the less serious and younger athlete consuming steroids as casually as he would select a new pair of running shoes. There is an absence of expert medical supervision and rigorous experimental design necessary to evaluate steroid use; instead, athletes at all levels in several sports, some of them quite young (17-21), are self-administering massive doses of different types of steroids.

A second problem is the loss of credibility of the medical and coaching professions. The athletes dismissed local doctors and coaches as naive and ignorant about the technology and pharmacology of contemporary sport, acquiring information from popular magazines and local gym gurus/pushers. It appears that athletes of the 1980s are no more likely to heed the warnings about the dangers of steroid use than youths of the 1960s were to heed the warnings about marijuana.

The haphazard self-administration of steroids and the repudiation of traditional experts (coaches and doctors) has led athletes to adopt a new line of justifications for the way in which they participate in their sport. The vocabulary of motives adopted by the athletes closely resembles the techniques of neutralization noted by Sykes and Matza (1957) to explain deviant behavior of juvenile delinquents.

The modes of rationalization used by these athletes have important implications. On one level, the potential deleterious effects on health are sufficient cause for concern. The athletes interviewed did not appear to have adequate knowledge to be self-administering these drugs. On another level, the effects of drugs on the way we participate in sports are important considerations. Sports require a certain amount of cooperation to ensure fair play and even competition. To the extent that performance-enhancing steroids provide an advantage, the time may come (the interviewees claimed it is already here) when it must be used in order to be competitive. Escalation of the sacrifice involved in sports participation is clearly getting out of hand, and if drug use becomes more popular, inevitably the socialization process will expand to include adolescents.

At yet another level, a serious question of policy arises as to whether youths who use steroids are in fact deviants or criminals. This paper has tried to display the mindsets of young athletes and their relationship to the institutions of society, i.e., education, sports, medicine, media, and government. This has been done by focusing on the symbolic and actual language of steroid users (techniques of neutralization). What happens in the lives of the athletes is intimately connected with, and reflective of, the order of society. In order to alter the actions of youths, administrators, coaches, and families must reflect on society's values and institutions as they relate to the current philosophy of games and winning that is generating this form of drug abuse.

REFERENCES

Brubaker, B. (1985, Jan. 21). A pipeline full of drugs. *Sports Illustrated*, pp. 18-21.

Goldman, B. (1984). *Death in the locker room: Steroids and sports*. South Bend, IN: Icarus Press.

Jacobs, J. B. (1977). *Stateville: The penitentiary in mass society*. Chicago: University of Chicago Press.

Luckenbill, D. (1977). Criminal homicide as a situated transaction. *Social Problems*, 25(2), 176-187.

McCaghy, C. (1968). Drinking and deviance disavowed: The case of child molesters. *Social Problems*, 16(1), 43-49.

Mills, C. W. (1940). Situated actions and vocabularies of motive. *American Sociological Review*, 33(1), 46-62.

Scully, D., & Marolla, J. (1984). Convicted rapists' vocabulary of motive: Excuses and justifications. *Social Problems*, 31(5), 530-544.

Stone, R., & Lipner, H. (1980, summer). The use of anabolic steroids in athletics. *Journal of Drug Issues*, 10(3), 351-360.

Sykes, G. M., & Matza, D. (1957). Techniques of neutralization. *American Sociological Review*, 22(6), 644-670.

Taylor, W. N. (1982). *Anabolic steroids and the athlete*. Jefferson, NC: McFarland & Company.

Taylor, W. N. (1985a). *Hormonal manipulation: A new era of monstrous athletes*. Jefferson, NC: McFarland & Company.

Taylor, W. N. (1985b). Super athletes made to order. *Psychology Today*, 19(5), 63-66.

Todd, T. (1984, Oct. 15). The use of human growth hormone poses a grave dilemma for sport. *Sports Illustrated*, pp. 10-18.

12. *Out of Bounds: The Truth about Athletes and Rape*

JILL NEIMARK

Meg Davis was gang-raped in the spring of her freshman year by seven members of the university's football team—guys she used to hang out with at fraternity parties. "I knew the guys I 'buddied' with sometimes had group sex, and that they even hid in a closet and took pictures of the event," she says now, "but I never thought it would happen to me." She was sexually assaulted for nearly three hours. She blacked out as she was being sodomized, and came to later with a quarterback's penis in her mouth. When she tried to push him off, he shouted, "Hey, what are you doing? I haven't come yet!" Back at the dorm that night, she says, "I took shower after shower. I stayed in until there was no hot water left. I felt so dirty. Even so, I didn't call what happened to me rape. These were guys I knew. It wasn't until I went to a woman's center in town that someone explained I'd been gang-raped."

Men have been raping in gangs for centuries, from Russian soldiers in Germany and American soldiers in My Lai, to the infamous gang of boys "wilding" in New York's Central Park two years ago. When we think of group rape, it is exactly those packs of men who come to mind. But these days a disproportionate number of gang rapes are being committed by men whom we look to as our heroes, whom we laud and look up to for their grace and power and seeming nobility: young male athletes.

Psychologist Chris O'Sullivan, Ph.D., of Bucknell University in Lewisburg, Pennsylvania, studied 26 alleged gang rapes that were documented between 1980 and 1990, and found that fraternity groups committed the highest number, followed by athletic teams. In addition, she found that "the athletes who do this are usually on a star team, not just any old team. It was the football team at Oklahoma, the basketball team at Minnesota, the lacrosse team at St. John's." It seems to be our most privileged athletes—the ones, by the way, most sought after by women—who are often involved in gang rape.

From June 1989 to June 1990, at least 15 alleged gang rapes involving about 50 athletes were reported. Among the most publicized cases: At

SOURCE: *Mademoiselle* (May 1991), pp. 196-199, 244-248. This article was originally published in *Mademoiselle*. Reprinted by permission of Jill Neimark.

Berkeley, a freshman claimed she was raped and sodomized in a dark stairwell, among shards of a shattered light bulb, and then dragged by her assaulter—a member of the football team—to his room, where three teammates join him. In Glen Ridge, New Jersey, four high-school athletes—all of them former football teammates—have been charged with wielding a small baseball bat and a broomstick to rape a 17-year-old slightly retarded girl. In Washington, D.C., a 17-year-old girl maintained, four members of the Washington Capitals hockey team assaulted her after the team was eliminated at the Stanley Cup play-offs (but none were indicted by a grand jury); and at St. John's University in New York, five members of the lacrosse team (plus one member of the rifle club) were accused of raping a student.

In spite of surging publicity about the phenomenon, athletes accused of rape usually escape with little more than a reprimand. Virtually every athlete accused of participating in a gang rape insists that it was not rape: He says the victim wanted group sex. *She asked for it.* Juries and judges seem to agree, for charges are often dropped. Pressing charges is crucial for rape victims' recovery. "A guy gets suspended for half a season and then he's back," notes Ed Gondolf, Ed.D., a sociologist at the Indiana University of Pennsylvania and author of *Man Against Woman: What Every Woman Should Know About Violent Men* (Tab Books, 1989). In the occasional gang-rape cases that proceed to prosecution, notes Claire Walsh, Ph.D., director of Campus and Community Consultation, an organization in St. Augustine, Florida, that specializes in presenting rape-prevention workshops across the country, "convictions are very difficult and rare."

"This act is so heinous," explains Dr. Walsh, "that we don't want to admit we have this kind of brutality in our culture. We don't want to believe our athletes are capable of this. So we immediately rename it, call it group sex, and perform a character assassination on the victim. It's her fault—no matter what the circumstances." What professionals involved in studying gang rape are beginning to understand is that there seems to be something very specific about the gloriously physical, sometimes brutal camaraderie of team sports that can set the stage for a brutal act.

One clue to the trigger for such an act may lie in the dynamics of the team experience itself: You don't find gang rape among tennis players or swimmers or those who participate in other solo sports. According to Bernice Sandler, Ph.D., director of the Project on the status and Education of Women at the Association of American Colleges, it is athletes on football, basketball and hockey teams who are most prone to group rape. Athletes who work and play together—hours each day, for months and years—become profoundly bonded. I remember my first, and only, outsider's taste of this bond: I was the sole woman attending a stag party for former rowers on the Yale crew team. I was to play waitress. The men wore nothing but loincloths. They were told to gulp down as many shots of whiskey as they could when they walked in the door. Then they slathered one another with mud and beer and spent much of the evening wrestling with a kind of wild, erotic joy. These guys never once talked about women. I went home shaken but, I admit, also envious. I knew I would never experience that raw, physical abandon with my own sex.

One rape victim recalls a similar experience. The group of athletes and fraternity brothers who later raped her, she said, used to dance a tribal dance in a darkened room, finally collapsing on one another in a heap. The "circle" dance, as it was called, was ecstatic and violent. "They'd be jumping up and pounding the ceiling and singing a song that began, 'When I'm old and turning gray, I'll only gang-bang once a day.'"

Most psychologists believe that powerful male bonding is the essence of gang rape—that, in fact, the men are raping for one another. Peggy R. Sanday, Ph.D., University of Pennsylvania anthropologist and author of *Fraternity Gang Rape* (NYU Press, 1990), explains: "They get a high off doing it with their 'brothers.'" The male bonding in these groups is so powerful and seductive that, says Dr. Walsh, "one man leads and the others follow because they cannot break the male bonds." Those men present who don't rape often watch—sometimes even videotaping the event. And, explains Gail Abarbanel, L.C.S.W., director of the Rape Treatment Center at Santa Monica Hospital in California, "There has never been a single case, in all the gang rapes we've seen, where one man tried to stop it." Even the voyeur with a stab of guilt never reports his friends. "That's the crux of group rape," explains Abarbanel. "It's more important to be part of the group than to be the person who does what's right."

But there is more to team-gang rape than male bonding. These athletes see the world in a special way—a way that actually legitimizes rape. They develop a powerful subculture founded on aggression, privilege and the scapegoating of women. Friendship is expressed through hostile teasing one player calls "busting." And, according to Dr. O'Sullivan, "Sports fosters this supermasculine attitude where you connect aggression with sexuality. These men see themselves as more sexual because they're more aggressive. I talked to one pro-basketball player who says that for years he raped women and didn't know it. Sex was only satisfying if it was a conquest."

According to Dr. Gondolf, who was also a football player, "For some athletes, there's an aggression, a competition, that's heightened in team sports. You come off the field and your adrenaline is still flowing, you're still revved up, and some of these guys may expect to take what they want by force, just like they do on the field." Dr. Gondolf says that he recalls certain moments from his time as a player, "where the whole team was moving as one, where we became part of a collective whole, rather than individuals."

Within that collective whole, according to experts and some athletes themselves, one way the men can demonstrate their power is by scapegoating women. "There was a lot of classic machismo talk," recalls Tommy*, now 24, who played on the football team at Lafayette College in Pennsylvania. "The talk was very sexist, even threatening. I recall some guys sharing that they were really drunk as a big excuse for having sex with a girl everyone thought was a dog. The guy would say, 'I had my beer goggles on.' He'd act like he was embarrassed, but the fact was he did have sex, so it was a bragging kind of confession."

The pressure to score is powerful. Months after one gang rape had taken place, one of the men who had participated in it was still uneasily lamenting his impotence that night. Dr. Gondolf recalls how some men tended to talk about scoring on and off the field as if they were the same thing: "Abuse of women became the norm—not necessarily out of meanness, but because we saw the person as an opponent, an object to be maneuvered. Because the camaraderie among us was so important, we never questioned or challenged one another when these things came up. I remember hearing about forced sex, group sex, naked showers with women, and the tendency was to shrug your shoulders or chuckle. The locker-room subculture fed on itself."

And when the adrenaline rush of the field does get translated to a sexual assault, Dr. Gondolf theorizes, "a high definitely takes over during the rape, and it has a neutralizing effect. There is enough momentum present that it negates any guilt, fear or doubt. The man thinks to himself, 'Oh, we're just having a good time, nobody's gonna get hurt.' It's the same rationalization men use when they beat or abuse their wives: 'She had it coming, she asked for it, she didn't get hurt that bad, I was drunk, it wasn't my fault.'"

What is perhaps most difficult to comprehend about gang rape is that the men involved *don't* feel guilty; they don't see this act of group violence as rape. Mary Koss, Ph.D., a University of Arizona psychologist, studied over 6,000 students at 32 universities and found that 1 of 12 college males admits to acts legally defined as rape or attempted rape, and yet only 1 out of 100 admits they have raped or attempted rape. "Of the one hundred thirty-one men who had committed what we would legally define as rape," says Dr. Koss, "eighty-four percent argued that what they did was definitely not rape."

In many of the team-gang-rape cases around the country, the athletes involved readily, almost eagerly, admitted they'd had sex with the victim. In fact, they seemed to offer up their confessions as juicy tidbits. One witness in a case against members of the Kentucky State football team, in which all the men were found not guilty, testified that guys had lined up in the hall holding their crotches and saying, "Me next." And in an Oklahoma case, a player testified that he saw three former teammates—who were also subsequently acquitted—take turns having sex with a screaming girl, saying, "If we have to, we're going to take some from her." In many of the cases the athletes described how they viewed their victim as different from other women: cheap, a slut, a whore. Many quoted the old cliché, "When she says no, she really means yes." Usually they'd heard she was "easy"—sometimes because a teammate had already slept with her. At Kentucky, a teammate testified that he'd had oral sex with the victim three days before the alleged rape. "Any woman who would do that would do anything," he'd said. In fact, according to Dr. O'Sullivan, "Some of these guys are really sweet. They can be very nice to other women in their lives. But once a woman is in this category, it's almost as if she isn't a human being. All their beliefs say it's okay to abuse her."

I found the same disturbing paradox when I interviewed athletes. When confronted with the abstract idea of rape, these men use words like "shattering, disgusting, immoral." (Jay*, 25, a former football player at the University of Rochester, said, "I'll tell you something, I'd never even dream of doing anything like that, it makes me sick to my stomach.") But if they personally know of a case involving their teammates, they're curiously lenient and forgiving. A former starting quarterback at Lafayette College recalled rumors of a gang rape by his teammates on campus. "From what I understand she came on to one of the guys. Not that this justifies it, but she did like one of the guys who allegedly raped her, and she was willing to come up to the room with him." Even when I interviewed an old friend of mine, formerly on an Ivy League track team, he mentioned offhandedly that some members of his team had shared a girl with a baseball team in Alabama, which "offered" her to the visitors. My friend never questioned whether it might have been rape: He assumed the girl was willing.

One possible reason for the astounding lack of guilt among athletes who rape is the special privilege accorded a star athlete—and the constant female adoration he attracts. "The 'hotshot syndrome' is inevitably part of team sports," says Dr. Gondolf. "If you're an athlete in college, you're given scholarships, a nice dorm, doctors, trainers, a lot of support and attention and fans and cheerleaders who ogle you. That sense of privilege influences you, and some guys may then think, 'I deserve something for this, I can take women, the rules don't apply to me.' They feel they're above the law."

"I used to have girls call me up" says former quarterback Jay, "and say, 'I go to football games and watch you, I look at your picture in the program, I'm writing a paper on you.' It happened all the time. You get this attitude where you can do anything you want and nobody is ever going to say anything to you."

Coaches and universities contribute to the athlete's unique sense of entitlement. As Dr. Walsh notes, "When we're talking about athletic teams and gang rape, we see how, time after time, the entire community comes to the support of the team. Athletes are very important in the fabric of a campus or town. They keep alumni interested, and produce money for the community."

Says one outraged father of a 17-year-old rape victim, "The college threatened her. They told her if she went to the police her name would be in the paper, and her grandparents, who lived in a neighboring town, would see it. She went to the assistant dean, who never told the dean. He simply made an investigation himself, and wrote her a few months later saying the investigation had led nowhere and he was going to close the matter. The police chief even bragged to me that he'd worked hard to cover it up. As for the boys who raped her, they admitted having sex, but said she was a slut–she'd asked for it. It didn't matter that she'd gone on less than a dozen dates in her life."

Coaches also do their best to help their "boys" slip through the adverse publicity unpunished. Perhaps that's not too surprising, since the coaches themselves are often former players. "Twenty years ago someone could have talked to *me* about all this stuff," confessed Ray Tellier, former football coach and facilitator of campus discussions on rape at the University of Rochester. And three years ago, Bobby Knight, basketball coach at Indiana University, created an uproar by telling broadcaster Connie Chung: "I think that if rape is inevitable, relax and enjoy it."

The attitude of juries is often similarly lenient: Sergeant Danny Conway, a detective in Frankfort, Kentucky, who prosecuted the gang-rape case at Kentucky State University, recalls his fury when the five players prosecuted for rape were set free. "We charged five men on the football team–although there must have been more, because there were semen samples that didn't belong to any of the five. All of them said she was a willing participant, because she had snuck into the dorm with one of them. And all of them were dismissed. These guys made sport of it. In the trial they were giving one another high-fives and holding their fists up in the air and saying, 'First I got her, then he got her,' and they were smiling at one another in open court. The jury didn't seem fazed at all. Their decision tore me to pieces. It never seemed to faze them that this was a young lady whose life was probably ruined."

In the past few years those entrenched attitudes have finally, slowly, begun to be challenged. "At least now we recognize how often gang rape occurs," notes Dr. Walsh. Many universities and fraternities have begun education programs about rape, and Santa Monica's Rape Treatment Center offers an educational video that is being distributed across the country, starring Susan Dey and Corbin Bernsen of *L.A.Law*. At Syracuse University in New York, where last year six rapes were reported in the first five weeks of the school year, activists have formed a group called SCARED (Students Concerned About Rape Education). And New York recently passed a law that requires freshman rape orientation for schools receiving state funds.

New studies are showing that there is no such thing as a typical rape victim. Many women who are raped in college are virgins, according to Mary Koss's study–and the vast majority (75 to 91 percent) of rape victims cannot be differentiated from nonvictims in terms of risk factors like personality or circumstance. Women are often raped in the "honeymoon" period, however: those first few months of school when they're learning to negotiate their new world. And drinking is almost always involved; in fact, states Dr. Walsh, "alcohol is used deliberately to impair the woman." At parties, punch is massively spiked with liquor—to the point where some rape victims complain that they had only two drinks before they passed out drunk. One victim at San Diego State University recalls asking for a nonalcoholic beverage. Instead she was brought punch spiked with Everclear, a 95-percent-alcohol drink that is illegal in California.

But if outside observers have difficulty finding common attributes among victims of team rape, it seems clear that the men themselves have an unspoken code that divides women into classes—the nice-girl girlfriend and the party-girl rape victim. The scary part is that the cues are so hidden most women are completely unaware of them—and the rules may be different among different teams, different campuses, different locker rooms. Athletes will sometimes let drop a few clues: Usually a woman is more vulnerable if she's had sex with one of the group before; if she's buxom, wears tight clothes and lots of makeup; if she's from a college that has a certain reputation. One fraternity actually stuck colored dots on women's hands as they came to a party, color-coded to indicate how "easy" each woman was. It's that kind of hidden code that has more and more colleges warning young women to stay away altogether from the fraternity and house parties where athletes and their buddies gather—just as one must avoid dark alleys at night. Dr. Gondolf explains: "Athletes are so tangled up in their glory and their privilege, and they get such big benefits for it. We need women to prompt them to check up on one another." But that is only half the answer.

In the case of gang rape, almost all college women are so devastated they drop out of school. "These are overwhelming rapes, and the trauma is profound," explains Abarbanel. "A lot of these women are freshmen who are just beginning to test their independence. They have hopes and dreams about college and achievement, meeting new people, a career, a future. After gang rape, everything that college means is lost to them. They're afraid to be alone, afraid of a recurrence. And since these are often men they know, the sense of betrayal is very profound."

In some cases, says Dr. Sanday, a woman may have subconsciously been courting danger. She knows she should avoid certain parties, be careful about her drinking, come and leave with friends. But she's looking for power, on male territory. "We all, at certain times in our life, test ourselves. It's like going into the inner city on a dare. These women are using the men that way. They want to court and conquer danger. And legally and morally, they have a right to go and have sex with whomever they want, without being gang-raped."

One of the most important ways to prevent rape may be to understand what the word means. Many men and women don't know that the law *requires* that a woman give consent to sexual intercourse. If she's so inebriated that she can't say yes, or so frightened that she won't say no, the act is rape.

But just knowing that distinction is not quite enough; the seeds of team gang rape are buried deep, even subconsciously, in the athletic culture. Dr. O'Sullivan tells of an incident outside the courtroom of the Kentucky State football-team trial. According to her, "We were all standing by the candy machine, and some guy mentioned that it was broken. And Big Will, a huge man who had charmed everybody, and who was testifying in behalf of his dormmate, said, 'I'll make it work. Everybody always does what I want.' And everybody laughed. I couldn't believe it. This is exactly the kind of attitude that can lead to the rape." The perception that force is "okay," that it is masculine and admirable, is really where gang rape begins—and where the fight against it will have to start.

NOTE

* Names have been changed.

FOR FURTHER STUDY

Berkow, Ira. "The Abundance of Skullduggery in Baseball." *The New York Times* (August 23, 1987):20.

Brady, Erik. "Craftsmen Ply Tricks of the Trade." *USA Today* (August 5, 1987):C1.

Chaiken, Tommy, with Rick Telander. "The Nightmare of Steroids." *Sports Illustrated* (October 24, 1988):82-102.

Chass, Murray. "True Confessions: A Pitcher Tells How to Cheat." *The New York Times* (July 26, 1987):18.

Frey, James H., ed. "Gambling in Sports." *Arena Review* 11 (May 1987): entire issue.

Mottram, D. R., ed. *Drugs in Sport*. Champaign, IL: Human Kinetics, 1988.

Simon, Robert L. *Fair Play: Sport, Values & Society*. Boulder, CO: Westview Press, 1991.

Sociology of Sport Journal. "Ethics and Morality in Sport: Annotated Bibliography." *Sociology of Sport Journal* 6 (1989):84-91.

Stack, M. F., ed. special issue on "Drugs and Sport." *Arena Review* 12 (May 1988).

Swift, E. M. "Dangerous Games: In the Age of AIDS, Many Pro Athletes are Sexually Promiscuous, Despite the Increasing Peril." *Sports Illustrated* (November 18, 1991):40-43.

Todd, Terry. "Anabolic Steroids: The Gremlins of Sport." *Journal of Sport History* 14 (1987):87-107.

Voy, Robert, with Kirk D. Deeter. *Drugs, Sport, and Politics*. Champaign, IL: Leisure Press, 1991.

Wadler, Gary I., and Brian Hainline. *Drugs and the Athlete*. Philadelphia: F. A. Davis, 1989.

Wright, James E., and Virgina S. Cowart. *Anabolic Steroids: Altered States*. Carmel, IN: Benchmark Press, 1990.

Part Five

Big-Time College Sport

Interschool sports are found in almost all American schools and at all levels. There are many reasons for this universality. Sports unite all segments of a school and the community or neighborhood they represent. School sports remind constituents of the school, which may lead to monetary and other forms of support. School administrators can use sport as a useful tool for social control. But the most important reason for the universality of school sports is the widespread belief that the educational goals are accomplished through sport. There is much merit to this view; sports do contribute to physical fitness, to learning the value of hard work and perseverance, and to being goal-oriented. There is some evidence that sports participation leads to better grades, higher academic aspirations, and positive self-concept.

However, there also is a negative side to school sports. They are elitist, since only the gifted participate. Sports often overshadow academic endeavors (e.g., athletes are disproportionately rewarded and schools devote too much time and money to athletics that could be diverted to academic activities). Where winning is paramount—and where is this not the case?—the pressure becomes intense. This pressure has several negative consequences, the most important of which is that participants are prevented from fully enjoying sport. The pressure is too great for many youngsters. The game is work. It is a business.

The pressure to win also contributes to abuse by coaches, poor sportsmanship, dislike of opponents, intolerance of losers, and cheating. Most significant, although not usually considered so, is that while sport is a success-oriented activity, it is fraught with failure (losing teams, bench warmers, would-be participants cut from teams, the humiliation of letting down your teammates and school, and so on). For every ego enhanced by sport, how many have been bruised?

While this description fits all types of schools, big-time college sports deserve special attention for they have unique problems. Athletes in these settings are athletes first and students second; thus they are robbed of a first-class education. They are robbed by the tremendous demands on their time and energy. This problem is further enhanced by athletes being segregated from the student body (in special classes, housed in athletic dorms); thus they are deprived of a variety of influences that college normally facilitates.

Another problem of college sports is that they tend to be ultraelitist. The money and facilities go disproportionately to the *male* athletes in the revenue-producing sports rather than to intramurals, minor sports, and club sports.

The greatest scandal involving college sports is the illegal and immoral behavior of overzealous coaches, school authorities, and alumni in recruiting athletes. In the quest to bring the best athletes to a school, players have been given monetary inducements, sexual favors, forged transcripts, and surrogates to take their entrance exams. In addition to the illegality of these acts, two fundamental problems exist with these recruiting violations: (1) Such behaviors have no place in an educational setting, yet they are done by some educators and condoned by others, and (2) these illicit practices by so-called respected authorities transmit two major lessons—that greed is the ultimate value and that the act of winning supersedes how one wins.

Finally, the win-at-any-cost ethic that prevails in many of America's institutions of higher learning puts undue pressure on coaches. They must win to keep their jobs. Hence, some drive their athletes too hard or too brutally. Some demand total control over their players on and off the field. Some use illegal tactics to gain advantage (not only in recruiting but also in breaking the rules regarding the allowed number of practices, ineligible players, and unfair techniques). But coaches are not the problem. They represent a symptom of the process by which school sports are big business and where winning is the only avenue to achieve success.

The articles in Part Five reflect on these problems and offer some solutions. The first article, by Indiana University English professor and former sports writer Murray Sperber, demythologizes college sport. In doing so he shows, among other things, how the athletic establishment is *not* part of the educational mission of academic institutions. The second selection, by physical educator George H. Sage, examines the efforts made by the regulatory body of college sports—the NCAA—to solve the problems of big-time sports. As Sage points out, the NCAA typically focuses its attention on the "problem" athletes (thereby blaming the victims) rather than addressing the structural sources of the problems. The final selection by D. Stanley Eitzen provides a clear set of policy recommendations for cleaning up college sport.

13. *Myths about College Sports*

MURRAY SPERBER

> In interviews with UK [University of Kentucky] students, faculty members and administrators, a picture of two UKs emerges. One is a top-of-the-line $14-million-a-year athletic program, run largely by and for off-campus supporters; the other is a chronically underfinanced, "fair-to-middlin" academic institution that seems to languish in the shadow of the "Big Blue" [athletic] monolith.
>
> Item in the *Louisville Courier-Journal*

A great number of myths shield college sports from casual scrutiny and burden any discussion of the subject. The following refutations of the most common myths should introduce the reader to the reality of contemporary sports. . . .

Myth: College sports are part of the educational mission of American colleges and universities.

Reality: The main purpose of college sports is commercial entertainment. Within most universities with big-time intercollegiate programs, the athletic department operates as a separate business and has almost no connection to the educational departments and functions of the school—even the research into and teaching of sports is done by the physical education department.

The reason elite athletes are in universities has nothing to do with the educational missions of their schools. Athletes are the only group of students recruited for entertainment—not academic—purposes, and they are the only students who go through school on grants based not on educational aptitude, but on their talent and potential as commercial entertainers.

SOURCE: From "College Sports Inc.: The Athletic Department vs. The University" by Murray Sperber. Copyright 1990 by Murray Sperber. Reprinted by permission of Henry Holt and Company.

If colleges searched for and gave scholarships to up-and-coming rock stars so that they could entertain the university community and earn money for their schools through concerts and tours, educational authorities and the public would call this "a perversion of academic values." Yet every year, American institutions of higher education hand out over a hundred thousand full or partial athletic scholarships, worth at least $500 million, for reasons similar to the hypothetical grants to rock performers.

Myth: The alumni support–in fact, demand–that their alma maters have large and successful college sports programs.

Reality: Studies indicate that most alumni–people who were students at a particular school–contribute to the academic units of their colleges and universities and that only 1 to 2 percent of them donate to athletic programs. In fact, alumni often withhold contributions from their alma maters when the athletic teams are too successful or are involved in sports scandals: they are embarrassed by their schools' becoming "jock factories" and/or are angered by the bad publicity from scandals, and they believe that their college degrees are being devalued.

Other research indicates that the major donors to athletic programs actually are boosters–people who never attended the school, who give money only to the athletic department and in proportion to its teams' success on the field or court, and who refuse to contribute to the institution's academic programs.

Myth: College sport is incredibly profitable, earning huge sums of money for American colleges and universities.

Reality: One of the best-kept secrets about intercollegiate athletics–well guarded because athletic departments are extremely reluctant to open their financial books–is that most college sports programs lose money. If profit and loss is defined according to ordinary business practices, of the 802 members of the NCAA (National Collegiate Athletic Association), the 493 of the NAIA (National Association of Intercollegiate Athletes), and the 1,050 nonaffiliated junior colleges, only 10 to 20 athletic programs make a consistent albeit small profit, and in any given year another 20 to 30 break even or do better. The rest–over 2,300 institutions–lose anywhere from a few dollars to millions annually.

Because athletic departments are allowed to engage in "creative accounting," covering many of their expenses with money from their schools' general operating funds and other university sources, it is difficult to ascertain the full extent of their losses. One expert, Don Canham, longtime athletic director at the University of Michigan, estimated that "about 99 percent of the schools in this country don't balance their budgets in athletics." Canham balanced his, but the year after he retired (1988-89), Michigan's athletic program was, according to an NCAA official, "$2.5 million in the red."

Myth: The NCAA Division I men's basketball tournament makes millions of dollars for American colleges and universities.

Reality: Of the total revenue from the tournament, the NCAA keeps at least half or more for itself; for example, of the millions received from the 1987 tourney, the association distributed only 44 percent directly to the schools involved.

The new NCAA contract with CBS Sports will increase tournament revenue but, rather than share the pot o' gold, the NCAA plans to exclude a large number of schools from reaching it. According to Tom Hansen, commissioner of the Pac-10, the NCAA may soon drop a many as 50 schools from Division I basketball, including four or five conferences. In addition, if past performance is any indication, the richer pot will increase lottery fever among the remaining 240 Division I basketball programs, with coaches engaging in "checkbook recruiting" and sparing no cost to build winning teams.

In the 1990s, Final Four squads will win the lottery (probably the perennial powers will triumph most often), the 60 other teams invited to the tournament will break even on their basketball program expenses, and the hundreds of also-rans will either pay large sums of money to purchase losing lottery tickets or be shut out entirely.

Myth: Schools receive millions of dollars when their teams play in football bowl games.

Reality: Often the numbers given in newspaper articles are for the "projected payout," whereas the actual payout can be much lower. Moreover, most participating schools must split their bowl revenue with other members of their conferences. As a result, when the headline announces that a Pac-10 team received $1 million for a bowl appearance, that school kept only $100,000 because of the conference's ten-way split.

In addition, athletic departments like to turn bowl and tournament trips into all-expenses-paid junkets for hundreds of people, including their employees and friends. Their travel, hotel, and entertainment costs often eat up the actual bowl or tourney payouts and transform post-season play into a deficit item!

Myth: The money earned from college sports helps other parts of the university.

Reality: Because athletic department expenses usually exceed revenues, any money earned by college sports teams stays in the athletic department. Moreover, athletic departments admit that they have no intention of sharing their revenue; an NCAA survey reported that fewer than 1 percent of all athletic programs defined their "fiscal objective" as earning money "to support nonathletic activities of the institution."

Rather than financially help the university, most athletic programs siphon money from it: for example, the enormous maintenance costs of stadiums and other facilities—used exclusively for athletic program events and by their elite athletes—are often placed in the "Building-and-Grounds" line in the university-wide budget, and the multimillion-dollar debt servicing on these facilities is frequently paid by regular students in the form of mandatory "Fees."

To cover athletic program losses, schools must divert money from their budgets and other financial resources. Thus funds that could go to academic programs, student scholarships, faculty and staff salaries disappear into the athletic department deficit.

Myth: College coaches deserve their high annual incomes because they generate huge profits for their athletic programs.

Reality: A few years ago, the athletic director at the University of South Carolina commented: "For someone to make $250,000 in the business world, he'd have to generate $60 million to $70 million in sales. When coaches say they're worth it, they don't know what's going on out there."

John Wooden, the most successful men's basketball coach in NCAA history, was never paid more than $25,000 a year by UCLA. Today, only a few coaches generate as much revenue for their schools as Wooden did for his, and the vast majority direct programs that lose money for their institutions. Nevertheless, the annual incomes of at least one hundred NCAA Division I men's basketball coaches, and seventy-five Division I-A football coaches, approach or top $100,000, and many program heads in the "nonrevenue sports" (so termed because they always lose money) like soccer, baseball, track, and swimming earn over $75,000 a year.

Myth: College coaches deserve their high annual incomes because they are the key to producing winning teams and are irreplaceable.

Reality: Sonny Smith, a longtime Division I men's basketball coach, commented, "It's a make-it-while-you-can thing. . . . If I quit tomorrow, there'd be three hundred names in the ring." Except for a handful of truly outstanding and innovative coaches, most of the others are interchangeable and can be replaced by any number of the "three hundred names in the ring." When Bill Frieder, making over $400,000 a year, quit the University of Michigan on the eve of the 1989 NCAA men's basketball tournament, an unheralded assistant, earning a fraction of Frieder's income, was given the top job. Under Steve fisher, Michigan swept through the tourney and won the national championship.

Myth: Hired to be fired—that's the fate of most college coaches.

Reality: Firings are not the reason most college coaches change jobs. Coaches leave schools for a variety of reasons, most often to take better-paying positions, to quit jobs that are not working out, or to keep one step ahead of the NCAA sheriff. Only in a minority of cases are they asked to leave.

An analysis of the major coaching appointments listed weekly in the *Chronicle of Higher Education* over the last decade reveals the following typical sequence: the head man at Bigtime Sports U. quits in midcontract to go to the pros or to become an AD; the coach at Southern Jock State leaves his school to take the more lucrative package at Bigtime U.; the coach at Western Boondock sees a chance to move up and grabs the job at Southern; finally, if Western cannot hire another head coach, it offers its smaller package to an assistant at a major program or, in desperation, promotes one of its own assistants. When this Coach in Motion Play ends, at least three head coaches, as well as innumerable assistants, have changed jobs—not one of them fired by a college or university.

Myth: College athletic programs provide a wonderful opportunity for black coaches.

Reality: White athletic directors and program heads keep college coaching lily white by hiring their duplicates. In a 1987 study of the racial backgrounds of head coaches in football, basketball, baseball, and men's track at 278 Division I schools, only 4.2 percent were black. However, the real surprise was the percentage of black assistant coaches—3.1, lower that the percentage of black head coaches. On the other hand, another study of big-time programs found that over 50 percent of the football players and 70 percent of the men's basketball players, as well as a high percentage of baseball and track athletes, were black. Since 1987, the percentage of black head and assistant coaches in college sports has not changed significantly.

Myth: College athletic programs provide a wonderful opportunity for women coaches.

Reality: Women coaches, unlike blacks, once had a strong position in college sports. However, in the 1970s and early 1980s, male athletic directors and program heads took over women's college sports as well as the jobs of female ADs and many coaches. The most comprehensive study of this phenomenon shows that in the early 1970s, 90 percent of the athletic directors of women's college sports programs were female, whereas by 1988, the percentage had dropped to 16. In the same time span, the percentage of female coaches of women's sports teams went from the mid-90s to 48.

Paralleling the male takeover of individual jobs was the NCAA's cynical demolition of the main women's college sport group, the AIAW (Association of Intercollegiate Athletics for Women), and the NCAA's subsequent control of women's athletic programs.

Myth: Talented athletes, like other high school graduates, should enroll in higher education.

Reality: Only about 30 percent of American high school students go on to four-year colleges and universities; one subsection of these students, with little interest in and preparation for higher education, is nevertheless required to attend university—aspiring professional athletes in football and men's basketball.

An anomaly of American history—that intercollegiate football and basketball began before the professional versions of those games and excluded viable minor leagues in those sports—has created a situation that is unknown and unthinkable in other countries: *To become a major-league player in a number of sports, an athlete must pass through an institution of higher learning.* And to compound the problem, American schools now take on the training of young athletes in sports, particularly baseball and hockey, for which there *are* excellent minor professional leagues, as well as Olympic sport athletes for which there is a strong club system.

Myth: College athletes are amateurs and their athletic scholarships do not constitute professional payment for playing sports.

Reality: A school gives an athlete a "full ride" grant worth $5,000 to $20,000 a year in exchange for the athlete's services in a commercial entertainment venture, namely, playing on one of the school's sports teams. If the athlete fails to keep his or her part of the agreement and quits the team, the institution withdraws the financial package—even if the athlete continues in school as a regular student. Moreover, once the athlete's playing eligibility ends, the grant is usually terminated.

At one time in NCAA history, athletic scholarships were for four years and, once awarded, could not be revoked. In 1973, under pressure from coaches who wanted greater control over their players and the ability to "fire" them for poor athletic performances, the NCAA instituted one-year scholarships, renewed annually at the athletic department's discretion.

Under their current terms, athletic scholarships appear indistinguishable from what the IRS calls "barter payment for services rendered," thus making college athletes professional wage earners. In addition, a number of courts have found that the one-year grants constitute an employer-employee relationship between a school and an athlete.

Myth: College sports provide an excellent opportunity for black youngsters to get out of the ghetto and to contribute to American society.

Reality: Research by Harry Edwards, professor of sociology at the University of California, Berkeley, indicates that many athletic programs treat black athletes as "gladiators," bringing them to campus only to play sports, not for an education. The low graduation rates of black college athletes supports Edwards' thesis.

Most schools with major athletic programs, as well as many with smaller ones, recruit black athletes much more intensively and systematically than they do regular black students. Moreover, some schools fund their "black gladiators" by diverting money from scholarship sources, such as opportunity grants, earmarked for academically motivated minority students. Thus, not only do the "black gladiators" fail to receive college educations, but many black high school graduates—whose academic potential is far greater than the athletes—are deprived of the chance of entering university.

Myth: For college athletes, the opportunity for a university education is as important as playing intercollegiate sports.

Reality: Formal and informal studies indicate that most college athletes in big-time programs hope to play their sport at the professional or Olympic level, and they regard college as their path to the pros or the national team. That very few of these athletes ever achieve their dream is irrelevant to its power over them and its role in shaping their college careers, especially their willingness to devote as many as sixty hours a week to their sports and their inability to sustain a serious course of studies. Jim Walden, head football coach at Iowa State University, says that in his sport, "Not more than 20 percent of the football players go to college for an education. And that may be a high figure."

Myth: Athletes, like Bill Bradley and Tom McMillen, who were outstanding in sports and in the classroom prove that college sports works.

Reality: In any large sample of people in any endeavor, there are always a few at the end of the bell curve. In fact, the widespread notice taken of Bradley's and McMillen's success in both sports and academics suggests that intercollegiate athletics is a system that works for only a few. No one bothers to name all of the outstanding Americans who were once top college students but not athletes, because they are not unusual; higher education is supposed to produce them.

From their first day of college, however, athletes face a conundrum—how to be a "student-athlete"—that few can solve. Their only response is to erase one of the terms and to highlight the other: neglect a meaningful education and pursue sports fulltime, or, in a few cases, drop out of intercollegiate athletics and seriously go to school.

Most big-time athletic programs try to finesse this problem by sheltering their athletes in special "hideaway curricula" and having them major in eligibility (the NCAA has minimal rules for "good academic standing" and playing eligibility). But time spent in a school's Division of Ridiculous Studies does not constitute a real college education. For the vast majority of athletic scholarship holders, the current system does not work; it also corrupts the host institutions and makes faculty, regular students, and the public cynical about the entire academic enterprise.

Myth: The high graduation rates of athletes announced each year by the NCAA and the College Football Association are accurate.

Reality: These rates are manipulated by the NCAA and CFA to produce the appearance of athletes doing well academically. Instead of basing the percentage of athlete-graduates at a school on the total number who began in an athletic program as freshmen, the NCAA and CFA do not count all those who transferred or who dropped out of school in "good academic standing." Because leaving in "bad academic standing"—i.e., flunking out—usually takes a grade point average *below D*, the NCAA and CFA exclude large numbers of academically marginal athletes from their pools, among them those who drop out after using up their college eligibility but have a D or better average. Not counting transfers has a similar statistical effect: many transfers do not graduate from their next institution, but their absence from the original pools raises the graduation rates.

Some schools even base their rates on only their senior class of athletes: such common pronouncements as "Of our senior student-athletes in football, 90 percent graduated this June" can mean "We based our rates on those ten football players who made it to the senior class—out of the thirty who started in our program as freshmen." Not surprisingly, after this numerical sleight of hand, the NCAA and CFA graduation rates reflect their propaganda, not reality.

Myth: The NCAA represents the will of its member colleges and universities and it tries to keep intercollegiate athletics in line with their educational objectives.

Reality: The NCAA functions mainly as a trade association for college coaches and athletic directors, implementing their wishes regardless of whether these are in the best interests of the member schools. Real power in the association resides in the forty-four-person Executive Council and the twelve-member Executive Committee; for many years, a large majority of Executive Council and Executive Committee members have been athletic directors. These two groups control NCAA legislation, choose future council and committee members, and supervise the executive director of the association, currently Dick Schultz, a former coach and AD.

Myth: NCAA athletic programs sponsor teams in many sports, including Olympic events, because they want to give those sports a chance to grow.

Reality: Most athletic directors and program heads are empire builders. Through their control of the NCAA, they have instituted key legislation that ensures expansion—even though costly athletic department growth is not in the financial or academic interest of most of their schools.

The NCAA requires a minimum number of teams for participation in its various divisions, for example, for Division I-A, thirteen teams (men's and women's) in seven sports. If an institution fails to meet the requirement, the NCAA drops it to "unclassified membership," bars all of its teams from NCAA play, and penalizes it in various other ways.

The NCAA's rationale for the sports and team minimums is that schools should have "well-balanced athletic programs." In practice, these regulations serve the college sports establishment's self-interest: ADs and coaches want their programs to be as large as possible, and to employ as many administrators, assistant coaches, and athletes as possible. The NCAA, by locking athletic departments into a high number of sports and teams, deprives member institutions of a large degree of autonomy over their athletic budgets.

Myth: The NCAA can correct the problems in college sports.

Reality: The athletic directors and coaches who control the NCAA deny the existence of any significant problems in college sports. For them, the present system works well—after all, it provides them with extremely comfortable livings—and they see no need to repair it, except for some minor tinkerings.

Bo Schembechler, when head football coach at the University of Michigan, speaking for his fellow coaches and most ADs, once shouted at an audience of reform-minded college presidents, "*We are not the enemy.*" Bo was wrong. But he was true to the NCAA's self-serving denials of any responsibility for the current problems.

The bottom line on meaningful NCAA reform is clear: the NCAA cannot solve the systemic problems in college sports because the coaches and ADs who control it are a central source of those problems. Moreover, the association will fight any attempts at real reform, even if—as is probable in the 1990s—College Sports Inc. begins to destroy the academic and fiscal integrity of some member institutions.

14. *Blaming the Victim: NCAA Responses to Calls for Reform in Major College Sports*

GEORGE H. SAGE

In his insightful volume *Blaming the Victim* (1976), William Ryan describes a scene in which a well-known American actor, impersonating a Southern Senator conducting an investigation into the reasons why the American military was unprepared for the attack by the Japanese on December 7, 1941, and wanting to find a way to exonerate the military, suspiciously booms out, "And what was Pearl Harbor *doing* in the Pacific?" Here is a humorous, but classic, example of blaming the victim. We laugh at the obviously convoluted reasoning that leads to such a question, but I shall argue in this [selection] that the same process is employed by the NCAA and its member universities in their responses to the many outcries for reform in major college athletics; they repeatedly engaged in classic examples of blaming the victim. The victims, in this case, are student-athletes.

Blaming the victim is an ideological process; meaning it is a more or less integrated set of ideas and practices held by a social group about how things should and do work. Social mechanisms for the promotion of an ideology are typically in the hands of the most powerful sector of the group and functions to maintain the existing social order (Mannheim, 1936; Zeitlin, 1968). According to Mannheim (1936), and ideology is formed from the "collective unconscious" of a group and is rooted in the interest of the powerful sector in maintaining the status quo. Similarly, Ryan (1976) says: "Victim blaming is cloaked in kindness and concern, and . . . it is obscured by a perfumed haze of humanitarianism" (p. 6).

This is not the place to describe in detail the numerous scandals that have beset intercollegiate athletics over the past few years (Brooks, 1985; Looney, 1985 a,b,c; Nack, 1986; Ostow, 1985; Shuster, 1985; Sanoff & Johnson, 1986; Wolff & Sullivan, 1985; Underwood, 1980). One outrage is followed by another one of greater proportions. Hardly a week goes by without new revelations about violations of NCAA rules by major univer-

SOURCE: George H. Sage, "Blaming the Victim: NCAA Responses to Calls for Reform in Major College Sports," *Arena Review* 11 (Fall 1987), pp. 1-11.

sity football or basketball programs. Each revelation is followed by righteous promises by university authorities and the NCAA that change is on the way—that collegiate athletics are going to be "cleaned up." But, as Padilla & Weistart (1986) note: "Scandals develop with a frequency that is astonishing even to the most cynical of observers, and the major regulatory body, the NCAA, seems unable to stop them or the conditions from which they breed." And Cramer (1986), after a thorough study of the NCAA and major college athletics contended: "A glimpse at the workings of college sports programs and at the efforts of the NCAA to reform them is not exactly a pretty sight" (p. 6).

The most recent NCAA effort to do something about the endemic problems of major college sports has been the creation of a university Presidents Commission. It has promised to re-direct the destiny of intercollegiate athletics. But it, too, seems to be floundering; in summarizing its fall 1986 meeting Sullivan (1986a) reported that the Commission "gave no firm evidence of any commitment to reform" (p. 17).

For all of the chest pounding about reform by the NCAA, university athletic departments, and the Presidents Commission, an analysis of changes that have been made or proposed over the past few years clearly shows that the structure of college athletics has been left intact; there have been no substantive changes in the *structure* of college sports—a structure that is largely responsible for the corruption and abuses. Hope for meaningful reform by the NCAA is a chimera.

By structure of college athletic programs I am referring to its rigidly authoritarian organization in which rules and policies affecting student-athletes are enacted and imposed without any input from the largest group in college sports—the student-athletes. I am also referring to the now common practice of keeping athletes involved in one way or another with their sport during the season for 20 to 40 hours per week practicing, watching film, skull sessions, travel from one coast to another for games, and to being away from campus and missing classes.[1] I'm referring to weight training programs, film analysis, and "informal" practice sessions in the "off season" period; indeed, athletes are expected to remain in training year-round. I'm referring to the pressures brought on by mass media attention and the expectations of alumni and boosters who demand championship teams. I'm referring to universities who use athletes as an arm of the public relations department. This is the essential structure of major university athletics, especially in football and basketball.

Instead of addressing structural issues that perpetuate scandals, the NCAA has identified student-athletes as the major cause of the continuing problems suffered by collegiate sports, and various forms of legislation have been passed which are designed to evoke a public image of student-athletes as the real culprits. As rules have been enacted to further control and restrict student-athletes, the NCAA and university authorities claim that they are attempting to solve the problems of college sports. What they have done, instead, is blame the student-athlete for the massive failure of college athletic authorities to address the real causes of corruption, cheating, and unethical behavior that are now well-documented in major college athletics—they have engaged, clearly and directly, in a classic display of "blaming the victim." This has been accomplished with such intensity and persistence that alternative images have been unthinkable.

Proposition 48 (bylaw 5-1-[j] in the NCAA *Manual*) is a good example of focusing the blame for problems in college sports on student-athletes. By requiring that student athletes achieve certain minimum high school grades and standardized test scores to be eligible for participation, the NCAA can publicly proclaim its interest in having qualified students as college athletes, and, of course, no one in his right mind can really quarrel with holding athletes to academic standards. Even many black leaders who recognized the unequal and adverse effects that the legislation would have on black athletes supported the passage of Proposition 48 because to have been against it would have seemed to have implied that they were not for academic standards.[2]

Actually, what all this charade for academic standards has done is deflect attention away from the commercialized structure of major college athletic programs and focused it on the athletes. The only reason that there is an academic standards problem in college sports is that coaches and other university officials have been willing to admit academically unqualified students and, through various ingenious methods,have been able to keep them eligible for one purpose: to help the university athletic teams maintain competitive success in the world of commercialized sport. Moreover, for athletes who are academically qualified and seriously interested in the pursuit of a college degree, the structure of major college sports leads them to become progressively detached from academics and gradually resigned to inferior academic achievement (Adler & Adler, 1985). Proposition 48, then, does nothing to alter the major cause of poor academic performance of many athletes.

Other recent examples of blaming athletes for collegiate sports ills are the imposition of drug testing programs and the punishment of football athletes for improper distribution of complimentary tickets (Latimer, 1986; Looney, 1986; "NCAA authorizes testing for drugs," 1986). In the first case, student-athletes' personal rights are infringed upon and in the second place they are characterized as ungrateful liars because they violated NCAA rules for distributing their game tickets. In both cases, the athletes are defined as the problem and measures are taken to punish them.

It does not take any in-depth investigating into equitable treatment provisions in college sports to see how blatantly athletes are victimized by the drug testing system. While athletes must undergo mandatory, random drug testing, there is no provision for coaches, athletic directors, sports information directors, athletic trainers, athletic secretaries, and various sundry others who are part of the big business of college sports to undergo the same testing. Instead, the public is encouraged to dwell on all the alleged defects of athletes. Moreover, there seems to be no understanding or acknowledgement that the social conditions of big time college sports may actually contribute to drug abuse by athletes. Several recent studies have documented the pressures and the incredible time demands that go with being a major university athlete (Adler & Adler, 1985). It does not seem to be stretching the imagination to think that some of this contributes to drug use by athletes.

As for the distribution of game tickets, NCAA rules forbid athletes from giving their complimentary tickets to anyone except "family members, relatives, and fellow students designated by the student-athlete." At the same time, it is common practice for football and basketball coaches to receive a liberal allotment of complimentary game tickets—LSU football coach Bill Arnsparger receives 26 tickets per game—with no restrictions on their distribution.

But there is an even larger, but related, issue here. Collegiate athletes cannot endorse products or engage in any commercialization of their athletic talent or name recognition. Meanwhile, football and basketball coaches can engage in an incredible variety of commercial activities to supplement their salary. Some of the common perks and benefits of being a major college coach are television and radio shows, worth up to $80,000, free use of a car, university provided housing, and use of university facilities for summer camps. A few coaches have quite lucrative sporting equipment endorsement contracts. For some coaches the perks and benefits push their annual income over $200,000 (*USA Today*, Special Report, September 24, 1986). It is NCAA rules like this that led Congressman John Moss, during a Congressional investigation of the NCAA, to say: "I have been writing law in this House for 26 years and I've never seen anything approaching the inequality of NCAA procedures" (Good, 1979, p. 35).

The generic process of Blaming the Victim can be seen most clearly in the unwillingness of the NCAA to permit the payment of a salary to college athletes. Here is a reform that has been suggested by a wide spectrum of persons both inside and outside the collegiate sport industry, but it is a reform the NCAA has steadfastly refused to consider.[3] Instead, by a clever manipulation of euphemisms student-athletes are provided a "scholarship" which is said to be a "free ride" to a college education.[4] This clever definition of the situation on the NCAA's terms makes it sound like student-athletes are the beneficiaries of a generous philanthropy by institutions of higher education. In addition, leaders of intercollegiate sport promote an ideology-based doctrine of the adequacy and legitimacy of amateurism, further obviating outright payment.

The college sports establishment uses the acquisition of a highly valued source of human capital—a college education—which, ironically, can be obtained at a relatively low cost (about $5000 per year at state supported universities) as compensation to athletes. The subtle impression that is conveyed that athletes are well-rewarded; what is created is an interpretation of reality that serves the interests of the college sports establishment.

The problem is that the total domination of major college athletics by commercial concerns and the undisguised salience of the profit motive make it quite obviously a business enterprise. The athletic director at Michigan accurately summarized the state of major college sports. He said: "This is a business, a big business. Anyone who hasn't figured that out by now is a damned fool" (Denlinger & Shapiro, 1975, p. 252). Today many major universities have athletic budgets over $12 million, football games generate over $33 million for competing teams, and the NCAA has an annual budget in excess of $57 million ("Big Bucks," 1984; McCallum, 1986; "NCAA to spend," 1984).

The main employers in the collegiate sport business are the various colleges and universities, under the control of the NCAA. Employee groups are coaches, athletic directors, athletic trainers, sports information directors, and sundry secretaries and equipment managers, all of whom negotiate in an open market for salaries and wages, and all of whom may be said to make a livable income. As noted above, coaches make a *very good* income, when all the perks and benefits are added to their salary.

The largest single employee group in the big business of college sports—the student-athletes—does not receive a salary or wage, per se. Indeed, NCAA rules prohibit athletes from accepting an offer of a salary or any other money under penalty of permanent debarment from collegiate sports participation. Although athletes are the key in the financial success of big-time college sports through their indispensability in the production process, they are victimized by a system that conceals the deception of extremely low remuneration with references to "scholarships" and "free rides." Thus, while the NCAA preaches the virtues of amateurism and a spartan existence to student-athletes, it lavishly rewards coaches, athletic directors, and some of the other ancillary employees in the college sport enterprise.[5]

In the case of major college sports, enacting legislation that focuses on the control, restrictions, monitoring, and punishment of student-athletes is a brilliant strategy for justifying a perverse system of social action by the NCAA and its member universities. Meanwhile the exploitation of collegiate athletes can continue unabated. Far from desiring to change the basic structure of major college sports, the NCAA and member universities strive for a change in social conditions by means of which existing patterns will be made as tolerable and comfortable as possible.

Blaming the student-athlete, and refusing to change the fundamental structure that perpetuates the continuing series of scandals, is an evasion of the responsibility that collegiate authorities have for either treating athletes as equal members of a commercial enterprise or withdrawing from commodified sports and returning to the promotion of an education model of college sports, where sports are used as a medium for the individual development of the participants.

NOTES

1. An analysis of the time the average BYU football player devoted to football was 2,202 hours per year, or 275 8-hour days, and it has been estimated that college football players devote 60 hours per week and basketball players 55 hours per week during their respective season (Eitzen & Purdy, 1986). A study by Sack & Thiel (1979) found that 68% of the Notre Dame football players who later played NFL football reported that playing at Notre Dame had been as physically and psychologically demanding as professional football.
2. There is a large literature dealing with the pros and cons of Proposition 48; see, for example, Sack (1984) and Edwards (1984).
3. See statement made by Dale Brown, head men's basketball coach at Louisiana State University, on pg. 3 of *The NCAA News*, February 27, 1985; see statement by Don Canham, athletic director at Michigan, on pg. 2 of *The NCAA News*, March 13, 1985; see statements by coaches in "Agents Don't Play By the NCAA Rules," 1984. Nationally renowned philosophers (Weiss, 1986) and economists (Becker, 1985) have called for the payment of major university athletes. Ernie Chambers, Nebraska State Senator, has introduced a bill into the Nebraska legislature to put University of Nebraska football players on the state payroll and pay them an appropriate salary.
4. In lieu of a salary or wage, college athletes are given "scholarships" which are basically coupons redeemable only at a university accounting office for educational expenses incurred by athletes in exchange for playing on an intercollegiate sports team. The scholarship is for a prescribed set of educational expenses and can only be used to pay those expenses. In most cases, the athletes do not actually handle the money themselves. Paper transactions between the athletic department and the university accounting office consummates the financial arrangement.
5. The strong hold of amateurism on the public conscience is a thing of the past. The International Olympic Committee has already dropped the word amateur from its rule book, and it has indicted that it will allow the entry of professionals in the 1980 Games ("IOC to allow," 1985; Sullivan, 1986b).

REFERENCES

Adler, P. & Adler, P. A. "From idealism to pragmatic detachment: The academic performance of college athletes." *Sociology of Education*. 58: 241-250, 1985.

"Agents don't play by the NCAA rules." *Greeley* (Colo.) *Tribune*. November 2, 1984, p. 81.

Becker, G. S. "College athletes should get paid what they're worth." *Business Week*. September 30, 1985, p. 18.

"Big bucks." *Sports Illustrated*. 61 (September 5):148, 1984.

Brooks, B. G. "A self-inflicted football injury." *Rocky Mountain News*. August 26, 1985, p. 18-G.

Cramer, J. "Winning or learning? Athletics and academics in America: Kappan special report." *Phi Delta Kappan*. 67: 1-8, 1986.

Denlinger, K. & Shapiro, L. *Athletes for sale*. New York: Thomas Y. Crowell, 1975.

Edwards, H. "The collegiate athletic arms race: Origins and implications of the 'Rule 48' controversy." *Journal of Sport and Social Issues*. 8 (Winter/Spring): 4-22, 1984.

Eitzen, D. S. & Purdy, D. A. "The academic preparation and achievement of black and white collegiate athletes." *Journal of Sport and Social Issues*. 10 (Winter/Spring): 15-27, 1986.
Good, P. "The shocking inequities of the NCAA." *Sport*. 68 (January): 35-38, 1979.
"IOC to allow limited entry of pros in '88." *Rocky Mountain News*. March 1, 1985, p. 96.
Latimer, C. "CU reports 21 misuse tickets." *Rocky Mountain News*. September 26, 1986, p. 113.
Looney, D. S. "Tickets, please." *Sports Illustrated*. 64 (September 15): 65, 1986.
Looney, D. S. "Big trouble at Tulane." *Sports Illustrated*. 62 (April 8): 34-39, 1985a.
Looney, D. A. "Troubled times at Memphis State." *Sports Illustrated*. 62 (June 24): 36-41, 1985b.
Looney, D. S. "Deception in the heart of Texas." *Sports Illustrated*. 63 (September 30): 28-35, 1985c.
McCallum, J. "In the kingdom of the solitary man." *Sports Illustrated*. 65 (October 6): 64-78, 1986.
Mannheim, K. *Ideology and utopia*. New York: Harcourt Brace Jovanovich, 1936.
Nack, W. "This case was one for the books." *Sports Illustrated*. 64 (February 24): 34-42. 1986.
"NCAA authorizes testing for drugs." *Rocky Mountain News*. January 15, 1986, p. 73.
"NCAA to spend $41.6 million this year: Budget balanced by shifting surplus." *The Chronicle of Higher Education*. 29 (September 5): 34, 1984.
Ostow, R. "Sanctions against Florida might be just the beginning." *USA Today*. January 14, 1985, p. 4C.
Padilla, A. & Weistart, J. C. "National commission needed to improve college athletics." *The Washington Post*. July 6, 1986.
Ryan, W. *Blaming the Victim*. (Revised edition.) New York: Vintage Books, 1976.
Sack, A. "Proposition 48: A masterpiece in public relations." *Journal of Sport and Social Issues*. 8 (Winter/Spring): 1-3, 1984.
Sack, A. L. & Thiel, R. "College football and social mobility: A case study of Notre Dame football players." *Sociology of Education*. 52: 60-66, 1979.
Sanoff, A. P. & Johnson, K. "College sports' real scandal." *U.S. News & World Report*. September 15, 1986, pp. 62-63.
Shuster, R. "Drug scandal at Clemson linked to 'obsession to win.'" *USA Today*. March 12, 1985,p. 4C.
Sullivan, R. "Barely touching the platter." *Sports Illustrated*. 65 (October 13): 17, 1986a.
Sullivan, R. "Toward an open olympics." *Sports Illustrated*. 65 (October) 60: 15, 1986b.
Underwood, J. "The writing is on the wall." *Sports Illustrated*. 52 (May 19): 36-72, 1980.
USA Today, Special Report, "Money and college athletics." September 24, 1986.
Weiss, P. "Pro sports in college." *U.S. News & World Report*. March 10, 1986.
Wolff, A. & Sullivan, R. "Blowing a fuse over the news." *Sports Illustrated*. 63 (November 11): 52-53, 1985.
Zeitlin, I. M. *Ideology and the development of sociological theory*. Englewood Cliffs, N.J.: Prentice Hall, 1968.

15. *The Reform of Big-Time College Sport*

D. STANLEY EITZEN

Big-time college sports pose a fundamental dilemma for educators. On the positive side, the games provide entertainment, spectacle, excitement, and festival, along with excellence in athletics. On the negative side, as we have seen, big-time athletics have severely compromised academe.

Pursuit of educational goals has been superseded by the quest for big money. And since winning programs realize huge revenues from television, gate receipts, bowl and tournament appearances, and even legislatures, many athletic departments and coaches are guided by a win-at-any-cost philosophy.

Can this fundamental dilemma be resolved? Can the corporate and corrupt sports programs at colleges and universities be changed to redress the wrongs that are making a mockery of their educational goals? Can the abuses be eliminated without sacrificing the high level of achievement by the athletes and the excitement of college sports?

It seems to me that reform must be directed at three crucial areas: the way sports are administered, the education of athletes, and the treatment of athletes. I suggest the following reforms.

THE ADMINISTRATION OF COLLEGE SPORTS

As a beginning, athletic departments must not be separated from their institutions in self-contained corporate entities. They must be under the direct control of university presidents and boards of regents. Presidents, as chief executive officers, must be accountable for the actions of their athletic departments. They must set up mechanisms to monitor athletic programs to detect illegal and unethical acts. They must determine policies to maximize the educational experiences of student-athletes.

Coaches must be part of the academic community and the tenure system, to provide them with reasonable job security and to emphasize that they, too, are teachers. As educators with special responsibilities, they should earn salaries similar to those of academic administrators. They should not receive bonuses for winning championships. Such performance incentives overemphasize winning and increase the likelihood of cheating. The outside incomes of coaches should be sharply curtailed. In particular, they should not be allowed to participate, as coaches, in commercial ventures. If coaches fail to keep their programs ethical, they should lose their tenure and be suspended from coaching at *any* institution for a specified period, even, in special cases, forever. Among the important criteria for evaluating a coach's performance should be the proportion of athletes who graduate in five years.

One problem with college sport is that it is run by the NCAA, which in turn has been run by athletic directors, representing their institutions, rather than by academicians. This is changing somewhat as university presidents, guided by a President's Commission, have, since 1984, become more involved. The presidents must take over the NCAA's rule-making to ensure fairness in the distribution of television and tournament revenues (we favor an equal distribution to all members to lessen the extraordinary rewards of winning and the accompanying pressures) and the fair treatment of student-athletes. The 1991 NCAA convention agenda was controlled somewhat by presidents and some encouraging rules were passed (e.g., the elimination of athletic dorms by 1996 and the limitation of in-season practice time to a maximum of four hours a day and 20 hours a week) but for the most part the presidents' efforts were timid and did not attack the problems endemic to big-time intercollegiate sport. But, the presidents' recent increased involvement is encouraging.

It is crucial that athletic departments be monitored and, when warranted, sanctioned externally. The NCAA is not, however, the proper external agent, since it has a fundamental conflict of interest. The NCAA is too dependent on sports-generated television money and bowl contracts to be an impartial investigator, judge, and jury. Accrediting associations should oversee all aspects of educational institutions, including sports, to assess whether educational goals are being met. If an institution is not meeting those goals because of inadequacies in the sports program, then it should lose accreditation, just as it would if the library were below standard or too few professors held doctorates. Also, since big-time sports are engaged in interstate commerce, the investigation and prosecution of wrongdoing–such as fraud, bribery, and the falsification of official records–in college sports should be pursued by federal district attorneys and the courts.

EMPHASIZING THE EDUCATION OF STUDENT-ATHLETES

Academic institutions worthy of the name must make a commitment to their athletes as students. This requires, first, that only athletes who have the potential to compete as students be admitted. A few, very few, may be admitted as exceptions, but they and other academically marginal students must receive the benefits of a concerted effort by the university to improve their skills through remedial classes and tutorials, so that they can earn a degree.

Second, freshmen should be ineligible for varsity sports. Such a requirement has symbolic value, because it shows athletes and the whole community that academic performance is the highest priority of the institution. More important, it allows freshman athletes time to adjust to the demanding and competitive academic environment before they also take on the pressure that comes from participating in big-time sports.

Third, colleges must insist that athletes make satisfactory progress toward a degree. There should be internal academic audits to determine whether athletes are meeting the grade-point and curriculum requirements for graduation. Schools must now provide the NCAA with graduation rates based on how many athletes graduate in five years. Schools must be required to make these rates public, including giving them to each potential recruit.

Fourth, the time demands of sports must be reduced. In-season practice time, travel, team meetings must be kept to reasonable minimums. Mandatory off-season workouts should be abolished. Spring football practice should be eliminated.

And, finally, colleges should grant athletic scholarships on a four-year basis, no strings attached (instead of the one-year commitment that is the present rule). Doing so would dramatically demonstrate the institutions' commitment to their athletes as students. In addition–and this is critical–if scholarship athletes participate in a sport for three years, the scholarship commitment by the institution should be extended automatically from four to five years.

COMMITMENT TO ATHLETES' RIGHTS

The current asymmetrical situation, where schools have the power and athletes do not, must be modified. First, student-athletes should have the right to counsel from agents, accountants, attorneys or whatever, just as any other student.

Second, athletes should have the right to fair compensation from the revenues they generate. By already receiving room, board, books, and tuition, athletes are not amateurs. Neither are they well-paid professionals. They should be adequately compensated by a modest monthly stipend–say $300 a month. Moreover, they should be allowed to have a job in the off-season (currently forbidden by the NCAA except for summer employment), just as any other student. Also, because scholarship athletes are in effect employees of the institution, they should be eligible for workmen's compensation if injured. Most assuredly, they must be fully insured by their institutions for injuries.

If players are dissatisfied with their situation at a school and want to transfer without losing eligibility, they should be able to submit their case to an arbitration panel independent of the NCAA, which should be established to hear such cases and make binding decisions. Athletes should also have the right to legal assistance and due process in disputes with athletic departments and coaches. Coaches are sometimes right, but when they are wrong they must not be protected at the expense of the athletes, as is the usual case.

■ FOR FURTHER STUDY

Academe. "The Commercialization of College Sport." *Academe* 73 (July/August 1987), entire issue.

Adler, Patricia A., and Peter Adler. *Backboards & Blackboards: College Athletics and Role Engulfment*. New York: Columbia University Press, 1991.

Adler, Peter, and Patricia A. Adler. "From Idealism to Pragmatic Detachment: The Academic Performance of College Athletes." *Sociology of Education* 58 (October 1985): 241-250.

Adler, Peter, and Patricia A. Adler. "Role Conflict and Identity Salience: College Athletics and the Academic Role." *The Social Science Journal* 24, No. 4(1987): 443-455.

American Association for Higher Education. "Ethics and Intercollegiate Sport." *AAHE Bulletin* 42 (February 1990), entire issue.

American Institutes for Research. "Report No. 1: Summary Results from the 1987-88 National Study of Intercollegiate Athletics." Palo Alto, CA: Center for the Study of Athletics, 1988.

Baumann, Steven, and Keith Henschen. "A Cross-Validation Study of Selected Performance Measures in Predicting Academic Success among Collegiate Athletes." *Sociology of Sport Journal* 3 (December 1986): 366-371.

Brede, Richard M., and Henry J. Camp. "The Education of College Student-Athletes." *Sociology of Sport Journal* 4 (September 1987): 245-257.

Case, Bob, H. Scott Greer, and James Brown. "Academic Clustering in Athletics: Myth or Reality." *Arena Review* (Fall 1987).

Chu, Donald. *The Character of American Higher Education and Intercollegiate Sport*. Albany: State University of New York Press, 1989.

Edwards, Harry. "The Collegiate Athletic Arms Race: Origins and Implications of the 'Rule 48' Controversy." *Journal of Sport and Sport Issues* 8 (Winter/Spring 1984): 4-22.

Eitzen, D. Stanley. "How We Can Clean Up Big-Time College Sports." *The Chronicle of Higher Education* (February 12, 1986): p. 96.

Eitzen, D. Stanley, and Dean A. Purdy. "The Academic Preparation and Achievement of Black and White Collegiate Athletes." *Journal of Sport and Social Issues* 10 (Winter/Spring 1986): 15-29.

Feinstein, John. *A Season on the Brink*. New York: Macmillan, 1986.

Frey, James H., ed. *The Governance of Intercollegiate Athletics*. West Point, NY: Leisure Press, 1982.

Gerdy, John R. "No More 'Dumb Jocks.'" *The College Review Board* 143 (Spring 1987): 2-3, 40-41.

Glasner, David. "Cheap Labor on Campus." *Newsweek* (November 9, 1987): 12.

Greendorfer, Susan L., and Elaine M. Blinde. "‹Retirement' from Intercollegiate Sport: Theoretical and Empirical Considerations." *Sociology of Sport Journal* 2 (June 1985): 101-110.

Hart-Nibbrig, Nand, and Clement Cottingham. *The Political Economy of College Sports*. Lexington, MA: D.C. Heath, 1986.

Hochfield, George. "The Incompatibility of Athletics and Academic Excellence." *Academe* 73 (July/August 1987): 39-43.

Kiger, Gary, and Deana Lorentzen. "The Relative Effects of Gender, Race, and Sport on University Academic Performance." *Sociology of Sport Journal* 3 (1986): 160-167.

Knapp, Terry J., and Joseph F. Raney. "Looking at Student-Athletes' Transcripts: Methods and Obstacles." *Arena Review* 11 (Fall 1987): 41-47.

Knoppers, Annelies, Barbara Bedker Meyer, Martha Ewing, and Linda Forrest. "Gender and Salaries of Coaches." *Sociology of Sport Journal* 6 (December 1989): 348-361.

Lapchick, Richard E., with Robert Malekoff. *On the Mark: Putting the Student Back in Student-Athlete*. Lexington, MA: D.C. Heath, 1987.

Lapchick, Richard E., and John B. Slaughter. *The Rules of the Game: Ethics in College Sport*. New York: Macmillan, 1989.

Leonard, Wilbert Marcellus II. "The Sports Experience of the Black College Athlete: Exploitation in the Academy." *International Review for the Sociology of Sport* 21 (1986): 35-49.

Meyer, Barbara Bedker. "From Idealism to Actualization: The Academic Performance of Female Collegiate Athletes." *Sociology of Sport Journal* 7 (March 1990): 44-57.

Montville, Leigh. "Thou Shalt Not Lose." *Sports Illustrated* (November 13, 1989): 83-91.

Purdy, Dean A. (ed.). "Sport and the Student Athlete." *Arena Review* 11 (November 1987), entire issue.

Purdy, Dean A., D. Stanley Eitzen, and Rick Hufnagel. "Are Athletes Also Students? The Educational Attainment of College Athletes." *Social Problems* 29 (April 1982): 439-448.

Purdy, Dean A., D. Stanley Eitzen, and Rick Hufnagel. "The Educational Achievement of College Athletes by Gender." *Studies in the Social Sciences* 24 (1985): 19-32.

Sack, Allen L. "Are 'Improper Benefits' Really Improper? A Study of College Athletes' Views Concerning Amateurism." *Journal of Sport and Social Issues* 12 (Spring 1988): 1-16.

Sack, Allen L. "The Underground Economy of College Football." *Sociology of Sport Journal* 8 (March 1991): 1-15.

Sellers, Robert M. "Racial Differences in the Predictors for Academic Achievement of Student-Athletes in Division I Revenue Producing Sports." *Sociology of Sport Journal* 9 (March 1992): 48-59.

Sperber, Murray. *College Sports Inc.: The Athletic Department vs. The University*. New York: Henry Holt, 1990.

Stangl, Jane Marie, and Mary Jo Kane. "Structural Variables That Offer Explanatory Power for the Underrepresentation of Women Coaches Since Title IX: The Case of Homologous Reproduction." *Sociology of Sport Journal* 8 (March 1991): 47-60.

Stevenson, Christopher L. "College Athletics and 'Character': The Decline and Fall of Socialization Research." In *Sport and Higher Education*, Donald Chu,

Jeffrey O. Segrave, and Beverly J. Becker, eds. Champaign, IL: Human Kinetics Publishers, 1985, pp. 249-266.

Telander, Rick. *The Hundred Yard Lie: The Corruption of College Football and What We Can Do to Stop It*. New York: Simon & Schuster, 1989.

Weistart, John C. "Serious Reform of College Sports Must Go Beyond Fine Tuning." *The Chronicle of Higher Education* (January 10, 1990): A52.

Wheeler, Stanton, ed. "Knowns an Unknowns in Intercollegiate Athletics: A Report to the Presidents' Commission." *Journal of Sport and Social Issues* 11 (December 1987), entire issue.

Will, George. "Our Schools for Scandal." *Newsweek* (September 15, 1986): 84.

Wolff, Alexander, and Armen Keteyian. *Raw Recruits: The High Stakes Game Colleges Play to Get Their Basketball Stars–and What It Costs to Win*. New York: Pocket Books, 1990.

Yaeger, Don. *Undue Process: The NCAA's Injustice for All*. Champaign, IL: Sagamore, 1991.

Part Six

The Economics of Sport

A dilemma that characterizes contemporary professional sport and much of what is called amateur sport in the United States has been described by Roger Kahn: "Sport is too much a game to be a business and too much a business to be a game."[1] The evidence indicating a strong relationship between sport and money is overwhelming. Consider the following examples:

item: In 1990 General Motors paid $193,553,000 for television sports advertising, followed by Anheuser-Busch ($79,154,000) and Philip Morris ($66,020,000).[2]

item: The rights to televise the 1992 Summer Olympic Games cost NBC $401,000,000, up from the $7.5 million ABC paid for the 1972 Games.

item: Evander Holyfield made $60.5 million in winnings and endorsements. Other top boxers were also paid handsomely: Mike Tyson ($31.5 million); George Foreman ($14.5 million); and Razor Ruddock ($10.2 million).

item: An average outing for a family of four to attend a San Francisco 49ers' game was $197.50 in 1991 (four tickets at $35 each, two draft beers, four soft drinks, four hot dogs, two programs, two caps, and parking).[3]

item: Indianapolis-style automobile racing requires corporate sponsorships to pay for the expenses, which run between $5 million and $10 million annually per racing team.

item: In 1991, 233 major league baseball players had salaries in excess of $1 million.

item: It is estimated that the University of Arizona's football program generates an annual economic impact of $23.8 million to $28.9 million on Tucson.[4]

item: In fiscal 1989-90, $1.96 billion was wagered in the legal sports books in Nevada (up from $360 million in fiscal 1980-81).

item: In 1973 the New York Yankees were purchased for $10 million. In 1991 the value of that franchise was estimated at $225 million.

item: Each school participating in the Rose Bowl receives $6.5 million.

Although these examples are diverse, there is a common thread—money. Money is often the motivator of athletes. Players and owners give their primary allegiance to money rather than to play. Playing for high monetary stakes is exciting for fans, too. Modern sport, whether professional, big-time college, or Olympic, is "corporate sport." The original purpose of sport—pleasure in the activity—has been lost in the process. Sport has become work. Sport has become the product of publicity agents using superhype methods. Money has superseded the content as the ultimate goal. Illicit tactics are commonplace. In short American sport is a microcosm of the values of American society. Roger Angell has said of baseball what is applicable to all forms of corporate sport: "Professional sports now form a noisy and substantial, if irrelevant and distracting, part of the world, and it seems as if baseball games taken entirely—off the field as well as on it, in the courts and in the front offices as well as down on the diamonds—may now tell us more about ourselves than they ever did before."[5]

The essays in Part 6 have been selected to illustrate the problems and issues involving the impact of money on professional sports. The first selection, by Jacob Weisman, shows the massive infusion of corporate America into professional basketball. The second selection, from George H. Sage's book *Power and Ideology in American Sport,* examines professional sports leagues as monopolies. The third essay, by T. Keating Holland, investigates the community subsidization of professional teams. The final selection, by Anthony Baldo, provides the data from research by *Financial World* on the value of professional teams.

NOTES

1. Roger Kahn, quoted in CBS Reports, "The Baseball Business," television documentary, narrated by Bill Moyers (1977).
2. The Arbitron Company Report, Television Bureau of Advertising, 1991.
3. *Team Marketing Report*, cited in Lynn Bronikowski, "Mile High Broncos Game Tab: $146.17," *Rocky Mountain News* (September 1, 1991), p. 125.
4. University of Texas-Permian Basin newspaper (April 29, 1991), p. 16.
5. Roger Angell, "The Sporting Scene: In the Counting House," *The New Yorker* (May 10, 1976), p. 107.

16. *Big-Buck Basketball: Acolytes in the Temple of Nike*

JACOB WEISMAN

The business of sport, most of us are becoming aware, is not only a big business but one that is no longer the sole property of the teams involved—nor has it been for some time. A quick look around the Seattle Coliseum during a SuperSonics basketball game will quickly confirm this suspicion. A total of ten bulletin boards, advertising companies such as Alaska Airlines, Blockbuster Video, G.T.E. ("The smart business") and Safeway ("What a neighbor should be"), circle the outer reaches, blocking scoreboard visibility for fans sitting in the top rows.

Illuminated Coca-Cola signs hang above the four courtside exits. The scorer's table rotates a series of new ads every five minutes or so throughout the course of the game, continually catching one's attention with their sudden movements. No matter where the eyes might rest, no matter how trivial that spot might be, it seems someone, somewhere, coveted its commercial potential. The folding chairs used to seat the visiting players sport Coca-Cola logos. The sweats worn by the Sonics ball boys carry Avia logos (as do their caps and the backs of their shirts); there is also an honorary Coca-Cola ball boy at each game.

The scoreboard is a whirl of computer-generated graphics, advertising such products as Isuzu Motors, Miller beer, Oberto Sausage, Elephant Car Wash, Taco Bell, Tombstone Pizza, BP Oil and Ernst Hardware. In all, sixty-five different product lines flash across the big screen at least once every game—many accompanied by messages broadcast over the public address system. Full-blown advertisements for Coca-Cola, Subaru and Tim's Cascade Style Potato Chips ("The potato chip that goes crunch") fill the breaks between quarters. The Sonics Dance Team, brought to you courtesy of Nestlé Crunch, performs original dance numbers to popular hits between timeouts.

The National Basketball Association and the Sonics are reluctant to disclose the revenue generated by the vast whirlwind of sponsorships, claiming, as well they might, that they have no wish for one company to know what another might be paying for the same service. A more logical explanation for the N.B.A.'s reluctance, however, would in all probability

---

SOURCE: *The Nation* (June 17, 1991), The Nation Co., Inc. © 1991.

center around negotiations with the N.B.A.'s players' union, which is currently looking into the possibility of including sponsorships and endorsements in its revenue-sharing contract. The players now receive 53 percent of the total gross revenue from television contracts and ticket sales, which adds up to almost $1 million per player.

Whatever the precise amount, the income the Sonics produce from their various sponsorships must be staggering. According to the Sonics' sales manager, Scott Patrick, while twenty-five of the Sonics' seventy-three sponsors pay only between $10,000 and $30,000, thirty-three pay from $30,000 to $70,000, twelve pay at least $100,000 and three pay in the high six figures. Add to that the individual promotions and give-aways, which can cost companies $100,000 or more, as well as league sponsorships divided among all twenty-eight N.B.A. teams, and the total rises well above the large share the players now receive, depending on the accuracy of figures provided for the purpose of leaving a lot to speculation.

Eight or nine years ago, every player on every team, right down to the players on the injured reserve, could expect to make at least $30,000 a year merely from wearing on the court whatever brand of basketball shoes he was paid to endorse. More recently, however, the shoe companies have consolidated their endorsements, paying huge sums to the high-profile athletes while completely excluding those on the lower rungs. The best and most charismatic players, like Chicago's Michael Jordan or San Antonio's David Robinson, can expect to earn many times more than their already considerably large salaries strictly from endorsements. Jordan himself has endorsed at least nine products—two lines of Nike basketball shoes, Wheaties, Coca-Cola, McDonald's, Chevrolet, Guy Laroche watches, Wilson basketballs and Bigsby & Kruthers suits.

The stakes are high, and shoe companies, often at the front lines, begin wooing the players they believe will be the superstars of the future while those players are still in college or even high school. L.A. Gear recently signed Louisiana State University head coach Dale Brown for a rumored $250,000 to have him endorse—and, more important, to have his team wear—its brand of basketball shoes. One of Brown's players, 19-year-old sophomore Shaquille O'Neil, is perhaps the most coveted pro prospect in the country. He may join the N.B.A. as early as next year, but he'll wear L.A. Gear until he leaves L.S.U. to become a professional. L.A. Gear hopes O'Neil will like the shoes enough to give it the inside track in the competition to sign him to a contract when he does leave college.

The process of wooing potential stars often begins even earlier, with bribes of free shoes and athletic equipment to children not yet out of junior high or high school. If players show enough promise, their interests will often be looked after by a shoe company, which will try to convince them to go to the right college—one where their talents can be showcased and where, not coincidentally, the team's coach endorses that company's brand of footwear.

"The stakes are very high," says Ron Grinker, a sports agent representing several established N.B.A. players, including Danny Manning, the first player selected in the 1988 college draft. "It's a big, ugly business: the college recruiting, the shoe business, everything. It's very profitable, very competitive and very ugly."

We learn to see ourselves in our heroes. When we watch them auction off their reputations over and over again while the teams they play for turn their arenas into giant billboards, the message we get is one of unabashed commercialism. "It's the American way," says Grinker. "Michael Jordan is not held accountable because people will literally kill someone to get a warm-up suit with a likeness of Jordan dunking a basketball. Today's kids will do anything to wear a certain product. They're very cognizant of what they wear, and a lot of things happen in order to acquire enough money to procure those products."

Athletes' behavior, whether it involves drug use, the shoes they wear or their views on society, *will* be emulated. They are taught, very early in their careers, to be the best example of American manhood, or at the very least to escape with all their defects undetected. They are taught to frown on drug use, to not drink and drive, and to be respectable, dress well, support charity, work hard, advocate getting an education and so on. If they also blindly support whatever corporation will pay them the most, then that too must be something our society condones.

Athletes today have become almost superhuman, their abilities almost beyond belief. We've become accustomed to players like the Atlanta Hawks' Dominique Wilkins slashing through the foul lane, twisting his body well over 360 degrees in the air and jamming the ball so hard it bounces fifteen feet off the court after passing through the basket. Nothing less will do.

"Is it the shoes?" Spike Lee's character, Mars Blackmon, asks Michael Jordan after we've watched countless clips of a dunking Jordan in a recent television commercial for Nike.

"No, Mars," says Jordan.

"It's gotta be the shoes," replies Mars, unconvinced. The message is clear: Maybe you can't be Michael Jordan, but adding an inch or two onto your vertical leap couldn't hurt—if you can afford the $125 price tag, of course.

"We're not a fashion athletic company," says Nike spokesperson Melinda Gable (although the original Air Jordan's most distinguishing characteristic was its unusual black and red coloring). "We build serious basketball shoes for serious basketball players." In order to make serious basketball shoes, Nike employs what it calls a "Sports Research Lab stocked with sophisticated testing equipment" complete with "certified lab technicians who really understand biomechanical engineering." Scientific breakthroughs on the new Air Jordan model include a completely clear outsole (originally developed by Nike as the shoe of the future for the film

Back to the Future II); Durabuck, a synthetic material that Nike claims is lighter than leather and resists stretching; and a new ankle collar design (originally created as the prototype for the Batboot in the movie *Batman*).

Nor is the move toward high-technology basketball shoes a Nike exclusive. Reebok has the Pump, a shoe with a built-in air bladder that can be inflated to fit the size of your foot. L.A. Gear, meanwhile, has come out with a shoe called the Catapult (endorsed by Karl Malone of the Utah Jazz), for which it has coined the slogan, "It's not a shoe. It's a machine." The shoes often seem like military hardware. Even shoes in the lower price ranges are often strangely ornamented with brightly colored plastics, bendable rubber joins and interesting or unusual sole designs. The shoes, although not built to perform any particular function, are often designed to look as if they were.

We are entranced by all the high-flying, acrobatic moves, the high-tech mumbo jumbo. What we've come to idolize, above all else, though, is the slamdunk–the ultimate symbol of the domination of one athlete over another. The speed, the power, the suddenness of the attack, the helplessness of the victim are all parts of what appeals to us about the dunk. It's now no longer enough to be able simply to dunk the ball. Now the player must be able to dunk over another player, on the run, off the dribble or, in the case of Michael Jordan, over a crowd.

In the ads, Jordan, Robinson, Malone, Dee Brown, Patrick Ewing and Tom Chambers wear the shoes; those they dunk over, the faceless victims, wear the off-brands. It's kill or be killed. Buy or perish. We are no longer able to feel sympathy for the underdog. He is simply a part of the show–the fall guy in the American dream.

The ads feel the intensity, market it, control it. They do not, however, create the need for such images. There must already be something we find appealing about the sight of seven-feet-one-inch, 235-pound David Robinson dunking over Rudolf Firkusny, an elderly, white-haired, classical pianist sporting dress shoes and a tuxedo. After the dunk, Robinson picks up the ball and turns on the little man, points a finger in his face and yells, "Foul!"

As the ad starts, before they've begun their game of basketball, Robinson and Firkusny sit down at opposing pianos. They play; Firkusny is obviously the better of the two–Robinson plays "Chopsticks." Nike evidently wants to stress that Firkusny and Robinson are *both* the best at what they do, yet the nature of the dunk obscures Nike's intentions. Robinson does after all manage to play *something*. Firkusny, on the other hand, is completely befuddled and humiliated on the court as Robinson demonstrates his total physical superiority–not allowing the pianist to compete at any level, not even to perform the basketball equivalent of "Chopsticks," whatever that might be.

The Robinson ad, more than any other, appeals to our collective imagination. We identify closely with Robinson. Firkusny's expertise at the piano is seen as frivolous, highbrow, of no practical value. Robinson, meanwhile, is elemental in his destruction of the classical piano player.

The ideals that Robinson and Firkusny represent form a telling contrast, characterizing the aspirations of different generations. Robinson is young, strong, lightning quick—the invincible hero of the moment, relying on superior talent, waiting to be discarded when his knees give out at last and a new hero is brought in to take his place. Firkusny, on the other hand, has dedicated many more years to the perfection of his craft, honing it until he has finally risen to the ranks of the masters—a lifelong struggle for improvement. In the age of the CD player, the personal computer and automobiles that go from zero to sixty miles per hour in record time, it's no wonder that we've come to replace the older ideals represented by Firkusny with those of David Robinson.

It's the allure of basketball: strong, tall and powerful yet graceful athletes who soar high above the ground with what we choose to believe is primitive elegance, like a hand-woven blanket from Peru or India. It's not that the players don't work as hard as classical composers or pianists; they do, but we choose, for the most part, not to notice. It is not essential to our enjoyment of the game.

Basketball players are the heroes of the moment not just because they are replaceable parts but because at any moment any one of them is likely to do something so fantastic, so unbelievable, that the rest of the game slips into oblivion, leaving only the memory of that play to linger for weeks, sometimes even years. And everybody, from Nike to your local supermarket, wants a piece of that action.

17. *Sport Cartels*

GEORGE H. SAGE

Commenting on the organization of professional team sports, Freedman (1987) noted they "have in general operated apart from normal business considerations, and their rules of business conduct have not been subject to governmental scrutiny to the same extent as any ordinary business" (p.31). Actually, the basic organizational unit of professional sport teams is the league, not the individual franchise. As such, professional leagues are effectively cartels. A cartel is an organization of independent firms that has as its aim some form of restrictive or monopolistic influence on the production or sale of a commodity as well as the control of wages. Obviously, cartels increase the benefits for the powerful few at the expense of the many. As economist Roger Noll (1974) has argued, the purpose of cartel organization in pro sports is that "of restricting competition (for athletes) and dividing markets among firms in the industry" (p.2). Whatever other functions a professional sports league performs, it serves as a network of power.

THE CONSEQUENCES

A cartel acts to constrain individuals to behave in the interests of the group of firms as a whole. The actual consequences of cartelized industries are varied and complex, depending upon such factors as the commodity produced and sold and the amount of the market actually under the control of the cartel. But in most cases the negative consequences impact labor and consumers most heavily. With respect to labor, cartels are able to hold down wages, and with respect to consumers cartels typically restrict production and control sales and thus can set prices as high as they wish. The beneficiaries of cartel-wide control of wages and production should be obvious. The major benefits accrue to owners of individual firms through the maximization of joint profits. In the case of professional team sports, the cartel members are the owners of the various team franchises, all of whom are wealthy. One does not have to be an economist to understand that the advantages of cartel organization in sport go

---

SOURCE: Excerpt from *Power and Ideology in American Sport: A Critical Perspective* (Champaign, IL: Human Kinetics, 1990), pp. 142-151.

overwhelmingly to the powerful owners, while the powerless laborers (athletes) and consumers suffer the burdens of such organization.

Professional sport leagues operate as cartels in three major ways (Freedman, 1987):

1. They restrict interteam competition for players by controlling the rights of workers (players) through player drafts, contracts, and trades, thereby reducing competitive bidding between teams for player services.
2. They act in concert to admit or deny new teams, and they control the location and relocation of teams.
3. They divide local and regional media markets as well as negotiate, as a single entity, national media rights fees.

Most people recognize the economic and political power inherent in collective corporate organization, and they believe that there are laws prohibiting cartels, monopolies, and trusts. It is true that beginning in the late 19th century the U.S. government took steps designed to thwart large corporations who organized to restrict trade through such tactics. The Sherman Antitrust Act of 1890 forbade every contract, combination in the form of trust, or conspiracy in restraint of trade and all attempts to monopolize any part of an industry. Since then, much additional legislation has been passed in the government's effort to outlaw corporate conspiracies. Unfortunately, it has had limited effect in the corporate world. And, more importantly, in the case of professional team sports it has been judged generally not to apply.

In spite of numerous challenges to cartelization by athletes and rival leagues extending over the 20th century, professional sports have been able to sustain their position that a sport league is a single entity—some have called it a joint venture—and that there can be no restraint of trade as defined by the Sherman Act because that would require two independent firms. Several arguments have also been consistently advanced to justify collective organization:

- Teams have to cooperate in scheduling and playing games.
- Commercial sport events must involve fairly evenly matched teams to maintain uncertainty about the outcome of games and league championships (without evenly matched teams there will be no marketable competition, so the league needs control over the distribution of athletic talent).
- Revenue sharing is necessary to regulate economic competition between teams and to equalize the distribution of money, thus enabling resources to be similar among the various franchises and equalizing competition on the field.

Pete Rozelle (1964), the Commissioner of the NFL for over 25 years, spoke articulately concerning the essential need for a cartel system in professional sports. In what has become a classic defense of this system, he said this:

> On the playing field, member clubs are clearly competitors—and every effort must be made to promote this. But in their business operations, member clubs of a league are less competitors than they are partners or participants in a joint venture. There is nothing comparable to this relationship elsewhere on the American scene. Because of it, the application of ordinary antitrust principles to sports league operations is more likely to produce confusions and distortions than sound results (p. 94).

Although there are certainly ways in which professional team sports differ from most business enterprises and thus they need to structure their organization differently, it is the enormous advantages in terms of power and accumulation of profits that foster cartelized arrangements.

Restriction of Interteam Competition for Players. When professional team sports were in their formative stages, team owners and promoters competed with each other in an open market, vying for athletes and spectators. But it became gradually evident to a few promoters and potential owners of professional baseball teams that such competition was counter-productive to the interests of controlling sport labor and capital accumulation. They realized that labor and consumer issues could be better stabilized and joint profits more consistently realized by a collective, or cartel. Accordingly, they took the lead in bringing order from the chaos with the formation of the National League, which set a precedent for business organization in professional sports that ultimately became the standard.

Founders of the National League established cartelized practices in the marketplace, and within a few years they expanded this to include a practice that economists call *monopsony*, which merely means a one-buyer market. In the case of professional baseball, this meant that all rights to a player were held by one team and one team only. Once a player signed a National League standard player contract with a team, he was bound to that team for his entire playing career unless it sold him. Under this reserve clause system . . . , competitive bidding among teams for player services was forbidden. The reserve system was, then, basically an agreement among owners not to compete with one another for players.

A 1922 challenge to the reserve clause, standard in major league contracts, was settled by a U.S. Supreme Court ruling in favor of the baseball owners. Freedman (1987) has summarized the court's action in this way: "Professional baseball . . . was granted an exemption from the application of the federal antitrust laws upon the ground that this professional sport was not engaged in interstate commerce or trade, and furthermore baseball was in essence not a commercial activity" (p.32). By default other professional sports have used that decision, and more recent ones, to define their own special legal and economic positions; all have adopted monopsonistic practices as they have evolved.

THE FRANCHISE MARKET

Control of the number and location of franchises is one of the important advantages of cartel organization in professional sports; all of the leagues have policies that allow the owners to do this. By controlling the number of franchises within a league, the owners make them scarce commodities, which means their worth appreciates much faster than other investments (Goodman, 1988). Consider these financial returns:

- Edgar Kaiser bought the Denver Broncos in 1981 for $35 million and sold the franchise just 3 years later for $70 million.
- Larry Weinberg paid $3.5 million for the Portland Trail Blazers as an expansion franchise in 1970 and sold the franchise in 1988 for $70 million.
- Edward B. Williams paid $12 million for the Baltimore Orioles in 1979; Eli S. Jacobs bought the franchise in 1988 for $70 million.
- In 1984, the Murchison family sold the Dallas Cowboys to a group of Dallas investors for about $60 million. Five years later the franchise was sold to Jerry Jones for $140 million.
- In 1985 "Red" McCombs sold the Denver Nuggets to Sidney Shlenker for $20 million. In 1989 Shlenker sold the Nuggets to a group of businessmen from Chicago for $65 million.

Another example illustrates how scarcity has worked in the franchise market: The Seattle Mariners of major league baseball were bought for $13 million in 1981 by George Argyros; as of January 1, 1988, the franchise was appraised for $58.6 million, despite 12 straight losing seasons (Whitford, 1988). In 1988 the editors of *Sports inc.* estimated the value of all NFL franchises and claimed that "no NFL team is valued at less than $70 million" ("Buying low," 1988). . . . Predictions are that the values of franchises will continue to appreciate in the 1990s.

FRANCHISE EXPANSION

Team owners exercise great control over league expansion. Applicants for new franchises must secure the permission of three fourths of the existing owners in a particular league. Such permission is difficult to obtain because owners are typically reluctant to expand the league and further share athletic talent and profits. Moreover, the scarcity of existing franchises and the difficulty of securing permission for a new franchise drive up the cost of expansion franchises—when they are approved. For example, applicants for each of the four newest NBA franchises (Miami, Charlotte, Orlando, and Minneapolis) had to pay $32.5 million to obtain the franchise. The cost is made more burdensome for the applicant because he or she is often required to pay an indemnity fee if the new franchise is to be located near an existing one.

The only alternative for someone who wants to establish a professional sport franchise is to start a new league, and all four established professional team sports have experienced challenges from upstart rivals. The established leagues have used their enormous political and economic power to either destroy the new league or incorporate some of the teams into the established league on terms that were very favorable to the established team owners. In 1986 the USFL brought a suit against the NFL challenging several of the monopolistic advantages the NFL enjoyed over any new league. Although the court ruled that NFL was indeed a self-regulating monopoly committed to crushing rival leagues, the court set damages at $3, making it clear that it had no intention of changing this antitrust exemption.

FRANCHISE RELOCATION

In addition to controlling the number of franchises within a league, each league has policies about the movement of franchises. The basic policy is that a franchise may not be moved without the approval of at least three fourths of the owners. All the leagues have fought fiercely to maintain control over franchise movement or relocation. As Freedman (1987) noted, the reasons for this are that

> the stability of each franchise is important to the overall financial success. If franchises were permitted to move freely, such as a move into an existing franchise market or to a distant franchise market, the franchise movement or relocation could jeopardize the existing financial security of all professional teams in that league. Stability of franchise operations is also important to cities and states which support those franchises; public bonds are often utilized to construct stadiums and arenas for use of professional sports teams. (pp. 78-79)

Although these may sound like good defenses, the fact is that when faced with economic considerations, the hypothetically valid reasons for franchise stability have frequently been jettisoned. As shown in Table 17.1, since 1953 there have been over 60 franchise relocations in baseball, football, basketball, and hockey, attesting to the leagues' power to accomplish what they consider beneficial to the business of professional sports (Freedman, 1987). This movement of franchises vividly reveals the lie in the "your team" rhetoric advanced by pro team owners. During the 1980s efforts by fans of football's Oakland Raiders, Baltimore Colts, and St. Louis Cardinals to petition and plead to keep "their" teams fell on deaf (but powerful) ears, blatantly exposing the community facade promoted by the professional sport industry.

The dynamics of franchise movement are quite complex, involving owners, politicians, business leaders, and the mass media, to name only the major participants. In each specific situation, at the heart of the

Table 17.1 Professional Team Sport Franchise Movement Since 1953

Year	Movement
Major league baseball	
1953	Boston to Milwaukee (Braves)
1954	St. Louis (Browns) to Baltimore Orioles
1955	Philadelphia to Kansas City, MO (Athletics)
1958	Brooklyn to Los Angeles (Dodgers)
	New York to San Francisco (Giants)
1961	Washington (Senators) to Minnesota (Twins)
1966	Milwaukee to Atlanta (Braves)
	Los Angeles to Anaheim, CA (Angels)
1968	Kansas City, MO, to Oakland (Athletics)
1970	Seattle (Pilots) to Milwaukee (Brewers)
1972	Washington (Senators) to Arlington, TX (Rangers)
Professional football	
1953	Dallas (Texans) to Baltimore (Colts)
1960	Chicago to St. Louis (Cardinals)
1961	Los Angeles to San Diego (Chargers)
1963	Dallas (Texans) to Kansas City, MO (Chiefs)
1971	Boston to Foxboro, MA (Patriots)
	Dallas to Irvine, TX (Cowboys)
1973	Buffalo to Orchard Park, NY (Bills)
1975	Detroit to Pontiac, MI (Lions)
1976	New York to Rutherford, NJ (Giants)
1980	Los Angeles to Anaheim, CA (Rams)
1982	Bloomington, MN, to Minneapolis (Vikings)
	Oakland, CA, to Los Angeles (Raiders)
1984	New York to Rutherford, NJ (Jets)
	Baltimore to Indianapolis (Colts)
1988	St. Louis to Phoenix (Cardinals)
Professional basketball	
1956	Milwaukee (Blackhawks) to St. Louis (Hawks)
1958	Ft. Wayne, IN, to Detroit (Pistons)
	Rochester, NY, to Cincinnati (Royals)
1961	Minneapolis to Los Angeles (Lakers)
1963	Philadelphia to San Francisco (Warriors)
1964	Chicago (Zephyrs) to Baltimore (Bullets)
	Syracuse, NY (Nationals) to Philadelphia (76ers)
1969	St. Louis to Atlanta (Hawks)
	Anaheim, CA (Amigos) to Los Angeles (Stars)
	Teaneck, NJ (Americans) to Commack, NY (Nets)
	Minneapolis (Muskies) to Washington (Caps)
1970	Houston (Mavericks) to Charlotte, NC (Cougars)
	Minneapolis (Muskies) to Pittsburgh (Pipers)
1971	New Orleans (Buccaneers) to Memphis (Pros)

Table 17.1 (Continued)

Professional basketball (continued)	
1971	Los Angeles to Salt Lake City (Stars)
	Washington (Caps) to Norfolk, VA (Squires)
1972	San Diego to Houston (Rockets)
1973	Cincinnati (Royals) to Kansas City, MO (Kings)
1974	Baltimore to Landover, MD (Bullets)
1975	Charlotte, NC (Cougars) to St. Louis (Stars)
1976	Memphis (Tams) to Baltimore (Claws)
1978	Commack, NY, to Rutgers, NJ (Nets)
1979	Buffalo (Braves) to San Diego (Clippers)
1980	New Orleans to Salt Lake City (Jazz)
1983	San Diego to Los Angeles (Clippers)
1985	Kansas City, MO, to Sacramento, CA (Kings)
Professional hockey	
1973	Philadelphia to Vancouver (Blazers)
	Ottawa (Nationals) to Toronto (Toros)
	New York (Raiders) to Cherry Hill, NJ (Knights)
	Boston to Hartford, CT (Whalers)
1974	Detroit (Stags) to Baltimore (Blades)
	Cherry Hill, NJ (Knights) to San Diego (Mariners)
1975	Denver to Ottawa (67s)
	Oakland, CA (Seals) to Cleveland (Barons)
	Kansas City, MO (Scouts) to Denver (Rockies)
1976	Cleveland (Barons) to Minneapolis (North Stars)
	Toronto (Toros) to Birmingham, AL (Bulls)
1978	Houston (Aeros) to Winnipeg (Jets)
1980	Atlanta to Calgary (Flames)
1982	Colorado (Rockies) to Rutherford, NJ (Devils)

phenomenon is the exercise of subtle power by different combinations of these groups. A frequent underlying issue in franchise relocation,or threats of relocation, is the complaint by an owner that existing facilities are inadequate or that financial arrangements with the city for facility rental, division of concessions, and parking are unacceptable. Owner complaints are usually accompanied by threats to move the franchise: "Build a new facility/improve the existing one/give us a better financial package, or we will move" is the way the demands and threats are usually phrased. Sportswriters have begun to refer to this tactic as *sportmail* (a play on blackmail). Whatever it is called, it must be taken seriously by cities housing professional teams because there exist many examples of the mobility of pro franchises; a number have relocated when their demands were not satisfied; three teams in the NFL alone relocated during the 1980s. Furthermore, the threat to move is especially ominous because communities know that it will be extremely difficult to secure another franchise if one is lost. All in all, then, owners have considerable leverage for extracting concessions from cities desperate to retain their franchises.

Add to the instability of the franchise market the fact that some cities have appointed commissions whose sole task is to try to lure professional franchises. These commissions and their backers resort to an incredible array of enticements that exacerbate sport-franchise hopscotch. Encouraged by the success of Indianapolis, Indiana, which built a football stadium before the city had a professional football franchise and, once it was built, went out and lured the Baltimore Colts to move there, other cities are constructing facilities–most publicly financed–as bait to attract sport franchises.

PUBLICLY OWNED FACILITIES

Loss of a professional franchise is viewed by many people as having adverse consequences for a city, but another issue is frequently part of the relocation equation. Since the 1950s, cities have spent close to a *billion* dollars building municipal stadiums for professional sport teams; about 70% of professional sport stadiums and arenas have been built with public funds. This issue of public subsidies for professional sport owners was discussed, . . . but a few additional points deserve elaboration here.

Many cities are financially burdened with debt on municipal facilities built to accommodate local franchises. As I pointed out earlier, most of these public facilities have become a financial liability because rental income from pro teams typically covers only a fraction of the actual maintenance and construction costs, let alone debt reduction on the municipal bonds the community sold to build the facility. When a professional franchise leaves a city, an additional load is thrust on taxpayers by a facility with no tenant to provide income. A public trust given to franchise owners through provision of a playing facility comes back to burden the taxpayers, who all along have been subsidizing the accumulation of private capital by owners (Baade & Dye, 1988).

REFERENCES

Baade, R. A., and Dye, R. F. (1988). Sports stadiums and area development: A Critical Review. *Economic Development Quarterly* 2, 265-275.

Freedman, W. (1987). *Professional sports and antitrust.* New York: Quorum Books.

Goodman, M. (1988). The home team ["Sports Today" section] *Zeta Magazine* 1 (1), 62-65.

Noll, R. G. (1974). The U. S. team sports industry: An introduction. In R. G. Noll, ed. *Government and the sports business* (pp. 2-32). Washington, DC: Brookings Institution.

Rozelle, P. (1964, June 4). Antitrust law and professional sports. *Virginia Law Weekly*, pp. 94-97.

Whitford, D. (1988, April 4). Bottom line baseball. *Sports inc.*, pp. 19-21.

18. *Field of Dreams*

T. KEATING HOLLAND

They want a professional baseball team in St. Petersburg, Florida, so badly they can taste it. Even with its booming economy, the things the fourth-largest city in Florida can brag about sound a bit lame these days—particularly with Tampa just across the bay, putting on airs about its airport, its hotels, and its National Football League team.

But just give St. Pete a baseball team, and things would really turn around. People would want to come to St. Petersburg. St. Petersburg would be in every newspaper in America every day for six months. Millions of baseball fans from Buffalo to Denver would wish they lived there. Tampa would be jealous; Miami would be *steamed.* St. Petersburg wants all that. It wants to become a Big League city.

But the price is steep. Major-league baseball owners play a little game with cities desperate for the ultimate municipal status symbol. *Build a stadium,* baseball tells a hungry city. *Paint the seats. Pave the parking lot. Spend the money till it hurts. Then we'll talk.* For St. Petersburg, the multimillion-dollar price tag for a new stadium just represents the cost of being put on baseball's waiting list.

So city fathers went ahead and took out a $110-million mortgage to pay for the Florida Suncoast Dome, a 43,000-seat stadium in the middle of a nine-block waterfront area already slated for redevelopment. Increased resort and property taxes stand behind the bonds issued to build the ballpark.

Forty percent of the Pinellas (County) Sports Authority bonds are backed by local resort taxes, with the rest coming from excise taxes and revenue sharing from the state. About $22 million comes from "tax increment financing" on downtown St. Petersburg property that has become more valuable than initially projected. "The property taxes have risen faster, so we can bond the difference," notes sports authority spokesman Bill Bunker.

The Suncoast Dome's planners have hedged their bets a little, preparing for a long dry spell of conventions, tractor pulls, and rock concerts

---

SOURCE: Reprinted, with permission, from the May 1990 issue of *Reason* magazine.

until baseball comes to town. Rock star Billy Joel inaugurated the Dome with a concert in March. But the Dome "needs baseball to be economically feasible," Bunker says.

It's a gamble, but one that came close to paying off before the Dome had even been capped. In 1988 the Chicago White Sox were worried about the fate of rotting old Comiskey Park, a stadium so riddled with safety problems that the American League laid plans to forbid the White Sox to play there. Tired of negotiations with the Chicago government, the White Sox owners announced plans to move the team into the Suncoast dome.

The euphoria over the arrival of the "Florida White Sox" lasted a few weeks, just long enough for Chicago to come to terms with the White Sox. Alas, St. Petersburg was just a pawn in a larger game that sports magnates are fond of playing. The White Sox owners got to soak Illinois taxpayers for a stadium across the street from Comiskey's present site. St. Petersburg got nothing but a valuable lesson.

The lesson was this: If you have a stadium, you might get a team. No one would have returned St. Petersburg's phone calls if the Suncoast dome hadn't been fully funded and under construction. That was not lost on other cities which were jealous of St. Pete for having come even that close to The Show.

Burned once, St. Petersburg will probably stay out of the loony market for existing franchises and concentrate on convincing baseball to place an expansion franchise in the Dome. Will baseball comply? According to George Mason University economist Jerome Ellig, St. Petersburg ranks no higher than sixth on a list of the most profitable cities baseball has yet to move into.

St. Petersburg desperately wants to attain major league status. Baltimore just as desperately wants to keep it. In 1984 the city fathers played chicken with Bob Irsay, the owner of the NFL's Colts. Irsay wanted new facilities for his team; Baltimore said no. Late one night, Irsay packed his team's equipment into some moving vans and shipped everything to Indianapolis, home of the brand-new $77-million Hoosierdome.

Irsay's midnight departure earned his team the derisive nickname "the Bolts," but Baltimore was the real loser. Since the team had already lost a pro basketball franchise, only baseball's Baltimore Orioles stood between the city and sports-page oblivion.

So when then-Oriole owner and Washington legal sharpie Edward Bennett Williams heightened his longtime demands for a new stadium, the Maryland government said, *Let's talk*. It didn't hurt that the new governor of Maryland was William Donald Schaefer, Baltimore's mayor at the time the Colts bolted.

"You look at prestige, you look at jobs, you look at the things it generates in a city," Schaefer said about the baseball team. "You won't be able to replace them, and once they're gone, they're gone."

In 1988 Schaefer used that argument to justify signing what baseball insiders called a "sweetheart of a deal"—a new, publicly funded stadium for the Orioles in downtown Baltimore. The state government promptly issued $201 million in new bonds for a downtown stadium complex. The Orioles' only concession: The government did not have to pay for $11 million of hot dog cookers, beer taps, and other food stand equipment. Williams, who claimed he was holding the Orioles "in trust for the city," died after making the deal that will keep them there into the next century.

What will Maryland get for the lottery proceeds and state taxes used to back the 30-year bonds it had to float? The Orioles' new home will be a gem of a stadium, a throwback to the good old stadiums like Wrigley Field and Fenway Park, with an old-timey brick facade and excellent sight-lines within. The park—which will stand on land in the Camden Naval Yards once inhabited by warehouses—will sit near the Inner Harbor, the "festival marketplace" built on Baltimore's waterfront.

But such downtown amenities do not come cheap. Land acquisition alone will run $85 million; construction itself will cost about $75 million. For a paltry $72 million more, Maryland will build a football stadium next door, in the confident hope that the NFL will not be able to see a big stadium in a good media market stand empty.

A market for professional sports franchises exists today as never before, and the asking price is high. For over 40 years, city and county governments have traditionally been asked to pay for huge new stadiums in the hope of luring—or retaining—big-league baseball and football teams like the White Sox, Colts, and Orioles.

That tradition shows encouraging signs of change, but not before local citizens are tagged in the next few years for huge construction bills.

In addition to the stadiums in Baltimore and St. Petersburg, pro sports will spawn a number of expensive additions to city skylines around the country in the next few years:

- In San Antonio, voters approved a sales-tax increase to finance the construction of the $88 million Alamo Dome;
- Illinois tax revenue stands behind $150 million worth of bonds to construct that new baseball stadium for the Chicago White Sox;
- Atlanta passed a hotel tax increase last summer to pay for the $160-million Georgia dome, scheduled for completion by 1996;
- And in Sacramento, sports maven Gregg Lukenbill, in a switch, offered to spend up to $125 million of his own money for a stadium in the California capitol. He *did* ask the local government to put up a $50-million bribe, in the form of a "franchise loan," to lure the Los Angeles Raiders northward. But he was outbid by the city of Oakland.

All told, as many as 20 North American cities are laying plans for new football or baseball stadiums in the next few years. Over three-quarters of a billion dollars was spent for sports facilities in the past decade, most of that from the public purse.

What do these cities and counties get for their money? Many stadiums don't even earn back their yearly operating costs, and only one built in the past 30 years has paid back its original investment.

Local boosters claim that even stadiums operating in the red pump billions of dollars into flagging local economies. Indeed, pro sports may have some beneficial effects, but not nearly the ones claimed. As put by economist Robert A. Baade, who once chaired a panel investigating a new stadium for Chicago, "looking at *pure* economic benefit and *pure* economic costs, stadiums are not worth the limited resources put into them."

Cities do receive what Baade calls an incalculable "psychological dimension which we can't discount or completely ignore." And in order to host a pro team these days, a city has to build a stadium. It's as simple as that.

Intangible psychological benefits, however, sound suspiciously air-headed in times when most governments face yearly struggles to balance their budgets. So pro-stadium forces traditionally turn their arguments toward the bottom line.

In St. Petersburg, for example, stadium boosters commissioned a study showing the Suncoast Dome adding $750 million to the local economy each year. Numbers from Maryland's Department of Economic and Community Development put the Baltimore stadium's value to the state economy at a more modest $134 million a year. Indeed, everywhere a new stadium proposal pops up, someone will be churning out numbers to justify its economic existence.

The new Baltimore ballyard, says Governor Schaefer, "is one of the most important economic benefits to the state. There isn't any question about it."

Schaefer may not be a trustworthy source for hard facts on the stadium—it does, after all, primarily benefit his hometown and particularly the Inner Harbor, the small piece of Baltimore's downtown which was Schaefer's theme-park legacy to the future. But the governor was merely engaging in the same optimistic crystal-ball gazing that happens in every city about to build a stadium. In Sacramento, stadium forces crowed about the $1.6 billion that a baseball or football team would add to the Greater Valley economy—and that privately funded facility didn't even have to meet taxpayer approval.

In most cases, those rosy estimates come from consultants who add up all the money from tickets, food, beer, parking, and souvenirs, plus all construction wages, hotel receipts, new jobs, and other economic shifts. Then, the consultants assume those construction workers and hot dog vendors will spend this extra money somewhere else in the city, thus doubling or even tripling the benefits of this new infusion of cash and spreading it to local citizens who don't work at the stadium, even those who don't particularly like pro sports. The consultants usually conclude that the stadium will pay for itself *and* contribute mightily to the area.

But adding it up a different way—as some spoilsport economists have done—makes stadiums seem a much shakier investment. They may benefit the local economy (there is some dispute on that) but they rarely pay back that initial investment.

Stadiums fall short of their rosy predictions in a number of ways:

Covering their costs. One problem is that construction companies want their money *now*. But those tickets, hot dogs, and souvenirs won't be sold until the distant future. The $100 a family of four will plunk down at the ballpark some afternoon in the year 2000 has some value, but not as much as $100 spent today, when the concrete and steel bills are due. That smaller figure—the "present value"—is a number consultants rarely use when adding up how much money a stadium will earn.

But Pepperdine University economist Dean J. Baim did use those more realistic estimates in a study of 14 stadiums across the country, and he concluded that only one—privately owned Dodger Stadium in Los Angeles—has paid back its original cost. (Other stadiums in Anaheim, San Diego, and Oakland may one day reach that point.) "From a financial standpoint, the net present value of stadiums is invariably negative," Baim concluded. Indeed, based on net present value, his study's 14 stadiums are a collective $136 million in the red, with the New Orleans Superdome at the back of the pack with a whopping $70-million debt in current dollars.

Spreading the wealth. A common comeback from sports magnates is that government subsidies allow them to lower ticket prices, in effect passing on the savings to the consumer. But Baim found that little, if any, of those subsidies are passed on to the fans. If that government aid is coming from an urban tax base, it may wind up as a transfer payment from poorer taxpayers to rich team owners.

Boosting the local economy. Baade, the economist who helped Chicago wade through stadium proposals, has done his own nationwide study of claims that stadiums pump millions of dollars into the surrounding community. His conclusion: "Economic landscapes don't seem to change much."

Baade, a professor at Lake Forest College, found no significant changes in retail sales, personal income, or other economic indicators in his before-and-after look at cities with new stadiums. Much of that, in Baade's view, is because sports teams just soak up the money from local patrons who would have spent it on other leisure activities in the same city. "Spending for leisure activities is highly substitutable," he says. "What you're really seeing is an economic realignment rather than new spending."

Under certain circumstances, stadiums achieve limited economic benefits—but economists with different methods see different advantages. Baade noted some economic improvement in regionally isolated cities such as Seattle and Denver. Pepperdine's Baim found an increase in service and nonagricultural employment in many cities, though Baade saw no rise in manufacturing employment. Furthermore, expansion teams seem to need some assistance in getting their feet off the ground, according to George Mason's Ellig, who has followed the rise and fall of baseball franchises from an economic point of view.

But those conclusions don't really address another concern. Publicly built stadiums are saddled with regulations, guidelines, and political expectations like any other public project. Even those that improve the local economy might have produced greater benefits if they had been built by private interests. Ellig noted that "it is not clear whether public ownership of stadiums represents the lowest-cost way" of capturing the economic benefits a sports facility brings.

Making investment sense. Even if further research adds to the list of circumstances in which a subsidized stadium is a mild economic plus, cities should worry about whether these benefits are the best they can get for the money they spend.

Baade cautions that the millions of dollars sunk into stadiums might be better spent luring new businesses into town. "If you exhaust a large part of your city's capital budget on sports facilities, you might be losing the chance to promote the development of highly skilled, nonseasonal, nonwage jobs."

In other words, there is an opportunity cost to that investment, even if it pays off in the long run. A major-league city might become a town full of hot dog vendors while a cross-state economic rival might fill up with Ph.D.s. Even in the unlikely event that the stadium pays for itself, it would have crowded out more valuable investments of local tax dollars.

And yet, it is a fact of American life in the 20th century that the rich city full of Ph.D.s, for all its advantages, might envy the poorer city with the sports team.

The path from clown town to super city seems simple: Build. Build a few nice hotels. Build an airport. Build a convention center or a festival marketplace. Build a library, a concert hall, a university, if you have to. And, finally, build a stadium. Unfortunately, the number of ballet troupes is not limited and the number of baseball teams is. That makes the stadium the most expensive and riskiest proposition of all.

Perhaps the most sought-after brass ring is national exposure. "There's no other way a community can be in newspapers all across America," says Mike Seward of the Sacramento sports Association. Other sports officials compare the effect of a nationally televised game from their city to an hour-long commercial—but the publicity is free.

Sacramento is one of the most recent additions to the ranks of big-league cities with the arrival of a moribund National Basketball Association franchise from Kansas City. Since the Kings, a league doormat, have moved to Sacramento, "the self-image of the people has gone up tremendously. Someone planning a building is willing to build it 30 stories, not 10. [Contributors] will go with a first-rate museum. That's an attitude that we can never attach dollars and cents to," Seward reported recently. In fact, it is tough to prove or disprove the link between a new team like the Kings and new construction or downtown development. New teams and boom times usually arrive hand in hand, so it's a chicken-or-the-egg question—one that makes a city feel good about itself, regardless of the answer.

All nouveau major-league cities claim to get that same psychological shot in the arm, and all say that it cannot be measured in dollars and cents. The boost to civic pride is undeniable and highly prized. But city fathers have generally oversold the economic benefits in attempts to hide their edifice complexes, and that's what makes some people mad. "Taxpayers have a right to be leveled with," Baade says. "If the argument ultimately is that the city will feel better about itself, tell them that."

When taxpayers are not leveled with, they usually get the picture anyway. Stadium proposals put up for a vote in recent years have gotten the thumbs-down in referenda from Oklahoma City to Cleveland. The classic example is last November's referendum in San Francisco, when voters decided that they had better things to do with their money than pay for a new stadium for baseball Giants' owner Bob Lurie.

Lurie had threatened, for the second time in a decade, to move his Giants elsewhere unless the city coughed up enough money for a new stadium. But voters, unimpressed by the Giants' standard claim that the city would get its $115 million back in due time, saw more immediate uses for that money around them. The earthquake and AIDS funding were on the minds of the voters who by a 51-to-49-percent margin turned down a replacement for Candlestick Park. Rumors that the team would move near its spring training grounds in Arizona had died after Phoenix voters had rejected a baseball stadium there by a 59-to-41-percent vote in October.

Ironically, it was Candlestick, a 59,000-seat behemoth built in 1960, that ushered in the modern era of the "super stadium." Unfortunately, bitter cold and winds fierce enough to blow pitchers off the mound pushed attendance down. Yet after Candlestick withstood the earthquake that disrupted last year's World Series—and earned it the adoring nickname "Wiggly Field" in the process—voters saw no need to replace such an amazingly sturdy structure. The Giants may now move to Denver, Sacramento, or another sports-hungry area.

It wasn't always like this. For pro sports' first 70 years, constructing a ballpark was the responsibility of individual teams. Local governments, if anything, were hostile. When the Giants were still in New York a century ago, the city government broke down a wall of the original Polo Grounds and pushed 111th Street through the team's outfield. It was up to the Giants to find new quarters on the Harlem River and slap together a new grandstand.

In the past 30 years, however, only one man has been able to go it alone. The late Joe Robbie, owner of the Miami Dolphins, constructed an aqua-and-orange football palace in 1987 entirely with private funds. He called it Joe Robbie Stadium.

For years the Dolphins had played in the Orange Bowl, a stadium that no less an authority than Hunter S. Thompson described as "hell." It was dirty, it was old, and it was in the middle of a slum. (While Joe Robbie Stadium hosted 75,000 fat cats at last year's Super Bowl, the neighborhood around the Orange Bowl was cleaning up the debris from Miami's latest race riot.) After three attempts to improve the facilities had been turned down by Miami voters, Robbie stuck out on his own.

Robbie knew how unreliable local governments can be, possibly from his days as a state legislator back in South Dakota. An individualist who bragged about his "Irish dander" and "Lebanese tenacity," the Dolphins' owner decided it was time to play bet-the-franchise in the hope of getting his own way.

Robbie charged diehard Dolphins fans up to $650,000 for 10-year leases on luxury boxes, those moneymaking sky suites that almost all football owners are blackmailing their hosts to get. For less affluent fans, Robbie built 10,000 air-conditioned "club seats" which went for as much as $140,000 for a 10-year lease. With that revenue, Robbie was able to borrow the money for 432 acres 30 minutes north of the Orange Bowl and put up his $115-million football octagon.

"This stadium is a monument to a free, competitive enterprise system and showed that anything the government can do, we can do better," Robbie said at the stadium's dedication in 1987. "What I have done is caused the politicians to look toward the private sector to build what are essentially public facilities." Before his death early this year, Robbie was laying plans to bring a major-league baseball team to his city. His son, Tim Robbie, has taken over the team and the stadium.

Is Joe Robbie Stadium the wave of the future? Well, yes and no. Stadium experts say that other teams might find it hard to duplicate Robbie's economic position—specifically the presence of thousands of fans willing to pay new-house prices for football tickets. Florida's booming economy also helped. "This was a real estate play, in part," reports Sam Katz, a Philadelphia financier who helped Robbie find banks willing to front him money for the stadium.

A few sports bigwigs have talked about constructing their own stadiums, including Washington Redskins owner Jack Kent Cooke and Sacramento's Gregg Lukenbill. For Cooke, like Robbie, the advantage of actually owning a team makes his dream complex in the northern Virginia suburbs a possibility. Lukenbill, who owns no team, planned to recoup his investment by gathering in most of the "externalities" that usually benefit the local economy. With plans for owning the hotels, bars, restaurants, and parking garages within a wide radius of his facility, Lukenbill, in a sense, would have *been* the local economy.

But the wave of the future is probably best represented by the plans of the Milwaukee Brewers to build their own ballpark on $50 million worth of land secured by the county government. The reason for the private construction plans? A new Milwaukee stadium won't get the tax breaks that have underwritten so many stadiums of the past.

Through the 1980s, the federal government gave bonds issued for stadium construction the same tax-exempt status given to bonds for building roads or schools. Since debt service can represent three-quarters of a stadium's costs, that meant something to local governments. "Competition between cities for sports teams had been financed by the federal government," says one Wall Street analyst.

But three separate changes to the tax code in 1984 and 1986 changed all that. Stadium bonds now get tax-exempt status only if they meet difficult criteria, and the difference could mean an extra $100 million or so tacked onto the cost of a particularly expensive stadium. Sports-hungry cities have deep pockets, but none are that deep.

But so many sports projects were grandfathered into the 1986 tax reform bill that the effects of those changes are only being seen now in places like Milwaukee. Cities are serving notice that there is a limit to what they can be asked to pay for. "You'll see more public-private ventures. You'll see more cost sharing—and risk sharing," predicts Katz, a top sports financial consultant.

Most analysts note, however, that the private sector is probably better equipped to handle construction. "By keeping this private, we'll build a better stadium at a cheaper price," says Maurice Reed of the Sacramento Sports Association. "We think that's the new way to do things." And, as Baade notes, a team "is much less likely to leave a stadium built with its own funds."

Even the new breed of sports owners with dreams of owning their own stadiums are not diehard private-enterprisers. Redskins' owner Cooke is still negotiating with the Washington, D.C., government in the hopes of getting a sweetheart deal. Sacramento's Lukenbill had to turn to the city government to ante up the bribe the NFL's Raiders demanded. Robbie himself admitted in 1987 that he thought building arenas was still a "normal function of government," and he left the state to build $25 million in road improvements to end eight-hour traffic jams at the Dolphins' new home.

And even private development cannot make a stadium affordable to more than a handful of men. Only those who already own teams can contemplate taking that next step. "The prospects for doing another Joe Robbie are going to be somewhat limited," says Katz.

The wave of the future is some type of joint public-private venture in all but the biggest sports markets. By one count, at least six new stadiums on the drawing boards have both public and private funds committed to them. For the foreseeable future, local governments and private developers will continue the relationship they have found themselves in by chance if not by choice.

Cities in search of a new team will still think subsidy. A pro sports franchise can cost $50 million or more; some fat cats in San Antonio or St. Petersburg might shell out that kind of cash, but add the $100 million or so for a place to play and they will likely bow out. This means, for the cities that want the exposure and prestige of major-league status, that continued subsidies will be inevitable.

But the record argues that those subsidies bring intangible benefits rather than economic good times. The public should know this. And the public should also know that those intangibles come with a steep price tag that may never be worked off. "Put it that way," urges Baade. "Let's see if the taxpayers are willing to go along with the program."

19. *Secrets of the Front Office: What America's Pro Teams Are Worth*

ANTHONY BALDO

Forget the somber note recently sounded for the New York Yankees by one national sports weekly. Sure, the fabulous days of Ruth, Gehrig and Mantle are long gone. And the franchise hasn't won a World Series since 1978. Still, Don Mattingly is nothing to sniff at, and his young teammates have played some inspired ball in 1991.

But the real pride of the Yankees these days has nothing to do with whether they win or lose; instead, it is how principal owner George Steinbrenner plays the financial game. As a business, the Bronx Bombers are in undisputed first place. By FW estimates, the Yankees are worth $225 million, making the team the most valuable of America's professional sports franchises. Indeed, FW found that the $60.4 million that the Yankees derive from media rights fees alone is more than the *total* revenues of every other sports team except the New York Mets and Toronto Blue Jays.

In analyzing the Yankees and 101 other baseball, basketball, football and hockey teams, one thing becomes glaringly apparent: Sports has become a big business and today's franchises are valued as much for the revenues they generate as the wins and entertainment they produce. "There is so much at stake because the numbers now are so huge that owners have to be numbers-driven," says Larry Miller, owner of the Utah Jazz of the National Basketball Association. "People can't afford to get into [franchise ownership] and play with it."

The 10 most valuable franchises . . . offer a few surprises and a glimpse of sports' old and new guard. The Yankees and Boston Red Sox are valuable for the customary reason: excellent revenues from local media. On the other hand, the Miami Dolphins and the Los Angeles Lakers are part of the new breed, teams whose principals own or control their stadiums and the revenues from skyboxes, concessions and parking. The Dallas Cowboys and the Green Bay Packers also have attractive stadium situations. The Baltimore Orioles will have a lucrative stadium lease arrangement when they move into their new Camden Yards facility next

---

SOURCE: *Financial World* (July 9, 1991). Reprinted from *Financial World*, 1328 Broadway, New York, NY 10001.

year, and the Boston Celtics are likely to get a new arena in the not-too-distant future. The Mets have the best of both worlds: media revenues of $38.3 million and stadium revenues of $15.4 million. The Los Angeles Dodgers also do well: They own Dodger Stadium and they receive total media revenues of almost $30 million.

But challenging times are ahead for these teams and the others lower in the pecking order. The Big Three—the National Football League, the National Basketball Association and Major League Baseball—have been weaned on television revenues, a rich wellspring in the Eighties, when CBS's Larry Tisch and the other network execs bid up national TV contracts. In the Nineties, the national and local television revenues will diminish. As labor disputes with players loom in the coming years, sports owners in all four sports find themselves trying to find fresh revenue sources. They have found instant relief in new stadiums, with big luxury skyboxes that rent for tens of thousands of dollars. But as the Nineties wear on, stadium revenues may not be enough to sustain a reasonable rate of growth in the value of sports franchises.

Owners of these teams today also must face the grim fact that the vigorous Age of Expansion has passed and maturity has set in. FW estimates that the four sports leagues as an industry had an operating profit margin of 17% on $3.7 billion in revenues, an enviable benchmark. But much like an athlete in his prime, the three best-known leagues—the NFL, the NBA and Major League Baseball (MLB)—are steadily approaching middle age. And while the National Hockey League still has room to grow as a sport, its revenues aren't likely to experience the leaps and bounds that the other leagues have.

The sports expansion of the past three decades produced a golden age that even Andrew Carnegie would have smiled upon. At the start of 1967, there were 61 franchises in the major professional sports, compared with today's 102. The NHL had six teams; the NBA, 10. Teams were added in lumps throughout the late Sixties, Seventies and Eighties. Night games increased to fill prime-time television, and seasons and postseasons expanded. New leagues, spawned to compete with the old order, survived briefly before being squeezed out, and only the strongest of the upstart franchises were invited to join the sport establishment's party.

TV's importance to franchise profits has been well reported, but it becomes more pronounced when compared with revenue flow from other sources. Last year, national and local television, cable and radio broadcasting garnered $1.7 billion in revenues for all four leagues, followed by gate receipts ($1.4 billion) and stadium concessions, skyboxes and ads ($400 million). And the growth in broadcast revenues has been phenomenal. In 1980, each NFL team received about $5.9 million from national television, according to Paul Kagan Associates; in 1990, clubs got $26.5 million. Each baseball team's take ballooned from about $3.3 million in 1980 to $14 million a decade later. The $1.2 million that every

NBA team received 1982 quadrupled, to $5 million for the 1989-90 season. Hockey, on the other hand, has seen but a small increase, from just over $1 million per team in 1985 to $2 million for the 1989-90 campaign, pretty good considering hockey is a regional, rather than national, sport.

With TV revenues as the engine, franchise values found themselves on a two-decade ride. "For the past 20 years, baseball, football and basketball teams have had an annual compounded increase of 20% to 25% in their franchise values," says Timothy Mueller, director of KPMG Peat Marwick's sports industry consulting group.

In the 1980s, franchise values exploded right along with real estate and the stock market, both of which helped fuel the sports boom. Before the 1986 Tax Reform Act, the law permitted rich investors to shelter their winnings—and indulge their fantasies—by investing them in sports teams.

The Nordstrom family, hugely successful retailers, paid $8.2 million for a controlling interest in the National Football League's Seattle Seahawks in 1974; in 1989, the team was sold for $97 million. In 1981, Donald Sterling paid $12.5 million for the National Basketball Association's San Diego (now Los Angeles) Clippers, but by 1989, the NBA's Portland Trailblazers brought $70 million. Even the NHL experienced swift appreciation in values: In 1984, the Hartford Whalers sold for $31 million, just two years after the Detroit Red Wings fetched $8 million.

As values have escalated, sports owners have developed arcane accounting gimmicks to hide profits and even revenues. Paramount Communications, for example, owns the New York Knicks, the New York Rangers, Madison Square Garden (where both teams play) and Madison Square Garden Network (the local cable channel that televises their games), so the Knicks' and Rangers' revenues and expenses get hidden away in Paramount's corporate income statements through what are known as "interrelated party transactions."

Accounting gimmickry is not an uncommon business practice, but there are other things that do set sports apart. For decades, Congress has treated big-time sports as if they were games adults play, and has never imposed the usual regulatory restraints such as antitrust. In effect, this has permitted management of the teams in each of the four major sports leagues to work in concert, in what some critics, including players unions, maintain is anticompetitive and antiplayer.

By pooling the resources of its 28 teams, the NFL has been the most effective in using this special status. As much as 90% of the revenues are shared, thereby strengthening the financial grounding of the whole sport. The NFL negotiates national television contracts for all the teams, then disburses revenues of $26.5 million to each of them. Little is derived from local television and radio. And when it comes to gate receipts, the same rules apply to all: 60% for the home team, 40% for the visitors. Says Kansas City Chiefs owner Lamar Hunt: "By sharing so much revenue, we have stability across the board, which is something you don't have in other professional sports leagues."

That translates into higher overall values in the NFL. "Football teams are worth more, on average, than baseball teams," says Michael Megna, senior vice-president of American Appraisals Associates, a Milwaukee-based consulting firm. "But several baseball teams are worth more because of the market that they have."

FW's franchise values bear that out. For example, the top five baseball teams—the Yankees ($225 million), Orioles ($200 million), Dodgers ($200 million), Mets ($200 million) and Red Sox ($180 million)—are worth more than the NFL's top five: the Dolphins ($205 million), Packers ($200 million), Cowboys ($180 million), New York Giants ($150 million) and San Francisco 49ers ($150 million).

Overall, however, it's a different story. The average NFL team is worth $132 million, the average MLB club is worth $121 million, with the NBA ($70 million) and NHL ($44 million) bringing up the rear. And the gaps among franchises in baseball are a lot larger than in football. In the NFL, the New England Patriots' estimated value is $100 million. In MLB, there are 10 teams under that, the Seattle Mariners at $71.4 million lagging all others.

Small wonder that Jeff Smulyan, owner of the struggling Mariners—whose revenues of $34 million are the lowest in baseball—wants to imitate football and promote more revenue sharing. Smulyan would love a cut of the $42 million per year that the Yankees derive from a local cable deal with the Madison Square Garden Network—a figure strictly resulting from the huge New York City area market. "The basic operating costs are the same for everybody," says American Appraisals' Megna. "The operating margin differential is influenced largely by the market."

But the Yankees and other rich franchises treat Smulyan's sharing concept as verging on Marxism. "I've been at meetings where the owner of a small market team will stand up and tell the other owners that, 'If the big-market teams don't share revenues, you will only have yourself to blame.' Then one of the big-market teams will stand up and begin his address, 'Comrade,' and everybody will laugh," says Peter Bavasi, a former president of the Toronto Blue Jays and the Cleveland Indians.

The heart of the matter is that all four sports are labor-intensive businesses that must either stringently control payrolls or boost revenues. Of the four sports, baseball has been the least effective in dealing with this challenge. As a result, even as MLB adds two new franchises in Miami and Denver, some existing teams are barely afloat.

All this began in the 1970s, when pitchers Andy Messersmith and Dave McNally challenged the MLB restrictions on the free movement of players. They won, and so was born free agency in baseball, leading to higher payrolls.

By the late Eighties, even free-agent utility infielders were getting million-dollar contracts. The owners decided enough was enough and stopped the auction. They were slapped with a lawsuit charging collusion, lost, and settled with the players union to the tune of $280 million in damages. Now, the owners are right back where they started, bidding up salaries to incredible levels. MLB payrolls rose an average of 40% between last season and the present one. And only one team—the Houston Astros, which lost $2 million last year—had a payroll drop.

So revenue sharing won't be enough. Some kind of salary cap is also needed. Indeed, MLB's problems aren't new; the NBA experienced the same thing in the early Eighties. By 1983, several NBA teams were losing money and some were ready to go under. In an effort to control operating cost increases, the players and owners forged an agreement: a salary cap, in which 53% of the gate and television revenues go to the players. The system worked, and now the league is enjoying labor peace and heady profits.

That comfy combination in the NBA could soon be rudely disrupted because payrolls are growing faster than revenues. As a result, NBA teams will be exceeding the cap, hampering their ability to bid up for free agents. That situation is sure to cause problems by the end of the 1993-94 season, when the league's collective-bargaining agreement with the players expires. The players' association may respond by refusing to renew the cap agreement with management. "The reason the players did what they did [in 1983] was to stabilize the league," says Jerry Colangelo, owner of the Phoenix Suns. "If you pull out the carpet now, you go right back to where you were before." Adds Detroit Pistons CEO Tom Wilson: "There are still always going to be some teams in weaker markets that are really going to have a difficult time competing, even with revenue sharing."

The NFL, like the NBA, faces a falling rate of revenue growth, and it couldn't come at a worse time. Football has avoided unrestricted free agency. But that may change if the National Football Players Association has its way. The NFL draft agreement, which legally allows teams to divvy up college talent every year, expires in 1992. Say a college player in 1993 wants to sign with a team other than the one that drafts him. He, at that point, can sue the NFL on antitrust grounds if he is stopped from signing with whomever he wants. Such a possibility may push the league to settle the whole free agency issue with players. Says Chiefs owner Hunt: "You could make a reasonable case that a draft in some form is extremely important to the success of the league."

Beset by labor worries and anticipating an end to big TV contracts, franchise owners in all four sports are scrambling to find new sources of revenue. The answer: new stadiums and arenas. "Are you going to paint yourself into a corner where players are going to cost so much that you can't pass that on to the fan?" asks the Pistons' Wilson. "That's why we are seeing a lot of teams building their own arenas. We have to find new revenue streams that aren't related to the game."

The Pistons have set the standard. The team's owner, William Davidson, also owns the Palace, the Auburn Hills, Mich., facility where the Pistons play. The $13 million in revenues he derives from skyboxes alone services the facility's annual debt payments.

For owners, skyboxes and premium seating are the cash cows of the 1990s. Consider the Chicago White Sox. In the old Comiskey Park, the Chisox had fewer than 5,000 box seats that cost fans $10.50 apiece; in the new stadium, they have 21,000 at an average of $13 a pop. Then there are the suites. Thirty-seven in the old park, priced at $45,000 each, 82 in the new at $60,000 to $90,000. Is it any wonder that the Baltimore Orioles, Cleveland Indians, Texas Rangers, Atlanta Falcons and the Phoenix Suns are all planning to move to new facilities? Or that half the teams in the NHL are thinking about building new stadiums, including the Quebec Nordiques, Philadelphia Flyers and St. Louis Blues? Even the Super Bowl champion New York Giants, who moved into Giants Stadium only 15 seasons ago, are considered to be in an old facility. Preston Robert Tisch, who recently bought half the team, has already announced plans to add 70 skyboxes.

Owners like to point out that skyboxes, which are occupied mainly by corporations, help reduce the ticket price of the fan sitting in the bleachers. "You have to underwrite the average fan," says Richard Gordon, the owner of the Hartford Whalers. "How much can you keep raising ticket prices? There has to be a subsidy."

Leases in new facilities—or in new cities—typically offer other, little-noticed benefits that ultimately make a franchise more valuable. Again, consider the White Sox. Under its new lease, the team pays rent to the state of Illinois, which owns the stadium, on attendance over 1.2 million a year at a rate of no more than $2.50 per fan.

Understanding the lure of a new stadium to a professional franchise, some cities are building them to attract a team with an unsatisfactory lease elsewhere. Memphis, for example, is building the Great American Pyramid, a 20,000-seat arena set to open this fall. St. Petersburg, Fla., has the Florida Suncoast Dome, which, having lost out to Miami for a baseball expansion franchise, must rely on tractor pulls and the like to fill seats.

The gains from moving to a new stadium or a new city dramatically effect a franchise's value. FW estimates that the Utah Jazz is worth $45 million. But prospective buyers are willing to pay $100 million to move the team from Salt Lake City to a city where they can get favorable leases. Is the Jazz's owner selling? No way. Instead, he is enhancing the team's value by building his own stadium in Salt Lake City, with 56 luxury suites that will generate $3.2 million in revenues annually.

In fact, new facilities are what make expansion teams more valuable than some established ones. The $50 million that three new NHL teams—

the Ottawa Senators, Tampa Bay Lightning and the San Jose Sharks—must each pay to enter the league, and the $95 million that Denver and Miami will pay to join MLB, can't be considered floors for values in those leagues. Simply put, the two leagues have set rigorous standards on attendance and in-stadium revenues for those new teams that the established clubs don't have to meet. So it shouldn't come as any surprise why only six NHL teams—the Montreal Canadiens, Boston Bruins, New York Rangers, Calgary Flames, New York Islanders and Edmonton Oilers—are worth more than Ottawa, Tampa Bay or San Jose, which have yet to put skate to ice.

Nor will expansion—the big revenue producer of the 1960s and 1970s—provide the answer. In addition to the expansion teams already approved by MLB and the NHL, the NFL will add two teams by 1994. But that will be it, unless the leagues want to start franchises in third-tier American cities.

Faced with the dilemma of a plateauing revenue stream, which threatens all mature businesses, the NFL and the NBA are finding solutions in business-school case studies: When domestic markets dry up, expand overseas. The World League of American Football, sponsored by the NFL, has just completed its first spring season. NFL owners were so pleased with the interest in the league internationally that they will kick in another $13 million on top of the $6.5 million they initially invested. Meanwhile, the NBA already runs the preseason McDonald's Open, a tourney featuring three European professional teams along with one from the NBA. The idea is to develop new markets in Europe for sports merchandise and audiences for game broadcasts from the U.S.

Inevitably, all four leagues will have to stretch their imaginations to grow revenues. Team owners may have to become sporting goods retailers, or clothing manufacturers, using their teams as marketing agents for what are commodities otherwise. The leagues may have to resort to product differentiation; maybe stars-only teams and exhibitions for elite players. Imagine Michael Jordan playing night after night against only Magic Johnson-caliber players. Or Joe Montana constantly going against defenses with Lawrence Taylor, Reggie White and Ronald Lott all on the same side.

Failing that, franchise values are not likely to be driven by artificial stimuli. For instance, no force is likely to emerge in the sports world that will drive prices up as, say, corporate takeovers in the Eighties drove up the stock market.

Owners—including corporations—have purchased sports franchises for any number of reasons. Some, such as Hartford's Gordon and the Indiana Pacers' Herbert and Melvin Simon, bought teams for civic purposes. Others, such as Paramount Communications (Knicks, Rangers), Tribune Co. (Chicago Cubs) and Ted Turner (Atlanta Hawks, Atlanta Braves), use their sports franchises to provide programming for their television stations or cable channels.

But don't expect corporate owners to come in droves. Several provisions of the 1986 Tax Reform Act limited the attractiveness of owning teams that generate losses.

Even as active investments, sports franchises aren't worth a corporations's trouble, unless they have a related business. The return on investment just doesn't warrant a corporation's financial involvement. "Today, I'd want a little higher cash-on-cash [operating cash flow divided by purchase price] return than in the past, so I could afford to hold [the franchise], because I wouldn't want to have to bet solely on the future appreciation in value to make my return," says Don Erickson, the director of Southwest valuation services at Ernst & Young. "Before, I'd take 6% annually. Today, I'd want a higher return, say 10%."

That isn't likely as payrolls continue to increase and the growth in revenues slows. Moreover, the demand by corporations for a return on their investment are simply too lofty for sports franchises to meet. "Return on equity would be too little for a corporation to buy and run a sports franchise," says Erickson. "You'd get sued as a corporate board member because your return on investment would be so low."

All the more reason why the smaller businessman, who can make a good living on 6%-to-10% annual returns, can't just run a sports team for the fun of it. The whole process has become businesslike, out of necessity. "Owning a sports franchise has crossed the line where you have to look at it as an investment and whether you can get a return," says the Jazz's Miller. "I'm sure there are some exceptions, where there are people who can do otherwise. But I think those people are few and far between.

■ FOR FURTHER STUDY

Baade, Robert A., and Richard F. Dye. "Sports Stadiums and Area Development: A Critical View." *Economic Development Quarterly* 2 (August 1988): 265-275.

Berry, Robert C., and Glenn M. Wong. *Law and Business of the Sports Industries: Professional Sports Leagues*, vol. 1. Dover, MA: Auburn House, 1986.

Ebert, Allan. "Un-Sporting Multinationals." *Multinational Monitor* 6 (December 1985): 11-12.

Eitzen, D. Stanley. "The Sociology of Amateur Sport: An Overview." *International Review for the Sociology of Sport* 24 (1989): 95-104.

Flint, William C., and D. Stanley Eitzen. "Professional Sports Team Ownership and Entrepreneurial Capitalism." *Sociology of Sport Journal* 4 (March 1987): 17-27.

Garvey, Edward R. "From Chattel to Employee: The Athlete's Quest for Freedom and Dignity." *The Annals of the American Academy of Political and Social Science* 445 (September 1979): 102-115.

Goodman, Matthew. "Behind the Ball." *Zeta Magazine* 4 (January 1991): 86-87.

Gruneau, Richard S. "Elites, Class and Corporate Power in Canadian Sport." In *Sport, Culture and Society*, ed. John W. Loy, Gerald S. Kenyon, and Barry D. McPherson. Philadelphia: Lea & Febiger, 1981, pp. 348-371.

Guttmann, Allen. *Sports Spectators*. New York: Columbia University Press, 1986.

Jennings, Kenneth M. *Balls & Strikes: The Money Game in Professional Baseball*. New York: Praeger, 1990.

Koch, James V. "Intercollegiate Athletics: An Economic Explanation." *Social Science Quarterly* (June 1983): 360-374.

Lowenfish, Lee. *The Imperfect Diamond: A History of Baseball's Labor Wars*. New York: Da Capo Press, 1991.

Miller, Marvin. *A Whole Different Ball Game: The Sport and Business of Baseball*. New York: Birch Lane, 1991.

Stanton, Michael. "Playing for a Living: The Dream Comes True for Very Few." *Occupational Outlook Quarterly* 31 (Spring 1987): 2-15.

Taafe, William. "The Other Game in New York." *Sports Illustrated* (September 29, 1986): 32-33.

Underwood, John. *Spoiled Sport*. Boston: Little, Brown, 1984.

Welling, Brenton, Jonathan Tasini, and Dan Cook. "Basketball: Business Is Booming." *Business Week* 2918 (October 28, 1985): 73-82.

Part Seven

The Mass Media and Sport

The mass media have a tremendous impact on sports. Among these impacts are first, the popularity of sport is due in large measure to the enormous attention it receives from the mass media. Second, television has infused huge sums of money into sport, affecting franchise moves and salaries. Third, television (and the money it offers) have changed the way sports are played (for example, the scheduling of games, the interruption of the flow of games for commercial breaks, a shift from match play to medal play in tournament golf, the use of replays to determine controversial calls by referees in professional football, and rule changes such as liberalizing offensive holding in football to increase scoring and, therefore, viewer interest). Fourth, television has affected college sports by making recruiting more national than regional and by focusing the nation's attention (and heaping television's money) on the games by a relatively few schools. Thus, television has exacerbated the gap between the "haves" and the "have nots." Moreover, since television money goes to the successful, it has heightened the pressure to win and, for some, the necessity to cheat in order to win.

Another consequence of the media—the affect on perceptions—is the focus of this section. The media direct attention toward certain acts and away from others. While the media appear to simply report what is happening, or what has just happened, during a sporting event, they actually provide a constructed view by what they choose to cover, their focus, and the narrative themes they pursue.[1] As Alan and John Clarke have said:

> It select *between* sports for those which make "good television," and it selects *within* a particular event, it highlights particular aspects for the viewers. This selective highlighting is not "natural" or inevitable—it is based on certain

> criteria, certain media assumptions about what is "good television." But the media do not only select, they also provide us with definitions of what has been selected. They interpret events for us, provide us with frameworks of meaning in which to make sense of the event. To put it simply, television does not merely consist of pictures, but also involves a commentary on the pictures—a commentary which explains to us what we are seeing. . . . These selections are socially constructed—they involve decisions about what to reveal to the viewers. The presentation of sport through the media involves an active process of re-presentation: what we see is not the event, but the event transformed into something else—a media event.[2]

The three selections in this section focus on this theme. The first, by Lawrence A. Wenner, examines the made-for-television Super Bowl pregame show, extracting its cultural and political messages. The second selection, by Michael A. Messner, Margaret Carlisle Duncan, and Kerry Jensen, documents how live, play-by-play (therefore, unscripted) television commentators talk differently about women and men athletes. They find that while contemporary commentators are less overtly sexist than their predecessors, their language, nevertheless, tends to mark women's sports and women athletes as "other," infantilizes women athletes, and frames their accomplishments negatively or ambivalently. The final selection, by David A. Klatell and Norman Marcus from their book *Sports for Sale: Television, Money and the Fans*, shows why journalists tend to focus on the positive in sport rather than do investigative reports on the negatives. As they put it: "As a business proposition, why should a television company shell out astounding amounts of money as guaranteed payments in a speculative bid for future broadcast rights and then permit one of its own employees in any way to diminish the potential return on that investment?" The result, of course, is that the consumers of sports-related media receive a distorted view of sport.

NOTES

1. D. Stanley Eitzen and George H. Sage, *Sociology of North American Sport*, 5th ed. (Dubuque, IA: Wm. C. Brown, 1993), Chap. 9.
2. Alan Clarke and John Clarke, "Highlights and Action Replays—Ideology, Sport and the Media," in *Sport, Culture, and Ideology*, Jennifer Hargreaves, ed. (Boston: Routledge & Kegan Paul, 1982), pp. 69, 71.

20. *The Super Bowl Pregame Show: Cultural Fantasies and Political Subtext*

LAWRENCE A. WENNER

In the United States, when the Super Bowl comes on television, the world stops. The highways empty of traffic and the shopping malls become barren of customers. Year in and year out, the Super Bowl—more descriptively, the championship game of American professional football—is one of the highest rated of all television programs. This phenomenon has been going on for some time. The Super Bowl has passed out of childhood and adolescence, and in human form would be a number of years past voting age. And this young adult is a professional, well compensated for services rendered. The "million-dollar minute" is now a bargain rate for advertising not found in buying advertising time during the Super Bowl (Goodwin, 1986).

Fittingly, then, the most frequently cited study of mediated sports has been Real's (1975) study of a Super Bowl telecast. Using a cultural approach, Real looks at the Super Bowl telecast as a microcosm of American life, replete with myth, ritual, heroic archetypes, and interlocking story lines involving lifelike issues of labor, management, territoriality, and property ownership. Real concludes:

> The structural values of the Super Bowl can be summarized succinctly: *North American professional football is an aggressive, strictly regulated team game fought between males who use both violence and technology to gain control of property for the economic gain of individuals within nationalistic entertainment context.* The Super Bowl propagates these values by elevating one game to the level of a spectacle of American ideology collectively celebrated. (p. 42)

A football game, of course, starts with a kickoff. However, as a media event, the Super Bowl starts with a "pregame show," typically two hours in length. The pregame show is the culmination of two weeks of what

---

SOURCE: In *Media, Sports and Society*, Lawrence A. Wenner, ed. (Newbury Park, CA: Sage Publications, 1989), pp. 157-179.

Buell (1980) and others have called "superhype." As Buell has remarked: "The hyping of televised football seems to have no limits" (p. 66). All of the mediated scenarios, fantasies, rumors, couched predictions, psychological profiling, and the like have seemingly reached their saturation point by the time of the pregame show. This study looks at the "outer limits" of media hype—the saga of the pregame show that frames the Super Bowl broadcast with a set of values intricately developed in over two hours of fantasy theme chaining (Bormann, 1972). More specifically, the focus here is on NBC's pregame show for Super Bowl XX—a contest that featured the Chicago Bears playing the New England Patriots on January 26, 1986.

AN APPROACH TO SUPERHYPE: FANTASY THEME ANALYSIS

Bormann's (1972) fantasy theme analysis is a seemingly appropriate method to apply to the hodgepodge of themes that were bandied about during NBC's coverage of the preevent nonevent that the Super Bowl pregame show clearly is.[1] As a genre, the pregame show is notable in that it is very different from most sports programming on television. Commenting on the role of mediated sports in socialization, Goldstein and Bredemeier (1977) have noted that "one effect of the prevalence of sports on television has been an emphasis on outcome rather than process" (p. 155). One of the most distinguishing features of the pregame show is that it is exclusively composed of process. In a sense, it is the communication equivalent of being pregnant. It is a process in and of itself, and while there may be expert conjecture as to whether the pregnancy will be difficult or easy, the labor long or short, the child male or female, or the delivery simple or full of complications, a good many of the details of both the pregnancy and its outcome remain unknown. However, unlike pregnancy, the process of the Super Bowl pregame show is one of pure fantasy.

Bormann's approach hits at the heart of both process and fantasy. Derived from Bale's (1950) work in group interaction process analysis, Bormann's method uncovers the rhetorical visions that come out of group interactions. He goes about this by focusing on "how dramatizing communication creates social reality for groups of people" (p. 396). By "dramatizing communication," Bormann means the specific dramatic or story elements that appear as members of the group communicate with each other. For Bormann, as group communication progresses, the participants become less self-conscious and the tone of interaction becomes more lively, to a point where dramatizing accelerates into the building of a group fantasy or alternate reality. The content of the group fantasy "consists of characters, real or fictitious, playing out a dramatic situation in a setting removed in time and space from the here-and-now transactions of the group" (p. 397).

Bormann is interested in the fantasy themes that develop out of the dramatic elements in a group's fantasy because they tend to constitute the "reality" of a group posed with a problematic task. As Nimmo and Combs (1983) have put it, "for those who share them, the fantasies are real, the fantasy reality" (p. 13). The symbolic reality that results Bormann calls a "rhetorical vision" that is "constructed from fantasy themes that chain out in face-to-face interacting groups, in speaker-audience transactions, in viewers of television broadcasts, in listeners to radio programs, and in all diverse settings for public and intimate communication in a given society" (p. 398).

Thus the rhetorical vision of a sports program such as NBC's Super Bowl pregame show can be understood in terms of the fantasies chained by the group participants—sports announcers, commentators, coaches, athletes, and the like—and embraced by the audience that has chosen to enter the fantastic reality by becoming members of a larger fantasy group. In the case of the yearly Super Bowl event the fantasy group becomes so large that, in a sense, it defines a recurring fantasy that is at one with American culture.

LOOKING THROUGH A CHAIN LINK FENCE: THE POLITICAL FANTASY TYPE

The political implications of sport in a culture have been commented upon frequently in the sociology of sport (Eitzen & Sage, 1978; Jhally, 1984; Pooley & Webster, 1976; Snyder & Spreitzer, 1978). The relationship between politics and sport takes place on a two-way street. Sports contests are played within the political context of a given culture (Pooley & Webster, 1976), political values (e.g., conservatism, nationalism) are seen to abound in the playing of sports (Goldstein & Bredemeier, 1977; Nimmo & Combs 1983; Prisuta, 1979, Real, 1975), and sports themes are commonly used metaphorical devices in both the rhetoric of politics (Balbus, 1975) and the reporting of politics (Carey, 1976).

In short, the symbiotic relationship between politics and sports has yielded both recurring sports themes in politics and recurring political themes in sports. In Bormann's framework, such recurring themes in a body of discourse are "fantasy types" (Bormann, 1977; Bormann, Koester, & Bennett, 1978). Thus the political themes that make up part of the fantasy of mediated sports discourse constitute one such fantasy type. This study focuses on the web of political fantasies woven about the Super Bowl pregame show, setting the stage for the game itself. One may see the web of political fantasy as spun in the form of fantasy chains, linked together, surrounding the body of discourse and the public event to which it refers (in this case the Super Bowl game) as a fantasy "chain link fence."[2] To the degree to which the fantasy type is dominant in the body of discourse, the chain link fence becomes a somewhat distinct variant of a "frame" through which the event, and the body of discourse about it, is interpreted by the audience.

The chain link fence is a constructed entity, built by the participants in the discourse. So constituted, it inherits many of Goffman's (1974) notions about frame analysis, and Tuchman's (1978) application of it to the construction of reality in news. The difference here is the overt focus on fantasy. Frames, as they are used in news and everyday life, aim to "get things right," to construct reality accurately. Especially with regard to sports, fences constructed of fantasy chains are unlikely to have such a goal. More likely, the aim is to construct an altered reality that has intrinsic, but not necessarily practical, value. As such, chain link fences exist in the world of ritual, of which commentary on and spectatorship of sports play a part. As Stephenson (1967) might sum it up, frames have to do with work, and fantasy chains have to do with play.

Such fantasy construction is not without linkages to the real world. Nixon (1982) has noted that the "metaphorical interpretation of sport as an American 'fantasyland' of character, virtue, and the romanticized pursuit of the American Dream and embodiment of the Protestant ethic stands in striking contrast to the somewhat tarnished picture of the 'real world' outside the sports arena" (p. 2).

In noting this contrast, some critics have suggested studying sports and politics as a social dialectic. For instance, in looking at American sports, Jhally (1984) has observed:

> Sports are an explicit celebration of the *idealized* structures of reality—a form of capitalist realism. They mediate a vital social dialectic, providing both an escape from the alienated conditions of everyday life and a *socialization* into these very same structures. (p. 51)

This dialectic is at the heart of much cultural criticism in communication that attempts to understand the phenomenon of hegemony. Such inquiry is also basic to the sociology of sport. Sociologists such as Loy (1978) see the legitimation of sport in a society tied to such dialectically opposed functions:

> Sport fulfills the first and characteristically cultural function by mirroring the hegemony of the American success ideology; and . . . sport fulfills the second and characteristically expressive cultural function by providing a medium and a context for ecstatic experience in everyday life. (p. 79)

In short, the issue of looking at the political fantasies of mediated sport can be seen as central to understanding sport in culture.

STRUCTURE OF THE PREGAME FANTASY

One need not wield a fine-tooth comb between the lines of subtext to find political connections in the sports fantasy offered to the Super Bowl viewers who tuned into the pregame "festivities." From its opening seconds at 3 p.m. EST, NBC's pregame show was cast as "An American Celebration." The "celebration" began with the slick graphics and video effects that we have come to associate with American news and sports coverage. Just what "we" were "celebrating" was not so clear at the outset, but by the close of the two-hour lead-in to the game, it was clear "we Americans" were "celebrating America." The general idea seemed to be to bring the spirit of the Fourth of July to the middle of January. However, nowhere to be seen were Washington, Jefferson, Madison, and their contemporaries. This was a celebration of the American present. The only times a historical perspective intervened, we "learned" of the history of the Super Bowl spectacle in terms of the "great men" who fought the good fight in years gone by.

An overview of the pregame show is presented in Table 20.1 (page 204). Using the beginning of the program as time zero, this table pinpoints the starting time of each segment in the show in terms of hours, minutes, and seconds into the program. The program had 14 segments, each ending with a commercial break of varying duration. Commercial announcements filled slightly more than 30 minutes, over a quarter of the total running time of the program.

The typical program segment ran 4-7 minutes before a commercial interruption. The shortest segments (13 and 14) contained under a minute of program material. The longest segments (1 and 7) ran approximately 13 minutes before hitting a commercial. These segments served as the "kickoff" and "halftime show" in the structure of the pregame program.

The telecast was composed of three types of program elements. Of the first variety were the *studio reports*, which were anchored by announcer Bob Costas and featured live appearances by other reporters/commentators. The studio reports provided segues that held the rest of the program elements together. A second essential program element was the *field report*. Field reports featured "live commentary" from game announcers Dick Enberg and Merlin Olsen and color commentator Bob Griese. The third type of program element was the *feature segment*. Features were prerecorded (and edited) segments that focused on one of two things: (1) the upcoming game or (2) other things. These other things usually featured some aspect of professional football's history, football's role in American society, or both.

While all of the program elements have fantasy components that may be construed to have a political bent, the feature segments, especially those focusing away from the game, contained the most political fantasy.

The six features that contained the richest and most clearly defined political fantasies were singled out for analysis.

"FOREVER YOUNG" IN THE "UNITED NATION"

The pregame show begins with the full-screen graphic **"NBC SPORTS PRESENTS"** and dissolves to inspirational music and a second graphic showing an American flag and silver football trophy. Over this second graphic is superimposed: **"SUPER SUNDAY: AN AMERICAN CELEBRATION."** Announcer Dick Enberg begins speaking as a montage begins with an aerial shot of the stadium superimposed over crowds on city streets and fans in football stadiums. Enberg tells us:

> New Orleans, Louisiana. Super Bowl Sunday. Tens of thousands will watch in the Superdome as Chicago plays New England. A hundred million others will share the experience on television. Rich and poor, young and old, joining together on a day when a game makes our differences less important. While men play a boys' game, we stand and take sides.

Enberg's voice segues us into another set of visuals. We get a clue that this is a music video as the voice of Bob Dylan singing "Forever Young" is mixed in with Enberg's. The video (actually a short film by Bob Giraldi) superimposes the title "United Nation" as Dylan sings, and Enberg reads his last line of introduction: "Today we unite in an American celebration."

Dylan's song is interwoven throughout "United Nation," and provides the thematic base for the visuals. In this context, "Forever Young" is at once a symbol of a young nation, a celebration of strength and youth, and a call for a fountain of youth for those no longer young. Dylan amplifies the myth of America as a God-blessed country, a place where children may fulfill dreams of success through a climb to the top, and where righteousness, truth, courage, and strength win out. In short, the song paraphrases the American dream, and along with it the values that are at the heart of American existence.

"Forever Young" ties together three intercut stories in "United Nation." All of the stories take place on Super Sunday and all involve elements of American myth and ritual. The main story line finds a middle-aged Minnesotan father irked at two problems: (1) a broken television antenna, and (2) a daughter getting married. Both interfere with the father's watching the Super Bowl game, something he values highly. The groom comes to the rescue, grounding the television set's antenna to receive the game. The net result is twofold: (1) The father is happy that he can watch the game, and (2) the father now appreciates his future son-in-law. On the surface, this story line celebrates the tradition of marriage and its role in welcoming (integrating) new members into the fold of the family. However, what is different here is the relative devalua-

Table 20.1 Overview of the Super Bowl Pregame Show

1 00:00:00 Opening segment: An American Celebration
- 1.1 00:00:00 Field: announcer Dick Enberg introduces theme
- 1.2 00:00:49 Feature rock video: "United Nation"
- 1.3 00:07:26 Field: Enberg segue to studio anchor
- 1.4 00:07:26 Studio: anchor Bob Costas with game introduction
- 1.5 00:09:13 Bears Feature: reporter Ahmad Rashad
- 1.6 00:11:54 Studio: Costas/Rashad ponder Bears "overconfidence"
- 1.7 00:13:13 Commercial break 1

2 00:15:30 Pondering the Patriots
- 2.1 00:15:30 Studio: Costas segue to Patriots feature
- 2.2 00:15:56 Patriots feature: reporter Bill Macatee
- 2.3 00:18:02 Costas/Macatee ponder Patriots strategy
- 2.4 00:19:09 Commercial break 2

3 00:21:29 The Team That Time Forgot
- 3.1 00:21:29 Studio: Costas segue to "yesteryear" feature
- 3.2 00:22:16 1966 KC Chiefs feature: reporter Charley Scott
- 3.3 00:28:57 Studio: Costas segue to commercial
- 3.4 00:29:38 Commercial break 3

4 00:31:33 Game Announcers ponder key elements
- 4.1 00:31:33 Studio: Costas segue to game announcers
- 4.2 00:31:59 Field: announcers Enberg/Merlin Olsen
- 4.3 00:33:58 Studio: Costas-Enberg/Olsen Q&A interaction
- 4.4 00:34:54 Commercial break 4

5 00:37:16 Quaterbacks and Bill Cosby's Refrigerator
- 5.1 00:37:16 Studio: Costas segue to quarterback feature
- 5.2 00:37:37 Quarterback feature: Pete Axthelm reports
- 5.3 00:39:51 Studio: Costas/Axthelm ponder quarterbacks
- 5.4 00:40:53 Studio: Costas segue to Bill Cosby feature
- 5.5 00:41:10 Cosby feature: comedy relief
- 5.6 00:44:09 Commercial break 5

6 00:46:13 The Coaches
- 6.1 00:46:13 Studio: Costas segue to coaches feature
- 6.2 00:46:35 Coaches featue: Larry King reports
- 6.3 00:51:16 Studio: Costas/King ponder coaching style
- 6.4 00:52:35 Commercial break 6

7 00:54:53 Strategy and the Family Business
- 7.1 00:54:53 Studio: Costas segue to Bob Griese/Olsen
- 7.2 00:55:04 Field feature: Griese/Olsen ponder strategy
- 7.3 00:59:27 Studio: Costas segue to "intermission"
- 7.4 01:00:29 Intermission: movie theater cartoon ad for snack bar
- 7.5 01:01:19 Intermission: countdown minute with muzak
- 7.6 01:02:30 Studio: Costas segue to family feature
- 7.7 01:03:35 Family feature: Macatee reports on Sullivan family
- 7.8 01:07:48 Commercial break 7

8 01:09:08 The Bear Defense
- 8.1 01:09:08 Studio: Costas segue to Bear defense feature

Table 20.1 (continued)

Segment	Time	Content
8.2	01:09:59	Defense feature: Rashad reports on Buddy Ryan
8.3	01:13:19	Studio: Costas/Rashad ponder Bear defense
8.4	01:15:17	Commercial break 8
9	01:17:27	Rodney Dangerfield as Everyman
9.1	01:17:27	Studio: Costas segue to Dangerfield feature
9.2	01:18:10	Dangerfield feature: comedy relief
9.3	01:21:11	Studio: Costas/Axthelm segue to commercial
9.4	01:21:45	Commercial break 9
10	01:24:06	"Ain't That America"
10.1	01:24:06	Studio: Costas segue to Americana video
10.2	01:24:38	"Ain't That America" music video
10.3	01:27:49	Studio: Costas segue to commercial
10.4	01:28:20	Commercial break 10
11	01:30:15	The Great General
11.1	01:30:15	Studio: Costas segue to Vince Lombardi feature
11.2	01:30:48	Lombardi feature: Great man/more than football theme
11.3	01:37:59	Commercial break 11
12	01:40:59	Presidential Themes
12.1	01:40:59	Studio: Costas segue to President Reagan feature
12.2	01:41:23	Reagan interview: Tom Brokaw reports
12.3	01:49:29	Studio: Costas segue to commercial
12.4	01:49:50	Commercial break 12
13	01:51:51	Insider's Predictions
13.1	01:51:51	Studio: Costas with Axthelm game prediction
13.2	01:52:29	Commercial break 13
14	01:54:53	Closing Remarks and Credits
14.1	01:54:53	Studio: Costas with voice over credits
14.2	01:55:43	Commercial break 14
15	01:57:49	Game Show Begins: kickoff still 20 minutes off

tion of the marriage celebration in contrast to the Super Bowl celebration. There also seems to be a secondary theme of accepting outsiders into the family only if it helps one become further engrossed in a shared sports culture. As well, women are seen as peripheral in this story, as brides or mothers. It is clearly a male-oriented world we have entered.

The second story line in "United Nation" involves a more straightforward theme of integration. Here we see a New York businessman hurriedly getting into a cab to get to the airport so that he can meet his family in Hawaii. Again, we see the goal of bringing together the family. The businessman and his black cab driver get stuck in traffic. The "problem" is solved as the cabbie heads to Brooklyn, with the businessman in tow, to watch the Super Bowl game that is about to start. The white businessman looks unsure of himself as he enters the house and confronts a group of black friends and family members, but he then relaxes and calls his family, and the racially integrated group "unites" in watching the Super Bowl on television. The fantasy makes integration in America a simple matter.

The third story in "United Nation" is set in a veterans' hospital where the male patients are getting ready for the "biggest game of the year." The diverse mix of patients, apart from being male, symbolizes America as a "melting pot." An apparently greedy attendant named Julius is selling tickets so that the patients can see the game on television. The "problem" is that the television set is too small, and no one can see very well. The patients turn on Julius, who shrugs off their complaints because he "has work to do." The surprise ending has Julius taking the money he has collected to buy a large color set so that all can see the game. Julius becomes a hero, and the united patients watch the game. Here, as well, the fantasy theme involves integration. What may be most unfortunate is the stereotypical casting of Julius as the "Jewish businessman" who is the subject of group hate, even though the stereotype is broken later in the story. Apart from this, the fantasy of a "United Nation" under football is upheld.

In case viewers did not get such a thorough "reading" of the music video in viewing the program, announcer Dick Enberg tells them what they have seen:

> That's a symbolic tribute to the millions of you who share in the Super Bowl experience today. It's kind of unlike what you would expect at the start of a Super bowl telecast where normally there would be flying footballs and crashing padded bodies and touchdown celebrations. . . . We're going to pay tribute to what this day represents–an unannounced American holiday. For there is no time all year long where so many of us gather together around one event.

One doesn't need a magnifying glass to read the "meaning" of all this. Not only was NBC intermixing its vision of the American Dream with themes of integration, it was appealing to our sense of nationalism, and calling for a national holiday. And "unannounced" it certainly was not. The media hype had been building for two weeks at this point, and the Super Bowl pregame show had just begun.

QUARTERBACKS IN THE JUDICIAL SYSTEM

Approximately 35 minutes into the pregame show, reporter Pete Axthelm chooses to use an extended "legalistic" analogy in looking at different quarterbacks as lawyers with different styles. Axthelm's fantasy starts with the premise that "the Super Bowl can be a courtroom for quarterbacks, a chance to offer strong arguments and then deliver the proof." Axthelm has New York Jets quarterback Joe Namath overturning "the Supreme

Courts of football." Pittsburgh Steeler quarterback "Terry Bradshaw was a country lawyer, supposedly too dumb; he won his super case four times." Chicago Bears quarterback Jim McMahon is cast as "a young F. Lee Bailey, willing to flaunt tradition to win." In this fantasy, National Football League commissioner Pete Rozelle becomes the "NFL Chief Judge," and is seen on screen replete with gavel penciled in. According to Axthelm, Judge Rozelle "fined" the maverick McMahon "for wearing an advertising headband in court."

Thus the manifest fantasy that Axthelm presents takes note of differences in style, but values authority in the form of the judge (in this case, Pete Rozelle) even more. This is very much a traditional law-and-order scenario. What is most interesting about Axthelm's presentation is that it includes a latent fantasy that is almost directly in opposition to the normative values that the judicial system is there to enforce.

The oppositional fantasy is posed by the Jimmy Buffett song "Changes in Attitudes, Changes in Latitudes," which is used as a musical theme underneath Axthelm's narration. Buffett's song celebrates an alternative "partying" life-style that has little to do with following traditional rules, let alone laws. In Buffett's song, attitude changes are linked to alcohol use, and perhaps even abuse. One particular passage of the song that celebrates "craziness" is juxtaposed over Bears quarterback Jim McMahon. In the scene, McMahon is dressed in a football jersey, a head stocking, yellow gloves, and punk-style sunglasses—hardly traditional attire no matter how one looks at it. McMahon is jumping up and down, pointing, seemingly in a taunting manner, and the relative proximity of this shot to the one of "Judge Rozelle" suggests that McMahon is taunting Rozelle. As such, the oppositional fantasy celebrates yet another kind of American mythical hero—the maverick. With this added touch, Axthelm has made McMahon both more and less than a "young F. Lee Bailey." McMahon has become the crazy man defending himself in court—perhaps without a law degree—and winning the case. As well as celebrating the traditional values of the American criminal justice system, Axthelm seems to be celebrating its equally strong counterpart, the American maverick spirit.

AN IMMIGRANT FAMILY AND THE AMERICAN DREAM

America did not become a melting pot by chance. The notion that a family can come to America, work hard, and succeed is a basic component of the American Dream. The most basic of American political values concern equality, fairness, nondiscrimination, and the like. These values are heard in the retelling of the rags-to-riches stories of immigrant families. These stories have become part of American myth, as has the continued valuation of the family business in the age of multinational corporations. The modern-day continuation of that myth concerns the family that struggles to stay together and keep the family business alive.

Football mirrors these values, and in the past professional football teams were often family businesses. This has fallen by the wayside in a trend toward, corporate ownership of professional sports teams. In today's world evidence of the existence of a family-owned professional football team symbolizes that some part of that American Dream still lives.

The Super Bowl match-up between the Chicago Bears and the New England Patriots made the best of the myth that was left. It pitted two team with histories of family ownership. The Bears family history is legendary in football circles. The team was coached and owned for 60 years by "Papa" George Halas, and the team continues to be owned by his descendants. The Patriots are the family business of the Sullivan family. NBC decided to lead the second hour of its pregame show with a profile of the Sullivan family.

Reporter Bill MacAtee's feature on the "colorful and controversial" Sullivans typecasts the family as "an indomitable strain of Irish Catholics" with "fierce loyalty to one another." In MacAtee's fantasy, they are a family "battling for respect." This is graphically illustrated with film of a postgame "scuffle" that took place because of "bad blood" between Pat Sullivan, "the youngest of the Sullivan clan," and an opposing team's owner. After fisticuffs with a player on that opposing team, a bandaged and tough-talking Pat Sullivan says:

> Let me tell you something. We're just getting back for Jack Tatum and all the other crap that this football team has put on our football team for twelve years.

The way the family story is posed, Pat Sullivan is defending his family's honor and, specifically, the honor of the 70-year-old Billy Sullivan, who is cast as the "patriarch of Sullivan family." In fact, in this fantasy of protecting the family name, the patriarch later blames himself for provoking Pat's actions, because before that game he had said that he was tired of his family "being used as a punching bag."

As fantasy, the Sullivan family story serves as an analogy for the relatively recent turnabout in American nationalistic values. The fiefdom of Sullivan had been violated, and the young soldier in the clan had succeeded in restoring luster to the family crest. Like the Sullivans, many Americans have recently perceived their country as being the "punching bag" for the world. This feeling has stemmed from perceptions of a "no-win" war in Vietnam and national disgrace in Watergate, to Jimmy Carter's sense of political "malaise," and was brought to a head by the Iranian hostage crisis. To many observers, the "stand tall" image and resultant policies of the Reagan administration have replaced the symbol of "America as punching bag." The new image reflects the cinematic fantasies of Sylvester Stallone's Rocky and Rambo, and, like Pat Sullivan, restores the honor of the American "family." President Reagan's hopes for America seemingly parallel the Sullivans' hopes for the Super Bowl.

"AIN'T THAT AMERICA"

A John Cougar Mellencamp song focusing on the American Dream serves as the centerpiece for segment 10 of the pregame show. Coming at a point nearly an hour and a half into the program, Mellencamp's rock song is juxtaposed with NBC's two-pronged fantasy asking the audience to appreciate (1) America in a football context, and (2) football in an American context. The song is unabashedly introduced by studio anchor announcer Bob Costas:

> Super Sunday, an American celebration. As we said, it's almost like an undeclared national holiday and certainly our fascination with football in general and the Super Bowl in particular is a wonderful and sometimes curious piece of Americana–set now to the music of John Cougar Mellencamp.

The music video piece that follows is indeed a "curious" mixture of football images from stock footage intercut with NBC's visions of America.

The image we first see is a full-screen stylized American flag with equally stylized three-dimensional silver stars becoming larger as they move toward the viewer via special effects. Next to follow in this pattern of American stars zooming at us over red and white stripes is a larger, but equally silvered, logo for the National Football League. The logo comes at us until it fills the screen and is dissolved away as more silver stars continue to come at us. Next, the stars are interspersed with images of football "greats" that continue in a pattern of moving toward us over the backdrop of the flag's stripes. The net result is the equation of both the NFL and its "stars" with the stars and stripes that symbolize nationalistic values for all Americans. In doing this, NBC's fantasy has made professional football's heroes into American heroes. In the tautological reasoning of this fantasy, the NFL, as the organization responsible for bringing these heroes to us, is imbued with nationalistic sentiment in much the same way that the military's role is heightened at a time of celebrating war heroes.

The bulk of the visuals in the remainder of the video follow in the pattern of linking the flag to the playing of professional football. A frequent transitional device is a full-screen flag with sixteen dancing stars filling the frame. From this base, transitions are made to some of the more notable football players and coaches. In NBC's sense of football history, these are notable coaches and players because, for the most part, they have participated in a Super Bowl game. History "in the making" is shown by juxtaposing the players and coaches of the upcoming contest with their counterparts in the most significant of these games in the past. Thus, by participating in the construction of a hero-based history, the fantasy group is also allowed to participate in the making of history.

With John Cougar Mellencamp's lyrics relying on a chorus that is based on the "Star Spangled Banner" axiom of America as "home of the free," nationalistic values seem to dominate this song. However, this is still rock and roll, and there are some oppositional themes being posed as well. Beginning with the title of the song, "Pink Houses," Mellencamp provides a counterpoint to the idealized visions of Americana through football that NBC apparently seeks to emphasize. NBC avoids revealing the song's title, which Mellencamp uses in a secondary refrain as shorthand for the parceled-down dream that America leaves for its working class.

When such oppositional references come up in the song, NBC presents imagery that symbolically says these little houses are a thing of the past. We see short glimpses of stylized "color-tinted" houses that look like hand-painted postcards from an era predating color photography. We see romanticized country clapboard houses, log cabins, trailers, and even row houses and other small dwellings quickly mixed in with an occasional mansion. Mellencamp, however, is not talking about the past. For him, the problems that exist today call into question the myth of American Dream.

Debunking other American myths in the song, Mellencamp poses as absurd the common wisdom that anyone can grow up to be president. NBC wrestles with Mellencamp's assertions in an interesting fashion. When Mellencamp sings of a boy who is going to grow up to be president, NBC shows us the smiling Republican congressman from Buffalo, Jack Kemp, who just happened to be a former NFL quarterback. At the point of this telecast, Kemp was widely regarded in the press as a "presidential hopeful" of some promise. However, because of lines that follow in Mellencamp's song, it is ambiguous as to whether NBC is "endorsing" Kemp for the presidency. But clearly the association of Kemp with the main story line of football heroes in the land of the free did not injure his chances for the presidential nomination.

It is interesting to note that almost all of the nonfootball images accompanying Mellencamp's song look as though they were produced by artificial means, most likely by a sophisticated computer graphics machine. Only three scenes contain nonfootball people doing something in America. One is a two-shot sequence of bikini-clad young women—one shot showing a frontal view of two women "hanging out" at the beach and the other shot showing two women dancing together at what appears to be a party. Bikini-clad women may not be such an alarming novelty, but this is the first time we have focused on any women in this program since the "bride" in the "United Nation" video that opened the program. Thus it has taken an hour and a half to get from bride to bikini. Even on this "super" day dedicated to celebrating some of the strongest of male athletes, this is less than "super," especially if one is to take seriously NBC's themes concerning integration, family cohesiveness, and a system of American justice that stresses fairness and equality.

THE GREAT MAN THEORY OF COACHING

In closing out the last half hour of the pregame program, NBC continues to weave its nationalistic fantasy with two segments focusing on leadership. In recent presidential elections, "leadership" has become a political issue, one that is central to the success of a candidate. In developing themes about leadership, NBC first profiles Vince Lombardi, the late coach of the Green Bay Packers, and follows this segment with an "exclusive" interview with President Reagan.

Leading into the commercial break after which the Lombardi segment will appear, anchor announcer Bob Costas's "promo" sets a stage for "understanding" the Packer coach:

> When we come back an affectionate remembrance of the man for whom the Super Bowl trophy is named, the legendary and sometimes misunderstood figure—Vince Lombardi—of the Green Bay Packers.

After the commercial break, and as the segment nears, Costas continues:

> The Lombardi Trophy, that's what these Bears and Patriots are vying for. And the man whose name is inscribed on that trophy led the Packers to victory in the first two Super Bowls. The late Vince Lombardi, regarded by most as the finest coach of his era. Regarded by his players as something more than that.

As it turns out in this fantasy, that "something more" than a coach that Lombardi turned out to be was a "great leader" or "great man." As historian Daniel Boorstin (1961) has alluded to in his book, *The Image*, "great man" theories are a common, but uncomplex, way to explain history. In the fantasy here, great leaders are great leaders in more than one sphere. For NBC, Lombardi, the great coach, becomes one of the great philosophers of life. The feature segment is structured as a testimonial in which Lombardi's better-known players attest to the twofold "greatness" that their former coach possessed.

The clear-cut, or manifest, "greatness" in Lombardi was in his being a tough coach who demanded respect from his players. His coaching philosophy is summed up by the often-quoted Lombardi-ism: "Winning is not everything, it is the only thing." This "win at all costs" coaching philosophy is seen many times over in the course of the segment on Lombardi. However, in this Lombardi fantasy, winning comes about as a result of pride. Pride is stressed in a sequence where Lombardi introduces himself and his philosophy to the team. Shot from a low angle that emphasizes Lombardi as an authority figure, the strict "disciplinarian" tone of Lombardi's voice is embellished by a green tinge to the color film. Lombardi emerges as a symbolic Marine Corps sergeant speaking to his recruits:

> My name is Vince Lombardi. I want to welcome you to the Green Bay Packers. If you have the dedication, the total commitment, and the pride necessary to become part of this team that has been built around pride, you will stay here.

The less clear-cut, or latent, "greatness" in Lombardi is brought about largely through the hindsight of his former players. The extension of Lombardi's greatness beyond football and into life is best summed up by Bart Starr, a longtime quarterback on Lombardi's teams:

> The quality of coach Lombardi that enabled us to transcend the football field and be successful in other fields as well was the fact that he never talked in terms of football, he talked in terms of life.

In the fantasy that is passed along here, Lombardi's greatness in passing along the values for a successful life was "loved" by his players. As former player Fuzzy Thurston put it, "I sure loved him and I still miss him today as much as I ever missed anybody in my life."

Even though the major fantasy theme poses Lombardi as a multifaceted and loved leader, it can be seen that NBC's fantasy about Lombardi's "greatness" is based on a perception of him as a "common man." As the very beginning of the segment, we hear an inspirational musical theme as we see the silver Lombardi Trophy glimmering with light on a black background. It is the music that adds meaning to the trophy and carries the visual transition to an extreme close-up of Lombardi, who is about to speak. By no mere happenstance, the music that plays in the background is American composer Aaron Copland's "Fanfare for the Common Man." In this setting, we eagerly await Lombardi's first words:

> Unless a man believes in himself and makes a total commitment to his career and puts everything he has into it—his mind, his body, and his heart—what's life worth to him?

In total, the fantasy about Lombardi takes on mythlike proportions in the world of professional football. NBC's presentation of it chains the fantasy to the world outside. It is a world where a "great leader" or a "great man" is hard to find.

THE PRESIDENT AS THE PRESIDENT

A mythlike act like the Vince Lombardi segment is undoubtedly a difficult act to follow. In keeping with the overall theme of Super Bowl XX as "An American Celebration," NBC presents, as a closing act for the Super Bowl pregame show, a headliner whose mere presence on stage signifies the legitimacy of such a thematic choice. Symbolically riding on the coattails of the Lombardi myth, President Ronald Reagan appears on stage. The appearance of the president of the United States attaches national importance to any event. In this case, NBC presents a live interview with President Reagan at the White House. The appearance of the president on this program tautologically reifies the nationalistic themes that NBC has worked so hard to develop over the duration of the pregame program. Here is a living, breathing symbol of all that is American, and he is on this program "celebrating" America and the Super Bowl. In one fell swoop the rhetorical vision that has been constructed out of fantasy becomes reality.

Studio anchor announcer Bob Costas provides the background for the president's appearance:

> Like most of the rest of us, President Ronald Reagan is a football fan and he's got a varied background in the sport. The chief executive played some college football, was later a sportscaster in Iowa, and of course he had the role of the Gipper in the film biography of Notre Dame Coach Knute Rockne.

After this introduction, we see Tom Brokaw and the president sitting in comfortable chairs in the library of the White House. The tone of the interview is set by the benign nature of the opening series of questions. Brokaw inquires as to which team the president favors in the Super Bowl game. Amplifying the themes of fairness and equality posed in earlier segments, the president declines to pick a favorite. Shortly thereafter, a question about the national holiday status of Super Bowl Sunday is posed by Brokaw:

> Super Bowl Sunday has become a kind of undeclared national holiday. Do you think occasions like this help to shape our national character or are they just kind of entertaining diversions from things like the deficit and terrorism and Kadafi?

The president responds:

> Well I think it's typically American that we can have or be diverted by things like this from the serious problems. I think it's part of the American personality and I know that other countries take athletes seriously too, but there is something different about it in America. It's so much a part of American life that I think it's part of our personality.

In essence here, the president has endorsed the national holiday fantasy by giving the presidential seal of approval to being "diverted" from "serious problems" by the Super Bowl game. The president has extended the fantasy being chained here to some degree. Not only is such diversion officially endorsed with a stamp of nationalistic value, but such an official endorsement may raise questions about the patriotism of those Americans who choose not to participate in the Super Bowl fantasy. In total, the president had taken one more step in the direction of putting the Super Bowl fantasy at one with American culture.

Brokaw's interview with the president rambles on for over eight minutes, making it the longest feature segment in the pregame program. The bulk of the interview concerns Reagan's football playing days, his role playing the part of the Gipper and some related privy knowledge of Notre Dame coach Knute Rockne, and his days as a sports announcer. At only one time during the interview does Brokaw press the president with an overt political question. In this instance, Brokaw does so in such a creatively round-about fashion that he may succeed in further accelerating the fantasies being chained about football and politics:

> Mr. President, football is a metaphor for so many things in American life, including politics. Now at the end of this game today one team is going to be at a deficit situation and all those players are going to face a very taxing year in 1986. You're about to deliver the State of the Union Address. Are you going to put the American people through the same experience in 1986—a taxing year?

Brokaw's question so fully integrates football and political fantasies that it is nearly impossible to decipher what is football and what is politics. The president, however, easily distinguishes between the two and knows that this is a "holiday" and no time to answer questions about either the State of the Union Address or taxes. The heretofore blurred line between politics and sports is clearly redrawn by the president.

Other evidence of the president's "political" control over the pregame "sports" program can be seen in Brokaw's attempt to finish the interview. Brokaw poses to the president: "Final chance, do you want to pick a score or a team?" The president replies, "No, but do I have a second so I can tell you a little incident in my memories of football?" Brokaw responds, "Sure, absolutely," much as a person would respond to the proverbial 800 pound gorilla asking to sit in one's favorite easy chair. The president then launches into a story about his audition as a sports announcer that lasts approximately two more minutes.

This incident clarifies some of the more realistic aspects of the sports and politics fantasy. A president who knows the rules of broadcasting as well as the rules of politics can control the fantasy-building conduit, at least for a limited time. Also, any country having a president who has as one of his more visible attributes the fact that he is a former sportscaster, cannot help being fenced in by a fantasy chain link fence that surrounds politics with sports and sports with politics. The president is merely demonstrating which of the two elements in the fantasy hold the key to the reality gate. In this fantasy, as reality approaches, politics holds that key.

CLOSING THE GATE

The political fantasy type that pertains to sports programming has been chained out to a large degree in this limited analysis of six segments that appeared on NBC's 1986 Super Bowl pregame show. The nationalistic fantasy that was developed in the course of this program was based on themes central to the American Dream. Among the more prevalent of these were themes concerning racial and ethnic integration, national and family unity, due process of law, rugged individualism in the form of the maverick, hard work, family businesses, patriotism, heroism, simplicity in the form of the common man, equality, the multifaceted character of great leaders, commitment and pride, and last, but not least, the relationship of sports to American character. Taken together, this conglomeration of fantasy themes builds a chain link fence through which professional football, and perhaps all mediated portrayals of sports in America, may be better understood.

If this political chain link fence can be seen as formed by the program elements, NBC added a gate to that fence in the form of nationalistic promotional announcements for the network's sports programming. Peppered throughout the two hours of the program, these announcements were of varying lengths, but all shared a rapid-fire visual style highlighting well-known American athletes (especially Olympic athletes) to a bouncy tune proclaiming NBC as the American choice in sports programming. Through this, NBC was attempting to stake a claim on the political fantasies that were woven during the program itself. This rather parasitic relationship between the general network goals and the specific program was striking. If the fantasy chain link fence that was constructed in the program material was in any sense successful in containing our perceptions of the Super Bowl game in a nationalistic pen, then NBC wanted to close the gate and contain us within that fantasy for the long haul.

The only program element that could tamper with the political fantasy being constructed here was political reality in the form of the president. Symbolically holding the key to the gate, the president seized control over the pattern of fantastical discourse being fashioned by the media reporters and commentators. President Reagan opened the gate and walked in, adding his story to the political fantasy as the gate closed behind him. What lingered, however, was the knowledge that the president, and political reality generally, can intervene at any point in the political fantasies that mediated sports may conjure up.

The analyses here have shown the wide range of political fantasies embodied in the Super Bowl pregame show. These fantasies were sandwiched in at either end of the show by fantasies of youth, albeit slightly different ones. The show opened to the theme of Bob Dylan's "Forever Young," and essentially closed with a youthful-looking but nearly 75-year-old president one-upping NBC's senior news anchorperson in an interview setting.

The youthful "bread" holding together the political fantasy in this "sports" program helps to remind us that America is a young country, as well as a country that values and frequently celebrates youth. Professional sports are played by comparatively young people. Collegiate and Olympic sports typically feature even younger athletes. The new health and exercise consciousness is propelled, to some degree, by the desire to stay youthful looking and by fears of getting old. One of the major concerns about the presidential candidacy of Ronald Reagan was his age. However, as his youthful appearance belied stereotypes of old age, the issue seemingly disappeared into a fountain of youth.

Similarly, it is clear that the fantasy themes that grew with the participants of the Super Bowl pregame show had little to do with reality. This point was not lost on *Los Angeles Times* television critic Howard Rosenberg (1986), who bemoaned NBC's packaging of the Super Bowl with a double scoop helping of Americana:

> The Super Bowl? That's no American celebration. That's a marketing phenom, an incredibly successful sales job on Americans to convince us that there is something symbolically patriotic about a game between two professional football teams that have played previously and are playing again so that they, the National Football League, TV and sponsors can score a big payday. (p. 1)

In Rosenberg's cautioning against confusing the game with "America, the Beautiful" there is recognition that fantasy themes, chains, and the chain link fences that they yield may be full of contradictions. Also, they may fly in the face of reason or observable fact. The aim is to construct an altered reality that has intrinsic, but not necessarily practical, value. As Jhally (1984) has suggested, because sports celebrate idealized structures of reality in a ritualistic manner, they bridge an essential social dialectic of fantasy and reality. Mediated sport may accelerate the workings of such a dialectic by providing somewhat uniform fantasies. This study is merely suggestive of how the merger of political and sports fantasies breeds uniform interpretations about the significance of both elements in American culture.

NOTES

1. It is not my intention to fall into the great crevasse of disagreement about Bormann's (1972) fantasy theme analysis. Although it is admittedly applied in a playful way here, my reading of Bormann's approach is based on his seminal statement about it, not on the controversy that followed.
2. While the notion of a "fantasy chain link fence" is playfully inspired by Bormann's (1972) use of ambiguously overlapping terms, he is no way responsible for striking such a phrase.

REFERENCES

Balbus, I. (1975). Politics as sports: The political ascendancy of the sports metaphor in America. *Monthly Review*, 26, 26-39.

Bales, R. F. (1950). *Interaction process analysis: A method for the study of small groups*. Cambridge, MA: Addison Wesley.

Boorstin, D. J. (1961). *The image: A guide to pseudo-events in America.* New York: Atheneum.

Bormann, E. G. (1972). Fantasy and rhetorical vision: The rhetorical criticism of social reality. *Quarterly Journal of Speech*, 58, 396-407.

Bormann, E. G. (1977). Fetching good out of evil: A rhetorical use of calamity. *Quarterly Journal of Speech*, 63, 130-139.

Bormann, E. G., Koester, J., & Bennett, J. (1978). Political cartoons and salient rhetorical fantasies: An empirical analysis of the '76 presidential campaign. *Communication Monographs*, 45, 317-329.

Bryant, J., Brown, D., Comisky, P. W., & Zillmann, D. (1982). Sports and spectators: Commentary and appreciation. *Journal of Communication*, 32, 109-119.

Bryant, J., Comisky, P., & Zillmann, D. (1977). Drama in sports commentary. *Journal of Communication*, 27, 140-149.

Buell, J. (1980). Superhype. *Progressive*, 44, 66.

Buscombe, E. (1975). *Football on television.* London: British Film Institute.

Carey, J. 1976). How media shape campaigns. *Journal of Communication*, 26, 50-57.

Comisky, P., Bryant, J., & Zillmann, D. (1977). Commentary as a substitute for action. *Journal of Communication*, 27, 150-153.

Eitzen, S., & Sage, G. H. (1978). *Sociology of American sport.* Dubuque, IA: Wm. C. Brown.

Gantz, W. (1981). An explorations of viewing motives and behaviors associated with television sports. *Journal of Broadcasting*, 25, 263-275.

Goffman, E. (1974). *Frame analysis.* Philadelphia: University of Pennsylvania Press.

Goldstein, J. H., & Bredemeier, B. J. (1977). Socialization: Some basic issues. *Journal of Communication*,27, 154-159.

Goodwin, M. (1986, January 20). NBC's game plan is most extensive. *New York Times*, p. C15.

Jhally, S. (1984). The spectacle of accumulation: Material and cultural factors in the evolution of the sports/media complex. *Insurgent Sociologist*, 3, 41-57.

Loy, J. W. (1978). The cultural system of sport. *Quest Monograph*, 29.

Morse, M. (1983). Sport on television: Replay and display, In E. A. Kaplan (Ed.). *Regarding television: Critical approaches–an anthology* (pp. 44-66). Frederick, MD: University Publications of America.

Nimmo, D. & Combs, J. E. (1983). *Mediated political realities.* New York: Longman.

Nixon, H. L. (1982). Idealized functions of sport: Religious and political socialization through sport. *Journal of Sport and Social Issues*, 6, 1-11.

Nowell-Smith, G. (1981). Television football-the world. In F. Bennett (Ed.). *Popular television and film* (pp. 159-170). London: British Film Institute.

Parente, P. (1979). The interdependence of sports and television. *Journal of Communication*, 29, 94-102.

Pooley, J. C., & Webster, A. V. (1976). The interdependence of sports, politics and economics. In A. Yiannakis, T. McIntyre, M. Melnick, & D. Hardt (Eds.). *Sport sociology: Contemporary themes* (pp. 35-42). Dubuque, IA: Kendall-Hunt.

Prisuta, R. H. (1979). Televised sports and political values. *Journal of Communication*, 29, 94-102.

Real, M. R. (1975, Winter). Super Bowl: Mythic spectacle. *Journal of Communication*, 25, 31-43.

Rosenberg, H. (1986, January 28). NBC's Super Bowl runneth over 'n' over 'n' . . . *Los Angeles Times*, part VI, pp. 1, 8.

Sapolsky, B. S., & Zillmann, D. (1978). Enjoyment of a televised sport contest under different conditions of viewing. *Perceptual and Motor Skills*, 46, 29-30.

Snyder, E. E., & Spreitzer, E. (1978). *Social aspects of sport.* Englewood Cliffs, NJ: Prentice Hall.

Stephenson, W. (1967). *The play theory of mass communication.* Chicago: University of Chicago Press.

Trujillo, N., & Ekdom, L. R. (1985). Sportswriting and American cultural values: The 1984 Chicago Cubs. *Critical Studies in Mass Communication*, 2, 262-281.

Tuchman, G. (1978). *Making news: A study in the construction of reality*. New York: Free Press.
Vescey, G. (1986, January 20). Fans' moment of truth. *New York Times*, p. C15.
Williams, B. R. (1977). The structure of televised football. *Journal of Communication*, 27, 133-139.

21. *Separating the Men from the Girls: The Gendered Language of Televised Sports*

MICHAEL A. MESSNER, MARGARET CARLISLE DUNCAN, AND KERRY JENSEN

INTRODUCTION

Feminist scholars have argued that in the twentieth century, the institution of sport has provided men with a homosocial sphere of life through which they have bolstered a sagging ideology of male superiority.[1] Through the exclusion of women, and the association of males with physical competence, strength, power, and even violence, sport has provided a basis through which men have sought to reconstitute an otherwise challenged masculine hegemony (Bryson, 1987; Hall, 1988; Kidd, 1987; Messner, 1988; Theberge, 1981; Whitson, 1990)

But starting with the 1972 passage of Title IX in the U.S., athletic participation of school-age girls increased dramatically. In 1971, only 294,015 girls participated in high school sports, compared with 3,666,917 boys. By the 1989-90 academic year, there were 1,858,659 girls participating in high school sports, compared with 3,398,192 boys.[2] Increased numerical participation in sports by girls and women has been accompanied by changing attitudes as well. A nationwide survey found large majorities of parents and children agreeing that "sports are no longer for boys only" (Wilson & Women's Sports Foundation, 1988). With increases in opportunities for female athletes, including expanded youth programs, better and earlier coaching, and increases in scholarships for college women athletes, some dramatic improvements in female athletic performance have resulted. In fact, the "muscle gap"—the degree of difference between male and female athletic performance in measurable sports like swimming and track and field—has closed considerably in the past fifteen years (Crittenden, 1979; Dyer, 1983; Kidd, 1990). In short, the dramatic increase in female athleticism has begun to challenge the assumption that

SOURCE: Michael A. Messner, Margaret Carlisle Duncan, and Kerry Jensen, "Separating the Men from the Girls: The Gendered Language of Televised Sports," *Gender and Society*, 1992, Sage Publications. Reprinted by permission of Sage Publications.

sport is and should be a "male world." Organized sports, though still dominated by men at nearly all levels, has in the past two decades become a "contested terrain" of gender relations (Birrell, 1987/1988; Messner, 1988).

Much of the continued salience of sport as an institutional site for the construction and legitimation of masculine power lies in its role as mass-mediated spectacle (Clarke & Clarke, 1982; Hargreaves, 1986; Willis, 1982). There *has* been a boom in female athletic participation, but the sports media has been very slow to reflect it. Bryant's (1980) two-year content analysis of two newspapers revealed that only 4.4% of total column inches devoted to sports focussed on women's sports. Graydon (1983) observed that in the early 1980's, over 90% of sports reporting covered men's sports. Rintala and Birrell's (1984) analysis of *Young Athlete* magazine, and Duncan and Sayaovong's (1990) examination of *Sports Illustrated for Kids* magazine revealed that visual images of male athletes in these magazines tend to outnumber those of female athletes by a roughly two-to-one ratio. Moreover, text and visual images tend to frame female and male athletes "as fundamentally and essentially different," and thus to support stereotypical notions of natural differences between the sexes (Duncan & Sayaovong, 1990:91). In a part of our study (not dealt with in this paper), we examined four major metropolitan daily newspapers and found that over a three-month period in 1990, 81% of all sports column inches were devoted exclusively to men's sports, 3.5% covered women's sports, and 15.5% covered both men's and women's sports, or gender-neutral topics. We also examined six weeks of a leading television newscast, and found that 92% of sports news time was devoted exclusively to men's sports, 5% covered women's sports, and 3% covered gender-neutral topics. This sort of ignoring or underreporting of existing women's events contributes to the continuation of what Gerbner (1978) called "the symbolic annihilation" of women's sports.

Despite the paucity of coverage of women's sports by the media, there are some recent signs of increased coverage, especially on cable television (Eastman & Meyer, 1989). If there is indeed a "window of opportunity" for increased coverage of women's sports on television, the question of *how* women's and men's sports are covered becomes crucial. To date, very few analyses of the quality of live, televised, play-by-play coverage of women's sports have been conducted. Studies of 1970's and 1980's, revealed that women athletes (when they were reported on television at all) were likely to be overtly trivialized, infantilized, and sexualized (Boutilier & San Giovanni, 1983; Duncan, 1990; Dyer, 1987; Felshin, 1974). Even excellent performances by women athletes were likely to be framed "ambivalently" by sports commentators (Duncan & Hasbrook, 1988).

We were interested in comparing how live, play-by-play television sports commentators talk about women's sports and women athletes with how they talk about men's sports and men athletes. We constructed our research design, in part, from the now-vast feminist literature on gender and language. In short, this literature demonstrates that the ways men and women talk—and the ways we are talked about—are deeply gendered. For instance, a woman secretary would likely use the formal "Mr.," along with the last name, when speaking to her male boss, while he would probably feel free to refer to her by her first name. This kind of language convention tends to (often subtly) mark gender difference (and, in the above example, social class difference as well) in ways that support and reinforce the power and privilege of "dominants" over "subordinates." The micropolitical realm of face-to-face interaction and language both reflects and constructs the micropolitical realm of unequal power relations between groups (Henley, 1977, 1987; Lakoff, 1975; Miller & Swift, 1977; Thorne, Kramarae & Henley, 1985; Schultz, 1975; Spender, 1980).

DESCRIPTION OF RESEARCH

Our aim was to utilize feminist insights on gendered language to examine the ways that television commentators talk about women's and men's sports. We chose to examine two sports where televised coverage of women's and men's contests could be compared: basketball and tennis. For a number of years, women's tennis has been highly visible on television, but women's college basketball is only recently beginning to be televised (albeit mostly on cable t.v., and often on late-night tape delay). We reasoned that a comparison of the more "established" televised sport of tennis with the relative "newcomer" of women's basketball might be revealing.

Live televised coverage of the 1989 women's and men's NCAA final four basketball tournaments were compared and analyzed. (It should be noted that we chose the "final four," rather than regular-season games because there are so few women's regular season games actually broadcast on television.) This amounted to three women's games and three men's games, including introductions/lead-ins and halftime shows. We also examined the four final days of televised coverage of the 1989 U.S. Open tennis tournament. Televised coverage consisted of four men's singles matches (two quarterfinals, one semifinal, and the final), three women's singles matches (two semis and the final), one men's doubles match (the final), two women's doubles matches (a semi and the final), and one mixed doubles match (the final).

Three general questions guided our analysis: First, do commentators overtly trivialize and/or sexualize women's sports and individual women athletes in the ways that previous analysts have identified? Second, do sports commentators speak about women's and men's athletic contests differently? In particular, to what extent (if any) are women's and men's events verbally "gender marked" (e.g., "the *women's* national championship")? Third, do commentators speak of individual women and men athletes differently? For instance, are women athletes referred to as "girls" or as "women"? Are men athletes referred to as "boys" or as "men"?

First, we recorded the basketball games and tennis matches on videotape, and conducted a pilot study of the tapes. The pilot study had two outcomes: First the research design was fine-tuned. In particular, a preliminary list of specific qualitative and quantitative questions was constructed. Next, we developed standardized ways of analyzing the verbal commentary. Then, the research assistant viewed all of the tapes and compiled a detailed record of her observations. Next, all of the tapes were independently viewed and analyzed by one of the investigators, who then added her written analysis to that of the research assistant. Finally, the data was compiled and analyzed by the two investigators, using both sets of written descriptions of the tapes, and by viewing portions of the tapes once again.

Our data revealed very little of the overtly sexist commentary that has been observed in past research. Women's sports and women athletes were not overtly trivialized in tennis or in basketball commentary. And though camera angles at times may have subtly framed women athletes (especially in tennis) as sexual objects in ways that were not symmetrical with the ways men were framed, the verbal commentary did not frame women in this way. However, we did find two categories of differences in the verbal commentary: (1) Gender marking; (2) A "hierarchy of naming" by gender, and to a certain extent by race.

WOMEN MARKED AS OTHER

In women's basketball, gender was constantly marked, both verbally and through the use of graphics. We were continually reminded that we were watching the "*Women's* final four," the "NCAA *Women's* National Championship Game," that these were "some of the best *women's* college basketball teams," that coach Pat Summit "is a legend in *women's* basketball," that "this NCAA *women's* semifinal is brought to you by . . . ." Gender was also marked through the use of graphics in the women's games which CBS broadcasted, but not in the ESPN game. The CBS logo marked the women's championship game: "NCAA Women's National Championship," as did their graphics above game scores. ESPN's graphic did not mark gender: "NCAA Semifinal." As Table 21-1 indicates, over the course of the three women's games, there were 28 instances of graphic, and 49 cases of verbal gender marking, for a total of 77 instances of gender marking. This meant that gender was being marked an average of 25.6 times per women's game.

During the women's games, when commentators were discussing the next day's men's games, the men's games were sometimes gender marked (e.g.: "the *men's* championship game will be played tomorrow.") But

Table 21-1 Gender Marking in Basketball (three women's games, three men's games)

	Women	*Men*
Verbal	49	0
Graphic	28	0
Total	77 (25.6)	0

during the men's basketball games, we observed no instances of gender marking, either verbal or graphic. Men's games were always referred to as universal, both verbally and in on-screen graphic logos (e.g., "The NCAA National Championship Game," "The Final Four," etc.).

Women's and men's tennis matches were verbally gender-marked in a roughly equitable manner (e.g., "Men's doubles finals," "Women's singles semifinals," etc.). Verbal descriptions of athletes, though, revealed a tendency to gender mark women, not men. For instance, in the mixed doubles match, the commentators stated several times that Rick Leach is "one of the best doubles players in the world," while Robyn White was referred to as one of "the most animated girls on the circuit." An instance of graphic gender marking in tennis which we found notable was the tendency by CBS to display a pink on-screen graphic for the women's matches, and a blue on-screen graphic for the men's matches.

How might we interpret these observations? Stanley (1977) suggest that although *asymmetrical* gender marking tends to mark women as "other," *symmetrical* gender marking is not necessarily oppressive. In fact, she argues that the move toward a totally gender-neutral language may serve to further render women invisible. This would probably be the case if the language of sports reporting and commentary became gender neutral. In fact, in certain cases (in the daily television program, for instance) gender marking is probably necessary to clarify what the viewer will be tuning in to watch. We observed this sort of gender-marking in tennis, where women's and men's matches (though not always women and men *athletes*) were verbally gender-marked in a roughly symmetrical manner. The rough symmetry of gender-marking in tennis might be explained by the fact that the women's and men's tennis tournaments were being played in the same venue, with coverage often cutting back and forth to women's, men's, and mixed-doubles matches. In this context, symmetrical gender-marking probably provides a necessary sense of clarity for the viewers, though the pink (for women) and blue (for men) graphic on-screen logos tended to mark gender in manner which reinforced conventional gender stereotypes.

Table 21-2 Gender Marking in Basketball (three women's games, three men's games, including gender-marked team names)

	Women	*Men*
Verbal	98	0
Graphic	81	0
Total	179 (59.7)	0

By contrast, the women's and men's basketball games were played in different cities, on different nights. And our data revealed a dramatic asymmetry in the commentary: Women's games were verbally and graphically gender marked an average of 25.6 times per game, while men's games were never gender marked. We did not include gender-marked team names (e.g., "Lady Techsters, Lady Tigers, Lady Volunteers") in these tabulations because we reasoned that team names are the responsibility of their respective universities, not the networks or commentators. Nevertheless, gender-marked team names have recently been criticized as "contributing to the maintenance of dominance within college athletics by defining women athletes and women's athletic programs as second class and trivial" (Eitzen & Baca Zinn, 1989:362). In several colleges and universities in recent years, faculty and students have attempted to change gender-marked women's team names (Eitzen & Baca Zinn, 1990). In the three women's basketball games which we examine, team names were gender marked 53 times graphically, 49 times verbally (a total of 102 times). As Table 21-2 reveals, when we add these numbers to our original tabulations, we see that the combination of on-screen graphics, verbal commentary, and team names and logos amounted to a constant barrage of gender marking in the women's games: gender was marked in some fashion an average of 59.7 times per women's game. By contrast, the men's games were always simply referred to as "the national championship games," etc. As a result, the men's games and tournament were presented as the norm, the universal, while the women's were continually marked as the other, derivative (and by implication, inferior) to the men's.

A GENDERED HIERARCHY OF NAMING

There were stark contrasts between how men athletes and women athletes were referred to by commentators. This was true both in tennis and in basketball. First, and as we had expected, women were commonly referred to as "girls" as "young ladies," and as "women." (Often the naming of women athletes was ambivalent. For instance, Steffi Graf was

Table 21-3 First and Last Name Use in Tennis Commentary (totals [percentages], by sex)

	First Only	*Last Only*	*First & Last*
Women	304 (52.7)	166 (28.8)	107 (18.5)
Men	44 (7.8)	395 (69.8)	127 (22.4)

referred to as "the wonder girl of women's tennis.") By contrast, the male athletes, *never* referred to as "boys," were referred to as "men," "young men," or "young fellas." Second, when athletes were named, commentators used the first name only of the women far more commonly than for the men. This difference was most stark in tennis commentary, as revealed Table 21-3.

In basketball, the degree of difference in the use of first names of women and men players was not as dramatic, but the pattern was similar. In the three women's basketball games, we counted 31 incidents of women athletes being referred to by their first name only. This occurred 19 times in the men's games.

How do we interpret these differences in how commentators talk about male and female athletes? After these research findings were released at a national press conference, Diana Nyad, one of the USA Network tennis commentators, stated that the difference in first and last name use in women's and men's tennis commentary is not due to "sexism," but is simply a result of the fact that the women tennis players are more likely to be "teen-aged girls," while the men players are likely to be older (Herbert, 1990). This was an interesting response, given that in the tennis matches we examined in our study, the range of ages for the male players was 19-29, with the mean age 22.8, and the range of ages for female players was 19-32, with the mean age 24.0. In the NCAA basketball tournaments, all of the female and male players were college students, and roughly the same age. Clearly, actual age differences do not explain commentators' tendency to refer to women athletes as "girls," "young ladies," and by first name only.

Research has demonstrated that "dominants" (either by social class, age, occupational position, race, or gender) are more commonly referred to by their last names (often prefaced by titles such as "Mr."). "Dominants" generally have license to refer to "subordinates" (younger people, employees, lower class people, ethnic minorities, women, etc.) by their first names (Henley, 1977; McConnell-Ginet, 1978; Rubin, 1981; Wolfson & Manes, 1980). The practice of referring more "formally" to dominants, and more "informally" (or "endearingly") to subordinates linguistically grants the former adult status, while marking the latter in an infantilizing way. And research suggests that these linguistic differences both reflect and (re)construct inequality. For instance, Brannon (1978) had 462 college students read a story describing a female's application for a high-level executive position, in which she was referred to either as a "girl" or as a "woman." Students' ratings of personality traits described the "woman" as more tough, brilliant, mature, and dignified, more qualified to be hired, and more deserving of a higher salary than the "girl." Similarly, the term "lady" tends to "evoke a standard of propriety, correct behavior, and elegance" (Miller & Swift, 1977), and "carries overtones recalling the age of chivalry, implying that women are helpless and cannot do things for themselves," all of which are characteristics which are "decidedly unathletic" (Eitzen & Baca Zinn, 1990: 5-6). It can be concluded that tennis commentators' tendency to call women athletes "girls" and "young ladies," and their utilization of the first name only of women athletes (52.7% of the time) far more commonly than men athletes (7.8% of the time) reflects the lower status of women athletes. Moreover, it is reasonable to speculate that this language is likely to be received by viewers in such a way that it reinforces any already-existing negative attitudes or ambivalences about women's sports and women athletes.

We can speculate as to why the contrast in gendered patterns of naming was not as stark in basketball as it was in tennis. Perhaps since female tennis players have traditionally been stereotyped in more conventionally "feminine" ways than other female athletes, there is more of a (probably unconscious) tendency for commentators to view them (and talk about them) in an infantilizing manner. Moreover, women tennis players are often participating in the same venue as the men (and in the case of mixed doubles, in the very same *matches* with the men), and perhaps this contributes to an unconscious tendency to verbally separate them from the men by naming them differently. By contrast, female basketball players are participating in a traditionally defined "male" sport that requires a good deal of physically aggressive body-contact. Perhaps as a result, commentators are less likely to (again, probably unconsciously) view them and talk about them using conventionally "feminine" and infantilizing language. And since the women's basketball games are being constantly and thoroughly gender-marked, both graphically and verbally, there is little chance that their games will be confused with those of the men. There may therefore be less of an unconscious tendency on the part of commentators to verbally differentiate them from the men in terms of how they are named.

In addition to the tendency to linguistically infantilize women, while granting men athletes adult status, the quality of commentators' verbal attributions of strength and weakness, success and failure, for women's and men's events also tended to differ. In basketball, verbal attributions of strength to women were often stated in ambivalent language which undermined or neutralized the words conveying power and strength: "big girl," "she's tiny, she's small, but so effective under the boards," "her little jump hook," etc. A difference in descriptions of basketball coaches was also noted. Joe Ciampi (male) "yells" at his team, while Pat Summit (female) was described twice in the Auburn vs. Tennessee game as "screaming" off the bench. Men coaches were not described as "screaming," a term which often implies lack of control, powerlessness, even hysteria.

In tennis, "confidence" was very frequently used to describe strength for women, but not so often for men. We speculated that confidence is considered a "given" for men, but an attribute for which women players must constantly strive. Even very strong descriptors, for women, were often framed ambivalently: "That young lady Graf is relentless," or sexualized: "Sabatini has put together this first set with such naked aggression." And whereas for women, spectacular shots were sometimes referred to as "lucky," for the men, there were constant references to the imposition of their wills on the games (and on opponents). In men's doubles, for example, "You can feel McEnroe imposing his will all over this court. I mean not just with Woodford but Flach and Seguso. He's just giving them messages by the way he's standing at the net, the way he kind of swaggers between points."

There was little ambivalence in the descriptions of men: There are "big" guys with "big" forehands, who play "big games." There was a constant suggestion of male power and agency in the commentary. Even descriptions of men's weaknesses were commonly framed in a language of agency: "He created his own error. . . ." Discussion of men's "nervousness" was often qualified to make it sound like strength and heroism. For instance, early in the Becker/Krickstein match, the two commentators had this exchange: "They're both pretty nervous, and that's pretty normal." "Something would be wrong if they weren't." "It means you care." "Like Marines going into Iwo Jima saying they weren't nervous, something's a little fishy."

In both basketball and tennis, there were also qualitative differences in the ways that success and failure were discussed for women and men athletes. In fact, two formulae for success appeared to exist, one for men, the other for women. Men appeared to succeed through a combination of talent, instinct, intelligence, size, strength, quickness, hard work, and risk-taking. Women also appeared to succeed through talent, enterprise, hard work, and intelligence. But commonly cited along with these attributes were emotion, luck, togetherness, and family. Women were also more likely to be framed as failures due to some combination of nervousness, lack of confidence, lack of being "comfortable," lack of aggression, and lack of stamina. Men were far less often framed as failures—men appeared to miss shots and loss matches not so much because of their own individual shortcomings (nervousness, losing control, etc.), but because of the power, strength, and intelligence of their (male) *opponents*. This framing of failure suggests that it is the thoughts and actions of the male victor that wins games, rather than suggesting that the loser's lack of intelligence or ability is responsible for losing games. Men were framed as active agents in control of their destinies, women as reactive objects.

A HIERARCHY OF NAMING BY GENDER AND RACE

It was not simply women athletes who were linguistically infantilized and framed ambivalently. Our research suggests that black male basketball players shared some of this infantilization. Previous research revealed racial bias in televised commentary in men's sports. For instance, Rainville & McCormick (1977) found that white players received more praise and less criticism from football commentators than comparable black players. And Jackson (1989) reported that white male football and basketball players were much more likely to be credited with "intelligence and hard work," while the successes of their black male counterparts were more likely to be attributed to "natural athleticism." Our examination of basketball commentary occurred in the wake of widespread public discussion of Jackson's (1989) research. We observed what appeared to be a conscious effort on the part of commentators to cite both physical ability *and* intelligence when discussing successful black and white male and female players. However, this often appeared to be an afterthought. For instance, a commentator would note of a star white player that "He has so much court intelligence . . . **AND** so much natural ability!" And a typical comment about a black star player was "What a great athlete . . . **AND** he really plays the game intelligently!"

Though it appeared that television commentators were consciously attempting to do away with the "hard work/intelligence" (white) vs. "natural athlete" (black) dichotomy, we did find an indication of racial difference in naming of male basketball players. In the three men's basketball games, in each of the cases in which men were referred to by their first names only, the commentators were referring to men of color (e.g., Rumeal [Robinson], Ramon [Ramos]). Though there were several "star" white male basketball players (e.g., Danny Ferry and Andrew Gaze) in these games, they were *never* referred to by their first names only.

These findings suggest that T.V. sports commentators are (again, probably unconsciously) utilizing a "hierarchy of naming": At the top of the linguistic hierarchy sit the always last-named white "men," followed by (sometimes) first-named black "men," followed by (frequently) first-named "girls" and "young ladies." We found no racial differences in the ways that women athletes were named. We speculate that (at least within televised sports commentary) gender is the dominant defining feature of women athletes' shared subordinate status. By contrast, sports commentary tends to weave a taken-for-granted superordinate, adult masculine status around male athletes. Yet in the case of male athletes of color, the commentary tends to (subtly and partially) undermine their superordinate masculine status. This suggests, following the theory of gender stratification developed by Connell (1987) and applied to sport by Messner (1989), Messner & Sabo (1990) and Kidd (1987), that sports media reinforce the overall tendency of sport to be an institution which simultaneously (1) constructs and legitimizes men's overall power and privilege over women; and (2) constructs and legitimizes heterosexual, white, middle class men's power and privilege over subordinated and marginalized groups of men.

CONCLUSION

An individual who watches an athletic event constructs and derives various meanings from the activity. These meanings result from a process of interaction between the meanings that are built into the game itself (the formal rules and structure, as well as the history and accumulated mythology of the game), with the values, ideologies and presuppositions that the viewer brings to the activity of watching. But viewing an athletic contest on television is not the same as watching a contest "live." Televised sport is an event which is mediated by the "framing" of the contest by commentators and technical people (Clarke & Clarke, 1982; Duncan & Brummett, 1987; Gitlin, 1982; Gruneau, 1989; Jhally, 1989; Morse, 1983; Wenner, 1989). Thus, any meanings that a television viewer constructs from the contest are likely to be profoundly affected by the framing of the contest (Altheide & Snow, 1979; Antin, 1982; Conrad, 1982; Duncan & Hasbrook, 1988; Fiske & Hartley, 1978; Innis, 1951; McLuhan, 1964; Morse, 1983).

Televised sports are live and largely unscripted, but the language which commentators use to frame the events tends to conform to certain linguistic conventions which are themselves a result of "a complex articulation of technical, organizational, economic, cultural, political, and social factors" (Jhally, 1989: 84). And as Gruneau (1989) has argued, though commentators are often aware of themselves as "storytellers," they are not necessarily aware of the political and ideological ramifications of the linguistic conventions to which they—apparently unconsciously—conform.

Language is never neutral. An analysis of language reveals imbedded social meanings, including overt and covert social biases, stereotypes, and inequities. There is an extensive body of literature which documents how language both reflects and reinforces gender inequalities (Baron, 1986; Henley, 1977, 1987; Lakoff, 1975; Miller & Swift, 1977, 1980; Schultz, 1975; Spender, 1980; Thorne, Kramarae & Henley, 1985; Van Den Bergh, 1987). In a recent study of the gendered language of sport, sociologists D. Stanley Eitzen and Maxine Baca Zinn (1989: 364) argue that

> [Gendered] language places women and men within a system of differentiation and stratification. Language suggests how women and men are to be

> evaluated. Language embodies negative and positive value stances and valuations related to how certain groups within society are appraised. Language in general is filled with biases about women and men. Specific linguistic conventions are sexist when they isolate or stereotype some aspect of an individual's nature or the nature of a group of individuals based on their sex.

The media–and sports media in particular–tend to reflect the social conventions of gender-biased language. In so doing, they reinforce the biased meanings built into language, and thus contribute to the re-construction of social inequities.

Newspaper editors and television programmers often argue that they are simply "giving the public what it wants." Programming decisions are clearly circumscribed by market realities, and research does indicate that with few exceptions, men's athletic events draw more spectators than women's. But one question that arises concerns the reciprocal effect of, on the one hand, public attitudes, values and tastes, and on the other hand, the quantity and quality of coverage of certain kinds of athletic events. What comes first: public "disinterest" in televised women's athletics, or lack of quality coverage? Perhaps a more timely question now that women's sports are getting at least incrementally more coverage is: How do the ways that women and men's sports are covered on television effect the "interest" of the public in these events?

Our research on women's and men's tennis and basketball coverage indicated that commentators today are less likely than their predecessors to overtly sexualize or trivialize women athletes. However, the language used by commentators tends to mark women's sports and women athletes as "other," infantilize women athletes, and frame their accomplishments negatively or ambivalently. Our research also suggests that black male athletes share in some of the linguistic infantilization that is commonly used to describe women athletes. As a result, the language of sports commentary tends to (often subtly) reconstruct gender and racial hierarchies.

Though subtle bias is no less dangerous than overt sexism, the decline of overtly sexist language suggests that some commentators are becoming more committed to presenting women's athletics fairly. For instance, women's basketball commentator Steve Physioc re-named "man-to-man defense" as "player-to-player" defense. This is an example of a conscious decision to replace an androcentric language with language which is not gendered. Though Physioc did not do this consistently, the fact that he did it at all was an indication of his awareness of the gender biases built into the conventional language of sports. Critics might argue that changing language subverts the history or the "purity" of the game. But in fact, terminology used to describe sports is constantly changing. For instance, in basketball, the part of the court nearest the basket that used to be called "the key" through the 1950's was re-named "the lane" in the 1960's, and is more recently referred to as "the paint" or "the block." These changes have come about as a result of changes in the rules of the game, changes in the sizes and styles of players, and general changes in social values and mores. But language does not simply change as a "reflection" of social reality. Language also helps to construct social reality (Shute, 1981; Van Den Bergh, 1987). Thus the choice to use non-sexist language is a choice to linguistically affirm the right of women athletes to fair and equal treatment.

Viewed in this context, Physioc's use of "player-to-player defense" can be viewed as a linguistic recognition that something significant has happened to basketball: It is no longer simply a men's game. There are women players out there, and the language used to report their games should reflect and endorse this fact.

NOTES

1. This research is based on a larger study of gender and sports media which was commissioned by the Amateur Athletic Foundation of Los Angeles. The authors gratefully acknowledge the assistance of Wayne Wilson of the AAF, and of Barrie Thorne, who commented on an earlier version of this paper.
2. These statistics are compiled yearly by the National Federation of State High School Associations in Kansas City, MO. The 1989-90 statistics were received via a phone interview with the NFSHSA. For a discussion of the implications of this continuing trend of increasing high school athletic participation by girls, see D. Sabo (1988) "Title IX and Athletics: Sex Equity in Schools," in *Updating School Board Policies* 19 (10), November.

REFERENCES

Altheide, D. L., & Snow, R. P. (1979) *Media Logic.* Beverly Hills, CA: Sage.

Antin, D. (1982) "Video: The Distinctive Features of the Medium," Pp. 455-477 in H. Newcomb (Ed.) *Television: The Critical View* (3rd ed.). New York: Oxford University Press.

Baron, D. (1986) *Grammar and Gender.* New Haven: Yale University Press.

Birrell, S. (1987-1988) "The Woman Athlete's College Experience: Knowns and Unknowns," *Journal of Sport and Social Issues* 11: 82-96.

Brannon, R. (1978) "The Consequences of Sexist Language." Paper presented at the American Psychological Association Meetings, Toronto.

Bryant, J. (1980) "A Two-year Investigation of the Female in Sport as Reported in the Paper Media," *Arena Review* 4: 32-44.

Bryson, L. (1987) "Sport and the Maintenance of Masculine Hegemony," *Women's Studies International Forum* 10: 349-360.

Boutilier, M. A., & SanGiovanni, L. (1983) *The Sporting Woman.* Champaign, IL: Human Kinetics.

Clarke, A., & Clarke, J. (1982) "Highlights and Action Replays: Ideology, Sport, and the Media," pp. 62-87 in J. Hargreaves (Ed.) *Sport, Culture, and Ideology.* London: Routledge & Kegan-Paul.

Connell, R. W. (1987) *Gender and Power.* Stanford, CA: Stanford University Press.

Conrad, P. (1982) *Television: The Medium and Its Manners.* Boston: Routledge & Kegan-Paul.

Crittenden, A. (1979) "Closing the Muscle Gap," pp. 5-10 in S. Twin, (Ed.) *Out of the Bleachers: Writings on Women and Sport*. Old Westbury, NY: The Feminist Press.

Duncan, M. C. (1990) "Sports Photographs and Sexual Differences: Images of Women and Men in the 1984 and 1988 Olympic Games," *Sociology of Sport Journal* 7: 22-43.

Duncan, M. C., & Brummet, B. (1987) "The Mediation of Spectator Sport," *Research Quarterly for Exercise and Sport* 58: 168-177.

Duncan, M. C., & Hasbrook, C. A. (1988) "Denial of Power in Televised Women's Sports," *Sociology of Sport Journal* 5: 1-21.

Duncan, M. C. & Sayaovong, A. (1990) "Photographic Images and Gender in *Sports Illustrated for Kids*," *Play & Culture* 3: 91-116.

Dyer, K. (1983) *Challenging the Men: The Social Biology of Female Sport Achievement*. St. Lucia: University of Queensland.

Dyer, G. (1987) "Women and Television: An Overview," pp. 6-16 in H. Baeher & G. Dyer (Eds.) *Boxed In: Women and Television*. New York: Pandora Press.

Eastman, S. T., & Meyter, T. P. (1989) "Sports Programming: Scheduling, Costs, and Competition," pp. 97-119 in L. A. Wenner (Ed.) *Media, Sports, & Society*. Newbury Park, CA: Sage Publications.

Eitzen, D. S., & Baca Zinn, M. (1989) "The De-athleticization of Women: The Naming and Gender Marking of Collegiate Sport Teams," *Sociology of Sport Journal* 6: 362-370.

Felshin, J. (1974) "The Social View," pp. 179-279 in E. W. Gerber, J. Felshin, P. Berlin, & W. Wyrick (Eds.) *The American Woman in Sport*. Reading, MA: Addison-Wesley.

Fiske, J., & Hartley, J. (1978) *Reading Television*. New York: Methuen.

Gitlin, T. (1982) "Prime Time Ideology: The Hegemonic Process in Television Entertainment," pp. 426-454 in H. Newcomb (Ed.) *Television: The Critical View* (3rd ed.). New York: Oxford University Press.

Gruneau, R. (1989) "Making Spectacle: A Case Study in Television Sports Production," pp. 134-154 in L. A. Wenner (Ed.) *Media, Sports, & Society*. Newbury Park, CA: Sage Publications.

Hall, M. A. (1988) "The Discourse on Gender and Sport: From Femininity to Feminism," *Sociology of Sport Journal* 5: 330-340.

Hargreaves, J. (1986) "Where's the Virtue? Where's the Grace? A Discussion of the Social Production of Gender Through Sport," *Theory, Culture and Society* 3: 109-121.

Henley, N. M. (1977) *Body Politics: Power, Sex and Nonverbal Communication*. Englewood Cliffs, NJ: Prentice Hall.

Henley, N. M. (1987) "This New Species that Seeks New Language: On Sexism in Language and Language Change," pp. 3-27 in J. Penfield (Ed.). *Women and Language in Transition*. Albany: State University of New York Press.

Herbert, S. (1990) "Study Charges Sexism in Women's Sports Coverage," *Los Angeles Times*, Thursday, August 30, 1990, p. F-2.

Innis, H. A. (1951) *The Bias of Communication*. Toronto: University of Toronto Press.

Jackson, D. Z. (1989) "Sports Broadcasting: Calling the Plays in Black and White," *The Boston Globe* (Sunday, January 22).

Jhally, S. (1989) "Cultural Studies and the Sports/Media Complex," pp. 70-93 in L. A. Wenner (Ed.). *Media, Sports, & Society*. Newbury Park, CA: Sage Publications.

Kidd, B. (1987) "Sports and Masculinity," in M. Kaufman (Ed.), *Beyond Patriarchy: Essays by Men on Pleasure, Power, and Change*. Toronto and New York: Oxford University Press.

Kidd, B. (1990) "The Men's Cultural Centre: Sports and the Dynamic of Women's Oppression/Men's Repression," pp. 31-44 in M. A. Messner & D.F. Sabo (Eds.). *Sport, Men and the Gender Order: Critical Feminist Perspectives*. Champaign, IL: Human Kinetics Publishers.

Lakoff, R. (1975) *Language and Woman's Place*. New York: Harper & Row.

McConnell-Ginet, S. (1978) "Address Forms in Sexual Politics," pp. 23-35 in D. Butturff & E. L. Epstein (Eds.). *Women's Language and Style*. Akron, Ohio: L & S Books.

McLuhan, M. (1964) *Understanding Media: The Extensions of Man*. New York: Signet Books.

Messner, M. A. (1988) "Sports and Male Domination: The Female Athlete as Contested Ideological Terrain," *Sociology of Sport Journal* 5: 197-211.

Messner, M. A. (1989) "Masculinities and Athletic Careers," *Gender & Society* 3: 71-88.

Messner, M. A., & Sabo, D. F. (1990) "Toward a Critical Feminist Reappraisal of Sport, Men and the Gender Order," pp. 1-16 in M. A. Messner & D.F. Sabo (Eds.). *Sport, Men and the Gender Order: Critical Feminist Perspectives*. Champaign, IL: Human Kinetics Publishers.

Miller, C. & Swift, K. (1977) *Words and Women: New Language in New Times*. Garden City, NY: Doubleday/Anchor.

Miller, C., & Swift, K. (1980) *The Handbook of Nonsexist Writing*. New York: Lippincott & Crowell.

Morse, M. (1983) "Sport on Television: Replay and Display," pp. 44-66 in E. A. Kaplan (Ed.). *Regarding Television*. Los Angeles: American Film Institute/University Publications of America.

Rainville, R. E., & McCormick, E. (1977) "Extent of Covert Prejudice in Pro Football Announcers' Speech," *Journalism Quarterly* 54: 20-26.

Rintala, J., & Birrell, S. (1984) "Fair Treatment for the Active Female: A Content Analysis of *Young Athlete* Magazine," *Sociology of Sport Journal* 3: 195-203.

Rubin, R. (1981) "Ideal Traits and Terms of Address for Male and Female College Professors." *Journal of Personality and Social Psychology* 41: 966-974.

Sabo, D. (1988) "Title IX and Athletics: Sex Equity in Schools," *Updating School Board Policies* 19 (10), November.

Schultz, M. (1975) "The Semantic Derogation of Women," pp. 64-75 in B. Thorne & N. Henley (Eds.). *Language and Sex: Difference and Dominance*. Rowley, MA: Newbury House.

Shute, S. (1981) "Sexist Language and Sexism," pp. 23-33 in M. Vetterling-Braggin (Ed.). *Sexist Language: A Modern Philosophical Analysis*. Totowa, NJ: Littlefield, Adams.

Spender, D. (1980) *Man Made Language*. London: Routledge & Kegan-Paul.

Stanley, J. P. (1977) "Gender Marking in American English: Usage and Reference," pp. 43-74 in A. P. Nilsen et al. (Eds.). *Sexism and Language*. Urbana, IL: National Council of Teachers of English.

Theberge, N. (1981) "A Critique of Critiques: Radical and Feminist Writings on Sport." *Social Forces* 60: 387-394.

Theberge, N., & Cronk, A. (1987) "Work Routines in Newspaper Sports Departments and the Coverage of Women's Sports," *Sociology of Sport Journal* 3: 195-203.

Thorne, B., Kramarae, C., & Henley, N. (1985) "Language, Gender and Society: Opening a Second Decade of Research," pp. 7-24 in B. Thorne & N. Henley (Eds.). *Language, Gender and Society*. Rowley, MA: Newbury House.

Van Den Bergh, N. (1987) "Renaming: Vehicle for Empowerment," pp. 130-136 in J. Penfield (Ed.). *Women and Language in Transition*. Albany: State University of New York Press.

Whitson, D. (1990) "Sport in the Social Construction of Masculinity," pp. 19-30 in M. A. Messner, & D. F. Sabo (Eds.). *Sport, Men and The Gender Order: Critical Feminist Perspectives*. Champaign, IL: Human Kinetics Publishers.

Wenner, L. A. (1989) "Media, Sports and Society: The Research Agenda," pp. 13-48 in L. A. Wenner (Ed.). *Media, Sports an Society*. Newbury Park, CA: Sage Publications.

Willis, P. (1982) "Women in Sport in Ideology," pp. 117-135 in J. Hargreaves (Ed.). *Sport, Culture, and Ideology*. London: Routledge & Kegan-Paul.

Wilson Sporting Goods Co. and the Women's Sports Foundation (1988) "The Wilson Report: Moms, Dads, Daughters and Sports." (June).

Wolfson, N., & J. Manes (1980) "Don't 'Dear' Me!" pp. 79-92 in S. McConnell-Ginet, R. Borker, & N. Furman (Eds.). *Women and Language in Literature and Society*. New York: Praeger.

22. *Journalism and the Bottom Line*

DAVID A. KLATELL AND NORMAN MARCUS

The woeful state of television sports journalism should come as no surprise to the average fan. It has long been this way, and the fans themselves have been, both implicitly and explicitly, one of the most conservative influences restraining anything resembling unfettered journalism. For nearly forty years, television sports executives have shied away from the very tenets of free and enterprising reporting practiced by print journalists, and in doing so have cited their fear of upsetting either the viewing public on one hand, or the sports entrepreneurs and rights-holders they had to negotiate with, on the other. In short, the journalist, by nature a boat-rocker and disturber of the established order, is regarded with considerable suspicion, not only by his targets but by his employers as well.

No one likes to hear such bad news as the tragic, cocaine-induced death of University of Maryland basketball star Len Bias, payoff scandals at Southern Methodist University, academic "ghettoes" for athletes at the University of Georgia, or of the raft of athletes with drug, alcohol, and financial problems. Athletes and sports executives often react worst when the news is broken by a seemingly friendly source, a sports reporter. There is often a very real sense of betrayal, accompanied by a feeling that one's privacy has been violated by the very people who should have been guarding the secrets most assiduously, and who, in fact, have long benefitted from association with the sports business. It is as though an unwritten gentlemen's agreement has been violated by a member of the inner circle within the club.

All journalists face formidable barriers in their attempts to understand and describe the sports business. Teams and organizations are generally closed-mouthed and protective of their employees, suspicious of the motives of many in the press, and wont to regard all mass media as partners, or adjuncts to beneficial public relations. Television sports remains a most difficult environment for an honest journalist because so many of the support systems available to "straight" news reporters—

SOURCE: excerpt from David A. Klatell and Norman Marcus, *Sports for Sale: Television, Money, and the Fans* (New York: Oxford University Press, 1988), pp. 210-224.

demanding readers, experienced editors, financial resources, space in the newspaper or magazine, and most critically, independence from conflicts of interest or commercial entanglements—are thoroughly compromised in television sports.

Compared with most television program formats, sports journalism is not expensive to produce. The expenses entailed are relatively high, however, when measured against the rate of return the company might expect, as a result of low ratings. Good journalism anywhere is reasonably expensive, requiring as it does highly trained support personnel, considerable time to develop stories, extensive and careful research, and editing. Worse, only a few good stories can be generated in a year, and they are difficult to put into the predictable, prescribed program formats of commercial television: when a good serious story (e.g., "Drugs in High School Sports") is ready for air the choice is either to drop it into the middle of a ball game, or other essentially escapist programming, or to pre-empt the network schedule to air a sports journalism special. The former never seems appropriate to the subject matter, and the latter is a sure ratings disaster. Through the years, various journalistically minded reporters and producers have fought for, and received, their own time slot for enterprise reporting. The almost inevitable results have been a gaggle of awards, some attention-getting publicity, and a hearty pat on the back from the network programmers when they cancel the program due to low ratings.

It would be easy to state that the historical root of the problem is money: the financial partnership between television and sports, which binds the success of one to the other, as well as spawning a host of in-house inhibitions and prohibitions concerning the role, function, and range of journalism. In fact, the growth of financial interdependence has made the problems infinitely more intractable: as Huntington Williams points out in the "Gannett Center Journal," with the flow of TV money "sports progressed from relative penury into a complex world of free-agency and super-marketing, of legitimate and illegitimate betting, of drugs and the right-to-privacy issue, and of racism, antitrust law and eminent domain." However, the most basic problems stem from the earliest days of broadcasting and sports, and from the widely held belief that broadcast sports were (and are) entertainment programs, staged and performed for the amusement and interest of fans, and that as privately controlled entities they were immune from the usual intrusions of journalists into topics other than what took place on the playing field.

Despite the basically entertaining nature of sports, the early CBS and NBC radio networks assigned the "description and accounts" of the games to News, since it traditionally covered "live" events. Williams notes the distinction between news and sports was muddied by the fact that several of the most prominent on-air commentators covered both types of events interchangeably: Graham McNamee sandwiched the 1924 Democratic

National Convention and President Calvin Coolidge's inauguration between calls of the 1923 and 1925 World Series. At CBS, as always, tradition died hardest, lasting at least through 1960, when Walter Cronkite, looking slightly ill at ease, hosted the Squaw Valley Olympics. On the other hand, newborn ABC, having no tradition of covering much of anything in the fifties and early sixties, bought itself a Sports division by acquiring an independent production company; the result was a young and aggressive ABC Sports, independent of the stodgier News, which could cheerfully cover sports as entertainment. In an ironic turnabout, the later triumphs of ABC Sports would propel Roone Arledge to the presidency of News, where it must have seemed to many old hands that the tail was wagging the dog.

The public traditionally has demanded very little, if anything, in the way of journalism from broadcasting. Radio and television sports have always been described as the ultimate escapist fare—the kind of programming one tuned into precisely to escape the cares and troubles in the rest of the world. In an era in which athletes were regarded as heroes and role models for youth, very few people wished to hear about Babe Ruth's drinking and wenching, the gambling habits of players, owners' treatment of their employees, the obvious racism of sports, labor-management problems, salary disputes, or a host of issues we now take for granted. Neither newspapers nor broadcasters saw fit to mention these indelicate subjects, and many actively participated in hushing up scandals of one sort or another, "for the good of the game," but also because they were afraid of their own audience's reactions to such disclosures.

It was a very cozy relationship, as the writers and broadcasters traveled with (and sometimes lived with) the teams, frequently on the team's payroll. Expenses were covered, meals and lodging provided, and a host of other courtesies extended to the journalists, who saw themselves in many instances as extensions of the team itself. Players and managers, owners and fans could afford to lower their defenses in front of these reporters, secure in the knowledge that, as "one of the boys," the reporters would protect their image, thoroughly sanitizing the scruffy, roustabout realities of sports.

Nearly everyone involved in professional sports, including players, managers, and owners, was less attuned to the challenges and opportunities presented by the press, and hardly understood the role of the mass media in shaping imagery or in generating revenues. Many athletes were semi-educated and came from small towns throughout the country. Some, in fact, couldn't read the very newspapers that were writing about them. Unsophisticated, naive, but fiercely proud of their prowess and privacy, they expected reporters and broadcasters to act as public relations men; often they were not disappointed. Reporters rarely strayed from a formulaic presentation of the athlete as grizzled veteran or winsome youth, making his way through American society by dint of dedication, hard work, God-given talent, respect for the system which so blessed him, and a sense of obligation to the fans, the owners, and the nation.

Whatever real reporting was being done appeared in newspapers, but subject matter and content were vastly different from those of today. Sports pages were filled with detailed play-by-play reporting of games; some well-known columnists appeared frequently to comment on the proceedings. There were, however almost no feature articles, adversarial reports, "background stories," or investigations of anything save the on-field activities. Radio and television did not then have the technical capacity now taken for granted, which enables them to dissect a play, or entire game, through a series of replay, slow-motion, and still-frame devices. Nor did there exist the enormous local broadcast newscasts, each containing its own sports segment, complete with scoreboards, replays, highlights, and other breaking news. The sheer tonnage of material available through broadcasting, combined with its immediacy and ability to beat most newspaper deadlines by hours, eventually forced a change on newspaper sports sections.

Faced with the realization that any avid sports fan would already have seen and heard described virtually every important happening in a game long before he read the next morning's newspaper, print editors and reporters began to shift to a more analytic approach. Their stories started to delve into the behind-the-scenes aspects of sports, and they began to reveal the complexity and turmoil that had long been just below the surface. The newspapers and magazines eventually made a virtue of their long deadlines, and devoted themselves to the kind of story which broadcasters, in their relentless rush to be first and fastest, could not cover with any grace or comprehensiveness.

In the mid-eighties the "national" newspaper *USA Today* appeared, featuring a flashy sports section emphasizing colorful graphics, personality features, short, breezy stories, and an extensive statistical rundown of the previous day's events in sports. Some press critics were moved to comment that *USA Today* had successfully mimicked the stylistic elements which had made television sports so popular. In fact, an important element of the paper's format was its prominent coverage of television sports.

In many respects, the growth of the modern newspaper sports page, and magazines such as *Sports Illustrated*, can be credited to the broadcasters' pushing breaking sports news into the farthest reaches of the nation, greatly popularizing the topic, and spreading interest wherever their signals reached. Newspapers and magazines now give millions of readers a chance to reflect on the events they have already seen, and to do so armed with a fuller, more varied, and thoughtful assemblage of fact and opinion. Broadcasting sells a lot of newspapers and magazines. In what may seem a gentlemen's agreement to divide the territory, broadcasters frequently use the existence of newspapers and magazines as justification for their own abdication of much journalistic responsibility. They concede the superiority of print reporting, bemoan their own lack of air time, and usually leave the field without a fight.

Sports news is often controversial, since it commonly entails some elements of criticism about highly trained popular athletes, their performance in a very public arena, and other factors which might have bearing on their performance, including salaries, personal habits, family life, and relations with the fans. Encounters with reporters are often at very close quarters, as interviewers and their subjects may spend most of the year in proximity with each other. On very few other beats is the range so close, so sustained, and so directly personal. It is not difficult to understand why, inevitably, great friendships and great feuds spring up constantly between sports reporters and their subjects. Locker room confrontations are frequent, punctuated by the occasional punch-out.

The demands of modern journalism, dedicated as it is to changing the old ground rules and rattling all skeletons, have made the relationship particularly touchy. Perhaps, only a few years ago, it would have been possible for athletes or sports executives to evade reporters' inquiries, or brush them off with a laugh (or snarl)—or even by placing a call to the Sports Editor. Today such reactions would almost inevitably cause the reporters to redouble their efforts.

It is interesting to note that, while most newspaper and magazine readers appear to accept this inherently prickly relationship, television viewers are much less comfortable with their reporters and announcers acting in an aggressive or confrontational manner. Perhaps it is because they can actually see their reporters at work, experience the process of news-gathering, and hear the emotion contained in both questions and answers; newspaper readers only see the sanitized, printed results of that work. To the dismay of those few within broadcast sports who want to be regarded as serious journalists, their viewing audiences often seem offended when they act that way in pursuit of legitimate stories.

Television executives occasionally have resorted to a halfway solution: hiring print reporters to do the heavy work of broadcast reporting. At one time or another, excellent reporters such as Dick Schaap, Larry Merchant, Robert Lipsyte, Pete Axthelm, Will McDonough, and Frank Deford have been enlisted as on-air reporters and commentators. Unfortunately, their efforts have rarely earned a sustained audience, either because their own television skills are below those of full-time television announcers, or because of the audience's aversion to the material.

Perhaps this aversion can be traced to the drumbeat of promotional material which almost exclusively emphasizes the broadcaster's non-journalistic virtues: his enthusiasm, voice, appearance, comfort with the athletes, and, in the case of color commentators, his own athletic experience. It therefore seems very much out of character for these "good guys" to suddenly switch gears and come on like Ted Koppel. Television viewers of all sorts are eager to categorize the people they watch regularly, and to expect the on-air characters to remain true to form (or the script), and faithful to that character. Once you get a reputation as a friendly announcer, or conversely, a tough interviewer, viewers and television executives are reluctant to let you change roles. Newspaper reporters, however, can often switch from "straight" reporting to writing opinion columns, from supporting a team to knocking it, without readers' becoming unduly upset.

Perhaps, too, the viewing audience instinctively understands that much of the reporting and analysis offered up by on-air talent is simply not very good. Most announcers and commentators in sports are virtually without journalistic training, either in the mechanics and techniques of researching, writing, editing, interviewing, and reporting, or in the principles, attitudes, and philosophies of journalism. They often cannot identify and define a story, develop it, place it in an understandable context, or anticipate the audience's state of knowledge and mind. They get remarkably little training or support within their own organizations, and they face unremitting caution and wariness from their would-be subjects. Any cub reporter would be hard-pressed to survive under such conditions, and few sports announcers have had even that much journalistic preparation.

For many years, the audience had relatively little opportunity to compare broadcast announcers. Each city had its favorite, usually a veteran announcer who had broadcast the same team's games for years and who had developed a cult following for his unique, personalized presentation of events. The advent first of network, and later, cable television as national distributors of sports programming brought the voice and descriptions of many announcers from out-of-town teams into each other's markets. For the first time, for example, viewers could watch the same event on more than one cable channel simultaneously, or watch an event on television while listening to it on radio. The results are startling to the uninitiated. During the 1987 NBA Finals between the Boston Celtics and the Los Angeles Lakers, anyone wishing to hear a modulated, middle-of-the-road description of professional prowess could watch the CBS network broadcast, with its careful, balanced approach to the two teams. Those wishing to hear a description of the Lakers' natural, almost symphonic grace and coordination could tune to laid-back Chick Hearn. Those wishing to hear a morality play conducted against the background of a Pier Six brawl, with the fate of civilization as we know it at stake, could listen to the Celtics' legendary Johnny Most.

To say that the three descriptions were at some variance would be an insult to the hyperbolic talents of all three. And in each city, in each home, many members of the audience reveled in the clash of perceptions and realities; knowing they were being manipulated, flattered, appeased, and even lied to diminished the enjoyment not a whit. Biased reporting, especially at the local level, is accepted by the audience as a harmless part of the sports entertainment package.

In fact, the NBA and ABC Radio recognized the virtues of the dissonant gulf between Hearn and Most, pairing them for the broadcast of the 1988 All-Star Game. Perhaps attentive to the less distinctive tastes of a broad national audience, each tried to downplay the vocal idiosyncracies which had made him a regional favorite. Hearn perked up, brightening and sharpening his customary Californian placidity; Most, whose voice in full cry crackles, sputters, and screeches like a police scanner, contented himself with a dull roar. Both announcers opted for the middle of the road, thereby leaving many first-time listeners wondering just what all the fuss was about.

Audiences also distinguish between network announcers and reporters, and those employed by local stations. For the most part, the network announcers do not travel with, or establish personal relationships, with their subjects. They may fly to the site of an event the day before it takes place, and leave immediately thereafter for another assignment. Their role is really that of event host and announcer, and very little reporting is expected of them. However, the local station personnel not only follow the same teams all year, and report on them nightly, but are often the public's main link to the athletes and their organization. Additionally, they are working under the most adverse circumstances, as crowded locker rooms, planes, and buses are not the most congenial locations for serious reporting. Public relations specialists interpose themselves between reporters and their intended subject, often attempting to stage-manage the interviews, control their content, and influence the outcome. Players, coaches, and managers are instructed to be extremely cautious in their dealings with news media, and often receive coaching in interview techniques from specialists hired by their agents or employers.

This formidable list of obstacles and encumbrances to good reporting would discourage many a serious reporter in the best of circumstances. Given the meager journalistic qualifications of many broadcast on-air personnel, it is not surprising that so few have managed to assert themselves with sufficient professionalism and determination to establish reputations as television sports journalists. It requires toughness, an ability to break the conventions of attitude and behavior so ingrained in the sports business, the willingness to fight for resources and support within the relatively timid corridors of power in corporate television, and the preeminent ability to attract a sufficiently large and loyal audience to the effort. It may not require Howard Cosell per se, but his methods and personality were in many respects finely honed instruments completely appropriate for breaking the strictures others had long since learned to accept without quarrel.

Cosell was special, of course, for reasons of style, impact and precedence. Throughout his career, he tussled with his subjects, his employers, his on-air image, and his own true self. To those readers who only remember the later years of his remarkable career, when his ego and vainglorious pronouncements brought him into direct conflict with his employers and professional colleagues, it is important to restate the immense, seminal contributions he made to the field. Not only did he pioneer many journalistic techniques in broadcast sports, he widened the public agenda with his selection of topics, causes, and issues. He was controversial, but perhaps part of this was only in contrast to the pallid docility of so many others in the business. In addition, Cosell willingly took on the role that his employers felt most comfortable with—that of the outcast, the iconoclast, the crazed savant of ABC Sports. He was the man you hated to love, and loved to hate, and he stood out like a beacon amidst the somber gray landscape in network sports. Perhaps it could have been no other way: that to break through to the audience, to act as a journalist, he had first to accept the audience's discomfort with broadcast sports journalism, and become a character they could count on whenever he came on stage.

He spoke his mind and elevated many a debate by the force of his intellect and convictions. ABC always appeared somewhat baffled with his success and equally uncomfortable with his predilection for being an advocate, often of issues or personalities which made the television sports establishment edgy. Further, he was sometimes inconsistent, and rarely predictable, so that anticipating what he might say on the air, or in one of his books or columns, was always difficult for ABC; smoothing over the inevitable ruffled feathers among sports executives, advertisers, and rights-holders was a constant preoccupation. His feuds with the print press were many, heartfelt, and bitter; the television industry places enormous stock in the opinions of newspaper critics, and tries all manner of persuasion to effect favorable coverage.

Cosell violated this with impunity, bearding the lion in its own den with his unwillingness to cede the journalistic beat to newspapers, and by returning their criticism word for word (actually, Cosell rarely restrained himself, and usually returned ten words for every one flung his way). He broke all the rules for corporate deportment, and eventually paid the price of decline and exile. Perhaps his finest series of programs, ABC Sports-Beat, finally succumbed to low ratings after four years of good work.

One of the many complaints lodged against Cosell was that he was too negative about the sports scene and was always poking around, looking for problems, or even creating them. It was sometimes said he did not really enjoy sports at all but was just using them as a platform for his own views. This last intimation seems a patently false one, as Cosell enjoyed the beauties, intricacies, and human virtues of sports as much as any fan. In addition, he was possessed of that famous encyclopedic recall, which was trotted out in anecdotes during dull broadcasts, as he recalled some obscure statistic or fact from his immense memory. However, the impression that he was always poking around, making things difficult for people in the business, was essentially true. That it should surprise anyone reveals much more about the television sports business than it does about Cosell. Had he been covering any other business endeavor, such as banking or manufacturing, his behavior would be the absolute, expected, professional norm. Executives in those industries would not expect reporters covering them to be "fans," only dispassionate observers, dedicated to a truthful, balanced, and unbiased examination of the issues under discussion.

Too many sports executives and athletes expect a free ride from the press, especially broadcasting, and all too often they get it. In the majority of broadcast contracts, the selection of announcers is either shared with, or granted outright to, the rights-holder. They want to take no chances with an announcer who criticizes the team or its management, who raises embarrassing issues, or who lacks the requisite enthusiasm for what he is witnessing. As a result, the landscape is littered with "homers"—utterly biased observers in the employ of the event they are supposed to be covering. Many are current or former employees, or players themselves, retaining close personal ties to the players and management. All know exactly whom they have to please to retain their job in broadcasting, and most make certain they err on the side of caution, should any opportunity to rock the boat arise. By controlling the microphone (or, by extension, the camera shots) they effectively control the agenda for discussion, and can withhold praise and criticism with relative impunity. This often brings them scorn from newspaper writers, who are rightly offended by the one-sided presentation. However, among the broadcast audience itself, which is, after all, the final arbiter of taste in these matters, home-team announcers are a cherished ornament to the presentation of the game.

Advertisers, too, have preferences in the coverage of teams or sports with which they may be associated. Most advertising and sponsorship commitments are made well in advance (sometimes several years) of the actual sports season or event. Advertisers are rightfully nervous about the future performance of a team in which they have invested their clients' budgets. Bad news is not something they or their clients wish to be associated with, whether it is the poor on-field performance of a team hopelessly eliminated from contention; some public relations gaffe or major management error which turns the community against the team; an out-right scandal involving something like drug abuse; unforeseen roster changes involving players central to the advertising effort; or serious personal problems. They want the brightest, most optimistic face placed on everything, because, after all, they are not journalists, for they are trying to help sell their clients' products. Without satisfied clients, they have no business to bring to the rights-holders, stadium managers, or broadcast stations, all of whom are dependent to some degree on this crucial source of income.

In many instances, advertisers have some control over the selection of announcers, some of whom have their own endorsement contracts with the advertisers, or are featured as spokesman in the advertising campaign. This is not to say that advertisers directly muzzle aggressive reporters very often, because the situation only rarely occurs that such a move would be necessary. Very few announcers or reporters are ever hired in major local markets who do not already understand the rules, written and unwritten, of proper behavior and style. All the various parties with a financial stake in the success of the broadcasts help filter out the potential troublemakers.

And why not? As a business proposition, why should a television company shell out outstanding amounts of money as guaranteed payments in a speculative bid for future broadcast rights and then permit one of its own employees in any way to diminish the potential return on that investment? We would expect no different from any other industry group; General Motors isn't expected to hire Ralph Nader as spokesman after all. The business of television sports is selling advertising and gathering subscriber revenues, and that is best accomplished under controlled circumstances. A carefully orchestrated blend of entertainment, promotion, journalism, and controversy creates popularity, and the master blenders are loathe to rewrite this recipe, or bend to outsiders' demands that they do so. It is strongly felt along the corridors of power in television sports that the least they can get for their money is some control over the description and accounts of the events going out over their signals.

The networks have an understandable tendency to avoid criticism of their contractual partners—the league and team owners from whom they have bought the television rights. The 1987 strike by the National Football League Players Association illustrated the problem quite clearly. The three broadcast networks plus ESPN were, of course, offering coverage and commentary on an event and a league of which they were major financial partners. In fact, since the networks provided over 50 percent of total NFL team revenues, the were "the true owners and promoters of the game." Coverage of the strike was, at first, assigned to Sports, which proceeded to guilelessly carry the "scab" games (thus subsidizing them, and thereby the owners) while simultaneously offering commentary on the "news" angle of events. As negotiations to settle the strike dragged on, stadium attendance fell off sharply, but the NFLPA was declared the loser, because television ratings declined less sharply, and television, after all, was the more important factor. By the time the strike collapsed and the chastened players returned to work, the victorious league had indicated it would rebate approximately $60 million to its network partners for any damage done to ratings and advertising revenues.

The conflict of interest is apparent, freely admitted by sophisticated observers inside and outside the industry, and probably insoluble. So long as sports events are considered private performances, to be sold by their rights-holders at their discretion, the broadcasts of those events will in no way intentionally resemble unfettered journalism. The practice of placing rights on the table for competitive bidding means the rights-holder can use a range of criteria in deciding to whom the prize is awarded. Certainly money is a critical element, but so is the "cooperativeness factor," by which each contending bidder is judged: what will they do to help sell the product, to popularize the sport, to enhance its image? Who will have final say in the selection and assignment of announcers?

No newspaper of any stature would accede to these demands, nor would its editors even discuss with potential subjects the assignment of reporters or negotiate a rights fee to cover the very same story. It is one of the unique characteristics of our system of sports journalism that two reporters can be sitting side by side in the press box, one constrained only by his popularity with readers and editors, the other by an interlocking web of business interests and accommodations. Perhaps the sports public, which is made up of people who both watch television sports and read newspaper sports sections, has acclimated itself to the duality of the situation and makes mental adjustments in evaluating the two sources of information. The public may possess a more innate, flexible, and ultimately forgiving understanding of and comfort with the differences between the two industries than most observers believe.

If, then, the public seems in no way insistent that television sports take a more professional journalistic approach to its subjects, where then comes the pressure? Part of the demand for better, more independent reporting comes from the newspapers—both as competitive examples to the broadcasters, and as the source of many interesting stories—which have enlarged their sports sections to include copious reporting on all manner of off-field issues. The pressure on broadcasters to take note of stories involving the private lives of their players, is dramatic, particularly after they have appeared in print. Newspapers frequently set the agenda for broadcasting, and the broadcasters are hard pressed to respond when covering subsequent events. An aggressive, independent follow-up to the newspaper stories may leave them outside the good graces of the rights-holders with whom they have contracted, but failure to do so may damage their credibility as independent observers and lend further credence to the belief they have been bought off.

Another source of strain comes, surprisingly, from within their own television companies. More and more often, the News department of a local station—or the News division of a network—will attempt to assert its prerogatives to cover sports news, just as they would any other topic area. Institutional jealousies and turf-building are common in broadcasting, and no division of such a company would happily step aside for another under these circumstances, particularly given the implicit message of the News people: if you want a journalistic job done right, don't leave it to those amateurs in Sports. It is not unknown, therefore, to have more than one team of production personnel, representing News and Sports separately, cover an event or story of any magnitude. Sports, as we have noted earlier, has rapidly outgrown its formerly narrow confines in the public eye, and is frequently associated with international affairs, politics, social change, and other issues of complexity and importance. Wherever and whenever this seems to be the case, broadcast executives are faced with the choice of whether to cover it as Sports or News, and to whom to give the assignments.

Sometimes, events overtake any preplanning which may have taken place, and Sports production teams suddenly find themselves at a News event. Perhaps the most dramatic example of this was the 1972 Munich Olympiad, which rapidly became the focus of international attention not as a sports event but as the site of the kidnapping and massacre of Israeli athletes. ABC Sports was there in force, prepared to telecast the usual golden images of Olympic competition, international goodwill, and the ideals of amateur sport at its best. When the crisis erupted within the Olympic Village, it caught everyone totally off guard, scrambling for information. To its immense credit, ABC converted a Sports production into News in an almost seamless transformation, and relayed both description and accounts of the unfolding tragedy to a stunned world. When, finally, several crews of ABC News personnel arrived on the scene, and struggled to gain access to the suddenly high-security Olympic Village, they found their compatriots from Sports had already established so proficient and dedicated a team of deeply involved professionals, that there was little News could do, except step back, admire the job being done, and offer assistance as needed.

Such a confluence of events and the presence of Sports cameras are becoming more and more common. The greatly increased ability of portable equipment to travel virtually anywhere in the world and send back live, high-quality pictures, has virtually turned every Sports production crew into a potential News crew—at least in technical ability. Additionally, the knowledge that the cameras are, in fact, on scene, has encouraged a whole host of individuals and groups to seek out the cameras for the sake of demonstrating or publicizing their cause. The question of what to do in such a situation troubles Sports executives. They are torn between their responsibilities to the rights-holders, their contractual partners, and the Sports audience (which presumably tuned in only to be entertained) and the obligation to cover events taking place on their watch. It is really a question of self-definition: are they observers of specified, contracted events, or of the whole world around them, and on what basis do they distinguish events they want to cover, from those they feel they ought to cover, and those they (and News) feel they are capable of covering?

When NBC was preparing its coverage plans for the ill-fated 1980 Moscow Olympics, considerable debate erupted between News and Sports regarding the composition and mandate of the crews they planned to send to Moscow. Here was a unique, international Sports event of major importance to NBC Sports; it marked a hard-won victory over ABC. In exchange for which, it had entered into extensive and restrictive contracts with the Soviet Government. These agreements covered everything from the number and location of cameras, the amount of equipment NBC had to leave in Moscow permanently, and the hours of broadcasting, to the control of the necessary communications satellites (which rested firmly in the hands of the Soviets). And while the contract was, in theory, mutually enforceable, no one doubted that, should the worst come to pass, the Soviet Government held the upper hand: it could pull the plug whenever it wanted, expel NBC employees, or interfere in any number of ways. This was acknowledged by Sports, and by the most senior executives of the parent company who negotiated the contracts, but the opportunity was judged worth the risk.

To NBC News, the chance to insert dozens of personnel and scores of cameras in the very heart of the closed Soviet world, at a time when international tensions were high, and the prospects for potential news stories great, was irresistible. News was preparing to cover anything from demonstrations to dissidents, and within the company made no secret of its desire to be there in force, ready for anything. When the Soviets invaded Afghanistan, President Carter initiated a boycott of the Games, and pulled out the U.S. teams. This was quickly followed by a withdrawal of most American advertisers from the telecasts and a drastic cutback of NBC's ambitious plans. Only limited late-night weekend and early-morning highlights ever made it on the air in this country. News never got its chance to piggyback on Sports' hard-won window of opportunity, and some ill feelings persisted between the two divisions. These tensions are now common in all the networks, as international sports become more and more intertwined with international news, and often in most unexpected ways. Preplanning for future Olympics, in particular, involves careful assessment of the relative interests of News and Sports, sometimes as collaborators, sometimes as competitors. The 1988 Summer Games in Seoul were the focus of agonizing reappraisals and emergency planning at the seemingly star-crossed NBC when persistent anti-government riots broke out in early 1987.

Some sports events seem to take on a life of their own, far exceeding in public interest what they might "deserve" as news events, usually as a result of intense promotion. In these instances, television sometimes finds itself following public opinion, and covering events in detail because the public can't seem to get enough. The prime example of this phenomenon is the Super Bowl, which now dominates a two-week period of Sports and News attention even before the game itself is played. There are countless stories about even the most trivial aspects of team preparation, mob interviews with star players, individual interviews with everyone from the water-boy's parents to the man who paints the end zone. There are, naturally, plenty of stories about the explosion of coverage itself, and stories about the dearth of good stories. Reporters cover reporters covering other reporters, and newspaper critics cover them all. Much of the material is facile, shallow, and meant more to display each station or network's reporters hard at work on the scene than to provide any real reporting or insight. In short, the event has become a promotional showpiece for all involved, and it receives so much coverage because everyone in the television business benefits from that coverage.

The National Football League is, of course, the most skilled and experienced large-scale manipulator of television sports yet seen. Commissioner Pete Rozelle's legendary negotiating skills are augmented by a public relations apparatus that includes, in addition to the squads of helpful publicists, a marketing company, film outfit, archives, video production crews, technical advisers, writers, speech-makers, lobbyists, and lawyers. When he gets it all cranked up, as in the case of the Super Bowl, the cumulative effect is an irresistible tide of interest in the penultimate game of the year and all the hoopla surrounding it. Whether it is the tail wagging the dog, the television industry nevertheless turns out in full force to record the events, establishing by their presence the legitimacy of the whole process. In theory, anyway, ratings will rise if you cover Super Bowl Week (although how they can rise when everyone is covering the same thing is a mystery to statisticians), and the audience will be served. In fact, the prime beneficiary of all the publicity is the one network which will telecast the actual game itself, since all its competitors' attentions will build audience anticipation for the game. It may not be an accident that Rozelle's promotional efforts deliver increased audiences to that network, partly as a reward for having paid all that extra money for the broadcast rights, and partly to drive the next contract's price even higher.

■ FOR FURTHER STUDY

Birrell, Susan, and John W. Loy, Jr. "Media Sport: Hot and Cool." *International Review of Sport Sociology* 14 (January 1979): 5-19.

Chandler, Joan M. *Television and National Sport: The United States and Britain.* Urbana: University of Illinois Press, 1988.

Coulter, Jerry. "The Canadian Press and the Problem of Responsible Journalism: An Olympic Case Study." *Journal of Sport and Social Issues* 10 (1986): 27-47.

Duncan, Margaret Carlisle. "Sports Photographs and Sexual Difference: Images of Women and Men in the 1984 and 1988 Olympic Games." *Sociology of Sport Journal* 7 (March 1990): 22-43.

Duncan, Margaret Carlisle, and Barry Brummett. "The Mediation of Spectator Sport." *Research Quarterly for Exercise and Sport* 58 (1987): 168-177.

Duncan, Margaret Carlisle, and Cynthia A. Hasbrook. "Denial of Power in Televised Women's Sports." *Sociology of Sport Journal* 5 (1988): 11-21.
Eberhard, Wallace B., and Margaret Lee Myers. "Beyond the Locker Room: Women in Sport on Major Daily Newspapers." *Journalism Quarterly* 65 (1988): 595-599.
Garrison, Bruce, with Mark Sabljak. *Sports Reporting*. Ames: Iowa State University Press, 1985.
Jenkins, Sally. "Who Let Them In?" *Sports Illustrated* (June 17, 1990): 78-90.
Kane, Mary Jo. "Medias Coverage of the Female Athlete Before, During, and After Title IX: *Sports Illustrated* Revisited." *Journal of Sport Management* 2 (1988): 87-99.
Lumpkin, Angela, and Linda D. Williams. "An Analysis of *Sports Illustrated* Feature Articles, 1954-1987." *Sociology of Sport Journal* 8 (March 1991): 16-32.
Montville, Leigh. "Season of Torment." *Sports Illustrated* (May 13, 1991): 60-65.
O'Neil, Terry. *The Game Behind the Game: High Pressure, High Stakes in Televised Sports*. New York: Harper & Row, 1989.
Palmer, Melvin D. "The Heyday of the Football Novel." *Journal of Popular Culture* 16 (Summer 1982): 48-54.
Rader, Benjamin. *In Its Own Image: How Television Has Transformed Sports*. New York: Free Press, 1984.
Spence, Jim. *Up Close and Personal: The Inside Story of Network Television Sports*. New York: Atheneum, 1988.
Sociology of Sport Journal. "Gender and the Media: Annotated Bibliography." *Sociology of Sport Journal* 7 (December 1990): 412-421.
Smith, Garry J., and Terry A. Valeriote. "Ethics in Sports Journalism." *Arena Review* 7 (July 1983): 7-14.
Telander, Rick. "The Written Word: Player-Press Relationships in American Sports." *Sociology of Sport Journal* 1 (1984): 3-14.
Vanderwerken, David L., and Spencer K. Wertz, eds. *Sport Inside Out*. Fort Worth: Texas Christian Press, 1985.
Wenner, Lawrence A., ed. *Media, Sports & Society*. Newbury Park, CA: Sage, 1989.
Williams, Linda D. "An Analysis of *Sports Illustrated* Feature Articles, 1954-1987." *Sociology of Sport Journal* 8 (1991): 16-32.

Part Eight

Sport and Politics: International Dimensions

International sport is political.[1] Participants represent and show allegiance to their countries in international competitions. The rituals accompanying sporting events (music, colors, uniforms, flags) are aimed at symbolically reaffirming fidelity to one's country. Phillip Goodhart and Christopher Chataway have argued that there are four kinds of sport: sport as exercise, sport as gambling, sport as spectacle, and representative sport.

> [Representative sport] is a limited conflict with clearly defined rules, in which representatives of towns, regions, or nations are pitted against each other. It is primarily an affair for the spectators: they are drawn to it not so much by the mere spectacle, by the ritual, or by an appreciation of the skills involved, but because they identify themselves with their representatives. . . . Most people will watch [the Olympic Games] for one reason only: there will be a competitor who, they feel, is representing them. That figure in the striped singlet will be their man–running, jumping, or boxing for their country. For a matter of minutes at least, their own estimation of themselves will be bound up with his performance. He will be the embodiment of their nation's strength or weakness. Victory for him will be victory for them; defeat for him, defeat for them.[2]

This last point is important. Evidence from international competitions shows that for many nations and their citizens, victory is an indicator of that nation's superiority (in its politico-economic system and its culture).

Sport, then, is a source of national pride, a source of unity, and a mechanism used by ruling elites to impress its citizens and those of other countries as well. This use of sport to unify and as a propaganda vehicle is found in developing countries, in the nations emerging from what was once the Soviet Union, and from the nations of the West.

The first selection, by Bob Tedeschi, examines the sports potential internationally for the recently reunified Germany. In the 1988 summer Olympic Games the combined medal count by East and West Germany was 142, compared with 132 for the Soviet Union, and 94 for the United States in third place. Thus, it would appear that a combined Germany should dominate the Olympics in the near term. However, the East German sports bureaucracy with its excellent coaching and its identification and development of potentially elite athletes has been demolished. The use of performance enhancing drugs, now admitted by the East Germans, is no longer a state policy. Thus, the question of German athletic domination is an interesting question. More important sociologically is the role that sport will play in bringing about the shared identity that the new nation of Germany requires.

The second selection, by physical educator Bruce Kidd, shows how sport can be used as a mechanism of social change. Kidd chronicles the struggle by the world community to use sport to defeat the apartheid policies of South Africa. To update Kidd's article, in July 1991 the International Olympic Committee lifted its ban on South Africa's participation in the Olympics, which had been in place for twenty-one years. This sets the stage for the first black athletes to represent South Africa in the Olympics since 1904. The problem, of course, is that while South Africa's Parliament voted down the nation's apartheid laws (in June 1991), much of the society remains segregated.[3] Will the participation of whites and blacks as South Africans in the Olympics and in other sports events reduce racial tensions and help to bring about the full acceptance of all races in that society?

The final essay, by D. Stanley Eitzen, focuses on the political problems of the Olympics. He proposes concrete ways to minimize these problems.

NOTES

1. Of course, sport at all levels is inherently political. See D. Stanley Eitzen and George H. Sage, *Sociology of North American Sport*, 5th ed. (Dubuque, IA: Wm. C. Brown, 1993), Chap. 9.
2. Phillip Goodhart and Christoper Chataway, *War Without Weapons* (London: W.H. Allen, 1968), p. 3.
3. "Special Report: South African Sports in Transition," *Center for the Study of Sport Digest* 3 (Fall 1991), pp.3, 8.

23. *Will a Reunified Germany Continue to Dominate the International Sports Scene?*

BOB TEDESCHI

In the summer of 1989, Sybilli Schimmel's life was traveling along as if it were on autopilot. After all, the routine had been the same for years. An eight-year veteran of the East German women's handball team, Schimmel would rise early in the morning in her one-bedroom apartment in East Berlin, have a bite to eat, then climb into her exhaust-spewing Trabant automobile for the 10-minute ride to her sports club.

There, she would spend the entire day practicing with the team, lifting weights, running and listening to coaching lectures. At some point in the day Schimmel would also find herself flushing down the toilet the steroids that were routinely given to her by the coaching staff. It was business as usual for an East German athlete.

But even as that summer progressed, there were signs that Schimmel's autopilot life would change. The hushed voices of political dissenters grew in volume. And when autumn settled and the people gathered in the streets, demanding the end of communist rule, Schimmel and all her fellow East Germans decided to take control of the stick, and shut off the autopilot button for good.

"I have a whole new existence now," says 26-year-old Schimmel, in a room in her new sport club in West Berlin. "I have more money, a new car–no 'Trabby' anymore–and a new apartment [in West Berlin] with two bedrooms. A new existence of Sybilli Schimmel has begun."

It's telling that Schimmel defines her new life by discussing the basic changes in lifestyle rather than her athletic career. For years, East Germany showcased its athletes as the primary successes in a "successful" political system, only to neglect the everyday needs of its citizens. Now, as is the case with Schimmel, democracy seems destined to care for those needs. As for sports–and women's sports in particular–however, the story is different. With children's sports schools closing, private sponsorships for most women's sports lagging and state funding for athletes

---

SOURCE: *Women's Sports and Fitness* (January/February 1991), pp. 45-50. Reprinted with the permission of *Women's Sport and Fitness.*

diminishing, women's sports in a unified Germany face the unenviable task of living up to their lofty reputation without many of the factors that made that reputation possible.

As a member of the East German women's handball team, Schimmel's work was always a bit more strenuous than that of the other members of the socialist society, but it was also much more rewarding. In exchange for their athletic talent, women athletes were given educations in the nation's elite sports schools, a salary that was at least 50 percent higher than the average East German (often paid by the army or secret police, of which many athletes were ostensibly members), and monetary and material incentives for superior achievement in international competitions. The opportunities to travel throughout the world, too, were luxuries that only a handful of East Germans were permitted.

It was the promise of such luxuries that had attracted thousands of women to athletic careers ever since East Germany decided to use sports as a vehicle for promoting communism in the mid-60s. As long as the medals continued to roll in, they were told, the government would provide.

And roll they did. Since their first Olympic competition as an individual national team in 1968, East German athletes have won 192 gold medals. East German women garnered 95 of those golds. For a country with a population about equal to that of New York state (roughly 17 million), the results were staggering.

How did they do it? First of all, the East Germans had a plan. Knowing they had limited funds to work with, the government chose to promote sports that could return the most medals for every dollar invested. Thus, the so-called "medal-maximum" sports, such as swimming, track and field, luge and rowing, were given the most money. In these sports, not only could one superb athlete win several medals, but the athlete's training and equipment costs were relatively paltry. Team sports that could only garner one medal and that required more equipment and staff support, meanwhile, were virtually cut off from funding.

Women's athletics, on the other hand, were viewed as a veritable gold mine of "medal-maximum" sports, primarily because women's sports had yet to be brought into the era of modern training. "It was easier [to win medals] in a discipline like women's track and field than men's track and field, in which training had already been very [serious] for a long time," says Norbert Skowronek, the executive director of the Berlin Sports Federation.

And because the East German women were the first to jump headlong into extensive weight training and heavy aerobic training, they were able to develop more quickly and more completely than the women of other nations, who were still too leery of jeopardizing their femininity to experiment with such techniques.

"I remember the 1972 Olympics in Munich, there was a woman named Renate Stecher—a woman with such shoulders," says Skowronek, extending his hands beyond the width of his own shoulders. Stecher, the 100-meter and 200-meter Olympic champion in Munich "ran much faster than the other girls," he says. "To get such high quality you must train much more than the others."

To get such high quality, some would argue, you must also sometimes cheat. For years, the East German women were scrutinized for their oftentimes masculine appearance, while somehow always managing to pass drug tests. And although sports officials and athletes now acknowledge the widespread use of anabolic steroids, few are willing to speak openly about the extent to which such drugs were used.

"We didn't talk about it," says Sylvia Gerasch, a former world-record holder in the 100-meter breast-stroke, when asked about steroid use among her teammates. Gerasch, who admitted to taking steroids for a period of two years before setting the world record, was reluctant to discuss the use of steroids among her teammates. "It was more an individual thing," she said.

Schimmel, meanwhile, says all her teammates on the national handball team were given steroids by the coaching staff, but most chose to flush the steroids down the toilet, because they "did not want to look like men." She estimated, however, that 30 percent of the team did take drugs.

But neither steroids nor the incentive system nor the long hours of training could claim credit for the East German women's dominance of the '70s and '80s. Such credit belongs to two elements, according to the nation's sports leaders: an extensive system of finding and cultivating talent in the children's sports schools and the expertise and sheer numbers of coaches, trainers and sports scientists whose careers were devoted to athletic perfection.

Twenty-three children's sports schools were sprinkled throughout East Germany, each one catering to two or three different sports. Every child was tested for physical fitness and growth potential before he or she reached the age of eight and was either selected to go to a sports school or sent to regular school. The youngest children—most often gymnasts—would start at the sports schools at the age of 6, and all were paid a monthly salary from the age of 10.

Meanwhile, the supply of coaches at the schools and the training centers was inexhaustible. The East had about one coach for every three athletes (the ration in the West is one to 20). Because the coaches in the East worked closely with some of the world's best sports scientists, the level of expertise among East German coaches was often superior to that of the West.

Buoyed by the successes of the system, fans in East Germany rallied around the athletes and coaches for years. But the support was not ironclad. As the '80s brought economic stagnation throughout the Eastern Bloc nations, the VIP status of elite athletes became increasingly vexing to the general populus. Last fall, therefore, when the public cried out for democratic reforms, changes in the sports system were high among the list of demands. A $500 million-per-year sports system could no longer pacify a public that lacked basic necessities.

When the West German government agreed to absorb the East into its economic and political system, the final nails were put into the coffin of the East German sports machine. "It was a perfect system in the GDR," says Karlheinz Gieseler, who was the executive director of the West German Sports Federation for 25 years until his retirement last December. "But you cannot bring it into a democratic system. A democratic sports system is entirely different from a socialist one."

The primary difference is money. Finding the kind of money needed to sustain the East German sports system after unification was out of the question. Since the spring of last year, when the East German sports authority came under the control of the West German Sports Federation, money has been scarce. For the second half of this year, the West German government gave $60 million to the East German sports authority, in effect saying, "Here you are, don't spend it all in one place. And for good measure, you can disband the army and secret service teams, too."

What are the results of this austerity? Gone are most, if not all, of the children's sports schools. Gone are at least 85 percent of the 4,000 East German coaches who were often hailed as the world's best. Gone are the Olympic training centers. Gone, too, are many of the athletes who dominated their sports—"To other countries," says Werner Neumann, one of five executive directors of the East German sports authority. "We haven't the money [to keep them]."

Because of the anemia of the East German economy, the money may not be there in the future, either. The fate of the coaches, athletes and training centers is intrinsically linked to that of the East German economy, the prognosis of which is about as good as that of lasting peace in the Middle East. Nearly half of the nation's work force of nine million will be out of work by the spring of '91, economists say, as industries expected to invest in eastern Germany are balking.

Without a strong economy, the one thing that keeps a democratic sports system thriving—private sponsorship—is absent. When asked about the sponsorship possibilities for sports after unification, Neumann was exasperated. "We're coming from the Middle Ages here," says Neumann, adding, "Who is sponsoring a country that's going down?"

More important, perhaps is the question "who wants to sponsor sports that no one wants to watch?" When it comes to finding sponsors, women's sports in particular face a bleak future. East German sponsors and television stations have traditionally been interested in a woman athlete's looks just as much as—if not more than—her athletic performances. Because East German women have often forsaken femininity for medals, sponsors could be reluctant. "Most of the GDR girls were not a sight we'd describe as beautiful," says Skowronek. "So only from time to time will there be a chance for sponsorships."

One notable exception is Katarina Witt, the East German figure skater who captured gold medals at the '84 and '88 Olympics. But Witt has spoken out in defense of the old system, saying that sports in East Germany will "go a little down the ladder now."

The only survivor of the system could be women's track and field, which has so far been able to attract enough sponsors to remain strong. But even this East German sports mainstay could suffer from the same maladies as other sports. A spokesman for the largest TV network in West Germany says, "[East German] sports are not interesting to audiences or TV companies." With coaches leaving the country in droves and the sports schools closing, experts predict the East Germans can stay competitive only until the Barcelona Olympic Games in '92. Beyond that, they say, sponsors and TV stations won't even offer a fleeting glance at the East.

In the face of all this bleakness, however, are rays of sunlight. First, drugs will not be nearly as prevalent in a unified German sports system, because the West Germans have strict penalties for drug use and require regular testing. Plus, elite athletes will have to play by the same rules as the general populus when it comes to pool time or track time. Perhaps most important, eastern Germany will enter a new era in which mass sports take precedence over elite sports. Programs are already being developed to induce participation in mass sports activities throughout eastern Germany's five states, and the German Sports Federation is offering monetary incentives to those in the East who want to run private sports clubs that include mass sports programs.

There may also be a glimmer of hope for elite sports in eastern Germany. There are those in the West German Sports Federation who are pushing to retain some of the sports schools and coaches after unification. According to Norbert Wolf, the federation's executive director, the government is reviewing a '91 budget request of $200 million—double what it received last year. But with the eastern German population less than one-third of the west's, there is expected to be resistance—if not outright disdain—for the idea. Says Jurgen Aretz, a spokesman for the Ministry of Intra-German Affairs, "Sports will change [in the east] by making it possible for normal people to get involved. Top athletes will find ways anyway."

If spectator interest in East German sports is any indication, bureaucrats like Aretz could be justified in letting the entire East German sports system die. Bernd State, a press officer for the East German sports authority, sat in the stands at the recent East German Track and Field Championships in Dresden, shaking his head in dismay. The stadium, usually filled to capacity with screaming fans, was nearly empty as the finals of the women's 100-meter sprint got underway.

"Our view is much wider than before," he said, his hands forming a bracket around an imaginary horizon. "Now [instead of coming here], people are going to the other countries, visiting friends they couldn't meet before. People have many more possibilities to do all the things they couldn't before."

And in this region, where the people are still getting accustomed to having total control over their own lives, even those with a connection to East Germany's sports glory years understand that they must take a back seat. "You can't blame them," says Neumann of those who are dismantling eastern Germany's sports system. "There are more important things than sports at the moment. People are free now to do what they like."

24. *From Quarantine to Cure: The New Phase of the Struggle against Apartheid Sport*

BRUCE KIDD

The century-old struggle against racism and racist sport in South Africa has entered a new phase. During the last 18 months, in a series of dramatic breakthroughs few thought imaginable, the liberation movement has gained important new ground. The combined effect of the defeat of the south African Defense Force by joint Angolan-Cuban forces in Angola, the achievement of independence in Namibia, continuing international economic sanctions, and the growing mobilization of the mass democratic movement has forced the apartheid regime to abandon outright repression as a strategy of survival and to concede (at least in terms of its rhetoric) the necessity for the end of apartheid. In February, the De Klerk government released Nelson Mandela and lifted the ban on the African National Congress (ANC) and other liberation organizations. It has ended the draconian Emergency in most parts of the country and begun to negotiate (on negotiations) for restructuring state power. Though the government still uses the Internal Security act to detain opponents without trial, and the police tacitly condone murderous attacks on activists, it is now possible for the democratic forces to campaign more openly for the abolition of apartheid than at any time within the last 30 years.

In sport, the repression of antiapartheid sports leaders has been significantly curtailed. The white sports establishment has begun to seek negotiations with the nonracial bodies for the purpose of creating new, unified sport structures. A few of the white sport federations have even endorsed the nonracial movement's moratorium on international competition. In August 1990 the government allowed one of its most implacable enemies, Sam Ramsamy, to return after 18 years abroad to meet with his family and consult with comrades. Ramsamy is leader of the long-banned South African Non-Racial Olympic Committee (SANROC), the group of South African sportspersons-in-exile that has organized the

SOURCE: *Sociology of Sport Journal* 8, no. 1, (1991) pp. 33-46.

campaign to boycott apartheid South Africa. The Ramsamy visit set the stage for an historic meeting in Harare in November. At that meeting, Olympic leaders from the rest of Africa met with and informed the South African sports establishment that if they ever want to return to international competition they must meet the terms set by the nonracial movement.

The meeting was the result of increasing pressure. In the last few years the international campaign to isolate South Africa in sport has been intensified. The United Nations International Convention Against Apartheid in Sport has been ratified, the International Olympic Committee (IOC) has implemented a full ban against contact with South Africa, and a growing number of countries have denied entry to South African sportspersons. Today, white South African sport enjoys fewer international contacts than ever before. Such universal rejection has shown South African whites the international abhorrence to apartheid and has powerfully affirmed the resistance of the black majority.

In addition to breakthroughs at the political level and the success of the international quarantine, the mass democratic movement has brought the pressure against apartheid in sport to South Africa itself. In the past, no matter how much criticism and censure those athletes who flouted the international sanctions received in their own countries, once they stepped off the airplane in South Africa they could expect a hero's welcome, luxurious hospitality, and little contact with opponents of apartheid. In January 1990, opposition to the visiting British cricket team was so widespread that the tour had to be canceled prematurely. In many towns the cricketers and their white sponsors were directly confronted by thousands of demonstrators. In Johannesburg and Kimberley the players were forced to cook their own meals because the hotel staff would not wait on them (*Weekly Mail*, 1990, Feb. 2). Stopping the cricket tour has proven to be a watershed victory. The white sports establishment realized that it could no longer count on "rebel" tours and was forced to seek negotiations.[1]

The purpose of this paper is to discuss ongoing changes in South African sport, the new strategies and organizations developed by the liberation movement in response to the changes, and the promise and problems of the future. The campaign against apartheid in sport provides an illuminating case study of how shrewd intervention by sportspersons, under even the most difficult conditions, can effect significant change. It also points to the possibility that changes in sport can contribute to the transformation of society.

THE STATE OF PLAY WITHIN SOUTH AFRICA

South African sport has been deeply divided by apartheid and its opponents. Historically, the sharpest antagonisms have separated what is referred to as "establishment sport"—the white-dominated network of clubs, national bodies, and umbrella federations whose leaders have connections with the apartheid state—from the antiestablishment, antiapartheid, nonracial sector led by men and women of color. Each has its own facilities, competitions, champions, and publications. Rarely, until very recently, did the two communicate. On the contrary, establishment sport repeatedly spoke against their nonracial counterparts on the grounds that they had "politicized" sport. For its part, despite constant harassment and very meager revenues that have kept facilities poor and playing opportunities uneven, the nonracial movement has militantly opposed apartheid.

There are further demarcation lines within the establishment sector. The various governing bodies, leagues, and clubs are hierarchically organized by race. For example, the South African Rugby Board (SARB) is a membership organization of primarily white clubs that also incorporates and paternalistically controls the "colored" South African Rugby Federation (SARF) and the black South African Rugby Association (SARA).[2]

Under the reign of "petty" apartheid,[3] it was against the law for athletes from the different races to play against each other, and athletes of color had no chance to excel. Even spectators were rigidly segregated. But in the early 1970s, in response to South Africa's growing international isolation (the white South African National Olympic Committee, SANOC, was expelled from the Olympic Movement in 1970), the apartheid state sought to give establishment sport an integrated look in the hope that photographs of blacks and whites playing on the same fields would bring sanctions to an end. The policy that it developed, and which remains essentially in place to this day, was multinational or multiracial sport. In contrast, antiapartheid groups adopted the color-blind term, nonracial.

Under multiracial sport, the government created special occasions whereby athletes of different pigmentation could compete together. Initially, because of the apartheid premise that members of different races within South Africa are members of different nations, integrated competition was only allowed if international competitors were present. In the late 1970s, integrated competition among just South Africans was allowed if the players obtained a government permit. In the 1980s, as the sports boycott further restricted South African competition abroad, the government extended the policy of multiracial sport, dropping all direct legislative restrictions upon sport "mixing."

It is these changes that have enabled the propagandists of establishment sport to claim that they are autonomous from the apartheid state and that South African sport is fully integrated. This is clearly an improvement over petty apartheid. Athletes of all races have benefitted from a measure of integrated competition and some blacks have been able to enter and win at the highest levels of competition. In rugby, for example, some blacks are members of predominantly white clubs, and SARF and SARA teams play teams from the SARB.

However, it would be misleading to conclude that this represents significant change. When the totality of South African sport is considered, it is clear that the few concessions made by establishment sport have had little effect on grand apartheid. The ideology of multiracialism perpetuates the myth that differences in skin color require different—and grossly unequal—conditions of citizenship. Under autonomy, sports bodies are still free to differentiate by race, and most continue to do so. The overwhelming majority of athletes still train and play in racially segregated schools and clubs just as their parents did 30 years ago. One recent study found that only 4 of 56 surveyed establishment sports bodies had any antidiscrimination regulations (Booth, 1990). In many cities and towns, whites fiercely resist any attempt at integration. When the recent abolition of the Separate Amenities Act required the opening of public swimming pools, sports grounds, and libraries to all races, many town councils found new ways to continue segregation (Dunn, 1990). Even in the few sports where rules now prohibit racial discrimination, such as rugby, most athletes still compete in racially separate organizations. Most SARF and SARA teams play their games within their own leagues (Australia, 1988).

For establishment sport as a whole, less than 1% of competitions are actually integrated (*Financial Times*, London, 1990, Jan. 18). This is hardly surprising, given that players learned the game in racially segregated school systems, live in racially segregated, geographically separated areas, and enjoy vastly unequal resources. The reality is thus very different from that presented of effective segregation and the white establishment's claims of integration has become a source of great bitterness. In 1988, the Black Tournament Players' Association withdrew *en bloc* from the South African golf tour. Their president, Ben Kgantsi, told the press that,

> They tell visiting golfers that there is no apartheid in golf, but what they forget to tell them is the lack of facilities in the townships—where our players live.
>
> As soon as everything is over, blacks are not allowed to use white courses: it is back to square one on the dusty courses in Soweto and other townships. (*The New Nation*, Johannesburg, 1988, Aug. 18).

In 1989 the SARF president complained that,

> the presence of non-white clubs and teams in [SARB] competition is only outshined by their absence. The number of Federation players taken up in representative teams over the past decade can be numbered on the fingers of two hands. . . . Competitions and provincial teams are holy cows in which the occasional and symbolic presence of non-white players are intrusions to be tolerated rather than encouraged. (*Rugby World and Post*, 1989, June)

Continuing segregation is accompanied by persistent inequality. The Human Sciences Research Council (1982) reported that while whites make up just 15% of the population, they control 73% of all running tracks, 83% of the swimming pools, and 82% of the rugby fields. In Natal, the 330,000 blacks in the townships of Umlazi and Lamontville share six soccer fields and two swimming pools. The 212,000 whites living in nearby Durban share 146 soccer fields and 15 swimming pools. In 1984 a University of Potchefstroom study found that the annual per capita spending on white sport was between R7.13 and R19 while the expenditure for blacks was R0.82 (cited by Confederation of South African Sport, 1990). While the South African government continues to fund white sport (and major corporations are granted significant tax deductions for the sponsorship of rebel tours), it has used the excuse of "depoliticizing" sport to cut back on its already limited grants to black sport. In 1988 the director of sport in "coloured" areas estimated that it would cost R239 million to upgrade facilities. The government voted just R20 million. A civil servant responsible for sport in the townships reported that "the shortage of facilities will never be overcome. At present even essential maintenance has become a luxury" (Booth, 1990, p. 157).

Several establishment sports bodies have launched highly publicized coaching and development schemes for blacks. The best known is the heavily sponsored grassroots program started in the townships by the South African Cricket Union headed by Ali Backer. There are obvious benefits from the infusion of energy, expertise and money into township sport. But here too the political motivation seems dominant. Last year Backer tried to use the township program to justify the 1990 rebel tour. When the tour went ahead against their objections, many black leaders withdrew support for the program (Hill, 1990).

The Squash Rackets Association is quite open about the fact that it tries to convince the 8- to 12-year-olds it recruits that "sport and politics do not mix." Most programs are imposed from above with little if any consultation with black leaders and athletes. Some critics suggest that the white sports bodies "are introducing thousands of black children to sport only to discard them if they do not show potential for competition or if they cannot be transported to decent facilities in white areas" (Booth, 1990, p. 171).

Given the depths of racial separation and inequality underlying the surface change, black sport leaders continue to press for a full moratorium on international sport as a means of intensifying the pressures for change. Their call is supported by the major liberation organizations, the ANC, the United Democratic Front (UDF), the Pan African Congress, and the trade unions as well as student and women's organizations. Most international observers take the same position. A report by the Australian Embassy in Pretoria (1988) concluded that,

> as long as black South Africans do not have rough equality of opportunity in all aspects of life—health, education, housing, employment, welfare, access to leisure time and facilities—including equitable per capita expenditures by the government in all these areas, and underpinned by non-discriminatory laws, it will never be possible for them to participate in sport in a fair and equal basis. . . . The [Australian] Government continues to believe that sporting sanctions deliver a powerful message to white South Africans of the need for fundamental change.

After a tour of the SACU coaching scheme for black youngsters, David Sheppard, the Bishop of Liverpool (England) and a former national team cricket player, observed,

> however much "petty apartheid" has been removed, "grand apartheid" is firmly in place. Issues of policies about land, segregation, education, the police and how decisions are made all come to the surface. Any substantial numbers of boys cannot have facilities to play cricket, because the Group Areas Act confines black people, coloured people and Asian people to inadequate land. The crowding is such that it would be impossible to provide good cricket grounds until the Group Areas Act is removed and land is shared more equitably. . . .
>
> It is unthinkable that there should be any relaxing of sporting, political or economic pressure at this critical moment. (Sheppard, 1989, p. 26)

THE INTERNATIONAL RESPONSE

The international campaign against racism in South African sport has a long history. The first efforts actually preceded the imposition of apartheid by the Nationalist Government in 1948. In 1934 the British Empire games Federation (the predecessor to the Commonwealth Games Federation) refused to award its next Games to Johannesburg because the South Africans declared that black athletes from the other dominions and colonies would not be welcome (National Archives of Canada, 1934). But it took much longer for the international community to accept the need to isolate South Africa altogether as a means of combating racism in sport. It was not until 1956 that an international federation, Table Tennis, expelled white South Africa from membership. Although suspended by the IOC in 1963 and expelled in 1970, South Africa still enjoys membership in 15 Olympic federations (see Table 24-1). For the most part, international sport federations are controlled by white upper-class males from western countries with traditional ties to South Africa. The sports boycott goes against their impulse to compete whatever the circumstances, their belief in noninterference, and the admirable hope that sport could teach tolerance by example.

Gradually, through the leadership of the nonracial leaders (expressed through SANROC after 1963), the persistent lobbying and campaigning

Table 24-1 South Africa's Position in the Olympic Federations

Sport	*Status*
Archery	Member with voting rights only (i.e., not allowed in international competitions)
Badminton	Voting rights only
Baseball	Not a member
Basketball	Expelled in 1980
Bobsleigh	Not a member
Boxing	Expelled in 1968
Canoeing	Suspended in 1970
Cycling	Refused membership in 1970
Equestrian	Voting rights only
Fencing	Voting rights only
Gymnastics	Voting rights only
Handball	Refused membership in 1982
Hockey	Member but status unclear
Ice Hockey	Voting rights only
Judo	Not a member
Luge	Not a member
Pentathlon	Voting rights only
Rowing	Voting rights only
Shooting	Suspended
Skating	Member but status unclear
Skiing	Not a member
Soccer	Expelled in 1976
Swimming	Expelled in 1973
Table tennis	Expelled in 1956; antiapartheid SATTB a member
Tennis	Suspended in 1989
Track & Field	Expelled in 1976
Volleyball	Not a member
Weightlifting	Expelled in 1972
Wrestling	Expelled in 1970
Yachting	Member, but competition restricted

The International Olympic Committee (IOC) suspended the establishment South African Olympic Committee (SANOC) in 1963 and expelled it in 1970. On the other hand, it has officially recognized the South African Non-Racial Olympic Committee, giving it privileged status on its Commission on Apartheid and Olympism. The Association of National Olympic Committees of Africa (ANOCA) recently recognized the antiapartheid National Olympic and Sport Congress (NSC) of supporters in many countries, and the willingness of athletes and coaches from Africa, Asia, the Caribbean, and the socialist countries to sacrifice their own sporting opportunities in boycotts of solidarity, the international sports governing bodies agreed to sanctions. Three arguments have been particularly effective in this long and painstaking struggle: the moral claim that sport be free from racial discrimination, the arrogant refusal of the white South African sportsleaders to contemplate significant change, and the overwhelming evidence that the sports boycott has been effective. Every single Olympic federation has taken some action to resist South African participation. Governments have extended these prohibitions, by barring entry to South African athletes and officials and by requiring their own athletes and sports associations to boycott all sporting contact with South Africa as a condition of public support (Archer & Bouillon, 1982; Brickhill, 1976; Hain, 1971; Kidd, 1988; Lapchick, 1975; Ramsamy, 1982; Thompson, 1975).[4]

After 1986, as international opposition hardened with the introduction of the Emergency, the campaign has gone from strength to strength. The biggest victories were in cricket and tennis, both popular sports among South African whites. South Africa has always had influential contacts in English cricket. Many cricketers traveled to South Africa to play during the English winter, and some of the best-known players are active in the proSouth African lobby, Freedom for Sport. The governments of India, Pakistan, Sri Lanka, the Caribbean countries, and most recently New Zealand sought to discourage these exchanges by barring those with South African links. In 1988 for example, an English cricket tour of India, Pakistan, and New Zealand had to be canceled because the team included several members who had played in South Africa. However, efforts to force the governing International Cricket Conference (ICC; now Council) to ban contacts with South Africa repeatedly failed when English and Australian delegates used their founders' veto. But in 1989, as a result of lobbying by Asian and Caribbean cricket powers, the ICC unanimously established a ban from international competition for players who compete in South Africa. The decision seems to have significantly reduced the number who played in the South African season, from an estimated 70 (in the years before the ban) to 19 in 1989 (*The Times*, London, 1989, Jan. 25 and Sept. 26). It also resulted in the worldwide opposition to the 1990 rebel English tour.

In tennis, the campaign was helped by the IOC. In 1988 the Olympic governing body established a Commission of Apartheid and Olympism to intensify the isolation of apartheid South Africa. On the Commission's recommendation, the IOC decided that athletes who competed in South Africa would automatically be disqualified from taking part in any future Olympic Games. It was also made clear that federations seeking Olympic competition should remove South Africa from membership. The International Tennis Federation, seeking to upgrade its sport from the demonstration of Seoul, promptly suspended the South African Tennis Union. The Association of Tennis Professionals eliminated South African events from the Grand Prix tour (Cart, 1990, May 10).

The *cordon sanitaire* around South African sport has been tightened in other ways. The professional World Boxing Council (WBC) began to impose sanctions on promoters, boxers, and managers with South African ties. The governments of Belgium, Canada, New Zealand and Spain took steps to bar South African athletes from entry. The Swedish Sports Federation announced an even tougher stand, joining African, Asian, and Caribbean countries in barring athletes listed on the United Nations Register. In many cases the work of antiapartheid activists was instrumental in pressuring governments to take these decisions, and in reminding athletes who had been to South Africa that they could no longer play with apartheid without censure. In Australia, Britain, Canada, France, New Zealand, and the United States, activists protested apartheid links. A number of sportspersons, too, took positions of leadership. Former Commonwealth boxing champion Nigel Been of Britain turned down a $3 million offer to fight in South Africa (*The Star*, Johannesburg, 1989, Aug. 19). Between April 1, 1988, and April 1, 1990, 162 athletes took a United Nations pledge not to return to South Africa (United Nations, 1990).

But not all sportspersons and governments accept the need for a boycott. Despite the Gleneagles Agreement, which requires Commonwealth countries to stop sports ties, there is a constant two-way flow of British and South African athletes and officials. The Thatcher Government refused to take any action to prevent contact on the grounds that it would be "fundamentally objectionable in a free society."[5] When the ICC voted to penalize cricketers for playing in South Africa, 50 Conservative members of Parliament issued a declaration condemning the resolution. When the International Rugby Board gave South Africa permission to invite a world team for a series of matches in 1989, it was perhaps inevitable that the majority of players came from Britain. Neither the Thatcher Government nor the leaders of the British sports community nor Commonwealth officials were willing to discipline the offenders.

Attempts to expel South Africa from the international federations in badminton and squash failed despite majority support. In both cases, negative ballots from western countries left the vote short of the required majority. Despite the gains in tennis, South Africans can still compete in the Grand Slam of Wimbledon and the Australian, French, and U.S. Open and the professional circuits of those countries. A number of South Africans still circumvent sanctions through passports of convenience and false identification (Cart, 1990, May 8). But by all the measures employed–the shrinking contacts, the declining athletic ability of those rebels who flout the boycott, and the embarrassment heaped upon them at home–the international campaign is very effective.

THE NEW STRATEGY OF THE LIBERATION MOVEMENT

For most of the last two decades the nonracial sports movement has taken as its target the whole system of apartheid. Led by the South African Council on Sport (SACOS), it countered the cosmetic changes of multiracial sport with the slogan, "No normal sport in an abnormal society." Buoyed by the militancy of the post-Soweto resistance, it refused to have any dealings with establishment sport (and the various bantustan sports bodies). It urged SANROC and its allies to conduct a blanket boycott against all South African sportspersons, even those blacks who excelled under the policy of multiracialism.

Recently the movement has adopted a new strategy, one that maintains the pressure against the proapartheid sports bodies while strengthening the nonracial sector in preparation for the entry of democratic South Africa to international competition.[6] In a key shift, the movement opened the possibility of uncoupling the sports moratorium from the overall antiapartheid campaign and began to set sport-specific conditions for international competition and exchange. The most important of these is the creation of single, democratic, nonracial, and nonsexist governing bodies actively committed to the eradication of inequality; that is, establishment sport must join with the nonracial movement to build unified federations in every sport.

The new strategy actually predated the dramatic political breakthroughs of the last year. It grew out of the contradictions of multiracial sport and the harsh conditions of the Emergency, when virtually all political opposition was suppressed and critical discourse was censored. The cosmetic liberalization of sport created an opening whereby some critical public commentary was possible if coded in the language of sport. The democratic movement increased its efforts to agitate against apartheid sport and create new sports opportunities in the townships and rural areas where they have been particularly underdeveloped.

To extend the base of their support, liberation movement leaders sought to win over the black sports bodies that were collaborating with multiracial sport. To do this they had to reconsider the blanket boycott. In establishment track and field, rugby, soccer, and boxing, where the mines, the police, black sports entrepreneurs, and international companies like Adidas aggressively promote black players, the number of accomplished black athletes is growing. Many of these have no choice but to play within multiracial sport. Because careers are short, even a segment in the black community has criticized the international campaign's hard line. In 1988 SANROC persuaded the international soccer federation (FIFA) to bar professional soccer star Jomo Sono from an international fund-raising exhibition game in Harare. Soccer is the most popular sport for black South African males, and the intervention unleashed a fury of criticism against SANROC and the blanket boycott.

The two-track strategy took shape in response to these pressures, in consultation with SANROC and African sports leaders. Placing international assistance and competition on the agenda had several advantages. First, it offered strengthened communications and practical assistance to nonracial sport. These considerations have prompted a similar turn in the cultural and academic boycotts. Second, it created a powerful incentive for unity under the nonracial banner, helping solidify antiapartheid resistance in the black community and perhaps even drawing in white support. Third, and most tantalizingly, it raised the prospect of a new visibility for the antiapartheid movement as a whole. Sports usually reinforce the dominance of the powerful who control them, but they can also dramatize the worthiness and humanity of the powerless. An antiapartheid team in the Olympic Games, organized by the liberation movement under the banner of the liberation movement, while the representatives of establishment sport were forced to stay home, would demonstrate the illegitimacy of apartheid to the entire world. One can only imagine the excitement that this vision presented at the height of the Emergency!

The new strategy was first signaled in October 1988, when the ANC arranged a meeting between nonracial sports leaders and the officials of the National Soccer League, the powerful black organization that had not previously taken an active part in the antiapartheid movement. The ANC held out the prospect that a unified nonracial soccer body might send teams to international tournaments. Since then the nonracial movement has reasserted its link to the overall struggle, employing the language of the United Nations (1989) to insist upon full sanctions until the eradication of apartheid is "profound and irreversible." But it has taken the campaign to create unified, democratic, nonracial, and nonsexist governing bodies into many other sports. At the same time, through the auspices of SANROC, it has sent a growing number of black coaches and teachers to study abroad and accepted aid from sports groups and governments in Australia, Britain, Canada, and Sweden.

These steps have been coordinated by a new organization, the National Olympic and Sports Congress (NSC), created by the mass democratic movement when SACOS refused to contemplate any change in strategy (SACOS continues to advocate a blanket boycott under the slogan, "no normal sport in an abnormal society"). In July 1989, 475 persons from sports, the ANC and UDF, trade unions, women's groups, teachers' and students' organizations, and the churches attended the first national conference. The largest nonracial sports bodies in the country—in soccer, cricket, and rugby—and nonracial federations in 22 other sports are now involved with the NSC (National and Olympic Sports Congress, July 18, 1989, press release).

Since 1988 the NSC has been at the forefront of every major development. During the 1989 rugby tour it mounted the most effective protest against an international team ever seen in South Africa, demonstrating against games and local branches of the sponsoring National Bank, confronting the players and their manager in their hotel, all with favorable publicity. Later that spring it provided assistance to the democratic movement's mass trespass against "beach apartheid," which ultimately forced the De Klerk government to declare the beaches open to all races. These successful interventions culminated in the massive nationwide protest against the cricket tour in January 1990. Despite media manipulation, police charges, tear gas attacks, and threats of being declared illegal, the NSC and its allies turned the tour into a total failure. The message of these dramatic events was unmistakable: the old order of rebel tours, played out behind the protection of police dogs and baton charges, was finished. Henceforth the only hope of the sports establishment for international competition lay in negotiations with the NSC.

In recent months the NSC has met with establishment sports leaders in boxing, cricket, gymnastics, road running, soccer, and track and field, as well as the still functioning SANOC and some white schools sports associations, in an effort to draw them into a nonracial, antiapartheid alliance. The starting point for these negotiations has been acceptance of the sports moratorium by establishment organizations, an obligation to educate their members in the ethos of non-racialism, and a commitment to "actively participate in the process to destroy apartheid." The Congress has continued to bring the various black associations together. In addition, it has started its own developmental programs in cricket, tennis, and other sports. In each case it has challenged the South African breweries and the other large sport sponsors to make good on their antiapartheid rhetoric and invest in black sport (until now, 90% of all sponsorship money goes to white sports [National, 1990]). The NSC leadership is determined to extend and enrich opportunities, not only to athletes of color but also to the millions not presently engaged in sports, particularly girls and women and the oppressed peoples of the rural areas and bantustans. The NSC also seeks to transform sports from the self-assurance of the privileged to the empowerment of the powerless (Roberts, 1989).

These efforts have the support of the international community. Several western governments have contributed to the cost of NSC activities. The IOC has frequently said that South Africa must satisfy the African Olympic community before it can be accepted into international competition. The Association of African National Olympic Committees (ANOCA) has said that it is prepared to admit the NSC as the representative of nonracial South Africa "immediately the moratorium against international sporting contact is lifted" (Eley, 1990). At the recent meeting in Harare, ANOCA President Jean-Claude Ganga made it clear that "the total eradication of apartheid in all its forms" and nonracial unity must be achieved before the IOC will consider South Africa's membership. The Harare meeting established two committees to pursue these goals, one made up of South African sports leaders, the other a monitoring committee appointed by ANOCA (1990, Nov. 4, press release).

THE ROAD AHEAD

Recent breakthroughs have raised the worldwide hope that the demise of apartheid is near. While liberation leaders caution that grand apartheid remains in place, there is an undeniable spirit of optimism. Speculation about the normalization of relations with South Africa has become commonplace. In sports, where the desire to make friends and build bridges has always been strong, there is enormous curiosity (as well as admiration and solidarity) about the nonracial movement and a growing eagerness to see it in international competition. IOC President Samaranch (1990) has likened the sports boycott to a race and suggested that the "finish line is very, very near." He also said that since the Olympic movement was "the first to say 'no' to South Africa, it would be proud to be the first to welcome its return." Friends of white South Africa and a number of black South African sportspersons have encouraged these expectations, suggesting that a South African team might compete in the Olympics as early as 1992 in Barcelona (Osler, 1990).

But from the perspective of nonracial leadership, the gains of recent months only serve to illuminate the distance still to be covered. The minimum condition of unified, democratic, nonracial and nonsexist sports bodies has yet to be achieved in a single sport. Among the black communities, overcoming the ghettoization of forced separation and the jealousies created by multiracialism will take time. Trust has to be established, tentative agreements worked out, and the memberships consulted, invariably by volunteers from different regions, with scarce resources and countless other demands upon their time. The process has been advanced by the spirit of collective enterprise in recent years, but it cannot be hurried.

The path to unity with the white bodies will be more difficult. While SANOC, the track and field and road running bodies, and the promoters at Sun City have agreed to accept the NSC's conditions, including the moratorium on international competition, the powerful white golf, rugby, tennis, and cricket bodies refuse to do so. The establishment Confederation of South African Sport predicts that the white bodies will have to be coerced into opposing apartheid, and if that happens they "will be faced with breakaways to the right of the political spectrum" (1990, p. 12).

Even when unity is reached, the maximal goal of equality of opportunity will take years and millions of rands to achieve. South Africa remains a holiday camp for whites, a prison camp for blacks. Grand apartheid still condemns the black majority to separate living areas and housing, separate schooling, separate health care, and vastly inferior incomes and life chances. The Population Registration Act, which determines civil status by race, and the Land Acts, which give the white majority 87% of the land, are still firmly in place. Few whites are willing to grant a significant redistribution of sports facilities and other resources. Nor do all groups endorse the simultaneous commitment to gender equality. It will be difficult to overcome the legacy of discrimination and oppression under these conditions.

Much of course will depend upon the talks at the highest level between the apartheid government and the ANC. If they lead to a democratic reconstruction, then the hoped-for antidiscrimination legislation and redistribution of resources will accelerate the process in sports. But if the existing pattern of land ownership and a web of apartheid regulations, however amended, remains, then the possibilities for genuinely nonracial sport will be significantly reduced. Given the De Klerk government's refusal to contemplate an unrestricted "one person, one vote" franchise, the most likely scenario is protracted, possibly stalemated negotiations, with further advances only when mass mobilization and international pressure make them inevitable. It should not be forgotten that in both Namibia and Zimbabwe the liberation movements' ultimate successes at the negotiating table were enabled by military victories in the field.

Until there is major change, the NSC and its allies abroad will continue to insist upon a strong international boycott (e.g., Fourth International Conference Against Apartheid Sport, 1990). They strongly reject the idea that South Africa should be rewarded for the steps taken during last year, arguing that "if anybody needed to be 'rewarded' it was those that have for so long been on the receiving end of apartheid" (National and Olympic Sports Congress, Oct. 20, 1990, press release). Even when the moratorium is lifted, the NSC will insist upon nonracial and nonsexist unity as a condition for South Africa's entry into international competition.

In the meantime the NSC has stepped up its appeal for technical and financial international assistance, pointing out that the historic pattern of inequality ensures that white athletes will benefit disproportionately from international competition for many years to come.[7] If the effort to quarantine apartheid sport involves a commitment to the cure, the international community must not abandon the nonracial movement as it enters this next difficult stage.

Sports scholars have frequently debated the possibilities for effective human intervention (e.g., Ingham, Loy, & Swetman, 1979). The long campaign against apartheid in sport provides ample evidence that there is scope for human agency. It also shows how social structures both enable and constrain, in a manner that is frustratingly complex, unpredictable, and uneven. While waged in harmony with the overall struggle against apartheid, the sports boycott has set in motion dynamics of its own, often in response to pressures unique to the sports world. None of the other antiapartheid sanction campaigns (or other sports boycotts) have been as effective. It has brought about major changes to the international organization of sports and has assisted the liberation movement's advance in South African politics. Whether it can further the transformation of South African society awaits the next stage of the struggle.

POSTSCRIPT

On November 6, 1991, in Johannesburg, veteran anti-apartheid campaigner Sam Ramsamy announced before a national television audience that the new National Olympic Committee of South Africa (NOCSA) of which he is president will be sending a team to the 1992 Olympic Games in Barcelona.

The press conference was a careful showpiece for the inclusive non-racialism Ramsamy and his colleagues have long struggled to develop in sports. The Barcelona team will mark the first time that South Africa will be represented in Olympic competition, he said, pointing out that only "a section of South Africa" competed in the years prior to 1963 (when the International Olympic Committee suspended the all-white South African Olympic Committee; SANOC was expelled in 1970).

Rather than use the "inappropriate" symbols of apartheid, the team will march under a new "interim" blue, brown, green and grey flag and use the Olympic hymn, Beethoven's "Ode to Joy," as its anthem, to indicate a South Africa in transition towards democracy. (NOCSA is presently conducting a national competition for a new mascot to replace the Afrikaners' springbok.)

Ramsamy praised Nelson Mandela "for his vital role in opening the doors for the Olympic movement in South Africa." Mandela was the only non-sportsperson mentioned.

The announcement is the most concrete result of a deal worked out between the non-racial sports movement, the ANC, the white sports establishment and the apartheid regime during the early months of 1991. In it, the De Klerk government agreed to repeal the "pillars of apartheid" legislation and the white sports establishment to participate in the creation of "unified," non-racial governing bodies in every sport. They also committed to a series of anti-apartheid educational campaigns, and grass-roots development programs to address the tremendous inequalities created by apartheid. In return, the anti-apartheid movement agreed to take down the moratorium against international events, and to accelerate the schedule so that Olympic competition might begin with the Barcelona Games. Previously, Ramsamy and others had said that the first Olympics for a new South Africa would probably be in Atlanta in 1996.

The responsibility for monitoring implementation was given to NOCSA, an entirely new body made up of representatives from SANROC,

NSC, SACOS, SANOC and COSAS. (SACOS has since distanced itself from the agreement.) The IOC has given its blessing to the new arrangements.

The decision to send a team to Barcelona has not meant a complete end to the moratorium. NOCSA is determined to use whatever sting remains in the sanctions weapon to spur on sports bodies to meet the conditions for non-racial unity. It vetoed participation in the world track and field championships in Tokyo by the new "unified" body, on the grounds that there had been insufficient progress towards non-racialism.

One of the factors which led to the Barcelona timetable was the calculation that in the atmosphere of normalization that De Klerk has managed to create internationally, fewer and fewer federations and governments would continue to enforce the sports boycott. That has proven to be the case. NOCSA has found it increasingly difficult to obtain support even for a selective moratorium. In fact, the International Amateur Athletic Federation offered the largely white South African team an all-expenses paid invitation to the championships in Tokyo.

On this uncertain terrain, the non-racial leaders have played their hand well. Despite the fragility of their agreement with establishment sport and their declining international support, they continue to play a central role in determining the character and pace of change. They still use the lure of international sport to advance the process of creating fairer opportunities for participation. And they have gained decided ideological advantage on the symbols issue. None of this should surprise us given the tactical skill they developed during the long years of the international campaign.

To be sure, there are enormous risks ahead. It's unlikely that the non-racial leaders will be able to maintain the selective moratorium beyond Barcelona. Without the election of a progressive democratic government, they will need another "carrot and stick" to force the establishment bodies to deliver on their promises. Even in the best circumstances, they will find that international sport often drains energies and resources away from grassroots development. But Ramsamy & Co. recognize these–and other mine fields that could be mentioned–as the agenda for their movement for the next decade. In the meantime, the manner in which they negotiated their "coming out" inspires confidence.

NOTES

1. While South African whites in many other cultural fields–literature, music, film, and theatre–embraced the antiapartheid cause long ago, few did so in sport prior to 1990. For years the leaders of nonracial sport appealed to the establishment sector in vain for a common front against apartheid (Streek, 1985).
2. To add to the confusion of organizations and acronyms, there is also the nonracial South African Rugby Union (SARU).

3. "Petty" apartheid refers to the strict segregation of all aspects of South African society introduced by the Nationalist Government shortly after its election in 1948, and brutally enforced until the late 1970s. It has slowly been replaced by "grand" apartheid, under which some liberalization of contact between the races has occurred, while the "pillars of apartheid," such as the Group Areas Act, remain in place.
4. In addition, since 1980, annual summaries of the campaign have been published by the United Nations Center Against Apartheid, in its Register of Sports Contacts with South Africa.
5. These scruples did not prevent that same government from threatening with dismissal civil servants who wanted to compete in the 1980 Moscow Olympics.
6. Language is instructive here: nonracial leaders stress that the real South Africa has never competed in international competition, only the tiny white minority.
7. Because of similar circumstances, the first team that newly independent Zimbabwe entered in the Olympic Games–in Moscow in 1980–was entirely white. In newly independent Namibia, the white minority enjoys a virtual monopoly over the Olympic sports.

REFERENCES

Archer, R., & Bouillon, A (1982). *The South African Game*. London: Zed.

Australia, Minister for Foreign Affairs and Trade. (1988). Race and rugby in South Africa. Pretoria: Author.

Booth, D. (1990). South Africa's "autonomous sport" strategy: Desegregation apartheid style. *Sporting Traditions: Journal of the Australian Society for Sports History*, **6**(2), 155-179.

Brickhill, J. (1976). *Race against Race*. London: International Defense in Aid Fund.

Cart, J. (1990, May 8). Smuggling a banned commodity. *Los Angeles Times*.

Cart, J. (1990, May 10). Ban from Olympics turns into net loss. *Los Angeles Times*.

Confederation of South African Sport. (1990). *Contact, Unity, & Fair Play through Sport*. Johannesburg: Author.

Dunn, R. (1990, Oct. 14). Small-town whites outwit race reform. *The Sunday Times* (London).

Eley, H. (1990, June 10). Africa backs new body. *Sunday Star* (Johannesburg).

Fourth International Conference Against Apartheid Sport. (1990, Sept. 6). Declaration. Stockholm.

Hain, P. (1971). *Don't Play with Apartheid*. London: George Allen & Unwin.

Hill, D. (1990, Feb. 11). Mismatch of history and opportunism. *The Independent*.

Human Sciences Research Council. (1982). *Sport in the Republic of South Africa: Main Committee Report*. Pretoria.

Ingham, A., Loy, J. W., & Swetman, R. D. (1979). Sport, heroes, and society: Issues of transformation and reproduction. *Working Papers in the Sociological Study of Sport and Leisure*, **2**(4).

Kidd, B. (1988). The campaign against sport in South Africa. *International Journal*, **43**(4), 643-664.

Lapchick, R. (1975). *The Politics of Race and International Sport*. Westport, CT: Greenwood.

National Archives of Canada, Amateur Athletic Union of Canada. (1934). Minutes of the 1934 annual general meeting. Ottawa.

National and Olympic Sports Congress. (1990, June 1). *The Way Forward* (pamphlet). Johannesburg: Author.

Osler, S. (1990, Sept. 2). World sport eager for SA to return. *Sunday Star* (Johannesburg).

Ramsamy, S. (1982). *Apartheid: The Real Hurdle*. London: International Defense in Aid Fund.

Roberts, C. (Ed.) (1989). *Sport and Transformation: Contemporary Debates on South African Sport*. Capetown: Township Publ.

Samaranch, J. A. (1990, Sept. 4). Remarks to the 4th International Conference Against Apartheid Sports. Stockholm.

Sheppard, D. (1989, August). Little for your comfort. *The Cricketer*, pp. 26-27.

Streek B. (1985). Illusion and reality in South Africa sport policy. *South Africa International*, **16**(1), 29-41.

Thompson, R. (1975). *Retreat from Apartheid*. Wellington: Oxford.

United Nations, General Assembly. (1989, Dec. 14). Declaration on apartheid and its destructive consequences in southern Africa. New York.

United Nations, Special Committee Against Apartheid. (1990). Register of sports contacts with apartheid. New York.

25. *The Political Olympics: The Problem and Solution*

D. STANLEY EITZEN

The motto of the Olympic Games—"Citius, Altius, Fortius" ("Faster, Higher, Stronger")—implies that athletic performance is to supersede all other concerns (this essay depends in part on Eitzen and Sage, 1989:181-185). Ever since the revival of the Olympics in 1896, however, there has been an erosion of the prominence of athletic accomplishments and the corresponding ascendance of political, economic, and bureaucratic considerations. This paper addresses the political side of the Olympics and offers suggestions for reducing the corrosive effects of politics on the Olympic movement and its ideals.

POLITICAL PROBLEMS

Politics surrounding the Olympics is manifested in four major ways: (1) excessive nationalism within nations concerning the performance of their athletes in the Olympics; (2) decisions by ruling bodies to deny participation by certain nations; (3) decisions by nations to boycott the Games for political reasons; and (4) the political organization of the Olympics. Let's examine these in turn.

Excessive Nationalism within Nations

Nationalism related to the Olympics that goes beyond its appropriate boundaries is expressed several ways. Foremost, there is the use of athletics to promote political goals. Hitler, for example, turned the 1936 Games in Berlin into a propaganda show to legitimate Nazi Germany. Similarly, nations tend to use their showing in international athletic events as an indicator of the superiority of their politico-economic systems. The eastern bloc countries such as East Germany, Bulgaria, Romania, Cuba, and the Soviet Union, have traditionally conducted national efforts to identify, coach, and subsidize elite (or potential elite) athletes. Other nations, including the United States, use different methods to achieve international athletic success but with the same goal of demonstrating the superiority of their way-of-life. Thus, it was a shock to Americans when the United States came in third in total medal count at the 1988 Seoul Games (behind the Soviet Union and East Germany), and *ninth* in medals if population size is considered (behind East Germany, Bulgaria, Hungary, Romania, South Korea, West Germany, Soviet Union, and Great Britain.) This brought about considerable national concern about our poor performance. One representative headline read: "What Went Wrong for U. S.?" (Meyers, 1988). There were calls from various sectors for the U. S. to improve by increasing the subsidization of athletes (Holmes, 1988), emphasizing minor sports (Swift, 1988), and reorganization of the U. S. Olympic Committee (Rosner, 1988). As a result, commissions were formed to study the problem and make recommendations, government and corporate monies were raised, rules regarding amateurism overturned, and the athletes were provided with training, the latest in sports science and sports medicine, and the like. All of this to restore national pride, if our athletes won. Other countries are even more direct: in the 1988 Summer Games, The Philippines offered its athletes $100,000 for a medal; South Korea offered its gold medalists $1000 a month for life; and Taiwan offered $140,000 for a gold, $107,000 for a silver, and $70,000 for a bronze medal (Callahan, 1988).

A second manifestation of excessive nationalism is that in the zeal to win some nations may promote the use of performance enhancing drugs for their athletes.

A third indication of national chauvinism has to do with the reporting of international events. Members of the media in reporting the Olympics may let their politics distort their analysis. Some examples:

- During the opening ceremonies of the 1988 Winter Olympics in Calgary, as the Danes followed by the North Koreans paraded by the television cameras, ABC's Peter Jennings observed: "What a contrast between North Korea–remote, closed, hostile to Westerners–and Denmark, this peace-loving nation of Northern Europe where the emphasis is really on quality of life. . . ." (cited in Rosellini, 1988:64).
- During coverage of the pairs' figure-skating event in the 1988 Games, skating analyst Dick Button suggested that an East German judge had marked down the top American pair in order to boost East Germany's chances (Rosellini, 1988:64).

Political Decisions by National and International Olympic Committees

The following are a few examples from the last 55 years of decisions by ruling bodies made for political reasons (for a sample of the sources dealing with this aspect of the Olympics and the next section, see Espy, 1979; Mandell, 1979; Edwards, 1984; Guttmann, 1984; Lapchick, 1986):

1936: As a concession to the Nazis, the United States Olympic committee dropped two Jewish sprinters from the 400-meter relay.

1948: Israel was excluded from participation after a threat of an Arab boycott.
1952: East Germany was denied participation because it was not a "recognized state."
1960: The IOC decreed that North and South Korea should compete as one team, using the same flag, emblem, and uniform. Nationalist China was forced to compete under the name of Taiwan.
1964: South Africa was banned from the Olympics for its apartheid policies.
1968: Tommie Smith and John Carlos of the United States raised a black power salute during the American national anthem and were banned from Olympic competition for life by the U. S. Olympic Committee.
1972: The IOC ruled that Rhodesia would be allowed to participate. Many African nations were incensed by this action because of the racist policies of the ruling elite in Rhodesia and threatened a boycott of the Games unless Rhodesia was barred. The IOC bowed to this pressure and rescinded its earlier action.
1991: The International Olympic Committee agreed to let South Africa participate in the 1992 Olympics provided that it meet certain conditions regarding the dismantling of apartheid.

Political Decisions by Individual Nations regarding the Olympics

International incidents that have nothing to do with the Olympic Games have sometimes caused nations to withdraw their teams from competition. Some examples:

1952: Taiwan boycotted the Games when Communist China was admitted to the International Olympic Committee.
1956: Egypt, Lebanon, and Iraq boycotted the Olympics because of the Anglo-French seizure of the Suez Canal. Spain, Switzerland, and The Netherlands withdrew from the Olympics in protest after the Soviet Union invaded Hungary.
1976: Twenty-eight African nations boycotted the Games because New Zealand, whose rugby team had toured South Africa, was allowed to compete.
1980: Some fifty-four nations, including the United States, West Germany, Canada, and Japan, boycotted the Games because of the Soviet Union's invasion of Afghanistan.
1984: Fourteen nations, most notably the Soviet Union, East Germany, Cuba, Bulgaria, and Poland, boycotted the Games because they were held in the United States.

1988: Cuba boycotted the Summer Games because North Korea was not allowed to cohost the Games with South Korea. North Korea joined in the boycott.

The Political Organization of the Olympics

In addition to the corruptions of the Olympic ideals that I have just outlined, the very ways that the Games are organized are political. Nations select which athletes will perform (i.e., no athlete can perform without national sponsorship). The IOC provides ceremonies where athletes march behind their country's flag. After each event, the winner's national anthem is played and the flags of the three medal winners are raised at the awards ceremony. The IOC also considers political criteria in the selection of the site of the Olympics and in the choice of judges, ensuring in the latter case a balance between East and West, especially in the judging of events such as boxing, diving, ice skating, and gymnastics.

A PROPOSAL FOR CHANGE

To be fair in this appraisal, the Olympic Games do attempt to promote the idea of oneness with the use of the Olympic Hymn and the Olympic flag (five interlaced rings representing "the union of the five continents and the meeting of athletes from all over the world at the Olympic Games in a spirit of fair and frank competition"). But, as Gilbert Cranberg has pointed out, "nationalism not merely intrudes, it dominates." For him, another Olympiad, will be another "orgy of flag-waving. Not just literally, but in the way Olympic contests get the patriotic juices flowing" (Cranberg, 1988:6a).

Is there a way to organize the Olympics to accomplish the aim of neutralizing the crippling political problems that work to negate the Olympic ideals? I offer the following proposals to achieve that aim:

1. *Establish two permanent sites for the Games.* Each permanent site must be neutral for otherwise the Games will continue to be subject to the influence of power politics. The choices most often mentioned are Greece for the Summer Olympics and Switzerland for the Winter Games. Greece is a natural choice because the ancient Olympian Games were held there every four years for more than 1,000 years, ending in 393 A.D. Even better, each of these permanent sites should be in a free zone. A free zone would be land ceded to the International Olympic Committee and therefore land that no nation claims, just as the United Nations is located in a free zone in New York City.

2. *Restrict the events to competition among individuals.* All team sports must be eliminated because each team represents a nation, which makes political considerations inevitable. A second reason for eliminating team sports is that they are inherently unfair; the larger the population base of a nation, the more likely that country will be able to field a superior team.

3. *Athletes must represent only themselves.* Athletes, in actuality and symbolically, should not represent a country, nor should any nation-state be represented by uniforms, flags, national anthems, or political leaders. When an athlete is awarded his or her medal for winning an event, only the Olympic Hymn should be played. Athletes should also be randomly assigned to housing and eating arrangements at the Games to reduce national identification and to maximize cross-national interaction.

4. *All athletes (amateur and professional) are eligible for competition.* The nation-state should not be involved in the selection process because this encourages nationalistic feelings. To ensure that the best athletes of the world are able to compete, a minimum standard for each event should be set by the governing board. Athletes meeting this standard would have all expenses paid to meet in regional competition. At the regionals, another and higher standard of excellence would be set for athletes to qualify for the Olympics. Again, for those athletes qualifying for the Olympics, all expenses for travel and per diem would be paid by the Olympic Committee.

5. *Subsidize the cost of the Olympics from revenues generated from spectators' admissions to the regionals, admissions to the Games, and from television.* By establishing permanent sites and eliminating team events, the cost of the Olympics would be reduced significantly. Revenues from admissions and television should cover the costs after the Games are established. During the building of the permanent sites, though, the Olympic Committee may need a subsidy or loan from the United Nations. Television revenues present a particularly thorny problem because the revenue potential is great and this lends itself to threats of overcommercialization, the intrusion of corporations into the decision-making arena, and jingoism by chauvinistic television commentators. To reduce these potential dangers, the events could be televised and reported by a company strictly controlled by the Olympic Committee. The televising of the Olympics would be provided to each country at a cost determined by the existing number of television sets in that country. Each nation would decide how the fee would be paid, but the important point is that no country would have any control over what would be shown or the commentary emanating from the Games.

6. Establish an Olympic Committee and a secretary-general to prepare for and oversee the Games. The composition of this committee would be crucial. Currently the members of the IOC are taken from national committees, with an important criterion being the maintenance of a political balance between opposing factions. The concept of a ruling body is essential, but the committee should be reorganized to reduce political considerations. This is a baffling problem because the selection will inevitably involve politics. One possibility would be to incorporate the selection procedures used in the United Nations to select its Secretary-General. These procedures have worked, even during the darkest days of the Cold War, toward the selection of a competent, objective, and non-aligned (of neither a pro-Western or a pro-Eastern bloc) arbitrator. In addition to an Olympic secretary-general, a governing board, and a permanent staff would also have to be established.

CONCLUSION

Now is a propitious time to depoliticize the Olympics. The tensions and paranoia associated with the Cold War are receding. In the past two years we have seen cooperative efforts between the two superpowers that have not occurred since World War II. The Eastern bloc is no longer a force. East and West Germany are now Germany. The European Economic Community will break down nationalistic barriers further. Of course, there will be international tensions, wars, and acts of terrorism, but it appears they will not be as threatening as before. Could we take this turning point in history and reorganize the Olympics to eliminate as much of the politics from it as possible? The task is challenging but not impossible. The Olympic movement is important–that is why it must be altered radically from its present form if its lofty goals are to be realized. These proposals suggest some ways this might be accomplished. They are a beginning.

REFERENCES

Calahan, Tom. 1988. "Splashes of Class and Acts of Heroism." *Time* (October 3):56-57.

Cranberg, Gilbert. 1988. "Excess Nationalism Harms the Olympics." *USA Today* (September 23):6A.

Edwards, Harry. 1984. "Sportpolitics: Los Angeles 1984." *Sociology of Sport Journal* 1, no. 2:172-183.

Eitzen, D. Stanley and George H. Sage. 1989. *Sociology of North American Sport*, 4th ed. Dubuque, IA: Wm. C. Brown.

Espy, Richard. 1979. *The Politics of the Olympics*. Berkeley: University of California Press.

Guttmann, Allen. 1984. *The Games Must Go On: Avery Brundage and the Olympic Movement*. New York: Columbia University Press.

Holmes, John. 1988. "Keep a Top Track Record." *Insight* (July 25):8-12.

Lapchick, Richard E. 1986. "A Political History of the Modern Olympic Games." pp. 329-345 in *Fractured Focus*, Richard E. Lapchick (ed.). Lexington, MA: Lexington Books.
Mandell, Richard D. 1979. *The Nazi Olympics*. New York: Macmillan.
Meyers, Charlie. 1988. "What Went Wrong for U. S.?" *Denver Post* (February 28):1,9.
Rosellini, Lynn. 1988. "The Distorting Lens of Politics." *U. S. News & World Report* (February 29):64.
Rosner, David. 1988. "Robert Helmick." *Sports Inc.* (August 29):28-31.
Swift, E. M. 1988. "Mandate for Barcelona." *Sports Illustrated* (October 10):154.

■ FOR FURTHER STUDY

Edwards, Harry. "The Free Enterprise Olympics." *Journal of Sport and Social Issues* 8 (Summer-Fall 1984):i-iv.
Edwards, Harry. "Sportpolitics: Los Angeles, 1984—'The Olympic Tradition Continues.'" *Sociology of Sport Journal* 1, no. 2 (1984):172-183.
Edelson, Paula. "Sports During Wartime." *Zeta Magazine* 4 (May 1991):85-87.
Guttmann, Allen. *The Games Must Go On: Avery Brundage and the Olympic Movement.* New York: Columbia University Press, 1983.
Heinila, Kalevi. "Sport and International Understanding—A Contradiction in Terms?" *Sociology of Sport Journal* 2 (September 1985):240-248.
Hoberman, John M. *Sport and Political Ideology*. Austin: University of Texas Press, 1984.
Johnson, Arthur T., and James H. Frey, eds. *Government and Sport: The Public Issues.* Totowa, NJ: Rowman and Allanheld, 1985.
Kanin, David B. "The Olympic Boycott in Diplomatic Context." *Journal of Sport and Social Issues* 4 (Spring-Summer 1980):1-24.
Klein, Alan M. "Baseball as Underdevelopment: The Political Economy of Sport in the Dominican Republic." *Sociology of Sport Journal* 6 (June 1989):95-112.
Lapchick, Richard E. "Sports and Apartheid: The World Closes In," in *Fractured Focus: Sport as a Reflection of Society*, Richard E. Lapchick, ed. Lexington, MA: Lexington Books, 1986:369-376.
Mandell, Richard D. *The Nazi Olympics*. New York: Macmillan, 1971.
Redmond, Gerald, ed. *Sport and Politics*. Champaign, IL: Human Kinetics, 1986.
Reshef, Rurit, and Jeremy Paltiel. "Partisanship and Sport: The Unique Case of Politics and Sport in Israel." *Sociology of Sport Journal* 6 (December 1989):305-318.
Seppanen, Paavo. "The Olympics: A Sociological Perspective." *International Review for the Sociology of Sport* 19 (1984):113-128.
Sociology of Sport Journal. "Sport and Developing Nations: Annotated Bibliography." *Sociology of Sport Journal* 6 (June 1989):182-190.
Sociology of Sport Journal. "Social Policy/Law and Sport: Annotated Bibliography." *Sociology of Sport Journal* 6 (December 1989):397-405.

Part Nine

Sport and Religion

There are several facets to the relationship between sport and religion. The first is the strong possibility that sport is the functional equivalent of religion. Some striking similarities exist between the two phenomena that may allow individuals to receive the benefits from sport that are usually associated with religion. Some of these parallels include idols, proverbs, shrines, pilgrimages, fanatic believers, rituals, testimony, miracles, rules, judgment, and mysticism. Let us briefly consider two of these.

Ritual is basic to religion. Through the repetition of particular symbolic acts, worshippers are reminded of the supernatural and unified in a common belief with others sharing in the ceremony. Ritual is also very important to sport. Prior to, during, and after games, the faithful sing songs and recite chants that pledge fidelity to the team and implore the athletes to greater achievements. The national anthem is also part of every athletic event. For the athletes there are rituals such as the interlacing of hands with the coach to express team unity. There are also rituals common to particular sports, such as in baseball's "seventh inning stretch," or in boxing where the combatants touch gloves at the beginning of the first and last rounds.

Common to all religions is the element of mysticism. Belief in the mystical is to have faith in supernatural forces (powers that transcend normal human experience). The mystical is also found in sport. There is the belief that the individual with the greatest "heart" or "spirit" will win. There is also the intangible quality of team spirit, considered such an important ingredient of success. As a final example of the supernatural forces in sport, there is that elusive factor in a game known as momentum.

Although the parallels between religion and sport should not be overdrawn, the similarities are interesting and provide insight about the similar functions of these two institutions in society. The first two selections, by George H. Sage and Charles S. Prebish, examine the relatively strong ties among sport, religion, and society. The final selection, by Frank Deford, shows the close affinity between Catholic schools of higher education and basketball success. Deford raises the important question of ethical symmetry—Can religious schools "pursue the almighty dollar [of big-time college athletics] and answer to the Almighty at the same time?"

26. *Sport and Religion*

GEORGE H. SAGE

On the one hand, there may seem to be little in common between sport and religion; going to church on Sunday, singing hymns, studying the Bible, and worshiping God all seem quite alien to the activities that we associate with sport. On the other hand, like religion, contemporary sport symbolically evokes fervent commitment from millions of people. Sports fans worship their favorite athletes much as followers of various religions worship their special deities. And sports fans, like religious groups, consider themselves to be part of a community. Finally, the rituals and ceremonies common to religion are paralleled by rituals and ceremonies in sport. In both instances, these activities function to secure the loyalty and commitment of followers. Theologian-philosopher Michael Novak, in a moment of hyperbole, has claimed that "Sports are a form of religion. . . . Sports, in a word, are a form of godliness." And Charles S. Prebish of Pennsylvania State University's religious studies program claims that for growing numbers of North Americans "sport religion has become a more appropriate expression of religiosity than Christianity, Judaism, or any of the traditional religions." When he was President of the International Olympic Committee, Avery Brundage claimed that the Olympic Movement itself was a religion.

> The Olympic Movement is a Twentieth Century religion, a religion with universal appeal which incorporates all the basic values of other religions, a modern, exciting, virile, dynamic religion. . . . It is a religion for which Pierre de Coubertin was the prophet, for Coubertin has kindled a torch that will enlighten the world.[1]

While most social scientists and theologians believe it is superficial to suggest that sport equates with the complex phenomenon known as religion, it is nevertheless true that the two have become increasingly intertwined and that each is making inroads into the traditional activities and prerogatives of the other. For Christians of previous generations, Sunday was the day reserved for church and worship, but with the increase

SOURCE: Excerpt from *Sociology of North American Sport*, 5th ed., D. Stanley Eitzen and George H. Sage (Dubuque, IA: Wm. C. Brown, 1993). Reprinted by permission of Wm. C. Brown.

in opportunity for recreational pursuits—both for participants and for spectators—and the virtual explosion in televised sports, worship on weekends has been replaced by worship of weekends. As a result, sport has captured Sunday, and churches have had to revise their schedules to oblige sport. At most Roman Catholic churches, convenient Saturday late-afternoon and evening services are now featured in addition to traditional Sunday masses, and other denominations frequently schedule services to accommodate the viewing of professional sports events. In many respects churches have had to share Sundays with sports, and the idea that the Sabbath should be reserved for worship now seems merely an absurd idea of the past.

At the same time that sport seems to be usurping religion's traditional time for worship and services, many churches and religious leaders are attempting to weld a link between the two activities by sponsoring sports events under religious auspices and by proselytizing athletes to religion and then using them as missionaries to spread the Word and to recruit new members. Thus, contemporary religion uses sport for the promotion of its causes.

Sport uses religion as well and in more ways than just seizing the traditional day of worship. Those involved in sports—as participants or as spectators—employ numerous activities with religious connotations in connection with the contests. Ceremonies, rituals, taboos, fetishes, and so forth—all originating in religious practice—are standard observances in the world of sport.

In this [selection] we shall examine the multidimensional relationship between religion and sport.

RELIGION AND SOCIETY

Religion is the belief that supernatural forces influence human lives. There are many definitions of religion, but the one by French sociologist Emile Durkheim has perhaps been cited most. Durkheim said that "religion is a unified system of beliefs and practices relative to sacred things, that is to say, things set apart and forbidden—beliefs and practices which unite into one single moral community called a Church, all those who adhere to them."[2] As a social institution, religion is a system that functions to maintain and transmit beliefs about forces considered to be supernatural and sacred. It provides codified guides for moral conduct and prescribes symbolic practices deemed to be in harmony with beliefs about the supernatural. For all practical purposes we may assume that religious behavior among human beings is universal in that ethnologists and anthropologists have not yet discovered a human group without traces of the behavior we call "religious."[3]

Societies have a wide range of forms and activities associated with religion, including special officials (priests), ceremonies, rituals, sacred objects, places of worship, pilgrimages, and so forth. In modern societies, religious leaders have developed elaborate theories,or theologies, to explain the place of humans in the universe. Moreover, the world religions—Christianity, Hinduism, Buddhism, Confucianism, Judaism, and Islam—are cores of elaborate cultural systems that have dominated world societies for centuries.[4]

SOCIAL FUNCTIONS OF RELIGION

The term *social functions* as used here refers to the contribution that religion makes to the maintenance of human societies. The focus is on what religion does and what it contributes to the survival and maintenance of societies and groups.

One of the first sociologists to write from a functionalist perspective was Emile Durkheim. He was also the first to apply functionalism to religion in systematic way. According to Durkheim, religions exist because they perform important functions at several "levels" of human life—individual, interpersonal, institutional, and societal.

At the individual level, religious experience meets psychic needs by providing individuals with emotional support in this uncertain world. The unpredictable and sometimes dangerous world produces personal fears and general anxiety that revering the powers of nature or seeking cooperation through religious faith and ritual may alleviate. Fears of death, too, are made bearable by beliefs in a supernatural realm into which a believer passes. Also at the individual level religion gives meaning and makes comprehensible human experiences that might seem otherwise a "tale told by an idiot, full of sound and fury, signifying nothing." If one can believe in a God-given scheme of things, the universal quest for ultimate meaning is validated, and human strivings and sufferings seem to make some sense.

Religion functions at the interpersonal level as a form of human bonding. It unites a community of believers by bringing them together to enact various ceremonies and rituals, and it provides them with shared values and beliefs the bind them together. The need to proclaim human abilities and to achieve a sense of transcendence is met and indeed fostered by many religions through ceremonies and rituals that celebrate humans and their activities.

At the instructional level, religion serves as a vehicle for social control; that is, religious tenets constrain the behavior of the community of believers to keep them in line with the norms, values, and beliefs of society. In all the major religions, morals and religion are intertwined, and schemes of otherworldly rewards or punishments for behavior, such as those found in Christianity, become powerful forces for morality. The fear of hellfire and damnation has been a powerful deterrent in the control of Christian societies. The virtues of honesty, conformity to sexual codes, and all the details of acceptable, moral behavior in a society become merged with religious beliefs and practices.

For society, Durkheim argued that the paramount function of religion is social integration. It promotes a binding together both of the members of a society and of the social obligations that help to unite them because it organizes the individual's experience in terms of ultimate meanings that include but also transcend the individual. When many people share this ordering principle, they can deal with each other in meaningful ways and can transcend themselves and their individual egoisms, sometimes even to the point of self-sacrifice.

Religious ceremonies and rituals also promote integration, because they serve to reaffirm some of the basic customs and values of society. Durkheim noted that "before all, [religion is] a means by which the social group reaffirms itself periodically."[5] Here, the societal customs, folkways, and observances are symbolically elevated to the realm of the sacred. In expressing common beliefs about the supernatural, in engaging in collective worship activities, in recounting the lore and myths of the past, the community is brought closer together and linked with the heritage of the past.

Another important integrative function that religion performs is bringing people with diverse backgrounds into meaningful relationships with one another. To the extent that religious groups can reach individuals who feel isolated and abandoned and who are not being relieved of their problems elsewhere, to that extent religion is serving society.

Another social integrative role of religion is that it tends to legitimize the secular social structures within a society. There is a strong tendency for religious ideology to become united with the norms and values of secular structures, producing, as a consequence, religious support for the values and institutions of society. From its earliest existence, religion has provided rationales that serve the needs and actions of a society's leaders. It has legitimized as "God-given" such disparate ideologies as absolute monarchies and egalitarian democracies. Particularly when obedience to the social agents of control is interpreted as a religious duty and disobedience is interpreted as sinful, religion performs this social function well.

In contrast to sociologists who emphasize only the beneficial functions of religion for the individual and society, there are others who view the inclinations of people to create gods and believe in supernatural phenomena as instrumentally useful for powerful and wealthy groups to promote their privileged status and justify socially inequitable conditions. This latter approach to religion was articulated most clearly by Karl Marx who believed that religion was primarily a tool of the rich and powerful to produce a "false consciousness" in the masses of people. One of Marx's most well-known ideas was that religion is a means for legitimating the interests of the dominant class, justifying existing social injustices and inequalities, and, like a narcotic, lulling people into ready acceptance of the status quo. He said: "Religion is the sigh of the oppressed creature, the sentiment of a heartless world, and the soul of soulless conditions. It is the opium of the people."[6]

THE RELATIONSHIP OF RELIGION AND SPORT

Primitive Societies

According to Rudolph Brasch, sport began as a religious rite.[7] The ball games of the Mayans and Aztecs are examples of primitive societies that included physical activities as part of their religious rituals and ceremonies.[8] The purpose of many of games of primitive peoples was rooted in a desire to gain victory over foes seen and unseen, to influence the forces of nature, and to promote fertility among crops and cattle. The Zuni Indians of New Mexico played games that they believed would bring rain and thus enable their crops to grow. In southern Nigeria, wrestling matches were held to encourage the growth of crops, and various games were played in the winter to hasten the return of spring and to ensure a bountiful season. One Eskimo tribe, at the end of the harvest season, played a cup-and-ball game to "catch the sun" and thus delay its departure. In his monumental work on the Plains Indians, Stewart Culin wrote: "In general, games appear to be played ceremonially, as pleasing to the gods, with the objective of securing fertility, causing rain, giving and prolonging life, expelling demons, or curing sickness."[9]

Ancient Greece

The ancient Greeks, who worshiped beauty, entwined religious observance with their athletic demonstrations in such a way that to define where one left off and the other began is difficult. Greek gods were anthropomorphic (human-like), and sculptors portrayed the gods as perfect physical specimens who were to be both admired and emulated by their worshipers. The strong anthropomorphic conceptions of gods held by the Greeks led to their belief that the gods took pleasure in the same things that mortals enjoyed—music, drama, and displays of physical excellence. The gymnasia located in every city-state for all male adults (females were not allowed in the Greek gymnasia) provided facilities and places for sports training as well as for the discussion of intellectual topics. Furthermore, facilities for religious worship—an altar and a chapel—were located in the center of each gymnasium.

The most important athletic meetings of the Greeks were part of religious festivals. The Olympic Games were sacred contests, staged in a sacred location, and as a sacred festival; they were a religious act in honor of Zeus, king of the gods. Athletes who took part in the Olympics did so in order to please Zeus and the prizes they won came from him. Other Greek Panhellenic Games were equally religious in nature. The Nemean games were also held in honor of Zeus; the Pythian Games took place at a festival in honor of Apollo; and the Isthmian Games were dedicated to the god Poseidon. Victorious athletes presented their gifts of thanks upon the altar of the god or gods whom they thought to be responsible for their victory. The end of the ancient Olympic Games was a result of the religious conviction of Theodosius, the Roman emperor of A.D. 392-95. He was a Christian and decreed the end of the games as part of his suppression of paganism in favor of Christianity.[10]

The Early Christian Church

In Western societies, religious support for sport found no counterpart to that of the Greeks until the beginning of the twentieth century. The Roman Catholic church dominated society in western Europe from A.D. 400 until the Reformation in the sixteenth century, and since then Roman Catholicism has shared religious power with Protestant groups.

At first Christians opposed Roman sport spectacles such as chariot racing and gladiatorial combat because of their paganism and brutality, but later Christians opposed sport because they came to regard the human body as an instrument of sin. The early Christians did not view sports as evil per se, for the Apostle Paul wrote approvingly of the benefits of physical activity.[11] But the paganism prominent in the Roman sports events was abhorrent to the Christians. Moreover, early Christianity gradually built a foundation based on asceticism, which is a belief that evil exists in the body and that therefore the body should be subordinate to the pure spirit. As a result, church dogma and education sought to subordinate all desires and demands of the body in order to exalt the spiritual life. Twelfth century Catholic abbot, Saint Bernard, argued: "Always in a robust and active body the mind lies soft and more lukewarm; and, on the other hand, the spirit flourishes more strongly and more actively in an infirm and weakly body. Nothing could have been more damning for the promotion of active recreation and sport.

Spiritual salvation was the dominant feature of the Christian faith. Accordingly, the cultivation of the body was to be subordinated to the salvation of the spirit, especially since the body, it was believed, could obstruct the realization of this aim. An otherwise enlightened Renaissance scholar, Desiderius Erasmus, while a monk at a monastery (before he became a critic of Roman Catholicism), wrote an essay "On the

Contempt of the World," which articulately characterized the Christian attitude of his time toward body and soul:

> The monks do not choose to become like cattle; they know that there is something sublime and divine within man which they prefer to develop rather than cater for the body. . . . Our body, except for a few details, differs not from an animal's body but our soul reaches out after things divine and eternal. The body is earthly, wild, slow, mortal, diseased, ignoble; the soul on the other hand is heavenly, subtle, divine, immortal, noble. Who is so blind that he cannot tell the difference between body and soul? And so the happiness of the soul surpasses that of the body.[12]

The Reformation and the Rise of Protestantism

The Reformation of the early sixteenth century signaled the end of the viselike grip that Roman Catholicism had on the minds and habits of the people of Europe and England. With the Reformation, the pejorative view of sports might have perished wherever the teachings of Martin Luther and John Calvin prevailed. But Protestantism had within it the seeds of a new asceticism, and the Calvinism imported to England, in its Puritan form, became a greater enemy to sport than Roman Catholicism had been.

Puritan influence grew throughout the sixteenth century and by the early seventeenth century had come to have considerable influence on English life. Moreover, since Puritans were among the earliest English immigrants to America, they had considerable influence on the social life in the colonies. Perhaps no Christian group exercised a greater opposition to sport that the Puritans. Historian Dennis Brailsford asserted that "the Puritans saw their mission to erase all sport and play from men's lives.[13] They gave to England the "English Sunday" and to the United States its equivalent, the blue laws, which until a few decades ago managed to bar sports on the Sabbath and severely limit the kinds of sports played to those that were considered appropriate for Christians. As a means of realizing amusement and unrestrained impulses, sport was suspect for the Puritan; as it approached mere pleasure or involved physical harm to participants or to animals (e.g., boxing and cockfighting) or promoted gambling, sport was, of course, altogether evil. The renowned nineteenth century English historian Thomas B. Macaulay claimed that the Puritans opposed bearbaiting not so much because it was painful for the bear but because the bear's pain gave pleasure to the spectators.[14]

From the Seventeenth to the Twentieth Century

The principal relationship between the church and sport for the early North American settlers was one of restriction and probation, especially with regard to sports on the Sabbath. Soon after the first English settlement was established in the American colonies, a group of Virginia ministers enacted legislation prohibiting sports participation on Sunday. Such repressive acts are more commonly associated with the Puritans in New England who enacted similar legislation. Actually, most of the colonies passed laws against play and sport on the Sabbath, and it was not until the mid-twentieth century that industrial and economic conditions brought about the repeal of most of these laws, although most had been annulled by custom.[15]

There were a number of reasons for Protestant prejudice against play and sport among the early settlers. One prominent objection was that participation would divert attention from spiritual matters. There was also the belief that play and its resultant pleasure might become addictive because of the inherent weakness of human nature. The practical matter was that survival in the New World required hard work from everyone; thus, time spent in play and games was typically considered time wasted. Finally, the associations formed and the environment in which play and sport occurred conspired to cast these activities in a bad light. The tavern was the center for gambling and table sports; dancing had obvious sexual overtones; and field sports often involved gambling and cruelty to animals.

Churchly opposition to leisure pursuits was firmly maintained in the first few decades of the nineteenth century, and each effort to liberalize attitudes toward leisure pursuits was met with a new attack on sport as "sinful." Sports were still widely regarded by the powerful Protestant religious groups as snares of the devil himself. But in the 1830s social problems became prominent concerns of American social reformers, many of whom were clergy and intellectual leaders. There were crusades against slavery, intemperance, and poor industrial working conditions; widespread support for the emancipation of women, for public education, and for industrial reform; and indeed, scrutiny of every facet of American life. One aspect of this comprehensive social-reform movement was the concern for human health and physical fitness.[16]

Social conditions had begun to change rapidly under the aegis of industrialization–the population was shifting from rural to urban residence, and labor changed from agricultural toil to work for wages in squalid working and living conditions. The physical health of the population became a major problem, leading a number of reformers to propose that people would be happier, more productive, and healthier if they engaged in vigorous sports activities. Surprisingly, some of the leading advocates of play and sports were clerics, and from their pulpits they presented forceful arguments that physical prowess and sanctity were not incompatible. Intellectual leaders joined the movement. Ralph Waldo Emerson said, "Out upon the scholars . . . with their pale, sickly, etiolated indoor thought! Give me the out-of-door thoughts of sound men, thoughts all fresh and blooming."[17] The esteemed poet and novelist Oliver Wendell

Holmes joined the attack on the physical condition of the youth. He wrote:

> I am satisfied that such a set of black-coated, stiff-jointed, soft-muscled, paste-complexioned youth as we can boast in our Atlantic cities never before sprang from the loins of Anglo-Saxon lineage.[18]

Holmes argued that widespread participation in sport would make for a more physically fit citizenry, as well as create a more exciting environment.

The proposals of support for physical fitness and wholesome leisure had a profound effect on the church. Responding to the temporal needs of the people, the clergy began to shed much of the otherworldly emphasis and sought to alleviate immediate human problems. Recognizing the need for play and the health benefits of leisure amusements, the church began to soften its attitude toward play and sport. Sport historian Donald J. Mrozek summarized the change:

> Ministers and religiously enthusiastic laymen showed increasing concern over the behavior of young people . . . and they often turned to sport . . . [to guide them toward the right way of life]. In a broad range of denominations from Baptists to Congregationalists, there arose spokesmen who depicted Christ as primarily a man of action, thus seeking to appeal to the inclinations of the young by drawing out qualities which they believed most closely resembled those valued in their society.[19]

Although the development of a more liberal attitude by church leaders toward sport began to appear by the mid-nineteenth century, not all church authorities subscribed to the trend. A staid Congregationalist magazine, the *New Englander*, vigorously attacked sport:

> Let our readers, one and all, remember that we were sent into this world, not for sport and amusement, but for labor; not to enjoy and please ourselves, but to serve and glorify God, and be useful to our fellow men. That is the great object and end in life. In pursuing this end, God has indeed permitted us all needful diversion and recreation. . . . But the great end of life after all is work. . . . It is a true saying . . . "We come into this world not for sports." We were sent here for a higher and nobler object.[20]

In official publications and public speeches, some church leaders fought the encroaching sport and leisure mania throughout the late nineteenth century. Militant organizations, such as the American Sabbath Union, the Sunday League of America, and the Lord's Day Alliance, were visible proof of the vitality of the strong forces still mobilized in support of this phase of Protestant doctrine. But there was a growing awareness that disapproving churches were fighting a losing war. Church leaders gradually began to reconcile play and religion in response to pressure from medical, educational, and political leaders for games and sport. These activities were believed to aid in the development of physical, mental, and, indeed, moral health. City churches began to minister to the social, physical, and economic needs of their members and of residents in their neighborhoods, extending their role beyond just preaching salvation of the soul.

To meet the social needs of rural and city members, churches adopted sports and sponsored recreations to draw people together, and church leadership played an important part in the promotion of community recreation and school physical education in the latter part of the nineteenth century. Many clergy used their church halls and grounds as recreation centers. The playground movement in America began in 1885, when the sand gardens were opened in the yards of the West End Nursery and the Parmenter Street Chapel in Boston. The New York City Society for Parks and Playgrounds got its start in 1890 with the support of clergymen, who delivered sermons to their congregations on children's need for playgrounds.[21]

Support for physical education found its way into denominational journals and meetings, and religious support for physical education helped promote its acceptance by colleges and its eventual adoption by public school boards across the country. The Young Men's Christian College (now Springfield College) at Springfield, Massachusetts, made sport and physical fitness one of the cornerstones of a proper Christian education and life-style.

Increasingly, churches broadened their commitment to play and sport endeavors as means of drawing people together. Bowling leagues, softball leagues, and youth groups, such as the Catholic Youth Organization (CYO), were sponsored by churches for their young members. The church's prejudice against pleasure through play had broken down almost completely by the beginning of the twentieth century.

Twentieth-Century North America

Churches have been confronted with ever-increasing changes in the twentieth century; economic pressures, political movements, and social conditions have been the chief forces responsible for the drastically changed relationship between religion and sport. Increased industrialization turned the population into a nation of urban dwellers, while higher wages were responsible for an unprecedented affluence. The gospel of work (the Protestant work ethic) is less credible, and increased leisure has enhanced the popularity of sports. The story of changes in the attitudes of religionists in the twentieth century is largely one of increasing accommodation. Much of both Catholic and Protestant North America have come to view sport as a positive force and even as a useful means of promoting God's work. Sports and leisure activities have become an increasingly conspicuous part of the recreation programs of thousands of churches and many church colleges. The church has gradually moved further into recreation, and camping programs, athletic leagues, and even the employment of full-time recreation directors are all evidences of the close relationship between religion and play.

Clergy of many religions and denominations who over the centuries preached that sport is a handmaiden of the devil must be shifting uneasily in their graves at trends of the past half century. Times have certainly changed, the church as well, and the reconciliation between sport and organized religion has approached finality.

Sport as Religion

Emile Durkheim argued that while religion functions to ensure cohesion through a set of shared beliefs, other belief systems can serve as "functional equivalents" of religion. In the past generation the powers and influence of sport have increased enormously, while at the same time formalized religion and the institutional church have suffered a decline of interest and commitment, as society has undergone secularization. During this process of social change, sport has taken on so many of the characteristics of religion that some have argued that sport has emerged as a new religion, supplementing, and in some cases even supplanting, traditional religious expressions. Michael Novak, a noted Catholic theologian, claims that

> Sports are religious in the sense that they are organized institutions, disciplines, and liturgies; and also in the sense that they teach religious qualities of heart and soul. In particular, they recreate symbols of cosmic struggle, in which human survival and moral courage are not assured. To this extent, they are not mere games, diversions, pastimes. . . . Sports constitute the primary lived world of the vast majority of Americans. The holy trinity—baseball, basketball, and football . . . are not simply interludes but the basic substratum of our intellectual and emotional lives. Play provides the fundamental metaphors and the paradigmatic experiences for understanding the other elements of life.[22]

Charles Prebish is just as emphatic:

> For me, it is not just a parallel that is emerging between sport and religion, but rather a *complete identity*. *Sport is religion* for growing numbers of Americans, and this is no product of simply facile reasoning or wishful thinking. Further, for many, sport religion has become a more appropriate expression of personal religiosity than Christianity, Judaism, or any of the traditional religions. . . . It is reasonable to consider sport the newest and fastest growing religion, far outdistancing whatever is in second.[23]

There is no doubt that organized sport has taken on the trappings of religion. A few examples will illustrate this point. Every religion has its gods (or saints or high priests) who are venerated by its members.

Likewise, sports fans have gods (superstar athletes) whom they worship. They also have their saints, those who have passed to the great beyond (such as Jim Thorpe, Knute Rockne, Babe Ruth, Babe Didrikson Zaharias—and, of course, the legendary Vince Lombardi, who earned a place among the saints for his fierce discipline and the articulation of what has become for many athletes and fans alike the basic commandment of contemporary sport, "Winning is the only thing"). The high priests of contemporary sport are the professional, collegiate, and national amateur team coaches who not only direct the destinies of their athletes but also control the emotions of large masses of sports fans.

Sport also has its scribes, the sport journalists and sportscasters who disseminate the "word" of sports deeds and glories; its houses of worship, such as the Astrodome and Yankee Stadium; and masses of highly vocal "true believers." Numerous proverbs fill the world of sport: "Nice guys finish last"; "When the going gets tough, the tough get going"; "Lose is a four-letter word"; and so forth. These proverbs are frequently written on posters and hung in locker rooms for athletes to memorize.

The achievements of athletes and teams are celebrated in numerous shrines built throughout the country to commemorate and glorify sporting figures. These "halls of fame" have been established for virtually every sport played in North America, and some sports have several halls of fame devoted to them. They preserve the sacred symbols and memorabilia that direct us to rehearse the triumphs of the "saints" who have moved on. According to Gerald Redmond:

> Athletes become "immortal heroes" as they are "enshrined" in a sports hall of fame, when "devoted admirers" gaze at their "revered figures" or read plaques "graven in marble" before departing "often very moved" (or even "teary-eyed") from the many "hushed rooms, filled with nostalgia." This is the jargon of the churches of sport in the twentieth century.[24]

Symbols of fidelity abound in sport. The athletes are expected to give total commitment to the cause, including abstinence from smoking, alcohol, and in some cases, even sex. The devout followers who witness and invoke traditional and hallowed chants show their devotion to the team and add "spirit" to its cause. It is not unusual for these pilgrims to travel hundreds of miles, sometimes braving terrible weather conditions, to witness a game, thus displaying their fidelity.

Like religious institutions, sport has become a function of communal involvement. An article in the *Christian Century* entitled "The Super Bowl as Religious Festival" commented:

> There is a remarkable sense in which the Super Bowl functions as a major religious festival for American culture, for the event signals a convergence of sports, politics and myth. Like festivals in ancient societies, which made no distinctions regarding the religious, political and sporting character of certain

events, the Super Bowl succeeds in reuniting these now disparate dimensions of social life.[25]

Sociologist James A. Mathison said, "If I were to show a visitor to the United States a single recurring event which has come to characterize American folk religion, the Super Bowl would be it."[26]

Perhaps the most salient role that sport-as-religion plays for communal involvement is in the sense of belonging and of community that it evokes. In cheering for the Green Bay Packers, the New York Yankees, or the Montreal Canadiens, one belongs to a "congregation." The emotional attachment of some fans to their teams verges on the religious fanaticism previously seen in holy wars against heretics and pagans. Opposing teams and their fans, as well as officials, are occasionally attacked and brutally beaten.

In the past few years two popular motion pictures—"Field of Dreams" and "Bull Durham"—have used numerous religions themes and symbols suggesting baseball-as-religion. While they do not claim that baseball is a religion in a traditional theological way with Jesus present, they do suggest a symbiosis (an intimate association or close union) between the two. "Bull Durham" opens with gospel music in the background and the female lead, Annie, delivering the prologue:

> I believe in the church of baseball. I've tried all the major religions and most of the minor ones. . . . I gave Jesus a chance, but it just didn't work out between us. The Lord laid too much guilt on me. . . . There's no guilt in baseball, and it's never boring. . . . The only church that truly feeds the soul, day in and day out, is the church of baseball.

"Field of Dreams" makes clear its baseball-as-religion point of view. In the basic plot a supernatural voice of revelation tells a young farmer and baseball fanatic to plow up part of his corn fields and build a baseball stadium. The farmer does this, and soon baseball players from the past are playing on the baseball diamond, like saints from a land beyond the first rows of the cornfield. After the farmer has made a pilgrimage and faced his need for forgiveness, he is miraculously reconciled with his long-dead baseball-player father. At the end of the movie, the farmer's baseball field is a shrine that draws flocks of people seeking "the truth." The movie has many religious themes and symbols: Life after death, a seeker who hears a voice and has to go on a spiritual quest, an inner healing, becoming a child in order to enter the kingdom, losing your life to gain it.[27]

In spite of the many seeming parallels between sport and religion, sport does not fulfill what are considered by many to be the key functions of "churchly" religion. For example, why humans are created and continue to wrestle with their purpose here on earth and life hereafter are not addressed by sports. Furthermore, critics of the sport-as-religion emphasize that many activities that humans become deeply committed to can be referred to as a religion, when speaking metaphorically, but "when we include in 'religion' all meaningful or 'sacred' activities, we must include virtually any activity into which human beings pour their will, emotions and energy."[28] While sport does have some religious-like symbols, rituals, legends, sacred spaces and time, and heroes, it is organized and played by humans for humans without supernatural sanction. . . .

NOTES

1. Charles S. Prebish, "Heavenly Father, Divine Goalie: Sport and Religion," *The Antioch Review* 42, (1984), p. 312; *The Speeches of Avery Brundage*, Lausanne, Comite International Olympique, 1968, p. 80; Michael Novak, "The Natural Religion," in *Sport Inside Out*, ed. David L. Vanderwerken and Spencer K. Wertz, (Fort Worth: Texas Christian University Press, 1985), p. 358; for a different version of the sports-religion metaphor, see Robert J. Higgs, "Muscular Christianity, Holy Play, and Spiritual Exercises: Confusion About Christ in Sports and Religion," *Arete: The Journal of Sport Literature* 1, no. 1 (1983): 59-87.
2. Emile Durkheim, *The Elementary Forms of Religious Life*, trans. J. W. Swain (New York: Free Press, 1965), p. 62.
3. James A. Beckford and Thomas Luckman (eds.) *The Changing Face of Religion* (Newbury Park, CA: Sage, 1989); Martin E. Marty, *Pilgrims in Their Own Land: 500 Years of Religion in America* (Boston: Little, Brown, 1984).
4. Richard L. Rubinstein (ed.) *Spirit Matters: The Worldwide Impact of Religion on Contemporary Politics* (New York: Paragon, 1987).
5. Durkheim, *The Elementary Forms of Religious Life*, p. 387.
6. Karl Marx, *Selected Writings in Sociology and Social Philosophy* (translated and edited by Tom B. Bottomore and Maximilien Rubel) (New York: McGraw-Hill, 1964), pp. 26-27.
7. Rudolph Brasch, *How Did Sports Begin?* (New York: David McKay, 1970), p. 1.
8. Allen Guttman, "The Sacred and the Secular," in *Sport Inside Out*, pp. 298-308.
9. Steward Culin, *Games of the North American Indian* (Washington, DC: U. S. Government Printing Office, 1907), p. 34.
10. Noel Robertson, "The Ancient Olympics: Sport, Spectacle and Ritual," in *The Olympic Games in Transition*, eds. Jeffrey O. Segrave and Donald Chu (Champaign, IL: Human Kinetics Publishers, 1988), pp. 11-25; David Sansone, *Greek Athletics and the Genesis of Sport* (Berkeley: University of California Press, 1988).
11. See, for example, I Cor. 9:24-26. "Do you not know that those who run in a race, all indeed run, but one receives the prize? So run as to obtain it."
12. Quoted in Albert Hyma, *The Youth of Erasmus* (Ann Arbor: University of Michigan Press, 1930), p. 178.
13. Dennis Brailsford, *Sport and Society* (London: Routledge and Kegan Paul, 1969), p. 141.
14. Thomas B. Macaulay, *The History of England*, vol. 1 (London: Longman, Green, Longman, and Roberts, 1861), p. 162.
15. Nancy L. Struna, "Puritans and Sport: The Irretrievable Tide of Change," *The Sporting Image: Readings in American Sport History* ed. Paul J. Zingg (New York: University Press of America, 1988).
16. Kathryn K. Grover (Ed.) *Fitness in America: Images of Health, Sport and the Body, 1830-1940.* (Amherst, MA: University of Massachusetts Press, 1989; Harvey Green, *Fit for America: Health, Fitness, Sport, and American Society* (New York: Pantheon, 1986); James C. Whorton, *Crusaders for Fitness: The History of American Health Reformers* (Princeton: Princeton University Press, 1982).

17. Quoted in Van Wyck Brooks, *The Flowering of New England* (New York: Random House, Modern Library, 1936), p. 253.
18. Oliver Wendell Holmes, "The Autocrat of the Breakfast Table," *Atlantic Monthly* 1 (May 1858): 881.
19. Donald J. Mrozek, *Sport and American Mentality, 1880-1910* (Knoxville: University of Tennessee Press, 1983), p. 202; see also Green, *Fit for America* and Whorton, *Crusaders for Fitness.*
20. "Amusements," *New Englander* 9 (1851): 358.
21. Stephen Hardy, *How Boston Played* (Boston: Northeastern University Press, 1982), pp. 85-106; see also Dominic Cavallo, *Muscles and Morals: Organized Playgrounds and Urban Reform, 1880-1920* (Philadelphia: University of Pennsylvania Press, 1981).
22. Novak, "The Natural Religion," pp. 353, 363.
23. Prebish, "Heavenly Father, Divine Goalie," pp. 312, 318.
24. Gerald Redmond, "A Plethora of Shrines: Sport in the Museum and Hall of Fame," *Quest* 19 (January 1973): 41-48; see also Guy Lewis and Gerald Redmond, *Sporting Heritage: A Guide to Halls of Fame, Special Collections and Museums in the United States and Canada* (New York: Barnes, 1974); Eldon E. Snyder, "Sociology of Nostalgia: Sports Halls of Fame and Museums in America," *Sociology of Sport Journal*, 8, (1991), pp. 228-238.
25. Joseph L.Price, "The Super Bowl as Religious Festival," *Christian Century* 101 (22 February 1984): 190-91.
26. Quoted in "Sports: America's Newest Religion?" *The Denver Post*, 4 January 1987, p. 1A.
27. Terry Mattingly, "Hit Movie Played on a Religious Field," *Rocky Mountain News* 27 May 1989, p. 105.
28. Vance N. Scott, "Sport Is a Religion in America Controversial Professor Argues," *The Chronicle of Higher Education* 16 (May 1984), p. 27.

27. *Heavenly Father, Divine Goalie: Sport and Religion*

CHARLES S. PREBISH

Arnold Beisser begins his book *The Madness in Sports* with a reference to a famous Japanese World War II battle cry that was meant to demoralize American soldiers: "To hell with Babe Ruth!" Clearly, the attacking Japanese thought they knew what Americans valued most. In his landmark work on religion in sport, *Sports Illustrated* writer Frank Deford picked up on this same theme when he wrote, "The claim that sport has developed into a national faith may be linked to the nagging awareness that something has happened to Sunday." Deford knew just what it was that had happened, too. He correlated the decline in church attendance with the rise of professional football as the new darling of the American sportsman. For 1976, the year in which Deford's articles were published, he was quite correct: "Now, the trip out of the house on Sunday is not to visit a church, but to see a game or to play one. . . . So the churches have ceded Sunday to sports, to games." Later we shall see that, by 1982, sport had not only won the battle for Sunday, but for all other days as well. In sport religion, the sabbath is Everyday.

The response of the churches to the continually increasing American appetite for sport was to be as obliging as possible. On the one hand, the times of traditional worship services were adjusted so as to free the celebrant for his or her immersion in a Sunday of sport. Catholic churches offered Saturday afternoon services while Protestant denominations scheduled their services in harmony with *TV Guide* announcements of the sport specials of the week. For Jewish families it was somewhat easier. All that had to be sacrificed was the Friday Night Fight; Bar Mitzvah services were over on Saturdays long before the sport scene began to heat up for the day. Of course cable TV and ESPN have changed all that. On the other hand, religious groups, regardless of their specific affiliation, sought to cultivate sport as a means of keeping their clientele firmly in the fold. The holy alliance between religion and sport is not without precedent, however. By 1800, America had cast off the Puritan opposition to sport, and collectively began to realize that a life of physical inactivity was a

SOURCE: *The Antioch Review* 42 (1984), pp. 306-318.

liability rather than an asset. The American YMCA was founded in Boston in 1851, followed in 1858 by a YWCA chapter in New York. Needless to say, in the middle decades of the twentieth century, it was acknowledged by the various religious groups that participation in sport was healthy for their congregants and unifying for the congregations, and this was evidenced by the large number of church- or synagogue-sponsored athletic leagues, usually carrying the title YMCA, YWCA, CYO, JCC, or some similar identifying designation. Yet it was not until quite recently that churches and synagogues went into the sport business with a fury and passion that advertised *big-time* investments.

By the 1970s, religion was learning a valuable lesson from its secular counterpart. If lucrative television contracts were making club owners and athletes into fiscal wizards while providing ample exposure to an adoring public, then perhaps it was time for professional religion to imitate professional sport. In so doing, television evangelism was to become a hot franchise. The point here is twofold. First, religion was seeking new avenues of reaching the public that rivaled its successful sport adversary. Just like the NFL, NHL, or NBA, religion sought to catch John Q. Public's attention while he sat in his easy chair, newspaper or coffee in hand, and *before* he took his usual dose of O. J. Simpson or Walter Payton. Second, it sought to affirm sport, even champion its fundamental emphasis, in order to align itself with a proven winner.

Perhaps the most visible and well-known evangelist to utilize sport in his ministry is the Reverend Billy Graham. Following his appearance as grand marshal of the Rose Bowl parade in 1971, *Newsweek* ran an often cited article entitled "Are Sports Good for the Soul?" In citing Graham's use of sport as a basic metaphor in his preaching, the article quotes Graham's understanding of the role of sport in (at least his) religion: "The Bible says leisure and lying around are morally dangerous for us. Sports keep us busy; athletes, you notice, don't take drugs. There are probably more really committed Christians in sports, both collegiate and professional, than in any other occupation in America." Although less well-known generally than Billy Graham, on the sporting scene, the most conspicuous religious figure is the Reverend Billy Zeoli. A flashy dresser, he is flamboyant in appearance and speech. A sample from Deford's "Reaching for the Stars" demonstrates:

> By his own proud admission, the Zeoli theology is brutally simple. "I am a total liberal when it comes to methods, but very conservative in theology," he says. As he tells the Bills, as he will tell the Jets, as he always says, Jesus was either the Son of God or a cuckoo—take it or leave it. God and man are separated by sin, which is labelled "The Problem." "The Answer" is to employ Jesus as the intermediary. So there is "The Decision," and to avoid confusion Zeoli lays out the choices: "yes," "no," and "maybe." Taken as a whole, that is what Zeoli calls "God's Game Plan."

Perhaps Billy Zeoli is the extreme case in religion's attempt to use sport, but there are others like him in the arena. These so-called jock evangelists are rapidly becoming a fixture in the locker rooms throughout our land, and organizations are emerging through which athletes are able to take their religious message to the people, playing as much on their role as American heroes as on their ministerial acumen.

The attempt on the part of clergymen to deal with the spiritual needs of athletes is not nearly so altruistic as it might seem. By playing on the widespread appeal of well-known amateur and professional athletes, the ministers are able to expand their operations, numerically and financially, many times over. Frank Deford called this new movement "Sportianity," and to aid in this endeavor the athletes are utilized as amateur evangelists or, as *The Wittenberg Door* calls them, "Jocks for Jesus." There are primarily three organizations through which athletes are used to bring new members into the fold. The first of these is the Fellowship of Christian Athletes (FCA), founded in 1954. It intents "to confront athletes and coaches and through them the youth of our nation, with the challenge and adventure of following Christ and serving him through the fellowship of the church. . . . " In order to carry out its goals, the Fellowship of Christian Athletes uses older athletes (and coaches) to recruit younger ones to Christ.

The second group in athletic religion, Athletes in Action (AIA), is a division of the Billy Graham-inspired Campus Crusade for Christ. With special permission from the NCAA, Athletes in Action fields teams of former college athletes that are allowed to compete against current college squads in basketball, wrestling, gymnastics, track, and weight-lifting. During their various competitions against amateur teams, AIA members give religious speeches, often at half-time or after the match, and distribute materials for the parent organization. Although the organization claims that it relies on the "soft-sell," anyone who has ever attended an AIA event knows that the pitch is several steps up from gentle, with feverish a somewhat more accurate description.

As the FCA and AIA came into increasing competition for the "choice" athletes to serve in a missionary capacity, a third organization was founded to act as a buffer or intermediary between the two: Pro Athletes Outreach (PAO). An outgrowth of Sports World Chaplaincy, Inc., it is a prospering group that sends its professional athletes on what it calls "speaking blitzes" across the country. Like the other organizations, its members offer testimony sprinkled with group publicity.

What all of these groups have in common is that they are completely nondenominational, conservative in their theology, and fundamentalist in approach and lifestyle. They take no stands on questionable moral issues, exclude individuals of doubtful temperament, and insist on absolute fidelity. Everything is done for the glory of Christ, and in so doing, Deford claimed, "Jesus has been transformed, emerging anew as a holler guy, a give-it-100-percenter." Michael Novak, scholar-in-residence at the

American Enterprise Institute and a noted Catholic theologian, argues against the religious defensiveness of fundamentalism by boldly stating, "Sports is, somehow, a religion." And while he does not see sport as equal or identical to any of the world's religions, he does concede, ". . . sports flow outward into action from a deep natural impulse that is radically religious: an impulse of freedom, respect for ritual limits, a zest for symbolic meaning, and a longing for perfection. The athlete may of course be pagan, but sports are, as it were, natural religions." Further, despite the fact that each religious group boasts big numbers of fans and converts, all may not be so rosy as claimed. Young Christian athletes often seem to be interested in religion primarily as a means to get an edge, so to speak, to get God on their side. Although such an attitude is not sanctioned religiously, it prevails nonetheless, and though some athletes do indeed stop short of asking God for victory, many do not, thus prostituting the real basis for personal and religious growth. What emerges, then, is an unclear picture with the athletes trying to improve their religious and competitive field position.

On the college campuses today, the relationship between religion and sport is equally cloudy. Although college-level sport competition was originally intended to provide recreation for those who were hard at work cultivating the best that education had to offer, these programs of intercollegiate sport rapidly changed in nature and function in the early years of this century. A plethora of church-supported institutions of higher learning began to exploit the growing American interest in sport, first as a means of publicizing the university and later as a means of attracting funding and students. In many cases, sport as a growth industry within the university was a driving force in upgrading the academic reputation of the school as well. Father James Riehle of Notre Dame was unceremoniously blunt when he said: "Of course Catholic schools used athletics for prestige. Notre Dame would not be the great school it is today, the great academic institution, were it not for football. But the emphases have changed here. I think that now we realize the value of sport in more ways than just the financial, whereas I'm afraid once we didn't." Occasionally, the message does not filter down to the athlete on the field, for one recent Brigham Young quarterback remarked that classes were about the only thing he didn't like at BYU. Most recently, Oral Roberts University, founded in 1965, has utilized both sport and the gospel as a means of calling attention to itself. In fact, Roberts himself proclaims, "Athletics is a part of our Christian witness. . . . Nearly every man in America reads the sports pages, and a Christian school cannot ignore these people."

What effect does all this emphasis on winning, in the name of the Lord, have on individuals who are entrenched in the sports establishment? In the first place, if winning is the result of hard work, discipline, and dedication, as most coaches and athletes suppose, then such an emphasis is certainly consistent with the traditional Protestant work ethic that is such a shaping force in our culture. Some sport sociologists even argue that sport values mirror the core values of Protestantism. Over against this, however, is the growing protest of a rapidly expanding group of vocal clergy. Episcopal priest Malcolm Boyd, for example: "This sort of slick, stage-directed prayer alienates people from religion because anybody can see that it is as shoddy as anything else in the world. The gimmick use of prayer before a game for the purpose of getting psyched up, this use of prayer as *deus ex machina*—I find it simply immoral. To use God in this way—it isn't holy. Hell isn't a bunch of fires. I think that hell is when you're using anybody, even when you're trying to use God, as in this case." The last remark suggests that sport has used religion too, just as the reverse was true. Now we need to explore this other side of the coin.

Today, almost every team in professional sport holds chapel services on Sundays, both at home and away. Many college teams do the same. And the pregame prayer is customary even in the youth leagues of America. Why? Religion provides the athlete with a basis for reinforcement, both physical and spiritual. It allays his psychological anxieties. It enables him to face the competition at hand confident and peaceful, fully concentrated. In addition, an overwhelming number of athletes claim that religious conviction has been a profound factor in enhancing the development of their sport skills. Hardly an American boy of the 1950s or 1960s could escape watching the Reverend Bob Richards pole-vault his way out of a Wheaties box. Nor will we forget Sandy Koufax's refusal to pitch on a Jewish High Holy Day.

One researcher actually did a master's thesis at the University of California, Santa Barbara (in 1967) on "The Incidence of Prayer in Athletics by Selected California Collegiate Athletes and Coaches." It is clearly the case that when prayer is not private, or team sponsored, then it is institutionalized as part of the sporting event. Very often now, sport events, particularly if they are significant, employ *both* the playing of the National Anthem *and a religious invocation*. Perhaps the most dramatic of these invocations was delivered by Father Edward Rupp before the 1976 World Hockey Association All-Star game:

> Heavenly Father, Divine Goalie, we come before You this evening to seek Your blessing. . . . We are, thanks to You, All-Stars. We pray tonight for Your guidance. Keep us free from actions that would put us in the Sin Bin of Hell. Inspire us to avoid the pitfalls of our profession. Help us to stay within the blue line of Your commandments and the red line of Your grace. Protect us from being injured by the puck of pride. May we be ever delivered from the high stick of dishonesty. May the wings of Your angels play at the right and left of our teammates. May You always be the Divine Center of our team, and when our summons comes for eternal retirement to the heavenly grandstand, may we find You ready to give us the everlasting bonus of a permanent seat in Your coliseum. Finally, grant us the courage to skate without tripping, to

run without icing, and to score the goal that really counts—the one that makes each of us a winner, a champion, an All-Star in the hectic Hockey Game of Life. Amen.

From the above, we can see that sport and religion have been more than extensively related during the last generation of American history. The relationship has been so complete, in fact, that numerous critics, from each side of the fence, have responded to the phenomenon in a variety of ways.

By 1971, though, *Newsweek* was asking, "Are Sports Good for the Soul?" Its conclusion highlights the alarm apparently felt by more than a few Americans at the time: "It may be impossible to separate sports and religion in America. Nonetheless, more and more players and viewers are now asking themselves whether treating God as some kind of supercoach does not demean both faith and football." What this writer and others seemed to be saying, albeit in round-about fashion, is what sport sociologist Harry Edwards said directly in 1973: "If there is a universal popular religion in America it is to be found within the institution of sport." And, unlike his colleagues, Edwards included even the fan, noting that for the spectator, sport is a "quasi religion." In addition, what makes Edwards' treatment so important is that he demonstrated just where the parallels between religion and sport emerge and interpenetrate.

What I find overwhelmingly hard to understand is why Professor Edwards says, "In sum, sport is essentially a secular, quasi-religious institution. It does not, however, constitute an alternative to or substitute for formal sacred religious involvement." It is apparent that Edwards saw, or at least presented, far more material on the subject than his colleagues in any of the sub-disciplines of sport study. Yet he, too, like all other writers, insisted on stopping short of what is becoming notably obvious.

For me, it is not just a parallel that is emerging between sport and religion, but rather a *complete identity. Sport is religion* for growing numbers of Americans, and this is no product of simply facile reasoning or wishful thinking. Further, for many, sport religion has become a more appropriate expression of personal religiosity than Christianity, Judaism, or any of the traditional religions.

Many of the authors cited to this point made reference to the similarity of vocabulary in sport and religion. They suggested that sport has appropriated significant religious terminology as a means of expressing the sincerity, fervor, and seriousness of sport. All mentioned at least a few well-chosen examples of parallel nomenclature, resulting in a profusion of references to words like *sacred, faith, ritual*, and so forth. There are two problems obvious in such an approach. In the first place, it is only the surface of mutually shared terminology that is proverbially scratched. Even a cursory continuance of the procedure reveals that other, equally applicable expressions must be mentioned: *ultimate, dedicated, sacrifice, peace, commitment, spirit, suffering, worship, prayer, festival*, and *holiday*. With a little investigation, it would not be unreasonable to suppose that a list of fifty or more terms and phrases could be compiled. Yet it is the second problem that is critical, for we are not simply playing the numbers game here. Most authors presume a shared vocabulary with a *slightly altered meaning* for each enterprise. For Novak and others, words like *sacred, dedicated*, and *sacrifice* mean one thing for religion and another for sport. This bifurcation results from the axiom that religion is sacred while sport is secular. I would maintain, however, that in many cases there is absolutely no difference in the meaning that each term carries for the two traditions in question. Equally, the yearly Super Bowl is no less a religious holiday than Easter. The child's worship of Ted Williams is no less real than his reverential adoration of Christ, and to some, Williams's accomplishments and capabilities in baseball were unquestionably godly. And, judging from the sentiments it evoked, the Gold Medal victory of the U. S. Hockey team in the 1980 Winter Olympics was quite as ultimate as anything that occurs in a traditional house of worship.

The point of ritual is to approach purity through our actions in order that our attained purity brings us closer to the fulfillment of specific goals. Regarding practicality, these rituals are enacted both publicly and privately. Public expression requires attendance at formal, sanctioned, institutional services. In traditional religion, one attends church or synagogue, whereas in sport religion, one attends the gymnasium or arena. There are numerous examples of identity between religious and sport rituals in the public sphere. It would not be going far, I think, to suggest that in Christian services, communion may well be the most significant ritual activity. For sport religion, the ritual act of the game, its religious service would also not be complete without its respective act of communion. Richard Lipsky points out in straightforward fashion: "During the game, the social euphoria generates a festive communion and sense of solidarity between the players and fans." Finally, the post-game events explicitly replicate the rituals of traditional religion, replete with trying to catch a word with the religious professional, be he priest, rabbi, minister, or player. No religious service would be complete without ritual chants and hymns. These vary from tradition to tradition, but are utilized to some degree by all religions. We find the same ritual practice in sport as well, with each denomination in sport religion presenting its own specific assortment. Football, for example, might offer as its hymn, "You've Got to be a Football Hero"; baseball counter with "Take Me Out to the Ball Game." Chants range from the traditional "We want a touchdown" to the hopeless "Let's Go Cubs." Even the stadium organist is modeled on his counterpart in traditional religion. And the result is identical in each case: individuals go beyond their own ego bonds. In so doing, they open to the possibility of experiencing a different, non-ordinary reality.

No less analogous to public ritual expression is the private search for religious meaning through rites, whether the specific activity is the Muslim's daily domestic practices or the runner's solitary ten-miler at dawn. It is important to note that this is the point at which personal prayer, as a ritual activity, converges in sport and religion. The point is this: all of these ritual acts, both traditional and nontraditional, prepare the participant for what is to follow. Without proper ritual preparation, the game would be lost, a close call would be missed, the fan would feel just plain lousy, or religious catastrophe might occur. In other words, these singular, curious-looking acts bring forth the sacred; they are part of the sacraments of religion, the sport variety and otherwise.

Taken together, rituals are welded into festivals, and in sport religion, just as in its traditional counterpart, the festivals are obvious and seasonal. In each of the world's major religious traditions, it is possible to isolate and identify a series of important seasonal rituals that occur periodically throughout the calendar year, binding the devotees on a seasonal, continuing basis. Each major sport functions in quite the same way, culminating in the pinnacle of the tradition, the crowning of its national champion. The result is clear: from a combination of seasonal and personal ritual processes, sport activity provides a continual stream of resacralization and meaning for our everyday world, just as traditional religion offers.

No religious tradition would be complete or functional without a strong legendary basis to underline and accompany the historical data of the faith. It is the legends that reveal an individual in his or her depth and fullness. It is the legends that provide a three-dimensional glimpse of the person in question, generally manifesting all the characteristics considered exemplary in the particular tradition in question. It is the legends that give us a perspective rarely captured by the historical accounts. Thus, the legends offer the faithful what the history books cannot: a leader to emulate, to model themselves after, and, in some cases, to worship. Sport legends are no less imposing and function in just the same way. To be sure, even in modern times, where media gadgets, journalistic morgues, and computer banks offer instant access to accurate historical data, this is not the stuff of which sport legends are made. Sport legend captures the essence of the sporting figure, reporting little-known bits and pieces of the individual that often defy publication or widespread dissemination. It really doesn't matter whether the specific legendary figure is Babe Ruth, Mickey Mantle, Red Grange, Wilt Chamberlain, Roger Bannister, Babe Didrikson Zaharias, or numerous others. What does matter is that each provides for his or her respective sport an archetypal model that holds true and grows for future generations. As for some of the rather unsavory characteristics, one need only be reminded of similar religious circumstances in the papal line or in the lineage of the Dalai Lama in Tibetan Buddhism.

In *How We Play the Game*, Richard Lipsky tells us (of baseball), "The game takes place in an atmosphere of piety. In many ways the ballplayers themselves can be seen as priests who represent us in a liturgy (game) that is part of a sacred tradition." Lipsky's comment reveals that far too little has been said about the role of the player in sport religion. In other words, we need to reflect on the actors in sport religion. It would be incorrect, though, to suggest that it is only the actual players who fulfill the role of religious participants in sport. We must include the coaches and officials as well, in their role as functionaries in the religious process. They are not untrained, either. Sport, no doubt, has its own seminaries and divinity schools in the various minor leagues and training camps that school the participants in all aspects of the tradition, from theology to ritual. The spectators, as video viewers, radio listeners, or game-going die-hards, form the congregation of sport religion. Their attendance is not required for all religious observances, but they do attend at specified times to share in religious rites. And they bear the religious symbols of their faith: the pennants, emblems, hats, coats, gloves, and whatever other objects the media geniuses can promote to signify the glory of sport in general and the home team in particular. The sport symbol may not be the cross, rosary, or mezuzah, but it is no less valuable to the owner, and likely considered to be just as powerful as its traditional counterpart, or more so.

It is necessary to note here that one would be *incorrect in assuming that all sport is religion*. In fact, quite the opposite is true. Utilizing a definition of religion as "a means of ultimate transformation," the whole issue of sport as religion turns on the premise that sport is a religion only insofar as it brings its adherents to an experience of ultimate reality, radically alters their lives as a result of the experience of ultimacy, and then channels their positive gains back into society in a generally viable and useful fashion. This is not so simple as it sounds. In traditional religion, not everyone gets religious experience. That is to say, not everyone experiences God (or some other symbol for the ultimate), irrespective of how pious or devout in worship. Nor is the experience of the ultimate an occasion that repeats itself each time the worshiper attends church or synagogue. For the athlete, religious experience is not simply having a good time, an important win, or being "turned inward" on a run or in a workout. No less than in traditional religion, sport religion is actualized only when an aspirant genuinely experiences that which is considered to be ultimate. And it is no less awe-inspiring. Yet there is no so-called sport religion for the athlete who attains ultimate reality through sport as a means of worship or religious practice in traditional religion. For sport to be considered a religion, it must quite self-consciously attempt to be just that. It must present all the rituals, practices, holidays, myths, legends, shrines, and so forth that all traditional religions provide. The results of ultimate transformation through sport must be socially functional in a way that is consistent with sport and the ethical imperative that derives from its practice.

If the potential for experiencing ultimate reality is so readily available in sport, why is it that athletes have so far been relatively silent in affirming their personal religious encounters? There are two likely answers here. First, I think that athletes, for the most part, simply do not have the equipment to speak comfortably and intelligently about religion *or* sport. One hopes, however, that as people actively involved in sport gain some real measure of intellectual facility in these areas, they will be able to recount numerous occasions in which the case for religious experience in sport is made thoroughly and believably. In other words, we are trying to provide those engaged in all aspects of sport with a new way of looking at themselves and their religious world. The second reason for the relative silence in the sporting world is that athletes are simply afraid of being held up to public ridicule. Many in our culture will find the suggestion that sport has become a genuine and sacred religious tradition to be utterly blasphemous. For the average citizen, the person professing sport religion becomes the object of scorn and derision, but for the professional athlete, the repercussions are worse still. There are endorsements and public appearances to be lost, all of which quickly translates into loss of revenue, and we should not overlook the fact that professional sport is big business. It is both sad and unfortunate that when dollars are at stake, integrity all too often becomes an unprofitable luxury.

There are other problems in sport religion. Just who is it that gets religious experience in sport? Curiously, these experiences seem not to be specific to the athlete-participant, the specialist. Similar responses can be evoked from coaches, officials, and, not so surprisingly, spectators (present or otherwise). After all, each of the above advocates does participate in his or her own way. This latter point is particularly important, I think, because it indicates that *no special athletic talent is required in the quest for salvation in sport.* What is self-evident here, then, is that *religious experience in sport is open to anyone, at any time, anywhere*—just as it is in traditional religion. Consequently, religious experience in sport is no more confined to the participants on the playing field than is traditional experience confined to the priest, minister, or rabbi. Also problematic is the theology of sport religion. A most obvious concern is who this god of sport might be. Is it the God of ancient Israel? Is it consistent with the Trinitarian notion of Christianity? Does sport present us with a primitive polytheism in which we find a god of running, one of tennis, and still another of swimming? Is there some arena in which the pantheon of sport deities might gather? What is the gender of the sport god(s)? How much power and might is wielded? What is important in this rather lighthearted approach is the understanding that sport theology must face the same questions as traditional religious theology, and this is no simple dilemma. Conversations I have had with athletes indicate support for *each* of the above positions, including god as female with little, medium, or great powers. Still another complicating factor is that for some participants, ultimacy is defined in nontheistic terms, usually as a oneness with nature, union with an impersonal absolute.

Earlier, I suggested that if sport is to be considered a religion in the proper sense of that word, it must, in addition to bringing its followers to an experience of ultimacy, radically alter their lives and channel that positive change back into society in a useful way. Does the sport experience change lives? One need only look at the manner in which athletes persevere in increasing their training, sometimes at the expense of all else, and their religious zeal after experiencing the supremacy of union with the Absolute. Is the smile and fulfillment of the Monday-morning quarterback to be doubted when some inordinately significant "Eureka" occurred to him while watching Walter Payton's uncanny ability to succeed despite the ineptitude of the Bears' offensive line? The changes are far too diverse and numerous to document here, but they do occur—and with startling regularity. And as a result, everything changes: attitudes, values, frames of reference, interpersonal relationships, and social involvements. We have tacitly avoided any mention of social ethics to this point. There is no question that some sport figures today have been less than exemplary in their conduct. To be sure, sport religion faces the same series of ethical difficulties as traditional religion. The presumption is that as one's religious faith matures, so does one's ethical behavior. It is no wonder, then, that so many religious groups of all denominations emphasize charitable acts and social involvement in good works for their members. In addition, the leaders of the congregation are expected to be especially consummate in their behavior. Sport religion is no less responsive to social needs in requiring devout participation by its advocates. Well, it's no wonder. Social concern, charitable acts, and personal conduct are all founded on discipline, and it is precisely here that the follower of sport religion excels. It doesn't matter whether this discipline is expressed by a daily twelve-mile run or three hours glued to ESPN. It can be corralled and marshaled for good causes, both personal and collective.

A final problem must be noted. Is it possible to maintain multilateral religious affiliations? Can the proponent of sport religion also retain standing within his or her traditional religious affiliation? Ostensibly not! When one declares that one adheres to sport as a formal religious tradition, this implies a *constant pursuit* that is also the *most important pursuit* and a *religious pursuit*. If such individuals were to then state that they are also Jews or Protestants (or Catholics or whatever), they would be referring to their *cultural heritage only*, to the complex series of factors that are essentially ethnic and locational rather than religious.

What it all boils down to is this: if sport can bring its advocates to an experience of the ultimate, and this (pursuit and) experience is expressed through a formal series of public and private rituals requiring a symbolic language and space deemed sacred by its worshipers, then it is both proper and necessary to call sport itself a religion. It is also reasonable to consider sort the newest and fastest-growing religion, far outdistancing whatever is in second place.

28. *Heavenly Game?*

FRANK DEFORD

Three of the four finalists in the NCAA basketball championship last season were Roman Catholic colleges, and for the second year in a row a Catholic school won. Villanova, that champion, was also in the Final Four in 1939, the first year of the NCAAs, and since then 17 different Catholic institutions have achieved that level. In 1947 Holy Cross became the first Catholic college to win the NCAAs, and five more have also triumphed. Eleven other Catholic colleges won the NIT back in the quarter-century when it was still a genuine national championship. Thirty-nine of this year's 283 Division I basketball schools are Catholic; 12 of the 237 colleges with Phi Beta Kappa chapters are Catholic. . . .

For many Americans college basketball is the outward and visible sign of Catholicism in the United States. And because private schools of any stripe tend to be smaller and more focused than the sprawling public mega-universities that they play games against, basketball has become even more the cynosure on the Catholic campus.

The perception that education has become the token white at the end of the Catholic basketball bench may be all the more damaging because, historically, Catholic universities have never been accepted as intellectual company, neither with the private nondenominational elite nor with the great state schools. Some of this snubbing has come, reflexively, from cynical Protestants, but even many American Catholics themselves have long questioned whether the term *Catholic education* is an oxymoron, like military justice. At many Catholic schools, as one Catholic historian has written, "Original research became original sin."

Moreover, as Catholic school basketball has thrived, it has seemed all the more contradictory—hypocritical?—that the standard-bearers for white Catholic schools are, in the main, black Protestants. Most people who watched a nearly all-black Villanova team upset a totally black Georgetown squad in the championship game last spring would probably be startled to learn that, notwithstanding what appeared on the court, Villanova is so white (98%), so Catholic (86%) and so suburban preppie upper middle class that it is known in its own bailiwick as Vanilla-nova.

SOURCE: *Sports Illustrated* (March 3, 1986). The following excerpts reprinted courtesy of *Sports Illustrated* from the March 3, 1986 issue.

Of course, much of this Catholics can't help. Abroad in the land, the image of almost all American universities is related to athletics. Basketball and football—*programs*—attract more attention than chemistry and Romance languages—*departments*. The question is whether religious schools can really afford to strike this deal with . . . well, with the devil, the same as secular institutions. In other words, can the Catholic colleges pursue the almighty dollar and answer to the Almighty at the same time? What price prime time?

In 1971, the last year before 1985 that Villanova made the Final Four, the Wildcats had to forfeit their second-place finish when their star player was found to be a pro. The only fix disqualification in the history of the Final Four was leveled against another Philadelphia-area Catholic school, St. Joseph's in 1961. Boston College was caught in the fix trap four years ago. In 1982 San Francisco gave up basketball for three years after a succession of tawdry scandals that would have sorely tested even Jesus's inclinations toward forgiveness. The damage done to Creighton when one of its players had to go back to an elementary school to learn how to read after several years at the Omaha school remains incalculable. A scholar-athlete at Providence was charged with assaulting a teammate with a tire iron. Holy Cross's team took to racial skirmishing last year. Georgetown's reputation for fighting—at least half a dozen brawls in the last four years—is well established.

Now none of this is the peculiar province of Catholic higher education. Indeed, anybody even remotely familiar with football at Texas Christian and Southern Methodist can only draw the conclusion that the inherent problem with big-time college sports and religion is that the former is so pervasive, so rotten, so—let's say it—sinful that it is bound to soil any of the latter that lies down with it. Does religion need this? . . .

Religious schools, whatever the denomination, are forever torn about what sort of moral guidance they are mandated to provide. And, of course, there is also the perennial question: Where does house theology become propaganda and squeeze out open inquiry? Villanova's mission statement attempts to draw a line: "Although Villanova functions as an independent institution in the conduct of its own affairs, in matters theological it recognizes its obligation to the Magisterium of the Church."

Thus, last year the editor of *The Villanovan*, John Marusak, was censured for running a paid advertisement for a birth control device. More recently, the Villanova president, Father John Driscoll, rescinded the invitation of a pro-choice speaker who was to appear on campus for a theological symposium. "Within the framework of academic freedom," Driscoll says, drawing on his pipe, "anyone identified with a Catholic university has a right to teach the students the doctrine of its ruling body."

As suggested by the raging debates on many campuses over institutional investment in South Africa, universities must often make moral choices for themselves—and this is especially true if they feel their "explicit reason for existence," as Driscoll says is the case with Catholic schools, "is value orientation." But while big-time basketball is indisputably a rotten borough, Catholic schools have hardly been shy about residing there. When it comes to morality, they often seem to ask more of their students than of themselves. Of course, maybe they believe they haven't got any choice. Maybe they think if they want to compete in basketball, they've got to wink at the sinners. Praise the Lord and pass the ammunition. The one person at a Catholic institution who comes easily to mind for having spoken out courageously against the system in not a cleric, but Digger Phelps, the basketball coach at Notre Dame. And when he was derided, then, by both his coaching colleagues and the press for being a tattletale, who in Catholic education came to his side?

Questions about the direction of big-time intercollegiate athletics are regularly brought up by Catholic school presidents when they gather together, but apart from perfunctory nods toward goodness and light, no strong moral protests ever seem to be publicly ventilated. Driscoll shares what seems to be the benign, majority view. "In this country the tradition of athletics runs deep," he says. "And not only that of participating. Observing sports is also a strong part of our culture. Now we all must concern ourselves with overemphasis, and if abuses take place because of indifference on the part of coaches or the administration, then it's wrong. But if mistakes are made unintentionally, there's no reason to punish athletics. That's just the way human beings operate."

A championship such as that won by Georgetown or Villanova—or even just a nicely publicized winning season—can enlarge for a university what politicians call "the recognition factor." Villanova's applications rose almost 15% last year—although it's a safe guess that these are just more of the same sort of kids.

Villanova's vanillaness is not altogether of its own choosing, though. Like so many private schools just below the top rank, it is caught in a bind. With tuition and costs totaling in excess of $10,000 a year, it obviously is going to attract a high percentage of well-heeled applicants. Yet because Villanova is not generously endowed, it cannot offer the bountiful scholarship assistance that wealthier schools can. (Villanova's endowment totals $15 million as compared with $300 million for Notre Dame and more than $3 billion for Harvard.) The well-endowed Ivies routinely dip down the scale to accept reasonably well-qualified minority scholarship applicants. This leaves Villanova with, as Capone characterizes them, "second-round draft choices" and poses this dilemma: How do you justify offering aid to kids who don't project as graduates?

Contradictory as this may sound, the better academic schools—such as Georgetown among Catholic institutions—also seem more comfortable in practicing a form of noblesse oblige and granting admission to borderline students. East Cupcake State bends the rules; Harvard provides minority opportunity. Charles Deacon, Georgetown's dean of undergraduate admissions, says flatly, "We have no minimum averages or standards." So long as an applicant is projected as capable of graduating, who is to say that a 7-foot basketball player with a minimal SAT score isn't more deserving than a wimpy poet with an SAT score out of sight?

There was grousing on the Georgetown campus when Patrick Ewing was admitted in 1981, complaints that he was taking the place of some more deserving student. But as Father James Redington, a Georgetown theology professor who also serves as scorekeeper for the Hoya team, says, "After a year it was no longer an issue. The main way I see Georgetown—as a Catholic university, but as one with basketball—is in terms of the increased commitment by Catholic universities, and by Jesuits in particular, in support of social justice. Or, specifically, it's what we Jesuits call an option in favor of the poor." Cynics might suggest that the option is more likely to be exercised in favor of those among the poor who excel at basketball, but the fact is, long before Thompson arrived as a coach at Georgetown, the university had begun a "community scholars program" to help students with special educational needs. . . .

Almost all Catholic schools keep sports in better perspective than do their secular counterparts. At the same time, it is clear that in a period when Catholic universities are struggling for identity, even for justification, they are often mainly visible as accomplices in the big-time basketball mob. Even Georgetown, generally regarded as the finest academic Catholic institution, and with a perception of itself as being in competition with such colleges as Duke and Northwestern, acknowledges that abroad in the land it is viewed as "the Southern California of basketball." The fact is that Catholic colleges are playing somebody else's game, and even when they win, it is not clear that they do.

■ FOR FURTHER STUDY

Burhmann, H. G., and M. K. Zaugg. "Religion and Superstition in the Sport of Basketball." *Journal of Sport Behavior* 6 (October 1983), 146-151.

DeFord, Frank. "Religion in Sport." *Sports Illustrated* (April 19, April 26, and May 3, 1976): 88-100; 55-56, 68, 69, and 43-44, 57-60 respectively.

Fellowship of Christian Athletes. *The Christian Athlete* (any issue).

Frame, Randy. "Christianity Comes of Age in the NFL." *Christianity Today* 28 (January 1984): 36-37.

Gmelch, George. "Baseball Magic." *Trans-action* 8 (June 1971: 39-41, 54.

Guttmann, Allen. "The Sacred and the Secular." In *Sport Inside Out*, David L. Vanderwerken and Spencer K. Wertz, eds. Forth Worth: Texas Christian University Press, 1985: 298-308.

Higgs, Robert J. "Muscular Christianity, Holy Play, and Spiritual Exercises: Confusion about Christ in Sports and Religion." *Arete: The Journal of Sport Literature* (1983): 59-87.

Hoffman, Shirl J., ed. *Sport and Religion*. Champaign, IL: Human Kinetics, 1992.

Montville, Leigh. "Thou Shalt Not Lose." *Sports Illustrated* (November 13, 1989): 82-91.

Neil, Graham. "Demystifying Sport Superstition." *International Review of Sport Sociology* 17 (1982): 99-126.

Novak, Michael. *The Joy of Sports*. New York: Basic Books, 1976.

Price, Joseph L. "The Super Bowl as Religious Festival." *The Christian Century* (February 22,1984): 190-191.

Redmond, Gerald. "A Plethora of Shrines: Sport in the Museum and Hall of Fame." *Quest* 19 (January 1973): 41-48.

Rogers, Cornish. "Sports, Religion, and Politics: The Renewal of an Alliance." *The Christian Century* (April 5, 1972): 392-394.

Womack, Mari. "Why Athletes Need Ritual: A Study of Magic among Professional Athletes." In *Sport and the Humanities*, ed. W. J. Morgan. Knoxville: University of Tennessee Press, 1979, pp. 22-38.

Part Ten

Race/Ethnicity and Sport

By definition a *minority group* is one that (1) is relatively powerless compared with the majority group, (2) possesses traits that make it different from others, (3) is systematically condemned by negative stereotyped beliefs, and (4) is singled out for differential and unfair treatment (that is, discrimination). *Race* (a socially defined category on the basis of a presumed genetic heritage resulting in distinguishing social characteristics) and *ethnicity* (the condition of being culturally distinct on the basis of race, religion, or national origin) are two traditional bases for minority group status and the resulting social inequality. Sociologists of sport are interested in the question: Is sport an area of social life where performance counts and race or ethnicity is irrelevant? The three selections in this section examine three racial or ethnic minorities—Native Americans, Latinos, and African-Americans—to answer this question.

The first selection, by journalist Kevin Simpson, seeks an answer to the dilemma posed by the typical behaviors of excellent Native American athletes from reservations: Why do so many who are given scholarships either refuse them or return quickly to the reservation? These responses do not make sense to the Anglos because the reservation has high unemployment, a life of dependency, and disproportionate alcohol abuse. Simpson points to these young men being "pulled" by the familiar, by the strong bonds of family, and by their unique culture. They are also "pushed" back to the reservation by social isolation, discrimination, poor high school preparation for college, and little hope for a return on their investment in a college education.

The second selection, by anthropologist Douglas E. Foley, is from his study of a football season in a poor, rural South Texas community with a population that is 80 percent Latino. His thesis is that football is a cultural practice that socializes people into community structures of inequality (not just racial inequality, but also social class and gender inequalities).

The final selection, by Richard E. Lapchick and David Stuckey of the Center for the Study of Sport in Society, provides the data on the extent of racial discrimination (mostly against African-Americans because of their predominance numerically but indirectly against other racial categories as well because of underrepresentation) in professional sports.

29. *Sporting Dreams Die on the "Rez"*

KEVIN SIMPSON

Last season, basketball fans followed Willie White everywhere through the unforgiving South Dakota winter. Mesmerized by smooth moves and spectacular dunks, they watched the most celebrated product of the state's hoop-crazy Indian tribes secure his status as local legend by leading his high school to an undefeated season and state championship.

They would mob him after games in an almost frightening scene of mass adulation, press scraps of paper toward him and beg for an autograph, preferably scribbled beneath some short personal message. White would oblige by scrawling short, illegible phrases before signing. He made certain they were illegible for fear someone would discover that the best prep basketball player in South Dakota could barely read or write.

As the resident basketball hero on the impoverished Pine Ridge Reservation, where there was precious little to cheer about before the state title rekindled embers of Indian pride, White was allowed to slip undisturbed through the reservation school system until, by his senior year, he could read at only the sixth-grade level. Ironically, the same hero status moved him to admit his problem and seek help. The constant humiliation at the hands of autograph-seekers proved more than he could take.

"I had to face up to it," says White, a soft-spoken 6-foot-4 Sioux who looks almost scholarly behind his wire-rimmed glasses. "I couldn't go on forever like that. In school I didn't study. I cheated on every test they gave me. I couldn't read good enough to answer the questions."

After some intense individual help with his reading and writing, this fall White enrolled at Huron (S.D.) College, where he intends to continue his basketball career and take remedial reading courses. If he manages to play four years and complete his degree, he'll be the first schoolboy athlete from Pine Ridge to do so.

Other than his close friends, nobody thinks he stands a chance. Indians usually don't.

Every year, all over the western U.S., promising native American athletes excel in high school sports only to abandon dreams of college,

---

SOURCE: *The Denver Post* (September 6, 1987), pp. 1C, 19C. Reprinted by permission of *The Denver Post*.

return to economically depressed reservations and survive on their per capita checks, welfare-like payments from the tribal government, or the good will of more fortunate relatives. They waste away quietly, victims of alcohol, victims of inadequate education, victims of boredom, victims of poverty, but nearly always victims of their own ambivalence, caught between a burning desire to leave the reservation and an irresistible instinct to stay.

"We've had two or three kids get scholarships in the eight years I've been here," says Roland Bradford, athletic director and basketball coach at Red Cloud High School, just a few miles down the highway from Pine Ridge. "None have lasted. It's kind of a fantasy thing. In high school they talk about going to college, but it's not a reality. They have no goals set. They start out, things get tough and they come home."

At 6-foot-7 and 280 pounds, Red Cloud's Dave Brings Plenty inspired enough comparisons to the Refrigerator to lure a photographer from *People Magazine* out to the reservation. He went to Dakota Wesleyan to pursue his football career, but returned home after suffering a mild concussion in practice. He never played a game. Brings Plenty says he might enroll at a different school sometime in the future, but his plans are vague. For now, he's content to hang out on the reservation and work as a security guard at a bingo parlor.

Some of the athlete-dropouts have squandered mind-boggling potential. Jeff Turning Heart, a long-distance legend on South Dakota's Cheyenne River Reservation, enrolled at Black Hills State College in Spearfish, S.D., on a Bureau of Indian Affairs grant in 1980 amid great expectations. He left eight days later.

In 1982, he wound up at Adams State College in Alamosa. Longtime Adams State coach Joe Vigil, the U.S. men's distance coach for the 1988 Olympics, says that as a freshman Turning Heart was far more physically gifted than even Pat Porter, the Adams State graduate who now ranks as the premier U.S. runner at 10,000 meters. Both Porter and Vigil figured Turning Heart was on a course to win the national cross country title—until he left school, supposedly to tend to his gravely ill father in North Dakota. He promised to return in a few days. The story was bogus and Turning Heart never went back.

At Black Hills State, where in 19 years as athletic director and track coach, David Little has seen only one Indian track athlete graduate, Turning Heart wasn't the first world-class, native American runner to jilt him. Myron Young Dog, a distance man from Pine Ridge who once won 22 straight cross country races in high school, came to Black Hills after dropping out of Ellendale (N.D.) Junior College in 1969. Although he was academically ineligible for varsity sports and hadn't trained, Young Dog stepped onto the track during a physical conditioning class and ran two minutes in 9:30 "like it was Sunday jog," according to Little. Three weeks later he entered a 15-km road race and ran away from all the collegiate competition.

It was a tantalizing glimpse of talent ultimately wasted. Little still rates Young Dog as one of the top 10 athletes ever to come out of South Dakota, but in the spring of 1970 he returned to the reservation, never to run competitively again.

It doesn't take many heartbreaks before the college coaches catch on to the risky business of recruiting off the reservations. Although Indian athletes often are immensely talented and given financial backing from the tribe and the BIA—a budgetary boon to small schools short on scholarship funds—they suffer from a widespread reputation as high-risk recruits who probably won't stick around for more than a few weeks.

That's part of the reason so many schools backed off Willie White—that and his reading deficiency. Huron College coach Fred Paulsen, who made White his first in-state recruit in four years, thought the youngster's potential made him worth the risk.

"I hate to stereotype," says Paulsen, "but is he the typical Indian? If Willie comes and doesn't make it, nobody will be surprised. My concern is that he'll go home for the weekend and say he'll be back on Monday. Which Monday?"

Talented Indians are diverted from their academic and athletic career courses for many reasons, but often they are sucked back to subsistence-level life on the reservation by the vacuum created by inadequate education and readily available escapes like drugs and alcohol.

Ted Little Moon, an all-state basketball player for Pine Ridge High School in 1984 and '85, still dominates the asphalt slab outside the school. At 6-foot-6, he roams from baseline to baseline jamming in rebounds, swatting away opponents' shots and threading blind passes to teammates beneath the basket. He is unmistakable small-college talent.

But Little Moon missed his first opportunity to play ball in college when he failed to graduate from high school. By the following August, though, he had passed his high school equivalency exam and committed to attend Huron College. But when the basketball coach showed up at his house to pick him up and drive him to school, Little Moon said he couldn't go because he had gotten his girlfriend pregnant and had to take care of a newborn son.

He played independent basketball, a large-scale Indian intramural network, until last fall, when he planned to enroll at Haskell Junior College, an all-Indian school in Lawrence, Kan. He and some friends drank heavily the night before he was to take the bus to Kansas. Little Moon was a passenger in a friend's car when they ran a stop sign and hit another vehicle. He spent four days in jail, missed his bus and missed out on enrolling at Haskell.

Now he talks of going back to school, of playing basketball again, but there's ambivalence in his voice. He has become accustomed to cashing his bi-weekly per capita check for $28.50, drinking beer and growing his own marijuana at a secret location on the reservation. He distributes it free to his friends.

"I guess I'm scared to get away," Little Moon admits. "But also I'm afraid I'll be stuck here and be another statistic. You grow old fast here. If I get away, I have a chance. But I'm used to what I'm doing now. Here, your mom takes care of you, the BIA takes care of you. You wait for your $28.50 and then party. It's something to look forward to.

"I started drinking as a freshman in high school, smoking dope as a sophomore. I used to get high before practice, after practice. I still do it, on the average, maybe every other day. After I play, I smoke some. It makes you forget what you're doing on the reservation."

At home, alcohol offers whatever false comfort family ties cannot. Then it kills. Two years ago, Red Cloud's Bradford tallied all the alcohol-related deaths he had known personally and came up with some sobering statistics. In 13 years of teaching, 18 of his former students have died in alcohol-related tragedies. Aside from students, he has known an incredible 61 people under the age of 22 who have lost their lives in one way or another to the bottle.

Many died along a two-mile stretch of Highway 407 that connects Pine Ridge with Whiteclay, Neb., a depressing cluster of bars and liquor stores that do a land-office business. Three years ago, South Dakota's highway department began erecting metal markers at the site of each alcohol-related fatality. Locals say that if they's started 10 years ago, the signs would form an unbroken chain along the road. They'd have run out of signs before they ran out of death.

Among Indians nationwide, four of the top 10 causes of death are alcohol-related: Accidents, suicides, [cirrhosis] of the liver and homicide. Alcohol mortality is nearly five times higher among Indians, at 30 per 100,000 population, than for all other races. According to Dr. Eva Smith of the Indian Health Service in Washington, D.C., between 80 and 90 percent of all Indian accidents, suicides and homicides are alcohol-related.

Fred Beauvais, a research scientist at Colorado State University, points out that Indians not only start using drugs and alcohol earlier than the general population, but the rate of use also tends to be higher. According to a 1987 study of 2,400 subjects in eight western tribes Beauvais conducted with funding from the National Institute on Drug Abuse, 50 percent of Indian high school seniors were classified as "at risk" of serious harm because of drug and alcohol use. An amazing 43 percent are at risk by the seventh grade. The figure for seniors probably is too low, Beauvais explains, because by 12th grade many Indian students already have dropped out.

He attributes these phenomena not to racial or cultural idiosyncrasies, but socio-economic conditions on the reservations.

"Once it becomes socially ingrained, it's a vicious cycle," Beauvais says. "The kids see the adults doing it and they see no alternatives. It's a real trap. For some Indian kids to choose not to drink means to deny their Indian-ness. That can be a powerful factor."

Even those athletes who excel in the classroom are not necessarily immune to the magnetic pull of alcohol. Beau LeBeau, a 4.0 student at Red Cloud High who has started for the varsity basketball team since he was in eighth grade, recognizes the dangers but speaks of them as if they are elements quite out of his control. He estimates that 90 percent of his friends abuse alcohol.

"I'm going to the best academic school on the reservation," he says. "I should get a good education—if I don't turn to drugs and alcohol in the next few years and ruin it for myself. In my room before I go to sleep I think, 'Is this how I'm going to spend the rest of my life? On the reservation?' I hope not."

For all the roadside signs that stand as chilling monuments to death around Pine Ridge, the drinking continues, a false and addictive cure for boredom and futility.

"If they win they want to celebrate," offers Bryan Brewer, athletic director at Pine Ridge High School. "If they lose, that's another excuse to drink. People who didn't make it want to drag the good athletes down with them."

Consequently, the road to a college athletic career sometimes ends before it even begins.

"I'm not opposed to recruiting the Indian athlete," offers Black Hills State athletic director Little. "I'm selective about who I recruit, though. I don't have the answer to the problem and don't know I totally understand the situation. I do know that what's going on now is not working."

Something definitely isn't working Towoac (pronounced TOI-ahk), in southwestern Colorado, where Indian athletes don't even wait until after high school to see their careers disintegrate. There, on the Ute Mountain Ute Reservation, a multitude of Indian athletes compete and excel up to eighth grade and then quit rather than pursue sports at Montezuma-Cortez High, a mixed-race school 17 miles north of the reservation in the town of Cortez.

They drop out at the varsity level sometimes for academic reasons but often because of racial tension—or what they feel is bias on the part of white coaches. Pressed for particulars, current and former athletes make only vague accusations of negative attitudes and rarely cite specific instances. But how much of the discrimination is real and how much imagined is academic. The perception of discrimination remains, passed down among the athletes almost as an oral tradition.

For instance, today's athletes hear stories like those told by former Cortez High athlete Hanley Frost, who in the mid-1970s felt the wrath of the school administration when he was a sophomore on the basketball team and insisted on wearing his hair long, braided in traditional Indian style. He played four games with it tucked into his jersey but then was told school policy demanded that he cut it off. Eventually, he quit the team and began experimenting with drugs and alcohol.

Frost: "Really, it was the towns-people who didn't enjoy having a long-haired Indian on the team. There were a lot of people out there who would rather see their kids in a position on the team an Indian kid has."

"There's something about Towoac that just doesn't sit right," adds reservation athletic director Doug Call, a Mormon who came to the Ute Mountain Reservation from Brigham Young University. "I don't know if people are afraid or what, but there's a stigma if you live out here."

Those Indians who do participate in sports at the high school level tend to live in Cortez, not on the reservation. An invisible wall of distrust seems to surround Towoac, where most of the young athletes play what is known on reservations as "independent ball," a loosely organized kind of intramural basketball.

"They feel they're not getting a fair chance, I know they do," says Gary Gellatly, the Cortez High School athletic director who once served as recreation director on the reservation. "And I'm sure they have been discriminated against, directly or indirectly. It's tough to get them to compete. Yet you go out there on any weekend and watch those independent tournaments you'll see kids playing basketball that you've never seen before. But I'm afraid if we start an overt effort to get them to participate you crowd them into a tighter corner. In a sense, not participating because they think they might be discriminated against is a cop-out, but it's been perpetuated by circumstances. Somewhere, something happened that wasn't good."

After a massive turnover in the school's coaching staff, some new hires have expressed a desire to see more Indians become involved in the school's sports programs. Bill Moore, the new head football coach, heard the rumors that Indian kids wouldn't even try out for the squad and mailed tryout invitations to much of the student body—including as many Indian boys as he could find addresses for. Even so, the turnout hasn't been markedly different from previous years.

"The solution," says varsity basketball coach Gordon Shepherd, "is that something has to give. Cultural groups that remain within themselves don't succeed. For Indians to succeed in white society terms, they have to give up some cultural ethnicity."

Ethnic idiosyncrasies present a whole range of problems—from students' inclination or ability to perform in the classroom to conflicts such as the one currently under way at Jemez Pueblo, a small reservation north of Albuquerque, N.M. There, in a hotbed of mountain running, a cross country coach at a mixed-race school has struggled with athletes who reject modern training techniques for the less formal but highly traditional ways of their ancestors.

On some reservations, Indian student-athletes are merely ill-prepared to cope with the stringent academic demands of college. According to BIA statistics, the average Indian high school senior reads at the ninth-grade level. Of the 20 percent of high school seniors who go on to attempt college, 40 percent drop out.

And with some reservations approaching economic welfare states, students considering college confront a serious question about the value of an education: Why spend four years pursuing a college degree only to return to a reservation that has few or no private sector jobs?

Indians often find themselves without any real ethnic support system in college and become homesick for reservation life and the exceptionally strong bonds of an extended family in which aunts, uncles and grandparents often live under the same roof. In some tribal cultures, 18- or 19-year-olds still are considered mere children and haven't been pressed to formulate long-term goals. It's no coincidence, says an education administrator for the Arapahoe tribe on the central Wyoming's Wind River Reservation, that most successful Indian students are in their mid- to late-20s—when, incidentally, athletic eligibility has gone by the board.

Even the basic incentive of athletics tend to evaporate in a more intense competitive climate far removed from the reservation.

Myron "The Magician" Chavez, a four-time all-state guard from Wyoming Indian High School on the Wind River Reservation, enrolled at Sheridan (Wyo.) College last fall but left school during pre-season workouts when he was asked to redshirt. He felt he had failed because he didn't step immediately into a starting position. Jeff Brown, who preceded Chavez at WIHS, had a scholarship offer from the University of Kansas in 1982 but turned it down because he feared he would fail—academically if not athletically.

Dave Archambault, a Sioux who started the athletic program at United Tribes Junior College in Bismarck, N.D., has found the fear of failure to be a familiar theme among talented Indian athletes. On the reservations, he points out, athletes become heroes, modern extensions of the old warrior society that disappeared after defeat at the hands of the white man.

"They're kicking butt on the reservation," Archambault explains, "and then all of the sudden they're working out with juniors and seniors in college and getting their butts kicked. They're not held in that high regard and esteem. But they can go back to the reservation any time and get it."

They recapture their high school glory through independent ball, the intramural network among reservations that quenches an insatiable thirst for basketball competition among all age groups. There are tournaments nearly every weekend and an all-Indian national tournament each spring, where the best teams often recruit talent from a wide area by offering modest incentives like cash and expenses. At most levels, though, independent ball resembles extremely organized pickup basketball.

For most Indian athletes, it represents the outer limits of achievement, caught though it is in a void between the reservation and the outside world. It's in that limbo–socially as well as athletically–that most Indians play out their careers.

"There's no way to return to the old way, spiritually and economically," observes Billy Mills, the 1964 Olympic gold medalist at 10,000 meters who grew up on the Pine Ridge Reservation. "It's like walking death–no goals, no commitment, no accomplishment. If you go too far into society, there's a fear of losing your Indian-ness. There's a spiritual factor that comes into play. To become part of white society you give up half your soul. Society wants us to walk in one world with one spirit. But we have to walk in two worlds with one spirit."

30. *The Great American Football Ritual: Reproducing Race, Class, and Gender Inequality*

DOUGLAS E. FOLEY

This analysis of a football season is part of a larger study of the popular culture practices of youth in one South Texas town (Foley, 1990). Theoretically, it has a great affinity with a Gramscian perspective (Critcher, 1986; Deem, 1988; Gruneau, 1983; Hargreaves, 1986; McKay, 1986; Whitson, 1984) of sport as a site of contested popular cultural practices. Although there are significant differences between these authors, the Gramscian perspective advocated by the Birmingham Centre for Contemporary Cultural Studies (CCCS) generally informs many new critical studies of sports. The cultural studies perspective has been employed to study a wide array of popular or leisure practices (Bennett, Mercer, & Wollacott, 1986; Chambers, 1986; Fiske, 1989a, 1989b). Increasingly, sport sociologists are arguing that sports must also be studied as an autonomous cultural activity with the potential to challenge the commercialization and rationalization of sports activities.

This study seeks to ground recent critical perspectives of sports in the everyday cultural practices of one small, historical community. It explores the way high school sport reproduces social inequalities with the kind of detailed ethnographic data used in other microstudies of sport subcultures (Donnelly & Young, 1988; Fine, 1987). Like those microethnographic studies, this one is concerned with describing sports as a socialization process. Unlike other socialization studies, however, a historical[1] community with a social structure, not a group of people practicing a particular sport, is the focus. In addition, the reproduction and resistance perspective of popular culture theory is used rather than a functionalist or symbolic interactionist perspective (Donnelly & Young, 1988; Loy & Ingham, 1973).

The anthropological concept of a dramatic community ritual (Turner, 1974) is also used to give a holistic portrait of how major popular or leisure cultural practices (in this case, football) socialize people into community structures of inequality. The following description of the ritual complex

SOURCE: *Sociology of Sport Journal* 7, no. 2 (1990), pp. 111-135.

surrounding high school football games concentrates on the rites, ceremonies, and events that socialize youth in the community and that symbolically stage class, gender, and racial inequality. Two basic premises not generally used in anthropological studies of ritual, but commonly shared by critical theorists of sport, guided this study. First, capitalist societies and their sport scenes are marked by multiple systems of dominance (Birrell, 1984, 1989; Deem, 1988; Hall, 1984, 1985; Messner, 1988). Consequently, a multiple-system-of-dominance perspective was used to explore the intersections of class, gender, and racial practices and relations and the way in which they are dialectically related in local community sport rituals. Second, any ideological hegemony constructed by a capitalist class is never secure and is often contested through various popular culture practices. Consequently, this study also explores the extent to which community sport scenes are sites of resistance and counterhegemonic popular or leisure cultural practices.

The setting of this field study was "North Town," a small (8,000 population) South Texas farming/ranching community with limited industry, considerable local poverty, and a population that was 80% Mexican-American. North Town was one of three towns in this winter-vegetable-producing area where a Chicano third party emerged to challenge the segregated racial order. The third party, the Partido Raza Unida, has since disbanded, but their impact was felt in all walks of life and sport was no exception. "North Town High" had an enrollment of 600 students and its sport teams played at the Triple-A level in a five-level state ranking system.

During the football season described here, I attended a number of practices, rode on the players' bus, and hung out with the coaches at the fieldhouse and with players during extensive classroom and lunchtime observations. I also participated in basketball and tennis practices and interviewed students extensively about student status groups, friendship, dating, and race relations. The participant-observation and interviewing in the sports scene involved hundreds of hours of fieldwork over a 12-month period. The larger community study[2] also included three full-time research assistants, and the fieldwork took place over a 2-year period. The traditional anthropological field methods used in this study are reported in great detail in Foley, Mota, Post, and Lozano (1988) and Foley (1990).

THE RITUAL COMPLEX

The Weekly Pep Rally

Shortly after arriving in North Town I attended my first pep rally. Students, whether they liked football or not, looked forward to Friday afternoons. Regular 7th-period classes were let out early to hold a mass pep rally to support the team. Most students attended these events but a few used it to slip away from school early. During the day of this pep rally I overheard a number of students planning their trip to the game. Those in the school marching band (80) and in the pep club (50) were the most enthusiastic. Students were plotting secret rendezvous with boyfriends and girlfriends or were fantasizing about fateful meetings with their secret loves. Fewer students and townspeople than usual would follow the team on this first long road trip.

Nevertheless, as on most Fridays, teachers and students were talking about The Game. Some teachers engaged the players in lively banter during classes about "whipping" Larson City. In senior English class a long analysis of last year's bad calls, missed kicks, and fumbles ensued. The history of this event had already been reconstructed, and those students interested in it shared that moment with the players. Players and nonplayers collectively plotted and reveled in mythical feats of revenge. There was much brave talk about "kicking their asses this year."

Some high school students considered the idea of young males in padded armor crashing into each other as dumb and boring. Some adults also thought that the sport was silly or too rough or a waste of time. Generally, however, most North Town students, like the adults, looked forward to football season and the Friday night games. The games enlivened the community's social life. Adults, especially the local chamber of commerce types, articulated this view even more than the students. Community sports was the patriotic, neighborly thing to do. Many students felt deep loyalties to support their team, but others used these community events to express their disgust for the game and the players, hence for "respectable" mainstream society.

This Friday afternoon the pep rally started like most school pep rallies. As the last bell rang, the halls were crammed with students rushing to put books away and to find their friends. Various students claimed their rightful territory on the bleachers facing the microphones. Months later, when I knew them better, I could see the pattern to this mad scramble for seats: It was age-graded. The older, most prominent students took the center seats, thus signaling their status and loyalty. Younger first- and second-year students sat next to the leaders of the school activities if they were protégés of those leaders.

In sharp contrast, knots and clusters of the more socially marginal students, the "druggers," and "punks and greasers," usually claimed the seats nearest the exits, thus signaling their indifference to all the rah-rah speeches they had to endure. The "nobodies" or "nerds," those dutiful, conforming students who were followers, tended to sit in the back of the center regions. Irrespective of the general territory, students usually sat with friends from their age group. Teachers strategically placed themselves at the margins and down in front to assist in crowd control.

The pep rally itself was dominated by the coaches and players, who were introduced to the audience to reflect upon the coming contest. In this particular pep rally the team captains led the team onto the stage. All the Anglo players entered first, followed by all the Mexicano players. Coach Trujillo started out with the classic pep talk that introduced the team captains, who in turn stepped forward and spoke in an awkward and self-effacing manner, thus enacting the ideal of a sportsman—a man of deeds, not words. They all stuttered through several "uhs" and "ers," then quickly said, "I hope y'all come support us. Thanks." Generally students expected their jocks to be inarticulate and, as the cliché goes, strong but silent types. Coach Trujillo then elaborated upon how hard work, loyalty, and dedication would bring the school victory. He also brought up last year's defeat at the hands of Larson City to jibe the present seniors that this would be their "last chance to beat the Raiders."

Between the brief comments made by players and coaches, the cheerleaders and pep squad tried to involve the student body through cheers. A small contingent of the 80-piece marching band tooted and banged out the proper drum rolls for the speakers and cheerleaders. Other band members dispersed among the crowd and helped the pep squad lead cheers. Being a part of the band was also an important way of establishing one's loyalty to school and community. Later, during the game, the marching band would entertain the crowd at halftime while the players rested. Halftime performance also showcased the youth of North Town.

The Marching Band and Band Fags

The quality of the marching band was as carefully scrutinized as the football team by some community members. The band director, Dante Aguila, was keenly aware of maintaining an excellent winning band. Like sport teams, marching bands competed in local, district, and statewide contest and won rankings. The ultimate goal was winning a top rating at the state level. In addition, each band sent its best players of various instruments to district contests to compete for individual rankings. Individual band members could also achieve top rankings at the state level.

A certain segment of the student body began training for the high school marching band during their grade-school years. Band members had a much more positive view of their participation in band than the players did. The band was filled with students who tended to have better grades and came from the more affluent families. The more marginal, deviant students perceived band members as "goodie goodies," "richies," and "brains." This characterization was not entirely true because the band boosters club did make an effort to raise money to help low-income students join the band. Not all band students were top students, but many were in the advanced or academic tracks. Band members were generally the students with school spirit who were proud to promote loyalty to the school and community. The marching band was also a major symbolic expression of the community's unity and its future generation of good citizens and leaders.

The view that band members were the cream of the crop was not widely shared by the football players. Many female band members were socially prominent and "cool," but some were also studious homebodies. On the other hand, "real men" supposedly did not sign up for the North Town band. According to the football players, the physically weaker, more effeminate males tended to be in the band. Males in the band were called "band fags." The only exceptions were "cool guys" who did drugs, or had their own rock and roll band, or came from musical families and planned to become professional musicians. The males considered to be fags were sometimes derided and picked on as "sissies." Occasional gender jokes were made about their not having the "balls" to date the cute female band members.

The main masculinity test for band fags was to punch their biceps as hard as possible. If the victim returned this aggression with a defiant smile or smirk, he was a real man; if he winced and whined, he was a wimp or a fag. The other variations on punching the biceps were pinching the forearm and rapping the knuckles. North Town boys generally punched and pinched each other, but this kind of male play toward those considered fags was a daily ritual degradation. These were moments when physically dominant males picked on allegedly more effeminate males and reaffirmed their place in the male pecking order. Ironically, however, the players themselves rarely picked on those they called band fags. Males who emulated jocks and hoped to hang out with them were usually the hit men. The jocks signaled their real power and prestige by showing restraint toward obviously weaker males.

Cheerleaders and Pep Squads

As in most pep rallies, on the Friday I am describing, the cheerleaders were in front of the crowd on the gym floor doing dance and jumping routines in unison and shouting patriotic cheers to whip up enthusiasm for the team. The cheerleaders were acknowledged as some of the prettiest young women in the school and they aroused the envy of nobodies and nerds. Male students incessantly gossiped and fantasized about these young women and their reputations.

One frequently told story was about a pep rally when students started throwing pennies at Trini, a cheerleader. Initially this curious story made no sense to me. Trini struck me as the perfect all-American girl next door. She was widely acknowledged as cute and perky, got above average grades, and was on her way to college, a good career, and marriage. She also dated an Anglo from another town. That fact, and the relentless gossip about her being a "slut" and "gringo-loving whore," had hurt her; but being strong willed, she would not quietly accept these put-downs. She lashed back by criticizing people for being small-townish and small-minded.

The rest of the girls, four Mexicans and two Anglos, were more or less alike both physically and socially. One Anglo girl was particularly athletic, which often prompted Anglos to make negative remarks about a Mexicana who was popular but considered a bit plump. Students invariably had their favorites to adore and/or ridicule. Yet they told contradictory stories about the cheerleaders. When privately reflecting on their physical attributes and social status, males saw going with a cheerleader as guaranteeing their coolness and masculinity. Particularly the less attractive males plotted the seduction of these young women and reveled in the idea of having them as girlfriends. When expressing their views of these young women to other males, however, they often accused the cheerleaders of being stuck-up or sluts.

This sharp contradiction in males' discourse about cheerleaders makes perfect sense, however, when seen as males talking about females as objects to possess and dominate and through which to gain status. Conversations among males about cheerleaders were rhetorical performances that bonded males together and established their rank in this patriarchal order. In public conversations, males often expressed bravado about conquest of these "easy lays." In private conversations with intimate friends, they expressed their unabashed longing for, hence vulnerable emotional need for, these fantasized sexual objects. Hence, cheerleaders as highly prized females were dangerous, status-confirming creatures who were easier to relate to in rhetorical performances than in real life. Only those males with very high social status could actually risk relating to and being rejected by a cheerleader. The rest of the stories the young men told were simply male talk and fantasy.

Many young women were not athletic or attractive enough to be cheerleaders, nevertheless they wanted to be cheerleaders. Such young women often joined the pep squad as an alternative, and a strong esprit de corps developed among the pep squad members. They were a group of 50 young women in costume who came to the games and helped the cheerleaders arouse crowd enthusiasm. The pep squad also helped publicize and decorate the school and town with catchy team-spirit slogans such as "Smash the Seahawks" and "Spear the Javelinos." In addition, they helped organize after-the-game school dances. Their uniforms expressed loyalty to the team, and pep squad members were given a number of small status privileges in the school. They were sometimes released early for pep rallies and away games.

Teachers were often solicitous to pep squad members and labeled them good students. Pep squad members were usually students who conformed to the school rules and goals, thus were good citizens, but being in the pep squad also afforded them an opportunity to break home rules. Students and some teachers joked with pep squad members about "getting out of the house" to go to the games for romantic reasons. On road trips these young women momentarily escaped parental supervision and had opportunities to publicly attract and flirt with young men from other towns. This helped establish their gender status among other students as more "hip," even though being in the pep squad was a "straight" activity.

Homecoming: A Rite of Community Solidarity and Status

Ideally, North Town graduates would return to the homecoming bonfire and dance to reaffirm their support and commitment to the school and team. They would come back to be honored and to honor the new generation presently upholding the name and tradition of the community. In reality, however, few ex-graduates actually attended the pregame bonfire rally or postgame school dance. Typically, the game itself drew a larger crowd and the local paper played up the homecoming game more. College-bound youth were noticeably present at the informal beer party after the game. Some townspeople were also at the pregame bonfire rally, something that rarely happened during an ordinary school pep rally.

That afternoon, bands of Anglo males riding in pickup trucks began foraging for firewood. Other students not involved in hauling the wood gathered in the school parking lot. They wanted to watch what was brought for burning and meanwhile shared stories about stolen outdoor wooden outhouses, sheds, posts, and packing crates. It was important to the onlookers just which community members donated burnable objects, how cleverly objects were procured, and what outrageous objects were to be burnt this year. This was obviously a traditional event that entertained and bestowed status on both the procurers and donors of burnable objects.

Three groups of boys with pickup trucks eventually created a huge pile of scrap wood and burnable objects that had been donated. The cheerleaders, band, and pep squad members then conducted the bonfire ceremonies. Several hundred persons, approximately an equal number of Anglo and Mexicano students, showed up at the rally along with a fair sprinkling of older people and others who were not in high school. Nearly all of the leaders were Anglos and they were complaining that not enough students supported the school or them. The cheerleaders led cheers and sang the school fight song after brief inspirational speeches from the coaches and players. Unlike the school pep rally, the police arrived to survey the fire. Rumors circulated that the police were there to harass people because some crates might have been stolen from a local packing shed. It was also rumored that some of the football players were planning to get drunk after the bonfire died down.

The huge blazing fire in the school parking lot made this pep rally special. The fire added to the festive mood, which seemed partly adolescent high jinks and partly serious communion with the town's traditions. The collective energy of the youth had broken a property law or two to stage this event. Adults laughed about the "borrowed" packing crates and were pleased that others "donated" things form their stores and houses to feed the fire. The adults expressed no elaborate rationale for having a homecoming bonfire, which they considered nice, hot, and a good way to fire up the team.[3] Gathering around the bonfire reunited all North Towners, past and present, for the special homecoming reunion and gridiron battle. Whatever the deeper symbolic meaning, those attending seemed to enjoy the pep rally. Several of the organizers and friends remained behind to watch the fire burn down. They gossiped about friends and acquaintances and told sport stories.

After the homecoming game, a school dance was held featuring a homecoming court complete with king and queen. The queen and her court and the king and his attendants, typically the most popular and attractive students, were elected by the student body. Ideally they represented the most attractive, popular, and successful youth. They were considered the best of a future generation of North Towners. Following tradition, the queen was crowned during halftime at midfield as the band played and the crowd cheered. According to tradition, the lovely queen and her court, dressed in formal gowns, were ceremoniously transported to the crowning in convertibles. The king and his attendants, who were often football players and dirty and sweaty at that, then came running from their halftime break to escort the young women from the convertibles and to their crowning. The king and his court lingered rather uneasily until the ceremony was over and then quickly returned to their team to rest and prepare for the second half.

This particular homecoming halftime ceremony took place as it always did, but with one major difference. The customary convertibles for the queen and her court were missing; consequently, the queen and her court, on this occasion all Mexicanas, had to walk to their crowning. This evoked numerous criticisms among Mexicano students and parents in attendance. Many felt it was a "gringo plot" to rob them of their chance to be leaders in the community. The *Chicano Times*, a radical San Antonio newspaper, screamed out headlines that accused the school officials of blatant discrimination. The administrators and teachers in charge of organizing the event denied these charges but were left embarrassed and without any acceptable defense.

In this particular instance, this rite of solidarity became instead a source of divisiveness in North Town. A number of Better Government League (BGL) Anglos perceived the Mexicanos as politicizing the event and causing trouble. Another way of interpreting their criticism, however, was as an attempt to preserve the pomp and splendor of the ceremony that marked the social status of the town's future leaders. Those Mexicanos seeking to become integrated into and leaders of the community were not willing to be treated differently. They demanded that football and its homecoming ceremony serve its traditional purpose of creating continuity and unity. Mexicanos were trying to preserve a cultural tradition that would finally serve their children the way it had those of Anglos.

The Powder-Puff Football Game: Another Rite of Gender Reproduction

A powder-puff football game was traditionally held in North Town on a Friday afternoon before the seniors' final game. A number of the senior football players dressed up as girls and acted as cheerleaders for the game. A number of the senior girls dressed up as football players and formed a touch football team that played the junior girls. The male football players served as coaches and referees and comprised much of the audience as well. Perhaps a quarter of the student body, mainly the active, popular, successful students, drifted in and out to have a laugh over this event. More boys than girls, both Anglo and Mexicano, attended the game.

The striking thing about this ritual was the gender difference in expressive manner. Males took the opportunity to act in silly and outrageous ways. They pranced around in high heels, smeared their faces with lipstick, and flaunted their padded breasts and posteriors in a sexually provocative manner. Everything, including the cheers they led, was done in a very playful, exaggerated, and burlesque manner.

In sharp contrast, the females donned the football jerseys and helmets of the players, sometimes those of their boyfriends, and proceeded to huff and puff soberly up and down the field under the watchful eyes of the boys. They played their part in the game as seriously as possible, blocking and shoving with considerable gusto. This farce went on for several scores, until one team was the clear winner and until the females were physically exhausted and the males were satiated with acting in a ridiculous manner.

When asked why they had powder-puff football games, most male students could not articulate a very deep meaning for the event. Most said things like, "It's good for a laugh," "It's fun," "It's a good break from school; school's boring." Others hinted at something more than recreation and teenage fun:

> I don't know, I guess it gives guys a chance to have a little fun with the girls. . . . It makes the girls see how rough it is to play football. . . . The guys get to let off a little steam, tease their girlfriends a little, maybe show them who's the boss.

Some girls earnestly suggested the following meanings for the event:

> It gives us a chance to show the guys that we can compete too. We aren't sissies. We can take getting hit too. . . . We can show them that football isn't just for guys. . . . Girls are athletic, too. We can run and throw the ball pretty good, too. . . . God, I don't know, just to have a break from sixth period. . . . The guys get to have all the fun, why shouldn't we?

Teachers tended to look on the game as a silly, harmless event that helped build school spirit. One boldly suggested that maybe these big jocks were putting on bras because they secretly wanted to be girls. That tongue-in-cheek interpretation of football players has already been seriously proposed by one prominent folklorist (Dundes, 1978). Alan Dundes understands the butt-slapping and talk about "hitting holes" and "penetrating the other team's endzone" as a form of male combat that masks latent homosexuality. Such an interpretation would undoubtedly shock North Towners, who generally regarded this sort of thing as simply fun and silliness.

This interpretation also completely misses the cultural significance of such an event. Anthropologists have come to call such practices "rituals of inversion" (Babcock, 1978), specially marked moments when people radically reverse everyday cultural roles and practices. During these events people break, or humorously play with, their own cultural rules. Such reversals are possible without suffering any sanctions or loss of face. These moments are clearly marked so that no one familiar with the culture will misread such reversals as anything more than a momentary break in daily life.

Males of North Town High used this moment of symbolic inversion to parody females in a burlesque and ridiculous manner. They took great liberties with the female role through this humorous form of expression. The power of these young males to appropriate and play with female symbols of sexuality was a statement about males' social and physical dominance. Conversely, the females took few liberties with their expression of the male role. They tried to play a serious game of football. The females tried earnestly to prove they were equal. Their lack of playfulness was a poignant testimony to their subordinate status in this small town.

This moment of gender role reversal was a reflection of sexual politics, not of sexual preference. A psychological interpretation overlooks the historical pattern of patriarchy in the entire football ritual. The powder-puff football game, although seemingly a minor event, was an important part of the total football ritual. This ritual generally socialized both sexes to assume their proper, traditional gender roles. On the other hand, one could argue that the assertive, serious way they played the game may also be teaching these young women some new lessons in competing with males. Perhaps the girls were also trying to invert this inversion ritual, thus turning boys into real rather than symbolic buffoons. Generally, however, the women seemed to participate unwittingly in staging this expression of male dominance and privilege.

The Coach: A Mexicano Coach on the Firing Line

The North Town adult primarily responsible for making high school football an important, well-attended ritual was the head coach. Unfortunately, a good deal of local politics made it difficult for Coach Roberto Trujillo, North Town's first Mexicano head coach, to do his job. Coach Trujillo's father ran a dance hall that alternately hosted Anglo country and western as well as Mexicano "conjunto" (country, polka, and Caribbean) music. More important, his father had been a charter member in the new BGL political organization, which opposed North Town's new Chicano civil rights organization, Partido Raza Unida (PRU). The Trujillos' alliance with the Anglo BGL made both father and son "vendidos" (sellouts) in the eyes of most Raza Unida members. Coach Trujillo, in reality not a politically involved person, had a reputation as "a nice man but a little weak." He was the perfect compromise candidate for the BGL liberals who controlled the school board. He was a native son, college educated, polite, respectful, and generally mild mannered. His coaching record, though not exceptional, was considered acceptable. Most important, he was from a successful middle-class Mexicano family who renounced the extreme views of the PRU. Coach Trujillo was the BGL liberals' model of an accommodating, reasonable Mexican.

A number of other BGL Anglos were outraged, however, at his appointment over an Anglo coach, Jim Ryan, also a native son and one who had the distinction of leading North Town to their only regional finals. He was a likeable "good ole' boy" who was very approachable and had deep South Texas roots. Liberal BGLers viewed him as a poorly educated redneck who lacked the new ethnic tolerance they sought to project as school board leaders. Coach Ryan was a staunch conservative who constantly railed against what he termed communists, welfare loafers, and PRU radicals. Many Mexicano players actually considered him a good disciplinarian and coach, but a number of them also felt that he was indeed partial toward Anglo players.

Coach Trujillo, on the other hand, was considered too friendly and soft on the players. Stories circulated about his easy practices and indecisive play calling. What many of the critics wanted was a military-style coach, a stern disciplinarian. They constantly criticized the star North Town players as being lazy and too soft. Trujillo was in the proverbial coach's hot seat for all the classic reasons, and for uniquely racial ones as well. He had the double jeopardy of being neither manly enough nor white or brown enough to lead north Town youth into battle. He was constantly challenged to prove himself both to the Mexicano activists and to the more redneck Anglos.

Coaches as Storytellers: Reproducing and Resisting Inequality

The first out-of-town trip proved to be revealing on the subject of race relations. The players took their seats as if some crusading liberal had written the script. All the Mexicano players quietly seated themselves at the back of the bus. Then all the Anglo players brashly seated themselves in the front of the bus with the coaching staff. At first I was taken aback by this event, which seemed an unmistakable sign of Anglo racial dominance. Yet I wondered how such a seating arrangement could possibly signify subservience in a town full of politically assertive Mexicano adults. Before we reached Larson City, at least 10 racial jokes were hurled between the front and the back of the bus. One giant Anglo tackle, the high school principal's son, cracked perhaps the best joke. He bellowed out, "Shewt, if we lose this game, *we* are going to ride home in the back of the bus." This brought a nervous reply from Coach Trujillo that he might have to join them (the Anglos) there too. Having just heard the story of his compromised political position with Mexicanos, I thought the comment was his way of downplaying the controversy over him. Or perhaps he was as subservient to Anglos as the Raza Unida leaders claimed.

As we neared Larson City, to my great surprise Trujillo cracked the following joke with the Anglo players: "We are going to have to take some of you boys to Boystown to show you how the *other* half lives." Anyone familiar with Texas border culture knows that the whorehouse sections of Mexican border towns are called Boystown. The classic rite of passage for South and West Texas males[4] is to lose their virginity in one of these Boystowns. This embattled Mexicano coach was joking about Anglo males using Mexicano prostitutes. He was suggesting to the Anglo players that they were about to become men and friends with his race, if they would let him make men out of them. The coach was evoking a common male bonding ritual and using humor to displace the racial tensions. He was also saying that they were all heading for "the border" of race relations in search of a new understanding.

During the fieldwork, I spent a great deal of time watching for examples of coaches serving as mediators of racial conflict, and at least one other coach and Coach Trujillo did indeed take it upon themselves to mediate racial attitudes and images. They directly intervened as peacemakers in at least two incidents of conflict between players and students. More important, they often tried to redefine the reality of North Town race relations by telling a story or homily to their players. An excellent example of their role in redefining racial/ethnic relations was a story I overheard Coach Trujillo tell several Anglo players after practice one day. He had just finished putting the boys through a brutal 1-1/2 hour full-pads scrimmage. This occurred during the dog days of late September and the temperature on the playing field was at least 100°F. The boys were exhausted and began joking and complaining about what a dictator the coach was. One quipped, "Man, I thought Hitler was a German."

Coach Trujillo read this ethnic reference as an invitation to launch into a racial treatise on the sense of equality and character of the Mexicano people, and himself in particular. Trujillo had been the first Mexicano player with a scholarship to play for a "lily-white" West Texas college. He then recounted his own version of the brutal two-a-day summer practice story that all football players tell. Usually this tale is told to illustrate one's pain threshold and ability to survive hot, sweaty practices. Often such practices do seem like the nightmarish inventions of a sadistic coach. Only "real men" survive these hot summer practices, and the worse the practices, the better the telling of the tale. Young players usually recount these practices to older relatives and former players who hang out in local gas stations and restaurants.

Coach Trujillo created an interesting variant of this tale that also had a racial lesson. After the exhausted players returned to the locker room, one of the Anglo players had the gall to toss the coach's equipment away from the coach's locker, thus invading his hard-earned resting space. The coach confronted the offending lockermate and reminded him that they were all in it together. They were all survivors of the football wars; consequently he was deserving of equal respect and space. With a twinkle in his eye, the coach explained, "I was telling this guy in a nice way, 'Hey, redneck, that's my space.'" According to Coach Trujillo, this bold, honest confrontation with the Anglo, and by extension American society, brought instant respect from the other players sitting nearby. They could see that he was ready to fight for his rights, which he had earned the hard way. Seeing this hulking white monster of a lineman being cowed by this little brown bulldog was a new experience for the Anglo players. They purportedly responded with warmth and admiration, and this was the beginning of the coach's acceptance among the Anglo players.

In a way, Coach Trujillo's story was much like the miraculous conversion tales born-again Christians often tell. In a trying and difficult moment, he acted with courage and humility to be accepted as an equal. He risked everything and stood up for the ideal that the races should live together in harmony rather than discord. According to his tale, from that day forward a new era of race relations began for his college and their football team. He relived his past to model what he wanted for his own players. He was no Hitler, nor were his people any different from Anglos. Moreover, he and his people were ready to fight for their rights. The coach told several homilies like this one. It is not clear how effective such moral lessons were, but this was how he dealt with the race problem.

But in the end, Coach Trujillo said he "threw in the towel." Despite a good season, second in the conference, and a 7-4 record, he resigned and left his hometown feeling, in his own words, "sick of the strife and the pressure on my family." The coach claimed that he had "lost a lotta friends" and had gotten an ulcer. He compared the South Texas racial situation unfavorably to other places he had been, such as Colorado and Michigan, and feared that North Town might never change. Being a political centrist, he had very little good to say about either political group.

> My daddy wants out of the BGL. He can see that the Anglos just won't change. They just want to use him, and one or two Anglo board members still think I am just a Meskin'. They'll never change. They always overreact to a Mexicano getting ahead. Look at the school elections. They handled the whole thing very poorly. Some kids were left off the ballot by mistake, and they should get rid of the rule that disqualified some of our best kids. They are just trying to protect their kids and hold us back. And the Anglos should not have quit the band trying to pressure the new Mexican-American band director. I'm sick of the Raza Unida too. They use these pressure tactics and call people "vendidos" and shoot off their mouths. The indictments of voters is real bad, and the Anglos are pressuring to control the school board votes, but Raza Unida has gone too far. I believe they did try to steal the city election, and they did shoot a gun at the mayor's house.

When Coach Trujillo reflected on his past, he came across as a man trapped in a painful process of cultural change. Unlike the new generation of students, he was not part of the civil rights movement and remained unsure how much to assert himself. The movement left him filled with a longing for change but a certain fear about breaking the cultural rules he hated. In the end, Coach Trujillo decided the situation was impossible to change or live with, so he moved on, but not without a great deal of sadness. He was unable to develop the type of relationship with North Town community leaders that would solidify his place in the local power structure.

Prominent Citizens and Their Booster Club: Reproducing Class Privileges

North Town was the type of community in which male teachers who had athletic or coaching backgrounds were more respected than other teachers. For their part, the other teachers often told "dumb coach" jokes and expressed resentment toward the school board's view of coaches. North Town school board members, many of them farmers and ranchers—rugged men of action—generally preferred that their school leaders be ex-coaches. Consequently a disproportionate number of ex-coaches became school principals and superintendents. The superintendent, himself an ex-coach, sported a 1950s-style flattop and loved to hunt. The junior high principal, also a former coach, owned and operated a steak house. The high school principal was an ex-coach but he lacked the capital to start a business. Three of the present coaching staff had farms or small businesses. School board members invariably emphasized an ex-coach's ability to deal with the public and to discipline the youth.

Once gridiron warriors, coaches in small towns are ultimately forced to become organization men, budget administrators, and public relations experts. These administrative Minotaurs are half-man, half-bureaucrat who are paid a small sum of money for hundreds of hours of extra work. Ultimately they must appease local factions, school boards, administrators, booster clubs, angry parents, and rebellious teenagers. The successful North Town coaches invariably become excellent public relations men who live a "down home" rural lifestyle; they like to hunt and fish and join local coffee klatches or Saturday morning quarterback groups. They must be real men who like fraternizing with the entrepreneurs, politicians, and good ole' boys who actually run the town. This role as a local male leader creates a web of alliances and obligations that put most coaches in the debt of the prominent citizens and their booster club.

North Town's booster club, composed mainly of local merchants, farmers, and ranchers, had the all-important function of raising supplementary funds for improving the sports program and for holding a postseason awards banquet. The club was the most direct and formal link that coaches had with the principal North Town civic leaders. Some prominent merchants and ranchers were absent from these activities, however, because they disliked sports or because they left it to those with more time and enthusiasm. North Town had a long history of booster club and school board interference in coaching the team. One coach characterized North Town as follows: "One of the toughest towns around to keep a job. Folks here take their football seriously. They are used to winning, not everything, not the state, but conference and maybe bidistrict, and someday even regional. They put a lot of pressure on you to win here."

The booster club that coach Trujillo had to deal with was run by a small clique of Anglos whom the BGL liberals considered "good ole' boys and redneck types." They became outspoken early in the season against their "weak Mexican coach." They fanned the fires of criticism in the coffee-drinking sessions over which of the two freshman quarterbacks should start, the "strong-armed Mexican boy" or the "all-around, smart Anglo boy." The Anglo boy was the son of a prominent car dealer and BGL and booster club activist. The Mexican boy was the son of a migrant worker and small grocery store manager. The freshman coach, Jim Ryan, chose the Anglo boy, and the PRU accused him of racial prejudice. In a similar vein, conflict also surfaced over the selection of the varsity quarterback. Coach Trujillo chose the son of an Anglo businessman, an underclassman, over a senior, the son of a less prominent Anglo. The less educated Anglo faction lambasted the coach for this decision, claiming he showed his preference for the children of the more socially and politically prominent BGL types.

One of Coach Trujillo's former players, who was a coach and community political leader, eloquently recounted to me "what physical education courses never teach you" about coaching:

> I will never forget Coach Bowman. He was a hard-core sergeant-type who didn't give a damn about pleasing the booster club. During a real rough practice the Smith kid got beat up pretty bad by a Hispanic kid and Coach stopped starting him. His mother came into the office one day to chew out Coach Bowman, and she caught him sitting there in his shorts with his legs up on the desk puffing away on this stogie. He told her that her son was a "god-damned sissy and didn't deserve to start." From then on his days were numbered, and the booster club got him fired. . . . And it works both ways. Hispanics do the same thing. When we had the big school board change and Coach Fuentes was brought in, he gave me a list of three kids, a quarterback, line-backer, and running back, who he wanted me to play on the freshman team. They were all the kids of school board members or buddies of the politicos. It was bad, man. I threatened to walk off the field and let him coach, so he finally gave in.

The former player went on to explain how local pressures and influences on coaches get played out. He advised me to watch who got invited to the parties after the games and who got invited to hunt on certain ranches:

> I'll tell you where you really see all this stuff, Doc. You never got invited to the parties, so you didn't see this. Every Friday night after the games, the prominent people in this town throw a barbecue and invite us coaches. The whole staff has gotta go and behave right if you wanna keep your job. That is where a coach can make or break himself. . . . No there wasn't but one or two Mexicanos at these parties. It was all Anglos, until the Mexicano school board came in. Then everything changed. Nobody invited Coach Fuentes and his staff to these parties. They started going to parties on the other side held by the Mexicano politicos. Most Anglos also dropped out of the booster club at that time too. . . . Really, there is no way that this town can have a good football program without a good mix of kids and the Anglo parents ramrodding the booster club. It is sad to say, but the Mexicanos will probably always be too divided to run the thing right. The booster club was in bad shape when they ran it. . . . The other important thing is getting invited by the people who have got money to hunt bird or deer on their land. It is kind of an honor for you to do this, and for them to have you. And if you've got good connections with star players and name coaches from the university or the pro ranks, then you bring in to speak to the booster club. Local people like going hunting with a real sports celebrity even better. It's all part of the way it is down here, Doc. To survive, you gotta get along with certain people.

The pattern of community pressures observed in North Town was not particularly exceptional. A good deal of the public criticism and grumbling about choices of players had racial overtones. The debate over which Anglo varsity quarterback to play also reflected community class differences among Anglos. North Town students and adults often expressed their fears and suspicion that racial and class prejudices were operating. It would be an exaggeration, however, to portray the North Town football team as rife with racial conflict and disunity. Nor was it filled with class prejudice. On a day-to-day basis there was considerable harmony and unity. Mexicanos and Anglos played side by side with few incidents. A number of working-class Mexicano youths and a few low-income Anglos were also members of the football program. At least in a general way, a surface harmony and equality seemed to prevail.

The only rupture of such public accommodations came when Coach Trujillo and Coach Ryan exchanged sharp words and nearly got into a fistfight during practice. This led to Trujillo making what many Mexicano political activists considered a humiliating public apology to Ryan. The two coaches were also severely reprimanded by the principal and superintendent. Ultimately everyone, especially the two feuding coaches, tried to downplay the conflict for the good of the team. Powerful social pressures controlled any public expression of racial disunity and class conflict on the team.

Local sports enthusiasts are fond of arguing that coaches select players objectively, without class or racial prejudices, because their personal interest, and that of the team, is served by winning. Unfortunately, this free-marked view glosses over how sport actually functions in local communities. Small-town coaches are generally subjected to enormous pressures to play everyone's child, regardless of social class and race. Success in sport is an important symbolic representation of familial social position. Men can reaffirm their claim to leadership and prominence through the success of their offspring. A son's athletic exploits relive and display the past physical and present social dominance of the father. In displaying past and present familial prominence, the son lays claim to his future potential. Every North Town coach lived and died by his ability to win games *and* his social competence to handle the competing status claims of the parents and their children.

Socially prominent families, who want to maintain their social position, promote their interest through booster clubs. The fathers of future community leaders spend much time talking about and criticizing coaches in local coffee shops. These fathers are more likely to talk to the coaches privately. Coaches who have ambitions to be socially prominent are more likely to "network" with these sports-minded community leaders. A symbiotic relationship develops between coaches, especially native ones, and the traditional community leaders. Preferential treatment of the sons of prominent community leaders flows from this web of friendships, hunting privileges, Saturday morning joking, and other such exchanges.

Moreover, considerable pressure to favor the sons of prominent citizens comes from within the school as well. The school and its classrooms are also a primary social stage upon which students enact their social privilege. These youths establish themselves as leaders in academic, political, and social affairs, and teachers grant them a variety of privileges. This reinforces the influence of their parents in the PTA, the sports and band booster clubs, and the school board. Both generations, in their own way, advance the interests of the family on many fronts.

The Spectators: Male Socialization through Ex-players

Another major aspect of the football ritual is how the spectators, the men in the community, socialize each new generation of players. In North Town, groups of middle-aged males with families and businesses were influential in socializing the new generation of males. These men congregated in various restaurants for their morning coffee and conversation about business, politics, the weather, and sports. Those leading citizens particularly interested in sports could be heard praising and criticizing "the boys" in almost a fatherly way. Some hired the players for part-time or summer jobs and were inclined to give them special privileges. Athletes were more likely to get well-paying jobs as road-gang workers, machine operators, and crew leaders. Most players denied that they got any favors, but they clearly had more prestige than other high school students who worked. Nonplayers complained that jocks got the good jobs. On the job site the men regaled players with stories of male conquests in sports, romance and business.

Many players reported these conversations, and I observed several during Saturday morning quarterback sessions in a local restaurant and gas station. One Saturday morning after the all-important Harris game, two starters and their good buddies came into the Cactus Bowl Café. One local rancher-businessman shouted, "Hey, Chuck, Jimmie, get over here! I want to talk to you boys about that Harris game!" He then launched into a litany of mistakes each boy and the team had made. Other in the group chimed in and hurled jokes at the boys about "wearing skirts" and being "wimps." Meanwhile the players stood slope-shouldered and "uh-huhed" their tormentors. One thing they had learned was never to argue back too vociferously. The players ridiculed such confrontations with "old-timers" privately, but the proper response from a good kid was tongue-biting deference.

This sort of pressure on players began early in the week with various good-natured jests and comments. The most critical groups were the cliques of ex-players who had recently graduated. Those who went off to college usually came back only a few weekends to watch games. If they continued to play, they returned as celebrities and tended to say very little. Being college players, they tended to be above any carping criticism of high school players. Usually, the more relentlessly critical groups were those ex-players who had never left town.

Some ex-players led the romanticized life of tough, brawling, womanizing young bachelors. These young men seemed suspended in a state of adolescence while avoiding becoming responsible family men. They could openly do things that the players had to control or hide because of training rules. Many of these ex-players were also able to physically dominate the younger high school players. But ex-players no longer had a stage upon which to perform heroics for the town. Consequently they often reminded current players of their past exploits and the superiority of players and teams of their era. Current players had to "learn" from these tormentors and take their place in local sports history.

Players Talking about Their Sport: The Meaning of Football

The preceding portrayal of the community sports scene has already suggested several major reasons why young males play football. Many of them are willing to endure considerable physical pain and sacrifice to achieve social prominence in their community. Only a very small percentage are skilled enough to play college football, and only one North Towner has ever made a living playing professional football. The social rewards from playing football are therefore mainly local and cultural.

However, there are other more immediate psychological rewards for playing football. When asked why they play football and why they like it, young North Town males gave a variety of answers. A few openly admitted that football was a way for them to achieve some social status and prominence, to "become somebody in this town." Many said football was fun, or "makes a man out of you," or "helps you get a cute chick." Others parroted a chamber of commerce view that it built character and trained them to have discipline, thus helping them be successful in life. Finally, many evoked patriotic motives—to beat rival towns and to "show others that South Texas plays as good a football as East Texas."

These explicit statements do not reveal the deeper psychological lessons learned in sports combat, however. In casual conversations, players used phrases that were particularly revealing. What they talked most about was "hitting" or "sticking" or "popping" someone. These were all things that coaches exhorted the players to do in practice. After a hard game, the supreme compliment was having a particular "lick" or "hit" singled out. Folkloric immortality, endless stories about that one great hit in the big game, was what players secretly strove for. For most coaches and players, really "laying a lick on" or "knocking somebody's can off" or "taking a real lick" was that quintessential football moment. Somebody who could "take it" was someone who could bounce up off the ground as if he had hardly been hit. The supreme compliment, however, was to be called a hitter or head-hunter. A hitter made bone-crushing tackles that knocked out or hurt his opponent.

Players who consistently inflicted outstanding hits were called animals, studs, bulls, horses, or gorillas. A stud was a superior physical specimen who fearlessly dished out and took hits, who liked the physical contact, who could dominate other players physically. Other players idolized a "real stud," because he seemed fearless and indomitable on the field. Off the field a stud was also cool, or at least imagined to be cool, with girls. Most players expected and wanted strong coaches and some studs to lead them into battle. They talked endlessly about who was a real stud and whether the coach "really kicks butt."

The point of being a hitter and stud is proving that you have enough courage to inflict and take physical pain. Pain is a badge of honor. Playing with pain proves you are a man. In conventional society, pain is a warning to protect your body, but the opposite ethic rules in football. In North Town bandages and stitches and casts became medals worn proudly into battle. Players constantly told stories about overcoming injuries and "playing hurt." A truly brave man was one who could fight on; his pain and wounds were simply greater obstacles to overcome. Scars were permanent traces of past battles won, or at the very least fought well. They became stories told to girlfriends and relatives.

The other, gentler, more social side of football was the emphasis on camaraderie, loyalty, friendship between players, and pulling together. Players also often mentioned how much fun it was to hang out with the guys. Some of them admitted to being locker room and "gym rates," guys who were always hanging around the fieldhouse and gym. They told stories of their miraculous goal line stands, of last-minute comebacks against all odds, and of tearful, gut-wrenching losses on cold muddy fields. Most of the players talked about the value of teamwork and how satisfying it was to achieve something together with other guys. Difficult, negative experiences were also shared. Long grueling practices without water and shade, and painful injuries—these were part of being teammates. Only other football buddies who had been in the football wars could appreciate the sacrifice and physical courage demanded in practices and games.

There were also shining tales of good sportsmanship. Players told stories about being helped up and helped off the field by opponents. They also prided themselves in learning how to lose gracefully and be good sports. At the high school level, winning was still the most important thing, and most coaches drilled that into their players. But if you could not win, the very least you could do was try as hard as possible, give all of yourself to the cause. The one cliché that North Town players constantly parroted back to me was "winners never quit, and quitters never win." Most North Town players prided themselves on giving their best effort. If they did not, the townspeople would lose respect for them and grumble, as they did during two conference losses. As the chamber of commerce claimed, North Town youth acquire their aggressive, competitive spirit on the town's athletic fields.

Another positive, pleasurable part of the game that most players mentioned was the emotional thrill of performing before large crowds. Many stories were told about "butterflies" and "getting the adrenalin pumping." Players coming back to the bench during the game were quite aware of the crowd. They threw down their helmets in exaggerated anger and disgust. They shouted at each other, slapped high-fives, and smashed each others' shoulder pads. Meanwhile they cast furtive glances at girls in the pep squad or at older brothers prowling the sidelines. They had to constantly express their spirit and commitment to the game, even during sideline breaks. Others limped and ice-packed their injuries and grimaced broadly for all to see.

Many players, particularly the skilled ones, described what might be called their aesthetic moments as the most rewarding thing about football. Players sitting around reviewing a game always talked about themselves or others as "making a good cut" and "running a good route," or "trapping" and "blindsiding" someone. All these specific acts involved executing a particular type of body control and skill with perfection and excellence. Running backs made quick turns or cuts that left would-be tacklers gasping for thin air. Ends "ran routes" or a clever change of direction that freed them to leap into the air and catch a pass. Guards lay in wait for big opposing linemen or aggressive linebackers to enter their territory recklessly, only to be trapped or blindsided by them. Each position had a variety of assignments or moments when players used their strength and intelligence to defeat their opponents. The way this was done was beautiful to a player who had spent years perfecting the body control and timing to execute the play. Players talked about "feeling" the game and the ball and the pressure from an opponent.

Team sports, and especially American football, generally socialize males to be warriors. The young men of North Town were being socialized to measure themselves by their animal instincts and aggressiveness. Physicality, searching for pain, enduring pain, inflicting pain, and knowing one's pain threshold emphasizes the biological, animal side of human beings. These are the instincts needed to work together and survive in military combat and, in capitalist ideology, in corporate, academic, and industrial combat. The language used–head-hunter, stick 'em, and various aggressive animal symbols–conjures up visions of Wall Street stockbrokers and real estate sharks chewing up their competition.

Other Males: Brains, Farm Kids, and Nobodies

What of those males who do not play high school football? Does this pervasive community ritual require the participation of all young males?

Do all non-athletes end up in the category of effeminate "band fags"? To the contrary, several types of male students did not lose gender status for being unathletic. There were a small number of "brains" who were obviously not physically capable of being gridiron warriors. Some of them played other sports with less physical contact such as basketball, tennis, track, or baseball. In this way they still upheld the ideal of being involved in some form of sport. Others, who were slight of physique, wore thick glasses, lacked hand-eye coordination, or ran and threw poorly, sometimes ended up hanging around jocks or helping them with their schoolwork. Others were loners who were labeled nerds and weirdos.

In addition, there were many farm kids or poor kids who did not participate in sports. They were generally homebodies who did not participate in many extracurricular activities. Some of them had to work to help support their families. Others had no transportation to attend practices. In the student peer groups they were often part of the great silent majority called "the nobodies."

Resistance to the Football Ritual: The Working-Class Chicano Rebels

There were also a number of Mexicano males who formed anti-school oriented peer groups. They were into a "hip" drug oriented lifestyle. These males, often called "vatos" (cool dudes), made it a point to be anti-sports, an activity they considered straight. Although some were quite physically capable of playing, they rarely tried out for any type of team sports. They made excuses for not playing such as needing a job to support their car or van or pickup. They considered sports "kids' stuff," and their hip lifestyle as more adult, cool, and fun.

Even for the vatos, however, sports events were important moments when they could publicly display their lifestyle and establish their reputation. A number of vatos always came to the games and even followed the team to other towns. They went to games to be tough guys and "enforcers" and to establish "reps" as fighters. The vatos also went to games to "hit on chicks from other towns." During one road game, after smoking several joints, they swaggered in with cocky smiles plastered on their faces. The idea was to attract attention from young women and hopefully provoke a fight while stealing another town's women. Unlike stealing watermelons or apples from a neighbor, stealing women was done openly and was a test of courage. A man faced this danger in front of his buddies and under the eyes of the enemy.

Ultimately, only one minor scuffle actually occurred at the Larson City game. Some days after the game the vatos told many tales about their foray into enemy territory. With great bravado they recounted every unanswered slight and insult they hurled at those "geeks." They also gloried in their mythical conquests of local young women. For the vatos, fighting, smoking pot, and chasing females were far better sport than huffing and puffing around for "some fucking coach." As the players battled on the field, the vatos battled on the sidelines. They were another kind of warrior that established North Town's community identity and territoriality through the sport of fighting over and chasing young women.

The Contradiction of Being "In Training"

In other ways, even the straight young men who played football also resisted certain aspects of the game. Young athletes were thrust into a real dilemma when their coaches sought to rationalize training techniques and forbade various pleasures of the flesh. Being in training meant no drugs, alcohol, or tobacco. It also meant eating well-balanced meals, getting at least 8 hours of sleep, and not wasting one's emotional and physical energy chasing women. These dictates were extremely difficult to follow in a culture where drugs are used regularly and where sexual conquest and/or romantic love are popular cultural ideals. Add a combination of male adolescence and the overwhelming use of sex and women's bodies to sell commodities, and you have an environment not particularly conducive to making sacrifices for the coach and the team. North Town athletes envied the young bachelors who drank, smoked pot, and chased women late into the night. If they wanted to be males, American culture dictated that they break the rigid, unnatural training rules set for them.

Contrary to the vatos' caricature of jocks as straight and conformist, many North Town football players actually broke their training rules. They often drank and smoked pot at private teen parties. Unlike the rebellious vatos, who publicly flaunted their drinking and drugs, jocks avoided drinking in public. By acting like all-American boys, jocks won praise from adults for their conformity. Many of them publicly pretended to be sacrificing and denying themselves pleasure. They told the old-timers stories about their "rough practices" and "commitment to conditioning." Consequently, if jocks got caught breaking training, the men tended to overlook these infractions as slips or temptations. In short, cool jocks knew how to manage their public image as conformists and hide their private nonconformity.

One incident, when two of the players were caught drinking at a school livestock show, illustrates how many of the adults preferred to handle this cultural contradiction. The sons of two ranchers, Roddy, a senior tackle, and Bob, a senior linebacker, were suspended from school for this incident. Since football season was over, this only jeopardized their graduation, not the winning of a conference championship. The main line of argument made on their behalf was that "boys will be boys," and "these are good kids."[5]

Fathers who had experienced this training contradiction themselves made the boys-will-be-boys argument on behalf of their sons. They gave their sons and other players stern lectures about keeping in shape, *but* they were the first to chuckle at the heroic stories of playing with a hangover. They told these same stories about teammates or about themselves over a cup of coffee or a beer. As a result, unless their youth were outrageously indiscreet—for example passing out drunk on the main street or in class, getting a "trashy girl" pregnant—a "little drinking and screwing around" was overlooked. They simply wanted the school board to stop being hypocritical and acknowledge that drinking was all part of growing up to be a prominent male.

In the small sports world of North Town, a real jock actually enhances his public image of being in shape by occasionally being a "boozer" or "doper." Indeed, one of the most common genres of stories that jocks told was the "I played while drunk/stoned," or the "I got drunk/stoned the night before the game" tale. Olmo, a big bruising guard who is now a hard-living, hard-drinking bachelor, told me a classic version of this tale before the homecoming game:

> Last night we really went out and hung one on. Me and Jaime and Arturo drank a six-pack apiece in a couple of hours. We were cruising abound Daly City checking out the action. It was real dead. We didn't see nobody we knew except Arturo's cousin. We stopped at his place and drank some more and listened to some music. We stayed there till his old lady [mom] told us to go home. We got home pretty late, but before the sun come up, 'cause we're in training, ha ha.

Olmo told this story with a twinkle in his eye, especially the part about being in training. I asked him how it was possible to play well if he had "hung one on" the night before. This launched him into the story that he wanted to tell about drinking before and even during games. This story had become part of local sports lore because other players also told it to me. stories of players' sexual exploits were recounted in the same vein that drinking Stories were. A real man could be "in shape" because his extraordinary will could overcome these allegedly debilitating vices. A real man could have it all and become complete through drugs, sex, violence, and glory.

Most players secretly admired such rule-breaking behaviors. Olmo was a model of ideal male behavior and, to a degree, other players who were cool emulated him. Homebodies, the farm kids, and goodie-goodies rarely broke training, but the pressures on them to do so were enormous. Drinking parties, like North Town's post-homecoming bash, made celebrities out of the players. Kids clustered around the bonfire and around various pickups and shared beer and pot with their warriors who had beaten the enemy.

CONCLUSIONS: SOME THEORETICAL CONSIDERATIONS

A number of critical sports theorists have begun to ask whether the legitimation of the ruling elites of both capitalist and communist states through mass sports rituals actually does create an ideological hegemony. Moreover, they ask, if sport is some dehumanizing form of ideological dominance, why do so many people enjoy and increasingly participate in organized popular sports? This raises the issue of whether sport scenes also become the site for resistance to ideological hegemony.

The answer that sports theorists (Critcher, 1986; Gruneau, 1983; Hargreaves 1986) give, following a Gramscian perspective of popular culture studies, is that ruling-class cultural hegemony is never secure. These theorists generally argue that popular and leisure cultural practices such as sports always have the potential for autonomy and resistance to ruling-class hegemony. This is so, not because sport is inherently ludic but because the politicization and commercialization of local sports practices provoke some form of class consciousness and class resistance. In other words, the elite are never quite successful at appropriating popular cultural practices such as sport and recreation and turning them into mind-numbing, nationalistic forms of political conformity.

Other social theorists sympathetic to this perspective of class dominance (Birrell, 1984, 1989; Hall, 1984, 1985; McKay, 1986; Messner, 1988) suggest even more emphatically than the previously cited critical theorists that the ground of resistance to mass sport must be situated in multiple forms of dominance. In this view, the cultural practices of gender and racial dominance must *also* be included with a class theory perspective of sports. A multiple-dominance view of sports suggests that the commercializing and rationalizing tendencies in sports can at least be mediated and somewhat democratized through the more active participation of previously marginalized groups. Some feminists also argue that since women are more nurturing and humanistic, a massive new presence of women in organized sports will at least have a humanizing effect.

Finally, other popular culture theorists (Fiske 1989a, 1989b) suggest an additional ground for resistance and autonomy that is more general than class, gender, or racial consciousness. Fiske argues that all popular cultural forms have the potential to be pleasurable because they are profane, expressive cultural acts. Sport, like dance, music, or visual art, is a form of personal expression within a set of conventions or rules for self-expression. Within certain limits, these cultural performances manipulate the conventional symbols and expressive practices in new, self-gratifying ways. Students of popular cultural practices outside sport have shown a variety of creative resistance in the expressions of street graffiti, low-rider cars, pop art, informal clothes such as jeans, pop music, youth culture styles, and other unconventional popular expressive forms. This perspective generally suggests that the ultimate ground for resistance to the rationalization and commercialization of various expressive popular culture practices is the human preference to control and produce self-expression. Mass-produced overly standardized forms of self-expression such as commercialized art or sport will invariably run into some resistance because human beings are symbol-producing animals who invariably prefer to innovate with and invent expressive forms to represent themselves and create a social identity. Gruneau proposes some caution here that we "seem to have discovered resistance virtually everywhere in capitalist consumer cultures" (1988, p. 25).

This general question of how autonomous a cultural domain-organized sport is must be addressed, as Gruneau (1983) forcefully suggests, through historical studies of sport practices. Bourdieu (1988) also outlines a complementary programmatic statement for the sociology of sport that calls for intensive studies of the "habitus" of sport practices. I would add to these programmatic statements the addendum that a critical sociology of sport needs to conceptualize local studies of sorts as historical community studies. Whatever resistance exists against sport rituals of socialization, it must be understood within the context of the local traditions of structural dominance.

In this particular study there were definitely signs of working-class resistance to the way the football ritual socializes youths to enact various forms of social inequality. The most dramatic example was the way the rebellious vatos used the games to parody football as a ritual of class and racial privilege. According to them, football was not the only way to prove one was a real man and warrior. Moreover, even the most straight, conformist youths who played football, especially those who knew they would never play beyond the community level, did not simply go along with the increasing rationalization of their sport. They were far less likely to follow modern scientific training practices than coaches and the booster club hoped. As Fiske (1989a, 1989b) suggests, leisure culture practices such as football have pleasurable expressive and aesthetic moments. The real joy of playing hometown football is still some kind of ludic or expressive moment that may survive more on the local level than in big-time college and professionals sports.

In addition, in a town experiencing the Chicano civil rights movement, there were many signs of an ethnic resistance to the reproductive character of local sports. Many Mexicanos protested strongly when the Anglos enacted the homecoming ceremony in a way that marginalized them. The same could be said for the Mexicano players who defiantly sat in the back of the bus and who made it difficult for Anglo coaches to unquestioningly put Anglo players in high status positions. Moreover, Coach Trujillo clearly played a mediating role in resisting racial dominance until he was forced out. Finally, even the Mexicana cheerleader, Trini, was making her own statement about the reproductive character of the football ritual.

Yet, all of the previously mentioned signs of resistance notwithstanding, the football ritual remains a powerful metaphor of American capitalist culture. In North Town, football is still a popular cultural practice deeply implicated in the reproduction of the local ruling class of white males, hence class, patriarchal, and racial forms of dominance. The larger ethnographic study (Foley, 1990) details how the football ritual was also tied to student status groups, dating, friendship, and social mobility patterns. Local sports, especially football, are still central to the socialization of each new generation of youth and to the maintenance of the adolescent society's status system. In addition, this ritual is also central to the preservation of the community's adult status hierarchy. The local politics of the booster club, adult male peer groups, and Saturday morning coffee klatches ensnare coaches and turn a son's participation in the football ritual into an important symbolic reenactment of the father's social class and gender prominence.

Despite continuous claims about the autonomous and liberating effects of organized sports, this study appears to indicate that organized sports, as presently practiced at the community level, is still a rather archaic, conservative force in our society. This is not to claim that sport is an inherently conservative popular culture practice in the sense that Critcher (1986) seems to suggest. Following Gruneau (1983) and Bourdieu (1988), I would argue that sport, like all cultural practices, is never intrinsically reactionary or progressive. Each cultural context or habitus of practices has a history and set of traditions that can either endure or change, depending upon what the people living out that tradition choose to do. These data suggest the emergence of some forms of human agency and autonomy. There were Mexicano, female, and working-class challenges to the maintaining of traditional forms of dominance through local sports practices.

Nevertheless, it is clear that such challenges have done little to transform the everyday culture that this major community ritual enacts. The football ritual continues to stage North Town's contemporary system of class dominance and its archaic system of patriarchal dominance. The transformation of sports at the community level will require a deeper cultural change in this community socialization process that re-creates each new generation. Without political movements that are stronger than the Chicano civil rights movement, local sport scenes like North Town's will not easily become sites of progressive, counterhegemonic forces.

NOTES

1. The distinction here is between a community and a subculture or lifestyle group. A historical community is a geopolitical territory that has its own political, economic, and cultural systems—a collective of people who share a set of memories and traditions

about past political, economic, and cultural practices. A subculture of sports enthusiasts such as surfers or skiers do not live in and share a community mode of production and its traditional social structure of class, gender, and racial dominance.

2. The community study includes a historical analysis of how the county's political economy evolved into a fully capitalist mode of agricultural production and a major recomposition of social classes. This economic transformation engenders ethnic politics and the gradual dismantling of this capitalist racial order. The community study also analyzes how these broader transformations affect the local youth scene and race relations in the high school.
3. The firing-up-the-team pun was actually a fairly good explanation of the bonfire. It was a kind of tribal fire around which the community war dance was held. The event was preparing these young warriors for battle, and the cheerleaders and band replaced painted dancers and tom tom drums. In addition, the fire was a kind of community hearth. At least some people were literally returning to the "home fires" of their village and tribe.
4. This South Texas rite of passage was beautifully portrayed in Peter Bogdanovich's *The Last Picture Show*, which is based on a novel by Larry McMurtry.
5. This is of course the classic defense often used to condone the drinking and vandalism of privileged college fraternity kids.

REFERENCES

Babcock, B. (Ed.) (1978). *The reversible world: Symbolic inversion in art and society.* Ithaca, NY: Cornell University Press.

Bennett, T. C., Mercer, C., & Wollacott, J. (1986). *Popular culture and social relations.* Milton Keynes: Open University Press.

Birrell, S. (1984). Studying gender in sport: Issues, insights, and struggle. In N. Theberge & P. Donnelly (Eds.), *Sport and the sociological imagination* (pp. 125-135). Fort Worth: Texas Christian University Press.

Birrell, S. (1989). Race relations theories and sport: Suggestions for a more critical analysis. *Sociology of Sport Journal*, **6**, 212-227.

Bourdieu, P. (1988). Program for a sociology of sport. *Sociology of Sport Journal*, **5**, 153-161.

Chambers, I. (1986). Popular culture: The metropolitan experience. London: Methuen.

Critcher, C. (1986). Radical theorists of sport: The state of play. *Sociology of Sport Journal*, **3**, 333-343.

Deem, R. (1988). "Together we stand, divided we fall"; Social criticism and the sociology of sport and leisure. *Sociology of Sport Journal*, **5**, 341-354.

Donnelly, P., & Young, K. (1988). The construction and confirmation of identity in sport subcultures. *Sociology of Sport Journal*, **5**, 223-240.

Dundes, A. (1978). Into the endzone for a touchdown: A psychoanalytic consideration of American football. *Western Folklore*, **37**, 75-88.

Fine, G. A. (1987). *With the boys: Little League baseball and preadolescent culture.* Chicago: University of Chicago Press.

Fiske, J. (1989a). *Understanding popular culture.* Boston: Unwin Hyman.

Fiske, J. (1989b). *Reading the popular.* Boston: Unwin Hyman.

Foley, D. (1990). *Learning capitalist culture: Deep in the heart of Tejas.* Philadelphia: University of Pennsylvania Press.

Foley, D., with Mota, C., Post, D., & Lozano, I. (1988). *From peones to politicos: Class and ethnicity in a south Texas town, 1900-1987.* Austin: University of Texas Press.

Gruneau, R. (1983). *Class, sports, and social development.* Amherst: The University of Massachusetts Press.

Gruneau, R. (1988). Introduction: Notes on popular culture and political practice. In R. Gruneau (Ed.), *Popular cultures and political practices* (pp. 11-32). Toronto: Garamond Press.

Hall, M. A. (1984). Toward a feminist analysis of gender inequality in sport. In. N. Theberge & P. Donnelly (Eds.), *Sport and the sociological imagination* (pp. 82-103). Fort Worth: Texas Christian University Press.

Hall, M. A. (1985). Knowledge and gender: Epistemological questions in the social analysis of sport. *Sociology of Sport Journal*, **2**, 25-42.

Hargreaves, J. (1986). *Sport, power and culture: A social and historical analysis of popular sports in Britain*. London: St. Martin's Press.

Loy, J. W., & Ingham, A. G. (1973). Play, games, and sport in the psychosocial development of children and youth. In G. L. Rarick (Ed.), *Physical activity–Human growth and development* (pp. 257-302). New York: Academic Press.

McKay, J. (1986). Marxism as a way of seeing: Beyond the limits of current critical approaches to sport. *Sociology of Sport Journal*, **3**, 261-272.

Messner, M. (1988). Sports and male domination: The female athlete as contested ideological terrain. *Sociology of Sport Journal*, **5**, 197-211.

Turner, V. (1974). *Dramas, fields, and metaphors: Symbolic action in human societies*. Ithaca, NY: Cornell University Press.

Whitson, D. (1984). Sport and hegemony: On the construction of the dominant culture. *Sociology of Sport Journal*, **1**, 64-78.

31. *Professional Sports: The Racial Report Card*

RICHARD E. LAPCHICK WITH DAVID STUCKEY

Northeastern University's Center for the Study of Sport in Society, which has monitored the issue of race in sport since opening in 1984, today issued its second Racial Report Card designed to evaluate the racial factor in the National Basketball Association, the National Football League and Major League Baseball, the three major sports in which blacks compete most regularly [see page 356].

The NBA once again achieved an overall grade of "A" while the NFL held at a "C+" and Major League Baseball fell to a "C." The greatest problem areas remain front office management hiring practices and head coach or manager positions in both the NFL and Major League Baseball where barely passing grades were achieved.

In 1987, Al Campanis said blacks simply don't have the "necessities" to lead in sports; in 1988, Jimmy "The Greek" Snyder informed us that blacks were created differently than whites; in 1989, Roger Stanton wrote that white football players' IQs would be higher than blacks 100 percent of the time; in 1990, Hal Thompson told us that blacks weren't members of the club at Shoal Creek because "that's not done in Birmingham."

So the question becomes how good are the options for the black athlete in football, baseball and basketball? Is he treated equally in each sport? Is he viewed as the equal of his white counterparts by coaches, the front office and the fans? Is he paid the same? Are the stereotypes applied to him earlier in his career still assumed by whites? Is he limited to playing certain positions because of positional segregation (stacking)? Does his fame endure after his playing career? Will he become a coach in the pros or join the front office of his team?

The 1990 Racial Report card was decidedly upbeat but the 1991 version is less optimistic due to either stagnation or decline in key indicators aside from on the field play.

SOURCE: *Center for the Study of Sport in Society Digest* 3 (Summer 1991), pp. 1, 4-8. Reprinted by permission.

1991 Racial Report Card

Subject: Professional Sports vs. Society

	NBA	*NFL*	*MLB*	*Society*
Overall Grade	A	C+	C	D+
Improvement	A	B+	C	D
Overall GPA	3.8	2.5	2.1	1.5
Improve GPA	3.8	3.0	2.0	1.0
based on a 5.0 scale for A+; 4.0 for A; 3.5 for B+; 3.0 for B; 2.5 for C+; 2.0 for C; 1.5 for D+ and 1.0 for D				
Player Opportunities	A+	A	C	D-
Improvement	Same	A+	C+	D-
*Commissioner's Leadership	A+	A	C+	D+
Improvement	Same	A+	C+	C+
Players' Salaries	N/A	B	A	D+
Improvement	N/A	C+	A+	D+
Stacking	N/A	D+	D+	D+
Improvement	N/A	C+	B	D+
Subject: Hiring Practices—Front Office				
*Management	B	D+	D	D
Improvement	B+	C	D	C
Support Staff	B	C+	B	C
Improvement	C+	B+	B	C+
Subject: Hiring Practices—Coaches				
*Head Coach or Manager	B+	D+	C	N/A
Improvement	Same	Same	Same	N/A
Assistant Coaches	B+	B	N/A	N/A
Improvement	B	B-	N/A	N/A

*given double weight in overall grades

SPORT VERSUS SOCIETY

When compared to society-wide data compiled from various sources, blacks in all three sports are doing well.

Racial minorities, especially blacks, continue to see a deterioration, vis-à-vis whites in several key area: per-capita income, employment, percentage living in poverty, perceptions of whites toward blacks, college education and health factors.

According to the Census Bureau, the median income for white families rose from $32,713 in 1970 to $35,980 in 1989—a 10% increase; black median income barely changed, from $20,067 in 1970 to $20,210 in 1989.

According to the Joint Center for Political and Economic Studies, nearly half of all black children live in poverty today compared to 14.1% of white children.

According to a survey done by the National Opinion Research Center, more than half of all whites believe blacks are less hardworking, more violence prone, less intelligent, less patriotic, and live off welfare.

Police seem to sometimes act on stereotypical assumptions about blacks. While only 15% of drug users are black, 41% of those arrested for drugs are black.

Black males between 15-24 are 1% of the population but represent 13.7% of murder victims.

The number of black men in college is declining.

Blacks have a much higher incidence of heart disease, stroke, breast cancer and diabetes.

Given [these] discouraging data, across nearly all relevant indicators, the Center does not wish to present contradictory messages regarding the relative prospects of mobility in professional sports. Thus, while the sportsworld has made improvements, the number of blacks benefitting from this is minuscule compared to the general population. The disheartening socio-economic indicators for the larger society must not be looked upon as further evidence for the irrational pursuit of 10,000-to-1 odds of a high-school athlete becoming a professional athlete. The black high-school athlete still has a better chance of becoming an attorney or a doctor than a professional player.

OVERVIEW

The 1990-91 season was another year of improvement for the NBA which maintained the highest percentage of black head coaches and general managers in the history of pro sports while positions for blacks in front offices increased.

The NBA remains the most racially integrated of the major sports in hiring practices with respect to players, coaching staff, and front office ranks. The findings show that there are now clearly more opportunities for blacks as well as for women to obtain prominent positions in the NBA front offices. Thus, the NBA, where 72% of the players are black, has continued to show the most substantial progress for blacks and other minorities to achieve equal opportunities.

Baseball reversed a 10 year decline in the percentage of blacks playing the sport with a 1 percent increase. Salary equity also improved for minorities. There was, however, a decline in the already small number of blacks in the front offices and there were still only two black managers and no black general managers.

The NFL had more blacks playing (61% vs. 60% in 1989). However, the salary equity issue, reported as a gain in 1988 and 1989, was reversed as whites became the highest paid racial group. There were more black quarterbacks but stacking was still a reality for most of football. There was only one black head coach and no general managers.

The grades were given in certain areas where the question of race has been most frequently raised and includes leadership of Commissioners, player opportunities, salary differentials between black and white players, and positional segregation in baseball and the NFL. A special focus was placed on hiring practices for coaches and front office personnel since this has been the area of greatest controversy since Al Campanis' statement on *Nightline*.

THE COMMISSIONERS

NFL Commissioner Paul Tagliabue took a leadership role in the racial issue in 1990-91.

He took the lead in removing the Super Bowl from Phoenix after Arizona voters refused to make Martin Luther King's birthday an official holiday. The decision was a very controversial one in Arizona where many felt the NFL created a backlash that resulted in the defeat of the legislation. However, Commissioner Tagliabue's intervention marked the first time that an NFL Commissioner became actively involved in a racial issue. He had already created the Players Advisory Council which, among other things, is charged with the responsibility of developing career planning programs to smooth the transition into private life for professional football players. Tagliabue also helped make hiring minorities a priority in the World League of American Football to prepare minority coaches and front office employees for future positions in the NFL. This is discussed later in the Report Card.

Perhaps the biggest indicator of Commissioner Tagliabue's commitment was demonstrated by the appointment of blacks in three key posts: Dr. Lawrence Brown became the NFL Drug Advisor; Reggie Roberts was appointed Director of Information for the National Football Conference; and Harold Henderson was named Executive Vice President-Labor Relations for the NFL. Henderson became the highest ranking black in the history of the NFL.

The racial issue was hardly mentioned in the nearly four years since Al Campanis brought the reality of racism to baseball's front burner in his widely noted appearance on *Nightline*. However, a June 6 1991 *Nightline* updated the situation and served to bring attention to the issue again.

Commissioner Fay Vincent's public statements seemed to indicate a desire to follow the late Bart Giamatti's progressive leadership. However, his statements were not reflected by the record.

David Stern still has the best record of all the commissioners. His leadership has been consistent and NBA policies encouraging high level positions for minorities reflected those policies.

Blacks Playing Professional Sport

The integration of baseball, basketball, and football over the past four decades has been remarkable. There is no other area of the economy, with the exception of entertainment, where blacks play such a significant role. While opportunities for blacks in society seemed to be rolling back in the 1990's, blacks made up the majority of players in the NBA and NFL. As a result of their presence declining during the 1980's in favor of Hispanic-American and Latin players, black players continued to represent a minority of total players in Major League Baseball. That decline seemed to stop in 1991, when the number of blacks in Major League Baseball rose from 17% to 18%, marking the first increase in recent years. The percentage of Latins (11%) remained the same while the percentage of Hispanic-Americans rose to 3% and that of whites declined from 70% to 68%.

The percentage of blacks in the NBA dropped slightly to 72% and increased to 61% in the NFL. Table 31-1 shows the changes over the two Report Cards.

COACHING POSITIONS

This year 1991 marked the first time in the history of pro sports that there was a black head coach in all three sports for two consecutive years. The firing of Frank Robinson was "balanced" when Kansas City hired Hal McRae early in the 1991 season. McRae and Cito Gaston (Toronto) are the only two black baseball managers.

Table 31-1

Percentage of Blacks in the NBA, NFL, MLB

	NBA	*NFL*	*MLB*
1990:	75 ('89-90)	60 (1989)	17
1991:	72 ('90-91)	61 (1990)	18

Percentage of Hispanic and Latin Players in MLB

	Hispanic	*Latin*
1990:	2%	11%
1991:	3%	11%

Compiled by Northeastern University's Center for the Study of Sport in Society from the 1990-91 NBA and 1990 NFL media guides and the *1991 Who's Who in Baseball.*

Table 31-2 Major League Club On-Field Staff (includes managers, trainers, scouts, coaches and instructors)

	1989	*1990*
Total Employees	1588	1659
Asian	4 (.003%)	7 (.004%)
Black	102 (6%)	100 (6%)
Hispanic	207 (13%)	217 (13%)
Total	313 (20%)	324 (20%)

Source: Alexander and Associates

As Table 31-2 demonstrates, the percentage of blacks (6%) and Hispanics (13%) holding Major League jobs as manager, trainer, scout, coach or instructors has not changed between the 1989 and 1990 seasons.

The NBA has regularly had blacks leading teams since the 1970's and it remains the best by far of all pro sports at offering blacks accessibility in the coaching arena after their playing days are over.

The percentage of blacks in NBA head coaching positions remained the same since last year's Report Card. There have been six head coaches in each of the last two years. In 1990-91 they were Lenny Wilkins (Cavaliers), K. C. Jones (Supersonics), Don Chaney (Rockets), Stu Jackson (partial season with the Knicks), Gene Littles (Hornets) and Wes Unseld (Bullets).

Twelve of the 58 (21%) assistant coaches were black in 1990-91. As Table 31-3 shows, the percentage of black assistants has dropped slightly in 1990-91.

The NFL, which has historically had the poorest record in hiring blacks in head coaching positions, announced that its new World League of American Football could serve as a training ground for black coaches. Commissioner Tagliabue also created a special program to train black college coaches.

Table 31-3 Coaches in the NBA 1989-90 and 1990-91

	White	*Black*	*% Black*
Head Coaches			
1989-90	21	6	22%
1990-91	21	6	22%
Assistants			
1989-90	51	14	22%
1990-91	46	12	21%
Totals			
1989-90	72	20	22%
1990-91	67	18	21%

Compiled by Northeastern University's Center for the Study of Sport in Society from the 1989-90 and 1990-91 NBA media guides.

Table 31-4

Coaches in the NFL 1989 and 1990

	White	*Blace*	*% Black*
Head Coaches			
1989	21	1	3%
1990	27	1	3%
Assistants			
1989	247	50	17%
1990	258	50	16%
Totals			
1989	274	51	16%
1990	185	51	15%

Coaches in the WLAF in 1991

	White	*Black*	*% Black*
Head Coaches	10	0	0%
All Assistants[1]	44	13	28%
Coordinators	17	3	25%

[1]There is one Hawaiian Assistant.

Compiled by Northeastern University's Center for the Study of Sport in Society from the *1991 WLAF Media Guide.*

Of the 10 head coaching positions in the WLAF, none were held by blacks. Thirteen of the 44 (30%) assistant coaches in the WLAF were black, a full 15% above the NFL's average. Three blacks–Darrell "Pop" Jackson (New York), George Warhop (London) and Johnnie Walton (Raleigh)–served as coordinators. Fifty-seven percent of the players in the WLAF were black.

Art Shell of the Los Angeles Raiders remained the only black head coach in the NFL in 1990.

Like the NBA, the percentage of blacks as assistant coaches in the NFL dropped slightly in 1990. In the 1989 study, 17% (50 out of 247) of the assistants were black. In 1990, there were 50 black assistants listed for the 308 positions (16%). How the promise of the WLAF and the college program will translate into NFL jobs remains to be seen.

THE FRONT OFFICE

The year 1990-91 seemed to be one in which gains by minorities in front offices leveled off, or, in the case of the NBA, increased slightly.

Neither baseball nor the NFL has ever had a black general manager, while the NBA had five. Elgin Baylor (Clippers), Wayne Embry (Cavaliers), Willis Reed (Nets), Bill McKinney (Timberwolves) and Bernie Bickerstaff

(Nuggets) heading the operations of their franchises in 1990-91. This represented a remarkable 40% increase from 1989-90. Other blacks holding top management positions at the start of the season included Wes Unseld (Bullets) and Al Attles (Warriors).

Susan O'Malley was named President of the Washington Bullets, the first woman to hold this position in any sport.

Table 31-5 represents a breakdown of the NBA personnel for the 1989-90 season and the 1990-91 season. Minority advancement continues to take place in the NBA front offices. Blacks now hold 9% (vs. 7% in 1989-90) of front office management positions. Women now occupy 32% of all NBA front office positions (management and staff). Blacks hold 10% of NBA support staff positions, down from 16% in 1989-90.

An overview of NFL front office personnel has shown only slight improvement in recent years. Of the 235 management positions listed in the NFL media guides, 14 were held by blacks. That represented 6 percent, down from 1989's 7 percent. According to an NFL source, overall minority employment in the NFL dropped from 246 in 1989 to 244 in 1990 (14.9% to 14.7%).

Men who moved near the top last year included: Rod Graves, Assistant Director of Player Personnel-Chicago Bears; Patric Forte, Vice President for Administration-New England Patriots; Dick Daniels, Assistant General Manager-San Diego Chargers; and Bob Wallace, Assistant to the President and General Counsel-Philadelphia Eagles.

According to the NFL, 79 minorities have either been hired or promoted in the National Football League during the past three years. This number represents 32% of the total minority force. (NFL statistics are more expansive than those reflected in the Report since the NFL's records include blacks and other minorities.) The key appointments of Dr. Lawrence Brown, Reggie Roberts and Harold Henderson as noted in the section on "Commissioners" was a major step forward for the League office itself.

There was improvement below the management level. Blacks occupied 71 of the 826 support staff positions, representing a significant increase to 9% of the total (7% in 1989). The NFL official told the *CSSS Digest* that minority employment has had "modest, positive results."

Table 31-5 NBA Personnel

	1989-90			1990-91		
	White	*Black*	*Women*	*White*	*Black*	*Women*
Front Office	235/93%	19/ 7%	47/16%	258/91%	26/ 9%	27/10%
Support Staff	290/84%	56/16%	162/46%	678/90%	72/10%	308/41%
Total	525/87%	75/12%	209/35%	936/91%	98/ 9%	335/32%

Compiled by Northeastern University's Center for the Study of Sport in Society from the 1989-90 and 1990-91 NBA media guides.

The proposed promise of the WLAF for minorities in the front office did not hold beyond the key appointments of Reggie Williams and Michael Huyghue as general managers of the New York and Birmingham teams and Lionel Vital as Director of Player Personnel with Montreal. Mayfield Armstrong was the League's only black head trainer. Overall, five percent of all front office positions (support staff were not listed) were held by blacks.

There is much disparity existing in both the NFL, in which 61% of the players are black, and the WLAF in which 57% of its players are black. The percentage of blacks who are employed in front office positions of both leagues is small compared to blacks playing the game. However, an official of the NFL maintained that not many players, minorities or non-minorities, attain, or perhaps even seek, employment in an administrative capacity after they retire.

Former Secretary of the Army Clifford Alexander, who was hired as a consultant by Major League Baseball in the post-Campanis era to bring more blacks and minorities into the sport, annually provides information that shows opportunities for blacks and other minorities in baseball.

The Alexander report is released each December. The following tables (31-6 and 31-7) represent the 1989 and 1990 season. . . .

As can be seen, there has been no improvement by percentage between 1989 and 1990 while both represented a modest improvement over 1988. The percentage of women has remained at 38% each year.

There were no black or Hispanic executive or department heads in the Office of the Commissioner in either 1989 or 1990. The percentage of blacks employed there declined from 13% in 1989 to 10% in 1990 while the percentage of Hispanics rose from 6% to 11%.

The percentage of blacks and Hispanics among the 31 employees of Major League Baseball Properties declined from 35% in 1989 to 26% in 1990. There were no blacks and one Hispanic on the six person Player Relations Committee.

The percentage of blacks among the 18 employees of the National and American League Offices jumped from 18 percent in 1989 to 27% in 1990 with the addition of two blacks in the American League office. Bill White, as President of the National League, remained the highest ranking black executive in pro sports.

Table 31-6 NFL Personnel

	1989		1990		
	White	*Black*	*White*	*Black*	*Women*
Front Office	344/93%	25/7%	221/94%	14/6%	9/ 4%
Support Staff	570/93%	40/7%	755/91%	71/9%	273/34%
Total	914/93%	65/7%	976/92%	85/8%	282/27%

Compiled by Northeastern University's Center for the Study of Sport in Society from 1989 and 1990 NFL media guides.

Table 31-7

1991 Front Office Management Positions (held by Blacks)		
NBA	*NFL*	*MLB*
9%	6%	4%
1991 Front Office Support Staff (held by blacks)		
NBA	*NFL*	*MLB*
10%	9%	10%

Previously, those who were cynical about real progress in baseball pointed out that the Commissioner's Office did not provide a breakdown of the positions held by minorities. This year's department head data are very helpful. [Table 31-7] is a breakdown of executive and department heads for 1989 and 1990.

As can be seen there has been no change for blacks and Hispanics. Baseball is behind the NFL and far behind the NBA in these critical positions.

It is ironic that the issue of front office hiring practices is where all the concern began and it is in this area where progress is slowest. There can be little doubt that the decline of public pressure over the last two years has reduced the "need" for baseball to increase the number of minorities in the front office.

SALARIES AND ENDORSEMENTS

For the black superstars, life is secure. Their salaries are equal to white stars. According to *The Sports Marketing Letter*, 1991 saw both Magic Johnson and Bo Jackson join Michael Jordan among the top ten endorsement earners in 1991. Jordan topped the list with an estimated $11 million. It was the first time that Jordan wasn't the only black in the top 10, and showed positive movement since eight of the 10 most popular athletes in America were black.

It is more difficult to tell if better chances for minority endorsements apply across the board since companies rarely release the value of the endorsement packages.

Historically, information to compare salaries between blacks and whites has been very difficult to obtain. In the early 1980s, whatever information that was obtained showed whites consistently outearning blacks.

Data have been easier to obtain in recent years for the NFL and Major League Baseball.

In the 1990 NFL season, white salaries once again topped black salaries. According to the salaries published in *USA Today*, the NFL average for all players was $298,000. The average black player's salary was $287,000, compared to $313,000 for whites.

Most of this is explained by the salaries of quarterbacks, the highest paid position and one where whites outnumber blacks by nearly 10 to 1. In fact, if the salaries for quarterbacks were deleted the average salary for blacks ($281,000) would be greater than that for whites ($269,000).

This represented a reversal from the 1990 Report Card when average salaries of blacks topped those of whites (according to a *USA Today* survey) by $253,916 for blacks vs. $236,516 for whites (based on 1988 data).

There was a most dramatic development in Major League Baseball, where both black and Latin players topped whites in average salary for the first time. In 1991 whites made an average of $867,476 while blacks made $1,051,696. Latin players averaged $873,581 while Hispanic-American players remained at the rear making $552,887.

There is no doubt that pros today, black and white, are nearing salary equity in a stratospheric salary range that almost anyone else in society would envy. Therein, of course, lies the draw of the unrealistic dream of so many young athletes who think they can achieve the same status.

Table 31-8 Average Salary by Position by Race in the NFL

	Overall	*Off. Line*	*Kicker*
Overall	$298,000	$283,000	$241,000
Black	$287,000	$282,000	
White	$313,000	$280,000	$238,000
O.M.*	$322,000	$408,000	$310,000
	Quarterback	*Running Back*	*Tight End*
Overall	$608,000	$319,000	$233,000
Black	$673,000	$323,000	$223,000
White	$604,000	$248,000	$244,000
O.M.*		$358,000	
	Wide Receiver	*Defensive Back*	*Defensive Line*
Overall	$286,000	$249,000	$303,000
Black	$301,000	$249,000	$249,000
White	$190,000	$245,000	$314,000
O.M.*			$384,000
	Linebacker	*Punter*	
Overall	$295,000	$200,000	
Black	$300,000	$215,000	
White	$287,000	$199,000	
O.M.*	$271,000		

*O.M. = Other Minorities: Nigerians, Hawaiians, Samoans, and Hispanic-Americans.
Compiled by the Center for the Study of Sport in Society from 1990 NFL media guides and salaries published in *USA TODAY*.

Table 31-9 Average Salaries by Race in Major League Baseball

	Overall	*Second Base*	*Shortstop*
Overall	$896,376	$942,860	$808,687
White	$867,122	$1,131,492	$783,409
Black	$1,051,696	$693,852	$1,111,574
Latin*	$873,581	834,500	694,607
Hispanic*	$552,887	$306,250	$350,000
	Third Base	*Catcher*	*Outfield*
Overall	$691,677	$522,761	$989,408
White	$$795,970	$503,189	$806,149
Black	$603,519	$123,500	1,123,607
Latin	$250,000	$750,357	$1,143,750
Hispanic	$145,000	——	$442,500
	Pitcher	*First Base*	
Overall	$907,656	$1,408,971	
White	$902,449	$1,439,637	
Black	$1,102,910	$1,216,404	
Latin	$901,492	$1,302,500	
Hispanic	$564,204	$1,750,000	

* Hispanics are designated as American-born players of Spanish origin; Latins are foreign-born players of Spanish origin.
Compiled by Northeastern University's Center for the Study of Sport in Society from the *1991 Who's Who in Baseball* and salaries published in the *New York Times*

POSITIONAL SEGREGATION IN THE NFL AND MLB

Historically, much has been said about stacking (positional segregation) in professional football.

Is it a factor now in the NFL? Using the twenty-eight NFL 1990 team media guides, the statistics are overwhelming. On offense, 93 percent of the quarterbacks were white (versus 99 percent in 1983); 87 percent of the centers, 76 percent of the offensive guards, and 71 percent of the tackles were white (versus 97, 77 and 68 percent respectively in 1983).

Sociologist Jonathon Brower did a survey of coaches and asked them how they would characterize the three positions dominated by whites. They used the following words: intelligence, leadership, emotional control, decision making, and technique. Are coaches stereotyping positions they think only whites can handle?

The fact that Doug Williams led the Washington Redskins to a Super Bowl victory, coupled with the tremendous recent success of star quarterbacks like Warren Moon and Randall Cunningham and the emergence of others like Rodney Peete and Andre Ware in 1990, showed that there could be rapid progress in eliminating positional segregation at the club level. The wealth of fine black college quarterbacks should also hasten this.

But a note of caution to temper this optimism is sounded by the story of Rodney Peete. Prior to the 1989 draft, Peete was rated by most scouting combines as among the top three quarterbacks available. Charges of racism flared when he was picked in the sixth round and was the ninth quarterback chosen! Mike Wilbon of the *Washington Post* wrote that "The fact that eight other quarterbacks were chosen before Peete says one thing to me about NFL people and what they're looking for in a quarterback. If he's white and can stand up straight, he's a better prospect than a black quarterback with various and obvious talents."

Chosen by the Detroit Lions, Peete started some games as a rookie in 1989 and won the starting job in 1990 with Andre Ware behind him. The story recalled an earlier era when Warren Moon, who remained one of the NFL's highest paid players in 1990, was not even chosen in the draft and had to prove himself in Canada. Talent may not be totally blind to color.

The fact that the Redskins decided to go with younger quarterbacks one year after Williams' Super Bowl triumph and not one team was willing to pick up Doug Williams would have to be another reason to temper the optimism on a trend toward black quarterbacks in the NFL.

In spite of the cautionary notes it no longer seems impossible for a black to make it at quarterback in the NFL. However, it is still unlikely as the 93 percent white figure shows.

As another example, in 1990 90 percent of the running backs and 86 percent of the wide receivers were black (up from 88% and 77% respectively in 1983).

The defensive position that shows the most meaningful statistical difference by race is at cornerback. Ninety-six percent of the cornerbacks were black in 1990 (up from 92 percent in 1983).

The words used by the coaches for the positions of running back, wide receiver, and defensive back were: strength, quickness, and instinct. All three are black-dominated positions.

There were no black coaches in the NFL until Art Shell became the Raiders coach in 1989. If the white coaches hold traditional racial beliefs, then player assignments would easily be made according to race.

Table 31-10 was compiled from veterans listed in the 1990 media guides and demonstrates the pattern.

Baseball has its own positional segregation. The pitcher and the catcher are central to every play of the game. Of the 69 catchers listed in the New York Times 1991 opening day rosters, cross-referenced in the *1991 Who's Who in Baseball*, only one was black. Ten percent were Latins and Hispanics combined. Only thirteen (4 percent) of the 306 pitchers were black, down from 7 percent in 1983! Another 10 percent were Latins or Hispanics, up from 7.5% in 1983. It is not surprising that these pivotal "thinking positions" were held mostly by whites.

What was surprising was who was playing second base, shortstop, and third base. All three are also considered to be thinking positions. In 1991, blacks make up 22 percent of second basemen, 19 percent of shortstops, and 20 percent of third basemen (versus 21, 11, and 9 percent in 1983).

Table 31-10 Stacking in the NFL*

	Whites by %		Blacks by %	
Position	*1983*	*1990*	*1983*	*1990*
Offense				
Quarterback	99	92	1	8
Running Back	12	7	88	90
Wide Receiver	23	14	77	86
Center	97	87	3	13
Guard	77	76	2	24
Tight End	52	49	48	51
Tackle	68	71	32	29
Kicker	98	97	2	0
Defense				
Cornerback	8	4	92	96
Safety	43	17	57	83
Linebacker	53	31	47	66
Defensive End	31	28	69	72
Def. Tackle	47	50	53	50

*Figures don't add up to 100% due to "other minorities" playing some positions

Compiled by Northeastern University's Center for the Study of Sport in Society from 1983 and 1990 media guides.

These increases, which put blacks nearly on par with their overall percentage in the league, may be indicating a significant shift away from positional segregation in baseball. However, like the positive developments in football at quarterback, it is too soon to tell what the long term effects will be.

More cautionary notes: first basemen and outfielders mainly react to other players. Outfielders need quickness and instinct. Not as much skill and training is considered necessary to hold these positions as others. Seventy-six percent of all blacks listed as offensive players were either first basemen or outfielders. While the percent of blacks in the outfield decreased to 51 percent from 1983 when it was 65 percent, there was a slight increase at first base (20 percent in 1991 from 19 percent in 1983). In spite of being outnumbered in the league by more than five to one, blacks have a numerical superiority over whites in the outfield (81 to 56).

According to *Who's Who in Baseball* for 1983 and 1991 and the Opening Day rosters of 1991, the positional breakdown is as follows in Table 31-11.

As can be seen, the number of Hispanics and Latins have had major increases at first base (7 to 17 percent), second base (14 to 27 percent) and shortstop (16 to 34 percent). The decrease in the number of blacks in the league overall has more than been made up by the number of Hispanic and Latin ballplayers.

Table 31-11 Stacking in Major League Baseball

	Whites by Percentage		Blacks by Percentage		Latins and Hispanics by Percentage	
Position	*1983*	*1991*	*1983*	*1991*	*1983*	*1991*
Pitcher	86	86	7	4	7	10
Catcher	93	88	0	1	7	11
1B	55	63	38	20	7	17
2B	65	51	21	22	14	27
3B	82	76	5	21	13	13
SS	73	47	11	19	16	34
OF	45	35	46	51	9	13

Compiled by Northeastern University's Center for the Study of Sport in society from 1983 and 1991 opening day rosters and *1991 Who's Who in Baseball.*

It is no small irony that after Jackie Robinson blacks were let into sports largely to increase attendance. Their numbers in baseball have decreased over the past 10 years. Is it because it is perceived that too many blacks will hurt attendance? Shouldn't baseball have learned something from the NBA and NFL in this regard? Are more Hispanics and Latins playing now to promote baseball in those virtually untapped markets? Will the door swing closed on them sometime in the future?

CONCLUSION

While a sense of despair and hopelessness permeates many urban communities because of a general deterioration of life conditions, all three pro sports did better than society. However, in the key areas of employment in coaching and front offices in both the NFL and Major League Baseball minorities seemed to be losing ground.

The NBA remained at the top while the NFL showed improvement in the Commissioner's leadership, player opportunities, opportunities for black quarterback, and management and support staff hiring. Nonetheless, the greatest room for improvement was in on-the-field and front office hiring practices. Baseball improved in player opportunities, salary equity and in stacking. It still needed the greatest amount of improvement in front office hiring.

There was less of a feeling of hope expressed in baseball and football that the 1990s would bring steady improvement. It would seem that public pressure, especially from the civil rights groups, might be necessary to affect sweeping changes.

Whether sport can lead the way to improved race relations remains a question that is unanswered in the early 1990s.

■ FOR FURTHER STUDY

Allen, Maury. *Jackie Robinson: A Life Remembered.* New York: Franklin Watts, 1987.

Ashe, Arthur R., Jr. *A Hard Road to Glory: A History of the African-American Athlete,* 3 volumes. New York: Warner Books, 1988.

CSSS Digest, Center for the Study of Sport and Society, any issue.

Chalk, Ocania. *Pioneers of Black Sport.* New York: Dodd, Mead, 1975.

Cheska, Alyce Taylor. "Sport as Ethnic Boundary Maintenance: A Case of the American Indian." *International Review for Sociology of Sport* 19, no. 3/4 (1984): 241-258.

Chu, Donald, and David Griffey. "The Contact Theory of Racial Integration: The Case of Sport." *Sociology of Sport Journal* 2 (December 1985): 323-333.

Chu, Donald, and Jeffrey O. Segrave. "Leadership Recruitment and Ethnic Stratification in Basketball." *Journal of Sport and Social Issues* 5 (Spring-Summer 1981): 13-22.

Davis, Laurel R. "The Articulation of Difference: White Preoccupation with the Question of Racially Linked Genetic Differences among Athletes." *Sociology of Sport Journal* 7 (June 1990): 179-187.

DeFrantz, Anita. "We've Got to Be Strong." *Sports Illustrated* (August 12, 1991): 77.

Edwards, Harry. *The Revolt of the Black Athlete.* New York: Free Press, 1969.

Edwards, Harry. *The Struggle That Must Be.* New York: Macmillan. 1980.

Edwards, Harry. "Authority, Power, and Intergroup Stratification by Race and Sex in American Sport and Society." In *Handbook of Social Science of Sport,* Eds. Gunther Luschen and George H. Sage. Champaign, IL: Stipes, 1981,pp. 383-399.

Edwards, Harry. "Beyond Symptoms: Unethical Behaviors in American Collegiate Sport and the Problem of the Color Line." *Journal of Sport and Social Issues* 9 (Fall 1985): 3-22.

Eitzen, D. Stanley, and David M. Furst. "Racial Bias in Intercollegiate Volleyball." *Journal of Sport and Social Issues* 13 (Spring 1989): 46-51.

Fabianic, David. "Minority Managers in Professional Baseball." *Sociology of Sport Journal* 1, no. 2 (1984): 163-171.

Foley, Douglas E. *Learning Capitalist Culture: Deep in the Heart of Tejas.* Philadelphia: University of Pennsylvania Press, 1990.

Hallinan, Christopher J. "Aborigines and Positional Segregation in Australian Rugby League." *International Review for the Sociology of Sport* 26 (1991): 69-81.

Holwlay, John. *Black Diamonds: Life in the Negro Leagues from the Men Who Lived It.* Westport, CT: Meckler, 1989.

Hoose, Phillip M. *Necessities: Racial Barriers in American Sports.* New York: Random House, 1989.

Koch, James V., and C. Warren Vander Hill. "Is There Discrimination in the 'Black Man's Game'?" *Social Science Quarterly* 69 (March 1988): 83-94.

Lavoie, Marc. "Stacking, Performance Differentials, and Salary Discrimination in Professional Ice Hockey." *Sociology of Sport Journal* 6 (March 1989): 17-35.

Lavoie, Marc, and Wilbert M. Leonard II. "Salaries, Race/Ethnicity, and Pitchers in Major League Baseball: A Correction and Comment." *Sociology of Sport Journal* 7 (December 1990): 394-398.

Leonard, Wilbert M., II. "Salaries and Race/Ethnicity in Major League Baseball: The Pitching Component." *Sociology of Sport Journal* 6 (June 1989): 152-162.

Leonard, Wilbert M., II, Tony Ostrosky, and Steve Huchendorf. "Centrality of Position and Managerial Recruitment: The Case of Major League Baseball." *Sociology of Sport Journal* 7 (September 1990): 294-301.

Leonard, Wilbert M., II, Joe Pine, and Connie Rice. "Performance Characteristics of White, Black and Hispanic Major League Baseball Players: 1955-1984." *Journal of Sport and Social Issues* 12 (Spring 1988): 31-42.

Loy, John W., and Joseph F. McElvogue. "Racial Segregation in American Sport. *International Review of Sport Sociology* 5 (1970): 5-24.

McClendon, McKee, and D. Stanley Eitzen. "Interracial Contact on Collegiate Basketball Teams." *Social Science Quarterly* 55 (March 1975): 926-938.

McPherson, Barry D. "Minority Group Involvement in Sport: The Black Athlete." *Exercise and Sport Sciences Review* 2 (1974): 71-101.

McPherson, Barry D. "The Segregation by Playing Position Hypothesis is Sport: An Alternative Hypothesis." *Social Science Quarterly* 55 (March 1975): 960-966.

Maguire, Joe A. "Race and Position Assignment in English Soccer." *Sociology of Sport Journal* 5 (September 1988): 257-269.

Medoff, Marshall H. "Positional Segregation and the Economic Hypothesis." *Sociology of Sport Journal* 3 (December 1986): 297-304.

Melnick, Merrill. "Racial Segregation by Playing Position in the English Football League." *Journal of Sport and Social Issues* 12 (Fall 1988): 122-130.

Peterson, Robert. *Only the Ball Was White*. Englewood Cliffs, NJ: Prentice Hall, 1970.

Phillips, John C. "The Integration of Central Positions in Baseball: The Black Shortstop." *Sociology of Sport Journal* 8 (June 1991): 161-167.

Purdy, Dean, Wilbert M. Leonard, II, and D. Stanley Eitzen. "A Reexamination of Salary Discrimination in Major League Baseball by Race/Ethnicity." *Sociology of Sport Journal* (forthcoming).

Reed, William F. "Culture Shock in Dixieland." *Sports Illustrated* (August 12, 1991): 52-55.

Ruck, Rob. *Sandlot Seasons: Sport in Black Pittsburgh*. Urbana: University of Illinois Press, 1987.

Rust, Art, Jr. *Get That Nigger Off the Field!* New York: Delacorte Press, 1976.

Sammons, Jeffrey T. *Beyond the Ring: The Role of Boxing in American Society*. Urbana: University of Illinois Press, 1990.

Tygiel, Jules. *Baseball's Great Experiment: Jackie Robinson and His Legacy*. New York: Oxford University Press, 1983.

Women's Sports Foundation. "Minorities in Sports: The Effect of Varsity Sports Participation on the Social, Educational, and Career Mobility of Minority Students." New York: Women's Sports Foundation, 1989.

Yetman, Norman R. "Positional Segregation and the Economic Hypothesis: A Critique." *Sociology of Sport Journal* 4 (September 1987): 274-277; and the reply by Medoff (1986), pp. 278-279.

Part Eleven

Gender and Sport

Traditionally, gender role expectations have encouraged girls and women to be passive, gentle, delicate, and submissive. These cultural expectations clashed with those traits often associated with sport, such as assertiveness, competitiveness, physical endurance, ruggedness, and dominance. Thus, young women past puberty were encouraged to bypass sports unless the sport retained the femininity of participants. These "allowable" sports had three characteristics: (1) they were aesthetically pleasing (e.g., ice skating, diving, and gymnastics); (2) they did not involve bodily contact with opponents (e.g., bowling, archery, badminton, volleyball, tennis, golf, swimming, and running); and (3) the action was controlled to protect the athletes from overexertion (e.g., running short races, basketball where the offense and defense did not cross half-court).

In effect these traditional expectations for the sexes denied women equal access to opportunities, not only to sports participation but also to college and to various occupations. Obviously, girls were discriminated against in schools by woefully inadequate facilities—compare the "girls' gym" with the "boys' gym" in any school—and in budgets. The consequences of sexual discrimination in sport were that: (1) the femininity of those who defied the cultural expectations was often questioned giving them marginal status; (2) approximately one-half of the population was denied the benefits of sports participation; (3) young women learned their "proper" societal role (i.e., to be on the sidelines supporting men who do the actual achieving); and (4) women were denied a major source of college scholarships.

Currently, quite rapid changes are occurring. Unquestionably, the greatest change in contemporary sport is the dramatic increase in and general acceptance of sports participation by women. These swift changes have occurred for several related reasons. Most prominent is the societal-wide women's movement that has gained increasing momentum since the mid-1960s. Because of the consciousness-raising resulting from the movement and the organized efforts to break down the cultural tyranny of sex roles, court cases were initiated to break down sexual discrimination in a number of areas. In athletics, legal suits were successfully brought against various school districts, universities, and even the Little League.

In 1972, Congress passed Title IX of the Education Amendments Act. The essence of this law, which has had the greatest single impact on the move toward sexual equality in all aspects of schools, is: "No person in the United States shall, on the basis of sex, be excluded from taking part in, be denied the benefits of, or be subjected to discrimination in any educational program or activity receiving federal financial assistance."

Although the passage of Title IX and other pressures have led to massive changes, discrimination continues. The selections in this part show the progress and the difficulties that remain in achieving equality.

The first selection, by sociologist Don Sabo, identifies six myths about American women athletes and demythologizes each with the results from empirical research. The second selection, by physical educators Linda Jean Carpenter and R. Vivian Acosta, documents how the male-dominated NCAA fought to diminish the effectiveness of Title IX and its takeover of the female-dominated AIAW. They call for reform using a "female" model of sport rather than the "male" model provided by the NCAA.

The next essay, by sociologists D. Stanley Eitzen and Maxine Baca Zinn, examines a sexist practice—the differential naming of women's athletic teams—that is rarely considered a problem. The names, mascots, and logos for teams are important symbols, however. Those that are sexist, and over half of the colleges and universities have sexist symbols for their women's teams, serve to reproduce patriarchal relations by either making women invisible or trivial.

While sport has been limiting to females in so many ways, it presents problems of a different sort to males. Boys and men are expected to be successful in sports. They are expected to develop "masculine" traits from sports. But what are the effects of sports failure on the identities of boys and men? What are the consequences of developing the traits of traditional masculinity in intimate relationships? What happens to the identity of male athletes after they have left sport? These questions and issues are discussed perceptively by sociologist Michael Messner in the final selection.

32. *Psychosocial Impacts of Athletic Participation on American Women: Facts and Fables*

DON SABO

Patriarchal myths are encoded within American culture and transmitted through art and literature, religion and law, fables and folkways. These myths help to legitimate structured sex inequality in all sectors of society, including sport. Feminist theorists argue that patriarchal myths in American sport are more than mere cultural beliefs or "gender stereotypes." They are historically constructed ideologies that exaggerate and naturalize sex differences and, in effect, sustain men's power and privilege in [relation] to women (Messner and Sabo, in press; Birrell and Cole, 1986; Hargreaves, 1986). These same ideologies have also kept sport researchers from seeing women athletes as they really are as well as what they are capable of becoming.

This paper identifies six beliefs about American women athletes which are grounded more in myth than empirical reality. Each myth is examined in light of current sport research which includes findings from three recent nationwide surveys which the author helped to design and execute. The first of these latter studies, the *American High School Survey* (AHSS), is a longitudinal analysis of a national, two-state, stratified probability sample of 569 female students. This study is unique because it overcomes a critical defect present in most previous studies of the effects of athletic participation, namely, their reliance on cross-sectional rather than longitudinal analysis and the resulting inability to adequately discuss change (see Melnick, Sabo, & Vanfossen, 1988). The second study, the 1985 *Miller Lite Report on Women in Sports* (MLR), is the first nationwide survey of "active and committed" adult female athletes (Pollock, 1985). A random sample of 7,000 members of the Women's Sports Foundation were surveyed in fall of 1985 and questioned about participation in sports and fitness activities. Finally, *The Wilson Report: Moms, Dads, Daughters and Sports* (TWR) focused on how family factors influence girls' athletic participation (Garfield, 1988). Telephone interviews were conducted with

SOURCE: *Journal of Sport and Social Issues* 12 (Fall, 1988), pp. 83-96. Reprinted by permission.

a national random sample of 702 mothers, 302 fathers, and 513 of their daughters aged 7-18. Whereas the AHSS provides solid methodological grounds for making causal inferences, the data reported in the MLR and TWR are descriptive and interpretations are made with caution.

The goals of this paper are to (1) identify several "myth-conceptions" about women athletes, and (2) scrutinize their merit in light of sport research. The intent is to move sport research and theory away from androcentric assumptions and their resultant biases (Hall, 1987).

THE MYTH OF FEMALE FRAILTY

The "myth of female frailty" in sport holds that women lack the necessary physical strength and energy to full participate in athletics. As Lenskyj amply documents, such beliefs helped justify women's exclusion from sport and fitness activities. The belief in the fragility of female physiology is evident in 19th century medical writings which depict upper-class women as being inherently weak, sickly, hypochondriacal, and intellectually incapable of understanding medical matters and their own bodies. Well-to-do women were considered especially vulnerable to a variety of ailments. Because of their "innate" frailness, many medical scientists reasoned that women's activities had to be limited to the more moderate demands of motherhood and homemaking (Ehrenreich and English, 1979). Likewise, American sociologist W. I. Thomas argued in 1907 that women's peculiar anatomical traits were "very striking evidence of the ineptitude of woman for the expenditure of physiological energy through motor action" (1907).

The most recent evidence of the belief in female frailty issued in May of 1986 when the American College of Obstetricians and Gynecologists (ACOG) issued thirteen-pages of "Safety Guidelines for Women." Women were advised to consider 30 minutes of moderate exercise followed by a "day of rest" as a safe limit to avoid injury. These prescriptions were challenged by women's sports advocates and researchers who point out that ACOG's recommendations were not based on rigorously scientific studies of women athletes. In contrast to ACOG's medical prescriptions, studies show that very few physical obstructions stand in the way of women's full participation in sport and fitness activities (Harris 1973, 1986; Wilmore, 1974; Ryan 1975; Adrian and Brame 1977; Hudson 1978).

ACOG's recommendations also do not reflect the life experiences of active American women athletes who, according to MLS and TWR data, feel their health is bettered by participation. Seventy-four percent of the MLS respondents ranked "improved health" and "stress reduction" as main reasons for engaging in sports activity (Pollock, 1985:17). Fifty-five percent of the TWR parents interviewed cited fitness and health as chief benefits of their daughters' participation in sports (Garfield, 1988:15). Finally, data from both studies show that, while the exercise regimen of many of the female subjects exceeded ACOG's guidelines, there were no negative physiological effects other than a normal incidence of athletic injury.

Rather than "excessive" exercise, socialization for physical passivity and the more sedentary character of many women's roles may in fact be responsible for many of women's health problems. For example, about 43.4% of American women between the ages of 25-34 are obese (National Center for Health Statistics, 1983). American children are growing fatter. The National Children and Youth Fitness Study found significant increases in the percentage of body fat in young people since 1960 (U.S. Department of Health and Human Services, 1985). Obesity is a risk factor in the development of hyperlipidemia, hypercholesterolemia, hypertension, and diabetes, which are also cardiac risk factors (Schroeder, 1982). Obesity increases the risk of osteoarthritis, a crippling disease prevalent among elderly women (Braye, 1978; Mayer, 1968). Similarly, osteoporosis afflicts 25% of American women over age 60, a disease which is propitiated by sedentary lifestyles (Veninga, 1984). Moreover, emerging research shows that regular and strenuous exercise curtails or prevents the development of osteoarthritic symptoms (Larson & Shannon, 1984; Yeaker & Martin, 1984; Huddleston, *et al.*, 1980; Nilsson and Westlin, 1971).

In summary, both the increased number and apparent vitality of female athletes debunk the sexist assumptions of many health professionals. Feminist scholars are challenging the purportedly "objective" and "neutral" pronouncements of medical science, especially as regards to women's bodies (Lenskyj, 1986; MacPherson, 1985; Hubbard, 1983). Women athletes themselves, the MLS shows, want unbiased information about the effects of participation; 70% selected "Physiology of Women as Athletes" as one of the "most important areas for future research on women in sport" (Pollock, 1985:31). What appears to be needed is a more accurate assessment of women's athletic capabilities and the formation of sound health policy which encourages rather than squelches their physical potentials.

THE MYTH OF PSYCHIC DAMAGE

The "myth of psychic damage" contends that women do not have the necessary psychological assets for athletic competition and, in contrast to men, women do not reap psychological benefit from sport. These notions are partly rooted in psychological theory. Around 1900, the American school of functionalism developed the view that female psychology and behavior are molded by evolution and instincts. Within this biologistic framework, the observable differences between women and men's physiology, intellectual interests, and cultural achievements were interpreted as evidence of women's inferiority. Women's subordination to men thus found scientific legitimacy (Williams, 1977). These views (and their implicit values) became fused within the development of psychoanalytic theory and psychiatric practice (Efron, 1985; Smith, 1975). Within the framework of psychoanalytic theory, for example, nonconformity to traditional roles and stereotypes was considered pathological. Hence, women's interest and involvement in business, engineering, athletics, or other "masculine" activities were clinically suspect.

What does empirical research say about the psychological impacts of athletic participation on women? Generally, sport researchers have found sport involvement betters rather than worsens psychological health. Prior research suggests that, compared to nonathletes, female athletes are more achievement-motivated, independent, poised, and inner-controlled (Burke, *et al.*, 1977; Kleiber *et al.*, 1981). Some studies find that women athletes feel that their sport involvement contributes to their self-confidence, higher energy levels, better health and a general well-being (Snyder & Kivlin, 1977; Snyder and Spreitzer, 1983). Other research shows women are deriving elevated self-esteem, self-image, and self-actualization from athletic participation (Harris, 1975, 1973; Snyder and Kivlin, 1975; Snyder and Spreitzer, 1976). As regards to body image, a widely accepted index of overall psychological health, the 1985 MLR found that 62% of respondents felt much more positively about their bodies now than five years ago, and another 23% felt the same. Also, 41% of the TWR parents believed their daughters derived character benefits from athletic participation.

The AHSS findings, however, indicate that understanding the psychological impacts of athletic participation on women (and men) may be more complex than previously assumed. Earlier studies of both female and male athletes have mainly used convenient samples and cross-sectional data, hence it has been impossible to untangle the effects of selectivity into and out of the sport stream from the socialization that occurs within sport itself. Almost all studies to date, moreover, fail to systematically account for the confounding impacts of race and/or social class on psychological well-being. In contrast, the NHSS yielded no discernable psychological effects which were directly attributable to athletic participation itself (Melnick, Sabo, and Vanfossen, 1986). The researchers initially uncovered several correlations between athletic participation and self-esteem, self-mastery, and body-concept. When controls for socio-economic status and sophomore participation were introduced, however, these associations disappeared.

There are two interpretations of this outcome. First, since greater numbers of middle-class than working-class girls participate in high school athletic programs, the initial correlations may be picking up class differences rather than differential outcomes of athletic socialization. Secondly, the NHSS focused solely on athletic socialization between the sophomore and senior years. That no psychological effects accruing from athletic participation were found, therefore, might suggest that the impact of sport involvement upon overall personality development for many girls occurs before the sophomore year (Melnick, Sabo, & Vanfossen, 1986). In any event, contrary to patriarchal myth, no evidence of negative psychological outcomes emerged in any study!

THE MYTH OF THE "MACHO" FEMALE ATHLETE

The "myth of the 'macho' female athlete" holds that playing sports makes women think, act, and feel like men. It derives from the cultural assumption that sport is a "man's domain" and being an "athlete" means being "masculine." In this view, athletic participation is believed to exert a "masculinizing" effect on women's gender identities and, in turn, results in "abnormal" personality traits. This view was so well entrenched in American culture in the early 20th century that Dr. Dudley Sargent, a physician and physical educationist, created a stir in 1912 when he wrote in the *Ladies Home Journal* that women and men shared the same athletic potential. Sargent observed that "Many persons honestly believe that athletics are making girls bold, masculine and overassertive; that they are destroying the beautiful lines and curves of her figure, and are robbing her of that charm and elusiveness that has so long characterized the female sex" (quoted in Twin, 1979:53-54). Today, one often hears the assertion that sports turn women into lesbians which, according to some sexual stereotypes, means "masculine" women. Is there any empirical basis for these assumptions?

Research shows that athletic participation more probably "androgynizes" rather than "masculinizes" women's identities. Psychological androgyny means that a mixture or balance of feminine and masculine traits reside in the same personality (Bem, 1979). The outcomes of athletic socialization vis à vis androgyny are different for males and females (Sabo 1985). Traditional sport endorses stereotypical gender expectations and idealizes manliness. For boys, sport socialization represents a CONTINUATION of previous gender learning; traditionally masculine expectations often become exaggerated as boys spend more time in the athletic subculture. In contrast, when girls enter the "masculine" world of sport, their experiences are apt to have an androgynizing effect on gender identity development. Athletic involvement for girls is a source of social and psychological counterpoint but, for boys, just another variation on a theme. Theoretically, therefore, gender socialization in sport is often onesided and narrowing for boys and multifaceted and expansive for girls.

The expansion of women's gender identity in sport does not appear to produce psychological ill effects (Oglesby, 1983; Duquin, 1978). For example, Harris and Jennings (1977, 1978) studied college women athletes and found that those with androgynous identities also scored significantly higher on self-esteem than "masculine," "feminine," or "undifferentiated" individuals. These findings parallel studies of non-athletic subgroups which indicate that, regardless of their sex, androgynous individuals enjoy the highest level of self-esteem when compared with "masculine" (next highest), "feminine" (third highest) and "undifferentiated" (lowest) (Spence, Helmreich, and Stapp, 1974). Finally, data on female athletes and high achievers show they "are more likely than their male counterparts to possess masculine and feminine attributes without suffering any deficit to their femininity" (Harris, 1980:234). In other words, there does not appear to be any trade-off between women's sports involvement and "femininity" or self-esteem.

Sport researchers must recognize that the discussion of female athleticism within the conceptual framework of "androgyny" can be a form of psychological reductionism which actually reinforces patriarchal notions about gender differences. If athletic participation helps females to expand gender identity and behavior beyond narrow patriarchal standards (which include passivity, weakness, heterosexual appeal, etc.), then this means that the dominant cultural standard for femininity, or what Connell (1987) calls "emphasized femininity," is being challenged. Hence, the social construction of alternative definitions of femininity in sport depart from hegemonic views of gender which reflect and reinforce male dominance. So-called "psychological androgyny" in sport, therefore, is more accurately seen as a challenge to the social and political status quo. Indeed, data from the TWR show that most adults now accept sport as an appropriate cultural terrain for girls: 97% of parents were pleased with their daughters' involvement or want them to be more highly involved; 87% of parents believed that sports are just as important for daughters as sons; 85% of daughters felt sport is no more important for boys to play sports than it is for girls.

THE MYTH OF THE "FEMALE APOLOGETIC"

A variety of sport researchers have suggested that female athletes tend to espouse a more traditional or conventional view of the women's role in society, in effect, to "apologize" for their participation in a non-traditional and "manly" activity. More recently the usefulness of the "apologetic" concept has fallen into disfavor among researchers and it is sometimes vehemently denied by feminists who claim women athletes have nothing for which to apologize. Where does the truth lay?

Research on college samples has not demonstrated the existence of the apologetic (Colker and Widom, 1980; Del Ray, 1977; Snyder & Kivlin, 1977; Uguccioni & Ballantine, 1980). The AHSS found no evidence that the "female apologetic" is a pervasive reality among American female high school athletes; female athletes were no more apt to endorse conservative gender expectations than nonathletes. In addition, the MLS found that 94% of the respondents disagreed with the statement "Participation in sports diminishes a woman's femininity." However, at the same time, 57% of the sample agreed with the statement that "In this society, a woman forced to choose between being an athlete and being feminine." This latter finding may mean that, while women athletes are aware of other people's (especially men's) reservations or hangups about sports and femininity, they themselves are generally self-confident about their participation. Finally, the TWR findings revealed that, while some girls still feel that "boys will make fun of them" for playing sports (22% of the 7-10 year olds), this concern ebbs as they grow older (10% of 11-14 year olds and only 3% of 15-18 year olds).

On one hand, the data may indicate that generally favorable attitudes toward women's sports now exist among American girls and women. Negative attitudes toward female athletic participation were more pervasive and intense in earlier decades. In short, during the last two decades of women's increased participation in American sport, the "masculinizing" taint surrounding women's athletic involvements may have lost its former venom. On the other hand, the very existence of the apologetic in previous decades has never received unambiguous empirical documentation. Hence, the "apologetic" may have been more a figment of the social scientific imagination rather than a fixture in the psyche of women athletes. In any event, there is no evidence for its existence in the 1980s.

THE MYTH OF COED CATASTROPHE

The "myth of coed catastrophe" assumes that athletic competition between or among BOTH sexes is harmful to women, men, and society. Negative assumptions are that physiological disparities between the sexes (size and strength differences) would make females injury prone, that men's masculine self-esteem and women's feminine self-image would be destroyed, that any further erosion of gender differences would lead to individual pathology and social anarchy. In contrast, proponents of cross-sex sport see a potential for positive outcomes: e.g., destructive gender stereotypes would be eroded; greater contact between the sexes would translate into enhanced respect and empathy; girls would learn competitive and team skills which would help them function more effectively in adult occupational settings; boys would learn how to work WITH rather than against women and apply these lessons to other sectors of their lives; many women athletes would gain access to the higher levels of competition they desire. Where does the truth lay?

Chief among myth-conceptions about cross-sex sport is that it is a "totally new" and scarce phenomenon. In fact, many types of cross-sex sport have emerged during the last few decades; e.g., coed volley ball leagues, baseball and softball leagues, racquetball, touch or flag football, floor and ice hockey, and team tennis. Whereas some forms of cross-sex sport pit individual females against males, team-sports most often mix males and females on the same team; competitions between all-female and all-male teams are comparatively rare.

Reliable data on the actual extent of coed participation is scarce, but the MLR offers some intriguing descriptive statistics which may serve as a starting point for further theory and research. Table 32-1 shows the percentage of times the respondents participated in the 11 most popular athletic and fitness activities as either single-sex or coed participants. The overall data show that the subjects participate in coed sports about half of the time.

A second myth is that women do not want to participate in cross-sex sport. Emerging evidence only partly disconfirms this notion. On one hand, the desire for coed athletic alternatives is growing in some sectors. The TWR found that most girls (58%) would prefer to play coed sports while only 33% would prefer to play with girls only; no significant differences issued across age subgroups. Among the MLR respondents, 79% indicated that, when playing sports, they "seek out people with the same skill level REGARDLESS OF SEX." On the other hand, however, women's desire for male competitors with similar athletic skills NEED NOT stem from personal preferences as much as from social necessity. The fact is that women's athletic skills have greatly expanded in recent decades. For

Table 32-1 Percentage of Single-Sex and Cross-Sex Participation in the 11 Most Popular Athletic and Fitness Activities among Active, Committed Woman Athletes

	Single Sex %	*Cross Sex* %	*Total Number* N=
Calisthenics/Aerobics	66	34	987
Jogging/Running	66	34	1010
Softball/Baseball	56	44	874
Walking	55	45	1117
Bicycling	54	46	996
Weightlifting	53	47	821
Basketball	49	51	774
Tennis, Squash	41	59	1076
Swimming	40	60	1025
Volleyball	40	60	854
Dance	25	75	773

Adapted from the *1985 Miller Lite Report on Women in Sports*, in cooperation with the Women's Sports Foundation.

highly-skilled women athletes, it may be easier to find accessible and challenging competition among men than women simply for demographic reasons; i.e., there are more highly-skilled male athletes than women athletes within the general population.

Reservations about coed competition were also evident among the MLR respondents. For example, only about half (52%) of the sample were generally WILLING to play with members of the opposite sex, and 69% believed women's sports should be "kept separate from men's." Moreover, 78% felt that "women have something to teach men about humane competition" and 82% felt that "in coed sports men are often threatened by losing to a woman." Finally, though 82% disagreed that sports diminish a woman's PERSONAL SENSE of her femininity, 57% recognized that women are often forced by social pressures to choose between being athletes and being feminine. In summary, therefore, the issue of whether many women athletes actually prefer or simply settle for coed sport remains blurred. What does seem clear is that, for personal and socio-political reasons, they are wading rather than diving headlong into the waters of coed sport.

One final question clouded by patriarchal myth and sadly in need of empirical scrutiny is whether cross-sex participation eroticizes male-female relations. The argument is sometimes made that cross-sex sport would lead to sexual contact, especially where boys and girls are playing contact sports together such as wrestling or basketball. This position conjures up visions of sexually aroused adolescents spending their post-game hours in heated, coital clinches. There are reasons to suspect this kind of thinking. First of all, sex research consistently shows that physical familiarity usually de-eroticizes male-female relations; e.g., coital frequency decreases the longer a couple is married (Kinsey, 1948, 1953; Hunt, 1974). Secondly, the proposition that physical contact automatically leads to sexual arousal assumes that the human sexual response in physiologically or instinctually motivated. This is not so. For humans, sexual behavior is orchestrated by the mind's capacity to internalize cultural meanings rather than some primeval or genetically triggered instinctual program (Davis, 1971). It is culture that establishes what is sexual and what is not; e.g., hand-to-genital petting in a movie theater is sexual and a gynecological examination is not. Thirdly, there is no scientific evidence that SAME-SEX contact in sport results in excessive amounts of homosexual arousal or behavior. It is theoretically inconsistent, therefore, to assert that CROSS-SEX athletic activity would inflame heterosexual passion.

In summary, the "myth of coed catastrophe" reflects and shores up patriarchy's mandate for sex segregation. To propose that men and women enter direct competition with one another violates this structural imperative. Such a proposition also challenges patriarchal beliefs about men's athletic superiority and physical powers and women's athletic inferiority and physical vulnerability. Sport researchers can inject needed empirical clarity into current controversies surrounding cross-sex sport by separating fact from fancy, reason from sentiment, and theory from ideology.

THE MYTH OF IMMOBILITY

Many sport researchers conclude that, for males, athletic participation leads to increased status among peers, greater educational attainment and aspiration, and upward mobility (Curry & Jibou, 1984; Sack & Theil, 1979; Loy, 1969). In comparison, researchers are less contentious about whether sport involvement favorably impacts on the status and mobility of females. Whereas many researchers lean toward inferring upward mobility for men, they hesitate to do so for women. Are these dispositions based on social fact or patriarchal bias?

To begin with, most of the research on this question has focused on MALES and not FEMALES. This very disparity may reflect underlying and unconscious patriarchal norms which emphasize upward mobility and achievement for men but not women. Secondly, statements about upward mobility and male athletes remain methodologically suspect because most are based on studies using cross-sectional data and convenient samples.

Finally, the few studies of women athletes to date have produced mixed findings. For example, Feltz (1978) discovered that sports involvement ranked low among a variety of status criteria among high school students. She suggests that this is due to the stigma associated with female athletes in the high school subculture. Wells and Picow (1980), in contrast, found that among Louisiana high school females, athletes were more apt to be members of the college-oriented crowd and to hold higher educational aspirations than nonathletes. Finally, the MLR indicates that female athletes themselves endorse the view that sport involvement is related to social mobility for women. Ninety-three percent of the respondents agreed with the statement "if young girls compete successfully on the athletic fields, they will be better able to compete successfully in later life."

The AHSS generated several significant findings which may help dispel some of the current ambiguity. First, athletic participation exerted a modest impact on female athletes' self-reported popularity in the high school. Though socioeconomic status explained most of the variance in popularity, athletic participation exerted an independent effect between the sophomore and senior years. Findings also showed that athletic participation produced a slight but statistically significant effect on educational aspiration; athletes aspired toward greater educational attainment. Finally, athletic participation significantly increased the extent of girls' extracurricular activities; athletes were more involved in school and community activities that non-athletes. Melnick, Sabo, and Vanfossen (1986) infer that athletic participation expands the spectrum of activities which girls consider appropriate for self-expression. They add that, "As the high school career unfolds, the personal lessons learned through athletic socialization may interact with the status gains gleaned from sports activity thereby facilitating social experimentation and involvement within and outside the school social network" (p. 15).

CONCLUSION

This paper has identified six patriarchal myths about women athletes and examined them in light of current research knowledge. Several conclusions can be made.

[1] There is no evidence that women are too physiologically frail for athletic involvement. In fact, data indicate that strenuous exercise is a health asset while women's traditional socialization for physical passivity is a risk factor for several diseases.

[2] Contrary to the "myth of psychic damage," the evidence does not suggest that women are psychologically harmed by athletic participation.

[3] Rather than becoming "masculinized" by athletic participation, girls and women appear to be adopting a wider array of psychological traits and behaviors which goes beyond narrow, patriarchal definitions of femininity.

[4] Findings indicate that American girls and women in the 1980s no longer feel defensive or "apologetic" about their athletic involvement.

[5] Research on psychosocial impacts of coed sport on participants is so sparse at this time that inferences are not warranted. However, many young females prefer coed activities, and active and committed adult athletes frequently engage in coed sports and with no apparent negative social or psychological effects.

[6] The data show that, though participation in sport slightly heightens high school girls' educational aspirations, it significantly expands the extent of their involvement in extracurricular activities. In addition, athletic participation modestly increases girls' perceived status within the high school.

Patriarchal myths may be fading within American culture but they continue to influence perceptions of women athletes. All cultures defend their fictions and, ordinarily, we see only what we assume we know. When new information challenges mythic assumptions, two alternatives emerge: to discard the myths that establish the realities, or to cling unquestionably to the beliefs which emanate from and invigorate the status quo. Both women athletes and sport researchers now find themselves between these two alternatives. Simone de Beauvoir stated, "It is always difficult to describe a myth; it cannot be grasped or encompassed; it haunts the human consciousness without ever appearing before it in fixed form. The myth is so various, so contradictory, that at first its unity is not discerned" (1953).

The patriarchal myths described in this paper are only part of a larger, unified web of beliefs which not only contain and conceal the true abilities and potentials of women athletes, but women in ALL sectors of North American society. Empirical research will hopefully continue to play an important role in sifting fact from fable, and reality from sexist ideology.

REFERENCES

Adrian, M. & Brame, J. (eds.). 1977. National Association of Girls' and Women's sports. Research Reports, 3, Washington, DC: American Alliance for Health, Physical Education, and Recreation.

Aloia, J. F., Chn, S. H. & Ostunl, J. A. 1978. Prevention of involutional bone loss by exercise. *Annals of Internal Medicine*, 89 (3): 356-358.

Bem, S. 1975. Sex-role adaptability: One consequence of psychological androgyny. *Journal of Personality and Social Psychology*, 31: 634-43.

Birrell, S. & Cole, C. 1986. Resisting the canon: Feminist cultural studies and sport. Paper presented at NASSS meeting, Las Vegas, Oct.

Bray, G. A. (ed.) 1978. Obesity in perspective: Proceedings of the conference. Washington, DC: U.S. Government Printing Office.

Burke, E. J., Straub, W. F. & Bonney, A. R. 1975. Psycho-social parameters in young female long distance runners. *Movement. Actes du 7, Symposium en apopresntissage psycho-moteur et psychologie du sport*, 367-371.

Carpenter & Acosta. 1983. The status of women in intercollegiate athletics. Cited in P. Miller, The organization and regulation of sport proceedings of The New Agenda, Nov. 3-6, Washington, DC.

Colker, R. & Widom, C. S. 1980. Correlates of female athletic participation: Masculinity, femininity, self-esteem and attitudes toward women. *Sex Roles*, 6:47-58.

Connell, R. W. 1987. *Gender and power*. Stanford, CA: Stanford University Press.

Curry, T. J. & Jiobu, R. M. 1984. *Sports: A social perspective*. Englewood Cliffs, NJ: Prentice Hall.

Davis, K. 1971. The prostitute: Developing a deviant identity. In J. M. Harris, (ed.). *Studies in the sociology of sex*. New York: Appleton-Century-Crofts.

de Beauvoir, S. 1953. *The second sex*. New York: Knopf.

Duquin, M. 1978. Effects of culture on women's experience in sport. *Sport Sociology Bulletin*, 6:20-25.

Effron, A. 1985. The sexual body: An interdisciplinary perspective. *The Journal of Mind and Behavior*, 6: (1 & 2).

Ehrenreich, B. & English, D. 1979. *For her own good*. New York: Anchor Books.

Feltz, D. L. 1978. Athletics in the status system of female adolescents. *Review of Sport & Leisure*, 3:98-108.

Garfield, E. 1988. The Wilson report: Moms, dads, daughters and sport. Copies may be secured by writing Women's Sports Foundation, 342 Madison Avenue, Suite 728, New York, NY 10017.

Hall, M. A. 1987. The gendering of sport, leisure, and physical education. *Women's Studies International Forum*, 10 (4).

Hargreaves, J. A. 1986. Where's the virtue? where's the grace? A discussion of the social production of gender through sport. *Theory, Culture & Society*, 3: 109-121.

Harris, D. V. 1973. *Involvement in sport*. Philadelphia: Lea & Febiger.

Harris, D. V. 1975. Research studies on the female athletes: Psychosocial considerations. *Journal of Physical Education and Recreation*, 46: 32-6.

Harris, D. V. 1980. Femininity and athleticism: Conflict or consonance? pp. 222-239 in D. Sabo & R. Runfola (eds.) *Jock: Sports & Male Identity*. Englewood Cliffs, NJ: Prentice Hall.

Harris, D. & Jennings, S. E. 1977. Self-perception of female distance runners, in P. Milvy (ed.) *The marathon: physiological, medic, epidemiological, and psychological studies*. NY: New York Academy of Sciences.

Harris, D. & Jennings, S. E. 1978. Achievement motivation: There is no fear of success among female athletes. A paper presented at the Fall Conference of the Eastern Association of Physical Education of College Women. Hershey, PA. October.

Hubbard, R. 1983. Social effects of some contemporary myths about women. Pp. 1-8 in M. Lowe & R. Hubbard, (eds.). *Woman's nature: Rationalization of inequality*. New York: Pergamon Press.

Huddleston, A. L., Rockwell, D., Kulund, D. N. & Harrison, B. 1980. Bone mass in lifetime tennis athletes. *Journal of the American Medical Association*, 244 1107-1109.

Hudson, J. 1978. Physical parameters used for female exclusion from law enforcement and athletics. In C. A. Oglesby (ed.), *Women and Sport: From Myth to Reality*. Philadelphia: Lea & Febiger.

Hunt, M. H. 1974. *Sexual behavior in the 1970's*. New York: Dell Publishing Company.

Kinsey, A. 1948. *Sexual behavior in the human male. Philadelphia, PA: Saunders Publishing Company.*

——1948. *Sexual behavior in the human female*. Philadelphia, PA: Saunders Publishing Company.

Kleiber, D. A. & Hemmer, J. D. 1981. Sex differences in the relationship of locus of control and recreational sport participation. *Sex Roles*, 7: 801-810.

Larson, K. A. & Shannon, S. C. 1985. Decreasing the incidence of osteoporosis-related injuries through diet and exercise, Public Health Reports, 99 (6): 609-613.

Lenskyj, H. 1986. *Out of bounds: women, sport and sexuality*. Toronto: The Women's Press.

Loy, J. 1969. The study of sport and social mobility, Pp. 112-117 in G. S. Kenyon. *Aspects of Contemporary Sport psychology*. Chicago, IL: The Athletic Institute.

MacPherson, K. 1985. Osteoporosis and menopause: A feminist analysis of the social construction of a syndrome. *Advances in Nursing Science*, 7 (4): 11-22.

Mayer, J. 1968. *Overweight: causes, costs, controls*. Englewood Cliffs, NJ: Prentice Hall.

Melnick, M., Sabo, D., & Vanfossen, B. 1988. Developmental effects of athletic participation among high school girls. *Sociology of Sport Journal*, 5 (1): 22-36.

Messner, M. & Sabo, D. (In press.) *Sport, men, and the gender order: Critical feminist perspectives*. Champaign, IL: Human Kinetics Press.

Nilsson, D. E. & Westlin, N. E. 1971. Bone density in athletics. *Clinical Orthopedics and Related Research*, 77: 179-182.

Oglesby, C. 1973. Athleticism and sex role. A paper presented at The New Agenda Conference, Washington, D.C., November 3-6.

Pollock, J. 1985. *The 1985 Miller Lite report on women in sports*. Copies can be obtained from New World Decisions, Ltd., 120 Wood Avenue South, Iselin, NJ 08830.

Ryan, J. 1975. Gynecological considerations. *Journal of Physical Education and Recreation*, 46:40.

Sabo, D. & Runfola, R. (eds.). 1980. *Jock: Sports and male identity*. Englewood Cliffs, NJ: Prentice Hall.

Sabo, D. 1985. Sports, patriarchy & male identity. *Arena Review*, 9 (2): 1-30.

Sack, A. L. & Theil, R. 1979. College football and social mobility: A case study of Notre Dame football players. *Sociology of Education*, 52: 63.

Schroeder, M. A., (ed.). (1982). Symposia on obesity. *The Nursing Clinics of North America*, 17 (2): 189-251.

Smith, Dorothy. 1975. Women and psychiatry. Pp. 1-19 in D. Smith and S. David (eds.), *Women look at psychiatry*. Vancouver: Press Gange Publishers.

Snyder, E. E. & Kivlin, J. E. 1975. Women athletes and aspects of psychological well-being and body image. *Research Quarterly*, 46: 191-199.

Snyder, E. E. & Kivlin, J. E. 1977. Perceptions of the sex role among female athletes and nonathletes. *Adolescence*. 12: 23-29.

Snyder, E. D. & Spreitzer, E. A. 1976. Correlates of sport participation among adolescent girls. *Research Quarterly*, 47: 804-09.

Snyder, E. D. & Spreitzer, E. A. 1983. *Social aspects of sport*. Englewood Cliffs, NJ: Prentice Hall.

Spence J. T. & Helmreich, R. L. 1978. *Masculinity and femininity: Their psychological dimensions, correlates, and antecedents*. Austin: University of Texas Press.

Thomas, W. I. 1907. *Sex and society*. Chicago: University of Chicago Press.

Twin, S. 1979. *Out of the bleachers: Writings on women and sport*. New York: McGraw-Hill.

Uguccioni, S. M. & Ballantine, R. H. 1980. Comparison of attitudes and sex roles for female athletic participants and nonparticipants. *International Journal of Sport Psychology*, 11: 42-48.

U.S. Department of Health and Human Services. 1985. The national children and youth fitness study. Office of Disease Prevention and Health Promotion, Washington, D.C. 20201. This study is also published in the *Journal of Physical Education, Recreation & Dance*, 56 (1): NCYFS 1-NCYFS 48.

Veinga, K. S. 1984. Osteoporosis: Implications for community health nursing. *Journal of Community Health Nursing*, 1 (4): 227-233.

Wells, R. H. & Picou, J. S. 1980. Interscholastic athletes and socialization for educational achievement. *Journal of Sport Behavior*, 3: 119-128.

Williams, Juanita H. 1977. *Psychology of women: Behavior in a biosocial context*. New York: W. W. Norton.

Willhelm, S. 1983. *Black in a White America*. Cambridge, MA: Schenkman Publishing Company.

Wilmore, J. (ed.). 1974. Research methodology in the sociology of sport. *Exercise and Sport Sciences Review*, 2, New York: Academic Press.

Yeaker, R. A. & Martin, R. B. 1984. Senile osteoporosis: The effects of calcium. *Postgraduate Medicine*, 75 (2): 147-159.

33. *Back to the Future: Reform with a Woman's Voice*

LINDA JEAN CARPENTER AND R. VIVIAN ACOSTA

The deep and systemic problems of NCAA- and male-dominated college athletics may or may not have solutions. But a growing chorus urging reform is being heard—one to which women need to add their voices. As the brief, ultimately sad history of the Association of Intercollegiate Athletics for Women (AIAW) will show, a model of competitive but humane intercollegiate athletics once existed. Ironically, the NCAA demolished it in the wake of federal legislation intended to provide equity, including equity for women in sports. Those looking for ways to reform the NCAA—as well as reasons the NCAA will never reform itself—need look no further than recent history.

Through the 1960s, women involved in inter-scholastic and intercollegiate athletics programs were under the direction of an education-oriented organization made up mostly of women physical educators. Almost universally, athletics programs for females had female coaches and athletic directors. "Ladylike" participation and avoidance of intense competition had historically characterized the program. These characteristics existed to protect females from the perceived ills of men's athletics, and also because most people accepted that females should not, could not, or did not want to compete in sports as intensely as their male counterparts. Of course, times change.

In the early 1970s, two nearly simultaneous events fostered an explosion of interest and participation in women's sports. The AIAW was founded in 1971 by female physical educators who recognized that society's definitions of gender roles were changing. They saw a developing need for the option of more intense competition for the nation's college women as well as its men. Congress enacted Title IX a few months later, in 1972, and gave legislative support to the idea that sex discrimination had no place in educational institutions or in their gymnasia and on their playing fields.[1] Only 16,000 women participated in intercollegiate athletics in 1966. A decade later, the number had grown to 64,000, and

---

SOURCE: *Academe* 77 (January/February 1991), pp. 23-27. Reprinted by permission of the authors.

now stands at about 158,000. Growth in participation occurred both at the elite level and at the participation-for-its-own-sake level.

Female leaders in American athletics had always hoped to develop a participation model for women that was not necessarily bound by the male model of the NCAA. With the twin advances of the early 1970s, women seemed to have both the desire and the power to move forward in the construction of such a mode.

Although colleges and universities did not need to comply with Title IX until 1978, the six years between its enactment and the compliance date saw massive changes. In the name of Title IX, previously separate men's and women's departments of athletics were combined. Almost always, the head of the men's program became head of both the men's and women's programs in the newly combined department, relegating the previous female head administrator to a secondary or tertiary position. Thus, AIAW's and Title IX's anticipated enhancement of the role of women as leaders in athletics programs was not taking place in the 1970s.

During the early and mid-1970s, Title IX was also having an impact on national governance of athletics. Walter Byers, the NCAA executive director at the time, expressed fears held by many male athletic directors when he said that Title IX's call for equity would mean "the possible doom of [men's] intercollegiate sports."[2] These fears were grounded in the notion that establishing equity for women's programs would mean extracting funds and power from the men's programs. Accordingly, soon after the enactment of Title IX, the NCAA tried, through the judicial and legislative systems, to exclude athletics from Title IX.

The NCAA's intense lobbying efforts early in 1974 at the Department of Health, Education and Welfare were the beginning of a series of political strategies that supported very inconsistent and opportunistic points of view. First it lobbied for the exclusion of athletics from Title IX. When that effort failed, the NCAA launched a strong campaign supporting the Tower Amendment, which sought to exclude revenue sports from the jurisdiction of Title IX. The Tower Amendment passed the Senate, but died in committee in June 1974.[3]

The NCAA, however, redoubled its efforts. The intensity and questionable integrity of these efforts were remarkable, even among those who experienced lobbying every day. Title IX was an emotional issue, and feelings ran high. Gwen Gregory, an HEW attorney, said at the time that the NCAA "is determined to sabotage Title IX. . . . They're throwing in red herrings, asking us to be arbitrary. A good deal of the reaction so far to Title IX has been panicky and alarmist, and some of it deliberately distorted."[4] Turning to the courts, the NCAA in *NCAA v. Califano* argued the inapplicability of Title IX to athletics on constitutional grounds. It lost again.[5]

Even these losses did not stop the NCAA. Having argued unsuccessfully in Congress and the courts that Title IX should not apply to athletics, it tried a different tactic, portraying the issue as one of athletic governance. To do so, the NCAA had to interpret Title IX as a mandate for NCAA's governing both men's *and* women's athletics under the principle "If you can't beat them, take them over."

What would the NCAA be taking over? According to Charlotte West, AIAW's president in 1978, "The AIAW was serving 100,000 female student-athletes and offering seventeen national championships in twelve different sports. . . . the AIAW demonstrated that a progressive, humanistic concept of sport in an education framework is workable and viable."[6] Did the NCAA ploy to take over AIAW make sense? Again in the words of Charlotte West, "Against this background [of AIAW's success], it is difficult to justify the NCAA's repeated attempts to develop a competing program which would undermine this viable organization when women's inter-collegiate athletics programs are in an emerging state. Neither basic equity nor the legal requirements of equal opportunity call for the NCAA to start programs for women." But to the NCAA, it did make "cents." The takeover of the governance of women's athletics would guarantee the NCAA control of women's programs. It would thus limit the impact that moving toward equity for women would have on men's programs and budgets.

The beginning of the end came in 1980, when the NCAA established championships for women in some sports. The NCAA's decision, made at its annual convention, entailed little discussion; it was simply announced. A great cry of outrage came from the leaders of the AIAW and from many men who were delegates at the convention. But the AIAW never had a fighting chance. Over the next several years the NCAA offered incentives to institutions to join it rather than the AIAW—offers that the still-young AIAW could not match. These included free trips for women's teams participating in national championships, and free women's memberships for colleges whose men's teams joined the NCAA. Most damaging of all, the NCAA made a deal with TV networks to televise *both* men's and women's basketball finals on the same dates that the AIAW was holding its championship games, depriving the AIAW of its financial base. Although the AIAW filed an anti-trust suit against the NCAA and fought an honorable battle, it died and was laid to rest in 1982.

Thus the AIAW, which had a membership roll of 823 colleges and universities and a financial base that included television contracts for national championships, found itself defeated by the much stronger NCAA. Indeed, even before the 1984 *Grove City v. Bell*[7] case removed college athletics from Title IX jurisdiction for a time (jurisdiction was totally restored by the Civil Rights Restoration Act of 1988), the AIAW had lost its chance at designing an alternative pattern with a woman's voice for intercollegiate athletics.

The traditionally male-dominated, abuse-ridden NCAA became the governing body for both men's and women's intercollegiate athletics in

America. A male model of athletics was all that was left. This model has recognizable characteristics in practice, if not in print. If they *were* written, they might look like this:

- The *athlete* portion of the term *student-athlete* is the more important.
- Student governance of campus programs and student involvement via student athletic associations are extinct phenomena.
- Big is better; winning is everything; the quest for publicity is all-consuming.
- The greater the distance from academic control the better.
- The improvement of the student as an athlete is more important than the improvement of the student as a healthy, contributing member of society.
- Selection and fostering of a specific sport are based on the perception of its ability to churn dollars through the system as determined by television—not on participant interest or the sport's ability to provide positive experiences for the student.
- Women, women's sports, and men's minor sports are necessary evils that interfere with the proper development of the "athletic/commercial complex."

It is difficult to say what the female model, had it survived, would look like today, but it might be:

- The *student* portion of the term *student-athlete* is the more important.
- Student governance of campus programs and student involvement via student athletic associations are healthy, viable phenomena.
- Winning is great, but can be compatible with the growth of the individual.
- The greater the cooperation and mutual interest between the academic and athletic aspects of the college experience the better.
- The improvement of the student as an athlete is less important than the improvement of the student as a healthy contributing member of society.
- Selection and fostering of a specific sport are based on the perception of participant interest and the sport's ability to provide positive experiences for the student.
- Women, women's sports, and men's minor sports are necessary for the proper development of a balanced and responsible athletic/academic complex.

Some might say that it is not fair to label the two divergent models of intercollegiate athletics "male" and "female." However, the "male" model was fashioned by males, adopted by males, retained by males in the face of decades of calls to reform, and, with the death of the AIAW, forced upon females who wanted to continue to participate in intercollegiate athletics.[8]

Following the death of the AIAW (which many who witnessed it would describe as "murder at the hands of the NCAA"), women who wished to be leaders in intercollegiate athletics, particularly in Divisions I and II, had only one viable choice: to adopt the male model for athletics. If they sought significant institutional support they had to put *athlete* ahead of *student*. They had to redefine their own self-worth in terms of win/loss records. They had to consider whether their value systems allowed them to become as adept as their male counterparts at circumventing NCAA regulations when those regulations interfered with their attainment of a winning season. They sometimes had to search for athletes who could help the team win even if the athletes themselves had no chance of winning as students.

Of course, it is possible, even if the AIAW had survived and thrived, that the alternative paradigm it developed would have become more and more like the male model. Perhaps the "male" model of athletics simply reflects our society as a whole without regard to gender or pervasive male dominance. If so, the problems facing us as we call for the reform of intercollegiate athletics are even more overwhelming than we might have realized. For the sake of argument, and in the interest of maintaining hope for the future, let us assume that the abuses in athletics today are not symptomatic of a terminally ill society, but are a separate and distinct illness that might, just might, be treatable.

The mourning for the sound of a woman's voice in the design of women's athletics continued for some years. Some female leaders left the field, telling themselves the game was over and they had lost. Some stayed and tried to maintain their principles and vision within whatever circle of influence they might have. Some stayed and told themselves that the future for an alternative to the male model existed only by "working within the male system." Thus they sought or accepted positions within the NCAA while convincing themselves they could be agents for change from within. A price was paid by all.

Those who left athletics did so with unfulfilled dreams and a sense of loss.

Those who stayed and tried to maintain their principles have become more and more isolated.

Those who decided to work from within the NCAA have had less success than they might have wished. At best, they serve as an acknowledgment by the NCAA that women's athletics is part of the organization and must be given some degree of recognition and concern. Many of the women who are trying to bring about change from within the NCAA have struggled valiantly. Unfortunately, they are playing in a game that uses men's rules on a playing field designed for men with male referees who have a strong loyalty to the home team. The men have had decades more practice. Even if the women become more skillful than the men at the men's game, they might win only to find that winning has cost them their souls.

As early as the 1920s, reformers were sounding the call for change in athletics. Rules were made, regulations promulgated, enforcement committees formed, and compliance conferences convened. But changing rules and regulations does not cause reform. That will result only from changing basic principles.

It is unrealistic to believe that reform will come from the NCAA acting without external pressure. A paradigm of financial profit rules the NCAA and the athletic commercial complexes at Division I & II schools. Big-time football and big-time men's basketball do—or at least are perceived to—fit in. In reality, very, *very* few institutions see a profit from either. On most campuses, they churn a great deal of money through the system, but profit is almost always overtaken by production expenses.

Why are women's sports and men's minor sports expected to be financially profitable when the "premier" sports are not? Because those in control of the system structure their programs around the false expectation of financial gain. They say, "Perhaps it won't come this year, but if we spend more money, recruit more effectively, allocate more student time to practice, drop production costs from our accounting—maybe next year will be our year."

But perhaps the lack of profit results from following the wrong principle and therefore looking for the wrong kind of profit. Profit from intercollegiate athletics should be measured not in dollars but in the degree of benefit to the lives of the participants. If the athletic/commercial complex could change its guiding principles to those more appropriate for an academic/athletic complex, women's teams and men's minor sports would be considered potentially very profitable.

A word about reality: no real reform will occur while individual campuses as well as the NCAA define profit in terms of dollars. As long as big-time football and men's basketball continue to be pampered as potential profit makers, there will be more rules and regulations, but no significant change until or unless such programs collapse under the weight of their abuses. Having made this painful statement, let us hope for a change in principles. Let us consider why now, more than in the past, women's voices have a significant role to play in the call for reform.

The call being heard today differs from that of the past. More voices are calling in unison. The NCAA is highlighting reform, if only because the presidents of its member institutions are pressuring it to cut costs. The presidents are realizing that, no matter why they avoided accounting for their athletics programs, they have stayed away too long. Congress is realizing that it is obliged to be concerned about the education of the nation's youth, including those who are athletically skilled.

Should not women, who have long held the principles of an academic/athletic complex dear, add their voices too? The NCAA has turned a deaf ear to them in the past, but now other ears seem willing to listen. Women must extend their voices beyond the NCAA to those who will and need to hear: faculties, college presidents, and Congress.

Staying silent and placing trust in the NCAA to take steps toward the "rewomenization" of athletics will lead to nothing. History is clear:

- In 1972, women coached more than 90 percent of women's teams. Today only 47 percent of the coaches of women's teams are women. More than 99 percent of the coaches of men's teams are men.
- In 1972, women headed more than 90 percent of women's programs. Female administrators now direct only 16 percent.
- Today no women at all are involved in the administration of 30 percent of women's programs.[9]

The glass ceiling in the gymnasium is even lower than in the nation's business offices. Women in today's society have been increasingly encouraged to develop and carve out a future for themselves in all segments of the work force, but in athletics it appears that women are being carved out of the work force.

The current call for reform gives women a special opportunity to be more proactive concerning their future and that of intercollegiate athletics. However, overcoming the pervasiveness of gender discrimination and athlete abuse will require the collective efforts of men and women of courage and goodwill. If you are such a person, you should:

- Define "reform" in athletics to include full gender equity. The devaluation of *student* in *student-athlete* is compounded for women whose athletic participation is also discounted due to discrimination. Abusing student athletes on the basis of gender is at least as bad as abusing them because of their status as athletes.
- Encourage academic accrediting bodies to add a review of the institution's athletics programs for academic *and* equity accountability with respect to the institution's athletes.
- Call on Congress to require full disclosure of athletic budgets. Where secrecy starts, lying begins.
- Do not let budget constraints caused by cost-cutting "reforms" be used as an excuse for postponing progress on equity issues.
- Look and speak through the glass ceiling. Policies and agendas are influenced by all who share their voices. The presence or absence of female voices in the reformation eventually translates into athletic policies that will affect all who are involved.
- Beware of "reform" merely through the issuing of new rules and regulations. Many of the proposed "reform" changes are cosmetic at best and have a disparate impact on women at worst.
- Complement rules and regulations with principles, philosophy, and commitment.

The female model of sport has a great deal to offer for the future of intercollegiate athletics. Go back to the future and include women's voices for reform.

NOTES

1. Title IX of the Education Amendments provides that "No person in the United States shall, on the basis of sex, be excluded from participation in, be denied the benefits of, or be subjected to discrimination under any education program or activity receiving Federal financial assistance . . ." (U.S. Commission on Civil Rights, 180, Section 1681-1686).
2. Bart Barnes and N. Scannell, "No Sporting Chance: The Girls in the Locker Room," *The Washington Post*, May 12, 1974, A14.
3. Alan Chapman, Memorandum to the Chief executive Officers, Faculty Athletic Representatives and Athletic Directors of NCAA Member Institutions, June 14, 1974, 2.
4. Barnes and Scannell, A20.
5. *Memorandum to Presidents of AIAW Member Institutions*, February 21, 1978.
6. Ibid.
7. 104 S.Ct.1211 (1984).
8. For a complementary account of the NCAA takeover of the AIAW, see *Academe*, July-August 1987.
9. For a copy of the authors' 1990 thirteen-years summary of the *National Survey on the Status of Women in Intercollegiate Athletics*, from which these data come, send a self-addressed envelope with 45 cents postage to the authors at the Department of Physical Education, Brooklyn College, Brooklyn, NY 11210.

34. *The De-Athleticization of Women: The Naming and Gender Marking of Collegiate Sport Teams*

D. STANLEY EITZEN AND MAXINE BACA ZINN

Sport is an institution with enormous symbolic significance that contributes to and perpetuates male dominance in society (Hall, 1984, 1985). This occurs through processes that exclude women completely, or if they do manage to participate, processes that effectively minimize their achievements. Bryson (1987) has argued that sport reproduces patriarchal relations through four minimalizing processes: definition, direct control, ignoring, and trivialization. This paper examines several of these processes but focuses especially on how the trivialization of women occurs through the sexist naming practices of athletic teams.

THE PROBLEM

American colleges and universities typically have adopted nicknames, songs, colors, emblems, and mascots as identifying and unifying symbols. This practice of using symbols to achieve solidarity and community is a common group practice, as Durkheim showed in his analysis of primitive religions (Durkheim, 1947). Durkheim noted that people in a locality believed they were related to some totem, which was usually an animal but occasionally natural objects as well. All members of a common group were identified by their shared symbol, which they displayed by the emblem of their totem. This identification with an animal, bird, or other object is common in institutions of higher learning where students, former students, faculty members, and others who identify with the local academic community display similar colors, wave banners, wear special clothing and jewelry, and chant or sing together. These behaviors usually center around athletic contests. Janet Lever (1983, p. 12) connects these activities with totemism:

SOURCE: *Sociology of Sport Journal* 6, no. 4, pp. 362-370.

> Team worship, like animal worship, makes all participants intensely aware of their own group membership. By accepting that a particular team represents them symbolically, people enjoy ritual kinship based on a common bond. Their emblem, be it an insignia or a lapel pin or a scarf with team colors, distinguishes fellow fans from both strangers and enemies.

A school nickname is much more than a tag or a label. It conveys, symbolically as Durkheim posits, the characteristics and attributes that define the institution. In an important way, the school's symbols represent the institutions's self-concept. Schools may have names that signify the school's ethnic heritage (e.g., the Bethany College Swedes), state history (University of Oklahoma Sooners), mission (U.S. Military Academy at West Point Cadets), religion (Oklahoma Baptist College Prophets), or founder (Whittier College Poets). Most schools, though, use symbols of aggression and ferocity (e.g., birds such as Hawks, animals such as Bulldogs, human categories such as Pirates, and even the otherworldly such as Devils) (see Fuller & Manning, 1987).

While school names tend to evoke strong emotions of solidarity among followers, there is also a potential dark side. The names chosen by some schools are demeaning or derogatory to some groups. In the past two decades or so, Native American activists have raised serious objections to the use of Indians as school names or mascots because their use typically distorts Native American traditions and reinforces negative stereotypes about them by depicting them as savages, scalpers, and the like. A few colleges (e.g., Stanford and Dartmouth) have taken these objections seriously and deleted Indian names and mascots. Most schools using some form of reference to Indians, however, have chosen to continue that practice despite the objections of Native Americans. In fact, Indian or some derivative is a popular name for athletic teams. Of the 1,251 four-year schools reported by Franks (1982), some 21 used Indian, 13 were Warriors, 7 were Chiefs, 6 were Redmen, 5 were Braves, 2 were Redskins, and individual schools were Nanooks, Chippewas, Hurons, Seminoles, Choctaws, Mohawks, Sioux, Utes, Aztecs, Savages, Tribe, and Raiders. Ironically though, Native Americans is the only racial/ethnic category used by schools where they are *not* a significant part of the student body or heritage of the school. Yet the members of schools and their constituencies insist on retaining their Native American names because these are part of their collective identities. This allegiance to their school symbol is more important, apparently, than an insensitivity to the negative consequences evoked from the appropriation and depiction of Native Americans.

The purpose of this paper is to explore another area of potential concern by an oppressed group—women—over the names given their teams. The naming of women's teams raises parallel questions to the issues raised by Native Americans. Are the names given to university and college women's sport teams fair to women in general and women athletes in particular, or do they belittle them, diminish them, and reinforce negative images of women and their secondary status?

THEORETICAL BACKGROUND: LANGUAGE AND GENDER

Gender differentiation in language has been extensively documented and analyzed. An expanding body of literature reveals that language reflects and helps maintain the secondary status of women by defining them and their place (Henley, 1987, p. 3). This is because "every language reflects the prejudices of the society in which it evolved" (Miller & Swift, 1980, p. 3). Language places women and men within a system of differentiation and stratification. Language suggests how women and men are to be evaluated. Language embodies negative and positive value stances and valuations related to how certain groups within society are appraised (Van Den Bergh, 1987, p. 132). Language in general is filled with biases about women and men. Specific linguistic conventions are sexist when they isolate or stereotype some aspect of an individual's nature or the nature of a group of individuals based on their sex.

Many studies have pointed to the varied ways in which language acts in the defining, deprecation, and exclusion of women in areas of the social structure (Thorne, Kramarae, & Henley, 1985, p. 3). Our intent is to add to the literature by showing how the linguistic marking systems adopted by many college and university teams promote male supremacy and female subordination.

Names are symbols of identity as well as being essential for the construction of reality. Objects, events, and feelings must be named in order to make sense of the world. But naming is not a neutral process. Naming is an application of principles already in use an extension of existing rules (Spender, 1980, p. 163). Patriarchy has shaped words, names, and labels for women and men, their personality traits, expressions of emotion, behaviors, and occupations. Names are badges of femininity and masculinity, hence of inferiority and superiority. Richardson (1981, p. 46) has summarized the subconscious rules governing the name preference in middle-class America:

> Males names tend to be short, hard-hitting, and explosive (e.g., Bret, Lance, Mark, Craig, Bruce, etc.). Even when the given name is multisyllabic (e.g., Benjamin, Joshua, William, Thomas), the nickname tends to imply hardness and energy (e.g., Ben, Josh, Bill, Tom, etc.) Female names, on the other hand, are longer more melodic, and softer (e.g., Deborah, Caroline, Jessica, Christina) and easily succumb to the diminutive ie ending form (e.g., Debbie, Carrie, Jessie, Christie). And although feminization of male names (e.g., Fredricka, Roberta, Alexandra) is not uncommon, the inverse rarely occurs.

While naming is an important manifestation of gender differentiation, little research exists on naming conventions other than those associated with gender and given names. Only one study (Fuller & Manning, 1987) examines the naming practices of college sport teams, but it focuses narrowly on the sexism emanating from the violence commonly attributed to these symbols. Because of their emphasis Fuller and Manning considered only three sexist naming practices. The study presented here builds on the insights of Fuller and Manning by looking at eight sexist naming categories. The goal is to show that the naming traditions of sports teams can unwittingly promote the ideology of male superiority and sexual difference.

Our argument is that the names of many women's and men's athletic teams reinforce a basic element of social structure—that of gender division. Team names reflect this division as well as the asymmetry that is associated with it. Even after women's advances in sport since the implementation of Title IX, widespread naming practices continue to mark female athletes as unusual, aberrant, or invisible.

DATA AND METHODS

The data source on the names and mascots of sports teams at 4-year colleges and universities was Franks (1982). This book provides the required information plus a history of how the names were selected for 1,251 schools. Since our research focused on comparing the names for men's and women's teams, those schools limited to one sex were not considered. Also, schools now defunct were omitted from the present analysis. This was determined by eliminating those schools not listed in the latest edition of *American Universities and Colleges* (American Council of Education, 1987). Thus the number of schools in the present study was 1,185.

The decision on whether a school had sexist names for its teams was based on whether the team names violated the rules of gender neutrality. A review of the literature on language and gender revealed a number of gender-linked practices that diminish and trivialize women (Henley, 1987; Lakoff, 1975; Miller & Swift, 1980; Schulz, 1975; Spender, 1980).

1. Physical markers: One common naming practice emphasizes the physical appearance of women ("belle"). As Miller and Swift (1980, p. 87) argue, this practice is sexist because the "emphasis on the physical characteristics of women is offensive in contexts where men are described in terms of achievement."

2. Girl or gal: The use of "girl" or "gal" stresses the presumed immaturity and irresponsibility of women. "Just as *boy* can be blatantly offensive to minority men, so *girl* can have comparable patronizing and demeaning implications for women" (Miller & Swift, 1980, p. 71).

3. Feminine suffixes: This is a popular form of gender differentiation found in the names of athletic, social, and women's groups. The practice not only marks women but it denotes a feminine derivative by establishing a "female negative trivial category" (Miller & Swift, 1977, p. 58). The devaluation is accomplished by tagging words with feminine suffixes such as "ette" or "esse."

4. Lady: This label has several meanings that demean women athletes. Often "lady" is used to indicate women in roles thought to be unusual, if not unfortunate (Baron, 1986, p. 114). Lady is used to "evoke a standard of propriety, correct behavior, and elegance" (Miller & Swift, 1977, p. 72), characteristics decidedly unathletic. Similarly, lady carries overtones recalling the age of chivalry. "This makes the term seem polite at first, but we must also remember that these implications are perilous: they suggest that a 'lady' is helpless, and cannot do things for herself" (Lakoff, 1975, p. 25).

5. Male as a false generic: This practice assumes that the masculine in language, word, or name choice is the norm while the feminine is ignored altogether. Miller and Swift (1980, p. 9) define this procedure as, "Terms used of a class or group that are not applicable to all members." The use of "mankind" to encompass both sexes has its parallel among athletic teams where both men's and women's teams are the Rams, Stags, or Steers. Dale Spender (1980, p. 3) has called this treatment of the masculine as the norm as "one of the most pervasive and pernicious rules that has been encoded."

6. Male name with a female modifier: This practice applies the feminine to a name that usually denotes a male. This gives females lower status because it indicates inferior quality (Baron, 1986, p. 112). Examples among sports teams are the Lady Friars, Lady Rams, and Lady Gamecocks. Using such oxymorons "reflects role conflict and contributes to the lack of acceptance of women's sport" (Fuller & Manning, 1987, p. 64).

7. Double gender marking: This occurs when the name for the women's team is a diminutive of the men's team name and adding "belle" or "lady" or other feminine modifier. For example, the men's teams at Mississippi College are known as the Choctaws, while the women's teams are designated as the Lady Chocs. At the University of Kentucky the men's teams are the Wildcats and the women's teams are the Lady Kats. By compounding the feminine, the practice intensifies women's secondary status. Double gender marking occurs "perhaps to underline the inappropriateness or rarity of the feminine noun or to emphasize its negativity" (Baron, 1986, p. 115).

8. Male/female paired polarity: Women's and men's teams can be assigned names that represent a female/male opposition. When this occurs, the names for men's teams always are positive in that they embody competitive and other traits associated with sport while the names for women's teams are lighthearted or cute. The essence of sport is competi-

tion in which physical skills largely determine outcomes. Successful athletes are believed to embody such traits as courage, bravura, boldness, self-confidence, and aggression. When the names given men's teams imply these traits but the names for women's teams suggest that women are playful and cuddly, then women are trivialized and de-athleticized. Some egregious examples of this practice are, Fighting Scots/Scotties, Blue Hawks/Blue Chicks, Bears/Teddy Bears, and Wildcats/Wildkittens.

Although these eight categories make meaningful distinctions, they are not mutually exclusive. The problem arises with teams using the term lady. They might be coded under "lady" (Lady Threshers), or "male name with a female modifier" (Lady Rams), or "double gender marking" (Lady Kats). Since team names of all three types could be subsumed under the "lady" category, we opted to separate those with lady that could be included in another category. In other words, the category "lady" includes only those teams that could not be placed in either of the other two categories.

FINDINGS

The extent and type of symbolic derogation of women's teams were examined in several ways. We found, first, that of the 1,185 four-year schools in the sample, 451 (38.1%) had sexist names for their athletic teams. Examining only team logos (903 schools, or 76% of the sample, provided these data), 45.1% were sexist. For those schools with complete information on both names and logos, 493 of the 903 (54.6%) were sexist on one or both.We found that many schools have contradictory symbols, perhaps having a gender neutral name for both male and female teams (Bears, Tigers) but then having a logo for both teams that was clearly having stereotypical and therefore unathletic characteristics. The important finding here is that when team names and logos are considered, more than half of the colleges and universities trivialize women's teams and women athletes.

The data on names were analyzed by the mode of discrimination, using the naming practices elaborated in the previous section (see Table 34-1). This analysis reveals, first, that over half the cases (55.1%) fall into the category of using a male name as a false generic. This usage contributes to the invisibility of women's teams. The next popular type of sexism in naming is the use of "lady" (25.2% in Table 34-1, but actually 30.8% since some of the teams using lady are classified in what we considered more meaningful categories—see second footnote under Table 34-1). This popular usage clearly de-athleticizes women by implying their fragility, elegance, and propriety. This is also the consequence of the use of the feminine suffix (6.4%). Another 5.8% of the schools with sexist naming patterns use the male/female paired polarity where male teams have names with clear referents to stereotypically masculine traits while

Table 34-1 Naming Practices That De-Athleticize Women's Teams

Naming Practices	*N*	*%*	*Examples*
Physical markers	2	0.4	Belles, Rambelles
Girl or Gal[a]	1	0.2	Green Gals
Feminine suffix	29	6.4	Tigerettes, Duchesses
Lady[b]	114	25.3	Lady Jets, Lady Eagles
Male as false generic	248	55.0	Cowboys, Hokies, Tomcats
Male name with female modifier	21	4.7	Lady Rams, Lady Centaurs, Lady Dons
Double gender marking	10	2.2	Choctaws/Lady Chocs, Jaguars/Lady Jags
Male/Female paired polarity	26	5.8	Panthers/Pink Panthers, Bears/Teddy Bears
Totals	451	100.0	

[a]Several female teams were designated as Cowgirls but they were not included if the male teams were Cowboys. We assumed this difference to be nonsexist.

[b]Actually 139 of the 451 schools (30.8%) used Lady but we placed 25 of them in other, more meaningful categories.

the names for women's teams denote presumed feminine traits that are clearly unathletic. The other important category was the use of a male name with a female modifier (4.7%). This naming practice clearly implies that men are more important than women; men are represented by nouns whereas women are represented by adjectives. Few schools use the other linguistic categories (physical markers, girl or gal, and double gender marking).

The next question addressed was whether the institutions that diminished women through team naming were clustered among certain types of schools or in a particular geographical region. We thought perhaps that religious schools might be more likely to employ traditional notions about women than public schools or private secular schools (see Table 34-2). The data show that while religious colleges and universities are slightly more likely to have sexist naming practices than public or independent schools, the differences were not statistically significant.

Table 34-2 Prevalence of Sexist Team Names by Type of School

	Public[a]		Independent		Religious	
Naming Practice	*N*	*%*	*N*	*%*	*N*	*%*
Nonsexist	289	64.7	135	63.4	310	59.0
Sexist	158	35.3	78	36.6	215	41.0
Totals	447	100.0	213	100.0	525	100.0

$\chi^2 = 3.45$, $df = 2$, not significant

[a]The determination of public, independent, or religious was provided in the description of each school in American Council of Education (1987).

Table 34-3 Prevalence of Sexist Team Names by Region

	Non South		South[a]	
Naming Practice	*N*	%	*N*	%
Nonsexist	500	65.4	264	34.6
Sexist	264	34.6	187	44.4
Totals	764	100.0	421	100.0

$\chi^2 = 10.79$, corrected for continuity $df = 1$, $p < .001$.
[a]Included in the South are schools from Missouri, Arkansas, Virginia, West Virginia, Mississippi, Maryland, Texas, Oklahoma, Louisiana, Alabama, Georgia, Kentucky, Tennessee, North Carolina, South Carolina, Florida, and the District of Columbia.

We also controlled for region of the country, assuming that southern schools might be less likely than schools in other regions of the United States to be progressive about gender matters (see Table 34-3). The data show that the differences between schools in the South and the non South are indeed statistically different, with Southern schools more likely to use sexist names for their athletic teams. Table 34-4 (page 404) analyzes these data by type of discrimination. Three interesting and statistically significant differences are found. Southern schools are much more likely than non Southern schools to incorporate feminine suffixes and use lady in their naming of female teams. Both of these naming practices emphasize traditional notions of femininity. The other difference in this table is in the opposite direction–non Southern schools are more likely to use male names as a false generic than are Southern schools. This naming practice ignores women's teams. Southern schools on the other hand, with their disproportionate use of feminine suffixes and lady, call attention to their women's teams but emphasize their femininity rather than their athleticism.

DISCUSSION

This research has shown that approximately three eights of American colleges and universities employ sexist names and over half have sexist names and/or logos for their athletic teams. This means that the identity symbols for athletic teams contribute to the maintenance of male dominance within college athletics. As Polk (1974) has noted in an article on the sources of male power, since men have shaped society's institutions they tend to fit the value structure of such institutions. Nowhere is this more apparent than in sport. Since the traditional masculine gender role matches most athletic qualities better than the traditional feminine gender role, the images and symbols are male. Women do not fit in this scheme. They are "others" even when they do participate. Their team names and logos tend to perpetuate and strengthen the image of female

Table 34-4 Naming Practices That De-Athleticize Women's Teams by Region

	Non South		South		
Naming Practices	*N*	%	*N*	%	*Level of significance*
Physical markers	0	0.0	2	100.0	n.s.
Girl or Gal[a]	0	0.0	1	100.0	n.s.
Feminine suffix	10	34.4	19	65.6	$p < .025$
Lady[b]	47	41.2	67	58.8	$p < .001$
Male as false generic	173	70.0	75	30.0	$p < .001$
Male name with female modifier	14	66.7	7	33.3	n.s.
Double gender marking	5	50.0	5	50.0	n.s.
Male/female paired polarity	15	58.0	11	42.0	n.s.
Totals	264	58.5	187	41.0	

inferiority by making them either invisible or trivial and consistently nonathletic.

Institutional sexism is deeply entrenched in college sports. The mere changing of sexist names and logos to nonsexist ones will not alter this structural inequality, but it is nevertheless important. As institutional barriers to women's participation in athletics are removed, negative linguistic an symbolic imagery must be replaced with names and images that reflect the new visions of women and men in their expanding and changing roles.

In the past decade the right of women to rename or relabel themselves and their experiences has become a tool of empowerment. For feminists, changing labels to reflect the collective redefinition of what it means to be female has been one way to gain power. As Van Den Bergh (1987) explains, renaming can create changes for the powerless group as well as promoting change in social organization. Renaming gives women a sense of control of their own identity and raises consciousness within their group and that of those in power. Because language is intimately intertwined with the distribution of power in society, the principle of renaming can be an important way of changing reality.

Since language has a large impact on people's values and their conceptions of women's and men's rightful place in the social order, the pervasive acceptance of gender marking in the names of collegiate athletic teams is not a trivial matter. Athletes, whether women or men, need names that convey their self-confidence, their strength, their worth, and their power.

REFERENCES

American Council of Education. (1987). *American universities and colleges* (14th ed.). New York: Walter de Gruyter.

Baron, D. (1986). *Grammar and Gender*. New Haven: Yale University Press.

Bryson, L. (1987). Sport and the maintenance of masculine hegemony. *Women's Studies International Forum*, **10**, 349-360.

Durkheim, E. (1947). *The elementary forms of religious life* (J. W. Sivain, Trans.). New York: Free Press.

Franks, R. (1982). *What's in a nickname? Exploring the jungle of college athletic mascots*. Amarillo, TX: Ray Franks Publ.

Fuller, J. R., & Manning, E. A. (1987). Violence and sexism in college mascots and symbols: A typology. *Free Inquiry in Creative Sociology*, **15**, 61-64.

Hall, M. A. (1984). Feminist prospects for the sociology of sport. *Arena Review*, **8**, 1-9.

Hall, M. A. (1985). Knowledge and gender: Epistemological questions in the social analysis of sport. *Sociology of Sport Journal*, 25-42.

Henley, N. M. (1987). This new species that seeks a new language: On sexism in language and language change. In J. Penfield (Ed.), *Women and language in transition* (pp. 3-27). Albany: State University of New York Press.

Lakoff, R. (1975). *Language and woman's place*. New York: Harper & Row.

Lever, J. (1983). *Soccer madness*. Chicago: University of Chicago Press.

Miller, C., & Swift, K. (1977). *Words and women: New language in new times*. Garden City, NY: Doubleday/Anchor.

Miller, C., & Swift, K. (1980). *The handbook of nonsexist writing*. New York: Lippincott & Crowell.

Polk, B. B. (1974). Male power and the women's movement. *Journal of Applied Behavioral Sciences*, **10**(3), 415-431.

Richardson, L. W. (1981). *The dynamics of sex and gender* (2nd ed.). Boston: Houghton Mifflin.

Schulz, M. (1975). The semantic derogation of women. In B. Thorne & N. Henley (Eds.), *Language and sex: Difference and dominance* (pp. 64-75). Rowley, MA: Newbury House.

Spender, D. (1980). *Man made language*. London: Routledge & Kegan Paul

Thorne, B., Kramarae, C., & Henley, N. (1985). Language, gender, and society: Opening a second decade of research. In B.Thorne & N. Henley (Eds.), *Language, gender, and society* (pp. 7-24). Rowley, MA: Newbury House.

Van Den Bergh, N. (1987). Renaming: Vehicle for empowerment. In. J. Penfield (Ed.), *Women and language in transition* (pp. 130-136). Albany: State University of New York Press.

35. *The Meaning of Success: The Athletic Experience and the Development of Male Identity*

MICHAEL A. MESSNER

> Vince Lombardi supposedly said, "Winning isn't everything; it's the only thing," and I couldn't agree more. There's nothing like being number one.
>
> Joe Montana

> The big-name athletes will get considerable financial and social remuneration for their athletic efforts. But what of the others, the 99% who fail? Most will fall short of their dreams of a lucrative professional contract. The great majority of athletes, then, will likely suffer disappointment, underemployment, anxiety, or perhaps even serious mental disorders.
>
> Donald Harris and D. Stanley Eitzen

What is the relationship between participation in organized sports and a young male's developing sense of himself as a success or failure? And what is the consequent impact on his self-image and his ability to engage in intimate relationships with others? Through the late 1960s, it was almost universally accepted that "sports builds character" and that "a winner in sports will be a winner in life." Consequently, some liberal feminists argued that since participation in organized competitive sports has served as a major source of socialization for males' successful participa-

SOURCE: In *The Making of Masculinities: The New Men's Studies*, Harry Brod (ed.) (Winchester, MA: Allen & Unwin, 1987), pp. 193-209.

tion in the public world, girls and young women should have equal access to sports. Lever, for instance, concluded that if women were ever going to be able to develop the proper competitive values and orientations toward work and success, it was incumbent on them to participate in sports.[1]

In the 1970s and 1980s, these uncritical orientations toward sports have been questioned, and the "sports builds character" formula has been found wanting. Sabo points out that the vast majority of research does *not* support the contention that success in sports translates into "work success" or "happiness" in one's personal life.[2] In fact, a great deal of evidence suggests that the contrary is true. Recent critical analyses of success and failure in sports have usually started from assumptions similar to those of Sennett and Cobb and of Rubin:[3] the disjuncture between the *ideology* of success (the Lombardian Ethic) and the socially structured *reality* that most do not "succeed" brings about widespread feelings of failure, lowered self-images, and problems with interpersonal relationships.[4] The most common argument seems to be that the highly competitive world of sports is an exaggerated reflection of advanced industrial capitalism. Within any hierarchy, one can actually work very hard and achieve a lot, yet still be defined (and perceive oneself) as less than successful. Very few people ever reach the mythical "top," but those who do are made ultravisible through the media.[5] It is tempting to view this system as a "structure of failure" because, given the definition of *success*, the system is virtually rigged to bring about the failure of the vast majority of participants. Furthermore, given the dominant values, the participants are apt to blame themselves for their "failure." Schafer argues that the result of this discontinuity between sports values–ideology and reality is a "widespread conditional self-worth" for young athletes.[6] And as Edwards has pointed out, this problem can be even more acute for black athletes, who are disproportionately channeled into sports, yet have no "social safety net" to fall back on after "failure" in sports.

Both the traditional "sports builds character" and the more recent "sports breeds failures" formulas have a common pitfall: Each employs socialization theory in an often simplistic and mechanistic way. Boys are viewed largely as "blank slates" onto which the sports experience imprints values, appropriate "sex-role scripts," and orientations toward self and world. What is usually not taken into account is the fact that boys (and girls) come to the sports experience with an *already gendered* identity that colors their early motivations and perceptions of the meaning of games and sports. As Gilligan points out, observations of young children's game-playing show that girls bring to the activity a more pragmatic and flexible orientation toward the rules—they are more prone to make exceptions and innovations in the middle of the game in order to make the game more "fair" and maintain relationships with others.[7] Boys tend to have a more firm, even inflexible orientation to the rules of a game—they are less willing to change or alter rules in the middle of the game; to them, the rules are what protects any "fairness." This observation has profound implications for sociological research on sports and gender: The question should not be *simply* "how does sports participation affect boys [or girls]?" but should add "what is it about a developing sense of male identity that *attracts* males to sports in the first place? And how does this socially constructed male identity develop and change as it interacts with the structure and values of the sports world?" In addition to being a social-psychological question, this is also a *historical* question: Since men have not at all times and places related to sports the way they at present do, it is important to explore just what kinds of men exist today. What are their needs, problems, and dreams? How do these men relate to the society they live in? And how do organized sports fit into this picture?

THE "PROBLEM OF MASCULINITY" AND ORGANIZED SPORTS

In the first two decades of this century, men feared that the closing of the frontier, along with changes in the workplace, the family, and the schools, was having a "feminizing" influence on society.[8] One result of the anxiety men felt was the creation of the Boy Scouts of America as a separate sphere of social life where "true manliness" could be instilled in boys *by men*.[9] The rapid rise of organized sports in roughly the same era can be attributed largely to the same phenomenon. As socioeconomic and familial changes continued to erode the traditional bases of male identity and privilege, sports became an increasingly important cultural expression of traditional male values—organized sports became a "primary masculinity-validating experience."[10]

In the post-World War II era, the bureaucratization and rationalization of work, along with the decline of the family wage and women's gradual movement into the labor force, have further undermined the "breadwinner role" as a basis for male identity, thus resulting in a "problem of masculinity" and a "defensive insecurity" among men.[11] As Mills put it, the ethic of success in postwar America "has become less widespread as fact, more confused as image, often dubious as motive, and soured as a way of life [Yet] there are still compulsions to struggle, to 'amount to something.'"[12]

How have men expressed this need to "amount to something" within a social context that seems to deny them the opportunities to do so? Again, organized sports play an important role. Both on a personal-existential level for athletes and on a symbolic-ideological level for spectators and fans, sports have become one of the "last bastions" of traditional male ideas of success, of male power and superiority over—and separation from—the perceived "feminization" of society. It is likely that the rise of football as "America's number-one game" is largely the result of the comforting *clarity* it provides between the polarities of traditional male power, strength, and violence and the contemporary fears of social feminization.

But these historical explanations for the increased importance of sports, despite their validity, beg some important questions: Why do men fear the (real or imagined) "feminization" of their world? Why do men appear to need a separate male sphere of life? Why do organized sports appear to be such an attractive means of expressing these needs? Are males simply "socialized" to dominate women and to compete with other men for status, or are they seeking (perhaps unconsciously) something more fundamental? Just what is it that men really *want*? To begin to answer these questions, it is necessary to listen to athletes' voices and examine their lives within a social-psychological perspective.

Daniel Levinson's concept of the "individual life structure" is a useful place to begin to construct a gestalt of the life of the athlete.[13] Levinson demonstrates that as males develop and interact with their world, they continue to change throughout their lives. A common theme during developmental periods is the process of individuation, the struggle to separate, to "decide where he stops and where the world begins." "In successive periods of development, as this process goes on, the person forms a clearer boundary between self and world. . . . Greater individuation allows him to be more separate from the world, to be more independent and self-generating. But it also gives him the confidence and understanding to have more intense attachments in the world and to feel more fully a part of it."[14]

This dynamic of separation and attachment provides a valuable social-psychological framework for examining the experiences and problems faced by the athlete as he gropes for and redefines success throughout his life course. In what follows, Levinson's framework is utilized to analyze the lives of 30 former athletes interviewed between 1983 and 1984. Their *interactions* with sports are examined in terms of their initial boyhood attraction to sports; how notions of success in sports connect with a developing sense of male identity; and how self-images, relationships to work and other people, change and develop after the sports career ends.

BOYHOOD: THE PROMISE OF SPORTS

Given how very few athletes actually "make it" through sports, how can the intensity with which millions of boys and young men throw themselves into athletics be explained? Are they simply pushed, socialized, or even *duped* into putting so much emphasis on athletic success? It is important here to examine just what it is that young males hope to get out of the athletic experience. And in terms of *identity*, it is crucial to examine the ways in which the structure and experience of sports activity meets the developmental needs of young males. The story of Willy Rios sheds light on what these needs are. Rios was born in Mexico and moved to the United States at a fairly young age. He never knew his father, and his mother died when he was only 9 years old. Suddenly he felt rootless, and at this time he threw himself into sports, but his initial motivations do not appear to be based upon a need to compete and win. "Actually, what I think sports did for me is it brought me into kind of an instant family. By being on a Little League team, or even just playing with all kinds of different kids in the neighborhood, it brought what I really wanted, which was some kind of closeness."

Similar statements from other men suggest that a fundamental motivational factor behind many young males' sports strivings is a need for connection, "closeness" with others. But why do so many boys see *sports* as an attractive means of establishing connection with others? Chodorow argues that the process of developing a gender identity yields insecurity and ambivalence in males.[15] Males develop "rigid ego boundaries" that ensure separation from others, yet they retain a basic human need for closeness and intimacy with others. The young male, who both seeks and fears attachment with others, thus finds the rulebound structure of games and sports to be a psychologically "safe" place in which he can get (nonintimate) connection with others within a context that maintains clear boundaries, distance, and separation from others. At least for the boy who has some early successes in sports, some of these ambivalent needs can be met, for a time. But there is a catch: For Willy Rios, it was only after he learned that he would get attention (a certain kind of connection) from other people for being a good athlete—indeed, that this attention was *contingent* on his *being good*—that narrow definitions of success, based on performance and winning, became important to him. It was years before he realized that no matter how well he performed, how successful he became, he would not get the closeness that he craved through sports. "It got to be a product in high school. Before,it was just fun, and having acceptance, you know. Yet I had to work for my acceptance in high school that way, just being a jock. So it wasn't fun any more. But it was my self-identity, being a good ballplayer. I was realizing that whatever you excel in, you put out in front of you. Bring it out. Show it. And that's what I did. That was my protection. . . . It was rotten in high school, really."

This conscious striving for successful achievement becomes the primary means through which the young athlete seeks connections with other people. But the irony of the situation, for so many boys and young men like Willy Rios, is that the athletes are seeking to get something from their success in sports that sports cannot deliver—and the *pressure* that they end up putting on themselves to achieve that success ends up stripping them of the ability to receive the one major thing that sports really *does* have to offer: fun.

ADOLESCENCE: YOU'RE ONLY AS GOOD AS YOUR LAST GAME

Adolescence is probably the period of greatest insecurity in the life course, the time when the young male becomes most vulnerable to peer expectations, pressures, and judgments. None of the men interviewed for this study, regardless of their social class or ethnicity, seemed fully able to "turn a deaf ear to the crowd" during their athletic careers. The crowd, which may include immediate family, friends, peers, teammates, as well as the more anonymous fans and media, appears to be a crucially important part of the process of establishing and maintaining the self-images of young athletes. By the time they were in high school, most of the men interviewed for this study had found sports to be a primary means through which to establish a sense of manhood in the world. Especially if they were good athletes, the expectations of the crowd became very powerful and were internalized (and often *magnified*) within the young man's own expectations. As one man stated, by the time he was in high school, "it was *expected* of me to do well in all of my contests—I mean by my coach and my peers, and my family. So I in turn expected to do well, and if I didn't do well, then I'd be very disappointed."

When so much is tied to your performance, the dictum that "you are only as good as your last game" is a powerful judgment. It means that the young man must continually prove, achieve, and then *re*prove, and *re*achieve his status. As a result, many young athletes learn to seek and *need* the appreciation of the crowd to feel that they are worthy human beings. But the internalized values of masculinity along with the insecure nature of the sports world mean that the young man does *not* need the crowd to feel *bad* about himself. In fact, if one is insecure enough, even "success" and the compliments and attention of other people can come to feel hollow and meaningless. For instance, 48-year-old Russ Ellis in his youth shared the basic sense of insecurity common to all young males, and in his case it was probably compounded by his status as a poor black male and an insecure family life. Athletics emerged early in his life as the primary arena in which he and his male peers competed to establish a sense of self in the world. For Ellis, his small physical stature made it difficult to compete successfully in most sports, thus feeding his insecurity—he just never felt as though he belonged with "the big boys." Eventually, though, he became a top middle-distance runner. In high school, however: "Something began to happen there that later plagued me quite a bit. I started doing very well and winning lots of races and by the time the year was over, it was no longer a question for me of *placing*, but *winning*. That attitude really destroyed me ultimately. I would get into the blocks with worries that I wouldn't do well—the regular stomach problems—so I'd often run much less well than my abilities—that is, say, I'd take second or third."

Interestingly, his nervousness, fears, and anxieties did not seem to be visible to "the crowd": "I know in high school, certainly, they saw me as confident and ready to run. No one assumed I could be beaten, which fascinated me, because I had never been good at understanding how I was taken in other people's minds—maybe because I spent so much time inventing myself in their regard in my own mind. I was projecting my fear fantasies on them and taking them for reality."

In 1956 Ellis surprised everyone by taking second place in a world-class field of quarter-milers. But the fact that they ran the fastest time in the world, 46.5, seemed only to "up the ante," to increase the pressures on Ellis, then in college at UCLA.

> Up to that point I had been a nice zippy kid who did good, got into the *Daily Bruin* a lot, and was well-known on campus. But now an event would come up and the papers would say, "Ellis to face so-and-so." So rather than my being *in* the race, I *was* the race, as far as the press was concerned. And that put a lot of pressure on me that I never learned to handle. What I did was to internalize it, and then I'd sit there and fret and lose sleep, and focus more on not winning than on how I was doing. And in general, I didn't do badly—like one year in the NCAA's I took fourth—you know, in the *national finals*. But I was focused on winning. You know, later on, people would say, "Oh wow, you took fourth in the NCAA?—you were *that good*?" Whereas I thought of these things as *failures*, you know?

Finally, Ellis's years of training, hopes, and fears came to a head at the 1956 Olympic trials, where he failed to qualify, finishing fifth. A rival whom he used to defeat routinely won the event in the Melbourne Olympics as Ellis watched on television. "That killed me. Destroyed me. . . . I had the experience many times after that of digging down and finding that there was infinitely more down there than I ever got—I mean, I know that more than I know anything else. Sometimes I would really feel like an eagle, running. Sometimes in practice at UCLA running was just exactly like flying—and if I could have carried that attitude into events, I would have done much better. But instead, I'd worry. Yeah, I'd worry myself sick."

As suggested earlier, young males like Russ Ellis are "set up" for disappointment, or worse, by the disjuncture between the narrow Lombardian definition of success in the sports world and the reality that very few ever actually reach the top. The athlete's sense of identity established through sports is therefore insecure and problematic, *not simply* because of the high probability of "failure," but also because *success* in the sports world involves the development of a personality that *amplifies* many of the most ambivalent and destructive traits of traditional masculinity. Within the hierarchical world of sports, which in many ways mirrors the capitalist economy, one learns that if he is to survive and avoid being pushed off the ever-narrowing pyramid of success, he must develop certain kinds of relationships—to himself, to his body, to other people, and to the sport itself. In short, the successful athlete must develop a highly goal-oriented personality that encourages him to view his body as a tool, a machine, or even a weapon utilized to defeat an objectified opponent. He is likely to have difficulty establishing intimate and lasting friendships with other males because of low self-disclosure, homophobia, and cut-throat competition. And he is likely to view his public image as a "success" as far more basic and fundamental than any of his interpersonal relationships.

For most of the men interviewed, the quest for success was not the grim task it was for Russ Ellis. Most men did seem to get, at least for a time, a sense of identity (and even some happiness) out of their athletic accomplishments. The attention of the crowd, for many, affirmed their existence as males and was thus a clear motivating force. Gary Affonso, now 42 years old and a high school coach, explained that when he was in high school, he had an "intense desire to practice and compete." "I used to practice the high jump by myself for hours at a time—only got up to 5'3"—scissor! [Laughs] but I think part of it was, the track itself was in view of some of the classrooms, and so as I think back now, maybe I did it for the attention, to be seen. In my freshman year, I chipped my two front teeth in a football game, and after that I always had a gold tooth, and I was always self-conscious about that. Plus I had my glasses, you know. I felt a little conspicuous." This simultaneous shyness, self-consciousness, and conspicuousness *along with* the strongly felt need for attention and external validation (attachment) so often characterize athletes' descriptions of themselves in boyhood and adolescence. The crowd, in this context, can act as a distant, and thus nonthreatening, source of attention and validation of self for the insecure male. Russ Ellis's story typifies that what sports seem to *promise* the young male—affirmation of self and connection with others—is likely to be *undermined* by the youth's actual experience in the sports world. The athletic experience also "sets men up" for another serious problem: the end of a career at a very young age.

DISENGAGEMENT TRAUMA: A CRISIS OF MALE IDENTITY

For some, the end of the athletic career approaches gradually like the unwanted houseguest whose eventual arrival is at least *known* and can be planned for, thus limiting the inevitable inconvenience. For others, the athletic career ends with the shocking suddenness of a violent thunderclap that rudely awakens one from a pleasant dream. But whether it comes gradually or suddenly, the end of the playing career represents the termination of what has often become the *central aspect* of a young male's individual life structure, thus initiating change and transition in the life course.

Previous research on the disengagement crises faced by many retiring athletes has focused on the health, occupational, and financial problems frequently faced by retiring professionals.[16] These problems are especially severe for retiring black athletes, who often have inadequate educational backgrounds and few opportunities within the sports world for media or coaching jobs.[17] But even for those retiring athletes who avoid the pitfalls of financial and occupational crises, substance abuse, obesity, and ill health, the end of the playing career usually involves a crisis of identity. This identity crisis is probably most acute for retiring *professional* athletes, whose careers are coming to an end right at an age when most men's careers are beginning to take off. As retired professional football player Marvin Upshaw stated, "You find yourself just scrambled. You don't know which way to go. Your light, as far as you're concerned, has been turned out. You miss the roar of the crowd. Once you've heard it, you can't get away from it. There's an empty feeling—you feel everything you wanted is gone. All of a sudden you wake up and you find yourself 29, 35 years old, you know, and the one thing that has been the major part of your life is gone. It's gone."

High school and college athletes also face serious and often painful adjustment periods when their career ends. Twenty-six-year-old Dave Joki had been a good high school basketball player, and had played a lot of ball in college. When interviewed, he was right in the middle of a confusing crisis of identity, closely related to his recent disengagement from viewing himself as an athlete. "These past few months I've been trying a lot of different things, thinking about different careers, things to do. There's been quite a bit of stumbling—and I think that part of my tenuousness about committing myself to any one thing is I'm not sure I'm gonna get strokes if I go that way. [Embarrassed, nervous laugh.] It's scary for me and I stay away from searching for those reasons . . . I guess you could say that I'm stumbling in my relationships too—stumbling in all parts of life. [Laughs.] I feel like I'm doing a lot but not knowing what I want."

Surely there is nothing unusual about a man in his mid 20s "stumbling" around and looking for direction in his work and his relationships. That is common for men of his age. But for the former athlete, this stumbling is often more confusing and problematic than for the other men precisely because he has lost the one activity through which he had built his sense of identity, however tenuous it may have been. The "strokes" he received from being a good athlete were his major psychological foundation. The interaction between self and other through which the athlete attempts to solidify his identity is akin to what Cooley called "the looking-glass self." If the athletic activity and the crowd can be viewed as a *mirror* into which the athlete gazes and, in Russ Ellis's words, "invents himself," we can begin to appreciate how devastating it can be when that looking-glass is suddenly and permanently *shattered*, leaving the young man alone, isolated, and disconnected. And since young men often feel comfortable exploring close friendships and intimate relationships only *after* they have established their separate work-related (or sports-related) positional identity, relationships with other people are likely to become more problematic than ever during disengagement.

WORK, LOVE, AND MALE IDENTITY AFTER DISENGAGEMENT

Eventually, the former athlete must face reality: At a relatively young age, he has to start over. In the words of retired major league baseball player Ray Fosse, "Now I gotta get on with the rest of it." How is "the rest of it" likely to take shape for the athlete after his career as a player is over? How do men who are "out of the limelight" for a few years come to define themselves as men? How do they define and redefine success? How do the values and attitudes they learned through sports affect their lives? How do their relationships with friends and family change over time?

Many retired athletes retain a powerful drive to reestablish the important relationship with the crowd that served as the primary basis for their identity for so long. Many men throw themselves wholeheartedly into a new vocation—or a confusing *series* of vocations—in a sometimes pathetic attempt to recapture the "high" of athletic competition as well as the status of the successful athlete in the community. For instance, 35-year-old Jackie Ridgle is experiencing what Daniel Levinson calls a "surge of masculine strivings" common to men in their mid 30s.[18] Once a professional basketball player, Ridgle seems motivated now by a powerful drive to be seen once again as "somebody" in the eyes of the public. When interviewed, he had recently been hired as an assistant college basketball coach, which made him feel like he again had a chance to "be somebody."

> When I say "successful," that means somebody that the public looks up to just as a basketball player. Yet you don't have to be playing basketball. You can be anybody: You can be a senator or a mayor, or any number of things. That's what I call successful. Success is recognition. Sure, I'm always proud of myself. But there's that little goal there that until people respect you, then—[Snaps fingers.] Anybody can say, "Oh, I know I'm the greatest thing in the world," but *people* run the world, and when *they* say you're successful, then you *know* you're successful.

Indeed, men, especially men in early adulthood, usually define themselves primarily in terms of their position in the public world of work. Feminist literature often criticizes this establishment of male identity in terms of work-success as an expression of male privilege and ego satisfaction that comes at the expense of women and children. There is a great deal of truth to the feminist critique: A man's socially defined need to establish himself as "somebody" in the (mostly) male world of work is often accompanied by his frequent physical absence from home and his emotional distance from the family. Thus, while the man is "out there" establishing his "name" in public, the woman is usually home caring for the day-to-day and moment-to-moment needs of her family (regardless of whether or not she also has a job in the paid labor force). Tragically, only in midlife, when the children have already "left the nest" and the woman is often ready to go out into the public world, do some men discover the importance of connection and intimacy.

Yet the interviews indicate that there is not always such a clean and clear "before-after" polarity in the lives of men between work-success and care-intimacy. The "breadwinner ethic" as a male role *has* most definitely contributed to the perpetuation of male privilege and the subordination and economic dependence of women as mothers and housekeepers. But given the reality of the labor market, where women still make only 62 cents to the male dollar, many men feel very responsible for providing the majority of the income and financial security for their families. For instance, 36-year-old Ray Fosse, whose father left his family when he was quite young, has a very strong sense of commitment and responsibility as a provider of income and stability in his own family.

> I'm working an awful lot these days, and trying not to take time away from my family. A lot of times I'm putting the family to sleep, and working late hours and going to bed and getting up early and so forth. I've tried to tell my family this a lot of times: The work that I'm doing now is gonna make it easier in a few years. That's the reason I'm working now, to get that financial security, and I feel like it's coming very soon . . . but, uh, you know, you go a long day and you come home, and it's just not the quality time you'd like to have. And I think when that financial security comes in, then I'm gonna be able to forget about everything.

Jackie Ridgle's words mirror Fosse's. His two jobs and strivings to be successful in the public world mean that he has little time to spend with his wife and three children. "I plan to someday. Very seldom do you have enough time to spend with your kids, especially nowadays, so I don't get hung up on that. The wife does sometimes, but as long as I keep a roof over their heads and let 'em know who's who, well, one day they'll respect me. But I can't just get bogged down and take any old job, you know, a filling station job or something. Ah, hell, they'll get more respect, my kids for me, right now, than they would if I was somewhere just a regular worker."

Especially for men who have been highly successful athletes (and never have had to learn to "lose gracefully"), the move from sports to work-career as a means of establishing connection and identity in the world in a "natural" transition. Breadwinning becomes a man's socially learned means of seeking attachment, both with his family and, more abstractly, with "society." What is salient (and sometimes tragic) is that the care that a woman gives her family usually puts her into direct daily contact with her family's physical, psychological, and emotional needs. A man's care is usually expressed more abstractly, often in his absence, as his work removes him from day-to-day, moment-to-moment contact with his family.

A man may want, even *crave*, more direct connection with his family, but that connection, and the *time* it takes to establish and maintain it, may cause him to lose the competitive edge he needs to win in the world of work—and that is the arena in which he feels he will ultimately be judged in terms of his success or failure as a man. But it is not simply a matter of *time* spent away from family which is at issue here. As Dizard's research shows clearly, the more "success oriented" a man is, the more "instrumental" his personality will tend to be, thus increasing the psychological and emotional distance between himself and his family.[19]

CHANGING MEANINGS OF SUCCESS IN MIDLIFE

The intense, sometimes obsessive, early adulthood period of striving for work and career success that we see in the lives of Jackie Ridgle and Ray Fosse often begins to change in midlife, when many men experience what Levinson calls "detribalization." Here, the man "becomes more critical of the tribe—the particular groups, institutions, and traditions that have the greatest significance for him, the social matrix to which he is most attached. He is less dependent upon tribal rewards, more questioning of tribal values. . . . The result of this shift is normally not a marked disengagement from the external world but a greater integration of attachment and separateness."[20]

Detribalization—putting less emphasis on how one is defined by others and becoming more self-motivated and self-generating—is often accompanied by a growing sense of *flawed* or *qualified* success. A man's early adulthood dream of success begins to tarnish, appearing more and more as an illusion. Or, the success that a man *has* achieved begins to appear hollow and meaningless, possibly because it has not delivered the closeness he truly craves. The fading, or the loss, of the dream involves a process of mourning, but, as Levinson points out, it can also be a very liberating process in opening the man up for new experiences, new kinds of relationships, and new dreams.

For instance, Russ Ellis states that a few years ago he experienced a midlife crisis when he came to the realization that "I was never going to be on the cover of *Time*." His wife had a T-shirt made for him with the message *Dare to Be Average* emblazoned on it.

> And it doesn't really *mean* dare to be average—it means dare to take the pressure off yourself, you know? Dare to be a normal person. It gets a funny reaction from people. I think it hits at that place where somehow we all think that we're going to wind up on the cover of *Time* or something, you know? Do you have that? That some day, somewhere, you're gonna be *great*, and

everyone will know, everyone will recognize it? Now, I'd rather be great because I'm *good*—and maybe that'll turn into something that's acknowledged, but not at the headline level. I'm not racing so much; I'm concerned that my feet are planted on the ground and that I'm good.

[It sounds like you're running now, as opposed to racing?]

I guess—but running and racing have the same goals. [*Laughs, pauses, then speaks more thoughtfully.*] But maybe you're right—that's a wonderful analogy. Pacing myself. Running is more intelligent—more familiarity with your abilities, your patterns of workouts, who you're running against, the nature of the track, your position, alertness. You have more of an internal clock.

Russ Ellis's midlife detribalization—his transition from a "racer" to a "runner"—has left him more comfortable with himself, with his abilities and limitations. He has also experienced an expansion of his ability to experience intimacy with a woman. He had never been comfortable with the "typical jock attitude" toward sex and women,

but I generally maintained a performance attitude about sex for a long time, which was not as enjoyable as it became after I learned to be more like what I thought a woman was like. In other words, when I let myself experience my own body, in a delicious and receptive way rather than in a power, overwhelming way. That was wonderful! [*Laughs.*] To experience my body as someone desired and given to. That's one of the better things. I think I only achieved that very profound intimacy that's found between people, really quite extraordinary, quite recently. [*Long pause.*] It's quite something, quite something. And I feel more fully inducted into the human race by knowing about that.

TOWARD A REDEFINITION OF SUCCESS AND MASCULINITY

"A man in America is a failed boy," wrote John Updike in 1960. Indeed, Updike's ex-athlete Rabbit Angstrom's struggles to achieve meaning and identity in midlife reflect a common theme in modern literature. Social scientific research has suggested that the contemporary sense of failure and inadequacy felt by many American males is largely the result of unrealistic and unachievable social definitions of masculinity and success.[21] This research has suggested that there is more to it than that. Contemporary males often feel empty, alienated, isolated, and as failures because the socially learned means through which they seek validation and identity (achievement in the public worlds of sports and work) do not deliver what is actually craved and needed: intimate connection and unity with other human beings. In fact, the lure of sports becomes a sort of trap. For boys who experience early success in sports, the resulting attention they receive becomes a convenient and attractive means of experiencing attachment with other people within a social context that allows the young male to maintain his "firm ego boundaries" and thus his separation from others. But it appears that, more often than not, athletic participation serves only to exacerbate the already problematic, insecure, and ambivalent nature of males' self-images, and thus their ability to establish and maintain close and intimate relationships with other people. Some men, as they reach midlife, eventually achieve a level of individuation—often through a midlife crisis—that leads to a redefinition of success and an expansion of their ability to experience attachment and intimacy.

Men's personal definitions of success often change in midlife, but this research, as well as that done by Farrell and Rosenberg,[22] suggests that only a *portion* of males experience a midlife crisis that results in the man's transcending his instrumental personality in favor of a more affective generativity. The midlife discovery that the achievement game is an unfulfilling rat race can as easily lead to cynical detachment and greater alienation as it can to detribalization and expanded relational capacities. In other words, there is no assurance that Jackie Ridgle, as he ages, will transform himself from a "racer" to a "runner," as Russ Ellis has. Even if he does change in this way, it is likely that he will have missed participating in the formative years of his children's lives.

Thus the fundamental questions facing future examinations of men's lives should focus on building an understanding of just what are the keys to such a shift at midlife? How are individual men's changes, crises, and relationships affected, shaped, and sometimes contradicted by the social, cultural, and political contexts in which they find themselves? And what *social* changes might make it more likely that boys and men might have more balanced personalities and needs at an *early* age?

An analysis of men's lives that simply describes personal changes while taking social structure as a given cannot adequately *ask* these questions. But an analysis that not only describes changes in male identity throughout the life course but also critically examines the socially structured and defined meaning of "masculinity" can and must ask these questions.

If many of the problems faced by all men (not just athletes) today are to be dealt with, class, ethnic, and sexual preference divisions must be confronted. This would necessarily involve the development of a more cooperative and nurturant ethic among men, as well as a more egalitarian and democratically organized economic system. And since the sports world is an important cultural process that serves partly to socialize boys and young men to hierarchical, competitive and aggressive values, the sporting arena is an important context in which to begin to confront the need for a humanization of men.

Yet, if the analysis presented here is correct, the developing psychology of young boys is predisposed to be attracted to the present structure and values of the sports world, so any attempt *simply* to infuse cooperative and egalitarian values into sports is likely to be an exercise in futility. The need for equality between men and women, in the public realm as well as in the home, is a fundamental prerequisite for the humanization of men, sports, and society. One of the most important changes that men could make would be to become more equally involved in parenting. The development of early bonding between fathers and infants (in addition to that between mothers and infants), along with nonsexist childrearing in the family, schools, and sports would have far-reaching effects on society: Boys and men could grow up more psychologically secure, more able to develop balance between separation and attachment, more able at an earlier age to appreciate intimate relationships with other men without destructive and crippling competition and homophobia. A young male with a more secure and balanced personality might also be able to *enjoy* athletic activities for what they really have to offer: the opportunity to engage in healthy exercise, to push oneself toward excellence, and to bond together with others in a challenging and fun activity.

NOTES

1. J. Lever, "Sex Differences in the Games Children Play," *Social Problems* 23 (1976).
2. D. Sabo, "Sport Patriarchy and Male Identity: New Questions about Men and Sport," *Arena Review*, 9, no. 2, 1985.
3. R. Sennett and J. Cobb, *The Hidden Injuries of Class* (New York: Random House, 1973); and L. B. Rubin, *Worlds of Pain: Life in the Working Class Family* (New York: Basic Books, 1976).
4. D. W. Ball, "Failure in Sport," *American Sociological Review* 41 (1976); J. J. Coakley, *Sports in Society* (St. Louis: Mosby, 1978); D. S. Harris and D. S. Eitzen, "The Consequences of Failure in Sport," *Urban Life* 7 (July 1978): 2; G. B. Leonard, "Winning Isn't Everything: It's Nothing," in *Jock: Sports and Male Identity*, ed. D. Sabo and R. Runfola (Englewood Cliffs, NJ: Prentice Hall, 1980); W. E. Schafer, "Sport and Male Sex Role Socialization,: *Sport Sociology Bulletin* 4 (Fall 1975); R. C. Townsend, "The Competitive Male as Loser," in Sabo and Runfola, eds., *Jock*; and T. Tutko and W. Bruns, *Winning is Everything and Other American Myths* (New York: Macmillan, 1976).
5. In contrast with the importance put on success by millions of boys, the number who "make it" is incredibly small. There are approximately 600 players in major-league baseball, with an average career span of 7 years. Approximately 6-7% of all high school football players ever play in college. Roughly 8% of all draft-eligible college football and basketball athletes are drafted by the pros, and only 2% ever sign a professional contract. The average career for NFL athletes is now 4 years, and for the NBA it is only 3.4 years. Thus the odds of getting anywhere *near* the top are very thin—and if one is talented and lucky enough to get there, his stay will be brief. See H. Edwards, "The Collegiate Athletic Arms Race: Origins and Implications of the 'Rule 48' Controversy," *Journal of Sport and Social Issues* 8, no. 1 (Winter-Spring 1984); Harris and Eitzen, "Consequences of Failure," and P. Hill and B. Lowe, "The Inevitable Metathesis of the Retiring Athlete," *International Review of Sport Sociology* 9, nos. 3-4 (1978).
6. Schafer, "Sport and Male Sex Role," p. 50.
7. C. Gilligan, *In a Different Voice: Psychological Theory and Women's Development* (Cambridge: Harvard University Press, 1982); J. Piaget, *The Moral Judgment of the Child* (New York: Free Press, 1965); and Lever, "Games Children Play."
8. P. G. Filene, *Him/Her/Self: Sex Roles in Modern America* (New York: Harcourt Brace Jovanovich, 1975).

9. J. Hantover, "The Boy Scouts and the Validation of Masculinity," *Journal of Social Issues* 34 (1978): 1.
10. J. L. Dubbert, *A Man's Place: Masculinity in Transition* (Englewood Cliffs, NJ: Prentice Hall, 1979).
11. A. Tolson, *The Limits of Masculinity* (New York: Harper & Row, 1977).
12. C. W. Mills, *White Collar* (London: Oxford University Press, 1951).
13. D. J. Levinson, *The Seasons of a Man's Life* (New York: Ballantine, 1978).
14. Ibid., p. 195.
15. N. Chodorow, *The Reproduction of Mothering* (Berkeley: University of California Press, 1978).
16. Hill and Lowe, "Metathesis of Retiring Athlete," pp. 3-4; and B. D McPherson, "Former Professional Athletes' Adjustment to Retirement," *Physician and Sports Medicine*, August 1978.
17. Edwards, "Collegiate Athletic Arms Race."
18. Levinson, *Seasons of a Man's Life.*
19. J. E. Dizard, "The Price of Success," in *Social Change in the Family*, ed. J. E. Dizard (Chicago: Community and Family Study Center, University of Chicago, 1968).
20. Levinson, *Seasons of a Man's Life*, p. 242.
21. J. H. Pleck, *The Myth of Masculinity* (Cambridge: MIT Press, 1982); Sennett and Cobb, *The Hidden Injuries of Class*; Rubin, *Worlds of Pain*; and Tolson, *Limits of Masculinity*.
22. M. P. Farrell and S. D. Rosenberg, *Men at Midlife* (Boston: Auburn House, 1981).

■ FOR FURTHER STUDY

Acosta, R. Vivian, and Linda Jean Carpenter. "Women in Intercollegiate Sport: A Longitudinal Study–Thirteen Year Update 1977-1990." Brooklyn, NY: Brooklyn College (unpublished).

Beschoff, Judith A., ed. Special issue on "Females in sport: The Gendered Body." *Arena Review* 13 (November 1989).

Birrell, Susan. "Discourses on the Gender/Sport Relationship: From Women in Sport to Gender Relations." *Exercise and Sport Sciences Reviews* 16 (November): 459-502.

Birrell, Susan, and Cheryl L. Cole. "Double Fault: Renee Richards and the Construction and Naturalization of Difference." *Sociology of Sport Journal* 7 (March 1990): 1-11.

Blinde, Elaine. "Participation in a Male Sport Model and the Value Alienation of Female Intercollegiate Athletes." *Sociology of Sport Journal* 6 (March 1989): 36-49.

Boutilier, Mary A., and Lucinda San Giovanni. *The Sporting Woman*. Champaign, IL: Human Kinetics, 1983.

Bryson, Lois. "Sport and the Maintenance of Masculine Hegemony." *Women's Studies International Forum* 10 (1987): 349-360.

Carpenter, Linda Jean. "The Impact of Title IX on women's Intercollegiate Sports." In *Government and Sport*, ed. Arthur T. Johnson and James H. Frey. Totowa, NJ: Rowman and Allanheld, 1985, 62-78.

Curry, Timothy Jon. "Fraternal Bonding in the Locker Room: A Profeminist Analysis of Talk about Competition and Women." *Sociology of Sport Journal* 8 (June 1991): 119-135.

DiIorio, Judith A. "Feminism, Gender, and the Ethnographic Study of Sport." *Arena Review* 13 (May 1989): 49-60.

Eitzen, D. Stanley, and Stephen R. Pratt. "Gender Differences in Coaching Philosophy: The Case of Female Basketball Teams." *Research Quarterly for Exercise and Sport* 60 (June 1989): 152-158.

Felshin, Jan, and Carole A. Oglesby. "Transcending Tradition: Females and Males in Open Competition." *Journal of Physical Education, Recreation, and Dance* 57 (March 1986): 44-47, 64.

Greendorfer, Susan L. "Catch the Vision: Future Directions for Women in Sport." *Journal for Physical Education, Recreation, and Dance* 60 (March 1989): 31-32.

Hall, M. Ann. "Feminist Prospects for the Sociology of Sport." *Arena Review* 8 (July 1984): 1-2.

Hall, M. Ann. *Sport and Gender: A Feminist Perspective on the Sociology of Sport.* CAHPER monograph (no date).

Hall, M. Ann. "Knowledge and Gender: Epistemological Questions in the Social Analysis of Sport." *Sociology of Sport Journal* 2 (March 1985): 25-42.

Hall, M. Ann. "The Discourse of Gender and Sport: From Femininity to Feminism." *Sociology of Sport Journal* 5 (1988): 330-340.

Hall, M. Ann, and Dorothy A. Richardson. *Fair Ball: Toward Sex Equality in Canadian Sport.* Ottawa: Canadian Advisory Council on the Status of Women. 1984.

Howell, Reet, ed. *Her Story in Sport: A Historical Anthology of Women in Sports.* Champaign, IL: Human Kinetics, 1982.

Klein, Michael, ed. Special issue on "The Macho World of Sport." *International Review for the Sociology of Sport* 25 (1990): entire issue.

Knoppers, Annelies, Barbara Bedker Meyer, Martha Ewing, and Linda Forest, "Gender and the Salaries of Coaches." *Sociology of Sport Journal* 6 (December 1989): 348-361.

Knoppers, Annelies, Barbara Bedker Meyer, Martha Ewing, and Linda Forrest. "Dimensions of Power: A Question of Sport or Gender?" *Sociology of Sport Journal* 7 (December 1990): 369-377.

Lenskyj, Helen. *Out of Bounds: Women, Sport, and Sexuality.* Toronto: Women's Press, 1986.

Lenskyj, Helen. *Women, Sport and Physical Activity: Research and Bibliography,* 2nd ed. Canada Communication Group, 1991.

Lever, Janet. "Sex Differences in the Complexity of Children's Play and Games." *American Sociological Review* 43 (August 1978): 471-483.

Lopiano, Donna A. "A Political Analysis of the Possibility of Impact Alternatives for the Accomplishment of Feminist Objectives within American Intercollegiate Sport." *Arena Review* 8 (July 1984): 49-61.

Mangan, J. A., and R. J. Park, eds. *From "Fair Sex" to Feminism: Sport and the Socialization of Women in the Industrial and Post-Industrial Eras.* Totowa, NJ: F. Cass, 1987.

Mechekoff, Robert A., with Virginia Evans. *Sport Psychology for Women.* New York: Harper & Row, 1987.

Messner, Michael. "The Changing Meaning of Male Identity in the Lifecourse of the Athlete." *Arena Review* 9 (November 1985): 31-60.

Messner, Michael A. "Men Studying Masculinity: Some Epistemological Issues in Sport Sociology." *Sociology of Sport Journal* 7 (June 1990): 136-153.

Messner, Michael A., and Donald F. Sabo, eds. *Sport, Men, and the Gender Order: Critical Feminist Perspectives.* Champaign, IL: Human Kinetics, 1990.

Miedzian, Myriam. *Boys Will Be Boys: Breaking the Link Between Masculinity and Violence.* New York: Doubleday, 1991.

Nelson, Mariah Burton. *Are We Winning Yet? How Women Are Changing Sports and Sports Are Changing Women.* New York: Random House, 1991.

Pratt, Stephen R., and D. Stanley Eitzen. "Differences in Coaching Philosophies between Male and Female Basketball Teams." *International Review for the Sociology of Sport* 24 (1989): 151-162.

Rintala, Jan, and Susan Birrell. "Fair Treatment for the Active Female: A Content Analysis of *Young Athlete Magazine.*" *Sociology of Sport Journal* 1, no. 2 (1984): 231-250.

Slatton, Bonnie, and Susan Birrell. "The Politics of Women's Sport." *Arena Review* 8 (July 1984): entire issue.

Sociology of Sport Journal. "Gender and the Media: Annotated Bibliography." *Sociology of Sport Journal* 7 (December 1990): 412-421.

Stangl, Jane Marie, and Mary Jo Kane. "Structural Variables That Offer Explanatory Power for the Underrepresentation of Women Coaches Since Title IX: The Case of Homologous Reproduction." *Sociology of Sport Journal* 8 (March 1991): 47-60.

Theberge, Nancy. "Some Evidence on the Existence of a Sexual Double Standard in Mobility to Leadership Positions in Sport." *International Review for the Sociology of Sport* 19 (1984): 185-197.

Theberge, Nancy, and Alan Crook. "Work Routines in Newspaper Sports Departments and the Coverage of Women's Sports." *Sociology of Sport Journal* 3 (September 1986): 195-203.

Wilson, Wayne, ed. *Gender Stereotypes in Televised Sports.* Los Angeles: The Amateur Athletic Foundation, 1990.

Wilson Sporting Goods. *The Wilson Report: Moms, Dads, Daughters and Sports.* River Grove, IL: Wilson Sporting Goods (in cooperation with The Women's Sports Foundation), 1988.